R. Gupta's®

POPULAR MASTER GUIDE

Education Department

MANIPUR

Multi Tasking Staff

(MTS) GROUP-D

Recruitment Exam

- Specialised Study & Practice Material Prepared by Experts
- Numerous Solved Multiple Choice Questions

by
RPH Editorial Board

2019
EDITION

Ramesh Publishing House, New Delhi

Published by
O.P. Gupta *for* Ramesh Publishing House

Admin. Office
12-H, New Daryaganj Road, Opp. Officers' Mess,
New Delhi-110002 ☎ 23261567, 23275224, 23275124

E-mail: info@rameshpublishinghouse.com
Website: www.rameshpublishinghouse.com

Showroom
● Balaji Market, Nai Sarak, Delhi-6 ☎ 23253720, 23282525
● 4457, Nai Sarak, Delhi-6, ☎ 23918938

Book Code: R-1989

ISBN: 978-93-87918-61-0

HSN Code: 49011010

CONTENTS

□□□

The examination question paper will consist of 70 (seventy) Multiple Choice Questions (MCQs) carrying equal weightage consisting of 2 (two) parts.

Subject	Number of Questions	Total Duration of Examination
Mathematics	35	
General Knowledge	35	90 minutes

SYLLABUS

GENERAL KNOWLEDGE

Knowledge of current events and Everyday Science. Questions relating to state of Manipur and Our Country India and its neighboring countries especially pertaining to its People, History, Culture, Geography and Economy.

MATHEMATICS

Number Systems: Computation of Whole Number, Decimal and Fractions, Relationship between numbers

Fundamental Arithmetical Operations: Percentages, Ratio and Proportion, Square roots, Averages, Interest (Simple and Compound), Profit and Loss, Discount, Partnership Business (Marup), Mixture and Allegation, Time and distance, Time and work, Banking and Taxation.

Algebra: Basic algebraic identities of School Algebra and Elementary surds (simple problems), Graphs of Linear and Quadratic Equations.

Geometry : Familiarity with elementary geometric figures and facts: Triangle and its various kinds of centre, Congruence and similarity of triangles, Circle and its chords, tangents, angles subtended by chords of a circle, common tangents to two or more circles.

Mensuration: Triangle, Quadrilaterals, Regular Polygons, Circle, Right Prism, Right Circular Cone, Right Circular Cylinder, Sphere, Hemispheres, Rectangular Parallelepiped, Regular Right Pyramid with triangular or square Base and its applications

Trigonometry: Trigonometric ratios and identities, Complementary angles, Height and distances (simple problems only).

Statistics: Application of Mean, Median, Mode and analysis of Statistical Charts like Histogram, Frequency polygon, Bar-diagram, Pie-chart.

□□□

Education Department Manipur
MULTI TASKING STAFF (MTS)
Group-D, Recruitment Exam

MATHEMATICS

1. The value of $\left(\dfrac{x^b}{x^c}\right)^{\frac{1}{bc}} \cdot \left(\dfrac{x^c}{x^a}\right)^{\frac{1}{ca}} \cdot \left(\dfrac{x^a}{x^b}\right)^{\frac{1}{ab}}$ is equal to

   A. 1   B. −1
   C. 0   D. abc

2. The HCF of any two prime numbers a and b, is
   A. a B. ab
   C. b D. 1

3. The total two-digit numbers which are divisible by 5, are
   A. 17   B. 18
   C. 19   D. 20

4. If the roots of the equation $2x^2 + ax + b = 0$ are reciprocals to each other, then the value of b is
   A. −1   B. −2
   C. 2   D. 1

5. If $\sin(A + B) = \cos(A - B)$, then the value of $(A + B)$ is

   A. $\dfrac{\pi}{4}$ B. $\dfrac{\pi}{2}$

   C. $\dfrac{3\pi}{4}$ D. $\dfrac{\pi}{8}$

6. The mean of the first ten even natural numbers is
   A. 10   B. 11
   C. 12   D. 13

7. If the heights and radii of a cone and a hemisphere are same then the ratio of their volumes is
   A. 1 : 2   B. 2 : 3
   C. 1 : 3   D. 1 : 1

8. The lengths of two parallel chords of a circle are 6 cm and 8 cm. If the smaller chord is at distance 4 cm from the centre, then the distance of the other chord from the centre is
   A. 5 cm   B. 4 cm
   C. 3 cm   D. 2 cm

9. In the given figure, $\angle DBC = 22°$ and $\angle DCB = 78°$ then $\angle BAC$ is equal to

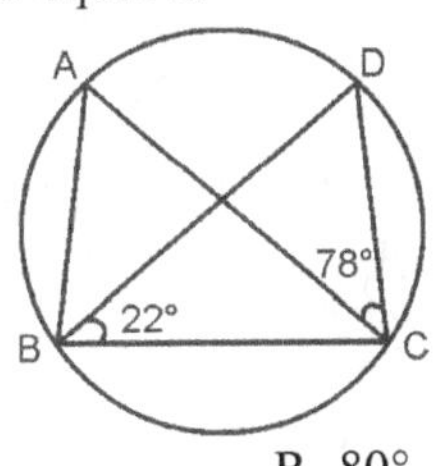

   A. 90°   B. 80°
   C. 78°   D. 22°

10. In the given figure, $\triangle ODC \sim \triangle OBA$, $\angle BOC = 115°$ and $\angle CDO = 80°$. Then $\angle OAB$ is equal to

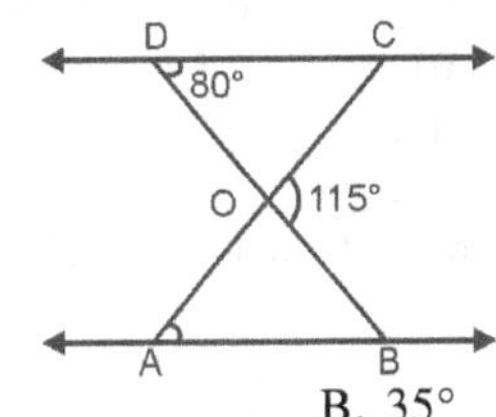

   A. 80°   B. 35°
   C. 45°   D. 65°

11. For the equation $|x|^2 + |x| - 6 = 0$
   A. There are four roots
   B. The sum of the roots is −1
   C. The product of the roots is −4
   D. The product of the roots is −6

12. In $\triangle ABC$, D is a point on BC such that $3BD = BC$. If each side of the triangle is 12 cm, then AD equals

   A. $4\sqrt{5}$ B. $4\sqrt{6}$

   C. $4\sqrt{7}$ D. $4\sqrt{11}$

13. If a, b, c be the 4th, 7th and 10th term of an AP respectively then the sum of the roots of the equation $ax^2 - 2bx + c = 0$

   A. $-\dfrac{b}{a}$

   B. $-\dfrac{2b}{a}$

C. $\dfrac{c+a}{a}$

D. can not be determined unless some more information is given about the AP.

14. If the sum of 60% of a fractional number and the number's square root is 5 greater than one fifth of the number, then the number is
A. 6.25
B. 0.25
C. 12.25
D. 2.25

15. If 12 persons working 12 hours a day dig 12 meters of a tunnel in 12 days, how many men are required to dig additional 04 meters of the tunnel (of the same dimension) given that they work 04 hours a day for 04 days?
A. 27
B. 4
C. 12
D. 36

16. Numerator of a fraction is increased by 60%, and at the same time its denominator is decreased by 60%. The new fraction is
A. 2.56 times the older fraction
B. Equal to the older fraction
C. 4 times the older fraction
D. 0.36 times the older fraction

17. In a triangle ABC, one of the angles is average of the remaining two angles. Which of the following is always true about the triangle ABC?
A. Isosceles triangle
B. Equilateral triangle
C. One of its angles measures 60°
D. Right angled triangle

18. If the area of a circle 'C' is equal to the area of a square 'S', then the ratio of the square of the perimeter of 'C' to the square of the perimeter of 'S' is nearly equal to
A. 22 : 7
B. 11 : 14
C. 88 : 7
D. 1 : 1

19. The last digit of the number 3^{2015} is
A. 1
B. 3
C. 5
D. 7

20. What is the square root of 49%?
A. 0.7%
B. 7.0%
C. 70%
D. Undefined

21. Twelve persons meet in a conference and each shakes hands with all the others. How many handshakes take place?
A. 66
B. 72
C. 144
D. 132

22. A man travels uphill to city C from city B in a car at the speed of 40 Km/hr, and returns to city B at a faster speed of 60 Km/hr. What is his average speed for the round trip?
A. 0
B. 48 Km/hr
C. 50 Km/hr
D. Data insufficient

23. (7 + 14 + 21 + 28 ..... + 700) is equal to:
A. 35350
B. 42714
C. 49420
D. 56707

24. A man decides to travel 80 kilometres in 8 hours partly by foot and partly on a bicycle. If his speed on foot is 8 km/hr and on bicycle 16 km/hr, what distance would he travel on foot?
A. 20 km
B. 30 km
C. 48 km
D. 60 km

25. Due to a 25% increase in the price of rice per kilogram, a person is able to purchase 20 kilograms less for ₹ 400. What is the increased price of rice per kilogram?
A. ₹ 5
B. ₹ 6
C. ₹ 10
D. ₹ 4

26. A toy weighing 24 grams of an alloy of two metals is worth ₹ 174, but if the weights of the two metals be interchanged, the toy would be worth ₹ 162. If the price of one metal be ₹ 8 per gram, find the price of the other metal used to make the toy.
A. ₹ 10/gram
B. ₹ 6/gram
C. ₹ 4/gram
D. ₹ 5/gram

27. Three bells chime at intervals of 48, 60 and 90 minutes respectively. If all the three bells chime together at 10 AM, at what time will all the three chime again that day?
A. 1 PM
B. 2 PM
C. 8 PM
D. 10 PM

28. Find the last two digits of:
15 × 37 × 63 × 51 × 97 × 17
A. 35
B. 45
C. 55
D. 85

29. After striking the floor, a ball rebounds to 4/5th of the height from which it has fallen. Find the total distance that it travels before coming to rest if it has been gently dropped from a height of 120 metres.
A. 540 metres
B. 960 metres
C. 1080 metres
D. 1120 metres

30. There is a 7-digit telephone number with all different digits. If the digit at extreme right and extreme left are 5 and 6 respectively, find how many such telephone numbers are possible.
A. 120
B. 1,00,000
C. 6720
D. 30,240

31. A speaks the truth 3 out of 4 times, and B 5 out of 6 times. What is the probability that they will contradict each other in stating the same fact?
A. 2/3
B. 1/3
C. 5/6
D. 1/21

32. A circle is inscribed inside an equilateral triangle touching all the three sides. If the radius of the circle is 2 cm, find the area of the triangle.

A. $15\sqrt{3}$ B. $18\sqrt{3}$

C. $12\sqrt{2}$ D. $12\sqrt{3}$

33. Five persons A, B, C, D and E are sitting in a row facing you such that D is on the left of C; B is on the right of E; A is on the right of C and B is on the left of D. If E has only one neighbour then who is sitting in the centre?

A. A   B. B

C. C   D. D

34. $\left(\sqrt{9}\right)^{3} \times \left(\sqrt{81}\right)^{5} \div \left(\sqrt{27}\right)^{2} = (3)^{?}$

A. $\dfrac{25}{12}$ B. $\dfrac{12}{25}$

C. $\dfrac{27}{16}$ D. $\dfrac{16}{27}$

35. 18 men can do a piece of work in 12 days. How many men would be required to do the same work in 8 days?

A. 12   B. 18

C. 24   D. 27

GENERAL KNOWLEDGE

36. Which element is always present in an amalgam?

A. Na   B. Mg

C. Hg   D. Ca

37. Which of the following is not a wetland site under Ramsar Convention?

A. Loktak Lake, Manipur   B. Bhitarkanika, Odisha

C. Jaisamand, Rajasthan   D. Rudrasagar, Tripura

38. Which metal is used for coating in Galvanization?

A. Copper   B. Zinc

C. Tin   D. Iron

39. Match List-I (Dance) with List-II (State) and select the correct answer:

List-I	*List-II*
(a) Bagurumba	1. Tripura
(b) Cheraw	2. Meghalaya
(c) Nongkrem	3. Mizoram
(d) Hojagiri	4. Sikkim
	5. Assam

Codes:

	(a)	(b)	(c)	(d)
A.	2	3	5	4
B.	5	3	2	1
C.	5	1	4	2
D.	2	1	3	4

40. Keilam Wildlife Sanctuary is located in:

A. Chandel   B. Churachandpur

C. Senapati   D. Tamenglong

41. Who was the King of Manipur when Burmese invasion, Chahi Taret Khuntakpa took place?

A. Marjit   B. Chourjit

C. Madhuchandra   D. Labanyachandra

42. ...., the Political Agent in Manipur was executed at Kangla on 24th March, 1891.

A. J.W. Quinton   B. Slim

C. St. Clair Grimwood   D. J. Johnstone

43. Which of the following correctly defines Nunggoibi?

A. Sacred place of worship of the Goddess of War

B. Abode of Lord Pakhangba

C. Cremation site of the kings of Manipur

D. Sacred place where the kings of Manipur performed their coronation

44. Which of the following pairs (Famous person-Title) is correctly matched?

A. Hijam Irabot – Jananeta

B. Bir Tikendrajit – Tarzan of Manipur

C. Laishram Mema Devi – Iron Lady of Manipur

D. Bheigyachandra – Melody King

45. Match List-I (Writ) with List-II (Meaning) and select the correct answer:

List-I	*List-II*
(a) Certiorari	1. To be certified
(b) Habeas Corpus	2. What is your authority
(c) Mandamus	3. You may have the body
(d) Quo Warranto	4. We command

Codes:

	(a)	(b)	(c)	(d)
A.	2	1	3	4
B.	3	1	2	4
C.	4	3	2	1
D.	1	3	4	2

46. 'Servants of India Society' was founded by:

A. Jyotiba Phule   B. G.K. Gokhale

C. V.D. Savarkar   D. G.V. Mavlankar

47. The Manipur Merger Agreement was signed by Maharaja Bodhchandra and V.P. Menon at Shillong on ....

A. 17th October, 1950   B. 21st September, 1949

C. 21st July, 1949   D. 23rd March, 1948

48. What is Khuba Kishei?

A. Devotional song in remembrance of Khamba Thoibi

B. A ritual associated with Poumai seed sowing festival

C. Collection of literary works of Maharajkumari Binodini Devi

D. A clap dance performed during Ratha Yatra

49. Clemency in Capital punishment may be granted by:
A. President of India
B. Chief Justice of India
C. Prime Minister of India
D. The Parliament

50. Disputes regarding the election of President of India are filed and settled:
A. In the Supreme Court of India
B. In the Parliament
C. In the Election Commission
D. Both in the Supreme Court & High Court

51. What is the correct sequence of the States in terms of the length of the International Border with Myanmar in descending order?
A. Arunachal Pradesh, Mizoram, Manipur, Nagaland
B. Nagaland, Manipur, Mizoram, Arunachal Pradesh
C. Mizoram, Nagaland, Arunachal Pradesh, Manipur
D. Manipur, Mizoram, Nagaland, Arunachal Pradesh

52. Who was the Chairman of Drafting Committee of the Indian Constitution?
A. N. Gopalaswamy
B. Dr. B.R. Ambedkar
C. K.M. Munshi
D. N. Madhava Rao

53. The member of Shivaji's Astha Pradhana who looked after foreign affairs was:
A. Peshwa
B. Sachiv
C. Pandit Rao
D. Sumant

54. The educated middle class in India:
A. Opposed the revolt of 1857
B. Supported the revolt of 1857
C. Remained neutral to the revolt of 1857
D. Fought against native rulers

55. The Sultan of Delhi who is reputed to have built the biggest network of canals in India was:
A. Iltutmish
B. Ghiyasuddin Tughlaq
C. Feroze Shah Tughlaq
D. Sikandar Lodi

56. The Hunter Commission was appointed after the:
A. Black-hole incident
B. Jalianwalla Bagh massacre
C. Uprising of 1857
D. Partition of Bengal

57. An increase in the bank rate generally indicates that the
A. Market rate of interest is likely to fall
B. Central Bank is no longer making loans to commercial bank
C. Central bank is following an easy money policy
D. Central Bank is following a tight money policy

58. In India, deficit financing is used for raising resources for
A. Economic Development
B. Redemption of Public Debt
C. Adjusting the balance of payments
D. Reducing the foreign debt

59. The game of Sepak Takraw originated in which place?
A. Thai Malay Peninsula
B. Mainland China
C. Philippines
D. Vietnam

60. What is the total area of Manipur?
A. 22223 sq. km
B. 22732 sq. km
C. 22327 sq. km
D. 22237 sq. km

61. The shrine at Kaina in Manipur was built during the reign of which king?
A. Shri Jai Singh Maharaja
B. Maharaja Bhagyachandra
C. Meidingu Nongdaa Lairen Paakhangba
D. Maharaja Pamheiba

62. Mahatma Gandhi undertook fast unto death in 1932, mainly because
A. Round Table Conference failed to satisfy Indian political aspirations
B. Congress and Muslim League had differences of opinion
C. Ramsay MacDonald announced the communal award
D. None of the statements A, B and C given above is correct in this context

63. In What way does the Indian Parliament exercise control over the administration?
A. Through Parliamentary Committees.
B. Through Consultative Committees of various ministries.
C. By making the administrators send periodic reports.
D. By compelling the executive to issue writs.

64. The 73rd Constitution Amendment Act, 1992 refers to the:
A. generation of gainful employment for the unemployed and the under employed men and women in rural area.
B. generation of employment for the able bodies adults who are in need and desirous of work during the lean agricultural reason.
C. laying the foundation for strong and vibrant Panchayati Raj Institutions in the country.
D. guarantee of right to life, liberty and security of person equality before law and equal protection without discrimination.

65. The Raga which is sung early in the morning is:
A. Todi
B. Darbari
C. Bhopali
D. Bhimpalasi

66. Which mountain range separates the Indo-Gangetic plain from the Deccan Plateau?
  A. The Aravalli   B. The Vindhyas
  C. The Satpura   D. The Sahyadri

67. Which of the following disturbances occurs only in the coastal regions?
  A. Cyclone   B. Tornado
  C. Gale   D. Tsunami

68. Keibul Lamjao National Park is famous for
  A. Brow Antlered deer
  B. Swamp deer
  C. Musk deer
  D. Barking deer

69. What is 'roaring forties'?
  A. Sub-tropical zone of high pressure on either side of the equator
  B. Westerly winds blowing over the southern hemisphere
  C. Group of forty small islands on the eastern coast of Florida
  D. Winds that blow towards equator

70. Which combination is not correct?
  A. The Gobi—Mongolia and China
  B. Mariana Trench—Atlantic Ocean
  C. Godwin Austen—Karakoram
  D. Ojos del Salado—Argentina-Chile

ANSWERS

1	2	3	4	5	6	7	8	9	10
A	D	B	C	B	B	A	C	B	B

11	12	13	14	15	16	17	18	19	20
C	C	C	A	D	C	C	B	D	C

21	22	23	24	25	26	27	28	29	30
A	B	A	C	A	B	D	A	C	C

31	32	33	34	35	36	37	38	39	40
B	D	D	A	D	C	C	B	B	B

41	42	43	44	45	46	47	48	49	50
A	C	A	A	D	B	B	D	A	A

51	52	53	54	55	56	57	58	59	60
A	B	D	C	C	B	D	A	A	C

61	62	63	64	65	66	67	68	69	70
A	C	A	C	A	B	D	A	B	B

EXPLANATORY ANSWERS

1. $\left(\dfrac{x^b}{x^c}\right)^{\frac{1}{bc}} \cdot \left(\dfrac{x^c}{x^a}\right)^{\frac{1}{ca}} \cdot \left(\dfrac{x^a}{x^b}\right)^{\frac{1}{ab}}$

$= \left(x^{b-c}\right)^{\frac{1}{bc}} \cdot \left(x^{c-a}\right)^{\frac{1}{ca}} \cdot \left(x^{a-b}\right)^{\frac{1}{ab}}$

$= x^{\frac{b-c}{bc}} \cdot x^{\frac{c-a}{ca}} \cdot x^{\frac{a-b}{ab}}$

$= x^{\frac{1}{c}-\frac{1}{b}} \cdot x^{\frac{1}{a}-\frac{1}{c}} \cdot x^{\frac{1}{b}-\frac{1}{a}}$

$= x^{\frac{1}{c}-\frac{1}{b}+\frac{1}{a}-\frac{1}{c}+\frac{1}{b}-\frac{1}{a}}$

$= x^{0} = 1.$

2. The HCF of any two prime numbers a and $b = 1$.

3. 10, 15, 20, ... 95

nth term of AP $= a + (n-1)d$

$\Rightarrow \qquad 95 = 10 + (n-1)5$

$\Rightarrow \qquad 95 = 10 + 5n - 5$

$\Rightarrow \qquad 95 = 5n + 5$

$\Rightarrow \qquad n = 18$

Hence, required numbers = 18.

4. $\qquad 2x^2 + ax + b = 0$

Let one root $= \alpha \therefore$ other root $= \dfrac{1}{\alpha}$

Sum of the roots $= \alpha + \dfrac{1}{\alpha} = \dfrac{-a}{2}$

Product of the roots $= \alpha \times \dfrac{1}{\alpha} = \dfrac{b}{2}$

$\Rightarrow \qquad 1 = \dfrac{b}{2}$

$\Rightarrow \qquad b = 2.$

5.
$$\sin(A+B) = \cos(A-B)$$
$$\Rightarrow \quad \sin(A+B) = \sin[90° - (A-B)]$$
$$\Rightarrow \quad A + B = 90° - A - B$$
$$\Rightarrow \quad 2A = 90°$$
$$\Rightarrow \quad A = 45° = \frac{\pi}{4}$$

If $B = 0$, then $A + B = \dfrac{\pi}{4}$

If $B = 45°$, then $A + B = 90° = \dfrac{\pi}{2}$.

6. Mean of first ten even natural numbers

$$= \frac{2+4+6+8+10+12+14+16+18+20}{10}$$

$$= \frac{2(1+2+3+4+5+6+7+8+9+10)}{10}$$

$$= \frac{2 \times 10 \times 11}{2 \times 10} = 11.$$

7. Required ratio $= \dfrac{\dfrac{1}{3}\pi r^2 h}{\dfrac{2}{3}\pi r^3} = 1:2.$

8.

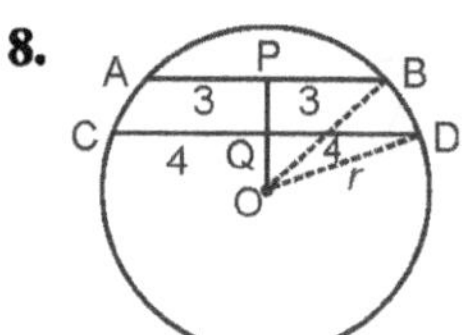

In Δ POB, $\qquad (OB)^2 = (3)^2 + (4)^2$
$$= 9 + 16 = 25$$
$\therefore \qquad OB = 5 = r$

In Δ OQD, $\qquad (OQ)^2 = (OD)^2 - (QD)^2$
$$= (5)^2 - (4)^2 = 25 - 16 = 9$$
$\therefore \qquad OQ = 3$ cm

Hence, the distance of the other chord from the centre
$$= 3 \text{ cm.}$$

9.

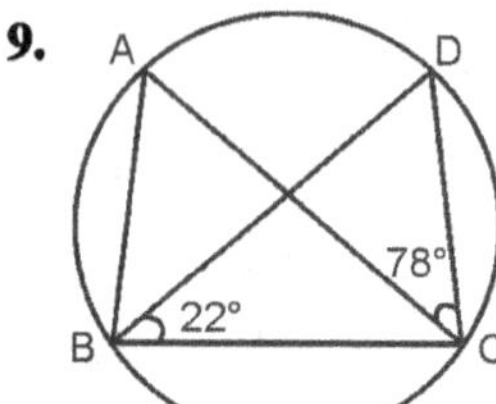

In Δ BDC, $\qquad \angle D = 180° - (22° + 78°)$
$$= 180° - 100° = 80°$$
$\therefore \qquad \angle BAC = 80°$

(Angle in the same segment).

10.

In Δ AOB, $\qquad \angle B = 80°$
$$\angle AOB = 180° - 115° = 65°$$
$\therefore \qquad \angle OAB = 180° - (80° + 65°)$
$$= 180° - 145° = 35°.$$

11. Let $|x| = y$
$$y^2 + y - 6 = 0$$
$$(y+3)(y-2) = 0$$
$$y = -3 \text{ or } y = 2$$
$$|x| = -3 \text{ which is not possible}$$
$$|x| = 2$$
$\therefore \qquad x = \pm 2$

Hence, the product of the roots is -4.

12. $\because \quad 3x = 12 \Rightarrow x = 4$

$$AE = \frac{\sqrt{3}}{2}(3x)$$

$$DE = AE - AD = \frac{3x}{2} - x = \frac{x}{2}$$

$$AD = \sqrt{AE^2 + DE^2} = \sqrt{\frac{27}{4}x^2 + \frac{x^2}{4}}$$

$$= \sqrt{\frac{28x^2}{4}} = \sqrt{7x^2} = \sqrt{7}x = 4\sqrt{7}.$$

13. Let,
$$\text{4th term} = x + 3d = a \qquad \qquad ...(i)$$
$$\text{7th term} = x + 6d = b \qquad \qquad ...(ii)$$
$$\text{10th term} = x + 9d = c$$

On solving (i) & (ii) we get
$$x = 2a - b$$
$$d = \frac{a - (2a-b)}{3}$$

10th term $= x + 9d = C$

$$2a - b + 9\left(\frac{a-(2a-b)}{3}\right) = C$$

$$2a - b + 3a - 6a + 3b = C$$
$$-a + 2b = C$$
$$2b = a + c$$

Sum of roots of equation
$$ax^2 - 2bx + c = 0$$

$$\text{sum of roots} = \frac{2b}{a} = \frac{a+c}{a}.$$

14. Let the number $= x$

$$\left(60\% \text{ of } x + \sqrt{x}\right) = \frac{1}{5}x + 5$$

$$\Rightarrow \quad \frac{60}{100} \times x + \sqrt{x} = \frac{x + 25}{5}$$

$$\Rightarrow \quad \sqrt{x} = \frac{x + 25}{5} - \frac{3x}{5}$$

$$\Rightarrow \quad \sqrt{x} = \frac{x + 25 - 3x}{5} = \frac{-2x + 25}{5}$$

$$\Rightarrow \quad x = \frac{4x^2 - 100x + 625}{25}$$

$$\Rightarrow \quad 4x^2 - 100x - 25x + 625 = 0$$
$$\Rightarrow \quad 4x(x - 25) - 25(x - 25) = 0$$
$$\Rightarrow \quad (x - 25)(4x - 25) = 0$$

either $\qquad\qquad x = 25$

or $\qquad\qquad x = \dfrac{25}{4} = 6.25$

Hence, required number $= 6.25$.

15. We have,

$$\frac{M_1 \times D_1 \times R_1}{W_1} = \frac{M_2 \times D_2 \times R_2}{W_2}$$

$$\Rightarrow \quad \frac{12 \times 12 \times 12}{12} = \frac{M_2 \times 4 \times 12}{16}$$

$$\therefore \quad M_2 = \frac{12 \times 12}{3} = 48$$

Hence, required no. of men
$$= 48 - 12 = 36.$$

16. Let the fraction $= \dfrac{x}{y}$

According to the question,

$$\frac{x + 60\% \text{ of } x}{y - 60\% \text{ of } y} = \frac{x + \dfrac{60}{100} \times x}{y - \dfrac{60}{100} \times y}$$

$$= \frac{160x}{100} \times \frac{100}{40y} = 4\frac{x}{y}$$

Hence, the new fraction is 4 times the older fraction.

17. One angle of a triangle $= 60°$

$\therefore$ Sum of two other angles
$$= 180 - 60 = 120°$$

Average of the other two angles
$$= \frac{120}{2} = 60°.$$

18. $\because \qquad$ Area of circle $=$ Area of square
$$\Rightarrow \qquad \pi r^2 = a^2$$

$$\Rightarrow \quad \frac{r^2}{a^2} = \frac{1}{\pi} = \frac{1}{\dfrac{22}{7}} = \frac{7}{22}$$

According to the question,

$$\frac{(2\pi r)^2}{(4a)^2} = \frac{4\pi^2 r^2}{16a^2}$$

$$= \frac{4}{16} \times \frac{22}{7} \times \frac{22}{7} \times \frac{7}{22} = \frac{11}{14}$$

Hence, required ratio $= 11 : 14$.

19. The last digit of the number $3^{2015} = 7$.

20. $\sqrt{\dfrac{49}{100}} = \dfrac{7}{10} \times 100 = 70\%.$

21. Required number of hand shakes take place

$$= {}^{12}C_2 = \frac{12!}{2! \times 10!}$$

$$= \frac{12 \times 11 \times 10!}{2 \times 1 \times 10!}$$

$$= 66.$$

22. $\qquad$ Required Speed $= \dfrac{2 \times 40 \times 60}{40 + 60}$

$$= \frac{2 \times 40 \times 60}{100} = 48 \text{ km/hr.}$$

23. $7 + 14 + 21 + 28 + ... + 700$
$$= 7(1 + 2 + 3 + 4 + ... + 100)$$

$$= \frac{7 \times 100 \times 101}{2}$$

$$= 7 \times 50 \times 101$$
$$= 707 \times 50 = 35350.$$

24. Let man travels x km by foot and $(80 - x)$ km by bicycle.

According to the question,

$$\frac{x}{8} + \frac{80 - x}{16} = 8$$

$$\Rightarrow \quad \frac{2x + 80 - x}{16} = 8$$

$$\Rightarrow \quad x + 80 = 128$$
$$\Rightarrow \quad x = 48$$

The distance travelled by the man on foot
$$= 48 \text{ km.}$$

25. Difference of price in ₹ 400

$$= 25\% \text{ of } ₹\ 400 = \frac{25}{100} \times 400 = ₹\ 100$$

Due to increase in the price of rice per kg

$$= \frac{100}{20} = ₹\ 5$$

$\therefore$ Increased price of rice = ₹ 5 per kg.

26. **Metal I**   **Metal II**

Let weight of $\therefore$ weight of metal II

metal I be x gram   is $(24 - x)$ gram

According to the question,

$$8(x) + 6(24 - x) = ₹\ 174$$
$$8x + 144 - 6x = 174$$
$$2x = 30 \Rightarrow x = 15$$

$\therefore$ weight of metal II = $24 - 15 = 9$ gram

Cost of metal II = $9 \times 6 = ₹\ 54$

$\because$ Cost of 9 gram metal = ₹ 54

Cost of 1 gram metal = $\dfrac{54}{9} = ₹\ 6$

Because $8 \times 9 + 15 \times 6 = 72 + 90 = ₹\ 162$.

27. L.C.M of 24, 60, 90 = 720

$$720 \text{ min} = \frac{720}{60} = 12 \text{ hrs}$$

At 10 PM all the three will chime again that day.

28. Last two digits of $15 \times 37 \times 63 \times 51 \times 97 \times 17 = 35$

29. Initial height from which the ball dropped = 120 m.

Now, In 1st rebounds & backing of ball to hit the floor, distance covered = $2 \times 120 \times \dfrac{4}{5}$

In 2nd rebound & backing of ball to hit the floor, distance covered = $2 \times 120 \times \dfrac{4}{5} \times \dfrac{4}{5}$

Similarly, In nth rebound & backing of ball to hit the floor distance covered

$$= 2 \times 120 \times \left(\frac{4}{5}\right)^n$$

In order to come to the rest, the ball complete infinite rebounding.

Hence, total distance covered

$$D = 120 + 2 \times 120 \left[\frac{4}{5} + \left(\frac{4}{5}\right)^2 \dots \infty\right]$$

$$= 120 + 2 \times 120 \times \frac{\dfrac{4}{5}}{1 - \left(\dfrac{4}{5}\right)}$$

$$= 180 + 960 = 1080 \text{ m}.$$

30. According to the question,

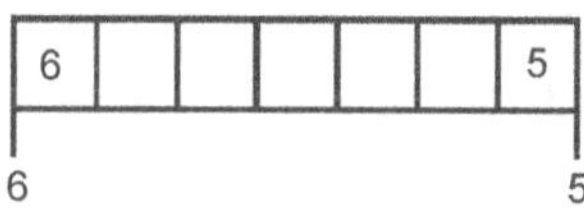

Number of way in which telephone numbers are possible

= Number of arrangement of 5 blank boxes by remaining 8 digits.

$$= {}^8P_5 = 6720.$$

31. $P(E_1) = \dfrac{3}{4}, \qquad P(\bar{E}_1) = 1 - \dfrac{3}{4} = \dfrac{1}{4}$

$P(E_2) = \dfrac{5}{6}, \qquad P(\bar{E}_2) = 1 - \dfrac{5}{6} = \dfrac{1}{6}.$

They will contradict each other if one speaks the truth and other does not.

Hence, $\quad P(E) = P(E_1) \times P(\bar{E}_2) + P(\bar{E}_1) \times P(E_2)$

$$= \frac{3}{4} \times \frac{1}{6} + \frac{1}{4} \times \frac{5}{6}$$

$$= \frac{1}{8} + \frac{5}{24} = \frac{3+5}{24} = \frac{8}{24} = \frac{1}{3}.$$

32. Let a be the side of the equilateral triangle. Radius of the circle = 2 cm

We have, $\qquad r = \dfrac{a}{2\sqrt{3}}$

$\Rightarrow \qquad\qquad 2 = \dfrac{a}{2\sqrt{3}}$

$\Rightarrow \qquad\qquad a = 4\sqrt{3}$

Area of triangle $= \dfrac{\sqrt{3}}{4}\left(4\sqrt{3}\right)^2$

$$= \frac{\sqrt{3}}{4} \times 48 = 12\sqrt{3} \text{ cm}^2.$$

33. A $\bullet$——$\bullet$——$\boxed{}$——$\bullet$ E
     C   D   B

$\therefore$ D is sitting in the centre.

34. $\left(\sqrt{9}\right)^3 \times \left(\sqrt{81}\right)^5 \div \left(\sqrt{27}\right)^2 = 3^{\frac{3}{2}} \times 3^{\frac{5}{4}} \div 3^{\frac{2}{3}}$

$$= 3^{\frac{3}{2} + \frac{5}{4} - \frac{2}{3}} = 3^{\frac{25}{12}}.$$

35. $\because$ To do a work in 12 days 18 men are required.

$\therefore$ To do a work in 1 day 18×12 men are required.

$\therefore$ To do a work in 8 days $\dfrac{18 \times 12}{8} = 27$ men.

MATHEMATICS

Number Systems

BODMAS - RULE

This rule is very important for the arithmetical simplification. When vinculum, brackets, of, division, multiplication, addition and subtraction all or two or more than two operations are present in any question, then we can find out the result (answer) with the help of **BODMAS** - rule. Details of BODMAS- rule are given below :

Order	Abbreviated Letter Used in rule	Meaning	Notation
1.	V	Vinculum or Bar	——
2.	B	Brackets	[ ], { }, ( )
3.	O	Of	of
4.	D	Division	÷
5.	M	Multiplication	×
6.	A	Addition	+
7.	S	Subtraction	−

Note :
- (*i*) Order of the letter which is used in BODMAS - rule is always fixed.
- (*ii*) Absence of any operation or more than one operations does not change the order of BODMAS.
- (*iii*) 'Of' means multiplication.

BRACKETS

When all brackets are present in a question, in that condition **ViCiCuSq-Rule** is applied. This ViCiCuSq-Rule stands for brackets and represents the order of calculation of brackets. Details are given below :

Order	Abbreviated Letter Used in rule	Meaning	Notation
1.	Vi	Vinculum	——
2.	Ci	Circular Bracket	( )
3.	Cu	Curly Bracket	{ }
4.	Sq	Square Bracket	[ ]

Note : This order of brackets (ViCiCuSq) is also fixed and not variable.

ADDITION

In the problem of addition we have two main factors (speed and accuracy) under consideration. We will discuss a method of addition which is faster than the method used by most people and also has a higher degree of accuracy. In the latter part of this chapter we will also discuss a method of checking and double-checking the results.

Meaning of Addition

Addition is the operation of finding a single number taken together. The result obtained by adding two or more numbers is termed as the sum or total. The numbers to be added are called 'addends'. The sign used for addition is '+' (*i.e.,* plus). We know that addition is a very simple process. Everybody knows to add but not many of those do know the correct way (time) to get the correct answer. Many of us have time consuming ways of adding numbers.

First of all while adding numbers, we avoid to say 7 plus 7 equal to 14 and 18 plus 12 equal to 30 etc. Instead as soon as we see 7 and 7 to be added , simply say '14'. Similarly for 18 and 12, merely say '30'.

It is also necessary that when we see a number like 151, we avoid saying one hundred and fifty one, simply say one fifty one.

As far as possible we use double columns method. But before going to use double columns method let us see how a single column method is used.

Rule I : Addition of Single Column Method

The time saving device is to place a dot (°) for each ten to be carried and add only units.

Example 1:

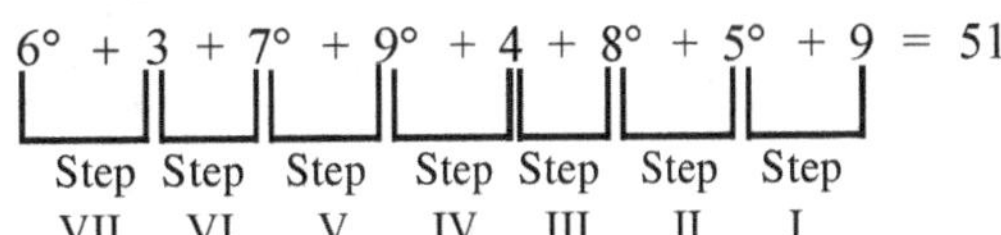

$$6° + 3 + 7° + 9° + 4 + 8° + 5° + 9 = 51$$

| | Step VII | Step VI | Step V | Step IV | Step III | Step II | Step I |

(*a*) 51   (*b*) 49
(*c*) 52   (*d*) 50
(*e*) None of these

Ans. (*a*)

Explanation : Starting from the right

Step I : $9 + 5 = 14$. Here, we say the unit figure only (only say 4). We place a dot for ten figure and take 4 for next step.

Step II : $4 + 8 = 12$. Again we take 2 for the next step and put a dot for ten figure.

Step III : $2 + 4 = 6$. We take only 6 because there is not a ten figure.

Step IV : $6 + 9 = 15$, We take 5 for the next step and put a dot for ten figure.

Step V : $5 + 7 = 12$. We take 2 for next step and place a dot for ten figure.

Step VI : $2 + 3 = 5$. Take 5 for next step.

Step VII : $5 + 6 = 11$. Here, we put a dot for ten figure and write only unit figure 1 in the answer.

There are five dots in (Step I + Step II + Step IV + Step V + Step VII), so, we place the number 5 at the ten figure digits. Thus, our answer will be 51.

Example 2 : Example 1 in another way

```
 6°
 3
 7°
 9°
 4
 8°
 5°
 9
―――
51
```

(*a*) 50   (*b*) 51
(*c*) 52   (*d*) 53
(*e*) None of these

Ans. (*b*)

Explanation : Here, starting from the bottom instead of 14, 22, 26. etc. we say the unit figure only placing a dot next to the number when we exceed 10. Thus, we say 4, 2, 6, 5, 2, 5, 1. The five dots indicate 50. Thus, 50 plus the last unit figure 1 is equal to 51.

Rule II : Addition of Double Columns Method

This method is very essential for quick work. Here, we add from 'tens' and then add its unit place as :

Example 1:
```
 98
 65
 32
 87
 54
 21
―――
357
```

(*a*) 355   (*b*) 356
(*c*) 358   (*d*) 357
(*e*) None of these

Ans. (*d*)

Explanation : The addition proceeds $21 + 50$ (of 54), *i.e.,* 71 and then 4 giving 75. 75 to 80 (of 87), *i.e.,* 155 and then 7 gives 162, $162 + 30$ (of 32), *i.e.,* 192 and then 2 giving 194, $194 + 60$ (of 65), *i.e.,* 254 and then 5 giving 259, $259 + 90$ (of 98) is 349 and then 8 giving 357.

Here, the figure which our eyes see and recognize should be 71, 75, 62, 94, 59, 57. The hundreds that we get during the process of addition can be placed beside the number where the total comes to a hundred.

Note : Starting from the top, we get the same process and same result.

Example 2 : We may apply the Double Columns Method for taking addition with more columns.

```
 4  6  9  7  8
 5  4  1  2  2
 2  8  5  7  9
 5  6  1  4  2
 4  5  2  1  3
―――――――――――――――
 2 3  1 0  3 4
```
Step III Step II Step I

(*a*) 231134   (*b*) 231034
(*c*) 231132   (*d*) 231032
(*e*) None of these

Ans. (*b*)

Explanation : Starting from the bottom right

Step I : First double column

     (*i.e.,* right 2 columns)

     $13 + 42 = 55, 55 + 79 = 134$

     $34 + 22 = 56, 56 + 78 = 134$

     Total = 234

     (*i.e.,* 34 written and 2 carried for next step)

Step II : Second double column

     $2 + 52 + 61 = 115, 15 + 85 = 100$

     $00 + 41 = 41 , 41 + 69 = 110$

     Total = 310

     (10 written and 3 carried for next step)

Step III : Last column

     $3 + 4 = 7, 7 + 5 = 12, 12 + 2 = 14,$

     $14 + 5 = 19, 19 + 4 = 23$

     Here, we write 23

        or

     $3 + 4 = 7 , 7 + 5 = 12, 2 + 2 = 4$

     $4 + 5 = 9, 9 + 4 = 13$ (3 for unit figure)

     Total 23

Thus, Result = 231034.

Rule III : Addition of Double Columns Method Horizontally

By double columns method, it is easy to add numbers horizontally even when the numbers of digits in each numbers are different.

Example :

$$36925 + 4563 + 321659 + 884 = ?$$

(a) 363140 (b) 364030
(c) 364031 (d) 364040
(e) None of these

Ans. (c)

Explanation :

Step I : First double column (starting from right hand side).

$84 + 59 = 143$, $43 + 63 = 106$,

$6 + 25 = 31$, Total = 231

(Here, we write 31 and carried 2 for next step)

Step II : Second double column is

$2 + 8 = 10$, $10 + 16 = 26$, $26 + 45 = 71$,

$71 + 69 = 140$ Total = 140

(We write 40 and carried 1 for next step)

Step III : Last double column is

$1 + 32 = 33$, $33 + 3 = 36$ (36 written)

The result is 364031.

Rule IV : Addition Including Decimal

For addition of numbers containing decimals addition should be used.

Example :

$$456.073 + 2.45 + 0.04 + 0.0004 + 485 = ?$$

(a) 943.5666 (b) 943.555
(c) 943.5634 (d) 943.56
(e) None of these

Ans. (c)

Explanation: Starting from right hand side of every term.

Step I : First double column is $04 + 30 = 34$

(Written 34, no carried)

Step II : Second double column is

$04 + 45 = 49 + 07 = 56$

(Written 56 and no carried)

Step III : Third double column is

$85 + 2 = 87$, $87 + 56 = 143$

(Written 43 and carried 1 for next step)

Step IV : Fourth column is

$1 + 4 = 5$, $5 + 4 = 9$

(Written 9 and no carried)

The decimal is placed after counting numbers from right hand side.

Thus, our result will be 943.5634.

Rule V : Sum of Consecutive *n*-natural Numbers

The sum of consecutive *n*-natural numbers

$$= \frac{n(n+1)}{2}$$

Example : $1 + 2 + 3 + 4 + 5 + 6 + 7 + 8 + 9 + 10 = ?$

Here, $n = 10$

Thus, sum $= \dfrac{10(10+1)}{2} = \dfrac{10 \times 11}{2} = 55$

Rule VI : Sum of X^{nth} Terms = ?

$$\boxed{\text{The sum of the } X^{nth} \text{ terms} = \frac{X.n(n+1)}{2}}$$

Example 1 : Give the sum of the 2^{10th}

Here, $X = 2$ and $n = 10$, then

$$\text{Sum} = \frac{2 \times 10(10+1)}{2} = 110$$

Example 2 : Give the sum of the 4^{20th} terms = ?

Here, $X = 4$ and $n = 20$ then

$$\text{Sum} = \frac{4 \times 20 \times (20+1)}{2} = \frac{4 \times 20 \times 21}{2} = 840$$

Rule VII : Sum of Squares of Consecutive *n*-natural Numbers

$$\boxed{\text{Sum of the squares of consecutive } n \text{ - natural numbers} = \frac{n(n+1)(2n+1)}{6}}$$

Example :

$$1^2 + 2^2 + 3^2 + 4^2 + 5^2 + ... + (10)^2 = ?$$

Here, $n = 10$, so

$$\text{sum} = \frac{10(10+1)(20+1)}{6} = \frac{10 \times 11 \times 21}{6} = 385$$

Rule VIII : Sum of Cubes of consecutive *n*-natural Numbers

$$\boxed{\text{Sum of the cubes of consecutive } n \text{-natural numbers} = \left[\frac{n(n+1)}{2}\right]^2}$$

Example : $1^3 + 2^3 + 3^3 + 4^3 + 5^3 + ... + (10)^3 = ?$

$$\text{sum} = \left[\frac{10(10+1)}{2}\right]^2 = 3025$$

Rule IX : Sum of Even Numbers

$$\boxed{\text{Sum of the consecutive } n\text{-even numbers} = X(X+1)}$$

Note : Here, $X = n/2$

Example : $2 + 4 + 6 + 8 + 10 = ?$

Here, $n = 10$, then $X = 5$

Thus, sum = $5 (5 + 1) = 30$

Rule X : Sum of Odd Numbers

$$\text{The sum of consecutive } n\text{-odd numbers} = \left[\frac{n+1}{2}\right]^2$$

Example : $1 + 3 + 5 + 7 + 9 + 11 = ?$

Here, $n = 11$, so sum $= \left[\frac{11+1}{2}\right]^2 = 36$

SUBTRACTION

Subtraction is the operation of finding what number is left when a smaller number is taken out from a greater number. The greater number is called minuend and the smaller number is called as the subtrahend and the number left is called the remainder or the difference. The sign used for this operation is '–'.

Rule 1 : Borrowing and Paying Back Method

This method is the quickest method of subtraction. This method is also called equal additions method.

Example : Suppose we have to subtract 55 from 91. Mentally, we have to increase the number to be subtracted to the nearest multiple of 10, *i.e.*, increase 55 to 60 by adding 5 to it. Mentally increase the other quantity by the same amount, *i.e.*, by 5. Therefore, the problem is 96 minus 60 *i.e.*, our answer is $96 - 60 = 36$.

Rule II : Vinculum Method

Note : But it is not necessary that we will get a positive number as we did this in the above example. Now, when we get the negative answer then, this method is :

$$
\begin{array}{r}
8\ 1\ 2 \\
-\ 5\ 3\ 4\ 2 \\
8\ 3\ 1\ 8 \\
-\ \underline{1\ 1\ 3\ 1} \\
\downarrow \mathrm{II}\ \downarrow \mathrm{I} \\
2\ 7\ 4\ 3
\end{array}
$$

or $\quad$ 2 6 5 7

  (*a*) 2547 $\qquad$ (*b*) 2678

  (*c*) 2657 $\qquad$ (*d*) 2675

  (*e*) None of these

Ans. (*c*)

Explanation : Starting from right top position.

Step I : $\quad$ First double column

$\quad$ $12 - 42 = - 30$ (or $\overline{30}$),

$\quad$ $-30 + 18 = -12$ (or $\overline{12}$)

$\quad$ $-12 - 31 = -43$ (or $\overline{43}$)

$\quad$ written $\overline{43}$, no carry.

Step II : Second double column

$\quad$ $8 - 53 = - 45$ (or $\overline{45}$), $- 45 + 83 = 38$

$\quad$ $38 - 11 = 27$, 27 written and no carry.

$\quad$ Here, we write $27\,\overline{43}$

The first double column total $= - 43$ or $\overline{43}$

and second double column total 27.

The answer is written as $27\,\overline{43}$. (The line above 43 is called a Vinculum). Then the value of this number is obviously,

$\quad$ $2700 - 43 = 2657$ which is our answer.

This method is known as VINCULUM METHOD.

Rule III : Double Column Addition and Subtraction Method

This method is useful when there is a series of additions and subtractions to be performed in a line.

$$
\begin{array}{r}
8\ 9\ 7\ 8 \\
-1\ 4\ 3\ 2 \\
+7\ 8\ 7\ 6 \\
-4\ 3\ 7\ 8 \\
+\underline{1\ 4\ 3\ 2} \\
1\ \underline{2\ 4\ 7}\ 6 \\
\downarrow\quad \downarrow \\
\mathrm{II}\quad \mathrm{I}
\end{array}
$$

  (*a*) 12380 $\qquad$ (*b*) 13380

  (*c*) 12476 $\qquad$ (*d*) None of these

Ans. (*c*)

Explanation : We should keep looking at the sign before the number and then adding and subtracting as the case may be starting from the top right position.

Step I $\quad$: First double column

$\quad$ $78 - 32 = 46$, $46 + 76 = \underline{122}$,

$\quad$ $22 - 78 = - 56$, $- 56 + 32 = - 24$

$\quad$ Total $1\,\overline{24}$, $1\,\overline{24}$ means $100 - 24 = 76$

$\quad$ So, 76 written and 0 carried.

Step II $\quad$: Second double column

$\quad$ $89 - 14 = 75$, $75 + 78 = \underline{153}$, $53 - 43 = 10$,

$\quad$ $10 + 14 = 24$

$\quad$ Total $\underline{124}$ which is written.

$\quad$ Thus, our answer will be 12476.

Example 2 :

$$
\begin{array}{r}
2\ 8\ 6 \\
-4\ 6\ 8\ 3 \\
+5\ 3\ 8\ 1 \\
-2\ 8\ 7\ 6 \\
+\underline{8\ 3\ 2\ 3} \\
6\ \underline{4\ 3\ 1} \\
\downarrow\quad \downarrow \\
\mathrm{II}\quad \mathrm{I}
\end{array}
$$

(a) 1634   (b) 3461
(c) 6431   (d) 5471
(e) None of these

Ans. (c)

Explanation : We should keep looking at the sign before the number and then adding and subtracting as the case may be.

Starting from the top right position.

Step I   : First double column
         $+ 86 - 83 = 3, 3 + 81 = 84,$
         $84 - 76 = 8$
         $8 + 23 = 31$ written 31 and no carry.

Step II   : Second double column
         $2 - 46 = - 44, - 44 + 53 = 9, 9 - 28 = -19$
         $- 19 + 83 = 64$ written 64 and no carry.
         Thus, our answer will be 6431.

Rule IV : Subtraction by Complementary Addition

This method is useful for those problems in which it is said that what should be added to a number to make a second number.

Example 1: $\underbrace{5748 + 3059 + ?}_{\text{I}} = \underbrace{9090}_{\text{II}}$

Step I   : Using double columns method
         Starting from right position
         $59 + 48 = 107 + 83 = 190$
         83 written and 1 carried.

Here, we add 83 because 83 is the lowest number which gives 190 when added to 107.

(190 because 90 is the last number of 9090).

Step II   : $1 + 57 = 58 + 30 = 88 + 2 = 90$
         Here, we write 2 and no carry.
         The answer will be 283.

Rule V : Austrian Method of Subtraction

Suppose we want to subtract a smaller number from a larger number then this method is useful for us. This is also very useful for those students who are appearing in the Banking Examination or Banking based Examination.

Example :

```
+ 6 3 2 4 8
-   1 7 6 5
-   2 4 3 2
-   3 1 8 7
-   8 8 7 6
T   S R Q P
↓   ↓ ↓ ↓ ↓
4   6 9 8 8
```

Mental Work : Different steps are involved.

Step I   : Starting from bottom right $6 + 7 + 2 + 5 = 20$. The number 8 is in front of 20. Here, we choose a number in which unit figure is

8 and this is nearest to 20 (Just greater than 20). Let this number be 28.

Then we subtract 20 from 28 $(28 - 20 = 8)$ and write this number below P and carry 2 for next step.

Step II   : $2 + 7 + 8 + 3 + 6 = 26$

The number 4 is in front of 26. Here, again we choose a number whose unit figure is 4 and is nearest to 26 (Just greater than 26). Let this number be 34. We subtract 26 from 34 $(34 - 26 = 8)$ and write this number below Q. Then we carry 3 for next step.

Step III : $3 + 8 + 1 + 4 + 7 = 23.$

The number 2 is in front of 23. Here, we choose such a number in which unit figure is 2 and is nearest to 23. This number is 32 (Just greater than 23). We subtract 23 from 32 $(32 - 23 = 9)$. Write this number below R and carried 3 for next step.

Step IV : $3 + 8 + 3 + 2 + 1 = 17.$

The number 3 is in front of 17. Here, again we choose such a number that unit figure will be 3 and is just nearest to 17. This number is 23. We subtract 17 from 23 $(23 - 17 = 6)$ and write this number below S and carried 2 for next step.

Step V   : $2 + 0 = 2.$ Here, 6 is in front of 2. We write $6 - 2 = 4$ below T.

Then the number below T S R Q P = 46988 is our required result.

Some Special Type Questions Based on Banking Examinations and their Tricky Solutions

If two given numbers are opposite, the unit digit (figure) of first is the tens digits (figure) of second and tens digit of first is the unit digit (figure) of second such that 34 and 43, then sum of the numbers is the addition of both figures of any number multiplied by 11 and difference of the numbers is the subtraction of higher figure minus lower figure of any number multiplied by 9.

Sum = (Addition of both the figures of any number) × 11

and

Difference = (Subtraction of higher figure – lower figure of any number) × 9

Example : Find the sum and difference of the numbers 43 and 34.

Here, 43 and 34 are opposite. The unit figure of first is 3 and is the tens figure of second. And tens figure of first is 4 and is the unit figure of second.

So, using the formula, sum = $(4 + 3) \times 11 = 77.$

And difference = $(4 - 3) \times 9 = 9$

MULTIPLICATION

We suggest you to remember the tables up to 30 because it saves some valuable time during calculation. Multiplication should be well commanded, because it is needed in almost every question of our concern.

Multiplication is the operation of finding the sum of a given number repeated as many times as there are units in the other given number. The sum thus obtained is called the 'product' of the two numbers. The number to be repeated or multiplied is called 'multiplicand'. The number which indicated how often the multiplicand is to be repeated is called the 'multiplier'.

DIFFERENT SHORT-CUT RULES FOR MULTIPLICATION

MULTIPLICATION BY 11

Step I : We prefix a zero to the multiplicand.

Step II : We write the answer one figure at a time, from right to left as in any multiplication. The figures of the answer are obtained by adding to each successive digit of the multiplicand its right neighbour.

If in the process of addition, we get a 2 digit number, we set down only the right digit thereof and carry the left digit. Some examples are here :

Example 1 : $5892 \times 11 = ?$

Solution :

Step I : Put down the last figure of 5892 as the right hand figure of the answer :

$$\frac{5892 \times 11}{2}$$

Step II : Each successive figure of 5892 is added to its right-hand neighbour. 9 plus 2 is 11, put 1 below the line and carry over 1. 8 plus 9 plus 1 is 18, put 8 below the line and carry over 1. 5 plus 8 plus 1 is 14, put 4 below the line and carry over 1.

$$\frac{5892 \times 11}{12}$$ (9 + 2 = 11, put 1 below the line and carry over 1)

$$\frac{5892 \times 11}{812}$$ (8 + 9 + 1 = 18, put 8 below the line and carry over 1)

$$\frac{5892 \times 11}{4812}$$ (5 + 8 + 1 = 14, put 4 below the line and carry over 1)

Step III : The first figure of 5892, 5 plus 1, becomes the left-hand figure of the answer :

$$\frac{5892 \times 11}{64812}$$. The answer is 64812.

As you see, each figure of the long number is used twice. It is first used as a 'number', and then, at the next step, it is used as a neighbour. Looking carefully, we can use just one rule instead of three rules, and this one rule can be called as "add the right neighbour" rule.

We must first write a zero in front of the given number, or at least imagine a zero there.

Then we apply the idea of adding the neighbour to every figure of the given number in turn :

$$\frac{05892 \times 11}{2}$$

As there is no neighbour on the right, so we add nothing.

$$\frac{05892 \times 11}{4812}$$ As we did earlier

$$\frac{05892 \times 11}{64812}$$ zero plus 5 plus carried over 1 to 6.

This example shows why we need the zero in front of the multiplicand. It is to remind us not to stop too soon. Without the zero in front, we might have neglected the last 6, we might then have thought that the answer was one 4812. The answer is longer than the given number by one digit, and the zero in front takes care of that.

MULTIPLICATION BY 12

This method is exactly the same as in the case of 11 except that we double each number before adding the right neighbour.

Example : 5324×12

Step I : $$\frac{05324 \times 12}{8}$$

(double the right hand figure and add zero, as there is no neighbour)

Step II : $$\frac{05324 \times 12}{88}$$ (double the 2 and add 4)

Step III : $$\frac{05324 \times 12}{888}$$ (double the 3 and add 2)

Step IV : $$\frac{05324 \times 12}{3888}$$

(double the 5 and add 3, put 3 below the line and carry over 1)

Step V : $$\frac{05324 \times 12}{63888}$$

(zero doubled is zero, plus 5 plus carried over 1)

The answer is 63888. If you go through it yourself you will find that the calculation goes very fast and is very easy.

Rule I : Short-Cut Method for Two-digit Multiplication

General Formula : A   B

          C   D

$A \times C/A \times D + B \times C/B \times D$

Here, there are three steps :

Step I : $B \times D$

Step II : $A \times D + B \times C$

Step III : $A \times C$

Example 1 : 35×72

$$\begin{array}{r} 35 \\ \times\ 72 \\ \hline 2520 \end{array}$$

Step I : $5 \times 2 = 10$ Here, write 0 and carry 1 for next step.

Step II : $(3 \times 2 + 7 \times 5) + 1 = 41 + 1 = 42$, we write 2 and again carry 4 for next step.

Step III : $(7 \times 3) + 4 = 21 + 4 = 25$, we write 25 and then we get our result $35 \times 72 = 2520$.

Example 2 : 41×75

Last step / Middle step / First step

30   7   5

So, $41 \times 75 = 3075$

Thus, we see that during the process of multiplication if the result obtained contains more than one digit, then we put down only the right digit and carry the remaining digit to the left.

MULTIPLICATION BY 13

To multiply any number by 13, we

" Treble each digit in turn and add its right neighbour".

This is the same as multiplying by 12 except that now we " treble" the " number" before we add its "neighbour".

If we want to multiply 9483 by 13, we proceed like this:

Step I : $\dfrac{09483 \times 13}{9}$

(treble the right hand figure and write it down as there is no neighbour on the right)

Step II : $\dfrac{09483 \times 13}{79}$

($8 \times 3 + 3 = 27$, write down 7 and carry over 2)

Step III : $\dfrac{09483 \times 13}{279}$

($4 \times 3 + 8 + 2 = 22$, write down 2 and carry over 2)

Step IV : $\dfrac{09483 \times 13}{3279}$

($9 \times 3 + 4 + 2 = 33$, write down 3 and carry over 3)

Step V : $\dfrac{09483 \times 13}{123279}$

($0 \times 3 + 9 + 3 = 12$, write it down)

The answer is 1,23,279.

Rule II : Multiplication of 2, Three digit Numbers

$$\begin{array}{r} A\ B\ C \\ \times\ D\ E\ F \\ \hline \end{array}$$

General Formula :

Step I : $C \times F$

Step II : $B \times F + C \times E$

Step III : $A \times F + C \times D + B \times E$

Step IV : $A \times E + B \times D$

Step V : $A \times D$

The required answer: $A \times D/A \times E + B \times D\ /A \times F + C \times D + B \times E/B \times F + C \times E/C \times F$

Example : 123×456

Solution :

$$\begin{array}{r} 123 \\ \times\ 456 \\ \hline 56088 \end{array}$$

Step I : $3 \times 6 = 18$, we write 8 and carry 1 for next step.

Step II : $(2 \times 6 + 3 \times 5) + 1 = 27 + 1 = 28$, we write 8 and carry 2 for next step.

Step III : $(1 \times 6 + 3 \times 4 + 2 \times 5) + 2 = 28 + 2 = 30$, we write 0 and carry 3 for next step.

Step IV : $(1 \times 5 + 2 \times 4) + 3 = 13 + 3 = 16$, we write 6 and carry 1 for next step.

Step V : $(1 \times 4) + 1 = 4 + 1 = 5$

Thus required answer is 56088.

Rule III : Multiplication of 2, Four digit Numbers

General Formula :

$$\begin{array}{r} AB\ \ CD \\ \times\ EF\ GH \\ \hline \end{array}$$

Step I : $D \times H$

Step II : $C \times H + D \times G$

Step III : $B \times H + F \times D + C \times G$

Step IV : $A \times H + E \times D + B \times G + C \times F$

Step V : $A \times G + C \times E + B \times F$

Step VI : $A \times F + B \times E$

Step VII : $A \times E$

The required answer : $D \times H/C \times H + D \times G/B \times H + F \times D + C \times G/A \times H + E \times D + B \times G + C \times F/A \times G + C \times E + B \times F/A \times F + B \times E/A \times E$

Example : $2\ 3\ 2\ 4$

$$\begin{array}{r} \times\ 5\ 2\ 6\ 7 \\ \hline 122\ 4\ 0\ 5\ 0\ 8 \end{array}$$

Step I : $4 \times 7 = 28$, We write 8 and carry 2 for Step II.

Step II : $2 \times 7 + 4 \times 6 + 2 = 40$
Again write 0 and then carry 4 for Step III.

Step III : $3 \times 7 + 4 \times 2 + 2 \times 6 + 4 = 45$.
We write 5 and carry 4 for Step IV.

Step IV : $2 \times 7 + 4 \times 5 + 3 \times 6 + 2 \times 2 + 4 = 60$.
We write 0 and carry 6 for Step V.

Step V : $2 \times 6 + 2 \times 5 + 3 \times 2 + 6 = 34$.
Write down 4 and carry 3 for Step VI.

Step VI : $2 \times 2 + 3 \times 5 + 3 = 22$
Write down 2 and carry 2 for Step VII.

Step VII : $2 \times 5 + 2 = 12$.
We write 12 finally and then get our result 12240508.

Rule VI : Special case when the units figures of the multiplicand and the multiplier together total 10 and the other figures are the same

Example : $45 \times 45 = ?$
Tens figure × (Tens figure + 1)
Unit figure × unit figure
$45 \times 45 = 4\,(4 + 1)\,(5 \times 5) = 2025$

Step I : To obtain the right part of the answer, multiply the unit (*i.e.*, the extreme right) digits of the two numbers.

Step II : To obtain the left part of the answer, multiply the other (*i.e.*, the tens digit) by one more than itself/themselves.

Rule VII : If the unit figure is same and the sum of tens figure is 10. Then the rule is

General Rule :

> | Tens figure × Tens figure + Unit figure |

> | (Unit figure)^2 ← Last two digits of the product. |

For Example : $86 \times 26 = 8 \times 2 + 6\,,\ 6 \times 6 = 2236$
$52 \times 52 = 5 \times 5 + 2\,,\ 2 \times 2 = 2704$

Rule VIII : The sum of unit figures is 5 and the tens figures are equal. Then the rule is :

General Rule :

> | (Tens figure)$^2 + \dfrac{1}{2} \times$ Tens figure |

> | (Unit figure)^2 ← Last two digits of the product. |

[**Note :** Tens digit must be an even number.]
Example: $83 \times 82 = 8^2 + \frac{1}{2} \times 8\,,\ 3 \times 2 = 6806$.

Rule IX : If the unit figures are same and the sum of tens figures is 5. Then

> | Rule = Tens figure × Tens figure + 1/2 × Unit figure |

> | (Unit figure)^2 ← Last two digits of the product. |

[**Note :** Ones digit must be an even number.]
For Example :

$36 \times 26 = \left(3 \times 2 + \dfrac{1}{2} \times 6\right),\ (6 \times 6) = 936$

Rule X : If the unit figures are 5 and difference between tens figure is 1, then the rule is

Rule = (Larger tens figure + 1) × (smaller tens figure), 75
Example : $35 \times 45 = (4 + 1) \times 3,\ 75 = 1575$.

Rule XI : If sum of the right digits (in sets of 2) of numbers is 50 and the other digits are the same

The method is

1   421
       <u>429</u>

    180609 $\left(4 \times 4 + \dfrac{1}{2} \times 4 \text{ and } 21 \times 29\right)$

2   9918
     <u>9932</u>
     9850 <u>1 0576</u> = 98505576
        2

$\left(99 \times 99 + \dfrac{1}{2} \times 99 \text{ and } 18 \times 32\right)$

Rule XII : The same method is useful for multiplying mixed fractions whose fractional parts together total 1 and whose integral parts are the same

$6\dfrac{1}{2} \times 6\dfrac{1}{2} = 42\dfrac{1}{4}$ (*i.e.*, 6×7 and $\dfrac{1}{4}$)

$5\dfrac{1}{4} \times 5\dfrac{3}{4} = 30\dfrac{3}{16}$

Rule XIII : Special Method for Squaring Numbers, Ending from 5

$(15)^2$	=	2<u>25</u>	$1 \times 2/25$
$(25)^2$	=	6<u>25</u>	$2 \times 3/25$
$(35)^2$	=	12<u>25</u>	$3 \times 4/25$
$(45)^2$	=	20<u>25</u>	$4 \times 5/25$
$(95)^2$	=	90<u>25</u>	$9 \times 10/25$
$(875)^2$	=	765<u>625</u>	$87 \times 88/25$
$(995)^2$	=	990<u>025</u>	$99 \times 100/25$
$(1005)^2$	=	1010<u>025</u>	$100 \times 101/25$
$(1245)^2$	=	1550<u>025</u>	$124 \times 125/25$

Rule XIV : In two numbers, if sum of fractional parts is 1/2 and integral parts of both numbers are same

$8\dfrac{1}{4} \times 8\dfrac{1}{4} = 68\dfrac{1}{16}$

$\left(8 \times 8 + \dfrac{1}{2} \times 8 \text{ for the integral part and } \dfrac{1}{4} \times \dfrac{1}{4} \text{ for the fractional part}\right)$

Rule XV : Multiplication of a given number by a power of 5.

We put as many zeros to the right of multiplicand as is the number of the power of 5 and we divide the number so formed by 2 to the same power as is the number of 5.

Example: $1478 \times 625 = ?$

We know $625 = 5^4$

$$\therefore \quad 1478 \times 625 = \frac{14780000}{2^4} = \frac{14780000}{16} = 923750$$

Rule XVI : Multiplication of a given number by 9, 99, 999, 9999, 99999 etc.

We place as many zeros to the right of the multiplicand as is the number of nines and from the number so formed, subtract the multiplicand to get the answer.

Example: $7832 \times 9999 = ?$

So, $7832 \times 9999 = 78320000 - 7832 = 78312168$

Rule XVII : Multiplication by Repeating Number 1

Example : $5423 \times 111 = ?$

Step I : We write down the first right side digit of 5423 *i.e.*, 3.

Step II : We write down the sum of two right side digit of 5423 *i.e.*, $2 + 3 = 5$.

Step III : Again write down the sum of the three right side digit of 5423 *i.e.*, $4 + 2 + 3 = 9$.

[Here, we never exceed from three because 111 is made of three numbers.]

Step IV : We write down the sum of next three right side digits 5423 *i.e.*, $5 + 4 + 2 = 11$.

Step V : We write down the sum of next two digits $5 + 4$ and add $1 = 10$ of the number 5423.

Step VI : At last we write the last digit $5 + 1 = 6$.

Required answer = 601953

$5423 \times 111 = ?$

V	U	T	Z	Y	X
$5 + 1$	$5 + 4 + 1$	$5 + 4 + 2$	$4 + 2 + 3$	$2 + 3$	3
6	10	11	9	5	3
↓	↓	↓	↓	↓	↓
6th Step	5th Step	4th Step	3rd Step	2nd Step	1st Step

Required answer = 601953.

Rule XVIII : Multiplication by Repeating Number 2

In this process the multiplication and general rule both are same, like Rule XVII but only difference is that we multiply every digit of XYZT..... by 2.

Example : $234 \times 22 = ?$

T	Z	Y	X
$2 \times 2 + 1$	$2 (2 + 3) + 1$	$2 (3 + 4)$	2×4
↓	↓	↓	↓
5	1	4	8
4th Step	3rd Step	2nd Step	1st Step

Required answer = 5148.

DIVISION

We now go on to the quicker Math's of at-sight division which is based on long-established Vedic process of mathematical calculations. Different from "for the special cases", it is capable of immediate application to all cases and it can be described as the "crowning gem of all" for the universality of its applications.

Rule I : Test of divisibility by 2

A given number is divisible by 2, if the unit digit in the number is any of 2, 4, 6, 8 and 0.

Example : The numbers 96712, 34504, 26436, 648, 243980 end in 2, 4, 6, 8 and 0 respectively so they all are divisible by 2.

Rule II : Test of Divisibility by 3

A given number is divisible by 3, if the sum of the digits of a number is divisible by 3.

Example : The number 537240 is divisible by 3 because sum of its digits = $5 + 3 + 7 + 2 + 4 + 0 = 21$ which is divisible by 3.

Rule III : Test of divisibility by 4

A given number is divisible by 4, if the number formed by last two digits is divisible by 4.

Example : The number 539624 is divisible by 4, since the number formed by last two digits is 24, which is divisible by 4.

And the number 674238 is not divisible by 4 since the number formed by last two digits is 38, which is not divisible by 4.

Rule IV : Test of Divisibility by 5

A given number is divisible by 5 if the unit digit is either 0 or 5.

Example : The number 5176580 and 672385 end in 0 and 5 respectively so both of them are divisible by 5.

Rule V : Test of divisibility by 6

A given number is divisible by 6 if this number is divisible by 2 and 3 both.

Example : 24 is divisible by 6 because 24 is divisible by 2 and 3 both.

Rule VI : Test of divisibility by 8

A given number is divisible by 8, if the number formed by last three digits is divisible by 8.

Example : The number 36597512 is divisible by 8, since the number formed by the last three digits is 512 which is divisible by 8. But the number 31527412 is not divisible by 8, since the number formed by the last three digits is 412, which is not divisible by 8.

Rule VII : Test of Divisibility by 9

A given number is divisible by 9, if the sum of the digits of a number is divisible by 9.

Example : The number 586431 is divisible by 9 because sum of its digits = 5 + 8 + 6 + 4 + 3 + 1 = 27 which is divisible by 9.

The number 586432 is not divisible by 9 because sum of digits 5 + 8 + 6 + 4 + 3 + 2 = 28, which is not divisible by 9.

Rule VIII : Test of Divisibility by 10

Any number that ends in zero is divisible by 10.

Example : The number 87670 is divisible by 10 because this number ends in zero.

Rule IX : Test of Divisibility by 11

A given number is divisible by 11, if the difference of the sum of its digits in odd places and the sum of its digits in even places, is either zero or divisible by 11.

Example : The number 4832718 is divisible by 11 because sum of digits in odd places = 8 + 7 + 3 + 4 = 22.

Sum of digits in even places = 1 + 2 + 8 = 11

Difference = 22 – 11 = 11, which is divisible by 11, Hence, 4832718 is divisible by 11.

Rule X : Test of Divisibility by 12

A given number is divisible by 12 if the number is divisible by 3 and 4 both.

Example : The number 96 is divisible by 12, because this number is divisible by 3 and 4 both.

Rule XI : Multiples of a Number

A number which is divisible by a given number *'a'* is called its multiple *i.e.,* 3, 6, 9, 12 etc. are all multiples of 3.

Rule XII : If in any number the digit repeats thrice then this number will be divisible by 3 and 37

Example : 222, 777, 131313, 212121

Rule XIII : If in a number any digit repeats six times then this number must be divisible by 3,7,11,13

Example : 222222, 777777,

Rule XIV : If any number is divided in three groups and the difference between the numbers at even places and odd places is 0 or divisible by 7 then this number must be divisible by 7.

Example : 231622342 divides into three groups as

231	622	342
1st	2nd	3rd
group	group	group
odd	even	odd

$$\frac{622}{even} - \frac{(231+342)}{odd} = 49$$

which is divisible by 7.

Other Points :

1. **Dividend :** The number to be divided is called the dividend.

2. **Divisor :** The number by which it is divided is called the divisor.

3. **Quotient :** The number which tells how many times the divisor is contained in the dividend is called the quotient.

4. **Remainder :** If the dividend does not contain the divisor on exact number of times and we take away from the dividend as many times the divisor as we can, what is left is called the remainder. When there is no remainder, the division is called to be exact.

5. In inexact division

   Dividend = (Divisor × Quotient + Remainder)

6. In exact division

   Dividend ÷ Divisor = Quotient

7. Quotient × Divisor = Dividend

8. Divisor = $\dfrac{\text{Dividend} - \text{Remainder}}{\text{Quotient}}$

9. True Remainder = (First Remainder) + (Second Remainder × First Divisor) + (Third Remainder × First divisor × Second Divisor) and so on.

If a given number is divided by another number using factors, then the true remainder is obtained from successive remainders by using the above formula.

Example : A number when divided by 899 gives a remainder 63. The remainder, when the same number is divided by 29 is

$$\text{Number} = 899 \times \text{Quotient} + 63$$
$$= 29 \times 31 \text{ Quotient} + 2 \times 29 + 5$$

So, the remainder obtained by dividing the number by 29 is clearly 5.

Rule I : Division by 9, 99, 999, ... etc.

Rule II : Division by 5, 15, 35 and 45

If we want to divide a number by 5, 15, 35 and 45 then first of all we multiply the given number by 2 and then divide it by 10, 30, 70, 90 respectively, after calculation we get the result.

Step I : The given number is multiplied by 2.

Step II : Divide the number (found from step 1) by 10, 30, 70, 90 for 5, 15, 35, 45, respectively.

Example : 285 ÷ 45.

Step I : Multiply the dividend by 2, *i.e.,* 285 × 2 = 570.

Step II : Divide the result of step 1 by 90 *i.e.,* 570 ÷ 90 = 6.3.

Rule III : Division by 100000, 10000, 1000, 100, 10

If we want to divide any number by 10, 100, 1000, 10000, 100000, ... etc., then first of all we count the zeros. Write the number which is to be divided, count the digits of the number from the right hand side which is equal to the number of zeros and put decimal at that point. The right hand side of the decimal is known as remainder and left hand side of the decimal is known as quotient.

Example : $66666 \div 100 = ?$

Step I : 'Count the zero'. There are two zeros here.

Step II : In the dividend a decimal is given as the digits of the number from R.H.S. which is equal to the number of zeros.

666.66

Step III : R.H.S. of the number is 66 which is known as Remainder.

Step IV : L.H.S. of the number is 666 which is required Quotient.

Rule IV : Division by 25 and 75

If we want to divide any number by 25 and 75 then first of all, we multiply the number by 4 and then divide by 100 and 300 respectively for finding real remainder, we divide the remainder by 4. The process same as Rule II.

Step I : Multiply the number by 4.

Step II : Divide the number (from step 1) by 100 or 300.

Step III : Divide remainder by 4 to get the real remainder.

Example : $7878 \div 25 = ?$

Step I : Multiply the number by 4

$7878 \times 4 = 31512$

Step II : Divide the number (from step 1) by 100

$31512/100 = 315.12$

Step III : Real remainder $12/4 = 3$.

Rule V : Division by two digit Number

Example : $1701 \div 21 = ?$

As before, separate the divisor 21 into parts as 2/1

This means that

(1) We have to put a decimal after one place from the right in the dividend, *i.e.,* as 170.1 and

(2) That we are going to divide only by the left digit 2 (of the divisor 21) and not by 21 itself.

Our 1st A.D. is the first digit 1 of 1701 but since 1 will not go in 2, we bring down the 1st 2 digits 17 as the A.D. (as in any conventional division). To indicate that 17 has been brought down, the 17 had been underlined in the working. The subsequent steps are shown below :

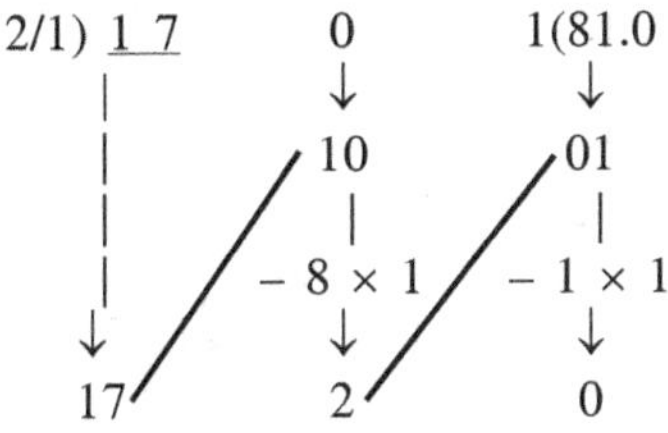

Rule VI : Three Digit divisors

Example : Divide 7031985 by 823.

Step I : Here, the divisor is of 3 digits. All the difference which we make is to put the last two digits (23) of divisor on top. And there are two flag-digits (23), We will separate two digits (85) for remainder.

$$8^{23} \mid \quad 70 \quad 3 \quad 1 \quad 9 \mid 85$$

Step II : We divide 70 by 8 and put down 8 and 6 in their proper places.

$$8^{23} \mid \quad 70 \quad {}_6 3 \quad 1 \quad 9 \mid 85$$
$$8$$

Step III : Now, our gross dividend is 63. From that we subtract 16, the product of the first of the flag-digits, *i.e.,* 2, and the first quotient-digit, *i.e.,* 8, and get the remainder $63 - 16 = 47$ as the actual dividend. And, dividing it by 8, we have 5 and 7 as Q and R respectively and put them at their proper places.

$$8^{23} \mid \quad 70 \quad {}_6 3 \quad {}_7 1 \quad 9 \mid 85$$
$$8 \quad 5$$

Step IV : Now our gross dividend is 71, and we deduct the cross-products of two flag-digits 23 and the two quotient digits (8 and 5), *i.e.,* $2 \times 5 + 3 \times 8 = 10 + 24 = 34$; and our remainder is $71 - 34 = 37$. We then continue to divide 37 by 8. We get $Q = 4$ & $R = 5$

$$8^{23} \mid \quad 70 \quad {}_6 3 \quad {}_7 1 \quad {}_5 9 \mid 85$$
$$8 \quad 5 \quad 4$$

Step V : Now our gross dividend is 59. And actual dividend is equal to 59 minus cross- product of 23 and 54, *i.e.,* $59 - (2 \times 4 + 3 \times 5) = 59 - 23 = 36$

Dividing 36 by 8, our $Q = 4$ and $R = 4$

$$8^{23} \mid \quad 70 \quad {}_6 3 \quad {}_7 1 \quad {}_5 9 \mid {}_4 85$$
$$8 \quad 5 \quad 4 \quad 4$$

Step VI : Actual dividend $= 48 - (3 \times 4 + 2 \times 4)$
$$= 48 - 20 = 28$$

Dividing it by 8, our $Q = 3$ and $R = 4$

$$8^{23} \mid \quad 70 \quad {}_6 3 \quad {}_7 1 \quad {}_5 9 \mid {}_4 8 {}_4 5$$
$$8 \quad 5 \quad 4 \quad 4 \mid 3$$

Step VII : Actual dividend $= 45 - (3 \times 4 + 2 \times 3)$
$$= 45 - 18 = 27.$$

Dividing 27 by 8, we have $Q = 3$ and $R = 3$.

$$8^{23} \mid \quad 70 \quad {}_6 3 \quad {}_7 1 \quad {}_5 9 \mid {}_4 8 {}_4 5 {}_3$$
$$8 \quad 5 \quad 4 \quad 4 \mid 3 \ 3$$

The vertical line separating the remainder from the quotient part may be a demarcation point for decimal.

Ans. 8544.33

Our answer can be 8544.33, but if we want the quotient and remainder, the procedure is somewhat different. In that case, we do not need the last two steps, *i.e.*, the calculation up to the stage

$$\begin{array}{c|cccc} 8^{23} & 70 & _6 3 & _7 1 & _5 9 \, | \, _4 85 \\ \hline & 8 & 5 & 4 & 4 \, | \end{array}$$

is sufficient to answer the question.

Quotient = 8544 ; Remainder = 485 – 10 × (Cross multiplication of 23 and 44) * – last digit of flag × last digit of quotient

$$= 485 - 10 \, (4 \times 2 + 4 \times 3) - 3 \times 4$$
$$= 485 - 200 - 12 = 273$$

APPLICATION OF ALGEBRAIC FORMULA IN SIMPLIFICATION

In competitive examinations some questions can be solved very easily maintaining speed and accuracy by using algebraic formulae than the use of the other method.

Example :

$$\frac{0.05 \times 0.05 \times 0.05 + 0.04 \times 0.04 \times 0.04}{0.05 \times 0.05 - 0.05 \times 0.04 + 0.04 \times 0.04} = ?$$

(*a*) 0.09 (*b*) 0.01
(*c*) 0.009 (*d*) 0.01
(*e*) None of these

Solution : General method

$$\frac{0.05 \times 0.05 \times 0.05 + 0.04 \times 0.04 \times 0.04}{0.05 \times 0.05 - 0.05 \times 0.04 + 0.04 \times 0.04} =$$

$$= \frac{0.000125 + 0.000064}{0.0025 - 0.002 + 0.0016} = \frac{0.000189}{0.0021}$$

$$= \frac{0.000189}{0.002100} = \frac{189}{2100} = \frac{189}{21 \times 100} = \frac{9}{100} = 0.09$$

By using Algebraic formula

$$\frac{0.05 \times 0.05 \times 0.05 + 0.04 \times 0.04 \times 0.04}{0.05 \times 0.05 - 0.05 \times 0.04 + 0.04 \times 0.04} = ?$$

$$= \frac{(0.05)^3 + (0.04)^3}{(0.05)^2 - 0.05 \times 0.04 + (0.04)^2}$$
$$= 0.09$$

$$\left[\frac{a^3 + b^3}{a^2 - ab + b^2} = a + b \right]$$

It is clear that this problem is solved in the minimum time by using algebraic formula.

So, algebraic formulae are very useful in the field of simplification. Therefore candidates are suggested to remember these important algebraic formulae for fast calculation and accuracy :

* Cross multiplication of two flag digits and last two digits of quotient.

1. $a^2 - b^2 = (a + b)(a - b)$

2. $\dfrac{a^2 - b^2}{a + b} = a - b$

3. $\dfrac{a^2 - b^2}{a - b} = a + b$

4. $(a + b)^2 + (a - b)^2 = 2 \, (a^2 + b^2)$

5. $(a + b)^2 - (a - b)^2 = 4ab$

6. $\dfrac{a^3 - b^3}{a^2 + ab + b^2} = a - b$

7. $\dfrac{a^3 + b^3 + c^3 - 3abc}{a^2 + b^2 + c^2 - ab - ac - bc} = a + b + c$

8. $(a + b)^3 = a^3 + 3ab \, (a + b) + b^3$
$= a^3 + 3a^2 b + 3ab^2 + b^3$

9. $(a - b)^3 = a^3 - 3ab \, (a - b) - b^3$
$= a^3 - 3a^2 b + 3ab^2 - b^3$

10. $a^3 - b^3 = (a - b) \, (a^2 + ab + b^2)$

11. $a^3 + b^3 = (a + b) \, (a^2 - ab + b^2)$

12. $(a + b)^2 = a^2 + 2ab + b^2$

13. $(a - b)^2 = a^2 - 2ab + b^2$

EXERCISE

1. ? % of 150 + 250 = 280
(*a*) 30 (*b*) 10
(*c*) 20 (*d*) 40
(*e*) None of these

2. 25 % of 40 ÷ 4 % of 25 = ?
(*a*) 10 (*b*) 1
(*c*) 0 (*d*) 2
(*e*) None of these

3. 75 % of 96 = ? × 12
(*a*) 72 (*b*) 6
(*c*) 12 (*d*) 96
(*e*) None of these

4. 73.85 + 215.345 – 167.2134 = ?
(*a*) 456.4084 (*b*) 121.2166
(*c*) 120.8296 (*d*) 121.6711
(*e*) None of these

5. 30 % of 270 + 5/8 of 64 = ?
- (*a*) 121
- (*b*) 81
- (*c*) 40
- (*d*) 242
- (*e*) None of these

6. $\dfrac{2.4 \times 3.2 + 4.32}{0.5 \times 24}$ = ?
- (*a*) 4
- (*b*) 0.5
- (*c*) 1.504
- (*d*) 1
- (*e*) None of these

7. 9.75 + 25.88 + ? = 41.18
- (*a*) 5.55
- (*b*) 5.75
- (*c*) 6.57
- (*d*) 4.23
- (*e*) None of these

8. $\dfrac{1344 \div 24 + 104}{202.1 - 198.9}$ = ?
- (*a*) 50
- (*b*) 500
- (*c*) 0.50
- (*d*) 25
- (*e*) None of these

9. $\dfrac{17.82 + 17.18 - 5}{(30)^2 \div 3}$ = ?
- (*a*) 10/1
- (*b*) 1/10
- (*c*) 10/100
- (*d*) 100/30
- (*e*) None of these

10. $22 + 5\dfrac{1}{3} + 1\dfrac{1}{2} - 9\dfrac{3}{5} \div \dfrac{2}{5}$ = ?
- (*a*) $4\dfrac{1}{2}$
- (*b*) $3\dfrac{1}{2}$
- (*c*) $2\dfrac{1}{3}$
- (*d*) $5\dfrac{1}{6}$
- (*e*) None of these

11. 3.6 − 1.2 ÷ 5.76 = ?
- (*a*) 3.381
- (*b*) 3.401
- (*c*) 4.391
- (*d*) 2.391
- (*e*) None of these

12. $\dfrac{11 - 4 \times 3 + 7}{20 - 5 \times 4 + 12}$ = ?
- (*a*) 0.1
- (*b*) 0.2
- (*c*) 0.3
- (*d*) 0.4
- (*e*) None of these

13. $\dfrac{\sqrt{324}}{36} \times \dfrac{\sqrt{729}}{9} \times \dfrac{\sqrt{25}}{196}$ = ?
- (*a*) 135/14
- (*b*) 18/5
- (*c*) 18/7
- (*d*) 9/17
- (*e*) None of these

14. 13.243 + 5.409 + ? = 24.71
- (*a*) 5.78
- (*b*) 4.718
- (*c*) 4.818
- (*d*) 5.818
- (*e*) None of these

15. 16 % of 40 = ? % of 1
- (*a*) 6.40
- (*b*) 0.640
- (*c*) 640
- (*d*) 450
- (*e*) None of these

16. 7.02 + 7.2 − 2.2 = ?
- (*a*) 12.2
- (*b*) 12.0
- (*c*) 12.02
- (*d*) 12.002
- (*e*) None of these

17. ? % of 346 = 10.38
- (*a*) 5
- (*b*) 7
- (*c*) 9
- (*d*) 4
- (*e*) None of these

18. $3\dfrac{1}{3} + ? - 2\dfrac{3}{4} = 2\dfrac{29}{36}$
- (*a*) $2\dfrac{7}{9}$
- (*b*) $\dfrac{7}{9}$
- (*c*) $1\dfrac{1}{7}$
- (*d*) $1\dfrac{17}{18}$
- (*e*) None of these

19. 288 ÷ 24 ÷ 0.12 = ?
- (*a*) 100
- (*b*) 12
- (*c*) 12.12
- (*d*) 1.44
- (*e*) None of these

20. $\dfrac{8 + 6 \times 2 - 9}{3 + 7 \times 3 - 9}$ = ?
- (*a*) $1\dfrac{1}{4}$
- (*b*) 4/9
- (*c*) 11/15
- (*d*) 19/21
- (*e*) None of these

21. 1/2 + 1/3 + ? = 3/2
- (*a*) $2\dfrac{1}{5}$
- (*b*) $1\dfrac{1}{10}$
- (*c*) $\dfrac{2}{3}$
- (*d*) $1\dfrac{1}{3}$
- (*e*) None of these

22. 60 % of 30 = ? % of 200
- (*a*) 18
- (*b*) 36
- (*c*) 40
- (*d*) 9
- (*e*) None of these

23. 5/4 × 200/67 ÷ 20/67 = ?
- (*a*) 0.125
- (*b*) 125
- (*c*) 12.5
- (*d*) 1250
- (*e*) None of these

24. $\dfrac{36 + 6 - 2 \times 2}{72 - 14 \times 5} = ?$

   (*a*) 1/2   (*b*) 1/240
   (*c*) 15/2   (*d*) 3
   (*e*) None of these

25. $\dfrac{\sqrt{625}}{5} \times \dfrac{\sqrt{144}}{3} \times 0.07 = ?$

   (*a*) 140   (*b*) 14.0
   (*c*) 0.140   (*d*) 1.40
   (*e*) None of these

EXPLANATORY ANSWERS

1. (*c*): x % of $150 + 250 = 280$

$$\therefore \quad \frac{x \times 150}{100} = 30$$

$$\therefore \quad x = \frac{30 \times 100}{150} = 20.$$

2. (*a*): $\dfrac{25 \times 40}{100} \times \dfrac{100}{25 \times 4} = 10.$

3. (*b*): $\dfrac{75}{100} \times 96 = 12\, x$

$$\therefore \quad x = \frac{96 \times 75}{12 \times 100} = 6.$$

4. (*e*): 121.9816.

5. (*a*): $\dfrac{30}{100} \times 270 + \dfrac{5}{8} \times 64 = 81 + 40 = 121$

6. (*d*): $\dfrac{2.4 \times 3.2 + 4.32}{0.5 \times 24} = \dfrac{7.68 + 4.32}{12} = \dfrac{12}{12} = 1$

7. (*a*): $X = 41.18 - 9.75 - 25.88 = 5.55.$

8 (*a*): $\dfrac{56 + 104}{3.2} = \dfrac{160}{32} \times 10 = 50.$

9. (*b*): $\dfrac{35 - 5}{900 \div 3} = \dfrac{30}{300} = \dfrac{1}{10}.$

10. (*e*): $22 + \dfrac{16}{3} + \dfrac{3}{2} - \dfrac{48}{5} \times \dfrac{5}{2} = \dfrac{29}{6} = 4\dfrac{5}{6}.$

11. (*e*): $3.6 - \dfrac{120}{576} = 3.6 - 0.208 = 3.392.$

12. (*e*): $\dfrac{11 - 12 + 7}{20 - 20 + 12} = \dfrac{6}{12} = 0.5.$

13. (*e*): $\dfrac{18}{36} \times \dfrac{27}{9} \times \dfrac{5}{196} = \dfrac{15}{392}.$

14. (*e*): 6.058.

15. (*c*): $x = \dfrac{16 \times 40}{100} \times 100 = 640.$

16. (*c*): $14.22 - 2.2 = 12.02.$

17. (*e*): $\dfrac{x}{100} \times 346 = 10.38$

$$\therefore \quad x = \frac{1038}{346} \times \frac{100}{100} = 3.$$

18. (*e*): $3\dfrac{1}{3} + x - 2\dfrac{3}{4} = 2\dfrac{29}{36}$

$$\Rightarrow \quad x = 2\dfrac{29}{36} + 2\dfrac{3}{4} - 3\dfrac{1}{3}$$

$$= 2 + 2 - 3 + (29/36 + 3/4 - 1/3)$$

$$= 1 + 44/36 = 1 + \frac{11}{9} = 1\frac{11}{9}$$

19. (*a*): $288 \div 24 \div 0.12$

$$= 288 \times \frac{1}{24} \times \frac{1}{0.12}$$

$$= \frac{12}{12} \times 100 = 100$$

20. (*c*): $\dfrac{8 + 12 - 9}{3 + 21 - 9} = \dfrac{20 - 9}{24 - 9} = \dfrac{11}{15}.$

21. (*c*): $1/2 + 1/3 + ? = 3/2$

$$\therefore \quad x = 3/2 - 5/6$$

$$= \frac{9 - 5}{6} = \frac{4}{6} = \frac{2}{3}.$$

22. (*d*): $\dfrac{60}{100} \times 30 = \dfrac{x}{100} \times 200$

$$\Rightarrow \quad 18 = 2\, x$$

$$\Rightarrow \quad x = 9$$

23. (*c*): $\dfrac{5}{4} \times \dfrac{200}{67} \times \dfrac{67}{20} = \dfrac{25}{2} = 12.5.$

24. (*e*): $\dfrac{36 + 6 - 4}{72 - 70} = \dfrac{38}{2} = 19.$

25. (*d*): $\dfrac{25}{5} \times \dfrac{12}{3} \times 0.07 = 1.40.$

Powers And Roots Square, Cube, Indices, Surds Squaring

Squaring of a number is largely used in mathematical calculations. There are so many rules for special cases. But we will discuss a general rule for squaring which is capable of universal application.

Squaring is multiplying the number by itself. For example,

$$25^2 = 25 \times 25 = 625$$

When the number is large, squaring by simple multiplication is obviously not very easy.

You should remember the following squares which will help you in taking square roots :

$1^2 = 1$	$11^2 = 121$	$21^2 = 441$
$2^2 = 4$	$12^2 = 144$	$22^2 = 484$
$3^2 = 9$	$13^2 = 169$	$23^2 = 529$
$4^2 = 16$	$14^2 = 196$	$24^2 = 576$
$5^2 = 25$	$15^2 = 225$	$25^2 = 625$
$6^2 = 36$	$16^2 = 256$	$26^2 = 676$
$7^2 = 49$	$17^2 = 289$	$27^2 = 729$
$8^2 = 64$	$18^2 = 324$	$28^2 = 784$
$9^2 = 81$	$19^2 = 361$	$29^2 = 841$
$10^2 = 100$	$20^2 = 400$	$30^2 = 900$

Short Methods in Squaring

Let a, b denote numbers

$$a^2 = a^2 - b^2 + b^2 = (a^2 - b^2) + b^2$$

or
$$a^2 = [(a + b)(a - b)] + b^2 \quad ...(I)$$
$$(a + b)^2 = a^2 + b^2 + 2ab \quad ...(II)$$
$$(a - b)^2 = a^2 + b^2 - 2ab \quad ...(III)$$

These are very useful as we can write the given number as sum or difference of two convenient numbers.

Example : Find $(1213)^2 = ?$
$$= [(1213 - 13)(1213 + 13)] + (13)^2$$
$$= (1200 \times 1226) + 169 = 1471200 + 169$$
$$= 1471369$$

Squaring of a number ending in 5

Multiply the number formed after deleting 5 at the units place with the number, one higher than it. Annex 25 on the right side of the product and you will get the square of the given number.

Example : Find $(165)^2 = ?$
Solution : $16 \times 17 = 272$
So, $(165)^2 = 27225$

Properties of Squares

1. It cannot be a negative number.
2. It cannot have odd number of zeros at its end.
3. It cannot end with 2, 3, 7 or 8.
4. Square of an even number is always an even number.
5. Square of an odd number is always an odd number.
6. Every square number is either a multiple of 3 or exceeds multiple of 3 by unity.
7. Every square number is either a multiple of 4 or exceeds multiple of 4 by unity.
8. If a square number ends in 9, the digit preceding 9 must be either zero or even.
9. 1, 5, 6 and 0 at the end of a number reproduce themselves as the last digit in their squares.

Square of Decimal Number

Find the square of the number ignoring the decimal point. Put the decimal point leaving double the number of digits (from the right) as compared to that in the given number. In other words, the position of decimal place in the square is double of that in the original number. The square will lie between the square of integral part and the square of the number, one higher than the integral part.

Example : Find the square of $14.52 = ?$
Solution : $(1452)^2 = 2108304$; $(14.52)^2 = 210.8304$
Square of Fraction :

$$\left(\frac{p}{q}\right)^2 = \frac{p^2}{q^2}$$

Square of $1\frac{1}{2}, 2\frac{1}{2}, 3\frac{1}{2}, 4\frac{1}{2}$ etc.

Multiply the integral part by one more than it. Add $\frac{1}{4}$ to the product and you will get the square of the given half fraction.

Example : Find the square of $4\frac{1}{2}$.

Solution : $\left(4\frac{1}{2}\right)^2 = 4 \times 5 + \frac{1}{4} = 20 + \frac{1}{4} = \frac{81}{4} = 20\frac{1}{4}$

Square of Number Consisting of 9s only

Let the number consists of n 9s.

Write down $(n - 1)$ 9s, followed by one 8, then $(n - 1)$ zeros and finally annex 1 at the end.

Example : Find $(99999)^2$.
Solution : The given number consists of five 9s.

So, we will write four 9s followed by 8, then four zeros and finally 1.

i.e., $(99999)^2 = 9999800001$.

SQUARE ROOT

Square root is inverse of square. Square root of a given number may be defined as the number whose square is equal to the given number. In other words, square root of a given number is the number, which when multiplied by itself, gives the product equal to the given number.

Example : $\sqrt{4}$ = 2 and 2 × 2 = 4,

$\qquad$ $\sqrt{9}$ = 3 and 3 × 3 = 9

There are two methods of finding square root of a number.

Method I : By Factorization

This method is generally used where the given number is a perfect square or when the number can be written as product of such factors whose square roots are known.

You should know following common square roots:

$\sqrt{0}$ = 0	$\sqrt{15}$ = 3.873
$\sqrt{1}$ = 1	$\sqrt{16}$ = 4
$\sqrt{2}$ = 1.414	$\sqrt{17}$ = 4.123
$\sqrt{3}$ = 1.732	$\sqrt{19}$ = 4.359
$\sqrt{4}$ = 2	$\sqrt{21}$ = 4.583
$\sqrt{5}$ = 2.236	$\sqrt{22}$ = 4.690
$\sqrt{6}$ = 2.449	$\sqrt{23}$ = 4.796
$\sqrt{7}$ = 2.646	$\sqrt{25}$ = 5
$\sqrt{9}$ = 3	$\sqrt{36}$ = 6
$\sqrt{10}$ = 3.162	$\sqrt{49}$ = 7
$\sqrt{11}$ = 3.317	$\sqrt{64}$ = 8
$\sqrt{13}$ = 3.606	$\sqrt{81}$ = 9
$\sqrt{14}$ = 3.742	$\sqrt{100}$ = 10

In factorization method, we write the given number as product of prime factors and take the product of prime factors, choosing one out of every pair.

Note :

1. Square root of a number greater than or equal to 1 but less than 100 consists of only one digit.

2. Square root of a number greater than or equal to 100 but less than 10000 consists of two digits.

3. In general, if the given number has 'n' digits, its square root will have n/2 digits when n is even and $\dfrac{n+1}{2}$ digits when n is odd. This holds good for the case of pure decimal fractions too.

Some properties of exact square roots (*i.e.,* square roots are whole numbers)

1. A pure square number ending in 1 must have 1 or 9 as the last digit in its square root.

For example, $\sqrt{81}$ = 9; $\sqrt{121}$ = 11.

2. If a square ends in 4, its square root must have 2 or 8 as the last digit.

For example, $\sqrt{64}$ = 8 ; $\sqrt{144}$ = 12.

3. If a square ends in 5 or 00, its square root must have 5 or 0 respectively as the last digit.

For example, $\sqrt{625}$ = 25 ; $\sqrt{100}$ = 10.

4. A square ending in 9 has 3 or 7 as the last digit in its square root.

For example, $\sqrt{169}$ = 13 ; $\sqrt{729}$ = 27.

Method II : By Division

It is the most general method of finding square roots and is applicable to all cases.

Step I : Mark-off groups of two digits, starting from right. The extreme group may be either single digit or a pair.

Step II : Start division process from the extreme left group.

Step III : For the second stage, add the quotient to the divisor. The divisor of this stage will be equal to this sum with the quotient for this stage suffixed to it. The next dividend is always obtained by annexing the next pair of digits (of the dividend) to the remainder.

Step IV : For the next stage, again add the divisor and the quotient of the previous stage. The divisor for this stage will be formed in the same manner as explained for the second stage in step III.

Step V : Continue step IV till all the groups get exhausted, in case a remainder is left, annex two zeros to it and put a decimal point in the quotient.

At every stage after this we will annex two zeros to the remainder.

Continue to the number of decimal places required in the result. The quotient is equal to the square root of the given number.

CUBE ROOTS

If $a^3 = x$, then $a = \sqrt[3]{x}$; a is the cube root of x

Cube root of $\qquad$ $8 = \sqrt[3]{2 \times 2 \times 2} = 2$

"Cube root of" $\qquad$ $27 = \sqrt[3]{27} = \sqrt[3]{3 \times 3 \times 3} = 3$

"Cube root of" $\qquad$ $216 = \sqrt[3]{6 \times 6 \times 6} = 6$

"Cube root of" $0.000064 = \sqrt[3]{0.04 \times 0.04 \times 0.04} = 0.04$

Example : Evaluate $\sqrt[3]{1325 + \sqrt{20 + \sqrt{256}}}$

Solution : $\sqrt[3]{1325 + \sqrt{20 + 16}}$ $\quad (\because \sqrt{256} = 16)$

$= \sqrt[3]{1325 + \sqrt{36}}$ $\; = \sqrt[3]{1325 + 6}$ $\quad (\because \sqrt{36} = 6)$

$= \sqrt[3]{1331}$ $\; = \sqrt[3]{11 \times 11 \times 11} = 11$

EXERCISE

1. The largest number of five digits which is a perfect square, is :
   (a) 99999   (b) 99764
   (c) 99976   (d) 99856
   (e) None of these

2. The value of $\sqrt{2}$ up to three places of decimals is :
   (a) 1.410   (b) 1.412
   (c) 1.413   (d) 1.414
   (e) None of these

3. $\dfrac{\left(\sqrt{7}+\sqrt{5}\right)}{\sqrt{7}-\sqrt{5}}$ is equal to :
   (a) $6+\sqrt{35}$ (b) $6-\sqrt{35}$
   (c) 2   (d) 1
   (e) None of these

4. The least number by which 294 must be multiplied to make it a perfect square, is :
   (a) 2   (b) 3
   (c) 6   (d) 5
   (e) None of these

5. The least number to be added to 269 to make it a perfect square, is :
   (a) 31   (b) 16
   (c) 7   (d) 20
   (e) None of these

6. What is the smallest number by which 3600 be divided to make it a perfect cube?
   (a) 9   (b) 50
   (c) 300   (d) 450
   (e) None of these

7. The smallest number of 4 digits, which is a perfect square is:
   (a) 1000   (b) 1016
   (c) 1024   (d) 1036
   (e) None of these

8. $\sqrt{10} \times \sqrt{250}$ = ?
   (a) 46.95   (b) 43.75
   (c) 50.25   (d) 50
   (e) None of these

9. $\sqrt{?}/200 = 0.02$
   (a) 0.4   (b) 4
   (c) 16   (d) 1.6
   (e) None of these

10. $\sqrt{.04}$ = ?
    (a) .02   (b) .2
    (c) .002   (d) 1.2
    (e) None of these

11. The greatest number of four digits which is a perfect square, is :
    (a) 9996   (b) 9801
    (c) 9900   (d) 9604
    (e) None of these

12. $\sqrt[3]{?}/200 = 0.02$
    (a) 0.4   (b) 64
    (c) 16   (d) 1/64
    (e) None of these

13. If $\sqrt{256} \div \sqrt[3]{x} = 2$, then x is equal to :
    (a) 64   (b) 128
    (c) 512   (d) 1024
    (e) None of these

14. $112/\sqrt{196} \times \sqrt{576}/12 \times \sqrt{256}/8$ = ?
    (a) 8   (b) 12
    (c) 16   (d) 32
    (e) None of these

15. $(2\sqrt{27} - \sqrt{75} + \sqrt{12})$ is equal to :
    (a) $\sqrt{3}$ (b) $2\sqrt{3}$
    (c) $3\sqrt{3}$ (d) $4\sqrt{3}$
    (e) None of these

16. $\sqrt{50} \times \sqrt{98}$ is equal to :
    (a) 65.95   (b) 63.75
    (c) 70.25   (d) 70
    (e) None of these

17. The largest four-digit number which is a perfect cube, is:
    (a) 9999   (b) 9261
    (c) 8000   (d) 8467
    (e) None of these

18. If $\sqrt{2}$ = 1.4142, the square root of $\dfrac{\left(\sqrt{2}-1\right)}{\sqrt{2}+1}$ is equal to :
    (a) 0.732   (b) 0.3652
    (c) 1.3142   (d) 0.4142
    (e) None of these

19. $\dfrac{\sqrt{121} \times 0.9}{1.1 \times 0.11}$ = ?
    (a) 2   (b) $\dfrac{900}{11}$
    (c) 9   (d) 11
    (e) None of these

20. $\sqrt{25}/15625 = \sqrt{?}/30625$
    (a) 2   (b) 3.5
    (c) 96.04   (d) 1225
    (e) None of these

21. $\sqrt{3.61/10.24}$ = ?
    (a) 29/32   (b) 19/72
    (c) 19/32   (d) 29/62
    (e) None of these

22. $\dfrac{\sqrt{32} + \sqrt{48}}{\sqrt{8} + \sqrt{12}} = ?$

   (a) $\sqrt{2}$ (b) 2

   (c) 4   (d) 8

   (e) None of these

23. $\dfrac{1}{\sqrt{9} - \sqrt{8}} = ?$

   (a) $1/2\,(3 - \sqrt{2})$ (b) $1/3 + 2\sqrt{2}$

   (c) $(3 - 2\sqrt{2})$ (d) $(3 + 2\sqrt{2})$

   (e) None of these

EXPLANATORY ANSWERS

1. (d) : Largest number of 5 digits is 99999.

$$3\,)\,\overline{99999}\,(316$$
$$-\,9$$
$$61)\,\overline{99}\,($$
$$-\,61$$
$$626)\,\overline{3899}\,($$
$$\underline{3756}$$
$$\underline{-\,143}$$

So, required number = (99999 − 143) = 99856.

2. (d) :

$$1)\,2.000000\,(\,1.414$$
$$-\,1$$
$$24\,)\,\overline{100}\,($$
$$-\,96$$
$$281\,)\,\overline{400}\,($$
$$-\,281$$
$$2824\,)\,\overline{11900}\,($$
$$\underline{-\,11296}$$

So, $\sqrt{2} = 1.414$.

3. (a) : $\dfrac{\sqrt{7} + \sqrt{5}}{\sqrt{7} - \sqrt{5}} = \dfrac{\sqrt{7} + \sqrt{5}}{\sqrt{7} - \sqrt{5}} \times \dfrac{\sqrt{7} + \sqrt{5}}{\sqrt{7} + \sqrt{5}}$

$= \dfrac{\left(\sqrt{7} + \sqrt{5}\right)^2}{7 - 5}$

$= \dfrac{7 + 5 + 2\sqrt{7} \times \sqrt{5}}{2}$

$= \dfrac{12 + 2\sqrt{35}}{2} = 6 + \sqrt{35}$.

4. (c) : $294 = 7 \times 7 \times 2 \times 3$. To make it a perfect square it must be multiplied by 2×3, *i.e.,* 6.

5. (d) :

$$1\,)\,\overline{269}\,(\,16$$
$$-\,1$$
$$26\,)\,\overline{169}\,($$
$$-\,156$$
$$\overline{13}$$

Required number to be added = $(17)^2 - 269 = 20$.

6. (d) : $3600 = 2 \times 2 \times 2 \times 2 \times 3 \times 3 \times 5 \times 5$.

To make it a perfect cube, we must divide it by $2 \times 5 \times 5 \times 3 \times 3 = 450$

7. (c) : Smallest number of 4 digits = 1000

$$3\,)\,\overline{1000}\,(\,31$$
$$-\,9$$
$$61\,)\,\overline{100}\,($$
$$-\,61$$
$$\overline{39}$$

So, required number = $(32)^2 = 1024$.

8. (d) : $\sqrt{10} \times \sqrt{250} = \sqrt{2500} = 50$.

9. (c) : Let $\sqrt{x}/200 = 0.02$

Then, $\sqrt{x} = 200 \times 0.02 = 4$

So, $x = 16$.

10. (b) : $\sqrt{.04} = \sqrt{4/100} = 2/10 = 0.2$

11. (b) : Greatest number of four digits = 9999

Now, $9999 = (99)^2 + 198$

So, $(99)^2 = 9999 - 198 = 9801$,

So, required number = 9801.

12. (b) : Let $\sqrt[3]{x}/200 = 0.02$

Then, $\sqrt[3]{x} = 200 \times 0.02 = 4$,

So, $x = 4 \times 4 \times 4 = 64$.

13. (c) : $\because \sqrt{256}/\sqrt[3]{x} = 2 \Rightarrow 16 = 2\sqrt[3]{x}$

$\Rightarrow \sqrt[3]{x} = 8 \Rightarrow x = 512$

14. (d) : Given expression

$= (112/14 \times 24/12 \times 16/8) = 32$

15. (c) : $2\sqrt{27} - \sqrt{75} + \sqrt{12}$

$= 2\sqrt{9 \times 3} - \sqrt{25 \times 3} + \sqrt{4 \times 3}$

$= 6\sqrt{3} - 5\sqrt{3} + 2\sqrt{3} = 3\sqrt{3}$

16. (d) : $\sqrt{50} \times \sqrt{98} = \sqrt{4900} = 70$

17. (b) : Clearly, 9261 is a perfect cube.

18. (d) : $\dfrac{\sqrt{2} - 1}{\sqrt{2} + 1} = \dfrac{\sqrt{2} - 1}{\sqrt{2} + 1} \times \dfrac{\sqrt{2} - 1}{\sqrt{2} - 1} = \dfrac{\left(\sqrt{2} - 1\right)^2}{1}$

So $\sqrt{\dfrac{\sqrt{2} - 1}{\sqrt{2} + 1}} = \sqrt{2} - 1 = 1.4142 - 1 = 0.4142$

19. (*b*) : Given expression

$$= \frac{\sqrt{121} \times 0.9}{1.1 \times 0.11} = \frac{11 \times 9 \times 1000}{11 \times 11 \times 10} = \frac{900}{11}$$

20. (*c*) : $\dfrac{\sqrt{25}}{15625} = \dfrac{\sqrt{x}}{30625} \Rightarrow \sqrt{x} = \dfrac{30625 \times 5}{15625} = 9.8$

$$\therefore \ x = 96.04.$$

21. (*c*) : $\sqrt{3.61/10.24} = \sqrt{361/1024}$

$$\frac{\sqrt{19 \times 19}}{\sqrt{32 \times 32}} = 19/32$$

22. (*b*) : $\dfrac{\sqrt{32} + \sqrt{48}}{\sqrt{8} + \sqrt{12}} = \dfrac{\sqrt{16 \times 2} + \sqrt{16 \times 3}}{\sqrt{4 \times 2} + \sqrt{4 \times 3}}$

$$= \frac{4\sqrt{2} + 4\sqrt{3}}{2\sqrt{2} + 2\sqrt{3}} = \frac{4\left(\sqrt{2} + \sqrt{3}\right)}{2\left(\sqrt{2} + \sqrt{3}\right)} = \frac{4}{2} = 2$$

23. (*d*) : $\dfrac{1}{\sqrt{9} - \sqrt{8}} = \dfrac{1}{\sqrt{9} - \sqrt{8}} \times \dfrac{\sqrt{9} + \sqrt{8}}{\sqrt{9} + \sqrt{8}}$

$$= \frac{3 + 2\sqrt{2}}{9 - 8} = 3 + 2\sqrt{2}\,.$$

LCM AND HCF

LEAST COMMON MULTIPLE (LCM)

LCM of two or more numbers is the least among the numbers which are common multiples of the given numbers. In other words, LCM of given numbers is the smallest number which is exactly divisible by each of them. In the above examples, the LCM for

2 and 5 is 10   2 and 3 is 6

4 and 6 is 12   We can find LCM by two methods.

Method 1:

Step I : Write the numbers as product of prime factors.

Step II : Find the product of the highest powers of the prime factors, which will be the LCM

Note : Do not repeat any factor while writing the product in Step II.

Example : Find the LCM of 36, 56, 105 and 108.

Step I :

$$36 = 2^2 \times 3^2$$
$$56 = 2^3 \times 7$$
$$105 = 3 \times 5 \times 7$$
$$108 = 2^2 \times 3^3$$

Step II : The LCM must contain every prime factor of each of the numbers. Also it must include the highest power of each prime factor which appears in any of them. So, it must contain 2 or it would not be a multiple of 56, it must contain 3 or it would not be a multiple of 108, it must contain 5 or it would not be a multiple of 105, and it must contain 7 or it would not be a multiple of 56 or of 105.

Therefore, the LCM $= 2^3 \times 3^3 \times 5 \times 7 = 7560$

Method 2:

This is quicker method to find the prime factors and hence LCM In this method there can be more than one arrangement for the same numbers.

Step I : Write the numbers in a row and strike out those numbers which are factors of any other number in the set.

Step II : Write the factor on the left hand side which can divide maximum of the numbers.

Step III: Write in the next row the quotients obtained and also those numbers (as they are) which are not divisible by that factor. You can strike out from any row 1, if it appears.

Step IV : Repeat steps II and III until we get a set where no two numbers have a common factor or divisor, *i.e.,* all the numbers in the row are prime to each other, though individually they may not be prime numbers.

Step V : Multiply all the factors or divisors and the numbers left in the last row. The product gives the LCM of the given numbers.

Let us now see how it works and how simple it is.

Example : Find LCM of 48, 108 and 140.

Method 1: Factorization Method

Factors of $48 = 2 \times 2 \times 2 \times 2 \times 3 = 2^4 \times 3$

Factors of $108 = 2 \times 2 \times 3 \times 3 \times 3 = 2^2 \times 3^3$

Factors of $140 = 2 \times 2 \times 5 \times 7 = 2^2 \times 5 \times 7$

LCM = Highest power of 2 × Highest power of 3 × Highest power of 5 × Highest power of 7

$$= 2^4 \times 3^3 \times 5 \times 7$$
$$= 15120$$

Method 2 : By Division Method

2	48, 108, 140
2	24, 54, 70
3	12, 27, 35
	4, 9, 35

So, LCM $= 2 \times 2 \times 3 \times 4 \times 9 \times 35 = 15120$.

L.C.M of Decimals

To find the LCM of decimal numbers first of all we find out the LCM of numbers without decimal. And then we see the number in which the decimal is given in the minimum digits from right to left. We put the decimal in our result which is equal to that number of digits.

Example : Find the LCM of 0.16, 5.4 and .0098.

First of all we find out the LCM of 16, 54, 98.

Here, LCM of 16, 54, 98 is 21168.

In numbers 0.16, 5.4, 0.0098, the minimum digits from right to left is 5.4. Here, in 5.4 the decimal is given of one digit from right to left is 5.4. So, we put decimal in our result such that: = 21168 = 2116.8.

Example : Find the LCM of 48, 10.8 and 0.140.

LCM of 48, 108 and 140 = 15120

So, LCM of 48, 10.8, and 0.140 = 1.5120.

L.C.M of Fractions

If a/b, c/d, e/f be the proper fractions then their LCM is

$$\text{given by} = \frac{\text{L.C.M of numerators } a, c, e}{\text{H.C.F of denominators } b, d, f}$$

Example : Find the LCM of 3^5, 3^8, 3^{12}, 3^{15}, 3^{20}

If the base of these numbers is same then LCM of these numbers will be equal to maximum power of these numbers.

So, LCM = 3^{20}

> **Imp :** If A and B be the two numbers then the product of their LCM and HCF is equal to the product of the two numbers. *i.e.*,
>
> LCM × HCF = A × B
>
> So, L.C.M = $\dfrac{A \times B}{\text{H.C.F}}$

To Find LCM By Multiples

If we want to find LCM of 3 and 4 then first of all we find the multiples of 3 and 4. Then the lowest common multiples of both of them is their LCM

Multiples of 3: 3, 6, 9, 12, 15, 18, ...

Multiples of 4: 4, 8, 12 , 16, 20, ...

Here, lowest common multiple is 12 which is our LCM.

HIGHEST COMMON FACTOR (HCF)

A number which is a factor of two or more numbers is said to be a common factor or common measure of the numbers. We exclude unity which is common measure of all numbers. The greatest number which will divide each of two or more numbers is called their Highest Common Factor or Greatest Common Measure and is denoted by the letters HCF or GCM(Greatest Common Measure).

Example: Find the HCF of 8 and 12.

Factors of 8 are 1, 2, 4, 8 and

Factors of 12 are 1, 2, 3, 4, 6, 12

The common factors are 1, 2, 4 but highest of these is 4. Hence, 4 is the HCF.

By Factorization Method

Factor method has discussed above or, we express each given number as the product of primes. Now, we take the product of common factors which is our required HCF.

Example : Find the HCF of 144, 336 and 2016.

Factors of 144 = $2^4 \times 3^2$

Factors of 336 = $2^4 \times 3 \times 7$

Factors of 2016 = $2^5 \times 7 \times 3^2$

So, HCF of given numbers = $2^4 \times 3 = 48$.

By Division Method

Step I : We divide the greater number by the smaller and find out the remainder.

Step II : Then divide the first divisor by remainder and find the second remainder.

Step III : Then divide the second divisor by the second remainder.

Step IV : We repeat this process till no remainder is left. The last divisor is our required HCF.

Example : HCF of 513 and 783.

```
513 ) 783 ( 1
      513
      270 ) 513 ( 1
            270
            243) 270 (1
                 243
                 27 ) 243 ( 9
                      243
So, HCF = 27.          ×
```

HCF of Decimals

Here, first of all we find HCF of the given numbers without decimals and then put decimal.

Example : Find the HCF of 0.0012, 1.6, and 28.

Here, HCF of 12, 16 and 28 is 4.

The decimal is given at maximum digits from right to left. So, HCF = 0.0004.

HCF of Fractions

If a/b, c/d, e/f be the proper fractions then their HCF is given by

$$= \frac{\text{H.C.F of numerators } a, c, e \ldots}{\text{L.C.M of denominators } b, d, f \ldots}$$

Example : Find the HCF of 2/5, 8/35, 4/15 and 6/25.

$$\text{HCF} = \frac{\text{H.C.F. of } 2, 8, 4, 6}{\text{L.C.M. of } 5, 35, 15, 25} = \frac{2}{525}.$$

EXERCISE

1. HCF of 11, 0.121, 0.1331 is :
   (a) 0.0011   (b) 0.121
   (c) 0.1331   (d) 12.21
   (e) None of these

2. The L.C.M of 22, 54, 108, 135 and 198 is :
   (a) 330   (b) 1980
   (c) 5940   (d) 11880
   (e) None of these

3. HCF of 8^{-2}, 8^{-3}, 8^{-4}, 8^{-5} is :
   (a) 8^{-2} (b) 8^{-3}
   (c) 8^{-4} (d) 8^{-5}
   (e) None of these

4. The sum of two numbers is 528, and their HCF is 33. How many pairs of such numbers can be formed?
   (a) 4   (b) 5
   (c) 8   (d) 2
   (e) None of these

5. HCF of 4^5, 4^{11} and 4^{15} is :
   (a) 4^5 (b) 4^{11}

   (c) 4^{15} (d) 4
   (e) None of these

6. The HCF of 2^3, 3^2, 4 and 15 is :
   (a) 2^3 (b) 3^2
   (c) 1   (d) 360
   (e) None of these

7. HCF of 15, 45, 90 is :
   (a) 12   (b) 13
   (c) 13   (d) 15
   (e) None of these

8. The GCM of 9/45, 15/20, 16/20 and 15/25 is :
   (a) 1/20   (b) 1/40
   (c) 1/60   (d) 1/15
   (e) None of these

9. GCM of 3556 and 3444 is :
   (a) 25   (b) 26
   (c) 27   (d) 28
   (e) None of these

EXPLANATORY ANSWERS

1. (a): HCF of 11, 121, 1331 is 11.
So, HCF of 11, 0.121 and 0.1331 is = 0.0011.

2. (c): Method 1

2	22,	54,	108,	135,	198
11	11,	27,	54,	135,	99
9	1,	27,	54,	135,	9
3	1,	3,	6,	15,	1
	1,	1,	2,	5,	1

So, LCM = $2 \times 11 \times 9 \times 3 \times 2 \times 5 = 5940$

Method 2

Factors of $22 = 2 \times 11$
Factors of $54 = 2 \times 3 \times 3 \times 3 = 2 \times 3^3$
Factors of $108 = 2 \times 2 \times 3 \times 3 \times 3 = 2^2 \times 3^3$
Factors of $135 = 5 \times 3 \times 3 \times 3 = 5 \times 3^3$
Factors of $198 = 2 \times 3 \times 3 \times 11 = 2^1 \times 3^2 \times 11^1$
So, LCM = Max. power of 2 × Max. power of 3 × Max. power of 5 × Max. power of 11
$= 2^2 \times 3^3 \times 5 \times 11 = 5940$

3. (d): HCF of the given numbers = 8^{-5}

4. (a): Trick : Let the numbers be $33\,a$ and $33\,b$
Now, $33a + 33b = 528$
$\Rightarrow 33(a + b) = 528 \qquad a + b = 16$
The possible values of a and b are (1, 15); (3, 13); (5, 11); and (7, 9).
So, the possible pairs of numbers are (33, 495); (99, 429); (165, 363); (231, 297).

5. (a): HCF of the given numbers = 4^5
Minimum power of 4.

6. (c): Trick : HCF of 2^3, 3^2, 4 and 15
Here by factorization method we see that 1 is the HCF of given numbers
$$2^3 = 2^3$$
$$3^2 = 3^2$$
$$4 = 2^2 = 1$$
$$15 = 3 \times 5$$
$= 1$

7. (d): By Factorization Method
Factors of $15 = 3 \times 5$
Factors of $45 = 3^2 \times 5$
Factors of $90 = 3^2 \times 5 \times 2$
So, HCF $= 3 \times 5 = 15$.

8. (a): GCM of the given fractions
$$= \frac{\text{G.C.M of } 9, 15, 16, 15}{\text{L.C.M of } 45, 20, 20, 25} = \frac{1}{900}$$

9. (d): Trick :

$$\text{HCF} = 3444 \overline{)\,3556\,}(\,1$$
$$\underline{-\;3444}$$
$$112\,\overline{)\,3444\,}(\,30$$
$$\underline{-360}$$
$$84\,\overline{)\,112\,}(\,1$$
$$\underline{-84}$$
$$28\,\overline{)\,84\,}(\,3$$
$$\underline{84}$$
$$\times$$

HCF = 28.

RATIO AND PROPORTION

RATIO

When we say that the length of a line *AB* is 5 centimetres, we mean that a unit of length called 1 centimetre is contained in *AB* five times. If we have two lines *AB* and *CD* and their lengths be 2 and 3 centimetres respectively, we say that the length of *AB* is 2/3 of the length of *CD*.

Ratio is a relation between two quantities in the same units which shows that one quantity is how many times of another quantity. Suppose A and B are two persons who have ₹ 50 and ₹ 100 respectively. Here 50 and 100 are two quantities in the same unit, rupees. It is clear that ₹ 50 is half of ₹100. Thus we can say in term of ratio that ratio of ₹ 50 and ₹ 100 is 1: 2.

A ratio may be expressed in the form of simplest fraction (If numerator and denominator have no common factor except 1, then fraction is in the simplest or lowest form).

Sign of ratio = (:) read as "Is To" So, ratio of two quantities ₹ 50 and ₹ 100 = 50/100 = 1/2 = 1 : 2 (Pronounced as 1 is to 2).

Memorable Points

1. Here in 1 : 2, '1' is called *Antecedent* of the ratio.
2. '2' is called *Consequent* of the ratio.

PROPORTION

The equality of two ratios is called *proportion.* Suppose, we have two ratios for example, 3 : 2 and 151:110. Here, 3 : 2 = 15 : 10. Thus this equality of these two given ratios is called proportion.

Sign of Proportion

Sign of proportion is : :

Therefore the above mentioned example is written as 3 : 2 : : 15 : 10 (it means 3/2 = 15/10)

The terms 3, 2, 15 and 10 are called proportional and named as the 1st, 2nd, 3rd and 4th proportional respectively.

In a proportion, the 1st and 4th terms are known as *extremes*, while 2nd and 3rd terms are known as *means.*

So, in given example 3 and 10 are extremes, while 2 and 15 are means.

In the concised way, all these terms are shown below :

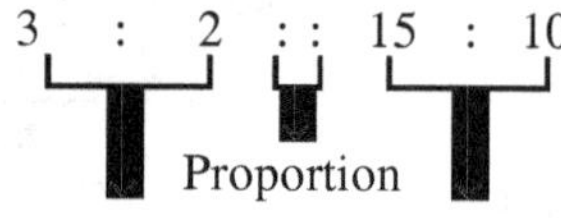

Note : (1) It is not necessary that all four terms (proportional) are in the same unit. But in this condition, 1st and 2nd and 3rd and 4th terms must have same unit.

(2) 3 : 2 : : 15 : 10 is also written as

3/2 = 15/10

Memorable Points

We can find out the value of a unknown proportional, when values of three proportional are known by applying the following methods :

1. 1st proportional $= \dfrac{2\text{nd} \times 3\text{rd}}{4\text{th}}$

Example : ? : 190 : : 840 : 40

Solution : ? (1st proportional)

$$= \dfrac{190 \times 840}{40} = 3990.$$

2. 2nd proportional $= \dfrac{1st \times 4th}{3rd}$

Example : 50/ ? = 20/60

Solution : 50/ ? = 20/60

50 : ? : : 20 : 60

$$? = \dfrac{50 \times 60}{20} = 150$$

3. 3rd proportional $= \dfrac{1\text{st} \times 4\text{th}}{2\text{nd}}$

Example : 3/4 = ? / 56

Solution : 3 : 4 :: ? : 56

$\Rightarrow \qquad ? = \dfrac{3 \times 56}{4} = 42$

4. 4th proportional $= \dfrac{2\text{nd} \times 3\text{rd}}{1\text{st}}$

Example : 500/1200 = 500/?

Solution : 500 : 1200 : : 500 : ?

$\Rightarrow \qquad ? = \dfrac{1200 \times 500}{500} = 1200$

SOME OTHER TERMS AND THEIR FORMULAE OF RATIO AND PROPORTION

1. Mean proportional of '*a*' and '*b*' = $\sqrt{ab}$

Example : Find the mean proportional between 0.32 and 0.02.

Solution : Mean proportional between 0.32 and 0.02

$= \sqrt{0.32 \times 0.02} = \sqrt{0.0064} = 0.08$

2. Duplicate Ratio of $a : b = a^2 : b^2$

Example : Find duplicate ratio of $7\sqrt{3} : 4\sqrt{2}$

Solution : Duplicate ratio of $7\sqrt{3} : 4\sqrt{2}$

$$= \left(7\sqrt{3}\right)^2 : \left(4\sqrt{2}\right)^2 = 49 \times 3 : 16 \times 2 = 147 : 32.$$

3. Sub-duplicate Ratio of $a : b = \sqrt{a} : \sqrt{b}$

Example : Find sub-duplicate ratio (S.D.R) of 200 : 392.

Solution : S.D.R of $200 : 392 = \sqrt{200} : \sqrt{392}$

$$= \frac{\sqrt{200}}{\sqrt{392}} = \sqrt{\frac{200}{392}}$$

$$= \sqrt{\frac{100}{196}} = \frac{10}{14} = \frac{5}{7} = 5 : 7$$

4. Triplicate Ratio of $a : b = a^3 : b^3$

Example : Find triplicate ratio of 4 : 5.
Solution : Triplicate ratio of 4 : 5
$$= 4^3 : 5^3 = 64 : 125$$

5. Sub-Triplicate Ratio of $a : b = \sqrt[3]{a} : \sqrt[3]{b}$

Example : Find sub-triplicate Ratio of 27 : 1.
Solution : S.T.R of $27 : 1 = \sqrt[3]{27} : \sqrt[3]{1}$
$$= \sqrt[3]{3^3} : \sqrt[3]{1} = 3 : 1.$$

6. Inverse or Reciprocal Ratio of $a : b = 1/a : 1/b$

Example : Find reciprocal ratio of 4 : 5.
Solution : Reciprocal ratio of $4 : 5 = 1/4 : 1/5$

7. Third Proportional to 'a' and 'b' = b^2/a

Example : Find the third proportional to 0.8 and 0.2.
Solution : Third proportional to 0.8 and 0.2
$$= \frac{(0.2)^2}{0.8} = \frac{0.04}{0.8} = \frac{4}{80} = 0.05.$$

8. Compound Ratio of $a : b, c : d, e : f$

$$= \frac{\text{Product of all first terms of all ratio}}{\text{Product of all second terms of all ratio}}$$

$$= \frac{a \times c \times e}{b \times d \times f}$$

Example : Find compound ratio of 8 : 2, 2 : 1 and 9 : 3.

Solution : Compound ratio $= \dfrac{8 \times 2 \times 9}{2 \times 1 \times 3}$

$$= \frac{24}{1} = 24 : 1.$$

9. If $A : B = x : y$ and $B : C = m : n$ then

$$\boxed{\begin{array}{l} (I)\ A : C = \dfrac{x \times m}{y \times n} \\[2mm] (II)\ A : B : C = mx : ym : yn \end{array}}$$

Example : If $A : B = 2 : 3$ and $B : C = 4 : 5$ then $C : A$ is equal to

$$A : C = \frac{2 \times 4}{3 \times 5} = \frac{8}{15} = 8 : 15$$

$$\left[\because \text{In Formula } A : C = \frac{x \times m}{y \times n} \right]$$

So, $C : A = 15 : 8$.

10. If $A : B : C = x : y : z$ and $C : D = m : n$
Then $A : B : C : D = m\ (x : y) : z\ (m : n)$

Example : If $A : B : C = 2 : 3 : 4$ and $C : D = 5 : 6$, then $A : B : C : D$ is equal to

Solution : $A : B : C : D = m(x : y) : z\ (m : n)$
So, $A : B : C : D = 5\ (2 : 3) : 4\ (5 : 6)$
  $= 10 : 15 : 20 : 24.$

EXERCISE

1. The students in three classes are in the ratio $2 : 3 : 5$. If 20 students are increased in each class, the ratio changes to $4 : 5 : 7$. What is the total number in the three classes before the increase?
   (a) 100 students   (b) 75 students
   (c) 150 students   (d) 50 students
   (e) None of these

2. The ratio between two numbers is 3 : 4. If each number be increased by 2, the ratio becomes 7 : 9. Find the numbers.
   (a) 12, 16   (b) 16, 12
   (c) 12, 15   (d) 13, 14
   (e) None of these

3. Divide ₹ 1540 among A, B, C so that A shall receive 2/9 as much as B and C together, and B 3/11 of what A and C together do. Find the share of A, B and C.
   (a) 285, 330, 830   (b) 280, 330, 930
   (c) 280, 330, 980   (d) 330, 380, 980
   (e) None of these

4. In a fort there is provision for 40 days for 275 persons. If after 16 days, 125 persons leave the fort, for how many more days the provision will now last?
   (a) 45 days   (b) 35 days
   (c) 44 days   (d) 53 days
   (e) None of these

5. A fort has provision for 35 days. If after 5 days 225 more persons joined and the food lasts 25 days, how many men are there in the fort?
(*a*) 1225 persons   (*b*) 1572 persons
(*c*) 1125 persons   (*d*) 1229 persons
(*e*) None of these

6. The ratio between the ages of Rahim and Karim is 3 : 5 and the sum of their ages is 56 years. What was the ratio of their ages 7 years ago?
(*a*) 1: 2   (*b*) 3 : 2
(*c*) 3 : 4   (*d*) 4 : 3
(*e*) None of these

7. The prices of a scooter and television set are in the ratio 3 : 2. If a scooter costs ₹ 6,000 more than the television set, what is the price of the television set?

(*a*) ₹ 12,000   (*b*) ₹ 8,000
(*c*) ₹ 10,000   (*d*) ₹ 5,000
(*e*) None of these

8. The prices of scooter and a moped are in the ratio of 9 : 5. If a scooter costs ₹ 4200 more than a moped, find the price of the moped.
(*a*) ₹ 5052   (*b*) ₹ 5250
(*c*) ₹ 5053   (*d*) ₹ 5060
(*e*) None of these

9. A sum of money is divided between two persons in the ratio of 3 : 5. If the share of one person is ₹ 20 less than that of the other, find the sum.
(*a*) ₹ 75   (*b*) ₹ 90
(*c*) ₹ 80   (*d*) ₹ 85
(*e*) None of these

EXPLANATORY ANSWERS

1. (*a*): $4 - 2 = 5 - 3 = 7 - 5 = 2$.

As we know 20 students are increased in each class.

So, $(2 + 3 + 5) = \dfrac{20}{2} \times 10$

$$= 100 \text{ students.}$$

2. (*a*): Let numbers are $3x$ and $4x$

$$\dfrac{3x+2}{4x+2} = \dfrac{7}{9}$$

$\Rightarrow \quad 27x + 18 = 28x + 14$

$\Rightarrow \qquad\quad x = 4$

Hence, numbers are $3 \times 4 = 12$ and $4 \times 4 = 16$.

3. (*b*): A's share : $(B + C)$'s share = 2 : 9   ... (1)

B's share : $(A + C)$'s share = 3 : 11   ... (2)

Now dividing ₹ 1540 in the ratio of 2 : 9 and 3 : 11

A's share 2/11 of ₹ 1540 = ₹ 280

B's share = 3/14 of ₹ 1540 = ₹ 330

C's share = ₹ 1540 – (₹ 280 + ₹ 330) = ₹ 930

4. (*c*): Reasoning

More men less days, less men more days

So, 275 : x : : (275 – 125) : (40 – 16)

So, $x = \dfrac{275 \times 24}{150} = 44$ days.

5. (*c*): Let the number of persons be x.

$(35 - 5)\, x = 25\,(x + 225)$

$\Rightarrow \quad 30\, x - 25x = 25 \times 225$

$\Rightarrow \qquad\qquad x = \dfrac{25 \times 225}{5}$

$\Rightarrow \qquad\qquad x = 1125$ persons.

6. (*a*): Present age of Rahim = 56/8 × 3 = 21 years

Present age of Karim = 56/8 × 5 = 35 years

So, ratio of ages 7 years ago

$$= (21 - 7) : (35 - 7)$$
$$= 14 : 28$$
$$= 1 : 2$$

7. (*a*): Let the price of a scooter = $3x$ and the price of a television set = $2x$.

$\because \qquad 3x - 2x = 6000$

$\Rightarrow \qquad\qquad x = 6000$

So, price of television set = $2x = 2 \times 6000$

$$= ₹ 12000$$

8. (*b*): We have, $9x - 5x = 4200$

$\Rightarrow \qquad\qquad 4x = 4200$

$\Rightarrow \qquad\qquad x = \dfrac{4200}{4} = 1050$

So, price of the moped = $5x = 5 \times 1050$

$$= ₹ 5250.$$

9. (*c*): $\dfrac{\text{Sum}}{\text{Difference}} = \dfrac{\text{Sum}}{20} = \dfrac{3+5}{5-3}$

$$\text{Sum} = \dfrac{8}{2} \times 20 = ₹ 80.$$

***

2

Fundamental Arithmetic Operation

TIME WORK, PIPE AND CISTERN

Solved Examples

Example 1: *A can complete a piece of work in 8 days, whereas A and B together can complete the same work in 6 days. How long will it take for B alone to complete the work?*

Solution: A's one day's work = $\dfrac{1}{8}$

(A + B)'s one day's work = $\dfrac{1}{6}$

B's one day's work = $\left(\dfrac{1}{6}-\dfrac{1}{8}\right)=\dfrac{1}{24}$

∴ B can complete the work in 24 days.

Example 2: *Two pipes A and B can separately, fill a cistern in 8 hours and 12 hours respectively while a third pipe C can empty it in 24 hours. In what time will the cistern be full, if all the pipes are opened together?*

Solution: In 1 hour, the pipe A fills $\dfrac{1}{8}$ th of the cistern.

In 1 hour, the pipe B fills $\dfrac{1}{12}$ th of the cistern.

In 1 hour, the pipe C can empty $\dfrac{1}{24}$ th of the cistern.

Net filling of the cistern in 1 hour

$$= \left(\dfrac{1}{8}+\dfrac{1}{12}\right)-\dfrac{1}{24}$$

$$= \dfrac{5}{24}-\dfrac{1}{24}=\dfrac{4}{24}=\dfrac{1}{6}$$

So, the cistern will be full in 6 hours.

EXERCISE

1. If 36 binders bind 900 books in 10 days, how many binders will be required to bind 1,200 books in 12 days?
A. 30
B. 32
C. 40
D. 42

2. If A can complete a work in 30 days and B can complete the same work in 25 days, then in how many days will 'A' and 'B' together complete the work?

A. $\dfrac{11}{150}$ days

B. $\dfrac{150}{11}$ days

C. 55 days

D. $\dfrac{1}{55}$ days

3. If 100 men can do 100 jobs in 100 days, then 1 man can do one job in:
A. 1 day
B. 100 days
C. 50 days
D. 10 days

4. Ajit can complete a job in 4 days, Manoj can complete the same job in 6 days and Ravi can complete it in 12 days. In how many days will Ajit, Manoj and Ravi together complete the same job?

A. 2 days
B. 3 days

C. $\dfrac{1}{2}$ day

D. 1 day

5. A and B can finish a work in 16 days while A alone can do the same work in 24 days. Therefore B alone can finish the same work in ...... days.
A. 24
B. 36
C. 48
D. 56

6. A, B and C undertake to complete a piece of work for ₹ 1,950. A works for 8 days, B for 9 days and C for 12 days to complete the work. If their daily wages are in the ratio of 3 : 5 : 4, what does C get?
A. ₹ 400
B. ₹ 750
C. ₹ 675
D. ₹ 800

7. Two taps A and B can fill a cistern in 30 minute and 45 minute respectively. There is third exhaust tap C at the bottom of the tank. If all the taps are opened at the same time the cistern will be full in 45 minute. In what time can exhaust tap C empty the cistern when full?
A. 10 min
B. 15 min
C. 18 min
D. 20 min

8. Two taps A and B can separately fill a cistern in 24 minute and 30 minute respectively. Both the pipes are opened together. Find when the pipe B must be turned off so that the cistern may be full in 18 minute.

A. $6\dfrac{1}{2}$ min   B. $6\dfrac{3}{4}$ min

C. 7 min   D. $7\dfrac{1}{2}$ min

9. Efficiency of B is 80% of A. If both can complete a work in 24 days, in how many days B alone will complete the same work?
A. 54   B. 50
C. 49   D. 56

10. The efficiency of A is twice that of B. A completes a work in 9 days less than taken by B. In how many days A alone will complete this work?
A. 12 days   B. 10 days
C. 9 days   D. 13 days

11. If 3 men or 6 boys can finish a work in 20 days, then 6 men and 8 boys finish twice the work in:
A. 9 days   B. 11 days
C. 3 days   D. 12 days

12. 6 boys and 4 girls together complete a work in 5 days. The same work is done in 5 days by 10 boys. How many girls would be required if only the girls can finish this work in 5 days?
A. 20   B. 10
C. 15   D. 12

13. A man and a boy can complete digging in 40 days. The ratio of their speed of digging is 8 : 5. How many days the boys alone will take to do this work?
A. 68 days   B. 52 days
C. 104 days   D. 80 days

14. 104 men are employed to complete a work in 56 days working 8 hours per day. After 30 days $\dfrac{2}{5}$th work is finished. How many more men should be employed to finish the remaining work within time working 9 hours per day?
A. 52   B. 54
C. 56   D. 58

15. 5 persons prepare an admission list in 8 days working 7 hours per day. If two more persons are included to finish the work in 4 days, how much hours per day they should do the work?
A. 10 hours   B. 9 hours
C. 12 hours   D. 8 hours

16. A and B take 15 days and 10 days respectively to complete a job. Both of them together started the job, but after 2 days B have to leave the job due to any reason and the remaining work was finished by A. In how many days the job was completed?
A. 10 days   B. 8 days
C. 12 days   D. 15 days

17. A work can be finished in 100 days by some persons, but due to the absence of 10 persons, the work is finished in 110 days. How many persons were employed initially?
A. 100   B. 110
C. 55   D. 56

18. The efficiencies of two workmen A and B are in the ratio of 5 : 4. If A can do a piece of work in 12 hours, then B can do it in:
A. 18 hours   B. 16.5 hours
C. 16 hours   D. 15 hours

19. A pipe can fill a cistern in 12 hours and another pipe can empty completely filled cistern in 18 hours. If both the pipes are opened together, the cistern will be filled in:
A. 30 hours   B. 36 hours
C. 40 hours   D. 44 hours

ANSWERS

1	2	3	4	5	6	7	8	9	10
C	B	B	A	C	D	A	D	A	C

11	12	13	14	15	16	17	18	19
D	B	C	C	A	C	B	D	B

EXPLANATORY ANSWERS

1. Less books, less number of binders (direct)
more days, less number of binders (indirect)

books   900 : 1,200 ⎫
days   12 : 10   ⎬ :: 36 : x

Compounding the ratio,
$(900 \times 12) : (1,200 \times 10) = 36 : x$

$\Rightarrow \quad x = \dfrac{1,200 \times 10 \times 36}{900 \times 12} = 40$

Hence, 40 binders will be required.

2. A's work for one day = $\dfrac{1}{30}$

B's work for one day = $\dfrac{1}{25}$

(A + B)'s work for one day = $\dfrac{1}{30} + \dfrac{1}{25} = \dfrac{11}{150}$

$\therefore$ A and B together can complete the work in $\frac{150}{11}$ days.

3. 100 men can do 100 jobs in days = 100
$\therefore$ 1 man can do 100 jobs in days
$$= 100 \times 100 \text{ days}$$
$\therefore$ 1 man can do 1 job in days
$$= \frac{100 \times 100}{100} \text{ days} = 100 \text{ days}.$$

4. Ajit's one day's work $= \frac{1}{4}$

Manoj's one day's work $= \frac{1}{6}$

Ravi's one day's work $= \frac{1}{12}$

(Ajit + Manoj + Ravi)'s one day's work
$$= \frac{1}{4} + \frac{1}{6} + \frac{1}{12} = \frac{1}{2}$$

$\therefore$ Ajit, Manoj and Ravi together can complete the work in 2 days.

7. Taps (A + B)'s one minute work
$$= \frac{1}{30} + \frac{1}{45} = \frac{5}{90} = \frac{1}{18}$$

Taps (A + B + C)'s one minute work $= \frac{1}{45}$

$\therefore$ Exhaust tap C's one minute work
$$= \frac{1}{45} - \frac{1}{18} = -\frac{1}{10}$$

Thus, tap C can empty $\frac{1}{10}$ th of tank in 1 minute. Tap C can empty the full tank in 10 minute.

9.

	A	B	A + B
Efficiency	100	80	
	5 :	4 :	9
		E_1 :	E_2
		D_1 :	$D_2 = 24$

$\therefore$ $\quad D_1 E_1 = D_2 E_2$
$\Rightarrow$ $\quad 4 \times D_1 = 9 \times 24$
$\therefore$ $\quad D_1 = \frac{9 \times 24}{4} = 54$ days.

10. Let A completes this work in x days.
Then B completes this work in $(x + 9)$ days.

	A	B
Efficiency	2 :	1
Days	x :	$x + 9$

$\Rightarrow \quad 2 : 1 :: x + 9 : x$
$\Rightarrow \quad 2 \times x = (x + 9) : x$
$\quad\quad 2 \times x = (x + 9) \times 1$
$\quad\quad 2x = x + 9 \quad \therefore x = 9.$

11. 3 men's work = 6 boy's work
$\therefore$ 6 men's work = 12 boy's work
6 men's + 8 boy's work = (12 + 8) boy's work
$$\textit{i.e., } 20 \text{ boy's work}$$
Now, 6 boys can do the work in 20 days.

$\therefore$ 20 boys can do the work in $\frac{20 \times 6}{20}$ days $\textit{i.e., }$ 6 days

$\therefore$ 20 boys can do twice the work in 12 days.
Thus, 6 men and 8 boys finish twice the work in 12 days.

12. $(6B + 4G) \times 5 = 10B \times 5$
$$6B + 4G = 10B$$
$$4B = 4G \textit{ i.e., } 1B = 1G$$
Thus, the work of 1 boy = The work of 1 girl
The work of 10 boys = The work of 10 girls
Hence the required number of girls = 10.

13.
$\quad\quad M : B = 8 : 5$ Efficiency
$\therefore \quad M : B = 5 : 8$ No. of days
Let the number of days be $5x$ and $8x$. Then

$$\frac{1}{5x} + \frac{1}{8x} = \frac{1}{40}$$

$$\frac{8 + 5}{40x} = \frac{1}{40} \quad\quad \therefore x = 13$$

Hence the required number of days
$$= 8 \times 13 = 104.$$

14. Formule : $\dfrac{M_1 D_1 H_1}{W_1} = \dfrac{M_2 D_2 H_2}{W_2}$

$\Rightarrow \quad \dfrac{104 \times 30 \times 8}{\dfrac{2}{5}} = \dfrac{M_2 \times (56 - 30) \times 9}{\left(1 - \dfrac{2}{5}\right)}$

$\Rightarrow \quad M_2 = \dfrac{3}{5} \times \dfrac{5}{2} \times \dfrac{104 \times 30 \times 8}{26 \times 9} = 160$

Required number of men = 160 – 104 = 56.

15. $\quad M_1 D_1 H_1 = M_2 D_2 H_2$
$\Rightarrow \quad 5 \times 8 \times 7 = (5 + 2) \times 4 \times H_2$

$\Rightarrow \quad H_2 = \dfrac{5 \times 8 \times 7}{7 \times 4} = 10$ hours.

16. Let A alone finish the remaining job in T days. Then

$$\frac{2}{15} + \frac{2}{10} + \frac{T}{15} = 1$$

$\Rightarrow \quad \dfrac{T}{15} = 1 - \left(\dfrac{2}{15} + \dfrac{2}{10}\right) = 1 - \dfrac{1}{3} = \dfrac{2}{3}$

$\therefore \quad\quad T = \dfrac{2}{3} \times 15 = 10.$

Hence the required number of days
$$= 2 + 10 = 12.$$

17.
$$M_1D_1 = M_2D_2$$
$$\Rightarrow \quad M_1 \times 100 = (M_1 - 10) \times 110$$
$$\Rightarrow \quad 10M_1 = 1100 \quad \therefore \ M_1 = 110.$$

18.
$$E_1 : E_2 :: D_2 : D_1$$
$$D_2 = \frac{E_1 D_1}{E_2} = \frac{5 \times 12}{4} = 15 \text{ hours.}$$

19.
$$\frac{1}{12} - \frac{1}{18} = \frac{1}{T}$$

or
$$\frac{T}{12} - \frac{T}{18} = 1$$

$$\Rightarrow \quad \frac{3T - 2T}{36} = 1 \quad \therefore \ T = 36 \text{ hours.}$$

SPEED, TIME AND DISTANCE

Solved Examples

Example 1: *In how much time will a car cover a distance of 4,500 m with a speed of 45 km/hour?*

Solution:
$$\text{Time} = \frac{\text{Distance}}{\text{speed}}$$
$$= \frac{4.5}{45} = 0.1 \text{ hour (or 6 min.)}$$
$$(\because \ 4,500 \text{ m} = 4.5 \text{ km})$$

Example 2: *A man travels a certain distance at the rate of 70 km/hour and returns the same point at the rate of 55 km/hour. What is his average speed of journey?*

Solution: Using formula,
$$\text{Average speed} = \frac{2xy}{x + y} = \frac{2 \times 70 \times 55}{70 + 55}$$
$$= 61.6 \text{ km/hour.}$$

Example 3: *A train 270 m long passes a standing man in 24 sec. What is the speed of the train?*

Solution: Required speed $= \dfrac{270}{24}$ m/sec

$$= \frac{270}{24} \times \frac{18}{5} \text{ km/hour}$$
$$= 40.5 \text{ km/hour.}$$

EXERCISE

1. A man travels a certain distance at the rate of 10 km per hour and returns the same point at the rate of 15 km per hour. His average rate for the whole journey is:

- A. 12 km/hour
- B. $12\dfrac{1}{2}$ km/hour
- C. 13 km/hour
- D. None of these

2. Walking at the rate of 4 km an hour, a man covers a distance in 2 hrs. 45 min. Running at a speed of 11 km per hour, the man will cover this much distance in:

- A. $\dfrac{1}{2}$ hour
- B. 1 hour
- C. $1\dfrac{3}{4}$ hour
- D. 2 hours

3. If a person takes as much time in running 20 metre as a car takes in covering 50 m; the distance covered by the person during the time car covers 1 km is:

- A. 100 m
- B. 140 m
- C. 400 m
- D. 500 m

4. A motorist travels a distance of 10 km at a speed of 50 km/hour in the onward journey and 60 km/hour while returning. His average speed is:

- A. $54\dfrac{6}{11}$ km/hr
- B. 55 km/hr
- C. $55\dfrac{6}{11}$ km/hr
- D. 54 km/hr

5. On a tour a man travels at the rate of 35 km an hour for the first 160 km, then travels the next 160 km at the rate of 45 km an hour. What is the average speed in km per hour for the first 320 km of the tour?

- A. $39\dfrac{1}{4}$
- B. $39\dfrac{1}{2}$
- C. $39\dfrac{1}{16}$
- D. $39\dfrac{3}{8}$

6. X and Y are 15 km apart. X can walk at the speed of 14 km/hr and Y at the speed of 16 km/hr. They start walking towards each other at 7 a.m. At what time will they meet:

- A. 7.15 a.m.
- B. 7.30 a.m.
- C. 7.45 a.m.
- D. 8.00 a.m.

7. A train 600 metre long is running with a speed of 54 km/hr. In what time will it pass a tunnel 200 metre long?

- A. 48 sec
- B. 50 sec
- C. $53\dfrac{1}{3}$ sec
- D. $55\dfrac{1}{4}$ sec

8. A man travels 3/4th of the distance of his journey by bus, 1/6th by rickshaw and 4 km on foot. How many km does he travel in the journey?

- A. 40 km
- B. 46 km
- C. 48 km
- D. 50 km

9. A man walks from his house at an average speed of 5 km/hr and reaches his office 6 minute late. If he walks at an average speed of 6 km/hr he reaches 2 minute early. What is the distance of the office from his house?

A. 4 km   B. 4.5 km

C. 5.0 km   D. 5.5 km

10. If a man can row 30 km downstream and 18 km upstream, each in 3 hours, what is the speed of boat in still water?

A. 8 km/hr

B. 10 km/hr

C. 12 km/hr

D. 15 km/hr

ANSWERS

1	2	3	4	5	6	7	8	9	10
A	B	C	A	D	B	C	C	A	A

EXPLANATORY ANSWERS

1. Using formula,

$$\text{Average speed} = \left(\frac{2\times10\times15}{10+15}\right) \text{ km/hr} = 12 \text{ km/hr}$$

2. 2 hours 45 min. $= 2\dfrac{3}{4}$ hours $= \dfrac{11}{4}$ hours

Distance covered by man = speed × time

$$= 4\times\frac{11}{4} = 11 \text{ km}$$

So, the time taken by man to cover 11 km distance when speed in 11 km/hr. is

$$= \frac{11}{11} = 1 \text{ hour}$$

3. Clearly, $20 : 50 = x : 1{,}000$, x being the distance covered the person.

So, $\qquad x = \dfrac{20}{50}\times1{,}000 = 400 \text{ m}$

4. Using formula,

$$\text{Average speed} = \frac{2\times50\times60}{50+60}$$

$$= \frac{6{,}000}{110} = 54\frac{6}{11} \text{ km/hour}$$

5. Using formula,

$$\text{Average speed} = \frac{2\times35\times45}{35+45}$$

$$= \frac{3{,}150}{80} = 39\frac{3}{8} \text{ km/hour}$$

6. X and Y are moving towards each other, so their relative speed

$$= (14 + 16) \text{ km/hour} = 30 \text{ km/hour}$$

$$\text{Time taken} = \frac{\text{Distance}}{\text{Speed}}$$

$$= \frac{15}{30} \text{ hour} = \frac{1}{2} \text{ hour}$$

Since, they start at 7 a.m., they will meet at 7.30 a.m.

7. Speed of train $= \left(54\times\dfrac{5}{18}\right)$ m/sec $= 15$ m/sec

In passing a tunnel, train will have to cover a distance of (200 + 600) m *i.e.,* 800 m.

$\therefore$ Time it will take to pass $= \dfrac{800}{15} = 53\dfrac{1}{3}$ sec.

8. Let the total distance be x km. Then,

$$\frac{3}{4}x + \frac{1}{6}x + 4 = x$$

$$\Rightarrow \quad \frac{9x + 2x + 48}{12} = x$$

$$\Rightarrow \quad 11x + 48 = 12x \quad \therefore \quad x = 48 \text{ km}$$

9. Let the distance of office from the house be x km. Difference of two timings = 6 + 2 = 8 min.

$$= \frac{8}{60} \text{ hour} = \frac{2}{15} \text{ hour}$$

Then, $\qquad \dfrac{x}{5} - \dfrac{x}{6} = \dfrac{2}{15}$

$$\Rightarrow \quad \frac{6x - 5x}{30} = \frac{2}{15}$$

$$\therefore \qquad x = \frac{2\times30}{15} = 4 \text{ km}$$

10. Let speed of boat $= x$ km/hr and speed of stream $= y$ km/hr

Then, $\qquad \dfrac{30}{x+y} = 3$

and $\qquad \dfrac{18}{x-y} = 3$

$\Rightarrow \qquad 3x + 3y = 30 \qquad\qquad …(i)$

and $\qquad 3x - 3y = 18 \qquad\qquad …(ii)$

Adding (*i*) and (*ii*),

$$6x = 48 \quad \therefore \quad x = 8$$

$\therefore$ Speed of boat in still water is 8 km/hr.

PERCENTAGE

Solved Examples

Example 1: *35% of a number is 315. What is the number?*

Solution: Let the number be x. Then,

$$35\% \text{ of } x = 315$$

or

$$\frac{35}{100}x = 315$$

$$\therefore \quad x = \frac{315 \times 100}{35} = 900$$

Thus, the required number is 900.

Example 2: *Mohan spent 20% of his income on food, 30% on house rent and 25% on clothes. If he saved ₹ 750, then find his income.*

Solution:

$$750 = I\left(1 - \frac{20 + 30 + 25}{100}\right)$$

$$= \frac{I[100 - (20 + 30 + 25)]}{100}$$

$$\Rightarrow \quad I = \frac{750 \times 100}{100 - 75} = 750 \times \frac{100}{25} = ₹ \ 3,000$$

Example 3: *Rakesh spends 20% on food, 25% of the rest on education and 10% of the remaining on house rent. If still he has ₹ 120 with him, find his income.*

Solution: Formula:

$$\text{Income} = \frac{\text{Saving} \times 100 \times 100 \times 100}{(100 - 20)(100 - 25)(100 - 10)}$$

$$= \frac{120 \times 100 \times 100 \times 100}{80 \times 75 \times 90} = ₹ \ \frac{20,000}{9}$$

$$= ₹ \ 2,222.22$$

EXERCISE

1. What per cent is 25 paise of ₹ 100?
 A. 250%
 B. 25%
 C. 2.5%
 D. 0.25%

2. In a co-educational school 35% of the students are boys. If there are 416 girls in the school, the number of boys in the school is:
 A. 220
 B. 224
 C. 228
 D. 230

3. In an examination a candidate has to secure 40% of the marks to pass. If a candidate secures 190 marks and fails by 10 marks, the total number of marks in the examination is:
 A. 600
 B. 500
 C. 400
 D. 360

4. If Ram's salary is 50% more than Shyam's, how much percent is Shyam's salary less than Ram's salary?
 A. 33.5%
 B. $33\frac{1}{3}\%$
 C. 50%
 D. 15%

5. Surinder appears in an examination, in which a student has to secure 36% of the marks to pass. If he secures 198 marks and fails by 18 marks, find the total marks in examination:
 A. 800
 B. 600
 C. 700
 D. 900

6. If 2 litre of water are evaporated on boiling 8 litre of sugar solution containing 6% of sugar, the % of sugar in the remaining solution is:
 A. 0.6%
 B. 0.8%
 C. 6%
 D. 8%

7. The population of a city is 15,00,000. It increases by 10% during 1st year, decreases by 20% in 2nd year and increases by 30% in the 3rd year. The population after 3 years is:
 A. 17,16,000
 B. 17,50,000
 C. 16,50,000
 D. 16,00,000

8. A man spends 80% of his income. His income is increased by 20% and his expenditure is also increased by 15%. What is the % increase/decrease in his savings?
 A. 40% increase
 B. 10% decrease
 C. 5% increase
 D. 20% decrease

9. If the price of sugar is increased by 1%, what percentage should be the reduction in the consumption so that there is no extra expenditure:
 A. 1%
 B. 10%
 C. $\frac{101}{100}\%$
 D. $\frac{100}{101}\%$

10. The ratio of boys and girls in a school is 3 : 2. 20% boys and 25% girls get scholarship. How many students do not get scholarship?
 A. 22%
 B. 40%
 C. 60%
 D. 78%

ANSWERS

1	2	3	4	5	6	7	8	9	10
B	B	B	B	B	D	A	A	D	D

EXPLANATORY ANSWERS

1. Required $\% = \dfrac{25}{100} \times 100 = 25\%$

2. Let the total number of students $= x$

$\qquad$ % of boys $= 35$,

$\therefore \qquad$ % of girls $= 100 - 35 = 65\%$

So, $\qquad 65\%$ of $x = 416$

or $\qquad \dfrac{65}{100} \times x = 416$

$\therefore \qquad x = \dfrac{416 \times 100}{65} = 640$

Hence, no. of boys $= 35\%$ of 640

$\qquad\qquad = \dfrac{35}{100} \times 640 = 224$

3. Let the total marks in the examination $= x$

$\qquad$ Pass marks $= 190 + 10 = 200$

So, $\quad 40\%$ of $x = 200$

or $\qquad \dfrac{40}{100} \times x = 200$

$\therefore \qquad x = \dfrac{200 \times 100}{40} = 500$

4. Let Ram's salary $= ₹\ 100$

Then,

$\qquad$ Shyam's salary $= ₹\ 100 + 50\%$ of 100

$\qquad\qquad = ₹100 + \dfrac{50}{100} \times 100 = ₹\ 150$

$\therefore$ Ram's salary is $₹\ 50$ less from Shyam's salary.

Required percentage $= \dfrac{50}{150} \times 100 = 33\dfrac{1}{3}\%$

6. Sugar in 8 litre of solution $=$ sugar in $(8 - 2)$ *i.e.,* 6 litre of solution

So, $\quad 6\%$ of $8 = x\%$ of 6

or $\qquad \dfrac{6}{100} \times 8 = \dfrac{x}{100} \times 6 \quad \therefore \ x = \dfrac{6 \times 8}{6} = 8\%$

7. Required population

$\qquad = \dfrac{15,00,000 \times (100+10)(100-20)(100+30)}{100 \times 100 \times 100}$

$\qquad = 17,16,000$

8. Let the monthly income be $₹\ 100$. Then, the man spends $₹\ 80$ and saves $₹\ 20$.

His increased income $= ₹\ 120$

His increased expenditure $= ₹\ 80 + 15\%$ of $₹\ 80$

$\qquad\qquad = ₹\ 80 + ₹\ \dfrac{15}{100} \times 80 = ₹\ 92$

New savings $= ₹\ 120 - ₹\ 92 = ₹\ 28$

% increase in savings $= \dfrac{28-20}{20} \times 100 = 40\%$

10. Let number of boys $= 3x$ and number of girls $= 2x$

Total number of students $= 3x + 2x = 5x$

Students who get scholarship

$\qquad = \dfrac{3x \times 20}{100} + \dfrac{2x \times 25}{100} = \dfrac{110x}{100} = \dfrac{11x}{10}$

Number of students who do not get scholarship

$\qquad = 5x - \dfrac{11x}{10} = \dfrac{39x}{10}$

$\therefore$ Required Percentage $= \dfrac{39x}{10} \times \dfrac{1}{5x} \times 100 = 78$

Alternative Method:

Let the number of students be 100. Then

B	:	G	Total
3	:	2	5
↓ × 20		↓ × 20	↓ × 20

Note : 20% of 60 + 25% of 40 = 12 + 10 = 22

$\therefore$ Required percentage $= 100 - 22 = 78$

PROFIT AND LOSS

Solved Examples

Example 1: *A person buys an article at $\dfrac{3}{4}$ of its value and sells it for 20% more than its value. What is his gain %?*

Solution: Let the value of the article $= ₹\ x$

$\therefore$ The person buys it for $₹\dfrac{3}{4}x$

and sells it for $₹\ (x + 20\%$ of $x)$

i.e., $\left(x + \dfrac{20}{100}x\right) = ₹\dfrac{6x}{5}$

$\qquad$ Gain $= \dfrac{6}{5}x - \dfrac{3}{4}x = \dfrac{24x-15x}{20} = \dfrac{9}{20}x$

$\qquad$ Gain $\% = \dfrac{\dfrac{9}{20}x}{\dfrac{3}{4}x} \times 100 = 60\%$

Example 2: *Manu buys a radio at 20% discount of its value and sells it for 20% more than its value. What will be his profit %?*

Solution: Let List price of radio be $₹\ x$.

C.P. of radio = ₹ $(x - 20\%$ of $x)$

$$= ₹\left(x - \frac{x}{5}\right) = ₹\frac{4}{5}x$$

S.P. of radio = ₹ $(x + 20\%$ of $x)$

$$= ₹\left(x + \frac{x}{5}\right) = \frac{6}{5}x$$

$$\text{Profit} = \frac{6}{5}x - \frac{4}{5}x = \frac{2}{5}x$$

$$\text{Profit\%} = \frac{\frac{2}{5}x}{\frac{4}{5}x} \times 100 = 50\%$$

EXERCISE

1. Surabhi sold a washing machine for ₹ 9,499 at a gain of 15%. Find the cost price of the washing machine:
   A. ₹ 8,000   B. ₹ 8,100
   C. ₹ 8,260   D. ₹ 8,300

2. A fruit seller buys mangoes at the rate of 15 for ₹ 12 and sells them at the rate of ₹ 15 per dozen. Find his gain %:
   A. 25.65%   B. 32.25%
   C. 51.35%   D. 56.25%

3. Raj Kumar sold 2 calculators for ₹ 990 each. On one calculator he gained 10% and on the other he lost 10%; find his gain or loss in the transaction:
   A. no loss-no gain   B. 1% gain
   C. 1% loss   D. 5% loss

4. Mickey sells an article to Minnie at a profit of 20% and Minnie sells it to Meha at a profit of 25%. If Meha pays ₹ 450 for it, the cost price for Mickey is:
   A. ₹ 300   B. ₹ 325
   C. ₹ 350   D. ₹ 375

5. A shopkeeper buys 2 varieties of rice, one costing him ₹ 26 per kg and another ₹ 30.50 per kg. He mixes them in the ratio of 3 : 4 and this blended variety of rice is sold off at rate of ₹ 30 per kg. Gain % is:
   A. 2%   B. 3%
   C. 4%   D. 5%

6. Mudit purchases 5 shirts and 10 trousers for ₹ 5,000. He sells the shirts at 15% profit and trousers at 10% loss. Thus he gets ₹ 375 as profit. The cost of one shirt is:
   A. ₹ 650   B. ₹ 675
   C. ₹ 700   D. ₹ 725

7. Shobit marks his goods 25% above cost price, but allows 17.5% discount for cash payment. If he sells the article for ₹ 825, find the cost price of the article:
   A. ₹ 800   B. ₹ 810
   C. ₹ 820   D. ₹ 823

8. The selling price of two cows is ₹ 500 each. There is a gain of 20% on one and a loss of 10% on the other. Total gain or loss is:
   A. $1\frac{5}{9}\%$ B. $3\frac{4}{5}\%$
   C. 1.44%   D. $2\frac{6}{7}\%$

9. By selling an article in ₹ 480, the loss is 20%. The selling price for gaining 20% is:
   A. ₹ 720   B. ₹ 600
   C. ₹ 620   D. ₹ 700

10. Mohan sells a radio at 10% profit. If the purchasing price would be 10% less and selling price ₹ 132 less, then there is a loss of 10% to him. The purchasing price of the radio is:
    A. ₹ 264   B. ₹ 728
    C. ₹ 1,200   D. ₹ 2,100

ANSWERS

1	2	3	4	5	6	7	8	9	10
C	D	C	A	D	C	A	D	A	C

EXPLANATORY ANSWERS

1. Cost Price = ₹ $\dfrac{100}{100+15} \times 9,499$ = ₹ 8,260

2.   C.P. of 15 mangoes = ₹ 12

   ∴   C.P. of 1 mango = ₹ $\dfrac{12}{15}$

   ∴   C.P. of 12 mangoes = ₹ $\dfrac{12}{15} \times 12$ = ₹ $\dfrac{48}{5}$ = ₹ 9.60

   Given, S.P. of 12 mangoes = ₹ 15

   $$\text{Gain} = ₹\left(15 - \frac{48}{5}\right) = ₹\frac{27}{5} = ₹\ 5.40$$

   $$\text{Gain\%} = \frac{5.40}{9.60} \times 100 = 56.25\%$$

3. Loss% = $\left(\dfrac{\text{Common loss and gain}}{10}\right)^2 = \left(\dfrac{10}{10}\right)^2 = 1$

4. Cost Price for Mickey $= ₹\,450 \times \dfrac{100}{120} \times \dfrac{100}{125}$

$$= ₹\,300$$

Another Method:

Since it is a case of successive profit,

resultant profit $= x + y + \dfrac{xy}{100}$,

formula for $x\%$ and $y\%$ profit

$$= 20 + 25 + \dfrac{20 \times 25}{100} = 50\%$$

$\therefore \qquad$ C.P. $= ₹\,450 \times \dfrac{100}{150} = ₹\,300$

5. Let the shopkeeper boys 3 kg of the 1st variety and 4 kg of the 2nd variety of rice.

C.P. of 3 kg of rice at the rate ₹ 26 per kg
$$= ₹\,26 \times 3 = ₹\,78$$

C.P. of 4 kg of rice at the rate of ₹ 30.50 per kg
$$= ₹\,30.50 \times 4 = ₹\,122$$

$\therefore$ C.P. of 7 kg of rice $= ₹\,78 + ₹\,122 = ₹\,200$

S.P. of 7 kg of rice $= ₹\,30 \times 7 = ₹\,210$

Gain $= ₹\,210 - ₹\,200 = ₹\,10$

$\therefore \quad$ Gain % $= \dfrac{10}{200} \times 100 = 5\%$

6. Let the cost of one shirt be ₹ x.

Then, total S.P.

$$= 5x\left(\dfrac{115}{100}\right) + (5,000 - 5x)\left(\dfrac{90}{100}\right)$$

$$= 5,375 \text{ (given)}$$

$\Rightarrow \quad 5\dfrac{3}{4}x + 4,500 - 4\dfrac{1}{2}x = 5,375$

$\Rightarrow \qquad \dfrac{5}{4}x = 875 \quad \therefore x = 700$

$\therefore$ Cost of one shirt $= ₹\,700.$

7. $\quad$ Market Price $= ₹\,825 \times \dfrac{100}{100 - 17.5}$

$$= ₹\,825 \times \dfrac{100}{82.5} = ₹\,1000$$

$\qquad$ C.P. $= ₹\,1000 \times \dfrac{100}{100 + 25} = ₹\,800$

8. Percentage gain or loss $= \dfrac{100(P - L) - 2PL}{200 + P - L}$

$$= \dfrac{100(20 - 10) - 2 \times 20 \times 10}{200 + 20 - 10}$$

$$= \dfrac{1,000 - 400}{210} = \dfrac{600}{210} = \dfrac{20}{7} \text{ positive}$$

$\therefore$ Total percentage gain $= \dfrac{20}{7}\%$ or $2\dfrac{6}{7}\%$

9. $100 - 20 = 80$

When SP ₹ 80 then CP = ₹ 100

When SP ₹ 480 then CP $= \dfrac{100}{80} \times 480 = ₹\,600$

Again $100 + 20 = ₹\,120$

When CP ₹ 100 then SP ₹ 120

When CP ₹ 600 then SP $= \dfrac{120}{100} \times 600 = ₹\,720$

$\therefore$ SP $= ₹\,720$

10. Let purchasing price be ₹ 100.

Then selling price $= ₹\,100 + 10 = ₹\,110$

New purchasing price $= 100 - 10 = ₹\,90$

and new selling price $= 90\left(1 + \dfrac{10}{100}\right)$

$$= 90 \times \dfrac{11}{10} = ₹\,99$$

Difference in the two selling prices
$$= 110 - 99 = ₹\,11$$

When difference is ₹ 11, then P.P. = ₹ 100

When difference is ₹ 132, then P.P.

$$= \dfrac{100}{11} \times 132 = ₹\,1,200.$$

RATIO, PROPORTION AND VARIATION

EXERCISE

1. What should be added to each of the numbers 12, 30, 40 and 86, so that they are in proportion:

A. 6 $\qquad\qquad$ B. 4

C. – 6 $\qquad\qquad$ D. – 4

2. The mean proportional to $6 + \sqrt{27}$ and $6 - \sqrt{27}$ is:

A. 3 $\qquad\qquad$ B. 9

C. 10 $\qquad\qquad$ D. $\sqrt{10}$

3. If $x : y = 9 : 11$, the value of $\dfrac{5x + 3y}{3x + 5y}$ is:

A. 45 : 55 $\qquad\qquad$ B. 18 : 22

C. 37 : 41 $\qquad\qquad$ D. 39 : 41

4. The ratio of males and females of a village is 5 : 3. If there are 800 males in the village, females are :

A. 240 $\qquad\qquad$ B. 480

C. 840 $\qquad\qquad$ D. 488

5. In a mixture of 60 litre, the ratio of ethanol to ether is 4 : 1. How much ether must be added to the mixture to make this ratio 2 : 1?
A. 10 litre   B. 12 litre
C. 18 litre   D. 24 litre

6. A mixture of 45 litre of spirit and water, contains 20% of water in it. How much water must be added to it make the water 25% in the new mixture?
A. 5 litre   B. 3 litre
C. 4 litre   D. 6 litre

ANSWERS

1	2	3	4	5	6
A	A	D	B	B	B

1. Let x be added to each of the numbers. Then,
$(12 + x) : (30 + x) :: (40 + x) : (86 + x)$
$\Rightarrow (86 + x)(12 + x) = (30 + x)(40 + x)$
$\Rightarrow 1{,}032 + 86x + 12x + x^2$
$\qquad = 1{,}200 + 30x + 40x + x^2$
$\Rightarrow \qquad 28x = 168 \therefore x = 6$

2. Mean proportion $= \sqrt{(6+\sqrt{27})(6-\sqrt{27})}$
$\qquad\qquad\qquad = \sqrt{36 - 27} = \sqrt{9} = 3$

3. $\dfrac{5x+3y}{3x+5y} = \dfrac{5\left(\dfrac{x}{y}\right)+3}{3\left(\dfrac{x}{y}\right)+5}$, dividing both num. and denom.

by y

$= \dfrac{5\left(\dfrac{9}{11}\right)+3}{3\left(\dfrac{9}{11}\right)+5}, = \dfrac{\dfrac{45+33}{11}}{\dfrac{27+55}{11}} = \dfrac{78}{82} = \dfrac{39}{41}$

4. $5 : 3 = 800 : x$, where x represent females of the village.
$\therefore \qquad x = \dfrac{800 \times 3}{5} = 480$

5. Quantity of ethanol in the mixture
$$= \frac{4}{5} \times 60 = 48 \text{ litre}$$
Quantity of ether in the mixture
$$= \frac{1}{5} \times 60 = 12 \text{ litre}$$
Let x litre of ether be added to mixture to get the desired ratio. Then,
$$\frac{48}{12+x} = \frac{2}{1} \Rightarrow 24 + 2x = 48$$
$\Rightarrow \qquad 2x = 24 \qquad \therefore x = 12$
$\therefore$ 12 litre of ether is to be added.

6. Quantity of water in the mixture
$$= \frac{20}{100} \times 45 \text{ litre} = 9 \text{ litre}$$
Quantity of spirit in the mixture
$$= \frac{80}{100} \times 45 \text{ litre}$$
$$= 36 \text{ litre}$$
Let x litre of water be added to make the water 25% in the new mixture. Then,
$$\frac{9+x}{36} = \frac{25}{75} \quad \therefore x = 3 \text{ litre}$$

INTEREST

Solved Examples

Example 1: *What sum of money will produce ₹2,430 interest in 3 years at 3% simple interest?*
Solution: We have,
$$\text{S.I.} = \frac{PRT}{100}$$
Here, S.I. = ₹ 2,430, R = 3%, T = 3 years
So, $P = \dfrac{SI \times 100}{R \times T} = ₹\dfrac{2{,}430 \times 100}{3 \times 3} = ₹ 27{,}000$

Example 2: *In what time does a money becomes double at simple interest rate of 5% per annum?*
Solution: Let the money be ₹ 100.
After T years, it becomes ₹ 200, so interest = ₹ 100
$\therefore$ Time, $T = \dfrac{100 \times (\text{S.I.})}{\text{Principal} \times \text{Rate}} = \dfrac{100 \times (100)}{100 \times 5}$
$\qquad\qquad = 20 \text{ years}$

Example 3: *A sum of ₹ 300 amounts to ₹ 420 in 4 years. What will it amount to if rate of interest is increased by 2%?*
Solution: Rate of interest before increase

$$= \frac{100 \times 120}{300 \times 4} = 10\%$$

$\therefore$ New rate of interest = 12%

S.I. with new rate of interest

$$= \frac{300 \times 12 \times 4}{100} = ₹\ 144$$

Amount = ₹ 300 + ₹ 144 = ₹ 444

Example 4: *What annual instalment will discharge a debt of ₹ 1,326 due in 4 years at 7% simple interest?*

Solution: Let the annual payment be ₹ x. Then,

Amount of x for 3 years = $x + \dfrac{x \times 7 \times 3}{100}$

Amount of x for 2 years = $x + \dfrac{x \times 7 \times 2}{100}$

Amount of x for 1 year = $x + \dfrac{x \times 7 \times 1}{100}$

The three payments along with last payment of ₹ x will discharge the debt.

According to question,

$$\left(x + \frac{21x}{100}\right) + \left(x + \frac{14x}{100}\right) + \left(x + \frac{7x}{100}\right) + x = 1,326$$

or $\qquad\qquad\qquad\qquad 442x = 1,32,600$

$\therefore \qquad\qquad\qquad\qquad\qquad x = 300$

Hence, annual payment = ₹ 300

Example 5: *Find the compound interest on ₹ 8,000 at the rate of 5% p.a. for 2 years.*

Solution: Amount = ₹$\left[8,000 \times \left(1 + \dfrac{5}{100}\right)^2 \right]$

$\therefore \qquad$ Amount = ₹$\left[8,000 \times \dfrac{21}{20} \times \dfrac{21}{20} \right]$

$$= ₹\ 8,820$$

Compound interest = ₹ 8,820 – ₹ 8,000 = ₹ 820.

EXERCISE

1. In how many years will a sum of ₹ 1,500 yield an interest of ₹ 1,080 at 12 per cent per annum?

   A. 5 years   B. $5\dfrac{1}{4}$ years

   C. $5\dfrac{1}{2}$ years   D. 6 years

2. The principal which yields an interest of ₹ 2,500 in $2\dfrac{1}{2}$ years at 10% per annum at simple interest is:

   A. ₹ 8,000   B. ₹ 9,000

   C. ₹ 10,000   D. ₹ 11,000

3. A sum of ₹ 7,800 is lent out in 2 parts in such a way that the interest on one part at 10% for 5 years is equal to that on the other part at 9% for 6 years. The sum lent out at 10% is:

   A. ₹ 4,050   B. ₹ 3,750

   C. ₹ 4,500   D. ₹ 3,300

4. The simple interest on a sum of money is $\dfrac{1}{16}$ of the principal and the number of years is equal to the rate percent per annum. The rate percent per annum is:

   A. $2\dfrac{1}{2}\%$ B. $2\dfrac{1}{3}\%$

   C. $2\dfrac{1}{6}\%$ D. $6\dfrac{1}{4}\%$

5. What is the compound interest on ₹ 6,250 at 4% p.a. compounded annually for 3 years?

   A. ₹ 780.40   B. ₹ 789.00

   C. ₹ 788.80   D. ₹ 780.40

6. At what rate percent compound interest ₹ 800 amounts to ₹ 926.10 in $1\dfrac{1}{2}$ years interest compounded semi-annually?

   A. 8% p.a.   B. 10% p.a.

   C. 12% p.a.   D. 14% p.a.

7. A sum of money doubles itself at compound interest, compounded annually in 15 years. In how many years will it become 8 times, the remaining rate the same?

   A. 40 years   B. 45 years

   C. 50 years   D. 55 years

8. A loan ₹ 50,440 at 5% compound interest is to be paid in three equal annual instalments. What will be the amount of each annual instalment?

   A. ₹ 18,522   B. ₹ 2,089

   C. ₹ 2,689   D. ₹ 9,522

ANSWERS

1	2	3	4	5	6	7	8
D	C	A	A	D	B	B	A

EXPLANATORY ANSWERS

1. Here, P = ₹ 1,500; R = 12%; S.I. = ₹ 1,080

Time, T = $\dfrac{₹\,1,080 \times 100}{₹\,1,500 \times 12}$ = 6 years

3. $\dfrac{\text{I part} \times 5 \times 10}{100} = \dfrac{\text{II part} \times 9 \times 6}{100}$

or $\dfrac{\text{I part}}{\text{II part}} = \dfrac{9 \times 6}{5 \times 10} = \dfrac{27}{25}$

∴ I part = $\dfrac{7,800}{27 + 25} \times 27$ = ₹ 4,050

and II part = ₹ 7,800 – ₹ 4,050 = ₹ 3,750

4. Time = R years, P = the sum in ₹

$\dfrac{P}{16} = \dfrac{P \times R \times R}{100}$

or $R^2 = \dfrac{100}{16}$

or $R = \dfrac{10}{4} = 2\dfrac{1}{2}$ % p.a.

5. Amount = $₹\,6,250 \times \left(1 + \dfrac{4}{100}\right)^3 = ₹\,6,250 \times \left(\dfrac{26}{25}\right)^3$

= ₹ 7,030.40

∴ Compound Interest

= ₹ 7,030.40 – ₹ 6,250 = ₹ 780.40

8. Let the annual instalment be ₹ a. Then,

$a\left[\left(\dfrac{100}{100+5}\right) + \left(\dfrac{100}{100+5}\right)^2 + \left(\dfrac{100}{100+5}\right)^3\right] = 50,440$

$\Rightarrow a\left[\dfrac{100}{105}\left\{1 + \dfrac{100}{105} + \left(\dfrac{100}{105}\right)^2\right\}\right] = 50,440$

$\Rightarrow a = ₹\,18,522.$

DISCOUNT

EXERCISE

1. A suitcase of ₹ 240 is sold for ₹ 202. The rate of discount is:

A. $15\dfrac{5}{6}$% B. $15\dfrac{5}{8}$%

C. $18\dfrac{41}{50}$% D. $18\dfrac{5}{8}$%

2. A merchant allows a discount of 15% on the clothes purchased. Manohar purchases clothes worth ₹ 470. The money he will give is:

A. ₹ 70.50 B. ₹ 399.50
C. ₹ 469 D. ₹ 270

3. A trader allows 10% trade discount and 20% cash discount. If the list price is ₹ 500, then selling price is:

A. ₹ 360 B. ₹ 350
C. ₹ 355 D. ₹ 340

4. A retailer gains 20% after allowing 10% discount on the cost price. If the cost price is ₹ 100, then selling price is:

A. ₹ 120 B. ₹ 108
C. ₹ 95 D. ₹ 115

5. The printed price of an electric fan is ₹ 500. It is sold at 10% discount. But due to change of season the shopkeeper, declares 10% additional discount. The sale price of the fan is:

A. ₹ 455 B. ₹ 405
C. ₹ 450 D. ₹ 400

6. The true discount of ₹ 12,100 due to two years, hence at 10% per annum compound interest is:

A. ₹ 1,000 B. ₹ 1,100
C. ₹ 2,100 D. ₹ 1,200

ANSWERS

1	2	3	4	5	6
A	B	A	B	B	C

EXPLANATORY ANSWERS

1. Amount of Discount

= List price – Selling price

= 240 – 202 = ₹ 38

Rate of Discount = $\dfrac{\text{Discount} \times 100}{\text{List Price}}$

= $\dfrac{38 \times 100}{240} = \dfrac{95}{6} = 15\dfrac{5}{6}$

i.e., Discount = $15\dfrac{5}{6}$%

2.

$$\text{Cost price} = ₹\ 470$$
$$\text{Rate of Discount} = 15\%$$
$$\text{Amount of Discount} = \frac{470 \times 15}{100}$$
$$= \frac{141}{2}$$
$$= ₹\ 70.50$$
$$\therefore \quad \text{Amount Due} = 470 - 70.50$$
$$= ₹\ 399.50$$

3. Selling Price

$$= \text{List price}\left(1 - \frac{10}{100}\right)\left(1 - \frac{20}{100}\right)$$
$$= 500 \times \frac{9}{10} \times \frac{4}{5} = ₹\ 360$$

Alternative Method:

List price	500
Less : Trade Discount @ 10%	
$\left(\dfrac{500 \times 10}{100}\right)$	$\dfrac{50}{450}$
Less : Cash Discount @ 20%	
$\left(\dfrac{450 \times 20}{100}\right)$	$\dfrac{90}{360}$

4. Selling Price = Cost Price $\left(1 + \dfrac{20}{100}\right)\left(1 - \dfrac{10}{100}\right)$

$$= 100\left(1 + \frac{1}{5}\right)\left(1 - \frac{1}{10}\right)$$
$$= 100 \times \frac{6}{5} \times \frac{9}{10} = ₹\ 108$$

5. Sale price = Printed price $\left(1 - \dfrac{d_1}{100}\right)\left(1 - \dfrac{d_2}{100}\right)$

$$= 500\left(1 - \frac{10}{100}\right)\left(1 - \frac{10}{100}\right)$$
$$= 500 \times \frac{9}{10} \times \frac{9}{10}$$
$$= ₹\ 405$$

6. $\quad$ Present value $= \dfrac{12,100}{\left(1 + \dfrac{10}{100}\right)^2}$

$$= ₹\ 10,000$$
$$\therefore \text{ True Discount} = ₹\ 12,100 - ₹\ 10,000$$
$$= ₹\ 2,100$$

AVERAGE

EXERCISE

1. The heights of 7 buildings are 12 m, 13 m, 14 m, 15 m, 16 m, 17 m and 18 m. The average height of 7 buildings is:

  A. 15 m   B. 16 m
  C. 17 m   D. 18 m

2. The average height of 10 students is computed as 153 cm. But it was found later on that 151 cm was wrongly read as 141 cm. The correct average height is:

  A. 155 cm   B. 154 cm
  C. 152 cm   D. 151 cm

3. In a school 85 boys and 35 girls appeared in an examination. The average marks of the boys were found to be 40% whereas the average marks of the girls were 60%. The average marks percentage of the school is:

  A. $50\dfrac{3}{5}$ B. 45

  C. $45\dfrac{5}{6}$ D. 60

4. If the average of 5 observations x, $x + 2$, $x + 4$, $x + 6$, $x + 8$ is 11, then the average of the last three observations is:

  A. 11   B. 13
  C. 15   D. 17

5. The average age of 8 persons is 87 years. Of these the age of oldest is 2 years more than the one next. If these two persons are ignored, then the average age of the remaining 6 persons is 85 years. The age of the oldest person is (in years):

  A. 90
  B. 94
  C. 96
  D. 98

ANSWERS

1	2	3	4	5
A	B	C	B	B

EXPLANATORY ANSWERS

1. Average height

$$= \frac{12+13+14+15+16+17+18}{7}$$

$$= \frac{105}{7} = 15 \text{ m}$$

2. Wrong average $= \overline{x} = 153$ cm
Wrong sum of heights,

$$\Sigma x = n\overline{x} = 10 \times 153 = 1,530 \text{ cm}$$

Correct sum of heights

$$\Sigma' x = \Sigma x - 141 + 151$$
$$= 1,530 + 10 = 1,540 \text{ cm}$$

$\therefore$ Correct average height,

$$\overline{x}' = \frac{\Sigma' x}{n} = \frac{1,540}{10} = 154 \text{ cm}$$

3. Let the maximum marks be 100
Then average marks of boys $= 40$
and average marks of girls $= 60$

$\therefore$ Required average $= \dfrac{85 \times 40 + 35 \times 60}{85 + 35}$

$$= \frac{3,400 + 2,100}{120}$$

$$= \frac{5,500}{120} = 45\frac{5}{6}$$

4. $\overline{x} = \dfrac{x+(x+2)+(x+4)+(x+6)+(x+8)}{5} = 11$

$\Rightarrow \quad 5x + 20 = 11 \times 5 = 55$

$\therefore \qquad x = \dfrac{55-20}{5} = \dfrac{35}{5} = 7$

This average of the last three numbers

$$= \frac{(x+4)+(x+6)+(x+8)}{3}$$

$$= \frac{(7+4)+(7+6)+(7+8)}{3}$$

$$= \frac{11+13+15}{3} = \frac{39}{3} = 13$$

5. Let $x_1, x_2, x_3, x_4, x_5, x_6, x_7, x_8$ be the ages of 8 persons where x_8 is the age of the oldest person.
Thus, total of ages of the 8 persons
$$= 8 \times 87 = 696$$
Total of ages of the 6 persons
$$= 6 \times 85 = 510$$

$\therefore \qquad x_7 + x_8 = 696 - 510 = 186 \qquad ...(i)$

But $\quad x_8 - x_7 = 2$ (given) $\qquad ...(ii)$

Adding these two equations
$$2x_8 = 188$$

$\therefore \qquad x_8 = \dfrac{188}{2} = 94$ years

PARTNERSHIP

EXERCISE

1. A, B and C share the profit in the ratio of 3 : 5 : 7. If the gain is ₹ 2,040, then C's share is :
A. ₹ 360
B. ₹ 600
C. ₹ 840
D. ₹ 120

2. Mishra, Sharma and Shukla started a business with ₹ 47,000. Mishra puts ₹ 5,000 more than Sharma and Sharma ₹ 3,000 more than Shukla. The share of Mishra out of the profit of ₹ 14,100 will be:
A. ₹ 3,600
B. ₹ 4,500
C. ₹ 6,000
D. ₹ 6,300

3. A, B and C are three partners in a business. The profit share of A is $\dfrac{3}{16}$ of the profit and B's share is $\dfrac{1}{4}$ of the profit. If C receives ₹ 243, then the amount received by B will be:
A. ₹ 90
B. ₹ 96
C. ₹ 108
D. ₹ 120

4. A starts a business with ₹ 5,000. After 4 months B joins him with a sum of ₹ 4,000. In the end of the year there is a profit of ₹ 8,970. The share of A in the profit will be:
A. ₹ 3,120
B. ₹ 4,020
C. ₹ 5,850
D. ₹ 6,360

5. A, B and C share the profit in the ratio of 2 : 3 : 7. If the average gain is ₹ 8,000, then B's share is:
A. ₹ 2,000
B. ₹ 1,000
C. ₹ 1,500
D. ₹ 3,000

ANSWERS

1	2	3	4	5
C	C	C	C	A

EXPLANATORY ANSWERS

1. C's share = $\dfrac{7}{3+5+7} \times 2,040 = ₹\ 840$

2. Let Shukla's capital = ₹ x

Then Sharma's capital = ₹ $(x + 3,000)$

and Mishra capital = ₹ $(x + 3,000 + 5,000)$

$\Rightarrow x + (x + 3,000) + (x + 3,000 + 5,000)$
$$= 47,000$$

$\Rightarrow \qquad 3x = 47,000 - 11,000 = 36,000$

$\therefore \qquad x = ₹\ 12,000$

Thus, capitals of Mishra, Sharma and Shukla are:
$$₹\ 20,000;\ ₹\ 15,000;\ ₹\ 12,000$$

$\therefore$ Profit sharing ratio = 20 : 15 : 12
$$\text{Sum} = 47$$

$\therefore \qquad$ Profit of Mishra = $\dfrac{20}{47} \times 14,100 = ₹\ 6,000$

3. Let the profit be ₹ 1. Then

$$A : B : C = \frac{3}{16} : \frac{1}{4} : \left[1 - \left(\frac{3}{16} + \frac{1}{4}\right)\right] = \frac{3}{16} : \frac{1}{4} : \frac{9}{16}$$

$$= \frac{3}{16} : \frac{4}{16} : \frac{9}{16}, \ i.e.,\ 3 : 4 : 9$$

When C's share is ₹ 9, then B's share = ₹ 4

When C's share is ₹ 243, then B's share

$$= \frac{4 \times 243}{9} = ₹\ 108$$

4.
$$₹\ 5,000 \times 12 = ₹\ 60,000 \text{ for A}$$
$$₹\ 4,000 \times (12 - 4) = ₹\ 32,000 \text{ for B}$$

Ratio of profit sharing = 60,000 : 32,000
$$\text{or } 60 : 32 \text{ or } 15 : 8$$

$\therefore$ A's share = $\dfrac{15}{15+8} \times 8,970$

$$= 15 \times 390 = ₹\ 5850$$

5. B's share = $\dfrac{3}{2+3+7} \times 8,000$

$$= \frac{3 \times 8,000}{12} = ₹\ 2,000$$

STOCK AND SHARES

EXERCISE

1. The 6% stock at 125 which can be purchased to get an annual income of ₹ 4,320 will be:

A. ₹ 24,000   B. ₹ 48,000

C. ₹ 36,000   D. ₹ 72,000

2. The rate of interest obtained by investing in 8% stock at ₹ 160 will be:

A. $2\dfrac{1}{2}\%$ B. 5%

C. $7\dfrac{1}{2}\%$ D. 10%

3. The investment required in "5% stock at 102" to obtain an annual income of ₹ 600 will be:

A. ₹ 6,120   B. ₹ 12,240

C. ₹ 9,120   D. ₹ 12,000

4. Ramesh holds ₹ 2,100 of 3% stock. He sells them at ₹ 121 and invests the proceeds in 5% stock. Thereby, his income increases by ₹ 14. The market price of 5% stock is:

A. ₹ 125   B. ₹ 135

C. ₹ 155   D. ₹ 165

5. Mohan invests ₹ 3,467.25 in a company paying 4% per annum when its ₹ 35 shares are selling for ₹ 51.75 each. His annual income will be:

A. ₹ 93.80   B. ₹ 39.80

C. ₹ 98.30   D. ₹ 39.08

ANSWERS

1	2	3	4	5
D	B	B	D	A

EXPLANATORY ANSWERS

1. Stock = $\dfrac{\text{Income} \times 100}{\text{Rate}}$

$$= \frac{4,320 \times 100}{6} = ₹\ 72,000$$

2. $\because$ On an investment of ₹ 160, interest = ₹ 8

$\therefore$ On an investment of ₹ 100, interest

$$= \frac{8 \times 100}{160} = ₹\ 5$$

3. Investment = $\dfrac{\text{Income} \times \text{Market Value}}{\text{Rate}}$

$= \dfrac{600 \times 102}{5} = ₹\ 12,240$

4. Income from ₹ 100 stock = ₹ 3

Income from ₹ 2,100 stock = $\dfrac{3 \times 2,100}{100} = ₹\ 63$

The income from new stock = 63 + 14 = ₹ 77
The cost of ₹ 100 stock = ₹ 121

The cost of ₹ 2,100 stock = $\dfrac{121 \times 2,100}{100}$

$= ₹\ 2,541$

When the income is ₹ 77, then cost = ₹ 2,541
When the income is ₹ 5, then cost

$= \dfrac{2,541 \times 5}{77} = ₹\ 165$

5. Market value of a share of ₹ 35 = ₹ 51.75
∴ No. of such shares purchased by ₹ 3,467.25

$= \dfrac{3467.25}{51.75} = 67$

Face value of 67 shares = 35 × 67 = ₹ 2,345
Hence, divided @ 4% of the face value

$= 2,345 \times \dfrac{4}{100} = ₹\ 93.80$

PROBLEM ON AGE

Solved Examples

Example 1: *The ratio of ages of Kavya and Neha is 4 : 5. After 12 years, this ratio will become 5 : 6. What will be the age of Kavya after 2 years?*

Solution: Let the age of Kavya be $4x$ years and age of Neha be $5x$ years.

Age of Kavya after 12 years = $(4x + 12)$ years

Age of Neha after 12 years = $(5x + 12)$ years

Hence, $\dfrac{4x+12}{5x+12} = \dfrac{5}{6}$

$\Rightarrow$ $\qquad 24x + 72 = 25x + 60 \qquad \therefore\ x = 12$

Present age of Kavya = 4 × 12 = 48 years
Thus, age of Kavya after 2 years

$= 48 + 2 = 50$ years

Example 2: *The age of a father is four times the age of his son. If the age of father is x years, find the age of his son after 8 years.*

Solution: $\qquad$ Age of the father = x years

$\therefore \qquad$ Age of the son = $\dfrac{1}{4}x$ years

$\therefore$ Age of the son after 8 years = $\left(\dfrac{x}{4}+8\right)$ years

EXERCISE

1. A father's age is four times that of his son. Eight years before, the father's age was sixteen times that of the son. Father's age is:
A. 40 years
B. 35 years
C. 42 years
D. 36 years

2. A is older than B by 5 years. Seven years hence, thrice A's age shall be equal to four times that of B. The present age of A is:
A. 13 years
B. 8 years
C. 9 years
D. 7 years

3. The ages of Ram and Mohan are in the ratio of 5 : 7 and the difference between them is 12 years. The ages (in years) of Ram and Mohan are respectively:
A. 30, 42
B. 42, 30
C. 15, 21
D. 21, 15

4. The ages of A and B are in the ratio of 9 : 4. 7 years hence, the ratio of their ages will be 5 : 3. The age of A is:
A. 8 years
B. 18 years
C. 26 years
D. 52 years

5. The ratio between the present ages of X and Y is 4 : 5. The ratio between the present age of X and the age of Y before 3 years is 7 : 8. The ratio between the present age of X and his age after 7 years will be:
A. 5 : 4
B. 8 : 7
C. 7 : 8
D. 4 : 5

6. The ratio between Rahim's and Karim's ages two years ago was 3 : 2 and at present it is 7 : 5. The present age of Karim is:
A. 10 years
B. 14 years
C. 12 years
D. 16 years

7. The sum of the ages of Ram and Shyam is 40 years. 5 years hence, the ratio of their ages will be 3 : 7. The age of Ram is:
A. 10 years
B. 30 years
C. 15 years
D. 25 years

8. The ratio of ages of the mother and her daughter is 12 : 5. The difference of their ages is 28 years. The ratio between the present age of the mother and the age of the daughter 4 years after will be:
A. 2 : 1
B. 1 : 2
C. 3 : 2
D. 2 : 3

9. The ratio of present ages of Mahesh and Dinesh is 7 : 8. If 4 years ago the ratio of their ages be 5 : 6, then present age of Dinesh is:
A. 10 years   B. 12 years
C. 14 years   D. 16 years

10. Six years back Seema was half that of Rupa in age. Four years hence, the respective ratio of their ages would be 3 : 5. The present age of Rupa is:
A. 46 years   B. 40 years
C. 32 years   D. 16 years

ANSWERS

1	2	3	4	5	6	7	8	9	10
A	A	A	B	D	A	A	A	D	A

EXPLANATORY ANSWERS

1. Let the age of the son $= x$ years
Then age of the father $= 4x$ years
Before 8 years,
$\qquad$ Son's age $= x - 8$
$\qquad$ Father's age $= 4x - 8$
$\qquad 4x - 8 = 16(x - 8)$
$\Rightarrow \qquad 4x - 8 = 16x - 128$
$\Rightarrow \qquad 12x = 120 \quad \therefore \ x = 10$
Thus, father's age $= 4 \times 10 = 40$ years

2. Let the age of A be x years
$\therefore$ the age of B $= (x - 5)$ years
Seven years hence,
$\qquad$ Age of A $= x + 7$
$\qquad$ Age of B $= (x - 5) + 7$
$\qquad 3(x + 7) = 4(x - 5 + 7)$
$\therefore \qquad 3x + 21 = 4x - 20 + 28 = 4x + 8$
$\Rightarrow \qquad 3x + 21 = 4x - 20 + 28 = 4x + 8$
$\therefore \qquad x = 13$

3. Let the ages of Ram and Mohan be $5x$ and $7x$
Then, $7x - 5x = 12 \Rightarrow 2x = 12 \therefore x = 6$
$\qquad$ Age of Ram $= 5 \times 6 = 30$ years
$\qquad$ Age of Mohan $= 7 \times 6 = 42$ years

4. Let the ages of A and B be $9x$ and $4x$.
Then $\dfrac{9x + 7}{4x + 7} = \dfrac{5}{3}$
$\Rightarrow \quad 3(9x + 7) = 5(4x + 7)$
$\Rightarrow \quad 27x + 21 = 20x + 35$
$\Rightarrow \quad 7x = 35 - 21 = 14 \quad \therefore x = 2$
Hence, age of A $= 9 \times 2 = 18$ years.

5. Let the present ages of X and Y be $4x$ and $5x$
$\therefore \quad \dfrac{4x}{5x - 3} = \dfrac{7}{8}$
$\Rightarrow \quad 8 \times 4x = 7(5x - 3)$
$\Rightarrow \quad 32x = 35x - 21$
$\Rightarrow \quad 3x = 21 \qquad \therefore x = 7$
Thus, age of X $= 4 \times 7 = 28$ years
Age of X after 7 years $= 28 + 7 = 35$ years
$\therefore$ Required ratio $= \dfrac{28}{35} = \dfrac{4}{5}$ or 4 : 5

6. Let the present ages of Rahim and Karim be $7x$ and $5x$.
Then $\dfrac{7x - 2}{5x - 2} = \dfrac{3}{2}$
$\Rightarrow \qquad 14x - 4 = 15x - 6$
$\Rightarrow \qquad x = 2$
$\Rightarrow$ The present age of Karim is $5 \times 2 = 10$ years

7. Let the ages of Ram and Shyam 5 years hence be $3x$ and $7x$.
The sum of their present ages
$\qquad = (3x - 5) + (7x - 5) = 40$
$\Rightarrow \qquad 10x = 40 + 10 = 50 \quad \therefore x = 5$
Hence, age of Ram $= 3 \times 5 - 5 = 15 - 5$
$\qquad\qquad\qquad\qquad\qquad\qquad = 10$ years.

8. Let the ages of mother and her daughter be $12x$ and $5x$.
Then, $\quad 12x - 5x = 28$
$\Rightarrow \qquad x = \dfrac{28}{7} = 4$
$\therefore$ Present age of the mother
$\qquad\qquad = 12 \times 4 = 48$ years
and age of daughter after 4 years
$\qquad\qquad = 5x + 4$
$\qquad\qquad = 5 \times 4 + 4 = 24$
$\therefore$ Required ratio $= \dfrac{48}{24}$
$\qquad\qquad\qquad = \dfrac{2}{1}, \ i.e., \ 2 : 1$

9. Let present ages of Mahesh and Dinesh be $7x$ and $8x$.
4 years ago,
$\qquad$ Mahesh's age $= 7x - 4$
$\qquad$ Dinesh's age $= 8x - 4$
$\therefore \qquad \dfrac{7x - 4}{8x - 4} = \dfrac{5}{6}$
$\Rightarrow \qquad 6(7x - 4) = 5(8x - 4)$
$\Rightarrow \qquad 42x - 24 = 40x - 20$
$\Rightarrow \qquad 2x = 4$
$\therefore \qquad x = 2$
$\therefore$ Dinesh's present age $= 8 \times 2 = 16$ years.

10. Let the present ages of Seema and Rupa be x and y.
Six years back,

Seema's age = $x - 6$

Rupa's age = $y - 6$

$$(x - 6) = \frac{1}{2}(y - 6)$$

or $\qquad 2x - y = 6 \qquad \qquad ...(i)$

Four years hence,

Seema's age = $x + 4$

Rupa's age = $y + 4$

$$\frac{x+4}{y+4} = \frac{3}{5}$$
$$5x + 20 = 3y + 12$$
$$5x - 3y = -8 \qquad \qquad ...(ii)$$

Multiply equation (i) by 3,
$$6x - 3y = 18 \qquad \qquad ...(iii)$$

Subtract eq. (iii) from eq. (ii),
$$x = 26$$

Substitute this value of x in (i),
$$y = 2x - 6 = 2 \times 26 - 6$$
$$= 52 - 6 = 46.$$

ALLIGATION, MIXTURE

EXERCISE

1. In a mixture of 60 litre, the ratio of ethanol to ether is 4 : 1. The quantity of ether to be added to the mixture to make this ratio 2 : 1 will be:

A. 10 litre   B. 12 litre

C. 18 litre   D. 24 litre

2. The price of a variety of a commodity is ₹ 5 per kg and that of another is ₹ 8 per kg. The ratio in which two varieties should be mixed so that the price is ₹ 7 per kg will be:

A. 1 : 2   B. 2 : 1

C. 3 : 1   D. 8 : 5

3. A confectioner sells the milk after mixing some water in it at the same rate at which he bought. If he gains 25% in this way, the quantity of water mixed with per litre of milk is:

A. 0.25 litre   B. 2.5 litre

C. 1.5 litre   D. 0.35 litre

4. A milk seller bought some milk at the rate of ₹ 16 per litre. He mixed water $\frac{1}{4}$ th of it and sold the mixture at the cost price. Assuming the price of water as ₹ 0.00 per litre. The gain % is:

A. 16%   B. 20%

C. 25%   D. None of these

5. Ramesh has ₹ 3,600. He invests a part of it at 3% per annum and the remaining at 5% higher rate of simple interest. He gets in all ₹ 540 at the end of 3 years. The sum invested at 3% per annum is:

A. ₹ 1,440   B. ₹ 2,000

C. ₹ 2,160   D. ₹ 2,200

ANSWERS

1	2	3	4	5
B	A	A	C	C

EXPLANATORY ANSWERS

1. The quantity of ethanol = $\frac{4}{5} \times 60$ = 48 litre

The quantity of ether = $\frac{1}{5} \times 60$ = 12 litre

$$\therefore \quad \frac{48}{12 + x} = \frac{2}{1}$$
$$\Rightarrow \qquad 48 = 2(12 + x)$$
$$\Rightarrow \qquad 48 = 24 + 2x$$
$$\Rightarrow \qquad 2x = 48 - 24 = 24$$
$$\therefore \qquad x = 12$$

2.

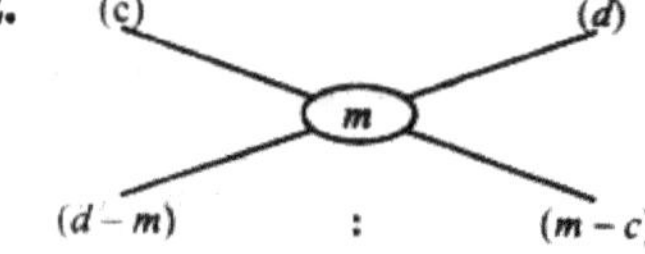

Required ratio = $\dfrac{d - m}{m - c} = \dfrac{\text{cheaper variety}}{\text{dearer variety}}$

$$= \frac{8 - 7}{7 - 5}$$
$$= \frac{1}{2} \quad i.e., \ 1 : 2$$

3. Let the cost price of 1 litre milk = ₹ 100

Profit on 1 litre = ₹ 25 ...(1)

Suppose he mixes x litre of water in 1 litre milk.

Then selling price of $(1 + x)$ litre milk

$$= (1 + x) \times 100$$

and Profit = Selling Price – Cost Price

$$= 100 (1 + x) - 100$$

$$= 100x \quad ...(2)$$

Comparing (1) and (2),

$$100x = 25$$

$$\therefore \qquad x = ₹ \ 0.25$$

4. Suppose he bought 1 litre of milk,

Cost price = ₹ 16/litre

Mixture = Milk + Water

$$= 1 + \frac{1}{4}$$

$$= \frac{5}{4}$$

Cost price of the mixture = ₹ 16

Selling price of the mixture = $\frac{5}{4} \times 16$ = ₹ 20

$$\therefore \qquad \text{Gain \%} = \frac{20 - 16}{16} \times 100$$

$$= \frac{4}{16} \times 100 = 25\%$$

5. Average rate of interest = $\dfrac{100 \times 540}{3,600 \times 3}$ = 5

By Rule of Alligation :

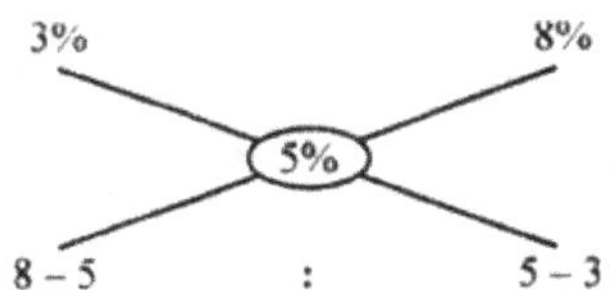

Investment at 3% per annum

$$= \frac{3}{3 + 2} \times 3,600 = ₹ \ 2,160$$

CLOCK AND CALANDER

EXERCISE

1. How many times the hands of a clock are at right angle in a day?
A. 24
B. 16
C. 44
D. 48

2. At what angle the hands of a clock are inclined at 15 minute past 5?
A. $58\frac{1}{2}°$
B. $64°$
C. $67\frac{1}{2}°$
D. $72\frac{1}{2}°$

3. What angle do the hands of a clock form at 20 past 7?
A. 70°
B. 80°
C. 90°
D. 100°

4. What will be the time when the hour hand makes an angle of 50° with the minute hand?
A. 1.15 hrs
B. 1.20 hrs
C. 1.10 hrs
D. 1.25 hrs

5. What is the time when the hands of the clock make an angle of 90° with each other?
A. 3.10 hrs
B. 3.30 hrs
C. 3.20 hrs
D. 3.25 hrs

6. What angle is formed when the hour hand is at 6.00 and the minute hand is at 12.00?
A. 100°
B. 120°
C. 180°
D. 90°

7. The angle subtended by the small hand of the clock in 20 minutes will be:
A. 10°
B. 15°
C. 20°
D. 25°

8. There are 5 Saturday in a month. The first day of the month will be:
A. Sunday
B. Friday
C. Wednesday
D. Monday

9. The first day of a year is Sunday what day of the week lies on the first day of the next year?
A. Saturday
B. Friday
C. Monday
D. Thursday

10. December 3, 1990 is Sunday; what day of the week will fall on Jan. 3, 1991?
A. Tuesday
B. Wednesday
C. Thursday
D. Friday

11. If 7th day of a month is a 3 days before Friday, then the 19th day of the same month will be:
A. Sunday
B. Monday
C. Wednesday
D. Friday

ANSWERS

1	2	3	4	5	6	7	8	9	10	11
C	C	D	A	B	C	A	B	C	B	A

EXPLANATORY ANSWERS

1. It is clear from the properties of the clock that both hands of a clock are at right angle twice in every hour, except at 3.00 o'clock and 9.00 o'clock. At 3.00 o'clock and 9.00 o'clock the positions are identical. So, they are at right angle 22 times in 12 hrs. Thus, in 24 hrs they are $22 \times 2 = 44$ times at right angles.

2. Whan the minute hand is at 3 and hour hand is slightly ahead of 5, only then the time is 15 past 3. The angle through which the four hand shifts in 15 minute =

$$15 \times \frac{1}{2}^\circ \ = \ 7\frac{1}{2}^\circ$$

Hence, angle at 15 minute past 5

$$= \ 60 + 7\frac{1}{2}^\circ \ = \ 67\frac{1}{2}^\circ$$

3. The hands of a clock form an angle of 100° at 20 past 7.

4. When the hour hand makes an angle of 50°, the time is 1.15 hrs.

5. The time is 3.30 hrs, when the hands make an angle of 90°.

6. An angle of 180° is formed when the hour hand is at 6.00 and the minute hand is at 12.00.

7. The small hand of the clock rotates 0.5° in one minute. Hence, required angle = $20 \times 0.5^\circ = 10^\circ$.

8. In a month of 31 days, there are 4 weeks + 3 days. The three days may be

> Thursday, Friday, Saturday
> Friday, Saturday, Sunday
> Saturday, Monday, Tuesday

The first day of the week may be
Thursday, *Friday* or Saturday

9. The answer depends on the year.
If the year is an ordinary year then next day.
If the year is a leap year then beyond 2 days.
Thus, possible answers are *Monday* or Tuesday.

10. No. of days from Dec. 3, 1990 to Jan. 3, 1991 = 31
No. of odd days in this period = 3
Hence, the required day is 3 days beyond Sunday, *i.e.,* Wednesday.

11. *Tuesday,* Wednesday, Thursday, Friday
7th day of the month = Tuesday
14th day of the month = Tuesday

15,	16,	17,
Wednesday,	Thursday,	Friday,
Saturday,	*Sunday*	
18,	19	

*** * ***

3
Linear Equation in Two Variables

1. Linear Equation in One Variable

Definition: A linear equation in one variable is an equation of the form $ax + b = 0$ or, $ax = c$ where, a, b, c are real numbers, $a \neq 0$ and x is a variable. Its graph is a straight line.

(*i*) If equation is on X-axis, then Y = 0

(*ii*) If equation is on Y-axis, then X = 0

2. Linear Equation in Two Variables

Definition: An equation of the form $ax + by + c = 0$ or, $ax + by = c$ where, a, b, c are real numbers, $a \neq 0$, $b \neq 0$ and x, y are variables, is called a linear equation in two variables.

For example: (*i*) $2x + 3y = 12$ (*ii*) $x + 2y = 8$

3. The System of Equations

$a_1 x + b_1 y + c_1 = 0$ and $a_2 x + b_2 y + c_2 = 0$ may be either unique solution or no solution or infinitely many solutions.

Unique solution is known as consistent or not parallel. No solution is known as inconsistent or parallel, while many solutions are known as coincident or dependent.

(*a*) **For unique solution:** $\dfrac{a_1}{a_2} \neq \dfrac{b_1}{b_2}$

(*b*) **For no solution:** $\dfrac{a_1}{a_2} = \dfrac{b_1}{b_2} \neq \dfrac{c_1}{c_2}$

(*c*) **For many solutions:** $\dfrac{a_1}{a_2} = \dfrac{b_1}{b_2} = \dfrac{c_1}{c_2}$

4. Algebraic Methods of Solving Simultaneous Linear Equations in Two Variables

(*a*) **Substitution Method :**

$$x + y = 14 \qquad \ldots(i)$$
$$x - y = 4 \qquad \ldots(ii)$$
$$\because \quad x + y = 14$$
$$\therefore \quad x = 14 - y$$

Putting the value of x in (*ii*)

$$x - y = 4$$
$$\Rightarrow \quad 14 - y - y = 4$$
$$\Rightarrow \quad -2y = 4 - 14 = -10 \Rightarrow y = 5$$

Substituting the value of y in (*i*)

$$x + y = 14$$
$$x + 5 = 14$$
$$x = 9$$

Hence, the solution is $\left.\begin{matrix} x = 9 \\ y = 5 \end{matrix}\right]$.

(*b*) **Elimination Method :**

$$2x + 3y = 12 \qquad \ldots(i)$$
$$3x + 4y = 14 \qquad \ldots(ii)$$

Multiply (*i*) by 3 and multiply (*ii*) by 2

$$6x + 9y = 36$$
$$\underline{6x + 8y = 28}$$
$$y = 8$$

Putting the value of y in (*i*)

$$2x + 3y = 12$$
$$2x + 3(8) = 12$$
$$2x = 12 - 24$$
$$2x = -12$$
$$x = -6$$

Hence, the solution is $\left.\begin{matrix} x = -6 \\ y = 8 \end{matrix}\right]$.

(*c*) **Cross Multiplication Method :**

$$3x + 4y = 10$$
$$2x - 2y = 2$$

$$\frac{x}{4 \times 2 - (-2 \times 10)} = \frac{y}{10 \times 2 - 3 \times 2} = \frac{-1}{3(-2) - 4(2)}$$

$$\frac{x}{8 + 20} = \frac{y}{20 - 6} = \frac{-1}{-6 - 8}$$

$$\frac{x}{28} = \frac{y}{14} = \frac{-1}{-14} = \frac{1}{14}$$

$$\frac{x}{28} = \frac{1}{14}$$

$$x = 2 \text{ and } \frac{y}{14} = \frac{1}{14}$$
$$y = 1$$

Hence, the solution is $\left.\begin{matrix} x = 2 \\ y = 1 \end{matrix}\right]$.

MULTIPLE CHOICE QUESTIONS

1. The system of linear equations $2x+3y=7$ and $4x+6y=10$ has :
A. no solution
B. unique solution
C. infinite solution
D. no conclusion can be drawn

2. The value of k for which the system of equations $x+2y+7=0$ and $2x+ky+14=0$ will have infinitely many solutions is :
A. 2   B. 4
C. 6   D. 8

3. For what value of α, the system of equations $\alpha x+3y=\alpha-3$ and $12x+\alpha y=\alpha$ will have a unique solution?
A. $\alpha \neq \pm 6$ B. $\alpha \neq \pm 3$
C. $\alpha \neq \mp 6$ D. None of these

4. For what value of k, the system of equations will represent the coincident lines $x+5y-7=0$ and $4x+20y+k=0$?
A. 28   B. –28
C. –26   D. None of these

5. A lady has 50 paise and ₹ 1 coins in her purse. If in all, she has 40 coins totally ₹ 25.50 how many of each type of coins does she have?
A. 26, 11   B. 11, 29
C. 29, 11   D. None of these

6. A father is three times as old as his son. After twelve years his age will be twice as the age of his son. Find their present ages in years.
A. 12, 26   B. 24, 36
C. 36, 12   D. None of these

7. Ten years ago, father was twelve times as old as his son. Ten years after, he will be twice as old as his son will be. Find their present ages in years.
A. 12, 36   B. 12, 24
C. 12, 34   D. None of these

8. The present age of a father is 3 years more than three times the age of son. Three years hence father's age will be 10 years more than twice the age of son. Determine their present ages in years.
A. 10, 33   B. 33, 10
C. 10, 30   D. None of these

9. In a triangle ABC, $\angle C = 3\angle B = 2(\angle A + \angle B)$. Find three angles in degrees.
A. 20°, 50°, 120°   B. 30°, 40°, 120°
C. 20°, 40°, 120°   D. None of these

10. The fraction becomes 2 when 1 is added to both the numerator and the denominator, and it becomes 3 when 1 is subtracted from both the numerator and denominator. The given fraction is :
A. $\dfrac{7}{3}$ B. $\dfrac{4}{7}$
C. $\dfrac{3}{7}$ D. $\dfrac{7}{4}$

11. In the system of equations $x + y = 13$ and $2x + 3y = 32$, the values of x and y are:
A. 5 and 6   B. 7 and 8
C. 7 and 6   D. 6 and 7

12. If $y = 4$, find the value of x in the equation $3x + 4y = 25$.
A. 3   B. 8
C. 5   D. 4

13. In the system of equations $5x - 7y = -13$ and $2x + 3y = 13$, the values of x and y will be:
A. $\dfrac{52}{29}$ and $\dfrac{91}{29}$ B. $\dfrac{31}{27}$ and $\dfrac{64}{27}$
C. $\dfrac{51}{29}$ and $\dfrac{87}{29}$ D. $\dfrac{52}{17}$ and $\dfrac{91}{17}$

14. For solving the system of equations $2x + y + 4 = 0$ and $x + 3y + 7 = 0$ by cross multiplication method, the equation obtained will be:
A. $\dfrac{x}{14-4} = \dfrac{y}{12-7} = \dfrac{1}{6-1}$
B. $\dfrac{x}{7-12} = \dfrac{y}{4-14} = \dfrac{1}{6-1}$
C. $\dfrac{x}{7-12} = \dfrac{y}{14-4} = \dfrac{1}{6-1}$
D. $\dfrac{x}{12-7} = \dfrac{y}{14-4} = \dfrac{1}{6-1}$

15. On eliminating y in the system of equations $6x - 5y = 11$ and $2x + y = 17$, the equation obtained in terms of x will be:
A. $13x - 95 = 0$ B. $17x - 85 = 0$
C. $19x - 91 = 0$ D. $16x - 96 = 0$

16. In the system of equations $\dfrac{x}{2}+\dfrac{y}{3} = 4$ and $x - y = -2$, the values of x and y will be:
A. 8 and 10   B. 4 and 6
C. 2 and 4   D. 6 and 8

17. In the given equation $\dfrac{x+3}{5} = \dfrac{8-y}{4} = \dfrac{3(x+y)}{8}$, values of x and y will be:
A. 4 and –8   B. 10 and –12
C. 8 and –4   D. 12 and –4

18. In the system of equations $\dfrac{2}{x}+\dfrac{3}{y}=6$ and $\dfrac{1}{x}+\dfrac{1}{2y}=2$, the values of x and y will be:

A. $\dfrac{2}{3}$ and 1   B. 1 and $\dfrac{2}{3}$

C. 3 and $\dfrac{1}{3}$ D. 2 and $\dfrac{1}{5}$

19. In the system of equations $\dfrac{6}{x+y}-\dfrac{3}{x-y}=2$ and $\dfrac{4}{x+y}+\dfrac{6}{x-y}=4$, the values of x and y will be:

A. 3 and $-\dfrac{1}{3}$ B. $\dfrac{5}{2}$ and $-\dfrac{1}{2}$

C. $\dfrac{4}{3}$ and $-\dfrac{2}{3}$ D. $\dfrac{5}{2}$ and $-\dfrac{1}{4}$

20. In the equation $\dfrac{x}{12-7}=\dfrac{y}{4-14}=\dfrac{1}{1-6}$, values of x and y will be:

A. -1 and 2   B. 2 and -1

C. 4 and -2 D. -1 and 4

21. The sum of two numbers is 80. If three times of one number is equal to five times of the other number, then the numbers are :

A. 20, 60   B. 50, 30

C. 10, 70   D. 25, 55

22. The solution of set of the system of equations :

$\dfrac{4}{x}+5y=7$, $\dfrac{3}{x}+4y=5$ is :

A. $\left(\dfrac{1}{3}, -1\right)$ B. $\left(\dfrac{-1}{3}, -1\right)$

C. $\left(\dfrac{-1}{3}, -1\right)$ D. $\left(\dfrac{1}{3}, 1\right)$

23. When one is added to each of two given numbers, their ratio becomes 3 : 4 and when 5 is subtracted from each, the ratio becomes 7 : 10. The numbers are:

A. 8, 11   B. 11, 15

C. 26, 35   D. 27, 36

24. If we add 1 to the numerator and subtract 1 from the denominator a fraction becomes 1. It also becomes $\dfrac{1}{2}$ if we only add 1 to the denominator what is the numerator of the fraction ?

A. 2   B. 4

C. 5   D. 3

25. In two digit number, the unit's digit is twice the ten's digit. If 27 is added to the number, the digits interchange their places. Find the number.

A. 36   B. 32

C. 34   D. 63

26. Points A and B are 70 km apart on a highway. A car starts from A and another car starts from B at the same time. If they travel in the same direction, they meet in 7 hours, but if they travel towards each other they meet in one hour. What are their speeds in km/hr?

A. 40, 20   B. 50, 30

C. 40, 30   D. None of these

27. The solution of the two simultaneous equations $2x+y=8$ and $3y=4+4x$ is :

A. $x=4, y=1$ B. $x=1, y=4$

C. $x=2, y=4$ D. $x=3, y=-4$

28. The solution of linear equations $3x-7y+10=0$ and $y-2x-3=0$ is :

A. $x=-1, y=1$ B. $x=1, y=-1$

C. $x=1, y=1$ D. $x=-1, y=-1$

29. The sum of the digits in a two digit number is 5. If 9 is subtracted from the number, the result is the number with the digits reversed. The number is :

A. 23   B. 32

C. 41   D. 14

30. A lady has only ₹ 2 and ₹ 1 coin in her purse. If in all, she has 60 coins, totalling Rs. 105, how many of each type of coins does she have?

A. 50, 15   B. 45, 20

C. 45, 15   D. None

31. In the system of equations $x + y = 4xy$ and $\dfrac{1}{x}+\dfrac{2}{y}=10$, the values of x and y will be:

A. $-\dfrac{1}{3}$ and $\dfrac{1}{6}$ B. $\dfrac{1}{5}$ and $\dfrac{1}{6}$

C. $-\dfrac{1}{2}$ and $\dfrac{1}{6}$ D. $+\dfrac{1}{3}$ and $-\dfrac{1}{2}$

32. In the system of equations $\dfrac{12}{x+y}+\dfrac{8}{x-y}=8$ and $\dfrac{27}{x+y}-\dfrac{12}{x-y}=3$, the values of x and y will be:

A. $\dfrac{5}{3}$ and $\dfrac{1}{3}$ B. $\dfrac{5}{2}$ and $\dfrac{1}{2}$

C. 2 and $\dfrac{1}{3}$ D. $\dfrac{5}{4}$ and $\dfrac{1}{4}$

33. On eliminating y in the system of equations $2x - y = 10$ and $3x + 2y = 22$, the equation obtained in terms of x will be:

A. $7x - 42 = 0$

B. $8x - 48 = 0$

C. $6x - 48 = 0$

D. $5x - 30 = 0$

34. In the system of equations $x + y = 7xy$ and $\dfrac{2}{x} + \dfrac{3}{y} = 17$, the values of x and y will be:

A. $\dfrac{1}{3}$ and $\dfrac{1}{4}$ 　　　 B. $\dfrac{1}{6}$ and 1

C. $\dfrac{1}{4}$ and $\dfrac{1}{3}$ 　　　 D. 2 and $\dfrac{1}{5}$

35. In the equations $x + y = 5xy$, $y + z = 7yz$ and $z + x = 6zx$, the values of x, y and z will be:

A. $\dfrac{1}{2}, \dfrac{1}{4}$ and $\dfrac{1}{3}$ 　　 B. $\dfrac{1}{3}, \dfrac{1}{4}$ and $\dfrac{1}{2}$

C. $\dfrac{1}{2}, \dfrac{1}{3}$ and $\dfrac{1}{4}$ 　　 D. $\dfrac{1}{2}, \dfrac{1}{3}$ and $\dfrac{1}{4}$

36. In the system of equations $\dfrac{1}{x} + \dfrac{1}{y} = \dfrac{5}{6}$, $\dfrac{1}{y} + \dfrac{1}{z} = \dfrac{7}{12}$ and $\dfrac{1}{z} + \dfrac{1}{x} = \dfrac{3}{4}$, values of x, y and z will be:

A. 4, 3 and 2

B. 3, 2 and 4

C. 2, 3 and 4

D. 3, 4 and 2

37. In the system of equations $8x = 5y$ and $13x = 8y + 1$, the values of x and y which satisfy the given equations are:

A. 8 and 5 　　　 B. 3 and 4

C. 10 and 16 　　 D. 5 and 8

38. In the system of equations $x(y + z) = 14$, $y(z + x) = 18$ and $z(x + y) = 20$, the values of x, y and z will be:

A. ±2, ±3 and ±4 　　 B. ±3, ±4 and ±2

C. ±2, ±4 and ±3 　　 D. ±4, ±2 and ±3

39. In the system of equations $\dfrac{3x}{x-1} + \dfrac{4y+20}{y-3} = 32$ and $\dfrac{5x}{x-1} - \dfrac{y+5}{y-3} = 15$, values of x and y which satisfy the given equations are:

A. 5 and 4/3 　　　 B. 4/3 and 5

C. 5/3 and 4 　　　 D. 4 and 5/4

40. If $\dfrac{x}{3} = \dfrac{y}{4} = \dfrac{z}{7}$, then the value of $\dfrac{x+y+z}{x}$ is:

A. $\dfrac{14}{5}$ 　　　 B. $\dfrac{14}{3}$

C. $\dfrac{13}{3}$ 　　　 D. $\dfrac{12}{7}$

ANSWERS

1	2	3	4	5	6	7	8	9	10
A	B	A	B	C	C	C	A	C	A
11	12	13	14	15	16	17	18	19	20
C	A	A	C	D	B	D	A	B	A
21	22	23	24	25	26	27	28	29	30
B	A	C	D	A	C	C	A	B	C
31	32	33	34	35	36	37	38	39	40
C	B	A	C	C	B	D	A	B	B

EXPLANATORY ANSWERS

1. $\dfrac{2}{4} = \dfrac{3}{6} \neq \dfrac{7}{10}$

$\Rightarrow \dfrac{1}{2} = \dfrac{1}{2} \neq \dfrac{7}{10}$

$\dfrac{a_1}{a_2} = \dfrac{b_1}{b_2} \neq \dfrac{c_1}{c_2}$

∴ There is no solution.

2. Since, it has many solutions.

∴ $\dfrac{a_1}{a_2} = \dfrac{b_1}{b_2} = \dfrac{c_1}{c_2}$

$\dfrac{1}{2} = \dfrac{2}{K} = \dfrac{7}{14}$

$\dfrac{1}{2} = \dfrac{2}{K}$

$\Rightarrow \quad K = 4$

3. Since, the given equations have unique solution.

∴ $\dfrac{a_1}{a_2} \neq \dfrac{b_1}{b_2}$

$\dfrac{\alpha}{12} \neq \dfrac{3}{\alpha}$

$\Rightarrow \quad \alpha^2 \neq 36 \Rightarrow \alpha \neq \pm 6$

4. Since, the given set of equations represent coincident lines.

then, $\dfrac{1}{4} = \dfrac{5}{20} = \dfrac{-7}{K} \Rightarrow K = -28.$

5. Let, x be the number of 50 paise coins and y be the number of ₹ 1 coins.

According to the question,

$$x + y = 40 \qquad \qquad ...(i)$$

and $\quad \dfrac{x}{2} + y = 25.50$

$$\Rightarrow \quad x + 2y = 51 \qquad \qquad ...(ii)$$

Subtracting equation (i) from (ii) and solving

we get, $\quad x = 29, y = 11$

6. Let, age of son $= x$ years.

$\therefore$ age of father $= 3x$ years.

According to the question,

$$2(x + 12) = 3x + 12$$
$$\Rightarrow \quad x = 12$$

$\therefore$ Son's age $= 12$ years

Father's age $= 36$ years.

7. Let ten years ago the age of son and father were x and $12x$ years.

Then, $2(x + 20) = 12x + 20$

$$\Rightarrow \quad 10x = 20 \Rightarrow x = 2$$

Their present ages are

$$x + 10 = 2 + 10 = 12 \text{ years}$$
$$12x + 10 = 24 + 10 = 34 \text{ years.}$$

8. Let the present age of son $= x$ years.

$\therefore$ Present age of father $= (3x + 3)$ years.

After 3 years,

Son's age $= (x + 3)$ years.

Father's age $= (3x + 3 + 3)$

$$= (3x + 6) \text{ years.}$$

According to the question,

$$3x + 6 = 2(x + 3) + 10$$
$$3x + 6 = 2x + 6 + 10$$
$$x = 10$$

$\therefore$ Son's present age $= 10$ years.

Father's present age $= 10 \times 3 + 3 = 33$ years.

9. $\therefore \angle C = 3\angle B = 2(\angle A + \angle B)$

$$\angle A + \angle B = \frac{\angle C}{2}$$

We have,

$\angle A + \angle B + \angle C = 180°$ (Sum of angles of a

triangle is 180°)

$$\frac{\angle C}{2} + \angle C = 180°$$

$$3\angle C = 2 \times 180°$$

$$\angle C = \frac{2 \times 180°}{3} = 120°$$

$$3\angle B = \angle C$$

$$\angle B = \frac{\angle C}{3}$$

$$= \frac{120°}{3} = 40°$$

$\therefore \qquad \angle A = 180° - (120° + 40°)$

$$= 180° - 160° = 20°$$

10. Let the fraction be $\dfrac{x}{y}$

$$\frac{x+1}{y+1} = 2$$

$$\Rightarrow \quad x + 1 = 2y + 2$$

$$\Rightarrow \quad x - 2y = 1 \qquad \qquad ...(i)$$

Again $\quad \dfrac{x-1}{y-1} = 3$

$$\Rightarrow \quad x - 1 = 3y - 3$$

$$\Rightarrow \quad x - 3y = -2 \qquad \qquad ...(ii)$$

from (i) and (ii)

$$\begin{aligned} x - 2y &= 1 \\ x - 3y &= -2 \\ \underline{- \quad + \qquad +} \\ y &= 3 \end{aligned}$$

Putting the value of y in (i) then we get

$$x = 7$$

$\therefore \qquad$ fraction $= \dfrac{x}{y} = \dfrac{7}{3}$

11. $\because \qquad x + y = 13 \qquad \qquad ...(i)$

$$2x + 3y = 32 \qquad \qquad ...(ii)$$

On multiplying equation (i) by 2 and subtracting this equation from equation (ii),

$2x + 3y - 2x - 2y = 32 - 26$ or $y = 6$

On substituting this value of y in equation (i),

$$x + 6 = 13$$

or $\qquad x = 13 - 6 = 7$

$\therefore \qquad x = 7, y = 6$

12. $\qquad 3x + 4y = 25$

$\Rightarrow 3x + 4 \times 4 = 25 \qquad \qquad (\because y = 4)$

or $\quad 3x + 16 = 25 \Rightarrow 3x = 25 - 16$

$\Rightarrow \qquad 3x = 9 \Rightarrow x = 9/3 = 3$

13. $\because \qquad 5x - 7y = -13 \qquad \qquad ...(i)$

$$2x + 3y = 13 \qquad \qquad ...(ii)$$

On multiplying equation (i) by 2 and equation (ii) by 5 and then subtracting the equation (ii) from equation (i),

$$10x - 14y - (10x + 15y) = -26 - 65$$

or $\quad 10x - 14y - 10x - 15y = -91$

or $\qquad -29y = -91 \Rightarrow y = \dfrac{91}{29}$

On substituting this value of y in equation (i),

$$5x - \frac{7 \times 91}{29} = -13$$

$$\Rightarrow \quad 5x = \frac{7 \times 91}{29} - 13$$

$$\Rightarrow \quad 5x = \frac{637 - 377}{29} = \frac{260}{29}$$

or, $\quad x = \frac{260}{29 \times 5} = \frac{52}{29}$

$\therefore \quad x = \frac{52}{29}, \ y = \frac{91}{29}$

14. $\because A = 2, B = 1, C = 4$ and $A^1 = 1, B^1 = 3, C^1 = 7$

$$\therefore \quad \frac{x}{1 \diagdown 4 \atop 3 \diagdown 7} = \frac{y}{2 \diagdown 4 \atop 1 \diagdown 7} = \frac{1}{2 \diagdown 1 \atop 1 \diagdown 3}$$

or $\dfrac{x}{7-12} = \dfrac{y}{14-4} = \dfrac{1}{6-1}$.

15. Value of y in terms of x in the first equation will be:

$\because \quad 6x - 5y = 11 \Rightarrow 5y = 6x - 11$

$$\Rightarrow \quad y = \frac{6x - 11}{5}$$

On substituting this value of y in the second equation,

$$2x + \frac{(6x - 11)}{5} = 17$$

$$\Rightarrow \quad 10x + 6x - 11 = 85$$

$$\Rightarrow \quad 16x - 96 = 0$$

16. $\because \quad \dfrac{x}{2} + \dfrac{y}{3} = 4 \quad \dots(i)$

and $\quad x - y = -2 \quad \dots(ii)$

Equation (i), $\dfrac{x}{2} + \dfrac{y}{3} = 4 \Rightarrow 3x + 2y = 24$

On multiplying equation (ii) by 2 and adding it to the equation (i),

$\therefore \ 3x + 2y + 2x - 2y = 24 - 4$

$\Rightarrow \quad 5x = 20 \Rightarrow x = 4$

On substituting this value of x in equation (i),

$4 - y = -2 \Rightarrow y = 6 \ \therefore \ x = 4, \ y = 6$

17. Suppose $\dfrac{x+3}{5} = \dfrac{8-y}{4} = \dfrac{3(x+y)}{8} = k$

$$\therefore \quad \frac{x+3}{5} = k \Rightarrow x = 5k - 3 \quad \dots(i)$$

$$\frac{8-y}{4} = k$$

$$\Rightarrow \quad y = 8 - 4k \quad \dots(ii)$$

and $\dfrac{3(x+y)}{8} = k$

$\Rightarrow \quad 3(x + y) = 8k \quad \dots(iii)$

On substituting the value of x and y from equation (i) and (ii) in equation (iii),

$$3(5k - 3 + 8 - 4k) = 8k$$

$\Rightarrow 3k + 15 = 8k \Rightarrow 5k = 15 \ \therefore \ k = \dfrac{15}{5} = 3$

On substituting this value of k in equation (i) and (ii),

$$x = 5 \times 3 - 3 = 12$$

and $\quad y = 8 - 4 \times 3 = -4$.

18. $\because \quad \dfrac{2}{x} + \dfrac{3}{y} = 6 \quad \dots (i)$

and $\quad \dfrac{1}{x} + \dfrac{1}{2y} = 2 \quad \dots (ii)$

On multiplying equation (ii) by 2 and subtracting it from equation (i),

$$\therefore \frac{2}{x} + \frac{3}{y} - \frac{2}{x} - \frac{1}{y} = 6 - 4 \Rightarrow \frac{2}{y} = 2 \Rightarrow y = 1$$

On substituting this value of y in equation (i),

$$\frac{2}{x} + \frac{3}{1} = 6 \Rightarrow \frac{2}{x} = 6 - 3 = 3$$

$\therefore \quad x = \dfrac{2}{3}$ Hence $x = \dfrac{2}{3}$ and $y = 1$.

19. $\because \quad \dfrac{6}{x+y} - \dfrac{3}{x-y} = 2 \quad \dots(i)$

and $\quad \dfrac{4}{x+y} + \dfrac{6}{x-y} = 4 \quad \dots(ii)$

If $\dfrac{1}{x+y} = a$ and $\dfrac{1}{x-y} = b$, then the equation will be:

$$6a - 3b = 2 \quad \dots(iii)$$

and $\quad 4a + 6b = 4 \quad \dots(iv)$

On multiplying equation (iii) by 2 and adding to equation (iv),

$2(6a - 3b) + 4a + 6b = 2 \times 2 + 4$

$\therefore \ 12a - 6b + 4a + 6b = 4 + 4$

$\Rightarrow \quad 16a = 8 \Rightarrow a = \dfrac{8}{16} = \dfrac{1}{2}$

On substituting this value of a in equation (iii),

$$6 \times \frac{1}{2} - 3b = 2 \Rightarrow 3b = 1 \Rightarrow b = \frac{1}{3}$$

Since $\quad \dfrac{1}{x+y} = a = \dfrac{1}{2} \Rightarrow x + y = 2 \quad \dots(v)$

and $\quad \dfrac{1}{x-y} = b = \dfrac{1}{3} \Rightarrow x - y = 3 \quad \dots(vi)$

On adding equations (v) and (vi),

$$2x = 5 \Rightarrow x = \frac{5}{2}$$

On substituting this value of x in equation (v),

$$\frac{5}{2} + y = 2$$

$$\Rightarrow y = 2 - \frac{5}{2} = -\frac{1}{2} \quad \therefore x = \frac{5}{2} \text{ and } y = -\frac{1}{2}.$$

20. $\because \quad \dfrac{x}{12-7} = \dfrac{1}{1-6} \Rightarrow \dfrac{x}{5} = \dfrac{1}{-5}$

$$\Rightarrow \quad x = -1$$

and $\quad \dfrac{y}{4-14} = \dfrac{1}{1-6} = \dfrac{y}{-10} = \dfrac{1}{-5}$

$$\Rightarrow \quad y = \frac{-10}{-5} = 2$$

$$\therefore \quad x = -1 \text{ and } y = 2.$$

21. $\quad x + y = 80 \hfill ...(i)$

and $\quad 3x = 5y \Rightarrow x = \dfrac{5y}{3}$

Putting the value of x in (i)

$$\frac{5y}{3} + y = 80$$

$$8y = 3 \times 80$$

$$y = 30$$

$$x = \frac{5 \times 30}{3} = 50.$$

22. Let, $\dfrac{1}{x} = m$

The given equation

$$4m + 5y = 7 \qquad ...(i)] \times 3$$
$$3m + 4y = 5 \qquad ...(ii)] \times 4$$
$$12m + 15y = 21$$
$$12m + 16y = 20$$
$$\underline{\quad - \quad - \quad - \quad}$$
$$-y = 1$$
$$\therefore \qquad y = -1$$
$$4m + 5(-1) = 7$$
$$4m = 12 \Rightarrow m = 3$$

$$\frac{1}{x} = m = 3$$

$$\Rightarrow \qquad 3x = 1$$

$$\therefore \qquad x = \frac{1}{3}.$$

23. $\quad \dfrac{x+1}{y+1} = \dfrac{3}{4}$

$$\Rightarrow \quad 4x + 4 = 3y + 3$$
$$4x - 3y = -1 \hfill ...(i)$$

$$\frac{x-5}{y-5} = \frac{7}{10}$$

$$\Rightarrow \quad 10x - 50 = 7y - 35$$
$$\Rightarrow \quad 10x - 7y = 15 \hfill ...(ii)$$
$$[4x - 3y = -1] \times 7$$
$$[10x - 7y = 15] \times 3$$
$$28x - 21y = -7$$
$$\underline{30x - 21y = 45}$$
$$\quad - \qquad + \qquad -$$
$$\overline{\qquad -2x = -52 \qquad}$$
$$\Rightarrow \qquad x = 26$$

Putting the value of x in (i)

$$4(26) - 3y = -1$$
$$-3y = -105$$
$$y = 35$$

$\therefore$ Numbers are 26, 35.

25. Let unit's digit $= x$ and ten's digit $= y$

$\therefore \qquad$ Number $= 10y + x$

Reverse number $= 10x + y$

According to the question

$$2y = x \hfill ...(i)$$
$$10y + x + 27 = 10x + y \hfill ...(ii)$$
$$\Rightarrow \quad 10y + 2y + 27 = 20y + y$$
$$12y - 21y = -27$$
$$-9y = -27 \Rightarrow y = 3$$
$$x = 6 \quad \therefore \text{ Number} = 36$$

29. Let ten's place digit $= x$ and unit place digit $= y$

Number $= 10x + y$

$$x + y = 5 \hfill ...(i)$$
$$10x + y - 9 = 10y + x$$
$$9x - 9y = 9$$
$$x - y = 1 \hfill ...(ii)$$

from (i) and (ii) we get,

$$x = 3, y = 2$$

$\therefore$ Number $= 10 \times 3 + 2 = 32.$

30. Let number of ₹ 2 coins $= x$

Number of ₹ 1 coins $= y$

$$x + y = 60 \hfill ...(i)$$
$$2x + y = 105 \hfill ...(ii)$$
$$\therefore \qquad x = 45$$

putting the value of x in eq. (i)

$$y = 15$$

Hence, Number of ₹ 2 coins = 45

Number of ₹ 1 coins = 15.

31. $\because x + y = 4xy \Rightarrow \dfrac{x+y}{xy} = 4 \Rightarrow \dfrac{1}{y} + \dfrac{1}{x} = 4$

$\therefore \dfrac{1}{y} + \dfrac{1}{x} = 4$ ..... (i) and $\dfrac{1}{x} + \dfrac{2}{y} = 10$ ...(ii)

On subtracting equation (ii) from equation (i),

$\therefore \dfrac{1}{y} + \dfrac{1}{x} - \dfrac{1}{x} - \dfrac{2}{y} = 4 - 10$

$\Rightarrow -\dfrac{1}{y} = -6 \Rightarrow y = \dfrac{1}{6}$

On substituting this value of y in equation (i),

$\dfrac{1}{1/6} + \dfrac{1}{x} = 4 \Rightarrow 6 + \dfrac{1}{x} = 4$

$\therefore \dfrac{1}{x} = 4 - 6 = -2 \Rightarrow x = \dfrac{-1}{2}$

$\therefore x = \dfrac{-1}{2}$ and $y = \dfrac{1}{6}$.

32. If $\dfrac{1}{x+y} = a$ and $\dfrac{1}{x-y} = b$, then the equations will be:

$\qquad 12a + 8b = 8$ ...(i)

and $\quad 27a - 12b = 3$ ...(ii)

On multiplying equation (i) by 3 and equation (ii) by 2 and adding the two equations,

$3(12a + 8b) + 2(27a - 12b) = 8 \times 3 + 3 \times 2$

$\therefore 36a + 24b + 54a - 24b = 24 + 6$

$\therefore \qquad 90a = 30 \Rightarrow a = \dfrac{30}{90} = \dfrac{1}{3}$

On substituting this value of a in equation (i),

$12 \times \dfrac{1}{3} + 8b = 8 \therefore 4 + 8b = 8$

$\Rightarrow 8b = 4 \Rightarrow b = \dfrac{1}{2}$

$\because \dfrac{1}{x+y} = a = \dfrac{1}{3} \Rightarrow x + y = 3$ ...(iii)

and $\dfrac{1}{x+y} = b = \dfrac{1}{2} \Rightarrow x - y = 2$ ...(iv)

On adding equation (iii) and (iv),

$\qquad 2x = 5 \Rightarrow x = \dfrac{5}{2}$

On substituting this value of x in equation (iii),

$\dfrac{5}{2} + y = 3 \Rightarrow y = 3 - \dfrac{5}{2}$

$\Rightarrow y = \dfrac{1}{2}$

$\therefore x = \dfrac{5}{2}$ and $y = \dfrac{1}{2}$.

33. From equation (i), value of y in terms of x will be:

$\because 2x - y = 10 \Rightarrow y = 2x - 10$

On substituting this value of y in equation (ii), we get

$\therefore 3x + 2(2x - 10) = 22$

$\Rightarrow \quad 3x + 4x - 20 = 22$

$\therefore \qquad 7x = 22 + 20$

$\Rightarrow \quad 7x - 42 = 0.$

34. $\because x + y = 7xy \Rightarrow \dfrac{x+y}{xy} = 7 \Rightarrow \dfrac{1}{y} + \dfrac{1}{x} = 7$

$\therefore \qquad \dfrac{1}{y} + \dfrac{1}{x} = 7$ ...(i)

and $\qquad \dfrac{2}{x} + \dfrac{3}{y} = 17$ ...(ii)

On multiplying equation (i) by 2 and subtracting it from equation (ii), we get

$\therefore \dfrac{2}{x} + \dfrac{3}{y} - 2\left(\dfrac{1}{y} + \dfrac{1}{x}\right) = 17 - 2 \times 7$

$\therefore \dfrac{2}{x} + \dfrac{3}{y} - \dfrac{2}{y} - \dfrac{2}{x} = 17 - 14$

$\Rightarrow \qquad \dfrac{1}{y} = 3 \Rightarrow y = \dfrac{1}{3}$

On substituting this value of y in equation (i), we get

$\dfrac{1}{1/3} + \dfrac{1}{x} = 7 \Rightarrow 3 + \dfrac{1}{x} = 7$

$\therefore \dfrac{1}{x} = 7 - 3 = 4 \Rightarrow x = \dfrac{1}{4}$

Hence $\qquad x = \dfrac{1}{4}$ and $y = \dfrac{1}{3}$

35. $\because \qquad x + y = 5xy \Rightarrow \dfrac{x+y}{xy} = 5$

$\Rightarrow \qquad \dfrac{1}{y} + \dfrac{1}{x} = 5$ ...(i)

$\therefore \qquad y + z = 7yz \Rightarrow \dfrac{y+z}{yz} = 7$

$\Rightarrow \qquad \dfrac{1}{y} + \dfrac{1}{z} = 7$ ...(ii)

and $\qquad z + x = 6zx \Rightarrow \dfrac{z+x}{zx} = 6$

$\Rightarrow \qquad \dfrac{1}{z} + \dfrac{1}{x} = 6$ ...(iii)

On adding equations (i), (ii) and (iii), we get

$2\left(\dfrac{1}{x} + \dfrac{1}{y} + \dfrac{1}{z}\right) = 5 + 7 + 6 = 18$

$$\Rightarrow \quad \frac{1}{x}+\frac{1}{y}+\frac{1}{z}=\frac{18}{2}=9 \qquad \qquad \ldots(iv)$$

On subtracting from equation (iv), the equation (i), (ii) and (iii) respectively,

$$\therefore \quad \frac{1}{z}=9-5=4 \Rightarrow z=\frac{1}{4}; \frac{1}{x}$$

$$=9-7=2 \Rightarrow x=\frac{1}{2}$$

$$\frac{1}{y}=9-6=3 \Rightarrow y=\frac{1}{3}$$

37. $\because \qquad 8x=5y \Rightarrow x=\frac{5y}{8} \qquad \qquad \ldots(i)$

and $\quad 13x=8y+1 \Rightarrow x=\frac{8y+1}{13} \qquad \ldots(ii)$

From equations (i) and (ii),

$$\frac{5y}{8}=\frac{8y+1}{13} \Rightarrow 65y=64y+8 \Rightarrow y=8$$

On substituting this value of y in equation (i), we get

$$x=\frac{5 \times 8}{8}=5$$

$$\therefore \qquad x=5 \text{ and } y=8$$

38. $\because \quad x(y+z)=14 \Rightarrow xy+zx=14 \qquad \ldots(i)$
$\because \quad y(z+x)=18 \Rightarrow yz+xy=18 \qquad \ldots(ii)$
and $\quad z(x+y)=20 \Rightarrow xz+yz=20 \qquad \ldots(iii)$
On adding equations (i), (ii) and (iii),
$\therefore \; 2(xy+yz+xz)=14+18+20=52$

$$\therefore \quad xy+yz+zx=\frac{52}{2}=26 \qquad \ldots(iv)$$

On subtracting from equation (iv), the equations (i), (ii) and (iii) respectively,

$$yz=26-14=12 \qquad \ldots(v)$$
$$xz=26-18=8 \qquad \ldots(vi)$$
$$xy=26-20=6 \qquad \ldots(vii)$$

On multiplying together the equations (v), (vi) and (vii),

$$x^2 y^2 z^2=12 \times 8 \times 6=24 \times 24$$

$$\therefore \qquad xyz=\sqrt{24 \times 24}=\pm 24 \qquad \ldots(viii)$$

On dividing equation $(viii)$ by the equations (v), (vi) and (vii) respectively,

$$x=\pm \frac{24}{12}=\pm 2;$$

$$y=\pm \frac{24}{8}=\pm 3;$$

$$z=\pm \frac{24}{6}=\pm 4.$$

39. $\because \qquad \dfrac{3x}{x-1}+\dfrac{4y+20}{y-3}=32$

$$\Rightarrow 3\left(\frac{x}{x-1}\right)+4\left(\frac{(y+5)}{y-3}\right)=32$$

and $\qquad \dfrac{5x}{x-1}-\dfrac{y+5}{y-3}=15$

$$\Rightarrow \; 5\left(\frac{x}{x-1}\right)-\left(\frac{(y+5)}{y-3}\right)=15$$

If $\qquad \dfrac{x}{x-1}=a$, and $\dfrac{y+5}{y-3}=b$,

then the given equations will be written as:
$\therefore \quad 3a+4b=32 \qquad \qquad \ldots(i)$
and $\quad 5a-b=15 \qquad \qquad \ldots(ii)$
On multiplying equation (ii) by 4 and then adding it to equation (i),
$\quad 3a+4b+20a-4b=32+60 \Rightarrow 23a=92$

$$\therefore \qquad a=\frac{92}{23}=4$$

On substituting this value of a in equation (i),
$\quad 3 \times 4+4b=32 \Rightarrow 4b=32-12=20$

$$\therefore \qquad b=\frac{20}{4}=5$$

Since, $\quad \dfrac{x}{x-1}=a=4 \Rightarrow x=4x-4 \Rightarrow 3x=4$

$$\therefore \qquad x=\frac{4}{3}$$

and $\quad \dfrac{y+5}{y-3}=b=5 \Rightarrow y+5=5y-15$

$$\Rightarrow \qquad 4y=20$$

$\therefore \; y=\dfrac{20}{4}=5$ Hence $x=\dfrac{4}{3}$ and $y=5$.

40. Suppose $\quad \dfrac{x}{3}=\dfrac{y}{4}=\dfrac{z}{7}=k$

$$\therefore \qquad x=3k, \; y=4k \text{ and } z=7k$$

$$\therefore \quad \frac{x+y+z}{x}=\frac{3k+4k+7k}{3k}=\frac{14k}{3k}=\frac{14}{3}.$$

★ ★ ★

4

Quadratic Equation

QUADRATIC EQUATION

Definition : A polynomial equation in which the highest power of the unknown variable is two. The general form of a quadratic equation in the variable x is

$$ax^2 + bx + c = 0$$

where, a, b and c are constant.

Solution of a Quadratic Equation

Consider the quadratic equation

$$ax^2 + bx + c = 0; \quad a \neq 0$$

Dividing by a both sides, we get

$$x^2 + \frac{b}{a}x + \frac{c}{a} = 0$$

$$x^2 + 2\frac{b}{2a}x + \left(\frac{b}{2a}\right)^2 - \left(\frac{b}{2a}\right)^2 + \frac{c}{a} = 0$$

or, $\quad \left(x + \frac{b}{2a}\right)^2 = \frac{b^2}{4a^2} - \frac{c}{a}$

or, $\quad \left(x + \frac{b}{2a}\right) = \pm\sqrt{\frac{b^2 - 4ac}{4a^2}}$

or, $\quad x = \frac{-b}{2a} \pm \frac{\sqrt{b^2 - 4ac}}{2a}$

or, $\quad x = \frac{-b \pm \sqrt{b^2 - 4ac}}{2a}$

$b^2 - 4ac = D$ is called discriminant.

(a) If $D > 0$ then there are real and distinct roots given by

$$\alpha = \frac{-b + \sqrt{b^2 - 4ac}}{2a}, \quad \beta = \frac{-b - \sqrt{b^2 - 4ac}}{2a}$$

(b) If $D = 0$, there are real and equal roots

$$\alpha = \beta = \frac{-b}{2a}$$

(c) If $D < 0$, there are no real roots.

Sum of the roots

$$\alpha + \beta = \frac{-b}{a}$$

Product of the roots

$$\alpha\beta = \frac{c}{a}$$

Expressions of the type $\alpha^2 + \beta^2$, $\alpha^3 + \beta^3$ etc. are called symmetric functions.

$$\alpha^2 + \beta^2 = (\alpha + \beta)^2 - 2\alpha\beta$$

and $\quad \alpha^3 + \beta^3 = (\alpha + \beta)^3 - 3\alpha\beta(\alpha + \beta).$

SOLVED EXAMPLES

Ex. 1 : The roots of the equation $6x^2 - 5x - 21 = 0$ are

  (a) $-\dfrac{7}{3}$ and $-\dfrac{3}{2}$ (b) $\dfrac{7}{3}$ and $\dfrac{3}{2}$

  (c) $\dfrac{7}{3}$ and $-\dfrac{3}{2}$ (d) $-\dfrac{7}{3}$ and $\dfrac{3}{2}$

Sol.
$$6x^2 - 14x + 9x - 21 = 0$$
$$\Rightarrow \quad 2x(3x - 7) + 3(3x - 7) = 0$$
$$\Rightarrow \quad (3x - 7)(2x + 3) = 0$$
$$\Rightarrow \quad x = \frac{7}{3}, \quad x = -\frac{3}{2}$$

Ex. 2 : The roots of the quadratic equation $abx^2 + (b^2 - ac)\,x - bc = 0$ are

  (a) $\dfrac{c}{b}, \dfrac{b}{a}$ (b) $\dfrac{c}{b}, -\dfrac{b}{a}$

  (c) $-\dfrac{c}{b}, \dfrac{b}{a}$ (d) $-\dfrac{c}{b}, -\dfrac{b}{a}$

Sol.
$$abx^2 + b^2x - acx - bc = 0$$
$$\Rightarrow \quad bx(ax + b) - c(ax + b) = 0$$
$$\Rightarrow \quad (bx - c)(ax + b) = 0$$
$$\Rightarrow \quad x = \frac{c}{b}, -\frac{b}{a}$$

Ex. 3 : If α and β are the roots of the quadratic equation $3x^2 + 3x + 2 = 0$ then $\alpha^3 + \beta^3 = $ ......

(a) $-\dfrac{1}{3}$ (b) -1

(c) 1 (d) None of the above

Sol. $a = 3,\ b = 3,\ c = 2$

$$\Rightarrow\ \ \alpha + \beta = -1,\ \alpha\beta = \frac{2}{3}$$

$$\alpha^3 + \beta^3 = (-1)^3 - 3 \times \frac{2}{3} \times (-1)$$

$$= -1 + 2 = 1$$

Ex. 4 : If α and β are the roots of the quadratic equation $x^2 - 7x + 3 = 0$ then the equation whose roots are 2α and 2β is

(a) $x^2 + 14x + 12 = 0$

(b) $x^2 + 14x - 12 = 0$

(c) $x^2 - 14x - 12 = 0$

(d) $x^2 - 14x + 12 = 0$

Sol. $\alpha + \beta = 7,\ \alpha\beta = 3$

$\alpha' = 2\alpha,\ \beta' = 2\beta$

$s' = \alpha' + \beta' = 2(\alpha + \beta) = 14$

$p' = \alpha'\beta' = 4\alpha\beta = 12$

Required equation : $x^2 - 14x + 12 = 0$

Ex. 5 : The value of p for which the quadratic equation $3x^2 - px + 5 = 0$ has no real roots

(a) $p \geq 2\sqrt{15}$ (b) $\dfrac{7}{3}\ p = \pm 2\sqrt{15}$

(c) $p \leq -2\sqrt{15}$ (d) None of these

Sol. $a = 3,\ b = -p,\ c = 5$

Equation has no real roots $\Rightarrow$ D < 0

$\Rightarrow\ \ (-p)^2 - 4 \times 3 \times 5 < 0$

$\Rightarrow\ \ p^2 < 60$

$\Rightarrow\ \ p^2 < \left(2\sqrt{15}\right)^2$

$\Rightarrow\ \ -2\sqrt{15} < p < 2\sqrt{15}$

Ex. 6 : The values of x satisfying the equation $4^x - 5(2^x) + 4 = 0$ are

(a) 0 and 2   (b) 0 and -2

(c) 2 and -2 (d) None of these

Sol. $\left(2^x\right)^2 - 5\left(2^x\right) + 4 = 0$

Let $2^x = y$

$\Rightarrow\ \ y^2 - 5y + 4 = 0$

$\Rightarrow\ \ (y - 1)(y - 4) = 0$

$\Rightarrow\ \ \ \ \ \ y = 1,\ 4$

$\Rightarrow\ \ \ \ \ \ 2^x = 1;\ 2^x = 4$

$\Rightarrow\ \ \ \ \ \ 2^x = 2^0;\ 2^x = 2^2$

$\Rightarrow\ \ \ \ \ \ x = 0,\ x = 2$

Ex. 7 : The values of x satisfying the equation

$$\left(\frac{x}{x+1}\right)^2 - 5\left(\frac{x}{x+1}\right) + 6 = 0;\ \text{are}$$

(a) $2,\ \dfrac{3}{2}$ (b) $2,\ -\dfrac{3}{2}$

(c) $-2,\ \dfrac{3}{2}$ (d) $-2,\ -\dfrac{3}{2}$

Sol. Let, $\dfrac{x}{x+1} = y$

$\Rightarrow\ \ \ \ \ \ y^2 - 5y + 6 = 0$

$\Rightarrow\ \ \ \ \ \ (y - 2)(y - 3) = 0$

$\Rightarrow\ \ \ \ \ \ y = 2,\ y = 3$

$\Rightarrow\ \ \dfrac{x}{x+1} = 2;\ \dfrac{x}{x+1} = 3$

$\Rightarrow\ \ x = 2x + 2;\ \ x = 3x + 3$

$\Rightarrow\ \ \ \ \ \ x = -2,\ x = -\dfrac{3}{2}$

Ex. 8 : A motor boat whose speed is 15 km/hr in still water goes 40 km downstream and comes back in a total of 6 hours. The speed of the stream is

(a) 9 km/hr   (b) 7 km/hr

(c) 5 km/hr   (d) 3 km/hr

Sol. Let speed of the stream be x km/hr.

Speed downstream = $(15 + x)$ km/hr

and speed upstream = $(15 - x)$ km/hr

$$\frac{40}{15+x} + \frac{40}{15-x} = 6$$

$$\Rightarrow\ \ \frac{40(15 - x + 15 + x)}{(15+x)(15-x)} = 6$$

$\Rightarrow\ \ 225 - x^2 = 200$

$\Rightarrow\ \ \ \ \ \ x^2 = 25$

$\therefore\ \ \ \ \ \ x = 5$

The speed of the stream = 5 km/hr

Ex. 9 : The length of a rectangle exceeds its breadth by 8 cm and the area of the rectangle is 240 cm^2. The dimension of the rectangle are

(a) 28 cm $\times$ 20 cm   (b) 20 cm $\times$ 12 cm

(c) 16 cm $\times$ 24 cm   (d) None of these

Sol. Let breadth be x cm

$\Rightarrow\ \ \ \ \ \ $ length = $(x + 8)$ cm

$\Rightarrow\ \ \ (x + 8)x = 240$

$\Rightarrow\ \ \ \ \ \ x^2 + 8x - 240 = 0$

$\Rightarrow\ \ \ (x + 20)\ (x - 12) = 0$

$\Rightarrow\ \ \ \ \ \ \ x = -20,\ x = 12$

$x = -20$ is impossible

Then, breadth = 12 cm

and length = 20 cm

$\therefore$ dimensions = 20 cm $\times$ 12 cm

MULTIPLE CHOICE QUESTIONS

1. The equation whose roots are 5, 9 is :
A. $x^2 - 5x + 14 = 0$ B. $x^2 - 14x + 14 = 0$
C. $x^2 - 45x + 14 = 0$ D. $x^2 - 14x + 45 = 0$

2. If α, β be the values of x satisfying the equation $x^2 - px + q = 0$, the value of $\frac{1}{\alpha} + \frac{1}{\beta}$ is :
A. $\dfrac{q}{p}$ B. $-\dfrac{p}{q}$
C. $\dfrac{p}{q}$ D. $\dfrac{1}{q}$

3. If one of the roots of the equation is $2+\sqrt{3}$, the other has to be :
A. $\sqrt{3}-2$ B. 2
C. $2-\sqrt{3}$ D. $\sqrt{3}$

4. If α, β are the roots of $2x^2 - x + 1 = 0$, the value of $\alpha^2 + \beta^2$ is :
A. 1 B. 0
C. $5/4$ D. $-3/4$

5. Find the values of 'p' for which the quadratic equation $px^2 + 4x + 1 = 0$ has real roots.
A. $p \le 4$ B. $p \ge 6$
C. $p \ge 4$ D. None of these

6. Determine 'k' such that the quadratic equation $x^2 + 7(3 + 2k) - 2x(1 + 3k) = 0$ has equal roots.
A. $2, -10/9$ B. $3, -10/9$
C. $2, 10/9$ D. None of these

7. For what value of 'k' the equation $(k + 3) x^2 - (5 - k)x + 1 = 0$ has coincident roots?
A. $1, 13$ B. $1, 12$
C. $3, 13$ D. None of these

8. Find the value of 'k' so that the sum of the roots of equation $3x^2 + (2x + 1) x - k + 5 = 0$ is equal to the product of roots.
A. 4 B. 2
C. 3 D. -6

9. Find the value of 'p' so that equation $4x^2 - 8px + 9 = 0$ has roots whose difference is 4.
A. ± 3 B. $\pm 2/5$
C. $\pm 5/2$ D. None of these

10. Find the value of 'm' so that the equation $9x^2 - 8mx - 9 = 0$ has one root as the negative of the other.
A. 0 B. 1
C. 2 D. None of these

11. If α and β are the roots of $x^2 - 2x - 1 = 0$, find the value of $\alpha^2\beta + \beta^2\alpha$.
A. -3 B. -2
C. 2 D. None of these

12. If a and b are the roots of the equation $x^2 - 5x + 6 = 0$, find the value of $(a^2 - b^2)$.
A. ± 3 B. ± 5
C. ± 4 D. None of these

13. For what values of 'p' for which the quadratic equation $px^2 - 4x + p$ has real linear factors?
A. $-2 \le p < 3$ B. $-2 \le p \le 2$
C. $-2 \ge p \le 2$ D. None of these

14. For what values of 'p' the equation $(1 + p) x^2 + 2(1 + 2p)x + (1 + p) = 0$ has coincident roots?
A. $2/3, 0$ B. $-2/3, 0$
C. $-3/2, 0$ D. None of these

15. If a and b are the roots of the quadratic equation $3x^2 + 8x + 2 = 0$, find the value of $a^3 + b^3$.
A. $368/27$ B. $-368/27$
C. $-368/24$ D. None of these

16. If a and b are the roots of the quadratic equation $6x^2 - x - 2 = 0$, from an equation whose roots are a^2 and b^2?
A. $36x^2 - 25x + 4 = 0$ B. $36x^2 + 25x + 4 = 0$
C. $6x^2 - 25x + 4 = 0$ D. None of these

17. If a and b are the roots of the quadratic equation $2x^2 - 6x + 3 = 0$, find the value of $a^3 + b^3 - 3ab (a^2 + b^2) - 3ab(a + b)$.
A. -27 B. -25
C. 27 D. None of these

18. $z^4 + 3z - 4 = 0$
A. 1 B. ± 1
C. -1 D. None of these

19. $x - \sqrt{25 - x^2} = 1$
A. 3 B. 4
C. -4 D. None of these

20. $\sqrt{3x-5} + \sqrt{x+2} = 3$
A. 2 B. 1
C. 3 D. None of these

21. If α, β are the roots of a quadratic equation such that $\alpha + \beta = 24$ and $\alpha - \beta = 8$, the quadratic equation is
A. $x^2 - 24x + 128 = 0$ B. $x^2 - 8x + 16 = 0$
C. $x^2 - 24x + 12 = 0$ D. $x2 - 16x + 20 = 0$

22. If α, β are the roots of a quadratic equation: $x^2 - 3kx + k^2 = 0$, find the values of k if $\alpha^2 + \beta^2 = \dfrac{7}{4}$.
A. $\pm \dfrac{1}{3}$.   B. $\pm \dfrac{1}{2}$
C. $\pm \dfrac{1}{4}$ D. $\pm \dfrac{1}{5}$

23. Find the value of k so that the sum of the roots of the quadratic equation $kx^2 + 2x + 3k = 0$ is equal to their product.

A. $\dfrac{2}{3}$ B. $\dfrac{-2}{3}$

C. $\dfrac{3}{2}$ D. $\dfrac{-3}{2}$

24. If α, β are the roots of the quadratic equation $x^2 - 8x + p = 0$, find the value of p if $\alpha^2 + \beta^2 = 40$.

A. 8   B. 10
C. 12   D. 6

25. Find the value of k such that the quadratic equation $x^2 - (k + 6)x + 2(2k - 1) = 0$ has sum of the roots as half of their product.

A. 1   B. 2
C. 3   D. 7

26. If the sum and product of roots of the quadratic equation $ax^2 - 5x + c$ are both equal to 10, find the value of a and c.

A. 2, 3   B. $\dfrac{1}{3}, 5$

C. $\dfrac{1}{2}, 5$ D. 3, 5

27. If α and β are the roots of $x^2 + x - 2 = 0$. find the value of $\alpha^{-1} + \beta^{-1}$.

A. 1   B. $\dfrac{1}{2}$

C. $\dfrac{1}{3}$ D. 3

28. If α, β are the roots of the equation $x^2 - x - 4 = 0$, find the value of $\dfrac{1}{\alpha} + \dfrac{1}{\beta} - \alpha\beta$.

A. $\dfrac{4}{15}$ B. $\dfrac{15}{4}$

C. $\dfrac{4}{5}$ D. $\dfrac{5}{4}$

29. Form a quadratic equation whose roots are −3 and 4.
A. $x^2 - x - 2 = 0$ B. $x^2 - 4x + 6 = 0$
C. $x^2 - x - 12 = 0$ D. $x^2 - x - 6 = 0$

30. For what value of k will the quadratic equation $2x^2 + 3x + k = 0$ have real equal roots?

A. $\dfrac{3}{8}$ B. $\dfrac{8}{3}$

C. $\dfrac{9}{8}$ D. $\dfrac{8}{9}$

31. $x(x + 5)(x + 7)(x + 12) + 150 = 0$

A. $\left\{6 \pm \sqrt{31}, 6 \pm \sqrt{6}\right\}$ B. $\left\{-6 \pm \sqrt{31}, -6 \pm \sqrt{6}\right\}$

C. $\left\{-6 \pm \sqrt{6}, -\pm \sqrt{31}\right\}$ D. None of these

32. $2^{2x} + 2^{x+1} = 4 - 2^x$
A. 2   B. 1
C. 0   D. None of these

33. $2^{2x+3} = 65(2^x - 1) + 57$
A. ±3   B. ±1
C. ±2   D. None of these

34. $7^{1+x} + 7^{1-x} = 50$
A. ±1   B. ±3
C. ±2   D. None

35. For what positive value of m, the equation $12x^2 + 4(m + 1)x + 3 = 0$ shall have equal roots?
A. 1   B. 4
C. 3   D. 2

36. If one root of $2x^2 + px + 3 = 0$ be 3. Find the value of p.
A. 6   B. −3
C. −7   D. 7

37. If the roots of $3x^2 + 5x + a = 0$ is four times the other, then the value of a is

A. $\dfrac{4}{3}$ B. $\dfrac{3}{2}$

C. $\dfrac{2}{3}$ D. $\dfrac{3}{4}$

38. Divide 16 into two parts such that the twice of the square of the greater part exceeds the square of the smaller part by 164.
A. 6, 10   B. 6, 4
C. 4, 10   D. None of these

39. The sides of a right triangle are $(x - 1)$, x and $(x + 1)$. Find the sides of the triangle.
A. 3, 4, 5   B. 4, 5, 6
C. 2, 3, 4   D. None of these

40. A two digit number is such that the product of its digit is 18 When 63 is subtracted from the number the digits interchange their places. Find the number.
A. 91   B. 92
C. 90   D. None of these

ANSWERS

1	2	3	4	5	6	7	8	9	10
D	C	C	D	A	A	A	D	C	A

11	12	13	14	15	16	17	18	19	20
B	B	B	B	B	A	A	B	B	A

21	**22**	**23**	**24**	**25**	**26**	**27**	**28**	**29**	**30**
A	B	B	C	D	C	B	B	C	C

31	**32**	**33**	**34**	**35**	**36**	**37**	**38**	**39**	**40**
B	C	A	A	D	C	A	A	A	B

EXPLANATORY ANSWERS

1. Roots are 5 and 9

Sum of the roots = 5 + 9 = 14

Product of roots = 5 × 9 = 45

$\therefore x^2$ – Sum of roots (x) + Product of roots = 0

$\Rightarrow x^2 - 14x + 45 = 0$

2. $\alpha + \beta = p, \quad \alpha\beta = q$

$\therefore \quad \dfrac{1}{\alpha} + \dfrac{1}{\beta} = \dfrac{\alpha+\beta}{\alpha\beta} = \dfrac{p}{q}$

5. For real roots $D \geq 0$

$\Rightarrow (4)^2 - 4.p.1 \geq 0$

$\Rightarrow 16 \geq 4p$

$\Rightarrow 4p \leq 16$

$\Rightarrow p \leq 4$

6. For equal roots $D = 0$

$\Rightarrow \left[2(1+3k)\right]^2 - 4.7(3+2k) = 0$

$\Rightarrow 4\left(1+6k+9k^2\right) - 28(3+2k) = 0$

$\Rightarrow 1+6k+9k^2 - 21 - 14k = 0$

$\Rightarrow 9k^2 - 8k - 20 = 0$

$\Rightarrow (k-2)(9k+10) = 0$

Hence, $k = 2, -\dfrac{10}{9}$

7. For coincident roots, $D = 0$

Now, $\left[-(5-k)\right]^2 - 4 \times (k+3) \times 1 = 0$

$\Rightarrow 25 + k^2 - 10k - 4k - 12 = 0$

$\Rightarrow k^2 - 14k + 13 = 0$

$\Rightarrow (k-13)(k-1) = 0$

$\therefore \quad k = 13, 1$

8. $\alpha + \beta = \alpha\beta$

$\dfrac{-(2k+1)}{3} = \dfrac{-k+5}{3}$

$-2k - 1 = -k + 5$

$k = -6$

9. $\alpha + \beta = \dfrac{8p}{4} = 2p; \quad \alpha\beta = \dfrac{9}{4}$

$\alpha + \beta = 2p$

$\alpha - \beta = 4 \,(\text{Given})$

Now, $(\alpha - \beta)^2 = (\alpha + \beta)^2 - 4\alpha\beta$

$\Rightarrow (4)^2 = (2p)^2 - 4 \times \dfrac{9}{4}$

$\Rightarrow 16 = 4p^2 - 9 \qquad \Rightarrow 25 = 4p^2$

$\Rightarrow p^2 = \dfrac{25}{4}$

$\Rightarrow p = \pm\dfrac{5}{2}$

10. Let α, β are roots

$\alpha + \beta = \dfrac{8m}{9}$

But, $\alpha = -\beta$

Thus, $\alpha + \beta = 0$

$\Rightarrow 8m = 0$

$\Rightarrow m = 0$

11. Here, $\alpha + \beta = 2, \alpha\beta = -1$

Now, $\alpha^2\beta + \alpha\beta^2 = \alpha\beta(\alpha + \beta)$

$= -1(2) = -2$

12. Here, $a + b = 5; \; ab = 6$

$a^2 - b^2$

$= (a+b)(a-b)$

$= (a+b)\sqrt{(a+b)^2 - 4ab}$

$= 5.\sqrt{5^2 - 4 \times 6}$

$= 5.(\pm 1) = \pm 5$

13. For real linear factors,

$\quad D \geq 0$

$\Rightarrow 16 - 4p^2 \geq 0$

$\Rightarrow p^2 \leq 4$

Thus, $-2 \leq p \leq 2$

14. For coincident roots,

$\quad D = 0$

$\Rightarrow \left[2(1+2p)\right]^2 - 4(1+p)^2 = 0$

$\Rightarrow 1 + 4p^2 + 4p - 1 - p^2 - 2p = 0$

$\Rightarrow 3p^2 + 2p = 0$

$\Rightarrow p(3p+2) = 0$

$\Rightarrow p = 0, -\dfrac{2}{3}$

15. Here, $a + b = \dfrac{8}{3}$ and $ab = \dfrac{2}{3}$

$a^3 + b^3 = (a+b)^3 - 3ab(a+b)$

$= \left(\dfrac{8}{3}\right)^3 - 3 \times \dfrac{2}{3} \times \dfrac{8}{3} = \dfrac{512}{27} - \dfrac{16}{3} = \dfrac{368}{27}$

16. $a + b = \dfrac{1}{6}$

$ab = -\dfrac{2}{6} = -\dfrac{1}{3}$

$\Rightarrow a^2 b^2 = \dfrac{1}{9}$

$a^2 + b^2 = (a+b)^2 - 2ab$

$= \left(\dfrac{1}{6}\right)^2 - 2 \times -\dfrac{1}{3} = \dfrac{1}{36} + \dfrac{2}{3} = \dfrac{25}{36}$

Thus, required equation

$= \quad x^2 - \dfrac{25}{36}x + \dfrac{1}{9} = 0$

$\Rightarrow \quad 36x^2 - 25x + 4 = 0$

17. Here, $a + b = 3$; $ab = \dfrac{3}{2}$

Now, $a^3 + b^3 - 3ab(a^2 + b^2) - 3ab(a + b)$

$= (a+b)^3 - 3ab(a+b) - 3ab\left[(a+b)^2 - 2ab\right]$

$\qquad\qquad\qquad\qquad\qquad - 3ab(a+b)$

$= (3)^3 - 3 \times \dfrac{3}{2} \times 3 - 3 \times \dfrac{3}{2}\left[3^2 - 2 \times \dfrac{3}{2}\right] - 3 \times \dfrac{3}{2} \times 3$

$= 27 - \dfrac{27}{2} - \dfrac{9}{2} \times 6 - \dfrac{27}{2} = -27$

18. $z^4 + 3z^2 - 4 = 0$

Let $x = z^2$

$x^2 + 3x - 4 = 0$

$(x+4)(x-1) = 0$

$x = -4 \quad x = 1$

Thus, $z^2 = -4$ (Impossible)

So, $z^2 = 1 \Rightarrow z = \pm 1$

19. $x - \sqrt{25 - x^2} = 1$

$\Rightarrow \quad x - 1 = \sqrt{25 - x^2}$

Squaring both sides,

$\Rightarrow \quad (x-1)^2 = 25 - x^2$

$\Rightarrow \quad x^2 + 1 - 2x = 25 - x^2$

$\Rightarrow \quad 2x^2 - 2x - 24 = 0$

$\Rightarrow \quad x^2 - x - 12 = 0$

$\Rightarrow \quad (x-4)(x+3) = 0$

$\Rightarrow \quad x = 4, -3$

20. $\sqrt{3x-5} + \sqrt{x+2} = 3$

$\Rightarrow \quad \sqrt{3x-5} = 3 - \sqrt{x+2}$

$\Rightarrow \quad 3x - 5 = 9 + x + 2 - 6\sqrt{x+2}$

$\Rightarrow \quad 2x - 16 = -6\sqrt{x+2}$

$\Rightarrow \quad x - 8 = -3\sqrt{x+2}$

$\Rightarrow \quad x^2 - 16x + 64 = 9(x + 2)$

$\Rightarrow \quad x^2 - 25x + 46 = 0$

$\Rightarrow \quad (x - 23)(x - 2) = 0$

$\Rightarrow \quad x = 23, 2$

21. $\because \qquad \alpha + \beta = 24 \qquad\qquad …(i)$

and $\qquad \alpha - \beta = 8 \qquad\qquad …(ii)$

Adding equation (i) and (ii), we get

$\qquad 2\alpha = 32 \Rightarrow \alpha = 16$

Subtracting equation (ii) from (i), we get

$\qquad 2\beta = 16 \Rightarrow \beta = 8$

$\therefore$ Product of the roots i.e.

$\qquad \alpha \cdot \beta = 16 \times 8 = 128$

We know that the quadratic equation whose roots are α and β is

$\qquad x^2 - (\alpha + \beta)x + \alpha \cdot \beta = 0$

$\Rightarrow \qquad x^2 - 24x + 128 = 0$

which is the required quadratic equation

22. The given quadratic equation is $x^2 - 3kx + k^3 = 0$.

Hence $a = 1$, $b = -3k$, $c = k^3$.

$\because$ α, β are the roots of the given quadratic equation:

$\therefore \qquad \alpha + \beta = -\dfrac{b}{a} = -\dfrac{-3k}{1} = 3k$

$\qquad\qquad \alpha \cdot \beta = \dfrac{c}{a} = \dfrac{k^2}{1} = k^2$

$\therefore \qquad (\alpha + \beta)^2 = \alpha^2 + \beta^2 + 2\alpha\beta$

$\Rightarrow \qquad (3k)^2 = \dfrac{7}{4} + 2k^2 \qquad \left[\because \alpha^2 + \beta^2 = \dfrac{7}{4}\right]$

$\Rightarrow \qquad 9k^2 - 2k^2 = \dfrac{7}{4}$

$\Rightarrow \qquad 7k^2 = \dfrac{7}{4} \Rightarrow k^2 = \dfrac{1}{4}$

$\therefore \qquad k = \pm\sqrt{\dfrac{1}{4}} = \pm\dfrac{1}{2}.$

23. $\left.\begin{array}{l} kx^2 + 2x + 3k = 0 \\ ax^2 + bx + c = 0 \end{array}\right\} \Rightarrow a = k, b = 2, c = 3k.$

Sum of roots $= \dfrac{-b}{a} = \dfrac{-2}{k}$

Product of the roots $= \dfrac{c}{a} = \dfrac{3k}{k}.$

Since sum of roots = Product of roots

$$\Rightarrow \quad \frac{-2}{k} = \frac{3k}{k}$$

$$\frac{-2}{k} = \frac{3}{1}$$

$$\Rightarrow \quad 3k = -2 \Rightarrow k = \frac{-2}{3}.$$

24. $\because$ α, β are the roots of the quadratic equation

$$x^2 - 8x + p = 0$$

Here $\qquad a = 1, b = -8, c = p$

$$\therefore \quad \alpha + \beta = -\frac{b}{a} = \frac{8}{1} = 8$$

and $\qquad \alpha \cdot \beta = \frac{c}{a} = \frac{p}{1} = p$

Now, $(\alpha + \beta)^2 = \alpha^2 + \beta^2 + 2\alpha \cdot \beta$

$$\Rightarrow \quad (8)^2 = 40 + 2p$$
$$\Rightarrow \quad 64 = 40 + 2p$$
$$\Rightarrow \quad 2p = 64 - 40 = 24$$
$$\therefore \quad p = \frac{24}{2} = 12$$

25. The given quadratic equation is :

$$x^2 - (k + 6)x + 2(2k - 1) = 0$$

Here, $a = 1, b = -(k + 6), c = 2(2k - 1)$

Sum of the roots $= \dfrac{-b}{a} = k + 6$

Product of the roots $= \dfrac{c}{a} = 2(2k - 1)$

According to the given condition :

Sum of the roots $= \dfrac{1}{2} \times$ Product of the roots

$$\Rightarrow \quad k + 6 = \frac{1}{2} \times 2(2k - 1)$$
$$\Rightarrow \quad k + 6 = 2k - 1$$
$$\Rightarrow \quad 6 + 1 = 2k - k$$
$$k = 7.$$

26. $ax^2 - 5x + c = 0$

Here, $\qquad b = -5$

Sum of the roots $= \dfrac{-b}{a} = \dfrac{-(-5)}{a} = \dfrac{5}{a}$

and product of the roots $= \dfrac{c}{a}$

According to the given, we have

$$\frac{5}{a} = 10 \Rightarrow a = \frac{5}{10} = \frac{1}{2}$$

and $\qquad \dfrac{c}{a} = 10 \Rightarrow c = 10.a = 10 \times \dfrac{1}{2} = 5$

Hence, $\qquad a = \dfrac{1}{2}$ and $c = 5$

27. $x^2 + x - 2 = 0$

$\therefore \qquad \alpha + \beta = -1, \alpha\beta = -2$

$$\alpha^{-1} + \beta^{-1} = \frac{1}{\alpha} + \frac{1}{\beta}$$

$$= \frac{\beta + \alpha}{\alpha\beta} = \frac{-1}{-2} = \frac{1}{2}.$$

28. $x^2 - x - 4 = 0$

Sum of the roots $= 1$

Product of the roots $= -4$

$$\alpha + \beta = 1$$
$$\alpha\beta = -4$$

$$\frac{1}{\alpha} + \frac{1}{\beta} - \alpha\beta = \frac{\beta + \alpha - (\alpha\beta)^2}{\alpha\beta}$$

$$= \frac{\alpha + \beta - (\alpha\beta)^2}{\alpha\beta}$$

$$= \frac{1 - (-4)^2}{-4} = \frac{1 - 16}{-4} = \frac{-15}{-4} = \frac{15}{4}.$$

29. Roots are -3 and 4.

Sum of the roots $= -3 + 4 = 1$

Product of the roots $= -3 \times 4 = -12$

Required equation is

$$x^2 - x$$

(Sum of the roots) + (Product of the roots) $= 0$

$$x^2 - x - 12 = 0.$$

30. $2x^2 + 3x + k = 0$

Here, $a = 2, b = 3, c = k$

$\because D = b^2 - 4ac = (3)^2 - 4 \times 2 \times k = 9 - 8k$

We know that a quardratic equation has real and equal roots if D $= 0$

$$\Rightarrow \quad 9 - 8k = 0 \Rightarrow -8k = -9$$

$$\therefore \qquad k = \frac{9}{8}.$$

31. $x(x+5)(x+7)(x+12) + 150 = 0$

$$\Rightarrow \quad x(x + 12)(x + 5)(x + 7) + 150 = 0$$
$$\Rightarrow \quad (x^2 + 12x)(x^2 + 12x + 35) + 150 = 0$$

Let, $x^2 + 12x = a$

Then, $a(a + 35) + 150 = 0$

$$\Rightarrow \quad a^2 + 35a + 150 = 0$$
$$\Rightarrow \quad (a + 30)(a + 5) = 0$$
$$\Rightarrow \quad a = -30, -5$$

Now, $x^2 + 12x = -30$

$$\Rightarrow \quad x^2 + 12x + 30 = 0$$

Thus, $x = \dfrac{-12 \pm \sqrt{144 - 4 \times 30}}{2}$

$$= \frac{-12 \pm \sqrt{24}}{2} = -6 \pm \sqrt{6}$$

Again, $x^2 + 12x = -5$

$\Rightarrow \quad x^2 + 12x + 5 = 0$

$x = \dfrac{-12 \pm \sqrt{144 - 20}}{2} = -6 \pm \sqrt{31}$

32. $2^{2x} + 2^{x+1} = 4 - 2^x$

$\Rightarrow \quad 2^{2x} + 2^x \cdot 2 = 4 - 2^x$

$\Rightarrow \quad 2^{2x} + 3 \cdot 2^x - 4 = 0$

Let, $2^x = y$

$\Rightarrow \quad y^2 + 3y - 4 = 0$

$\Rightarrow \quad (y+4)(y-1) = 0$

$\Rightarrow \quad y = -4 \qquad y = 1$

$\Rightarrow \quad 2^x = -4 \qquad 2^x = 1$

$\qquad\qquad\qquad\quad 2^x = 2^0$

$\qquad\qquad\qquad\quad x = 0$

33. $2^{2x+3} = 65(2^x - 1) + 57$

$\Rightarrow \left(2^x\right)^2 \times 2^3 = 65(2^x - 1) + 57$

Let, $2^x = y$

$8y^2 = 65y - 65 + 57$

$8y^2 - 65y + 8 = 0$

$8y^2 - 64y - y + 8 = 0$

$8y(y - 8) - 1(y - 8) = 0$

$(y - 8)(8y - 1) = 0$

$y = 8 \quad$ or, $\quad y = \dfrac{1}{8}$

$2^x = y = 8 = (2)^3 \Rightarrow x = 3$

$2^x = y = \dfrac{1}{8} = \dfrac{1}{2^3} = (2)^{-3} \Rightarrow x = -3$

34. $7 \cdot 7^x + 7 \times \dfrac{1}{7^x} = 50$

Let, $7^x = y$

$7y + \dfrac{7}{y} = 50 \quad \Rightarrow 7y^2 + 7 = 50y$

$\Rightarrow 7y^2 - 50y + 7 = 0$

$\Rightarrow 7y^2 - 49y - y + 7 = 0$

$\Rightarrow (y - 7)(7y - 1) = 0 \quad \Rightarrow y = 7, y = \dfrac{1}{7}$

$7^x = 7^1 \Rightarrow x = 1$ or, $7^x = 7^{-1} \quad \Rightarrow x = -1$

$\therefore \ x = \pm 1$

35. $12x^2 + 4(m + 1)x + 3 = 0$

$\because$ roots are equal

$\therefore \quad D = 0 \quad \Rightarrow b^2 - 4ac = 0$

$\{4(m + 1)\}^2 - 4(12)(3) = 0$

$\qquad 16(m + 1)^2 - 144 = 0$

$\Rightarrow \quad (m + 1)^2 = 9$

$\qquad\quad m + 1 = 3$

$\qquad\qquad m = 2$

36. $2x^2 + px + 3 = 0$

$\because$ one root $= 3$, Let other root $= \beta$

$3\beta = \dfrac{3}{2} \Rightarrow \beta = \dfrac{1}{2}$

$\alpha + \beta = \dfrac{-b}{a} = \dfrac{-p}{2}$

$3 + \dfrac{1}{2} = \dfrac{-p}{2}$

$\dfrac{7}{2} = \dfrac{-p}{2} \Rightarrow p = -7$

37. $3x^2 + 5x + a = 0$

Let, one root $= \alpha$

$\therefore$ Other root $= 4\alpha$

Sum of the roots $= \dfrac{-b}{a} = \dfrac{-5}{3}$

$5\alpha = \dfrac{-5}{3} \Rightarrow \alpha = \dfrac{-1}{3}$

Product of roots $= \dfrac{c}{a} = \dfrac{a}{3}$

$\alpha \times 4\alpha = \dfrac{a}{3}$

$\left(\dfrac{-1}{3}\right) \times 4\left(\dfrac{-1}{3}\right) = \dfrac{a}{3} \Rightarrow a = \dfrac{4}{3}$

40. Let ten's place digit number $= x$ and unit's place digit number $= y$

$\therefore \qquad$ Number $= 10x + y$

According to the question,

$\qquad\qquad xy = 18 \qquad\qquad\qquad ...(i)$

$\quad 10x + y - 63 = 10y + x$

$9x - 9y = 63 \quad \Rightarrow \quad x - y = 7 \qquad ...(ii)$

$\qquad (x + y)^2 = (x - y)^2 + 4xy$

$\qquad\qquad\qquad = 49 + 72 = 121$

$\qquad\qquad x + y = 11 \qquad\qquad ...(iii)$

From equation (ii) and (iii) we get,

$\qquad\qquad x = 9, y = 2$

$\therefore \qquad$ Number $= 92$

****

5

Arithmetic Progressions

An arithmetic progression is a list of numbers in which each term after the first differs from the preceeding term by a constant amount. *i.e.,* **an arithmetic progression is a list of numbers in which each next term is obtained by adding a fixed number to the preceeding term except the first term.**

This fixed number which is the difference between consecutive terms of the A.P. is called the **Common difference** of the A.P. The common difference, can be positive, negative or zero. The terms of an arithmetic progression (A.P.) with first term a and common difference d follow the pattern

$a, a + d, a + 2d, a + 3d$

This is called general form of an A.P. When an A.P. contains a finite number of terms, it is called a Finite Arithmetic Progression and these APs have a last term. When an AP is not finite, it is called **Infinite Arithmetic Progression**. Such APs do not have a last term.

In general, for an AP $a_1, a_2 \ldots\ldots a_n$, we have $d = a_{k+1} - a_k$ where, a_{k+1} and a_k are the $(k + 1)$th and the kth terms respectively.

To obtain d of a given AP find only one of $a_2 - a_1, a_3 - a_2, a_4 - a_3, \ldots\ldots$

nth Term of an AP

Suppose that a is the first term of an AP whose common difference is d.

$$\text{First term} \quad a_1 = a = a + 0.d = a$$
$$a_2 = a_1 + d = a + d$$
$$a_3 = a_2 + d = a + 2d$$
$$a_4 = a_3 + d = a + 3d$$
$$\ldots\ldots\ldots\ldots\ldots\ldots\ldots\ldots$$
$$\ldots\ldots\ldots\ldots\ldots\ldots\ldots\ldots$$
$$a_n = a_{n-1} + d = a + (n - 1)d$$

$\therefore$ For an AP whose first term is a and whose common difference is d, the nth term is determined by the formula

$$\boxed{a_n = a + (n-1)d}$$

Ex. 1 : Find common difference of the following

8, 15, 22, 29, ...

Sol. Common difference = 2nd term – first term

= 15 – 8 = 7

Ex. 2 : Find the 12th term of the A.P. whose first term is 9 and common difference is 10.

Sol. Here, $a = 9$

and $d = 10$

$$a_{12} = a + (n - 1)d$$
$$= 9 + (12 - 1)10$$
$$= 9 + 11(10)$$
$$= 9 + 110 = 119$$

Ex. 3 : 3, 7, 11, 15, 19, ... are in A.P. find 25th term.

Sol. $a = 3,$

$$d = 7 - 3 = 4$$
$$a_{25} = a + 24d = 3 + 24(4)$$
$$= 3 + 96 = 99$$

$\therefore$ 25th term = 99

If three numbers are in AP, then the middle one is called the Arithmetic mean between the other two.

A.M. between two given numbers

Let a and b are two numbers and A is the A.M. between them.

Then a, A, b are in A.P.

$\Rightarrow \quad A - a = b - A$

$\Rightarrow \quad A + A = a + b$

$\Rightarrow \quad 2A = a + b$

$$\boxed{\therefore \ A = \frac{a+b}{2}}$$

Sum of finite numbers of terms of an AP

Let a be the first term and d be the common difference of an AP, then the sum of the first n terms S_n of an A.P.

$$S_n = \frac{n}{2}[2a+(n-1)d] = \frac{n}{2}[a+l]$$

Three terms of A.P.

Three terms of AP are $\alpha - \beta,\ \alpha,\ \alpha + \beta$

Four Terms of AP

If we are to take four terms in AP, we take them as
$$\alpha - 3\beta,\ \alpha - \beta,\ \alpha + \beta,\ \alpha + 3\beta$$

SOLVED EXAMPLES

Ex. 1 : Find the Arithmetic mean between 24 and 36

Sol. A.M. $= \dfrac{a+b}{2} = \dfrac{24+36}{2} = \dfrac{60}{2} = 30$

Ex. 2 : If $1 + 6 + 11 + \ldots\ldots + x = 148$ then find the value of x.

Sol. : Let total terms $= n$

Then, $148 = S_n = \dfrac{n}{2}\{2 \times 1 + 5(n - 1)\}$

$\Rightarrow\quad 296 = n(5n - 3)$

$\Rightarrow\quad 5n^2 - 3n - 296 = 0$

$\Rightarrow\quad n = 8$

$\because\quad n = 8\qquad$ term $= 1 + 5(8 - 1)$

$\therefore\quad x = 36.$

MULTIPLE CHOICE QUESTIONS

1. Which term of the AP : 3, 8, 13, 18, ..., is 78?
   A. 12   B. 16
   C. 10   D. 18

2. Which term of the AP : 4, 9, 14, ..., is 89?
   A. 18   B. 14
   C. 12   D. 20

3. Which term of the AP : 3, 15, 27, 39, ..., will be 132 more than its 54th term?
   A. 60   B. 62
   C. 65   D. 63

4. Find the 20th term from the last term of the AP : 3, 8, 13, ..., 253.
   A. 100   B. 125
   C. 148   D. 158

5. Find the 6th term from end of the A.P.
   17, 14, 11, ..., –40
   A. 25   B. –25
   C. –28   D. 28

6. Find the 31st term of an AP whose 11th term is 38 and 16th term is 73.
   A. 150   B. 165
   C. 168   D. 178

7. 5th term of an AP is 26 and 10th term is 51. The 15th term is :
   A. 60   B. 76
   C. 55   D. 72

8. The arithmetic mean of 12 and 20 is :
   A. 12   B. 14
   C. 16   D. 18

9. The sum of first 20 natural numbers is :
   A. 55   B. 210
   C. 110   D. 215

10. The sum of 2, 7, 12, ... to 10 terms is :
   A. 240   B. 248
   C. 245   D. 250

11. The sum of first 100 natural numbers is :
   A. 5050   B. 6060
   C. 4040   D. 5500

12. The 10th term of A.P. 2, 7, 12, ... is :
   A. 35   B. 45
   C. 47   D. 50

13. The 11th term from the end of the A.P. 10, 7, 4, ..., –62 is :
   A. 25   B. 30
   C. –32   D. 35

14. The sum of the first 1000 positive integer is :
   A. 500500   B. 650650
   C. 300300   D. 700700

15. If 7th term of AP is 34 and 13th term is 64 them its 18th term is :
   A. 87   B. 88
   C. 89   D. 90

16. If 5, K, 11 are in A.P., the value of K is :
   A. 6   B. 8
   C. 7   D. 9

17. 30th term of the A.P : 10, 7, 4, ..., is :
   A. 97   B. 77
   C. –77   D. –87

18. The sum of the first 22 terms of the A.P. 8, 3, –2, ... is :
   A. –875   B. –979
   C. –717   D. 1072

19. The sum of the first 40 natural numbers is :
   A. 210   B. 820
   C. 610   D. 710

20. The 17th term of the series $3 + 7 + 11 + 15 + \ldots\ldots$ is :
   A. 63   B. 65
   C. 67   D. 69

21. The sum of 15 terms of the series 1, 3, 5, ... is :
   A. 225   B. 150
   C. 200   D. 250

22. The sum of three numbers of A.P. is 27 and their product is 504 then the numbers are :
   A. 4, 8, 14   B. 3, 8, 14
   C. 4, 7, 15   D. 4, 9, 14

23. If a, $(a - 2)$ and $3a$ are in AP, then the value of a is:
A. -3 B. -2
C. 3 D. 2

24. 8th term of an AP is 17 and its 14th term is 29. The common difference of the AP is :
A. 3   B. 2
C. 5   D. -2

25. Which term of the A.P. 20, 17, 14, ... is the first negative term?
A. 8th B. 6th
C. 9th D. 7th

26. 9th term of the A.P. 2, 4, 6, ... is :
A. 16   B. 18
C. 20   D. 14

27. Which term in the A.P. 5, 13, 21, ... is 181?
A. 21st   B. 22nd
C. 23rd   D. 24th

28. In the series 20, 18, 16, ..., -2 is the term :
A. 10th B. 11th
C. 12th D. 13th

29. The common difference of -2, -4, -6, -8, ... is :
A. -2 B. -1
C. 2   D. 3

30. The sum of $2 + 4 + 6 + 8 + ... + 80$ is :
A. 1540   B. 1640
C. 1740   D. 1440

31. If the nth term of the series is $3n - 1$, then the series is :
A. 2, 5, 8, ...   B. 1, 3, 5, ...
C. 2, 5, 9, ...   D. 1, 2, 4, ...

32. The sum of 20 terms of an A.P. whose n^{th} term $4n - 1$ is :
A. 820   B. 79
C. $80n - 1$ D. $80n + 1$

33. If sum of n terms of A.P. is 476, last term $= 20$ $n = 17$ then the first term is :
A. 32   B. 34
C. 36   D. 38

34. If $T_n = 2n$ of an AP then common difference is :
A. 1   B. 2
C. 3   D. 4

35. If the sum of n terms of A.P. is 476, $l = 20$, $a = 36$ then n is equal to :
A. 14   B. 15
C. 16   D. 17

36. 50th term of the A.P. 2, 5, 8, 11, ... is
A. 147   B. 149
C. 151   D. 153

37. The Arithmetic Mean of two numbers is 20, the sum of numbers is :
A. 40   B. 60
C. 80   D. 50

38. The 3rd term of an A.P. is -40 and 13th term is zero then d is equal to :
A. -4 B. 4
C. 0   D. -1

39. The sum of n natural number is :
A. $\dfrac{n(n+1)}{2}$ B. $\dfrac{n+1}{2}$
C. $(n + 2)$ D. $\dfrac{n+1}{2}$

40. If $l = 20$, $d = -1$, $n = 17$ then the first term is :
A. 30   B. 32
C. 34   D. 36

41. The nth term of the A.P. is $2n - 5$, then the series is:
A. -3, -1, 1, ...   B. 3, 1, -1, ...
C. 2, 5, 8, ...   D. 1, 7, 13, ...

42. If $a = 3$, $d = 2$, $l = 23$, then S_n is :
A. 143   B. 142
C. 141   D. 144

43. If $a = 3$, $n = 20$ and $S_n = 300$ then l is :
A. 30   B. 25
C. 27   D. 15

44. The four numbers in A.P. whose sum is 16 and sum of their squares is 84 are :
A. 3, 4, 5, 6   B. 2, 4, 6, 8
C. 1, 3, 5, 7   D. None of these

45. The sum of three A.M. between 2, 10 is :
A. 18   B. 16
C. 17   D. 15

46. The sum of the arithmetic series :
$5 + 11 + 17 + ... + 95$ is
A. 600   B. 700
C. 800   D. 500

47. How many terms of the arithmetic series $24 + 21 + 18 + 15 + ...$, be taken continuously so that their sum is -351?
A. 22   B. 24
C. 26   D. 28

48. If a, b, c are in A.P. then $\dfrac{a-b}{b-c}$ is equal to :
A. $\dfrac{a}{b}$ B. $\dfrac{b}{c}$
C. $\dfrac{a}{c}$ D. 1

49. The sum of the odd numbers between 0 and 50 is
A. 525   B. 625
C. 425   D. 725

50. How many two-digit numbers are divisible by 3?
A. 25   B. 27
C. 30   D. 33

ANSWERS

1	2	3	4	5	6	7	8	9	10
B	A	C	D	B	D	B	C	B	C

11	12	13	14	15	16	17	18	19	20
A	C	C	A	C	B	C	B	B	C

21	22	23	24	25	26	27	28	29	30
A	D	B	B	A	B	C	C	A	B

31	32	33	34	35	36	37	38	39	40
A	A	C	B	D	B	A	B	A	D

41	42	43	44	45	46	47	48	49	50
A	A	C	C	A	C	C	D	B	C

EXPLANATORY ANSWERS

1. Here, $a = 3$, $d = 8 - 3 = 5$ and $a_n = 78$

$$a_n = a + (n - 1)d$$
$$78 = 3 + (n - 1)5$$
$$\Rightarrow \quad 78 = 3 + 5n - 5$$
$$\Rightarrow \quad n = 16$$

2. Here, $a = 4$, $d = 9 - 4 = 5$, $a_n = 89$

$$a_n = a + (n - 1)d$$
$$\Rightarrow \quad 89 = 4 + (n - 1)5$$
$$\Rightarrow \quad 89 = 4 + 5n - 5 \Rightarrow n = 18.$$

3. Here, $a = 3$, $d = 15 - 3 = 12$

$$a_{54} = a + 53d = 3 + 53(12)$$
$$= 3 + 636 = 639$$
$$639 + 152 = 771$$
$$771 = a + (n - 1)d$$
$$\Rightarrow \quad 771 = 3 + (n - 1)12$$
$$\Rightarrow \quad 771 = 3 + 12n - 12$$
$$\Rightarrow \quad 771 = 12n - 9$$
$$\Rightarrow \quad 12n = 780$$
$$\Rightarrow \quad n = \frac{780}{12} = 65$$

4. The given A.P. is 3, 8, 13, ..., 253.

Here, $a = 3$, $d = 5$ and $n = 20$

$\because$ nth term from the end $= l - (n - 1)d$

$\therefore$ 20th term from the end $= 253 - (20 - 1)5$
$$= 253 - 95 = 158$$

5. The given A.P. is 17, 14, 11, ..., –40

Here, $a = 17$, $d = -3$, $n = 6$

$\because$ nth term from the end $= l - (n - 1)d$

$\therefore$ 6th term from the end $= -40 - (5)(-3)$
$$= -40 + 15 = -25$$

6.
$$a + 10d = 38 \qquad ...(i)$$
$$\text{and} \quad a + 15d = 73 \qquad ...(ii)$$
Solving eq. (i) and (ii) we get
$$5d = 35 \quad \Rightarrow \quad d = 7$$
$$a = -32$$
$$\therefore \quad a_{31} = a + 30d = -32 + 30(7)$$
$$= -32 + 210 = 178$$

$$a_5 = a + 4d = 26 \qquad ...(i)$$
$$a_{10} = a + 9d = 51 \qquad ...(ii)$$
Solving eq. (i) and (ii) we get
$$5d = 25 \Rightarrow d = 5 \text{ and } a = 6$$
$$\therefore \quad a_{15} = a + 14d = 6 + 70 = 76.$$

8. A.M. between 12 and 20 $= \dfrac{12 + 20}{2} = 16$

because A.M. $= \dfrac{a + b}{2}$

9. $\because$ Sum of the first n natural numbers of AP $= \dfrac{n(n+1)}{2}$

$\therefore$ Sum of first 20 natural numbers $= \dfrac{20 \times 21}{2} = 210$

10. $2 + 7 + 12 + ...$ to 10 terms

Here $a = 2$, $d = 7 - 2 = 5$, $n = 10$

$$\therefore \quad S_n = \frac{n}{2}\{2a + (n - 1)d\}$$

$$S_{10} = \frac{10}{2}\{4 + 45\} = 5 \times 49 = 245$$

11. Sum of the first 100 natural numbers

$$= \frac{100 \times 101}{2} = 5050$$

12. 2, 7, 12, ..., are in A.P.

$a = 2$, $d = 5$, $n = 10$

$a_n = a + (n - 1)d = 2 + (10 - 1)5 = 47$

13. $a = 10$, $d = -3$, $l = -62$, $n = 11$

$\because$ nth term from the end of A.P. $= l - (n - 1)d$

$\therefore$ 11th term from the end of A.P.
$$= -62 - (10)(-3) = -32$$

14. Sum of the first –1000 positive integers

$$= \frac{1000 \times 1001}{2} = 500500$$

15.
$$a + 6d = 34 \qquad ...(i)$$
$$a + 12d = 64 \qquad ...(ii)$$
Solving eq. (i) and (ii) then we get
$$6d = 30 \Rightarrow d = 5, a = 4$$
$$a_{18} = a + 17d = 4 + 85 = 89$$

16. $\because$ 5, K, 11 are in A.P.

$\therefore$ K $-$ 5 $=$ 11 $-$ K $\Rightarrow$ 2K $=$ 11 $+$ 5 $=$ 16 $\Rightarrow$ K $=$ 8.

17. 10, 7, 4, ... are in A.P.

Here, $a = 10$, $d = 7 - 10 = -3$

$a_{30} = a + 29d = 10 + 29(-3) = 10 - 87 = -77$

18. 8, 3, -2, ... are in A.P.

$a = 8$, $d = 3 - 8 = -5$, $n = 22$

$$S_n = \frac{n}{2}\{2a+(n-1)d\} = \frac{22}{2}\{16 + (21)(-5)\}$$
$$= 11\{16 - 105\} = -979$$

19. Sum of 40 natural numbers $= \dfrac{40 \times 41}{2} = 820$

20. $3 + 7 + 11 + 15 + \ldots$ are in A.P.

$a = 3$, $d = 4$, $n = 17$

$a_{17} = a + 16d = 3 + 64 = 67.$

21. $\because$ 1, 3, 5, ... are in A.P.

$\therefore$ $a = 1$, $d = 2$,

$$S_{15} = \frac{15}{2}\{2(1)+(15-1)(2)\}$$
$$= \frac{15}{2}\{2+28\} = \frac{15}{2}\times 30 = 225$$

22. Three numbers of A.P. are $\alpha - \beta$, α, $\alpha + \beta$

$\alpha - \beta + \alpha + \alpha + \beta = 27 \Rightarrow 3\alpha = 27 \Rightarrow \alpha = 9$

$(\alpha - \beta)(\alpha)(\alpha + \beta) = 504$

$\Rightarrow (9 - \beta)(9 - \beta) \times 9 = 504$

$81 - \beta^2 = 56 \Rightarrow 25 = \beta^2 \Rightarrow \beta = \pm\, 5$

$\therefore$ Numbers are 4, 9, 14

23. $\because$ a, $a - 2$ and $3a$ are in A.P.

$$\Rightarrow \quad a - 2 = \frac{a+3a}{2} = \frac{4a}{2} = 2a \left[\because \text{AM} = \frac{a+b}{2}\right]$$

$\Rightarrow \qquad a = -2$

24. $a_8 = a + 7d = 17$ ...(*i*)

$a_{14} = a + 13d = 29$ ...(*ii*)

Solving eq. (*i*) and (*ii*) then we get,

$6d = 12 \Rightarrow d = 2$, $a = 3$

25. Here, $a = 20$, $d = 17 - 20 = -3$

Let $T_n < 0$

then, $a + (n - 1)\, d < 0$

$$\therefore \ 20 + (n - 1)\,(-3) < 0 \Rightarrow (n - 1) > \frac{20}{3}$$

Hence, 8th term is the first negative term.

26. $\because$ 2, 4, 6, ... are in A.P.

Here, $a = 2$, $d = 4 - 2 = 2$, $n = 9$

$a_9 = a + 8d = 2 + 8(2) = 18$

27. $\because$ 5, 13, 21, ... 181 are in A.P.

Here, $a = 5$, $d = 13 - 5 = 8$, $n = ?$

$a_n = a + (n - 1)d \Rightarrow 181 = 5 + (n - 1)8$

$\Rightarrow 181 = 5 + 8n - 8 \Rightarrow n = 23$

28. 20, 18, 16, ... -2 are in A.P.

$a_n = a + (n - 1)d$

$\Rightarrow \qquad -2 = 20 + (n - 1)(-2)$

$\Rightarrow \qquad -2 = 20 - 2n + 2$

$\Rightarrow \qquad 2n = 24 \Rightarrow n = 12$

29. Common difference $= -4 - (-2) = -4 + 2 = -2$

30. Here, $a = 2$, $d = 4 - 2 = 2$, $a_n = 80$

$a_n = a + (n - 1)d$

$\Rightarrow \qquad 80 = 2 + (n - 1)2$

$\Rightarrow \qquad 80 = 2n \Rightarrow n = 40$

$$S_{40} = \frac{40}{2}\{2a+(n-1)d\}$$
$$= 20\{4 + 78\} = 20 \times 82 = 1640$$

31. $\because$ $a_n = 3n - 1$ putting $n = 1, 2, 3, \ldots$

$a_1 = 3 - 1 = 2$

$a_2 = 6 - 1 = 5$

$a_3 = 9 - 1 = 8$

$\ldots\ldots\ldots\ldots\ldots\ldots\ldots\ldots$

$\therefore$ Series is 2, 5, 8, ...

32. $\because$ $a_n = 4n - 1$ putting $n = 1, 2, 3, \ldots$

$a_1 = 3$, $a_2 = 7$, $a_3 = 11$, $a_4 = 15$

$\ldots\ldots\ldots\ldots$

$\therefore$ Series is 3, 7, 11, 15, ...

$$S_{20} = \frac{20}{2}\{2(3) + (20 - 1)4\}$$
$$= 10\{6 + 76\} = 10 \times 82 = 820$$

33. Here, $S_n = 476$, $n = 17$, $l = 20$

$$S_n = \frac{n}{2}(a+l) \quad [\because l = a + (n - 1)d]$$

$$476 = \frac{17}{2}(a + 20)$$

$$\Rightarrow \quad a + 20 = \frac{476 \times 2}{17}$$

$\Rightarrow \quad a + 20 = 56 \Rightarrow a = 36.$

34. $a_n = 2n$ putting $n = 1, 2, 3, \ldots$

$a_1 = 2$, $a_2 = 4$, $a_3 = 6$

$\therefore$ Series is 2, 4, 6, ...

$\therefore$ $d = 4 - 2 = 2$

35. $S_n = 476$, $l = 20$, $a = 36$, $n = ?$

$$\because \qquad S_n = \frac{n}{2}[a + l]$$

$$476 = \frac{n}{2}[36 + 20] = \frac{56n}{2} = 28n$$

$$\Rightarrow \qquad n = \frac{476}{28} = 17$$

36. $\because$ 2, 5, 8, 11, ... are in A.P.

$a = 2$, $d = 3$

$a_{50} = a + 49d = 2 + 49(3) = 2 + 147 = 149$

37. Let, a, b, c are in A.P.

$\because$ b is the A.M. of a and c

$$\text{A.M.} = b = \frac{a+c}{2}$$

$\Rightarrow \quad 20 = \frac{a+c}{2} \Rightarrow a + c = 40$

$\therefore$ Sum of numbers = 40

38. $\quad a_3 = a + 2d = -40 \qquad \qquad ...(i)$

$\quad a_{13} = a + 12d = 0 \qquad \qquad ...(ii)$

Solving eq. (i) and (ii) we get, $d = 4$.

39. The sum of first n natural numbers = $\frac{n(n+1)}{2}$.

40. $a_n = a + (n - 1)d$

$20 = a + (17 - 1)(-1) \Rightarrow 20 = a - 16$

$\Rightarrow a = 36$

41. $a_n = 2n - 5$ putting $n = 1, 2, 3, ...$

$a_1 = -3$

$a_2 = -1$

$a_3 = 1$

$a_4 = 3$

....

$\therefore$ Series is $-3, -1, 1, ...$

42. $a_n = a + (n - 1)d \Rightarrow 23 = 3 + (n - 1)2$

$\Rightarrow 23 = 3 + 2n - 2 \Rightarrow n = 11$

$S_{11} = \frac{n}{2}\{a + l\} = \frac{11}{2}(3 + 23) = \frac{11}{2} \times 26 = 143$

43. $S_n = \frac{n}{2}(a + l)$

$\Rightarrow 300 = \frac{20}{2}(3 + l) \Rightarrow l = 27.$

44. Four numbers of A.P. are

$\alpha - 3\beta, \alpha - \beta, \alpha + \beta, \alpha + 3\beta,$

$\alpha - 3\beta + \alpha - \beta + \alpha + \beta + \alpha + 3\beta = 16$

$\Rightarrow 4\alpha = 16 \Rightarrow \alpha = 4$

$(\alpha - 3\beta)^2 + (\alpha - \beta)^2 + (\alpha + \beta)^2 + (\alpha + 3\beta)^2 = 84$

$\alpha^2 + 9\beta^2 - 6\alpha\beta + \alpha^2 + \beta^2 - 2\alpha\beta + \alpha^2 + \beta^2 + 2\alpha\beta + \alpha^2 + 9\beta^2 + 6\alpha\beta = 84$

$\Rightarrow \quad 4\alpha^2 + 20\beta^2 = 84$

$\quad 4(4)^2 + 20\beta^2 = 84$

$\Rightarrow \quad 20\beta^2 = 84 - 64 = 20$

$\Rightarrow \quad \beta^2 = 1 \Rightarrow \beta = \pm 1$

$\therefore$ Numbers are 1, 3, 5, 7.

45. Let, A_1, A_2, A_3 be the three A.M.'s between 2 and 10 such that 2, A_1, A_2, A_3, 10 are in A.P.

$n = 3 + 2 = 5, a = 2$

$10 = 2 + (5 - 1)d$

$\Rightarrow 4d = 8 \Rightarrow d = 2$

$A_1 = a + d = 2 + 2 = 4$

$A_2 = a + 2d = 2 + 4 = 6$

$A_3 = a + 3d = 2 + 6 = 8$

$\therefore$ Sum of $4 + 6 + 8 = 18$

46. $95 = 5 + (n - 1)6 \Rightarrow 90 = 6(n - 1)$

$\Rightarrow n - 1 = 15 \Rightarrow n = 16$

$S_{16} = \frac{n}{2}\{a + l\} = \frac{16}{2}\{5 + 95\} = 800$

47. $\qquad S_n = -351, a = 24, d = -3$

$\qquad S_n = \frac{n}{2}\{2a + (n - 1)d\}$

$\quad -351 = \frac{n}{2}\{48 + (n - 1)(-3)$

$\Rightarrow -351 = \frac{n}{2}\{48 - 3n + 3\}$

$\qquad n(51 - 3n) = -702$

$\Rightarrow \qquad 51n - 3n^2 = -702$

$\qquad n^2 - 17n - 234 = 0$

$\Rightarrow \quad (n - 26)(n + 9) = 0$

$\therefore \qquad n = 26 \text{ or } n = -9$

Here $n = -9$ is not applicable.

Thus, 26 terms are needed to get the sum -351.

48. $\because$ a, b, c are in A.P.

$\therefore \qquad b - a = c - b$

$\Rightarrow \qquad a - b = b - c$

then, $\quad \dfrac{a-b}{b-c} = \dfrac{b-c}{b-c}$

$\qquad \qquad$ [Dividing both sides by $b - c$]

$\Rightarrow \qquad \dfrac{a-b}{b-c} = 1$

49. Odd numbers between 0 and 50 are 1, 3, 5, 7, 9, ..., 49

$\qquad 49 = a + (n - 1)d$

$\Rightarrow \qquad 49 = 1 + (n - 1)2$

$\Rightarrow \qquad 48 = 2n - 2$

$\Rightarrow \qquad 2n = 50 \Rightarrow n = 25$

$\because \qquad S_{25} = \frac{n}{2}(a + l)$

$\Rightarrow \qquad S_{25} = \frac{25}{2}(1 + 49)$

$\qquad \frac{25}{2} \times 50 = 625$

50. Two digit numbers divisible by 3 are 12, 15, 18, ... 99.

$\qquad 99 = 12 + (n - 1)3$

$\Rightarrow \qquad 99 = 12 + 3n - 3$

$\Rightarrow \qquad 99 = 3n + 9$

$\Rightarrow \qquad 3n = 90 \Rightarrow n = 30.$

✱ ✱ ✱

6
Trigonometry

Trigonometry is an important branch of mathematics. The word 'trigonometry' is derived from two Greek words 'trigon' meaning a triangle and 'metron' meaning measurement. Thus, the word 'trigonometry' literally means the science which deals with the measurement of triangles. The main purpose of trigonometry is to solve the following problem:

If any sides and angles of a right-angled triangle are known, how do we find the remaining sides and angles?

This problem is solved by using some ratios of the sides of a right-angled triangle with respect to its acute angles called trigonometric ratios of angles. Trigonometry is constantly used in surveying, engineering, physics, astronomy and navigation.

In order to define the trigonometric functions, we must define an angle first.

Angle

An angle is a figure formed by two rays (called the arms) with the common initial point (called the vertex).

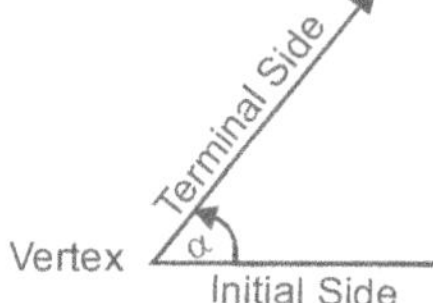

It is determined by rotating a ray about its end point.

The position of the ray before the rotation is called the **initial side** of the angle and the position of the ray after the rotation is called the **terminal side.** Angles will often be denoted by small Greek letters, such as α, β, γ, θ etc.

Positive and Negative Angles

Angles determined by a **counter clockwise** rotation are said to be **positive** and angles determined by **clockwise** rotation are said to be **negative**. One full turn of a ray about its end point is called **one revolution**. 1 revolution = 360°, one-half of a revolution is called a straight angle while one quarter of a revolution is called a right angle. Thus, a right angle is an angle that measures 90° and straight angle is an angle that measures 180°.

Trigonometric Ratios of Angles

There are six trigonometric ratios — sine, cosine, tangent, cotangent, secant and cosecant—upon which trigonometry is based.

ΔABC is a right- angled triangle in which $\angle$ACB = θ. The side AB is opposite to an angle θ and is called **opposide side**. BC is the **adjacent side** in relation to angle θ; AC is the **hypotenuse**.

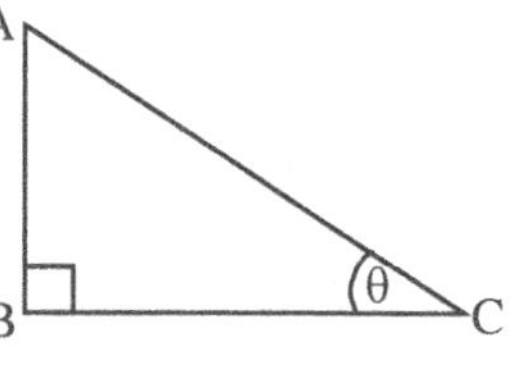

The six trigonometric ratios of the acute angle θ are defined as follows :

$$\sin\theta = \frac{p}{h} = \frac{AB}{AC}$$

$$\cos\theta = \frac{b}{h} = \frac{BC}{AC}$$

$$\tan\theta = \frac{p}{b} = \frac{AB}{BC}$$

$$\cot\theta = \frac{b}{p} = \frac{BC}{AB}$$

$$\sec\theta = \frac{h}{b} = \frac{AC}{BC}$$

$$\text{cosec}\theta = \frac{h}{p} = \frac{AC}{AB}$$

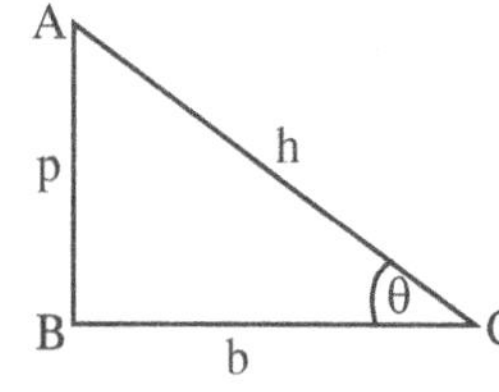

$$\begin{bmatrix} p = \text{perpendicular} \\ \quad \text{or opposite} \\ b = \text{base or adjacent} \\ h = \text{hypotenuse} \end{bmatrix}$$

Ex. 1 : If $\sin\theta = \dfrac{3}{5}$ find the values of $\cos\theta$, $\tan\theta$, $\cot\theta$, $\sec\theta$ and $\text{cosec}\theta$.

$$\because \quad \sin\theta = \frac{3}{5} = \frac{p}{h}$$

$$\therefore \quad b^2 = h^2 - p^2 \qquad [\because h^2 = p^2 + b^2]$$

$$= (5)^2 - (3)^2 = 25 - 9$$

$$b^2 = 16$$

$$\therefore \quad b = \sqrt{16} = 4$$

$$\cos\theta = \frac{b}{h} = \frac{4}{5}$$

$$\tan\theta = \frac{p}{b} = \frac{3}{4}$$

$$\cot\theta = \frac{b}{p} = \frac{4}{3}$$

$$\sec\theta = \frac{h}{b} = \frac{5}{4}$$

$$\csc\theta = \frac{h}{p} = \frac{5}{3}$$

IMPORTANT FORMULAE

A. (i) $\tan\theta = \dfrac{\sin\theta}{\cos\theta} = \dfrac{1}{\cot\theta}$

(ii) $\cot\theta = \dfrac{\cos\theta}{\sin\theta} = \dfrac{1}{\tan\theta}$

(iii) $\sec\theta = \dfrac{1}{\cos\theta}$

(iv) $\csc\theta = \dfrac{1}{\sin\theta}$

B. (v) $\sin^2\theta + \cos^2\theta = 1$

$\sin^2\theta = 1 - \cos^2\theta \Rightarrow \sin\theta = \sqrt{1-\cos^2\theta}$

$\cos^2\theta = 1 - \sin^2\theta \Rightarrow \cos\theta = \sqrt{1-\sin^2\theta}$

(vi) $1 + \tan^2\theta = \sec^2\theta$

$\sec^2\theta - \tan^2\theta = 1$

$\sec^2\theta - 1 = \tan^2\theta$

(vii) $1 + \cot^2\theta = \csc^2\theta$

$\csc^2\theta - \cot^2\theta = 1$

$\csc^2\theta - 1 = \cot^2\theta$

(viii) $\tan^2\theta = \dfrac{\sin^2\theta}{\cos^2\theta}$

(ix) $\cot^2\theta = \dfrac{\cos^2\theta}{\sin^2\theta}$

(x) $\sec^2\theta = \dfrac{1}{\cos^2\theta}$

(xi) $\csc^2\theta = \dfrac{1}{\sin^2\theta}$

C. (xii) $\sin(90 - \theta) = \cos\theta$

(xiii) $\cos(90 - \theta) = \sin\theta$

(xiv) $\tan(90 - \theta) = \cot\theta$

(xv) $\cot(90 - \theta) = \tan\theta$

(xvi) $\sec(90 - \theta) = \csc\theta$

(xvii) $\csc(90 - \theta) = \sec\theta$

D. (i) $\sin(A \pm B) = \sin A \times \cos B \pm \cos A \times \sin B$

(ii) $\cos(A \pm B) = \cos A \times \cos B \mp \sin A \times \sin B$

E. (i) $\sin 2\theta = 2\sin\theta \cdot \cos\theta$

(ii) $\cos 2\theta = \cos^2\theta - \sin^2\theta$

$\qquad = 1 - 2\sin^2\theta = 2\cos^2\theta - 1$

(iii) $\tan 2\theta = \dfrac{2\tan\theta}{1-\tan^2\theta}$

F. (i) $\sin 3\theta = 3\sin\theta - 4\sin^3\theta$

(ii) $\cos 3\theta = 4\cos^3\theta - 3\cos\theta$

T-Ratios of Standard Angles

θ	0°	30°	45°	60°	90°
$\sin\theta$	0	$\dfrac{1}{2}$	$\dfrac{1}{\sqrt{2}}$	$\dfrac{\sqrt{3}}{2}$	1
$\cos\theta$	1	$\dfrac{\sqrt{3}}{2}$	$\dfrac{1}{\sqrt{2}}$	$\dfrac{1}{2}$	0
$\tan\theta$	0	$\dfrac{1}{\sqrt{3}}$	1	$\sqrt{3}$	∞
$\cot\theta$	∞	$\sqrt{3}$	1	$\dfrac{1}{\sqrt{3}}$	0
$\sec\theta$	1	$\dfrac{2}{\sqrt{3}}$	$\sqrt{2}$	2	∞
$\csc\theta$	∞	2	$\sqrt{2}$	$\dfrac{2}{\sqrt{3}}$	1

TRIGONOMETRIC SIGNS OF T-RATIOS

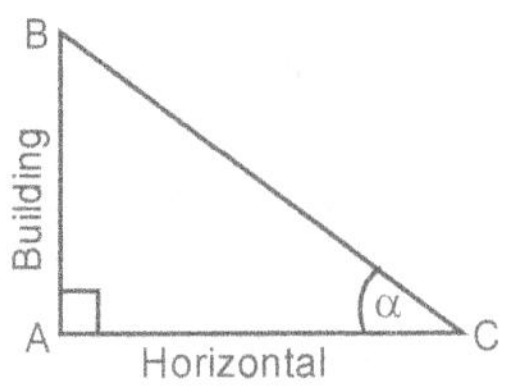

II Quadrant — $\sin\theta, \csc\theta$ (+ve)

I Quadrant — All(+ve)

III Quadrant — $\tan\theta, \cot\theta$ (+ve)

IV Quadrant — $\cos\theta, \sec\theta$ (+ve)

90°, 180°, 0°, 270°

HEIGHT AND DISTANCE

Our common use for trigonometry is to measure heights and distance that are either awkward or impossible to measure by ordinary means. One of the biggest triumphs of trigonometry is being able to find the size of an object or the distance to an object (such as the moon) without going to the object. In trigonometry, we develop methods for measuring sides and angles as well as for solving related applied problems. Because of the extensive use of these concepts, trigonometry is considered one of the most practical and relevant branches of mathematics.

The Angle of Elevation

If a person is looking up at an object, the acute angle measured from the horizontal to a line of sight observation of the object is called the angle of elevation. In the given figure, α is the angle of elevation.

The Angle of Depression

The angle β for a point below a horizontal line is the angle formed by the horizontal line and the observer's line of sight through the point. In the following figure, β is the angle of depression.

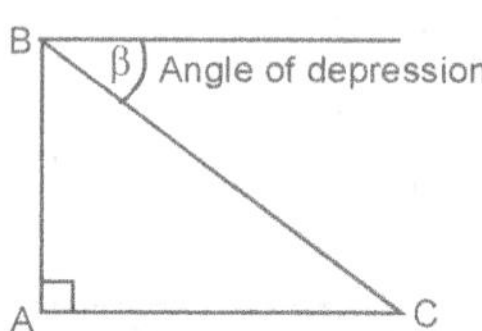

MULTIPLE CHOICE QUESTIONS

1. If $\cos\theta = \dfrac{1}{2}$, find the value of $\dfrac{2\sec\theta}{1+\tan^2\theta}$

A. 1   B. 2
C. 3   D. 4

2. If $\sin\theta = \dfrac{5}{13}$ and $0 < \theta < 90°$, find out the value of $\cos\theta$.

A. $\dfrac{5}{12}$ B. $\dfrac{12}{13}$

C. $\dfrac{13}{12}$ D. $\dfrac{12}{5}$

3. If $5\tan\theta = 4$, find the value of $\dfrac{5\sin\theta - 3\cos\theta}{5\sin\theta + 2\cos\theta}$

A. 2   B. $\dfrac{3}{2}$

C. $\dfrac{1}{6}$ D. $\dfrac{2}{3}$

4. If $3\cot\theta = 2$, find the value of $\dfrac{4\sin\theta - 3\cos\theta}{2\sin\theta + 6\cos\theta}$

A. $\dfrac{2}{3}$ B. $\dfrac{3}{2}$

C. $\dfrac{1}{3}$ D. 3

5. If $3\tan\theta = 2$, find the value of $\dfrac{4\sin\theta - \cos\theta}{2\sin\theta + \cos\theta}$

A. $\dfrac{3}{2}$ B. $\dfrac{5}{7}$

C. $\dfrac{3}{7}$ D. 1

6. If $3\cot\theta = 4$, find the value of $\dfrac{5\sin\theta - 3\cos\theta}{5\sin\theta + 3\cos\theta}$

A. $\dfrac{1}{9}$ B. $\dfrac{2}{7}$
C. 3   D. 4

7. If $\tan\theta = \dfrac{3}{4}$, find the value of $\dfrac{4\sin\theta - 2\cos\theta}{4\sin\theta + 3\cos\theta}$

A. $\dfrac{2}{3}$ B. $\dfrac{4}{3}$

C. $\dfrac{1}{6}$ D. $\dfrac{5}{6}$

8. If $\tan A = \dfrac{5}{12}$, find the value of $\sin A + \cos A$, where A is an acute angle.

A. $\dfrac{13}{17}$ B. $\dfrac{17}{13}$

C. $\dfrac{12}{5}$ D. $\dfrac{5}{17}$

9. If $\tan\theta = \dfrac{2}{3}\,(0° < \theta < 90°)$, then find the value of $\sin\theta$

A. $\dfrac{2}{\sqrt{13}}$ B. $\dfrac{3}{\sqrt{12}}$
C. 1   D. 0

10. If $2\tan\theta = 1$, find the value of $\dfrac{3\cos\theta + 2\sin\theta}{2\cos\theta - \sin\theta}$

A. $\dfrac{8}{3}$ B. $\dfrac{5}{3}$

C. $\dfrac{2}{3}$ D. 2

11. Evaluate
$(\csc\theta - \sin\theta)(\sec\theta - \cos\theta)(\tan\theta + \cot\theta)$
A. 1   B. 2
C. 3   D. 0

12. Evaluate
$(\sin A + \cos A)(\tan A + \cot A)$
A. $\sin A + \cos A$
B. $\sec A + \csc A$
C. $\sin A$
D. $\cos A$

13. Evaluate $\dfrac{\sin\theta}{1+\cos\theta} + \dfrac{1+\cos\theta}{\sin\theta}$
A. $2\sin A$ B. $2\csc A$
C. $2\tan A$ D. $2\cos A$

14. Evaluate $\dfrac{\tan A + \sec A - 1}{\tan A - \sec A + 1}$

A. $\sec A + \tan A$ B. $\sin A$
C. 1   D. 0

15. If $\sin x + \sin^2 x = 1$, then $\cos^2 x + \cos^4 x$ is :
   A. 1   B. 2
   C. 3   D. 4

16. If $\cos\theta - \sin\theta = \sqrt{2}\sin\theta$, then $\cos\theta + \sin\theta$ is:
   A. $\sqrt{2}\sin\theta$ B. $\sqrt{2}\cos\theta$
   C. $\sin\theta$ D. $\cos\theta$

17. Find the value of
$4(\sin^4 30° + \cos^4 60°) - 3(\sin^2 45° - 2\cos^2 45°)$.
   A. 1   B. 2
   C. 0   D. 3

18. Express $\cos 79° + \sec 79°$ in terms of angles between $0°$ and $45°$
   A. 1
   B. 2
   C. $\sin 11° + \operatorname{cosec} 11°$
   D. $\cos 11° + \sec 11°$

19. Using the formula
$\cos (A - B) = \cos A \cos B + \sin A \sin B$,
find the value of $\cos 15°$.
   A. $\dfrac{\sqrt{3}-1}{2\sqrt{2}}$ B. $\sqrt{3}-1$
   C. $\dfrac{\sqrt{3}+1}{2\sqrt{2}}$ D. $\sqrt{3}+1$

20. Using the formula
$\sin (A - B) = \sin A \cos B - \cos A \sin B$,
find the value of $\sin 15°$
   A. $\sqrt{3}$ B. $\sqrt{3}+1$
   C. $\dfrac{\sqrt{3}-1}{2\sqrt{2}}$ D. $\dfrac{\sqrt{3}+1}{2\sqrt{2}}$

21. If $\cos\theta = \dfrac{12}{13}$ and θ is an acute angle, then
$\sqrt{\left(1+\dfrac{\sin\theta}{\cos\theta}\right)(1-\tan\theta)}$ is :
   A. $\dfrac{\sqrt{115}}{12}$ B. $\dfrac{\sqrt{116}}{12}$
   C. $\dfrac{\sqrt{119}}{12}$ D. $\dfrac{\sqrt{117}}{12}$

22. $\sin\theta \cos (90° - \theta) + \cos\theta \sin (90° - \theta)$ equal to :
   A. 0   B. 1
   C. −1   D. 2

23. $\cos^2 72° + \cos^2 18° = ?$
   A. 0   B. 1
   C. −1   D. 2

24. $\sqrt{\dfrac{1+\cos 60°}{2}} = \ldots\ldots$
   A. $\dfrac{\sqrt{3}}{2}$ B. 1
   C. $\dfrac{1}{2}$ D. $\dfrac{1}{4}$

25. $3\tan^2 30° + \sec^4 45° - \tan^2 60°$ is equal to :
   A. 0   B. 1
   C. 2   D. 3

26. If $\cos\theta = \dfrac{3}{5}$, then the value of $\dfrac{\sin\theta \tan\theta + 1}{2\tan^2\theta}$ is :
   A. $\dfrac{88}{160}$ B. $\dfrac{91}{160}$
   C. $\dfrac{92}{160}$ D. $\dfrac{93}{160}$

27. If $\cos (A + B) = \sin (A - B) = \dfrac{1}{2}$, where A and B are positive, then smallest positive value of A + B (in degrees) is :
   A. $45°$ B. $60°$
   C. $105°$ D. $150°$

28. The value of $\sin^2 30° \cos^2 45° + 4\tan^2 30° + \dfrac{1}{2}\sin^2 90° - 2\cos^2 90°$ is :
   A. $\dfrac{45}{24}$ B. $\dfrac{46}{24}$
   C. $\dfrac{47}{24}$ D. $\dfrac{49}{24}$

29. The value of $\sin 79° \cos 11° + \cos 79° \sin 11°$.
   A. 1   B. 0
   C. 2   D. −2

30. If $\dfrac{x\operatorname{cosec}^2 30° \sec^2 45°}{8\cos^2 45° \sin^2 90°} = \tan^2 60° - \tan^2 45°$ then x is :
   A. 1   B. −1
   C. 2   D. 0

31. $(\sin\theta + \cos\theta)(1 - \sin\theta \cos\theta)$ can be written as :
   A. $\sin\theta + \cos\theta$ B. $\sin^3\theta - \cos^3\theta$
   C. $\sin^3\theta + \cos^3\theta$ D. $\sin\theta - \cos\theta$

32. $(\operatorname{cosec}\theta - \sin\theta)(\sec\theta - \cos\theta)(\tan\theta + \cot\theta)$
   A. 0   B. 1
   C. $\tan\theta$ D. $\cot\theta$

33. $(1 + \cot A - \operatorname{cosec} A)(1 + \tan A + \sec A)$
   A. 0   B. 1
   C. 2   D. 3

34. If $x^2 + y^2 + z^2 = r^2$, where $x = r\sin A \cos B$, $y = r\sin A \sin B$, then z has one of the following values :
   A. $r\sin B$ B. $r\cos A$
   C. $r\tan A \cos B$ D. $r\tan A \tan B$

35. If $\cot^2\theta = \dfrac{7}{8}$ and $0 < \theta < 90°$, then the value of
$\dfrac{(1+\sin\theta)(1-\sin\theta)}{(1+\cos\theta)(1-\cos\theta)}$ is equal to :

A. $\dfrac{7}{8}$ B. $\dfrac{7}{6}$

C. $\dfrac{7}{5}$ D. $\dfrac{7}{4}$

36. If $\sin \theta = \dfrac{8}{17}$ and $90° < \theta < 180°$, then the value of the expression $\dfrac{2\sin \theta + \cos \theta}{3\cos \theta + 5\sin \theta}$ is :

A. $\dfrac{1}{5}$ B. $-\dfrac{1}{5}$

C. $\dfrac{31}{85}$ D. $-\dfrac{31}{85}$

37. The value of the expression
$(\sin^2 30° + \cos^2 30°) - (\sin^2 60° + \cos^2 60°) + (\sin^2 45° + \cos^2 45°) =$

A. 0.25   B. 0.5
C. 0.75   D. 1

38. $\sin 40° . \sec 50° - \dfrac{\tan 40°}{\cot 50°} + 1 =$

A. 0   B. 1
C. -1 D. 2

39. In $\triangle ABC$, $\angle A + \angle B = 90°$,
then $\sin A = $ ......
A. $\sin A$ B. $\cos A$
C. $\sin B$ D. $\cos B$

40. If $\cos A - \sin A = 0$, then the value of $\operatorname{cosec} A$ is :
A. $\sqrt{2}$ B. $\sqrt{3}$
C. 2   D. 3

41. The value of $\dfrac{\sin 10°}{\cos 80°}$ is :

A. 0   B. 1
C. 2   D. 3

42. The value of $\sin 20° - \cos 70°$ is :
A. 1   B. 2
C. 3   D. 0

43. The value of $\dfrac{\cos 59°}{\sin 31°}$ is :
A. 1   B. 0
C. 2   D. None of these

44. The value of
$\sin(90° - A) \cdot \cos A + \cos A(90 - A) \cdot \sin A$ is:
A. 0   B. 1
C. 2   D. 3

45. The value of $\operatorname{cosec}^2 (90° - \theta) - \tan^2 \theta$ is
A. 2   B. 3
C. 0   D. 1

46. The value of $\cos^2 (90° - \theta) + \cos^2 \theta$ is :
A. 3   B. 0
C. 2   D. 1

47. If $\theta = 45°$ then $\sin 2\theta$ is :
A. 0   B. 1
C. 2   D. None of these

48. If $\theta = 45$ then $\dfrac{2\tan \theta}{1 + \tan^2 \theta}$ is :

A. 1   B. 0
C. 2   D. 3

49. If $\theta = 30°$ then $\cos 2\theta$ is :
A. 0   B. 1

C. $\dfrac{1}{2}$ D. $\dfrac{\sqrt{3}}{2}$

50. If $\tan A = \dfrac{5}{12}$ then $\sin A$ is :

A. $\dfrac{5}{13}$ B. $\dfrac{12}{13}$

C. $\dfrac{13}{5}$ D. $\dfrac{13}{12}$

51. If $\sin (A + B) = \sin A \cdot \cos B + \cos A \cdot \sin B$ then the value of $\sin 75°$ is :

A. $\dfrac{\sqrt{3}}{2}$ B. $\dfrac{\sqrt{3}-1}{2\sqrt{2}}$

C. $\dfrac{\sqrt{3}+1}{2\sqrt{2}}$ D. $\dfrac{1}{\sqrt{2}}$

52. The value of $\dfrac{\sin 60°}{\cos^2 45°} - \cot 30° + 5\cos 90°$ is :

A. 0   B. 1

C. 2   D. $\dfrac{1}{2}$

53. The value of $(\sin 72° + \cos 18°) (\sin 72° - \cos 18°)$ is :

A. 1   B. $\dfrac{1}{2}$

C. 0   D. 2

54. The value of $\left(\dfrac{\sin 49°}{\cos 41°}\right)^2 + \left(\dfrac{\cos 41°}{\sin 49°}\right)^2$ is :

A. 1   B. 2
C. 0   D. None of these

55. What is the value of $\sin^2 35° + \sin^2 55°$?
A. 0   B. 1

C. $\dfrac{1}{2}$ D. 2

56. What is the value of $\dfrac{\cos 80°}{\sin 10°} + \dfrac{\cos 59°}{\sin 31°}$?

A. 2   B. 1
C. 0   D. 3

57. If $5 \sin A = 3$ then value of $\sec^2 A - \tan^2 A$ is :
   A. 0   B. 5
   C. 3   D. 1

58. If $\cos \theta = \dfrac{3}{5}$, then value of $\tan \theta$ is :
   A. $\dfrac{1}{5}$ B. $\dfrac{2}{3}$
   C. $\dfrac{4}{5}$ D. $\dfrac{4}{3}$

59. If $\tan \theta = \dfrac{a}{b}$ then $\dfrac{\cos\theta + \sin\theta}{\cos\theta - \sin\theta}$ is
   A. $\dfrac{b+a}{b-a}$ B. $\dfrac{b-a}{b+a}$
   C. $\dfrac{a}{b}$ D. $\dfrac{b}{a}$

60. The value of
$\tan 5° \cdot \tan 85° \cdot \tan 31° \cdot \tan 59° \cdot \tan 45°$ is :
   A. 0   B. 2
   C. 1   D. $\dfrac{1}{2}$

61. If $\dfrac{\sin^2 \theta}{7} + \dfrac{\cos^2 \theta}{7} = \dfrac{x}{21}$, then x is :
   A. 1   B. 2
   C. 3   D. 4

62. If $\cos A = \dfrac{7}{9}$, then $\cot^2 A$
   A. $\dfrac{49}{72}$ B. $\dfrac{49}{52}$
   C. $\dfrac{49}{32}$ D. $\dfrac{49}{62}$

63. $\cos(90° - A) \cdot \tan(90° - A) \sec(90° - A)$
   A. $\cot A$ B. $\tan A$
   C. $\cos A$ D. $\cosec A$

64. $\sqrt{\dfrac{1+\sin A}{1-\sin A}}$ is equal to :
   A. $\dfrac{\cot A}{\sin A + \cos A}$ B. $\dfrac{\cot A}{\cosec A - 1}$
   C. $\dfrac{\cot A}{\sec A - 1}$ D. $\dfrac{\cot A}{\tan A - 1}$

65. If $\cos \theta - \sin \theta = \sqrt{2} \sin \theta$, then $\cos \theta + \sin \theta$ is equal to :
   A. $\sqrt{2} \cosec \theta$ B. $\sqrt{2} \sin \theta$
   C. $\sqrt{2} \tan \theta$ D. $\sqrt{2} \cos \theta$

66. $\tan 5° \cdot \tan 40° \cdot \tan 45° \cdot \tan 50° \cdot \tan 85°$ is equal to:
   A. 1   B. 0
   C. 2   D. -1

67. The value of
$\dfrac{\cos(90° - A)}{1+\sin(90° - A)} + \dfrac{1+\sin(90° - A)}{\cos(90° - A)}$ is equal to :
   A. $\dfrac{2}{\cos A}$ B. $\dfrac{2}{\sin A}$
   C. $\dfrac{2}{\sec A}$ D. $\dfrac{2}{\cosec A}$

68. If $\sqrt{3} \tan \theta = 3 \sin \theta$, then the value of $\sin^2\theta - \cos^2\theta$ is :
   A. $\dfrac{1}{3}$ B. $\dfrac{2}{3}$
   C. $\dfrac{1}{4}$ D. $\dfrac{2}{5}$

69. $\dfrac{\cos^2 25° + \cos^2 65°}{\sin^2 59° + \sin^2 31°}$
   A. 0   B. 1
   C. 2   D. 3

70. $\dfrac{\cos(90° - A)}{\cosec(90° - A)} \times \dfrac{\cot(90° - A)}{\sin A} = \ldots\ldots$
   A. $\cos A$ B. $\sin A$
   C. $\tan A$ D. $\sec A$

71. If $\cos \theta = \dfrac{3}{5}$, then $\cot \theta$ is equal to :
   A. $\dfrac{4}{3}$ B. $\dfrac{3}{4}$
   C. $\dfrac{5}{4}$ D. $\dfrac{3}{5}$

72. If $\tan \theta = \dfrac{10}{24}$, then $\sin \theta$ is equal to :
   A. $\dfrac{24}{26}$ B. $\dfrac{26}{10}$
   C. $\dfrac{10}{26}$ D. $\dfrac{10}{24}$

73. Which of the following is not correct :
   A. $\tan 30° = \dfrac{1}{\sqrt{3}}$ B. $\sin 60° = \dfrac{\sqrt{3}}{2}$
   C. $\cos 60° = 1$ D. $\tan 45° = 1$

74. If $\tan \theta = \dfrac{3}{4}$, $\sec \theta = \ldots\ldots$
   A. $\dfrac{1}{2}$ B. $\dfrac{3}{5}$
   C. $\dfrac{5}{4}$ D. $\dfrac{4}{3}$

75. If $3 \tan \theta = 4$ then $\sin \theta$ is :
   A. $\dfrac{4}{5}$ B. $\dfrac{3}{5}$
   C. $\dfrac{3}{4}$ D. $\dfrac{4}{3}$

76. sin 90° is :
A. 0
B. –1
C. 1
D. –2

77. If $\tan \theta = \dfrac{5}{12}$, then $\sec \theta = $ ......

A. $\dfrac{13}{12}$
B. $\dfrac{12}{13}$

C. $\dfrac{12}{5}$
D. $\dfrac{5}{12}$

78. The value of tan 45° × cot 45° is :
A. 0
B. 1

C. 2
D. $\dfrac{1}{2}$

79. The value of $\sin^2 60° + \cos^2 60°$ is :
A. 1
B. –1
C. 0
D. None of these

80. The value of cos 45° · cos 30° – sin 45° · sin 30° is equal to :

A. $\dfrac{\sqrt{3}-1}{2\sqrt{2}}$
B. 0

C. $\dfrac{\sqrt{3}-1}{\sqrt{3}+1}$
D. $\dfrac{\sqrt{3}+1}{2\sqrt{2}}$

81. $\dfrac{\sin A}{1+\cos A}+\dfrac{\sin A}{1-\cos A}$ is equal to :
A. sin A
B. 2 cosec A
C. cos A
D. None of these

82. The value of sin(90° – θ) is :
A. cos θ
B. sin θ
C. –cos θ
D. None of these

83. What is the value of sin 30° × cosec 30°
A. 1
B. 0

C. $\dfrac{1}{2}$
D. 2

84. sin(90 – θ) · cos θ + sin θ · cos(90 – θ) is :
A. 0
B. 1
C. 2
D. None of these

85. sin θ + cos θ = 1 where θ = ...
A. 30°
B. 45°
C. 60°
D. 90°

86. tan θ tan(90° – θ) + cos θ cosec(90° – θ) = ...
A. 0
B. –1
C. 1
D. 2

87. In $\tan \theta = \dfrac{40}{9}$ then sec θ is :

A. $\dfrac{41}{9}$
B. $\dfrac{9}{41}$

C. $\dfrac{9}{40}$
D. None of these

88. tan 45° × tan 82° is
A. 1
B. 0
C. 2
D. 3

89. $\dfrac{\sec \theta}{\operatorname{cosec}(90°-\theta)} - \dfrac{\sin \theta}{\cos(90°-\theta)} + \cos 0°$ equal to :
A. 1
B. 3
C. 2
D. 0

90. If cos 2θ = 2 cos² θ – 1 then value of cos 60° is :

A. 1
B. $\dfrac{1}{2}$

C. 0
D. 2

91. The shadow of a vertical tower on level ground increases by 10 metres when the altitude of the sun changes from the angle of elevation 45° to 30°. Find the height of the tower correct to one place of decimal.

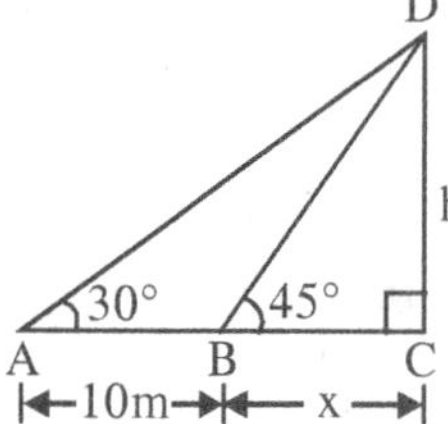

(Take $\sqrt{3}$ = 1.732)
A. 13.67 m
B. 15 m
C. 18.67 m
D. 20 m

92. A tree breaks due to storm and the broken part bends so that the top of the tree touches the ground making an angle 30° with it. The distance between the foot of the tree to the point where the top touches the ground is 8 m. The height of the tree is:

A. $5\sqrt{3}$ m
B. $8\sqrt{3}$ m

C. $10\sqrt{3}$ m
D. $6\sqrt{3}$ m

93. The angle of elevation of the top of a tower from a point on the ground, which is 30 m away from the foot of the tower is 30°. The height of the tower is :

A. $8\sqrt{3}$ m
B. $9\sqrt{3}$ m

C. $10\sqrt{3}$ m
D. $12\sqrt{3}$ m

94. A kite is flying at a height of 60 m above the ground. The string attached to the kite is temporarily tied to a point on the ground. The inclination of the string with the ground is 60°. Find the length of the string, assuming that there is no slack in the string.

A. $40\sqrt{3}$ m
B. $30\sqrt{3}$ m

C. $20\sqrt{3}$ m
D. $10\sqrt{3}$ m

95. From a point on the ground, the angles of elevation of the bottom and top of a transmission tower fixed at the top of a 20 m high building are 45° and 60° respectively. The height of the tower is :

A. $25(\sqrt{3}-1)$ m
B. $20(\sqrt{3}-1)$ m

C. 20 m
D. 10 m

ANSWERS

1	2	3	4	5	6	7	8	9	10
A	B	C	C	B	A	C	B	A	A

11	12	13	14	15	16	17	18	19	20
A	B	B	A	A	B	B	C	C	C

21	22	23	24	25	26	27	28	29	30
C	B	B	A	C	D	B	C	A	A

31	32	33	34	35	36	37	38	39	40
C	B	A	B	A	C	D	B	D	A

41	42	43	44	45	46	47	48	49	50
B	D	A	B	D	D	B	A	C	A

51	52	53	54	55	56	57	58	59	60
C	A	C	B	B	A	D	D	A	C

61	62	63	64	65	66	67	68	69	70
C	C	A	B	D	A	D	A	B	B

71	72	73	74	75	76	77	78	79	80
B	C	C	C	A	C	A	B	A	A

81	82	83	84	85	86	87	88	89	90
B	A	A	B	D	D	A	A	A	B

91	92	93	94	95
A	B	C	A	A

EXPLANATORY ANSWERS

1. $\cos\theta = \dfrac{1}{2}$ (given)

Also $\sin^2\theta = 1 - \cos^2\theta$

$$= 1 - \left(\frac{1}{2}\right)^2 = 1 - \frac{1}{4} = \frac{3}{4}$$

$$\sin\theta = \pm\frac{\sqrt{3}}{2}$$

$$= \frac{\sqrt{3}}{2}, \text{ taking only the positive value.}$$

$$\therefore \tan\theta = \frac{\sin\theta}{\cos\theta} = \frac{\frac{\sqrt{3}}{2}}{\frac{1}{2}} = \sqrt{3}$$

and $\sec\theta = 2$

$$\therefore \frac{2\sec\theta}{1+\tan^2\theta} = \frac{2\times 2}{1+3} = \frac{4}{4} = 1.$$

2. $\sin\theta = \dfrac{5}{13}$

Since $0 < \theta < 90°$, therefore $\cos\theta$ and $\tan\theta$ are positive

As $\cos^2\theta = 1 - \sin^2\theta$

$$\therefore \cos^2\theta = 1 - \left(\frac{5}{13}\right)^2 = 1 - \frac{25}{169}$$

$$= \frac{144}{169} = \left(\frac{12}{13}\right)^2$$

$$\therefore \cos\theta = \frac{12}{13}.$$

3. Given that $5\tan\theta = 4$ $\therefore \tan\theta = 4/5$

$$\therefore \frac{5\sin\theta - 3\cos\theta}{5\sin\theta + 2\cos\theta} = \frac{\frac{5\sin\theta}{\cos\theta} - 3}{\frac{5\sin\theta}{\cos\theta} + 2}$$

[Dividing both the numerator and denominator by $\cos\theta$]

$$= \frac{5\tan\theta - 3}{5\tan\theta + 2}$$

$$= \frac{5\times\frac{4}{5} - 3}{5\times\frac{4}{5} + 2} \qquad \left[\because \tan\theta = \frac{4}{5}\right]$$

$$= \frac{4-3}{4+2} = \frac{1}{6}.$$

4. $\dfrac{4\sin\theta - 3\cos\theta}{2\sin\theta + 6\cos\theta}$

[Dividing both numerator and denominator by sin θ]

$$= \dfrac{4\dfrac{\sin\theta}{\sin\theta} - \dfrac{3\cos\theta}{\sin\theta}}{4\dfrac{\sin\theta}{\sin\theta} + \dfrac{6\cos\theta}{\sin\theta}}$$

$$= \dfrac{4 - 3\cot\theta}{2 + 6\cot\theta} = \dfrac{4 - 3\times\tfrac{2}{3}}{2 + 6\times\tfrac{2}{3}} \qquad [\because 3\cot\theta = 2]$$

$$= \dfrac{4-2}{2+4} = \dfrac{2}{6} = \dfrac{1}{3}. \qquad \left[\because \cot\theta = \dfrac{2}{3}\right]$$

5. Dividing the numerator and denominator of

$\dfrac{4\sin\theta - \cos\theta}{2\sin\theta + \cos\theta}$ by cos θ, we get

$$= \dfrac{4\sin\theta - \cos\theta}{2\sin\theta + \cos\theta} = \dfrac{4\dfrac{\sin\theta}{\cos\theta} - \dfrac{\cos\theta}{\cos\theta}}{2\dfrac{\sin\theta}{\cos\theta} + \dfrac{\cos\theta}{\cos\theta}}$$

$$= \dfrac{4\tan\theta - 1}{2\tan\theta + 1} \qquad \ldots(i)$$

Also   3 tan θ = 2 (given)

∴   tan θ = 2/3.

Substituting the value of tan θ in (*i*) we get

$$\dfrac{4\tan\theta - 1}{2\tan\theta + 1} = \dfrac{4\times\tfrac{2}{3} - 1}{2\times\tfrac{2}{3} + 1} = \dfrac{\tfrac{8}{3} - 1}{\tfrac{4}{3} + 1}$$

$$= \dfrac{5/3}{7/3} = \dfrac{5}{3}\times\dfrac{3}{7} = \dfrac{5}{7}.$$

6. 3 cot θ = 4 (given)

$$\therefore \ \dfrac{5\sin\theta - 3\cos\theta}{5\sin\theta + 3\cos\theta} = \dfrac{5\dfrac{\sin\theta}{\sin\theta} - \dfrac{3\cos\theta}{\sin\theta}}{5\dfrac{\sin\theta}{\sin\theta} + \dfrac{3\cos\theta}{\sin\theta}}$$

(Dividing both numerator and denominator by sin θ)

$$= \dfrac{5 - 3\cot\theta}{5 + 3\cot\theta} = \dfrac{5 - 3\times 4/3}{5 + 3\times 4/3}$$

$$= \dfrac{5-4}{5+4} \qquad [\because 3\cot\theta = 4]$$

$$= \dfrac{1}{9}. \qquad \left[\because \cot\theta = \dfrac{4}{3}\right]$$

7. $\dfrac{4\sin\theta - 2\cos\theta}{4\sin\theta + 3\cos\theta} = \dfrac{\dfrac{4\sin\theta}{\cos\theta} - 2\dfrac{\cos\theta}{\cos\theta}}{\dfrac{4\sin\theta}{\cos\theta} + 3\dfrac{\cos\theta}{\cos\theta}}$

(Dividing both numerator and denominator by cos θ)

$$= \dfrac{4\tan\theta - 2}{4\tan\theta + 3}$$

$$= \dfrac{4\times 3/4 - 2}{4\times 3/4 + 3} \qquad \left[\because 3\tan\theta = \dfrac{3}{4}\right]$$

$$= \dfrac{3-2}{3+3} = \dfrac{1}{6}.$$

8. AC $= \sqrt{AB^2 + BC^2}$

AC $= \sqrt{5^2 + (12)^2}$

AC $= \sqrt{25 + 144} = 13$

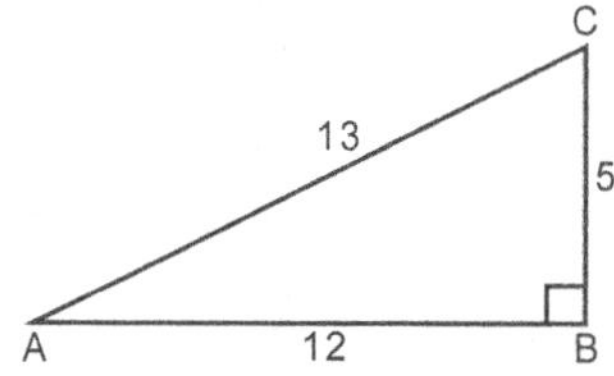

Now   Sin A $= \dfrac{5}{13}$,   cos A $= \dfrac{12}{13}$

$$\sin A + \cos A = \dfrac{5}{13} + \dfrac{12}{13}$$

$$= \dfrac{17}{13}.$$

9. As 0° < θ < 90°, therefore the value of all the T-ratios have positive values

∴ $\sec^2\theta = 1 + \tan^2\theta$

$$\therefore \quad \sec^2\theta = 1 + \left(\dfrac{2}{3}\right)^2 \qquad \left[\because \tan\theta = \dfrac{2}{3}\right]$$

$$= 1 + \dfrac{4}{9} = \dfrac{13}{9}$$

$$\therefore \quad \sec\theta = \pm\sqrt{\dfrac{13}{9}} = \dfrac{\sqrt{13}}{3}$$

Taking only the positive sign

$$\therefore \quad \cos\theta = \dfrac{3}{\sqrt{13}}$$

Also $\sin^2\theta + \cos^2\theta = 1$

$$\therefore \quad \sin^2 + \left(\dfrac{3}{\sqrt{13}}\right)^2 = 1 \quad \text{or} \quad \sin^2\theta + \dfrac{9}{13} = 1$$

$$\therefore \quad \sin^2\theta = 1 - \dfrac{9}{13} = \dfrac{4}{13}$$

$\therefore \quad \sin\theta = \pm\sqrt{\dfrac{4}{13}} = \dfrac{2}{\sqrt{13}}$

Taking only the positive sign.

10. $\dfrac{3\cos\theta + 2\sin\theta}{2\cos\theta - \sin\theta} = \dfrac{3\dfrac{\cos\theta}{\cos\theta} + 2\dfrac{\sin\theta}{\cos\theta}}{2\dfrac{\cos\theta}{\cos\theta} - \dfrac{\sin\theta}{\cos\theta}}$

[Dividing both the numerator and denominator by $\cos\theta$]

$= \dfrac{3 + 2\tan\theta}{2 - \tan\theta} = \dfrac{3 + 2\times\dfrac{1}{2}}{2 - \dfrac{1}{2}}$

$\left[\text{Given } 2\tan\theta = 1 \ \therefore \ \tan\theta = \dfrac{1}{2}\right]$

$= \dfrac{3 + 1}{3/2} = 4\times\dfrac{2}{3} = 2\dfrac{2}{3}.$

11. $(\text{cosec }\theta - \sin\theta)(\sec\theta - \cos\theta)(\tan\theta + \cot\theta)$

$= \left(\dfrac{1}{\sin\theta} - \sin\theta\right)\left(\dfrac{1}{\cos\theta} - \cos\theta\right)\left(\dfrac{\sin\theta}{\cos\theta} + \dfrac{\cos\theta}{\sin\theta}\right)$

$= \left(\dfrac{1 - \sin^2\theta}{\sin\theta}\right)\left(\dfrac{1 - \cos^2\theta}{\cos\theta}\right)\left(\dfrac{\sin^2\theta + \cos^2\theta}{\cos\theta\sin\theta}\right)$

$= \left(\dfrac{\cos^2\theta}{\sin\theta}\right)\left(\dfrac{\sin^2\theta}{\cos\theta}\right)\dfrac{1}{\sin\theta\cos\theta} = 1$

12. $(\sin A + \cos A)(\tan A + \cot A)$

$= (\sin A + \cos A)\left(\dfrac{\sin A}{\cos A} + \dfrac{\cos A}{\sin A}\right)$

$= (\sin A + \cos A)\left(\dfrac{\sin^2 A + \cos^2 A}{\cos A \sin A}\right)$

$= \dfrac{\sin A + \cos A}{\cos A \sin A}$

$= \dfrac{\sin A}{\cos A \sin A} + \dfrac{\cos A}{\cos A \sin A}$

$= \dfrac{1}{\cos A} + \dfrac{1}{\sin A} = \sec A + \text{cosec } A.$

13. $\dfrac{\sin\theta}{1 + \cos\theta} + \dfrac{1 + \cos\theta}{\sin\theta}$

$= \dfrac{\sin^2\theta + (1 + \cos\theta)^2}{\sin\theta(1 + \cos\theta)}$

$= \dfrac{\sin^2\theta + 1 + \cos^2\theta + 2\cos\theta}{\sin\theta(1 + \cos\theta)}$

$= \dfrac{1 + (\sin^2\theta + \cos^2\theta) + 2\cos\theta}{\sin\theta(1 + \cos\theta)}$

$= \dfrac{1 + 1 + 2\cos\theta}{\sin\theta(1 + \cos\theta)} = \dfrac{2 + 2\cos\theta}{\sin\theta(1 + \cos\theta)}$

$= \dfrac{2(1 + \cos\theta)}{\sin\theta(1 + \cos\theta)} = \dfrac{2}{\sin\theta} = 2\text{ cosec }\theta.$

14. $\dfrac{\tan A + \sec A - 1}{\tan A - \sec A + 1}$

$= \dfrac{\tan A + \sec A - (\sec^2 A - \tan^2 A)}{\tan A - \sec A + 1}$

$= \dfrac{(\tan A + \sec A) - (\sec A + \tan A)(\sec A - \tan A)}{\tan A - \sec A + 1}$

$= \dfrac{(\tan A + \sec A)(1 - \sec A + \tan A)}{(\tan A - \sec A + 1)}$

$= \tan A + \sec A$

$= \dfrac{\sin A}{\cos A} + \dfrac{1}{\cos A} = \dfrac{\sin A + 1}{\cos A} = \dfrac{1 + \sin A}{\cos A}.$

15. $\sin x + \sin^2 x = 1$

$\sin x = 1 - \sin^2 x$

$\sin x = \cos^2 x$

$\sin^2 x = \cos^4 x$

$1 - \cos^2 x = \cos^4 x$

$\cos^2 x + \cos^4 x = 1.$

16. $\cos\theta - \sin\theta = \sqrt{2}\sin\theta$

$\cos\theta = \sqrt{2}\sin\theta + \sin\theta = (\sqrt{2} + 1)\sin\theta$

$\sin\theta = \dfrac{\cos\theta}{\sqrt{2} + 1}$

$\sin\theta = \dfrac{\cos\theta(\sqrt{2} - 1)}{(\sqrt{2} + 1)(\sqrt{2} - 1)}$

$\sin\theta = \dfrac{\cos\theta(\sqrt{2} - 1)}{2 - 1}$

$\sin\theta = \sqrt{2}\cos\theta - \cos\theta \ \text{ or } \ \sin\theta + \cos\theta$

$\qquad = \sqrt{2}\cos\theta.$

17. $4(\sin^4 30° + \cos^4 60°) - 3(\sin^2 45° - 2\cos^2 45°)$

$= 4\left[\left(\dfrac{1}{2}\right)^4 + \left(\dfrac{1}{2}\right)^4\right] - 3\left[\left(\dfrac{1}{\sqrt{2}}\right)^2 - 2\left(\dfrac{1}{\sqrt{2}}\right)^2\right]$

$= 4\left[\dfrac{1}{16} + \dfrac{1}{16}\right] - 3\left[\dfrac{1}{2} - 2\times\dfrac{1}{2}\right]$

$= 4\times\dfrac{2}{16} - 3\left(-\dfrac{1}{2}\right) = \dfrac{1}{2} + \dfrac{3}{2} = 2.$

18. $\cos 79° + \sec 79°$
$= \cos (90° - 11°) + \sec (90° - 11°)$
$= \sin 11° + \operatorname{cosec} 11°$.

19. $\cos (A - B) = \cos A \cos B + \sin A \sin B$
$\therefore \cos 15° = \cos(45° - 30°) = \cos 45° \cos 30° + \sin 45° \sin 30°$

$= \dfrac{1}{\sqrt{2}} \times \dfrac{\sqrt{3}}{2} + \dfrac{1}{\sqrt{2}} \times \dfrac{1}{2}$

$= \dfrac{\sqrt{3}}{2\sqrt{2}} + \dfrac{1}{2\sqrt{2}} = \dfrac{\sqrt{3}+1}{2\sqrt{2}}$.

20. $\sin 15° = \sin (45° - 30°) = \sin 45° \cos 30° - \cos 45° \sin 30°$

$= \dfrac{1}{\sqrt{2}} \times \dfrac{\sqrt{3}}{2} - \dfrac{1}{\sqrt{2}} \times \dfrac{1}{2}$

$= \dfrac{\sqrt{3}}{2\sqrt{2}} - \dfrac{1}{2\sqrt{2}} = \dfrac{\sqrt{3}-1}{2\sqrt{2}}$.

21. $\because \cos \theta = \dfrac{12}{13} = \dfrac{b}{h}$

$\therefore p = \sqrt{(13)^2 - (12)^2} = 5$

$\therefore \sin \theta = \dfrac{p}{h} = \dfrac{5}{13}$, $\tan \theta = \dfrac{p}{b} = \dfrac{5}{12}$

$\sqrt{(1 + \tan \theta)(1 - \tan \theta)} = \sqrt{1 - \tan^2 \theta}$

$= \sqrt{1 - \dfrac{25}{144}} = \sqrt{\dfrac{119}{144}}$.

22. $\sin \theta \times \sin \theta + \cos \theta \times \cos \theta = \sin^2 \theta + \cos^2 \theta = 1$.

23. $\cos^2 72° + \cos^2 18° = \cos^2 (90 - 18°) + \cos^2 18°$
$= \sin^2 18° + \cos^2 18° = 1$.

25. $3\left(\dfrac{1}{\sqrt{3}}\right)^2 + (\sqrt{2})^2 - (\sqrt{3})^2$

$= 3 \times \dfrac{1}{3} + 4 - 3 = 2$.

26. $\because \quad \cos \theta = \dfrac{3}{5} = \dfrac{b}{h}$

$\therefore \quad p = \sqrt{25 - 9} = 4$

$\sin \theta = \dfrac{4}{5}$, $\tan \theta = \dfrac{4}{3}$

$\dfrac{\sin \theta \cdot \tan \theta + 1}{2 \tan^2 \theta} = \dfrac{\dfrac{4}{5} \times \dfrac{4}{3} + 1}{2 \times \dfrac{16}{9}} = \dfrac{\dfrac{16 + 15}{15}}{\dfrac{32}{9}}$

$= \dfrac{31}{15} \times \dfrac{9}{32} = \dfrac{93}{160}$.

27. $\cos (A + B) = \dfrac{1}{2} = \cos 60°$

$\Rightarrow \qquad A + B = 60° \qquad\qquad ...(i)$

$\sin (A - B) = \dfrac{1}{2} = \sin 30°$

$\Rightarrow \qquad A - B = 30° \qquad\qquad ...(ii)$
Solving eq. (*i*) and (*ii*) we get
$\quad A = 45°$, $B = 15°$
$\Rightarrow \qquad A + B = 60°$.

28. $\left(\dfrac{1}{2}\right)^2 \times \left(\dfrac{1}{\sqrt{2}}\right)^2 + 4\left(\dfrac{1}{\sqrt{3}}\right)^2 + \dfrac{1}{2}(1)^2 - 2(0)^2$

$= \dfrac{1}{4} \times \dfrac{1}{2} + \dfrac{4}{3} + \dfrac{1}{2} = \dfrac{1}{8} + \dfrac{4}{3} + \dfrac{1}{2}$

$= \dfrac{3 + 32 + 12}{24} = \dfrac{47}{24}$.

29. $\sin (90 - 11°) \cdot \cos 11° + \cos(90 - 11°) \cdot \sin 11°$
$= \cos 11° \times \cos 11° + \sin 11° \times \sin 11°$
$= \cos^2 11° + \sin^2 11° = 1$.

30. $\dfrac{x(2)^2 \times (\sqrt{2})^2}{8\left(\dfrac{1}{\sqrt{2}}\right)^2 \times \sin^2 \theta} = (\sqrt{3})^2 - (1)^2$

$\dfrac{8x}{8 \times \dfrac{1}{2} \times 1} = 3 - 1 = 2$

$\qquad 2x = 2$

$\qquad x = 1$.

31. $(\sin \theta + \cos \theta)(\sin^2 \theta + \cos^2 \theta - \sin \theta \cdot \cos \theta)$
$= \sin^3 \theta + \cos^3 \theta$.

32. $\left(\dfrac{1}{\sin \theta} - \sin \theta\right)\left(\dfrac{1}{\cos \theta} - \cos \theta\right)\left(\dfrac{\sin \theta}{\cos \theta} + \dfrac{\cos \theta}{\sin \theta}\right)$

$= \left(\dfrac{1 - \sin^2 \theta}{\sin \theta}\right)\left(\dfrac{1 - \cos^2 \theta}{\cos \theta}\right)\left(\dfrac{1}{\sin \theta \cdot \cos \theta}\right)$

$= \dfrac{\cos^2 \theta \times \sin^2 \theta}{\sin^2 \theta \times \cos^2 \theta} = 1$.

33. $\left(1 + \dfrac{\cos A}{\sin A} - \dfrac{1}{\sin A}\right)\left(1 + \dfrac{\sin A}{\cos A} + \dfrac{1}{\cos A}\right)$

$= \left(\dfrac{\sin A + \cos A - 1}{\sin A}\right)\left(\dfrac{\cos A + \sin A + 1}{\cos A}\right)$

$= \dfrac{(\sin A + \cos A)^2 - 1}{\sin A \cdot \cos A}$

$$= \frac{\sin^2 A + \cos^2 A + 2\sin A \cdot \cos A - 1}{\sin A \cdot \cos A}$$

$$= \frac{1 + 2\sin A \cdot \cos A - 1}{\sin A \cdot \cos A} = \frac{2\sin A \cdot \cos A}{\sin A \cdot \cos A} = 2.$$

34. $\because x^2 + y^2 + z^2 = r^2 \Rightarrow x^2 + y^2 = r^2 - z^2$

$\qquad x^2 = r^2 \sin^2 A \cos^2 B,$

$\qquad y^2 = r^2 \sin^2 A \sin^2 B$

$r^2 \sin^2 A \cdot \cos^2 B + r^2 \sin^2 A \cdot \sin^2 B = r^2 - z^2$

$r^2 \sin^2 A (\cos^2 B + \sin^2 B) = r^2 - z^2$

$\qquad r^2 \sin^2 A = r^2 - z^2$

$\Rightarrow \qquad z^2 = r^2 - r^2 \sin^2 A = r^2 (1 - \sin^2 A)$

$\Rightarrow \qquad z^2 = r^2 \cos^2 A \Rightarrow z = r \cos A.$

35. $\dfrac{1 - \sin^2 \theta}{1 - \cos^2 \theta} = \dfrac{\cos^2 \theta}{\sin^2 \theta} = \cot^2 \theta = \dfrac{7}{8}.$

36. $\because \sin \theta = \dfrac{8}{17} = \dfrac{p}{h}$

$\therefore b = 15, \cos \theta = \dfrac{b}{h} = \dfrac{15}{17}$

$$\frac{2\sin \theta + \cos \theta}{3\cos \theta + 5\sin \theta} = \frac{2\left(\dfrac{8}{17}\right) + \dfrac{15}{17}}{3\left(\dfrac{15}{17}\right) + 5\left(\dfrac{8}{17}\right)}$$

$$= \frac{\dfrac{16}{17} + \dfrac{15}{17}}{\dfrac{45}{17} + \dfrac{40}{17}} = \frac{\dfrac{31}{17}}{\dfrac{85}{17}} = \frac{31}{85}.$$

37. $1 - 1 + 1 = 1 \quad (\because \sin^2 \theta + \cos^2 \theta = 1)$

38. $\sin 40° \times \sec(90° - 40°) - \dfrac{\tan 40°}{\cot(90° - 40°)} + 1$

$\qquad = \sin 40° \times \cosec 40° - \dfrac{\tan 40°}{\tan 40°} + 1$

$\qquad = 1 - 1 + 1 = 1.$

39. $\because \angle A + \angle B = 90°$

$\therefore \qquad \angle C = 90°$

$\qquad \sin A = \dfrac{BC}{AB}$

$\qquad\qquad = \cos B.$

40. $\because \cos A - \sin A = 0$

$\Rightarrow \qquad \cos A = \sin A$

$\qquad \dfrac{\cos A}{\sin A} = 1 \Rightarrow \cot A = \dfrac{1}{1} = \dfrac{b}{p}$

$$h = \sqrt{(1)^2 + (1)^2} = \sqrt{2}$$

$\therefore \qquad \cosec A = \dfrac{h}{p} = \dfrac{\sqrt{2}}{1} = \sqrt{2}.$

41. $\dfrac{\sin 10°}{\cos(90° - 10°)} = \dfrac{\sin 10°}{\sin 10°} = 1.$

42. $\sin 20° - \cos(90° - 20°) = \sin 20° - \sin 20° = 0.$

43. $\dfrac{\cos(90° - 31°)}{\sin 31°} = \dfrac{\sin 31°}{\sin 31°} = 1.$

44. $\cos A \cdot \cos A + \sin A \cdot \sin A = \cos^2 A + \sin^2 A = 1.$

45. $\sec^2 \theta - \tan^2 \theta$

$\quad = \dfrac{1}{\cos^2 \theta} - \dfrac{\sin^2 \theta}{\cos^2 \theta} = \dfrac{1 - \sin^2 \theta}{\cos^2 \theta} = \dfrac{\cos^2 \theta}{\cos^2 \theta} = 1.$

46. $\sin^2 \theta + \cos^2 \theta = 1.$

47. $\sin 2(45°) = \sin 90° = 1.$

48. $\dfrac{2\tan 45°}{1 + \tan^2 45°} = \dfrac{2 \times 1}{1 + 1} = \dfrac{2}{2} = 1.$

49. $\cos 2(30°) = \cos 60° = \dfrac{1}{2}.$

50. $\because \tan A = \dfrac{5}{12} = \dfrac{p}{b}$

$\therefore \qquad h = \sqrt{5^2 + (12)^2} = \sqrt{25 + 144}$

$\qquad\qquad = \sqrt{169} = 13$

$\qquad \sin A = \dfrac{p}{h} = \dfrac{5}{13}.$

51. $\sin (45° + 30°) = \sin 45° \times \cos 30° + \cos 45° \times \sin 30°$

$\sin (75°) = \dfrac{1}{\sqrt{2}} \times \dfrac{\sqrt{3}}{2} + \dfrac{1}{\sqrt{2}} \times \dfrac{1}{2} = \dfrac{\sqrt{3} + 1}{2\sqrt{2}}.$

52. $\dfrac{\dfrac{\sqrt{3}}{2}}{\dfrac{1}{2}} - \sqrt{3} + 0 = \sqrt{3} - \sqrt{3} = 0.$

53. $\sin^2 72° - \cos^2 18°$

$\qquad = \sin^2 72° - \cos^2(90° - 72°)$

$\qquad = \sin^2 72° - \sin^2 72° = 0.$

54. $\left(\dfrac{\sin(90° - 41°)}{\cos 41°}\right)^2 + \left(\dfrac{\cos 41°}{\sin(90° - 41°)}\right)^2$

$\qquad = \left(\dfrac{\cos 41°}{\cos 41°}\right)^2 + \left(\dfrac{\cos 41°}{\cos 41°}\right)^2 = 1 + 1 = 2.$

55. $\sin^2 35° + \sin^2(90° - 35°)$

$= \sin^2 35° + \cos^2 35° = 1.$ $[\because \sin^2\theta + \cos^2\theta = 1]$

56. $\dfrac{\cos(90° - 10°)}{\sin 10°} + \dfrac{\cos(90° - 31°)}{\sin 31°}$

$= \dfrac{\sin 10°}{\sin 10°} + \dfrac{\sin 31°}{\sin 31°} = 1 + 1 = 2.$

57. $\sin A = \dfrac{3}{5} = \dfrac{p}{h}$

$\therefore \quad b = \sqrt{25 - 9} = \sqrt{16} = 4$

$\sec A = \dfrac{h}{b} = \dfrac{5}{4},$

$\tan A = \dfrac{p}{b} = \dfrac{3}{4}$

$\sec^2 A - \tan^2 A = \left(\dfrac{5}{4}\right)^2 - \left(\dfrac{3}{4}\right)^2$

$= \dfrac{25}{16} - \dfrac{9}{16} = \dfrac{16}{16} = 1.$

58. $\cos \theta = \dfrac{3}{5} = \dfrac{b}{h}$

$\therefore p = \sqrt{25 - 9} = \sqrt{16} = 4.$

$\tan \theta = \dfrac{p}{b} = \dfrac{4}{3}.$

59. $\because \tan \theta = \dfrac{a}{b}$

$\dfrac{\dfrac{\cos\theta}{\cos\theta} + \dfrac{\sin\theta}{\cos\theta}}{\dfrac{\cos\theta}{\cos\theta} - \dfrac{\sin\theta}{\cos\theta}} = \dfrac{1 + \tan\theta}{1 - \tan\theta}$

$= \dfrac{1 + \dfrac{a}{b}}{1 - \dfrac{a}{b}} = \dfrac{\dfrac{b+a}{b}}{\dfrac{b-a}{b}} = \dfrac{b+a}{b-a}.$

60. $\tan 5° \cdot \tan (90° - 5°) \cdot \tan 31° \cdot \tan (90° - 31°) \cdot \tan 45°$

$= \tan 5° \cdot \cot 5° \cdot \tan 31° \cdot \cot 31° \times 1$

$= 1 \times 1 \times 1 = 1.$

61. $\dfrac{\sin^2\theta + \cos^2\theta}{7} = \dfrac{x}{21}$

$\Rightarrow \quad \dfrac{1}{7} = \dfrac{x}{21}$

$\Rightarrow \quad x = 3.$

62. $\because \cos A = \dfrac{7}{9} = \dfrac{b}{h}$

$\therefore \quad p = \sqrt{81 - 49} = \sqrt{32} = 4\sqrt{2},$

$\cot A = \dfrac{b}{p} \quad \therefore \cot^2 A = \dfrac{49}{32}.$

63. $\sin A \times \cot A \times \operatorname{cosec} A = \cot A.$

64. $\sqrt{\dfrac{1 + \sin A}{1 - \sin A}} = \sqrt{\dfrac{1 + \sin A}{1 - \sin A}} \times \sqrt{\dfrac{1 + \sin A}{1 + \sin A}}$

$= \dfrac{1 + \sin A}{\cos A}$

$= \dfrac{1 + \sin A}{\cos A} \times \dfrac{\cos A}{\cos A} = \dfrac{\cos A(1 + \sin A)}{\cos^2 A}$

$= \dfrac{\cos A(1 + \sin A)}{(1 + \sin A)(1 - \sin A)} = \dfrac{\cos A}{1 - \sin A}$

$= \dfrac{\dfrac{\cos A}{\sin A}}{\dfrac{1 - \sin A}{\sin A}} = \dfrac{\cot A}{\operatorname{cosec} A - 1}.$

65. $\because \cos \theta - \sin \theta = \sqrt{2} \sin \theta$

Squaring both sides

$\cos^2 \theta + \sin^2 \theta - 2 \cos \theta \cdot \sin \theta = 2 \sin^2 \theta$

$\cos^2 \theta - \sin^2 \theta = 2 \sin \theta \cdot \cos \theta$

$(\cos \theta + \sin \theta)(\cos \theta - \sin \theta) = 2 \sin \theta \cdot \cos \theta$

$(\cos \theta + \sin \theta)(\sqrt{2} \sin \theta) = 2 \sin \theta \cdot \cos \theta$

$\therefore \cos \theta + \sin \theta = \sqrt{2} \cos\theta.$

66. $\tan 5° \cdot \tan (90° - 5°) \cdot \tan 40° \cdot \tan (90° - 40°) \tan 45° = \tan 5° \cdot \cot 5° \cdot \tan 40° \cdot \cot 40° \cdot 1 = 1 \times 1 \times 1 = 1.$

67. $\dfrac{\sin A}{1 + \cos A} + \dfrac{1 + \cos A}{\sin A} = \dfrac{\sin^2 A(1 + \cos A)^2}{\sin A(1 + \cos A)}$

$= \dfrac{\sin^2 A + 1 + \cos^2 A + 2\cos A}{\sin A(1 + \cos A)}$

$= \dfrac{2 + 2\cos A}{\sin A(1 + \cos A)} = \dfrac{2(1 + \cos A)}{\sin A(1 + \cos A)}$

$= 2 \operatorname{cosec} A.$

68. $\dfrac{\sqrt{3} \sin \theta}{\cos\theta} = 3 \sin \theta$

$\sec \theta = \sqrt{3}$

$\cos \theta = \dfrac{1}{\sqrt{3}} \Rightarrow \cos^2 \theta = \dfrac{1}{3}$

$\sin^2\theta - \cos^2\theta = 1 - \cos^2\theta - \cos^2\theta = 1 - 2\cos^2\theta$

$= 1 - 2\left(\dfrac{1}{3}\right) = 1 - \dfrac{2}{3} = \dfrac{1}{3}.$

69. $\dfrac{\cos^2 25° + \cos^2(90° - 25°)}{\sin^2(90° - 31°) + \sin^2 31°}$

$= \dfrac{\cos^2 25° + \sin^2 25°}{\cos^2 31° + \sin^2 31°} = \dfrac{1}{1} = 1.$

70. $\dfrac{\sin A}{\sec A} \times \dfrac{\tan A}{\sin A} = \dfrac{\tan A}{\sec A} = \dfrac{\dfrac{\sin A}{\cos A}}{\dfrac{1}{\cos A}} = \sin A.$

71. $\cos\theta = \dfrac{3}{5} = \dfrac{b}{h}$

$\therefore \quad p = \sqrt{25 - 9} = \sqrt{16} = 4$

$\cot\theta = \dfrac{b}{p} = \dfrac{3}{4}.$

72. $\tan\theta = \dfrac{10}{24} = \dfrac{p}{b}$

$\therefore \quad h = \sqrt{100 + 576} = \sqrt{676} = 26.$

$\sin\theta = \dfrac{p}{h} = \dfrac{10}{26}$

73. $\cos 60° = \dfrac{1}{2}$

Hence $\cos 60° = 1$ is not correct.

74. $\tan\theta = \dfrac{3}{4} = \dfrac{p}{b}$

$\therefore \quad h = 5,\ \sec\theta = \dfrac{h}{b} = \dfrac{5}{4}.$

75. $\because 3\tan\theta = 4 \therefore \tan\theta = \dfrac{4}{3}$

$\therefore \quad h = 5,\ \sin\theta = \dfrac{p}{h} = \dfrac{4}{5}.$

76. $\sin 90° = 1.$

77. $\tan\theta = \dfrac{5}{12} = \dfrac{p}{b}$

$\therefore \quad h = 13,\ \sec\theta = \dfrac{h}{b} = \dfrac{13}{12}.$

78. $\tan 45° \times \cot 45° = 1 \times 1 = 1.$

79. $\sin^2 60° + \cos^2 60° = 1.$

80. $\dfrac{1}{\sqrt{2}} \times \dfrac{\sqrt{3}}{2} - \dfrac{1}{\sqrt{2}} \times \dfrac{1}{2} = \dfrac{\sqrt{3}}{2\sqrt{2}} - \dfrac{1}{2\sqrt{2}} = \dfrac{\sqrt{3}-1}{2\sqrt{2}}.$

81. $\dfrac{\sin A}{1 + \cos A} + \dfrac{\sin A}{1 - \cos A}$

$= \sin A\left[\dfrac{1 - \cos A + 1 + \cos A}{(1 + \cos A)(1 - \cos A)}\right]$

$= \sin A\left(\dfrac{2}{\sin^2 A}\right) = \dfrac{2}{\sin A} = 2\operatorname{cosec} A.$

82. $\sin(90° - \theta) = \cos\theta.$

83. $\sin 30° \times \operatorname{cosec} 30° = \dfrac{1}{2} \times \dfrac{2}{1} = \dfrac{1}{1} = 1.$

84. $\sin(90° - \theta) \cdot \cos\theta + \sin\theta \cdot \cos(90° - \theta)$

$= \cos\theta \cdot \cos\theta + \sin\theta \cdot \sin\theta = \cos^2\theta + \sin^2\theta = 1.$

85. Put $\theta = 90°$ then $\sin\theta + \cos\theta = \sin 90° + \cos 90° = 1 + 0 = 1.$

88. $\tan 45° \times \tan 8° \cdot \tan(90° - 8°)$

$= \tan 45° \times \tan 8° \times \cot 8° = 1 \times 1 = 1.$

90. Put $\theta = 30°$, $\cos 2(30°) = 2\cos^2 30° - 1$

$\therefore \quad 2\left(\dfrac{\sqrt{3}}{2}\right)^2 - 1 = 2 \times \dfrac{3}{4} - 1$

$= \dfrac{3}{2} - 1 = \dfrac{3-2}{2} = \dfrac{1}{2}$

$\therefore \quad \cos 60° = \dfrac{1}{2}.$

91. Let height of tower CD be h metres.

Now in right-angled ΔBCD,

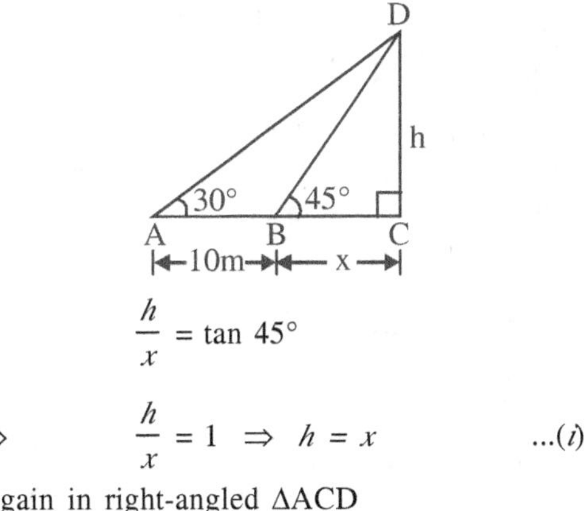

$\dfrac{h}{x} = \tan 45°$

$\Rightarrow \quad \dfrac{h}{x} = 1 \Rightarrow h = x \qquad \ldots(i)$

Again in right-angled ΔACD

$\dfrac{h}{x + 10} = \tan 30°$

$\Rightarrow \quad \dfrac{h}{x + 10} = \dfrac{1}{\sqrt{3}}$

$\Rightarrow \quad \sqrt{3}\,h = x + 10$

$\Rightarrow \quad \sqrt{3}\,h = h + 10 \qquad [\because \text{Using } (i)]$

$h(\sqrt{3} - 1) = 10$

$\Rightarrow \qquad h = \dfrac{10}{\sqrt{3}-1} \times \dfrac{\sqrt{3}+1}{\sqrt{3}+1}$

$\qquad\quad = \dfrac{10\left(\sqrt{3}+1\right)}{\left(\sqrt{3}\right)^2 - (1)^2} = \dfrac{10(1.732+1)}{3-1}$

$\qquad\quad = 5 \times 2.732 = 13.67 \text{ m}.$

92. Let AB be the tree.

Let it be broken by the wind at the point C and CB taking the position CD strikes the ground at D.

Now, $\angle ADC = 30°$

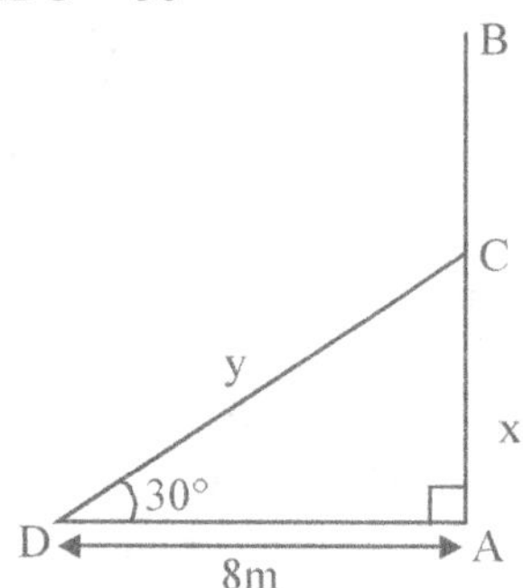

Let AC = x and CD = y

In right $\triangle ADC$, we have $\dfrac{AC}{AD} = \tan 30°$

$\Rightarrow \dfrac{x}{8} = \dfrac{1}{\sqrt{3}} \Rightarrow x = \dfrac{8}{\sqrt{3}}$

Again $\dfrac{AD}{CD} = \cos 30° \Rightarrow \dfrac{8}{y} = \dfrac{\sqrt{3}}{2} \Rightarrow y = \dfrac{16}{\sqrt{3}}$

$\therefore$ Height of the tree = $(x + y)$ metres.

$\qquad = \dfrac{8}{\sqrt{3}} + \dfrac{16}{\sqrt{3}} = \dfrac{24}{\sqrt{3}} = 8\sqrt{3}$ metres.

93. Let AB be the tower. The angle of elevation of the top A of the tower from a point C on the ground which is 30 metres away from the foot of the tower is 30°.

$\therefore \qquad \angle ACB = 30°$

and $\qquad BC = 30$ m.

From right $\triangle ABC$, we have

$\qquad \dfrac{AB}{BC} = \tan 30°$

$\Rightarrow \quad AB = BC \tan 30°$

$\qquad\quad = 30 \times \dfrac{1}{\sqrt{3}} = 10\sqrt{3}$ m.

94. Let AB = height of kite = 60 m and the inclination of the string AC is 60°.

From right-angled $\triangle ABC$, we have

$\qquad \dfrac{AC}{AB} = \operatorname{cosec} 60°$

$\Rightarrow \quad \dfrac{AC}{60} = \dfrac{2}{\sqrt{3}}$

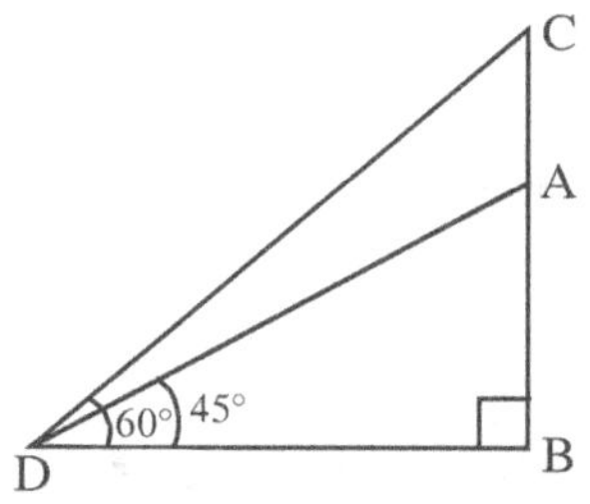

$\Rightarrow \quad AC = 60 \times \dfrac{2}{\sqrt{3}} = 40\sqrt{3}$ m.

95. Let AB = 20 m be the building and AC be the transmission tower fixed at the top of building. From a point D on the ground, the angle of elevation of the bottom and top of transmission tower are 45° and 60°.

$\therefore \ \angle ADB = 45°$ and $\angle CDB = 60°$

From right $\triangle ABD$, we have

$\qquad \dfrac{AB}{BD} = \tan 45° = 1$

$\therefore \qquad AB = BD$

$\Rightarrow \qquad BD = 20$ m $\qquad [\because AB = 20 \text{ m}]$

From right-angled $\triangle CBD$, we have

$\qquad \dfrac{BC}{BD} = \tan 60°$

$\Rightarrow \qquad BC = BD \tan 60°$

$\qquad\qquad = 20 \times \sqrt{3}$

$\qquad\qquad = 20\sqrt{3}$ m

Now $\ AC = BC - AB = 20\sqrt{3} - 20$

$\qquad\qquad = 20(\sqrt{3}-1)$ m.

Hence the height of the tower = $20(\sqrt{3}-1)$ m.

✱ ✱ ✱

Co-ordinate Geometry

The Co-ordinate Geometry deals with the geometrical figures with due regard their location in the plane by uniquely representing every point in the plane in terms of fixed number.

IMPORTANT FORMULAE

1. Distance between two points:

If (x_1, y_1) and (x_2, y_2) are two points then

$$\text{Distance} = \sqrt{(x_2 - x_1)^2 + (y_2 - y_1)^2}$$

$$= \sqrt{(\text{Diff. of abscissas})^2 + (\text{diff. of ordinates})^2}$$

$$\text{Distance from origin} = \sqrt{x_1^2 + y_1^2}$$

2. (*a*) Point (x, y) which divides the joint of two given points (x_1, y_1) and (x_2, y_2) in a given ratio $m_1 : m_2$ (internally and externally)

$$x = \frac{m_1 x_2 + m_2 x_1}{m_1 + m_2}, \quad y = \frac{m_1 y_2 + m_2 y_1}{m_1 + m_2} \quad \text{(internally)}$$

$$x = \frac{m_1 x_2 - m_2 x_1}{m_1 - m_2}, \quad y = \frac{m_1 y_2 - m_2 y_1}{m_1 - m_2} \quad \text{(Externally)}$$

$\therefore$ Co-ordinates of any point on the joint of (x_1, y_1) and (x_2, y_2) can be taken as $\left(\dfrac{\lambda x_2 + x_1}{\lambda + 1}, \dfrac{\lambda y_2 + y_1}{\lambda + 1}\right)$ this point divides the given line in the ratio $\lambda : 1$.

(*b*) Mid-point $\left(\dfrac{x_1 + x_2}{2}, \dfrac{y_1 + y_2}{2}\right)$

3. Area of triangle whose vertices are (x_1, y_1), (x_2, y_2) and (x_3, y_3)

$$= \frac{1}{2}\left\{x_1(y_2 - y_3) + x_2(y_3 - y_1) + x_3(y_1 - y_2)\right\}$$

$$= \frac{1}{2}\begin{vmatrix} x_1 & y_1 & 1 \\ x_2 & y_2 & 1 \\ x_3 & y_3 & 1 \end{vmatrix}$$

If one vertex (x_3, y_3) is at the origin $(0, 0)$, then

$$\text{Area} = \frac{1}{2}(x_1 y_2 - x_2 y_1) \qquad \because x_3 = 0, y_3 = 0$$

Particular Case

(*a*) If two vertices be on *x*-axis say $(a, 0)$, $(b, 0)$ and third vertex is (h, k) then area

$$= \frac{1}{2}\text{base} \times \text{height} = \frac{1}{2}(a - b)k$$

(*b*) Similarly, if two vertices be on *y*-axis say $(0, c)$, $(0, d)$ and third vertex is (h, k), then area

$$= \frac{1}{2}(c - d). h \quad \text{as above}$$

(*c*) $\triangle OAB$ where O is $(0, 0)$, A is $(a, 0)$ on *x*-axis and B is $(0, b)$ on *y*-axis, then

$$\Delta = \frac{1}{2}ab$$

4. Condition for three points to be collinear:

If the area of the triangle is zero, then the three points will be collinear.

5. Properties of geometrical figures:

(*i*) **Equilateral triangle:** All sides are equal.

(*ii*) **Isosceles triangle:** Two sides are equal.

(*iii*) **Rhombus:** All sides are equal and no angle is a right angle, but diagonals are at right angles and unequal.

(*iv*) **Square:** All sides are equal and each angle is right angle. The diagonals are also equal.

(*v*) **Parallelogram:** Opposite sides are parallel and equal, diagonals bisect each other.

(*vi*) **Rectangle:** Opposite sides are equal and each angle is a right angle, diagonals are equal.

6. Co-ordinates of standard points:

(*i*) *Centroid of a triangle:*

The point is the intersection of the medians. This point divides each median in the ratio 2 : 1, its co-ordinates are

$$G_1\left(\frac{x_1 + x_2 + x_3}{3}, \frac{y_1 + y_2 + y_3}{3}\right)$$

(*ii*) *Incentre of a triangle:*

This is the centre of the circle which touches the sides of a given triangle, it is the point of intersection of the internal bisectors of the angles of the triangle, its co-ordinates are given by the formula

$$I = (x, y) \text{ where } x = \frac{ax_1 + bx_2 + cx_3}{a+b+c}$$

$$y = \frac{ay_1 + by_2 + cy_3}{a+b+c}$$

where (*a*, *b*, *c*) are the lengths of the triangle

(*iii*) *Orthocentre of a triangle:*

The point *H* is the intersection of the altitudes.

(*iv*) The points *O, G, H* are collinear and *G* divides *OH* in the ratio 1 : 2.

MULTIPLE CHOICE QUESTIONS

1. The triangle formed by the points A $(2a, 4a)$, B $(2a, 6a)$ and C $\left(2a+\sqrt{3}a, 5a\right)$ is :
A. right angled
B. isosceles
C. equilateral
D. None of these

2. Vertices of a $\Delta\ ABC$ are $A\ (2, 2)$, $B\ (-4, -4)$ and $C\ (5, -8)$, then the length of the median through C is :
A. $\sqrt{65}$
B. $\sqrt{117}$
C. $\sqrt{85}$
D. $\sqrt{113}$

3. The points (0, 8/3), (1, 3) and (82, 30) are the vertices of :
A. obtuse angled triangle
B. right angled triangle
C. isosceles triangle
D. None of these

4. The straight lines $x + y - 4 = 0, 3x + y - 4 = 0, x + 3y - 4 = 0$ form a triangle which is :
A. isosceles
B. right angled
C. equilateral
D. None of these

5. The points $(-a, -b)$, $(0, 0)$, (a, b) and (a^2, ab) are :
A. collinear
B. vertices of a rectangle
C. vertices of a parallelogram
D. None of these

6. Mid-points of the sides AB and AC of a ΔABC are (3, 5) and $(-3, -3)$ respectively, then the length of the side BC is :
A. 10
B. 20
C. 15
D. 30

7. The points $A\ (12, 8)$, $B(-2, 6)$ and $C(6, 0)$ are vertices of :
A. right angled triangle
B. isosceles triangle
C. equilateral triangle
D. None of these

8. The points $(1, 1)$ $(-1, -1)$ and $(-\sqrt{3}, \sqrt{3})$ are the angular points of a triangle, then the triangle is :
A. right angled
B. isosceles
C. equilateral
D. None of these

9. The area of the triangle with vertices at $(-4, 1)$, $(1, 2)$, $(4, -3)$ is :
A. 14
B. 16
C. 15
D. None of these

10. The area of the triangle with vertices at the points $(a, b + c)$, $(b, c + a)$, $(c, c + b)$ is :
A. 0
B. $a + b + c$
C. $ab + bc + ca$
D. None of these

11. The equation of the base of an equilateral triangle is $x + y = 2$ and vertex is $(2, -1)$ length of its side is :
A. $\sqrt{\left(\frac{1}{2}\right)}$
B. $\sqrt{\left(\frac{3}{2}\right)}$
C. $\sqrt{\left(\frac{2}{3}\right)}$
D. $\sqrt{2}$

12. The equation of the line, the reciprocal of whose intercepts on the axis are a and b is given by :
A. $\frac{x}{a} + \frac{y}{b} = 1$
B. $ax + by = 1$
C. $ax + by = ab$
D. $ax - by = 1$

13. If a straight line passes through (x_1, y_1) and its segment between the axes is bisected at this point, then its equation is given by :
A. $\frac{x}{x_1} + \frac{y}{y_1} = 2$
B. $2\ (xy_1 + yx_1) = x_1y_1$
C. $xy_1 + yx_1 = x_1\ y_1$
D. None of these

14. A line passes through the point $(2, 3)$ and perpendicular to the line joining $(-5, 6)$ and $(-6, 5)$ is given by :
A. $x + y + 5 = 0$
B. $x + y - 5 = 0$
C. $x - y - 5 = 0$
D. $x - y + 5 = 0$

15. A line passes through $(2, 2)$ and is perpendicular to the line $3x + y = 3$ its y intercepts is :
A. $\frac{1}{3}$
B. $\frac{2}{3}$
C. 1
D. $\frac{4}{3}$

16. The equation of the diagonal through origin of the quadrilateral formed by the lines $x = 0$, $y = 0, x + y - 1 = 0$ and $6x + y - 3 = 0$ is :
A. $4x - 3y = 0$
B. $3x - 2y = 0$
C. $x = y$
D. $x + y = 0$

17. If the lines $3y + 4x = 1$, $y = x + 5$ and $5y + bx = 3$ are concurrent, then the value of b is :
A. 1   B. 3
C. 6   D. 0

18. The distance between the lines $4x + 3y = 11$ and $8x + 6y = 15$ is :

A. $\dfrac{7}{2}$ B. $\dfrac{7}{3}$

C. $\dfrac{7}{5}$ D. $\dfrac{7}{10}$

19. Two vertices of a triangle are the points (1, 4) and (7, 2). Its centroid is the point (5, 3), then the third vertex is :
A. (3, 7)   B. (7, 3)
C. (1, 1)   D. (0, 0)

20. Let the vertices of a triangle be (0, 0), (3, 0) and (0, 4), then its orthocentre is :

A. (0, 0)   B. $\left(1, \dfrac{4}{3}\right)$

C. $\left(\dfrac{3}{2}, 2\right)$ D. None of these

21. The point (–5, 8) lies in the quadrant :
A. 2nd   B. 1st
C. 3rd   D. 4th

22. The point (0, –6) lies on :
A. y-axis (+ve)   B. x-axis
C. x-axis (–ve)   D. y-axis (–ve)

23. Distance of (K, 5) from x-axis is :
A. 4   B. K
C. $\sqrt{K^2 + 25}$ D. K + 5

24. Distance of (2, 3) from origin is :
A. 2   B. 5
C. –1   D. $\sqrt{13}$

25. If the point (x, y) is equidistant from (2, 2) and (4, 5) then :
A. $4x + 6y - 33 = 0$ B. $4x - 6y + 33 = 0$
C. $6x + 4y - 41 = 0$ D. $6x - 4y + 41 = 0$

26. A point on the x-axis is equidistant from (2, –5) and (–2, 9) is
A. (–7, 0)   B. (–6, 0)
C. (–9, 0)   D. (4, 0)

27. Find the values of y for which the distance between the points P(2, –3) and Q(10, y) is 10 units.
A. 8, 2   B. –9, 3
C. –9, 5   D. –8, 2

28. The distance between (2, 3), (4, 1) is :
A. $3\sqrt{2}$ B. $4\sqrt{2}$
C. $2\sqrt{2}$ D. $5\sqrt{2}$

29. The distance between (a, b), $(-a, -b)$ is :
A. $2\sqrt{a^2 + b^2}$ B. $3\sqrt{a^2 + b^2}$
C. $2a^2$ D. $2b^2$

30. The point of intersection of y-axis and the perpendicular bisector of line segment joining A (3, 6) and B (–3, 4) is:
A. (0, 3)   B. (0, 8)
C. (0, 5)   D. (0, 2)

31. The ratio in which the joint of (–3, 10), (6, –8) is divided by (–1, 6) :
A. 1 : 7   B. 2 : 7
C. 3 : 7   D. 4 : 7

32. The mid-point of line segment joining the points (3, 0) and (–1, 4) is :
A. 1, 2   B. 2, 3
C. –1, 2   D. None of these

33. The point which divides the line segment joining the points (3, 5) and (8, 10) internally in the ratio 2 : 3 is:
A. 3, 5   B. 5, 3
C. 5, 7   D. 7, 5

34. In what ratio does the point P(–2, 3) divide the line segment joining the points A(–3, 5) and B(4, –9) internally?
A. 1 : 2   B. 1 : 6
C. 1 : 4   D. 1 : 5

35. The centroid of the triangle whose vertices are A(4, –6), B(3, –2) and C(5, 2) is :
A. 3, 2   B. 4, 1
C. 4, –2   D. 4, 3

36. If (7, 3), (6, 1), (8, 2) and (P, 4) are the vertices of a parallelogram taken in order then the value of P is :
A. 4   B. 6
C. 7   D. 9

37. If the vertices of rhombus are (3, 0), (4, 5), (–1, 4) and (–2, –1) taken in order then area of rhombus is :
A. 20 square units   B. 24 square units
C. 22 square units   D. 26 square units

38. The area of a triangle whose vertices are (–5, –1), (3, –5), (5, 2) is :
A. 24 square units   B. 28 square units
C. 32 square units   D. None of these

39. If the points (7, –2), (5, 1), (3, K) points are collinear then the value of K is :
A. 2   B. 4
C. 6   D. 8

40. Determine the ratio in which the line $2x + y - 4 = 0$ divides the line segment joining A(2, –2) and B(3, 7)

A. $\dfrac{2}{5}$ B. $\dfrac{3}{5}$

C. $\dfrac{2}{9}$ D. $\dfrac{5}{9}$

41. In what ratio is a line segment joining the points (–2, –3) and (3, 7) divided by y-axis?

   A. $\dfrac{2}{3}$ B. $\dfrac{3}{2}$

   C. $\dfrac{4}{5}$ D. $\dfrac{5}{4}$

42. Find the value of P for which the points A(–1, 3), B(2, P) and C(5, –1) are collinear :

   A. 3   B. 1
   C. 2   D. 4

43. Find a point on x-axis which is equidistant from A(7, 6) and B(–3, 4)

   A. 2, 0   B. 4, 0
   C. 3, 0   D. 5, 0

44. The line joining A(2, 1) and B(5, –8) is trisected at the point P and Q. If P lies on the line $2x - y + K = 0$, the value of K is :

   A. –5   B. –4
   C. –3   D. –8

45. The area of a triangle whose vertices are (1, 2), (–3, 4) and (–5, 6) is :

   A. 20 sq. units   B. 22 sq. units
   C. 24 sq. units   D. 26 sq. units

46. If the area of a triangle is 68 sq. units and the vertices are (6, 7), (–4, 1) and (a, –9) then the value of a is :
   A. 1   B. 2
   C. 3   D. 4

47. If P(x, y) is any point on the line joining the points (a, 0) and (0, b) then the value of $\dfrac{x}{a}+\dfrac{y}{b}$ is :
   A. 1   B. 2
   C. 3   D. 4

48. The area of a quadrilateral (–4, –2), (–3, –5), (3, –2) and (2, 3) is :
   A. 20 sq. units   B. 24 sq. units
   C. 28 sq. units   D. 30 sq. units

49. Find the value of K if (2, 3), (4, K) and (6, –3) are collinear :
   A. 0   B. 1
   C. 2   D. 3

50. Find the value of K if A(8, 1), B(K, –4), C(2, –5) are collinear :
   A. 2   B. 3
   C. 4   D. 5

ANSWERS

1	2	3	4	5	6	7	8	9	10
C	C	D	A	A	B	A	C	A	A
11	**12**	**13**	**14**	**15**	**16**	**17**	**18**	**19**	**20**
C	B	A	D	D	B	C	D	B	A
21	**22**	**23**	**24**	**25**	**26**	**27**	**28**	**29**	**30**
A	D	A	D	A	A	B	C	A	C
31	**32**	**33**	**34**	**35**	**36**	**37**	**38**	**39**	**40**
B	A	C	B	C	D	B	C	B	C
41	**42**	**43**	**44**	**45**	**46**	**47**	**48**	**49**	**50**
A	B	C	D	B	B	A	C	A	B

EXPLANATORY ANSWERS

1. AB = BC = CA = 2a

2. C (5, –8) and D, mid-point of AB is (–1, –1)

   $\therefore\ CD = \sqrt{85}$.

3. $P = \left(0, \dfrac{8}{3}\right), Q = (1, 3), R = (82, 30)$

$$m_1 = \text{slope of } PQ = \dfrac{3 - \dfrac{8}{3}}{1 - 0} = \dfrac{1}{3},$$

$$m_2 = \text{slope of } QR = \dfrac{30 - 3}{82 - 1} = \dfrac{1}{3}$$

$m_1 = m_2$, the three points P, Q, R are collinear.

4. $A(0, 4), B(1, 1), C(4, 0), AB = BC = \sqrt{10}$, it follows that the triangle is isosceles.

5. The slopes of OA, OB, OC are $\dfrac{b}{a}$ each and hence the points are collinear.

6. The line joining mid-points is half of the opposite side BC

   $\therefore\ BC = 2(10)$.

7. $BC^2 + CA^2 = AB^2$.

10. The points are collinear as slopes of AB and BC are same.

   $\therefore \Delta = 0$.

11. $P = a \sin 60°$ or $\dfrac{1}{\sqrt{2}} = \dfrac{a\sqrt{3}}{2} \Rightarrow \sqrt{\left(\dfrac{2}{3}\right)} = a.$

13. (x_1, y_1) is mid-point of $(a, 0)$ and $(0, b)$

$$\therefore \qquad a = 2x_1,\ b = 2y_1.$$

15. $x - 3y + 4 = 0$, put $x = 0$.

16. $P + \lambda Q = 0$ and passes through $(0, 0)$.

17. The point of intersection $(-2, 3)$ of first two satisfied third.

18. Lines are parallel.

19. $5 = \dfrac{\Sigma x}{3},\ 3 = \dfrac{\Sigma y}{3}.$

20. The two altitudes *i.e.*, x-axis and y-axis of $\triangle OAB$ meet at origin.

21.

$(-, +)$	$(+, +)$
$(-, -)$	$(+, -)$

$\therefore\ (-5, 8)$ is in 2nd quadrant.

22. The point $(0, -6)$ lies on y-axis $(-ve)$.

24. A $\overset{(0,\,0)}{\rule{3cm}{0.4pt}}\overset{(2,\,3)}{}$ B

$AB = \sqrt{(2-0)^2 + (3-0)^2} = \sqrt{4+9} = \sqrt{13}$

25. If the point (x, y) is equidistant from $(2, 2)$ and $(4, 5)$ then

A $\overset{(x,\,y)}{\rule{3cm}{0.4pt}}$ B
$(2, 2)\qquad$ P $\qquad(4, 5)$

$AP = PB \Rightarrow PA^2 = PB^2$

$(x - 2)^2 + (y - 2)^2 = (4 - x)^2 + (5 - y)^2$

$x^2 - 4x + 4 + y^2 - 4y + 4$

$\qquad\qquad = 16 - 8x + x^2 + 25 + y^2 - 10y$

$4x + 6y - 33 = 0$

26. Let the point on the x-axis is $P(x, 0)$

$\because PA = PB \Rightarrow (PA)^2 = (PB)^2$

$(2 - x)^2 + (-5 - 0)^2 = (-2 - x)^2 + (9 - 0)^2$

$4 + x^2 - 4x + 25 = 4 + x^2 + 4x + 81$

$\Rightarrow 0 = 8x + 56 \Rightarrow x = -7$

$\therefore P(x, 0) = P(-7, 0)$

27. $\because \qquad PQ = 10$

$\Rightarrow \sqrt{(10 - 2)^2 + (y + 3)^2} = 10$

$\sqrt{64 + y^2 + 9 + 6y} = 10$

Squaring both sides,

$$y^2 + 6y - 27 = 0$$
$$\Rightarrow \quad y^2 + 9y - 3y - 27 = 0$$
$$\Rightarrow \quad y(y + 9) - 3(y + 9) = 0$$
$$\Rightarrow \quad (y + 9)(y - 3) = 0$$
$$\Rightarrow \quad y = -9,\ y = 3$$
$$\therefore \qquad y = -9,\ 3$$

28. A $\overset{(2,\,3)}{\rule{4cm}{0.4pt}}\overset{(4,\,1)}{}$ B

$AB = \sqrt{(4-2)^2 + (1-3)^2} = \sqrt{4+4} = 2\sqrt{2}$

29. A $\overset{(a,\,b)}{\rule{4cm}{0.4pt}}\overset{(-a,\,-b)}{}$ B

$AB = \sqrt{(-a - a)^2 + (-b - b)^2}$

$\qquad = \sqrt{4a^2 + 4b^2} = 2\sqrt{a^2 + b^2}$

30. Let y axis meets $\perp$ bisector of AB at the point $P(0, y)$

$\therefore \qquad\qquad PA = PB$

$\Rightarrow \qquad\qquad PA^2 = PB^2$

$\Rightarrow \ (3 - 0)^2 + (6 - y)^2 = (-3 - 0)^2 + (4 - y)^2$

$\Rightarrow \ 9 + 36 + y^2 - 12y = 9 + 16 + y^2 - 8y$

$\Rightarrow \qquad\qquad 4y - 20 = 0$

$\Rightarrow \qquad\qquad y = 5$

$\therefore$ The required point is $P(0, 5)$.

31. Let the required ratio be K : 1

$$-1 = \frac{6K - 3}{K + 1}$$
$$\Rightarrow \quad -K - 1 = 6K - 3$$
$$\Rightarrow \quad 7K = 2$$
$$\Rightarrow \quad K = \frac{2}{7}$$

and $\qquad\qquad 6 = \dfrac{-8K + 10}{K + 1}$

$\Rightarrow \qquad\qquad 14K = 4$

$\Rightarrow \qquad\qquad K = \dfrac{2}{7}$

Hence, the required ratio is 2 : 7.

32. A $\overset{}{\rule{4cm}{0.4pt}}$ B
$(3, 0)\qquad$ P (x, y) $\qquad(-1, 4)$

Mid point of the line segment

$$P(x, y) = P\left(\frac{3 - 1}{2}, \frac{0 + 4}{2}\right)$$

$$= P(1, 2)$$

33. 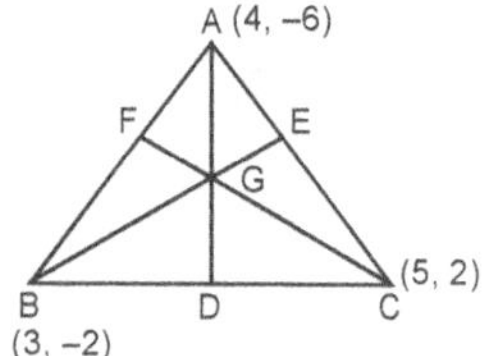

$$x = \frac{2(8)+3(3)}{2+3} = \frac{16+9}{5} = \frac{25}{5} = 5$$

$$y = \frac{2(10)+3(5)}{2+3} = \frac{20+15}{5} = \frac{35}{5} = 7$$

34. 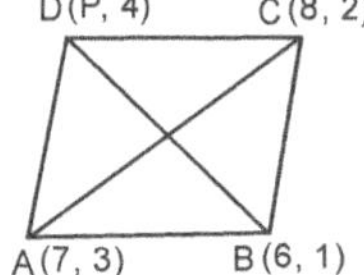

$$-2 = \frac{4K-3}{K+1} \Rightarrow -2K - 2 = 4K - 3$$

$$\Rightarrow \quad 6K = 1 \Rightarrow K = \frac{1}{6}.$$

35.

A (4, −6)

F   E

G

B   D   C (5, 2)

(3, −2)

The centroid of the triangle G(x, y)

$$= G\left(\frac{4+3+5}{3}, \frac{-6-2+2}{3}\right) = G(4, -2)$$

36.

D(P, 4)   C (8, 2)

A(7, 3)   B (6, 1)

We know that the diagonals of a parallelogram bisect each other. Mid-point of AC and BD coincide.

Hence, $\left(\dfrac{7+8}{2}, \dfrac{3+2}{2}\right) = \left(\dfrac{6+P}{2}, \dfrac{1+4}{2}\right)$

$$\Rightarrow \quad \left(\frac{6+P}{2}, \frac{5}{2}\right) = \left(\frac{15}{2}, \frac{5}{2}\right)$$

Equating the x-co-ordinate, we get

$$\frac{6+P}{2} = \frac{15}{2} \Rightarrow P = 9$$

37. We know that area of rhombus = $\dfrac{1}{2} \times AC \times BD$

$$= \frac{1}{2} \times \sqrt{(-1-3)^2 + (4-0)^2} \times \sqrt{(-2-4)^2 + (-1-5)^2}$$

$$= \frac{1}{2}\sqrt{32} \times \sqrt{72} = \frac{1}{2} \times 4\sqrt{2} \times 6\sqrt{2} = \frac{1}{2} \times 48$$

$$= 24 \text{ square units.}$$

38. Area of triangle

$$= \frac{1}{2}\,[x_1(y_2 - y_3) + x_2(y_3 - y_1) + x_3(y_1 - y_2)]$$

$$= \frac{1}{2}\,[-5(-5 - 2) + 3(2 + 1) + 5(-1 + 5)]$$

$$= \frac{1}{2}\,[35 + 9 + 20]$$

$$= \frac{1}{2}\,[64] = 32 \text{ square units.}$$

39. $\because$ Points are collinear $\therefore$ area = 0

$$\frac{1}{2}\,[7(1 - K) + 5(K + 2) + 3(-2 - 1)] = 0$$

$$\Rightarrow [7 - 7K + 5K + 10 - 9] = 0 \Rightarrow K = 4.$$

40.

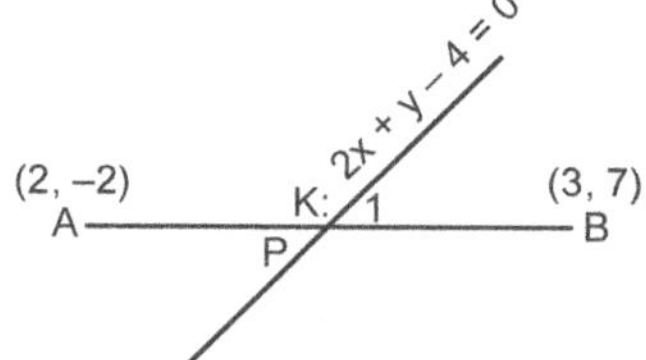

Let the line $2x + y - 4 = 0$ divide the line at P in ratio K : 1.

$$\therefore \ P\left(\frac{3K+2}{K+1}, \frac{7K-2}{K+1}\right) \text{ lies on } 2x + y - 4 = 0$$

$$\Rightarrow 2\left(\frac{3K+2}{K+1}\right) + \frac{7K-2}{K+1} - 4 = 0$$

$$\Rightarrow 6K + 4 + 7K - 2 - 4K - 4 = 0$$

$$\Rightarrow 9K = 2 \Rightarrow K = \frac{2}{9}.$$

41.

(−2, −3)   A   K : 1   (3, 7) B

C

(0, y)

$$(0, y) = \frac{3K-2}{K+1}, \frac{7K-3}{K+1}$$

$$\Rightarrow 0 = \frac{3K-2}{K+1} \Rightarrow 3K - 2 = 0 \Rightarrow K = \frac{2}{3}.$$

42. Points A, B, C are collinear

$$\Rightarrow \text{Area of } \triangle ABC = 0$$

$$\frac{1}{2}\,[-1\,(P + 1) + 2(-1 - 3) + 5(3 - P)] = 0$$

$$\Rightarrow \frac{1}{2}\,[-6P + 6] = 0 \Rightarrow 3P = 3 \Rightarrow P = 1.$$

43. Let P(x, 0) be the required point.

PA = PB $\Rightarrow$ PAV^2 = PB^2

$\Rightarrow (x - 7)^2 + (0 - 6)^2 = (x + 3)^2 + (0 - 4)^2$

$\Rightarrow x^2 - 14x + 49 + 36 = x^2 + 9 + 6x + 16$

$\Rightarrow 20x = 60 \Rightarrow x = 3$

$\therefore$ required point is P(3, 0).

44.

$$\frac{AP}{PB} = \frac{1}{2}$$

Here, $\dfrac{AP}{PB} = \dfrac{1}{2}$

$$P\left[\frac{(1)(5)+2(2)}{1+2}, \frac{(1)(-8)+2(1)}{1+2}\right]$$

$\Rightarrow P\left(\dfrac{9}{3}, \dfrac{-6}{3}\right) = P(3, -2)$ lies on $2x - y + K = 0$

$\Rightarrow 2(3) - (-2) + K = 0$

$\Rightarrow 6 + 2 + K = 0$

$\Rightarrow K = -8.$

45. Area of $\Delta = \dfrac{1}{2}[4 + 18 - 10 - (-6 - 20 - 6)]$

$$= \frac{1}{2}[12 + 32] = 22 \text{ square units.}$$

46. Area of $\Delta = \dfrac{1}{2}[(6 + 36 + 7a) - (-28 + a - 54)] = 68$

$\Rightarrow (42 + 7a) - (a - 82) = 136$

$\Rightarrow 6a = 12 \Rightarrow a = 2$

47. Now the points (x, y), (a, 0) and (0, b) are collinear.

$\therefore$ Area of $\Delta = 0$

$ab - bx - ay = 0$

$\therefore \quad bx + ay = ab$

Dividing by ab both sides, we get

$$\frac{x}{a} + \frac{y}{b} = 1.$$

48. $\because$ A(-4, -2), B(-3, -5), C(3, -2), D(2, 3)

Area of quadrilateral ABCD

$$= \frac{1}{2}[(20 + 6 + 9 - 4) - (6 - 15 - 4 - 12)]$$

$$= \frac{1}{2}[31 + 25] = \frac{56}{2} = 28 \text{ square units.}$$

49. Since the points are collinear

$\therefore$ Area of triangle formed by the points will be zero.

$$\therefore \frac{1}{2}[2(k + 3) + 4(-3 - 3) + 6(3 - k)] = 0$$

$$2k + 6 - 24 + 18 - 6k = 0$$

$$-4k = 0 \quad \therefore k = 0.$$

50. Since, points ABC are collinear

$\therefore \quad$ Area of ΔABC = 0

$$\therefore \frac{1}{2}[8(-4 + 5) + k(-5 - 1) + 2(1 + 4)] = 0$$

$$8 - 6k + 10 = 0$$

$$6k = 18 \quad \therefore k = \frac{18}{6} = 3.$$

✱ ✱ ✱

8

Geometry : Triangles

Two triangles are said to be similar, if

(*i*) their corresponding angles are equal and

(*ii*) their corresponding sides are in the same ratio (*i.e.* proportional).

Also, we know that :

(*i*) If corresponding angles of two triangles are equal, then they are known as equiangular triangles.

(*ii*) Two line segments are divided proportionally when the ratio of the lengths of the segments of one of them is equal to the ratio of the lengths of the segments of the other.

SOME IMPORTANT THEOREMS

Basic Proportionality Theorem: (Thalse Theorem)

Theorem 1: *In a triangle, a line drawn parallel to one side to intersect the other sides in distinct points divides the two sides in the same ratio.*

Given: A $\triangle ABC$ in which DE is drawn parallel to side BC.

To prove. $\dfrac{AD}{DB} = \dfrac{AE}{EC}$.

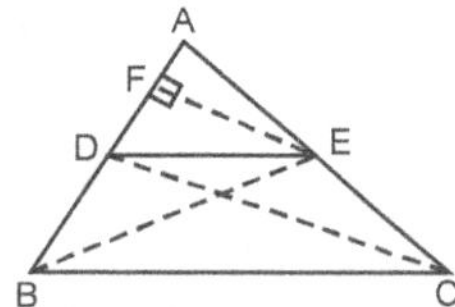

Const.: Join BE and CD. Draw EF $\perp$ AB.

Proof: ar.$(\triangle BDE)$ = ar.$(\triangle CDE)$ ...(1)

[$\because$ $\triangle s$ on the same base DE and between the same parallels are equal in area]

$$\frac{ar.(\triangle ADE)}{ar.(\triangle BDE)} = \frac{\frac{1}{2} \times AD \times EF}{\frac{1}{2} \times BD \times EF}$$

[$\because$ Area of $\triangle = \dfrac{1}{2}$ base $\times$ height]

$$\Rightarrow \quad \frac{ar.(\triangle ADE)}{ar.(\triangle BDE)} = \frac{AD}{DB} \qquad ...(2)$$

Similarly, $\dfrac{ar.(\triangle ADE)}{ar.(\triangle CDE)} = \dfrac{AE}{EC}$ ...(3)

$\therefore \quad \dfrac{ar.(\triangle ADE)}{ar.(\triangle BDE)} = \dfrac{AE}{EC}$

[from (1) and (3)] (4)

$\therefore \quad \dfrac{AD}{DB} = \dfrac{AE}{EC}$ [from (2) and (4)]

Corollary 1: $\dfrac{AD}{DB} = \dfrac{AE}{EC}$

Adding 1 to both sides, we get

$$\frac{AD}{DB} + 1 = \frac{AE}{EC} + 1$$

$$\Rightarrow \quad \frac{AD + DB}{DB} = \frac{AE + EC}{EC}$$

Corollary 2: $\dfrac{AD}{DB} = \dfrac{AE}{EC}$

$$\Rightarrow \quad \frac{DB}{AD} = \frac{EC}{AE}$$

Adding 1 to both sides, we get

$$1 + \frac{DB}{AD} = 1 + \frac{EC}{AE}$$

$$\Rightarrow \quad \frac{AD + DB}{AD} = \frac{AE + EC}{AE}$$

$$\Rightarrow \quad \frac{AB}{AD} = \frac{AC}{AE}.$$

Converse of Basic Proportionality Theorem

Theorem 2: *If a line divides any two sides of a triangle in the same ratio, prove that it is parallel to the third side.*

Given: A $\triangle ABC$, DE is st. line such that

$$\frac{AD}{DB} = \frac{AE}{EC}$$

To Prove. DE $\parallel$ BC

Const.: If DE is not ∥ BC, draw BK ∥ DE meeting AC produce in.

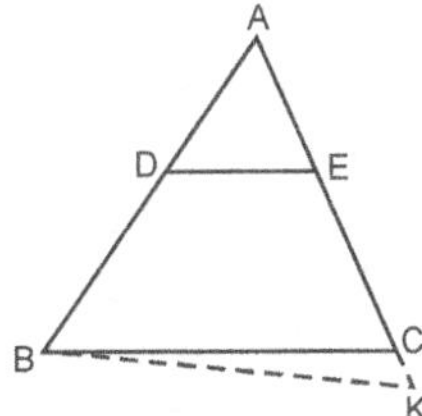

Proof: In DABK, DE ∥ BK

$$\therefore \quad \frac{AD}{DB} = \frac{AE}{EK} \qquad \ldots(1)$$

[∵ A line drawn ∥ to one side of a Δ divides the other two sides in the same ratio]

But, $\dfrac{AD}{DB} = \dfrac{AE}{EC}$ (given) $\qquad \ldots(2)$

From (1) and (2), we get

$$\frac{AE}{EK} = \frac{AE}{EC} \text{ or, } EK = EC$$

which is possible only when C and K coincides.

Hence, DE ∥ BC.

SOLVED EXAMPLES

Ex. 1 : M and N are points on the sides PQ and PR respectively of a ΔPQR. For each of the following cases, state whether MN ∥ QR.

(i) PM = 4 cm; QM = 4.5 cm;
PN = 4 cm; NR = 4.5 cm

(ii) PQ = 1.28 cm; PR = 2.56 cm,
PM = 0.16 cm; PN = 0.32 cm.

Sol. : (i) $\dfrac{PM}{QM} = \dfrac{4}{4.5}$ and $\dfrac{PN}{NR} = \dfrac{4}{4.5}$

$$\therefore \quad \frac{PM}{QM} = \frac{PN}{NR} \qquad \left[\text{Each ratio} = \frac{4}{4.5}\right]$$

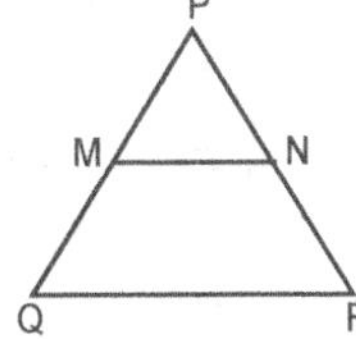

⇒ By the converse of Basic Proportinality theorem, we get, MN ∥ QR.

(ii) PQ = 1.28, PM = 0.16

⇒ MQ = PQ – PM = 1.28 – 0.16 = 1.12

NR = PR – PN = 2.56 – 0.32 = 2.24

Now, $\dfrac{PM}{MQ} = \dfrac{0.16}{1.12} = \dfrac{1}{7}$

$$\frac{PN}{NR} = \frac{0.32}{2.24} = \frac{1}{7}$$

$$\therefore \quad \frac{PM}{MQ} = \frac{PN}{NR} \qquad \left[\text{Each ratio} = \frac{1}{7}\right]$$

⇒ By the converse of Basic Proportionality Theorem,
MN ∥ QR.

Ex. 2 : If in fig. (i) and (ii), PQ ∥ BC, find QC in (i) and AQ in (ii).

Sol. : In fig. (i)

In ΔABC, PQ ∥ BC

∴ By basic Proportionality Theorem, we get

$$\frac{AP}{PB} = \frac{AQ}{QC}$$

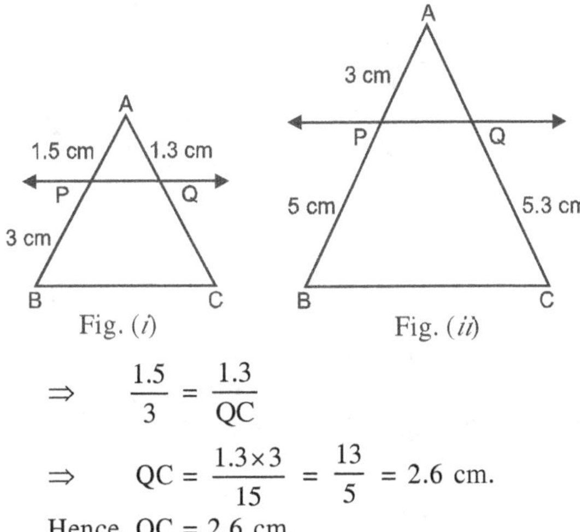

Fig. (i)   Fig. (ii)

$$\Rightarrow \quad \frac{1.5}{3} = \frac{1.3}{QC}$$

$$\Rightarrow \quad QC = \frac{1.3 \times 3}{15} = \frac{13}{5} = 2.6 \text{ cm.}$$

Hence, QC = 2.6 cm.

In fig. (ii) given above

In ΔABC, PQ ∥ BC

∴ By Basic Proportionality Theorem, we get

$$\frac{AP}{PB} = \frac{AQ}{QC} \Rightarrow \frac{3}{6} = \frac{AQ}{5.3}$$

$$\Rightarrow \quad AQ = \frac{3 \times 5.3}{6} = \frac{5.3}{2} = 2.65 \text{ cm.}$$

Ex. 3 : In given fig. (i) and (ii) DE ∥ BC. Find EC in (i) and AD in (ii).

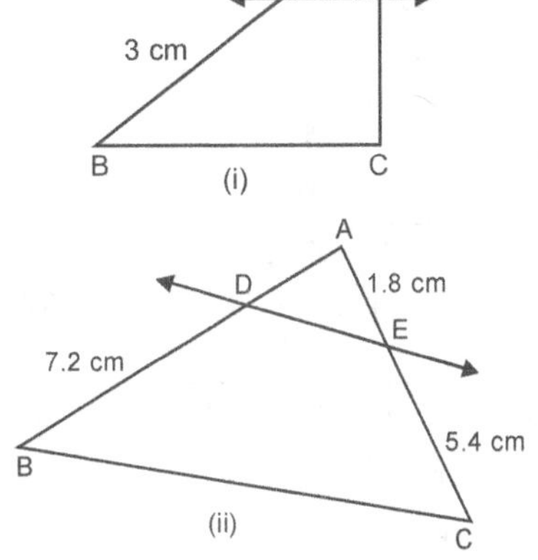

Sol. : In fig,... (*i*).

In $\triangle$ABC, DE ∥ BC

∴ By Basic Proportionality Theorem, we get

$$\frac{AD}{DB} = \frac{AE}{EC}$$

$$\Rightarrow \frac{1.5}{3} = \frac{1}{EC}$$

$$\Rightarrow EC = \frac{3 \times 1}{1.5} = 2 \text{ cm}$$

(*ii*) In Fig,... (*ii*)

In $\triangle$ABC, DE ∥ BC

∴ By Basic Proportionality Theorem, we get

$$\frac{AD}{DB} = \frac{AE}{EC}$$

Ex. 4 : In the given fig. DE ∥ BC. If AD = x, DB = $x - 2$, AE = $x + 2$ and EC = $x - 1$, find the value of x.

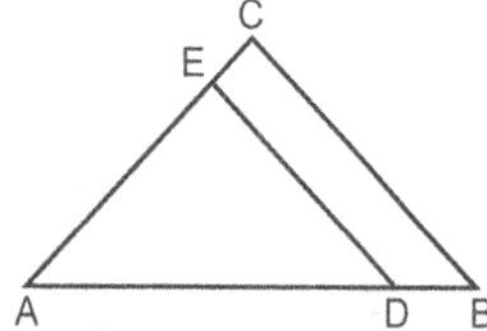

Sol. : In $\triangle$ABC, DE ∥ BC

∴
$$\frac{AD}{DB} = \frac{AE}{EC}$$

(By basic proportionality theorem)

$$\Rightarrow \frac{x}{x-2} = \frac{x+2}{x-1}$$

$$\Rightarrow x(x-1) = (x+2)(x-2)$$

$$\Rightarrow x^2 - x = x^2 - 4 \Rightarrow x = 4.$$

Ex. 5 : In the following fig. LM ∥ AB. If AL = $x - 3$, AC = $2x$, BM = $x - 2$, BC = $2x + 3$, find the value of x.

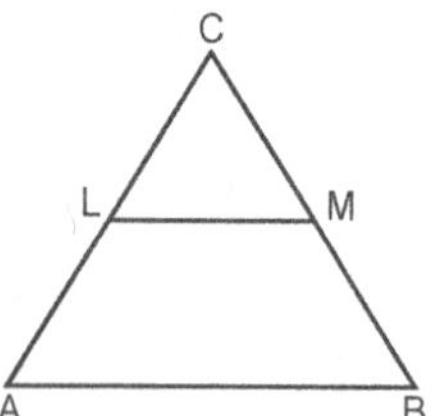

Sol. : In $\triangle$ABC, LM ∥ AB

∴
$$\frac{AL}{LC} = \frac{BM}{MC}$$

[By Basic Proportionality Theorem]

$$\Rightarrow \frac{x-3}{2x-(x-3)} = \frac{x-2}{(2x+3)-(x-2)}$$

$$\Rightarrow \frac{x-3}{x+3} = \frac{x-2}{x+5}.$$

Ratio of The Areas of Two Similar Triangles

Theorem 3: *Prove that the ratio of the areas of two similar triangles is equal to the ratio of squares on the corresponding sides.*

Given: $\triangle$ABC ~ $\triangle$DEF.

To Prove: $\dfrac{ar(\triangle ABC)}{ar(\triangle DEF)} = \dfrac{BC^2}{EF^2}$

$$= \frac{AB^2}{DE^2} = \frac{AC^2}{DF^2}$$

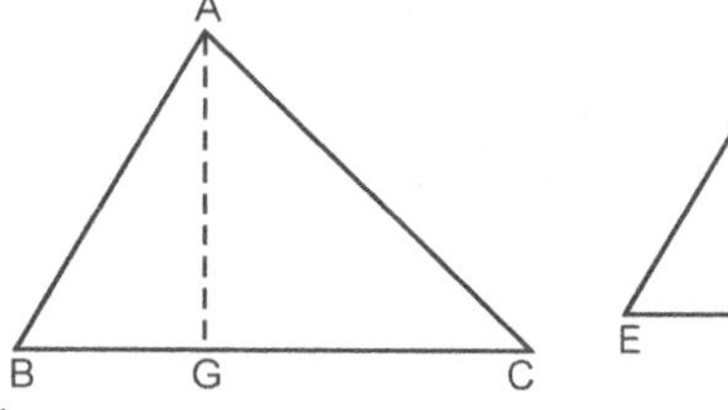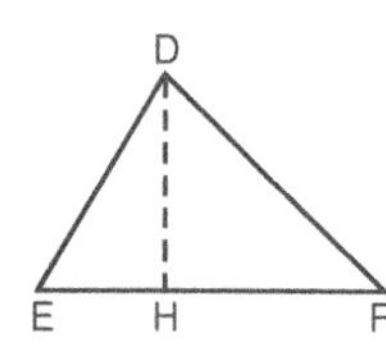

Const.: Draw AG $\perp$ BC and DH $\perp$ EF

Proof: $\dfrac{ar(\triangle ABC)}{ar(\triangle DEF)} = \dfrac{\frac{1}{2} \times BC \times AG}{\frac{1}{2} \times EF \times DH}$

$$\left(\because \text{area of } \triangle = \frac{1}{2} \text{ base} \times \text{height} \right)$$

$$= \frac{BC}{EF} \times \frac{AG}{DH} \qquad ...(i)$$

Now in $\triangle s$ ABG and DEH, we have

$$\angle B = \angle E \quad (\because \triangle ABC \sim \triangle DEF)$$

$$\angle AGB = \angle DHE \qquad (\text{each } 90°)$$

∴ 3rd $\angle$BAG = 3rd $\angle$EDH

therefore, $\triangle$ABG and $\triangle$DEH are equiangular and hence similar.

∴
$$\frac{AB}{DE} = \frac{AG}{DH}$$

($\because$ If $\triangle s$ similar, the ratio of their corresponding sides is same)

But, $\dfrac{AB}{DE} = \dfrac{BC}{EF}$ $\quad(\because \triangle ABC \sim \triangle DEF)$

∴ $\dfrac{AG}{DE} = \dfrac{BC}{EF}$ $\qquad ...(ii)$

Now, from (*i*) and (*ii*), we get

$$\frac{ar(\triangle ABC)}{ar(\triangle DEF)} = \frac{BC}{EF} \times \frac{BC}{EF} = \frac{BC^2}{EF^2}$$

Similarly, it can be proved that

$$\frac{ar(\triangle ABC)}{ar(\triangle DEF)} = \frac{AB^2}{DE^2} = \frac{AC^2}{DF^2}$$

Hence, $\dfrac{ar(\triangle ABC)}{ar(\triangle DEF)} = \dfrac{BC^2}{EF^2} = \dfrac{AB^2}{DE^2} = \dfrac{AC^2}{DE^2}.$

SOLVED EXAMPLES

Ex. 1 : The ratio of the corresponding sides of similar triangles ABC and A′B′C′ is 2 : 1. The altitudes, CD and C′D′, that we have drawn in these triangles are also in the same ratio 2 : 1.

Sol. :
$$\frac{CD}{C'D'} = \frac{24}{12} = \frac{2}{1}$$

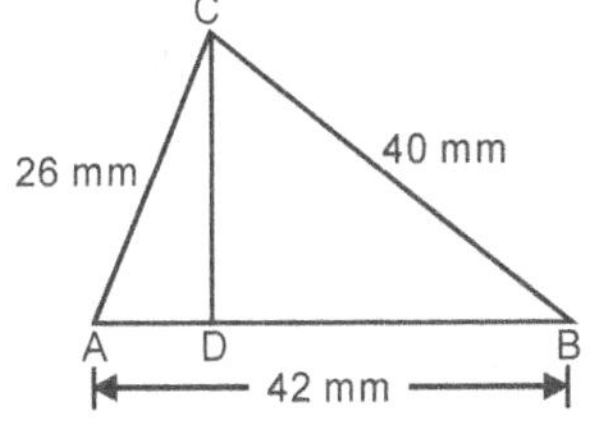

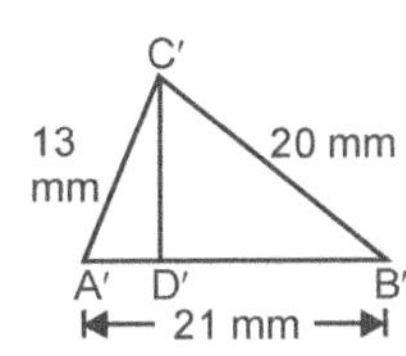

Area of a $\Delta = \dfrac{1}{2}$ base × altitude

$$\therefore \quad \frac{\text{Area of } \Delta ABC}{\text{Area of } \Delta\, A'B'C'} = \frac{\frac{1}{2}\times 42\times 24}{\frac{1}{2}\times 21\times 12}$$

$$= \frac{42\times 12}{21\times 6} = \frac{84}{21} = \frac{4}{1} = \left(\frac{2}{1}\right)^2$$

∴ The ratio of the areas of these similar triangles is the square of the ratio of the measures of the corresponding sides.

Ex. 2 : The areas of two similar triangles ABC and PQR are 64 cm² and 121 cm², respectively. If QR = 15.4 cm, find BC.

Sol. : We know that the ratio of the areas of two similar triangles is equal to the ratio of the squares of the corresponding sides.

$$\therefore \quad \frac{ar(\Delta ABC)}{ar(\Delta PQR)} = \frac{BC^2}{QR^2} \Rightarrow \frac{64}{121} = \frac{BC^2}{(15.4)^2}$$

$$\Rightarrow \quad \frac{8}{11} = \frac{BC}{15.4}$$

$$\Rightarrow \quad BC = \frac{8\times 15.4}{11} = 11.2 \text{ cm.}$$

Ex. 3 : ΔABC is similar to ΔPQR, ar(ΔABC) = 36 sq. cm. and ar(ΔPQR) = 49 sq. cm. If BC = 12 cm, find QR.

Sol. : ∵ ΔABC ~ ΔPQR

$$\therefore \quad \frac{ar(\Delta ABC)}{ar(\Delta PQR)} = \frac{BC^2}{QR^2}$$

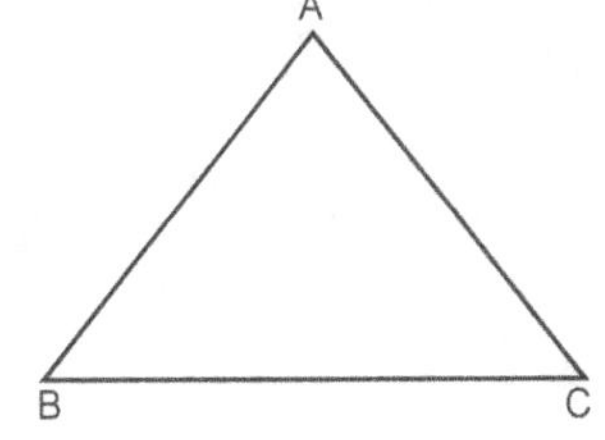

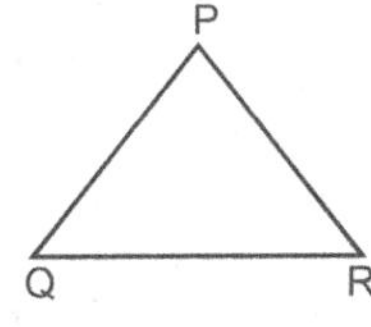

$$\Rightarrow \quad \frac{36}{49} = \frac{12^2}{QR^2}$$

$$\Rightarrow \quad (QR)^2 = \frac{12\times 12\times 49}{36} = 4\times 49$$

$$\Rightarrow \quad QR = +\sqrt{4\times 49}$$

$$= 2 \times 7 = 14 \text{ cm.}$$

Ex. 4 : In the given figure DE ∥ BC. If DE = 4 cm, BC = 8 cm and area (ΔADE) = 25 sq. cm, find the area of ΔABC.

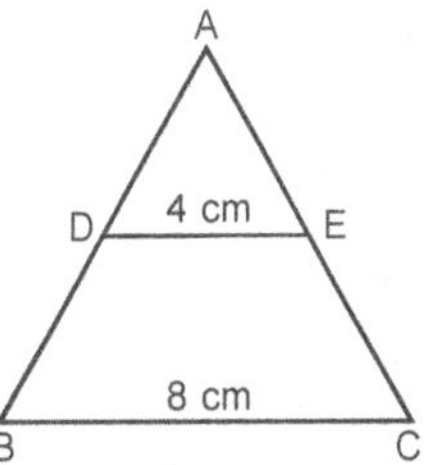

Sol. : ΔABC in which DE ∥ BC and DE = 4 cm, BC = 8 cm. and ar. (ΔADE) = 25 sq. cm.

In ΔADE and ΔABC

∠A = ∠A	[Common]
∠ADE = ∠ABC	[Corresponding angles]
∠AED = ∠ACB	[Corresponding angles]
∴ ΔADE ~ ΔABC	[AAA similarity]

Since ratio of areas of two similar Δs is equal to ratio of squares on the corresponding sides.

$$\therefore \quad \frac{ar(\Delta ADE)}{ar(\Delta ABC)} = \frac{(DE)^2}{(BC)^2}$$

$$\Rightarrow \quad \frac{25}{ar(\Delta ABC)} = \frac{(4)^2}{(8)^2} = \frac{16}{64} = \frac{1}{4}$$

Hence, ar (ΔABC) = 25 × 4 = 100 sq.m.

Ex. 5 : ΔABC ~ ΔPQR. Also ar(ΔABC) = 4 ar(ΔPQR). If BC = 12 cm, then find QR.

Sol. : ar(ΔABC) = 4 ar(ΔPQR)

$$\Rightarrow \quad \frac{ar(\Delta ABC)}{ar(\Delta PQR)} = \frac{4}{1}$$

$$\Rightarrow \quad \frac{BC^2}{QR^2} = \frac{4}{1}$$

[∵ The ratio of the areas of two similar Δs is equal to the ratio of the squares of any two corresponding sides]

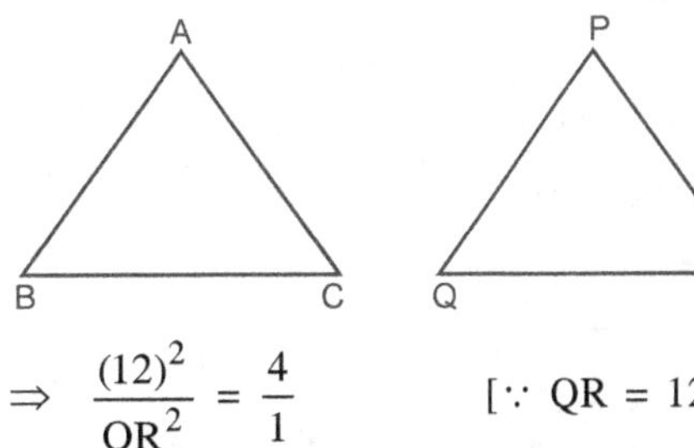

$$\Rightarrow \quad \frac{(12)^2}{QR^2} = \frac{4}{1} \qquad [\because QR = 12 \text{ cm}]$$

$\Rightarrow \quad QR^2 = \dfrac{12 \times 12}{4} = 36$

$\therefore \quad QR = +\sqrt{36} = 6$ cm.

Ex. 6 : In the following figure $\Delta ABC \sim \Delta APQ$ ar$(\Delta APQ) =$ 4ar(ΔABC). Find the ratio $\dfrac{BC}{PQ}$.

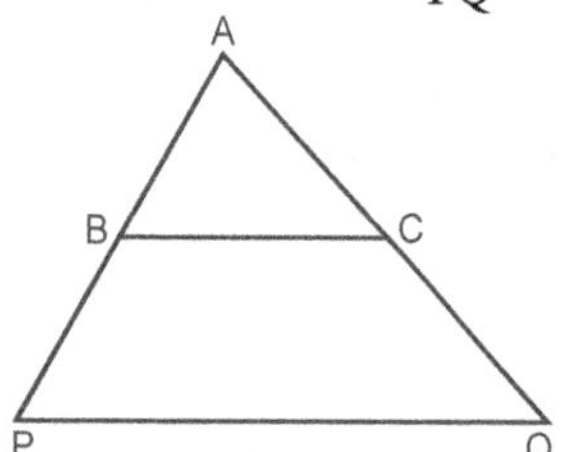

Sol. : $\Delta ABC \sim \Delta APQ$ (Given)

$\therefore \quad \dfrac{ar(\Delta ABC)}{ar(\Delta APQ)} = \dfrac{BC^2}{PQ^2}$ ...(i)

[$\because$ Ratio of the areas of two similar triangles is equal to the ratio of the squares of their corresponding sides]

But ar $(\Delta APQ) = 4$ ar (ΔABC) (Give)

$\therefore \quad \dfrac{ar(\Delta ABC)}{ar(\Delta APQ)} = \dfrac{1}{4}$ ...(ii)

$\therefore \quad \dfrac{BC^2}{PQ^2} = \dfrac{1}{4}$ [From (i) and (ii)]

Hence, $\dfrac{BC^2}{PQ^2} = \dfrac{1}{2}$.

Ex. 7 : (a) In the given figure ABCD is a trapezium in which AB ∥ CD and AB = 2CD. Find the ratio of the areas of triangles AOB and COD.

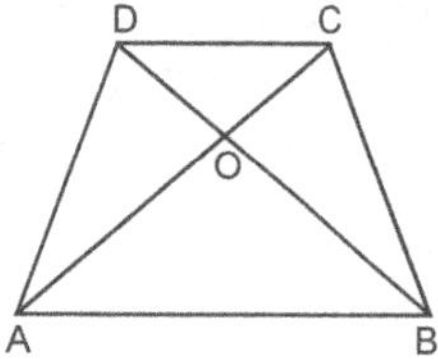

Sol. : In Δs AOB and ΔCOD.

$\angle AOB = \angle COD$ (Vert. opp. $\angle s$)

$\angle OAB = \angle OCD$

[Alternate $\angle s$ are equal as AB ∥ CD (Given)]

$\therefore \quad \Delta AOB \sim \Delta COD$

[By AA criterion of similarity]

$\Rightarrow \quad \dfrac{ar(\Delta AOB)}{ar(\Delta COD)} = \dfrac{AB^2}{CD^2} = \dfrac{(2CD)^2}{CD^2}$

[$\because$ AB = 2CD]

$= \dfrac{4CD^2}{CD^2} = \dfrac{4}{1}$

Hence, ar (ΔAOB) : ar $(\Delta COD) = 4 : 1$.

Ex. 8 : (b) In a trapezium ABCD, O is the point of intersection of AC and BD, AB ∥ CD and AB = 2 CD. If the area of $\Delta AOB = 84$ cm², find the area of ΔCOD.

Sol. : ABCD is a trapezium in which, AB ∥ CD and diagonals AC and BD intersect each other at O.

In ΔAOB and ΔCOD, we have

$\angle 1 = \angle 2$ [Alt. $\angle s$]

$\angle 3 = \angle 4$ [Vert. opp. $\angle s$]

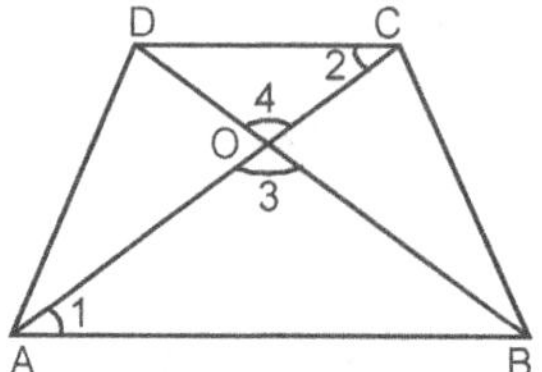

$\therefore \quad \Delta AOB \sim \Delta COD$

[By AA criterion of similarity]

$\Rightarrow \quad \dfrac{ar(\Delta AOB)}{ar(COD)} = \dfrac{AB^2}{CD^2}$

[The areas of two similar Δs are in the ratio of the squares of the corresponding sides].

$\Rightarrow \quad \dfrac{ar(\Delta AOB)}{ar(\Delta COD)} = \dfrac{(2CD)^2}{(CD)^2}$ [AB = 2CD (Given)]

$= \dfrac{4CD^2}{CD^2} = 4$

$= \dfrac{84}{ar(\Delta COD)} = 4;$

$\therefore \quad ar(\Delta COD) = 84 \div 4 = 21$ cm².

The Theorem of Pythagoras

Introduction. The figure at the right represents a right triangle. In right triangle ABC, side AB, which is opposite the right angle, is called by hypotenuse, The hypotenuse is the longest side of the triangle. The other two sides of the triangle BC and AC, form the right angle. They are called the legs of the right triangle.

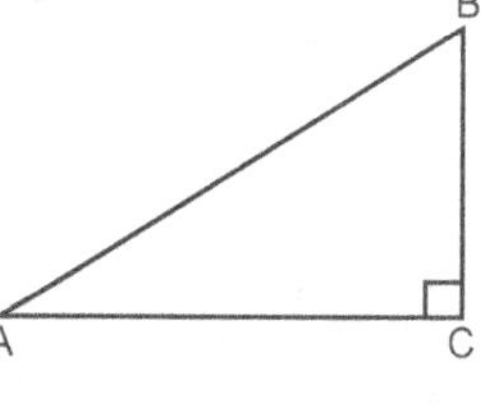

A very important property of a right triangle is given by Greek mathematician Pythagoras more than 2,000 years ago, which is called the **Pythagoras Theorem.**

The theorem states that

In a right triangles, the square of the length of the hypotenuse is equal to the sum of the squares of the lengths of the other two sides. If we rpresent the length of the

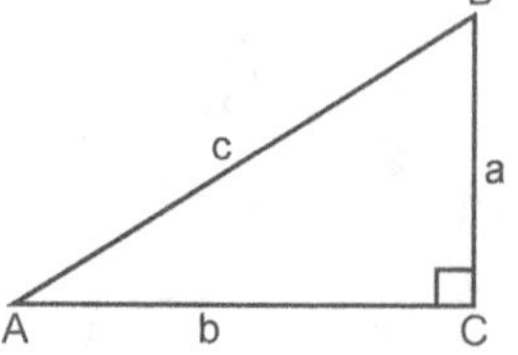

hypotenuse of right triangle ABC by C and the lengths of the other two sides by a and b, the theorem of Pythagoras, may be written as the following formula

$$c^2 = a^2 + b^2$$

Geometrically, this relation means that, if squares are built on the hypotenuse and on each leg of a right triangle, the area of the squares on the hypotenuse is equal to the sum of the areas of the squares on the legs.

In the following figure $\triangle ABC$ is a right triangle in which side AC = 4 cm, side BC = 3 cm and hyp. AB = 5 cm.

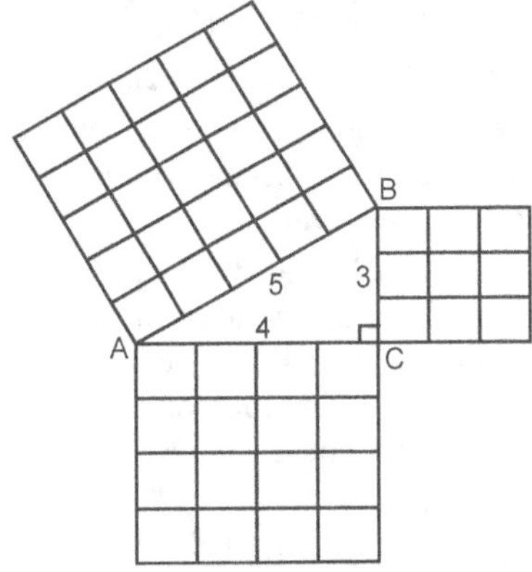

The area of the square on side BC = 9 cm^2

The area of the square on side AC = 16 cm^2

The area of the squares on hyp. AB = 25 cm^2

We see that

$$25 \text{ cm}^2 = 16 \text{ cm}^2 + 9 \text{ cm}^2$$
$$(5 \text{ cm})^2 = (4 \text{ cm})^2 + (3 \text{ cm})^2$$
$$AB^2 = AC^2 + BC^2$$

Another Approach to the Pythagoras Theorem

Similar triangles can be used to demonstrate the truth of the Pythagoras Theorem.

Theorem 4: *In a right triangle, the square of the hypotenuse is equal to the sum of the squares of the other two sides.*

Given: A right triangle ABC, right angled at B.

To Prove: $AC^2 = AB^2 + BC^2$.

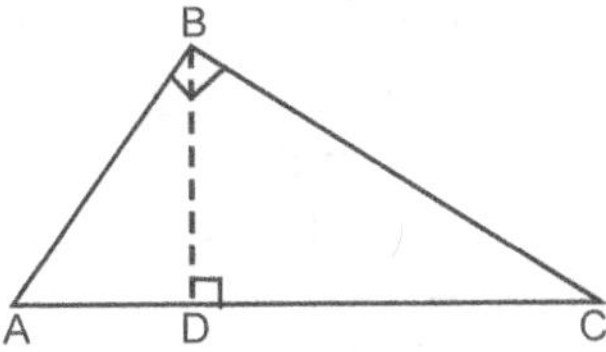

Construction: Draw BD $\perp$ AC.

Proof: In $\triangle ADB$ and $\triangle ABC$, we have

$$\angle ADB = \angle ABC \qquad \text{(Each} = 90°)$$
$$\angle A = \angle A \qquad \text{(Common)}$$
$$\therefore \quad \triangle ADB \sim \triangle ABC$$

(By AA criterion of similarity)

$$\therefore \quad \frac{AD}{AB} = \frac{AB}{AC}$$

[$\because$ Corresponding sides of similar triangles are proportional]

$$\Rightarrow \qquad AB^2 = AD \times AC$$

Similarly, $\quad \triangle BDC \sim \triangle ABC \qquad \qquad ...(i)$

$$\therefore \quad \frac{BC}{AC} = \frac{DC}{BC} \Rightarrow BC^2 = DC \times AC \qquad ...(ii)$$

Adding (i) and (ii), we get

$$AB^2 + BC^2 = AD \times AC + DC \times AC$$
$$AB^2 + BC^2 = (AD + DC) \times AC$$
$$= AC \times AC = AC^2$$

Hence, $\quad AC^2 = AB^2 + BC^2$.

Converse of The Pythagoras Theorem

Theorem 5: *In a triangle, if the square of one side is equal to the sum of the squares of the other two sides, then the angle opposite to the first side is a right triangle.*

Given: A triangle ABC such that

$$AB^2 + BC^2 = AC^2$$

To prove: $\quad ABC = 90°$

Construction: Construct a right triangle PQR, right angled at Q, such that PQ = AB and QR = BC.

Proof: $\because$ In $\triangle PQR$, $\angle PQR = 90°$

$$\therefore \quad PQ^2 + QR^2 = PR^2 \qquad \text{(Pythagoras Theorem)}$$

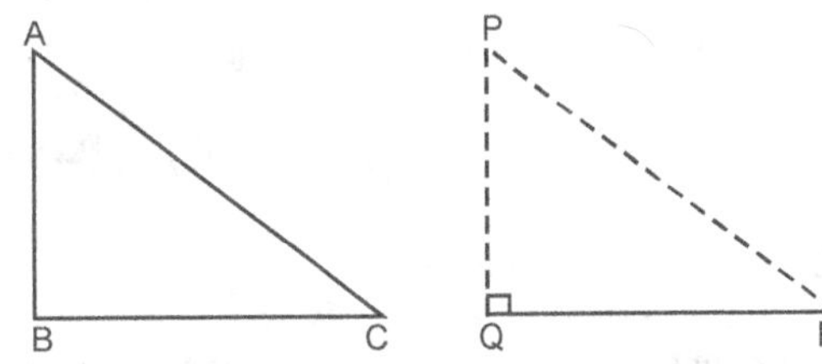

But PQ = AB and QR = BC (By construction)

$$\therefore \qquad AB^2 + BC^2 = PR^2 \qquad \qquad ...(i)$$

But, $\quad AB^2 + BC^2 = AC^2 \qquad \qquad ...(ii)$ (Given)

$\therefore$ From (i) and (ii), we get

$$PR^2 = AC^2$$

or $\qquad \qquad PR = AC$

Now in $\triangle ABC$ and $\triangle PQR$, we have

$$AB = PQ, \ BC = QR \text{ and } AC = PR$$

$$\therefore \qquad \triangle ABC \cong \triangle PQR$$

[By SSS congruence criterion]

$$\Rightarrow \qquad \angle ABC = \angle PQR \qquad \text{[c.p.c.t.c.]}$$

But, $\qquad \angle PQR = 90° \qquad$ [By construction]

Hence, $\qquad \angle ABC = 90°$

Note: Pythagoras triplet

If c is the length of the hypotenuse, and a and b are the lengths of other two sides, the Pythagoras theorem is

$$\boxed{c^2 = a^2 + b^2}$$

A set of Pythagoras triplet is a set of three natural numbers which satisfy the relation

$$c^2 = a^2 + b^2$$

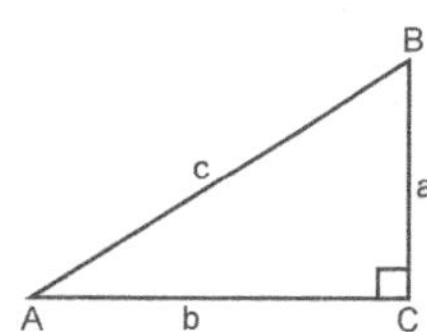

e.g., the relation is true for natural numbers 3, 4, 5 since $5^2 = 3^2 + 4^2$.

Other sets of Pythagoras triplet are

$\{5, 12, 13\}$ since $13^2 = 5^2 + 12^2$

and $\{8, 15, 17\}$ since $17^2 = 8^2 + 15^2$.

SOLVED EXAMPLES

Ex. 1 : The sides of some triangles are given below. Determine which of them are right triangles

(*i*) 7 cm, 24 cm, 25 cm

(*ii*) 3 cm, 8 cm, 6 cm

(*iii*) 50 cm, 80 cm, 100 cm

(*iv*) 13 cm, 12 cm, 5 cm.

Sol. : In a right triangle, the sum of the squares on two smaller sides is equal to the square on the largest side

(*i*) $(7)^2 + (24)^2 = 49 + 576 = 625$

$(25)^2 = 625$

Since $(7)^2 + (24)^2 = (25)^2$

Hence, the triangle is a right triangle.

(*ii*) $(3)^2 + (6)^2 = 9 + 36 = 45$

$(8)^2 = 64$

Since $(3)^2 + (6)^2 \neq (11)^2$, Hence the triangle is not a right triangle.

(*iii*) $(50)^2 + (80)^2 = 2500 + 6400 = 8900$

$(100)^2 = 10000$

Since $(50)^2 + (80)^2 \neq (100)^2$

Hence, the triangle is not a right triangle.

(*iv*) $(12)^2 + (5)^2 = 144 + 25 = 169$

$(13)^2 = 169$

Since $(12)^2 + (5)^2 = (13)^2$

Hence, the triangle is right angle.

Ex. 2 : A ladder 10 m long reaches a window 8 m above the ground. Find the distance of the foot of the ladder from base of the wall.

Sol. : Let BC = 8 m be the wall of a house, B being the window and AB = 10 m be the ladder, we are required to find the foot of the ladder from the house i.e., AC.

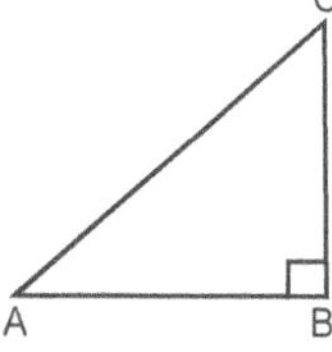

In right $\triangle$ACB,

$$AB^2 = AC^2 + BC^2$$

[By pythagoras theorem]

$\Rightarrow$ $(10)^2 = AC^2 + (8)^2 \cdot$

$\Rightarrow$ $AC^2 = (10)^2 - (8)^2 = 100 - 64 = 36$

$\Rightarrow$ $AC = \sqrt{36} = 6$ cm.

MULTIPLE CHOICE QUESTIONS

1. Two similar triangles have
A. equal sides
B. equal areas
C. equal angles
D. None of these

2. Two congruent triangles have
A. proportional sides
B. equal sides
C. equal corresponding sides
D. equal corresponding angles

3. Which of the following is false for two congruent triangles
A. Corresponding angles are equal.
B. Two sides and included angles are equal.
C. Corresponding sides are equal.
D. Two angles and one side are equal.

4. If the sides of a triangle are 8 cm, 12 cm and 15 cm then the angle is
A. Right angle
B. Obtuse angle
C. Acute angle
D. None of these

5. If two triangles are on the same base and between the parallel lines then they will be
A. equilaterals
B. right angled
C. equal in area
D. congruent

6. If the three heights of a traingle are equal then it is
A. right angled triangle
B. obtuse angled triangle
C. equilateral triangle
D. None of these

7. If two corresponding sides and the angle between them of a traingle are equal to another triangle. Then the angles are :
A. congruent but not similar
B. similar but not congruent
C. neither congruent nor similar
D. congruent and similar.

8. Ratio of areas of two similar triangles is equal to :
A. ratio of squares of the corresponding altitudes
B. ratio of squares of corresponding medians.
C. Either (A) or (B)
D. (A) and (B) both

9. If the areas of two similar triangles are equal then the triangles :
A. are congruent
B. have equal length of corresponding sides
C. (A) and (B)
D. None of these

10. Two isosceles triangles have equal vertical angles and their areas are in the ratio of 9 : 25 then the ratio between their corresponding heights is :
A. 5 : 3
B. 25 : 9
C. 3 : 5
D. 16 : 9

11. If in a Δ DEF, GH $\parallel$ EF and DG : EG = 2 : 3 then the value of $\dfrac{ar\,(\Delta\,DGH)}{ar\,(\Delta\,DEF)}$ is :

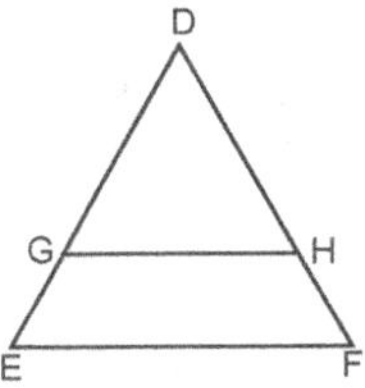

A. $\dfrac{2}{15}$
B. $\dfrac{4}{15}$
C. $\dfrac{4}{25}$
D. 2/25

12. Sides of two similar triangles are in the ratio of 5 : 11 then ratio of their areas is :
A. 25 : 11
B. 25 : 121
C. 125 : 121
D. 121 : 25

13. If ΔABC ~ ΔADE and ar (Δ ADE) = 9 ar (Δ ABC) then $\dfrac{BC}{DE}$ is equal to :

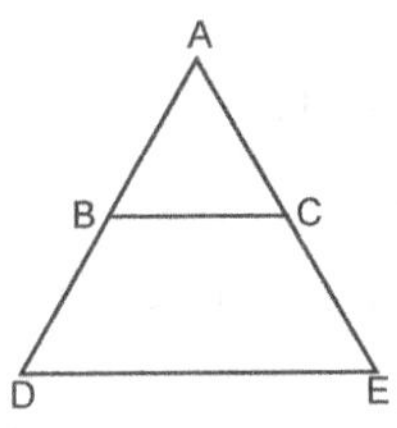

A. $\dfrac{1}{3}$
B. $\dfrac{1}{9}$
C. $\dfrac{3}{4}$
D. None of these

14. In a triangle a line is drawn from the mid-point of one side of and parallel to another side then
A. the line bisects the whole traingle
B. bisects the third side
C. bisects the opposite angle
D. None of these

15. If in a ΔABC, $\angle$B = $\angle$C and BD = CE then which of the following is true
A. DE = $\dfrac{1}{2}$ BC
B. DE $\parallel$ BC
C. (A) and (B)
D. None of these

16. If in ΔCAB, $\angle$A = $\angle$B and DE $\parallel$ AB then which of the following is true

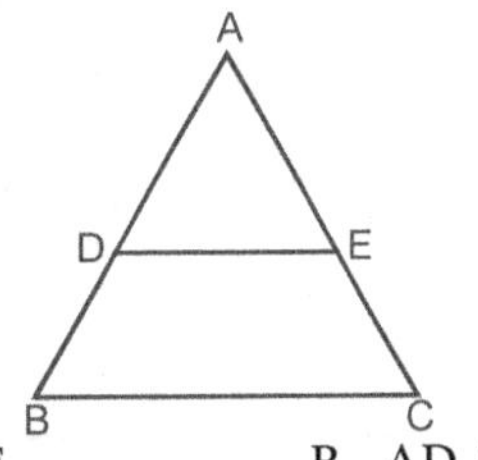

A. AD = BE
B. AD $\parallel$ BC
C. DE = $\dfrac{1}{2}$ AB
D. None of these

17. If in ΔABC, DE $\parallel$ BC and AD = 4x – 3, AE = 8x – 7, BD = 3x – 1 and CE = 5x – 3 then the value of x is :
A. 4
B. 3
C. 2
D. 1

18. If in ΔABC, DE $\parallel$ BC, AD = 2.4 cm, AE = 3.2 cm and CE = 4.8 cm then BD = ...
A. 3.6 cm
B. 6.3 cm
C. 4.8 cm
D. None of these

19. If in ΔABC, AD = 2.4 cm, AE = 3.2 cm, EC = 4.8 cm and DE $\parallel$ BC then AB = ...
A. 5.6 cm
B. 6.5 cm
C. 6 cm
D. None of these

20. In a ΔABC, AC = 5.6 cm, AD : DB = 3 : 5 and DE $\parallel$ BC then AE equals to :
A. 1.2 cm
B. 21 cm
C. 2.1 cm
D. 12 cm

21. If DE $\parallel$ BC and AD = 1.7 cm, AB = 6.8 cm and AC = 9 cm. Then length of AE is

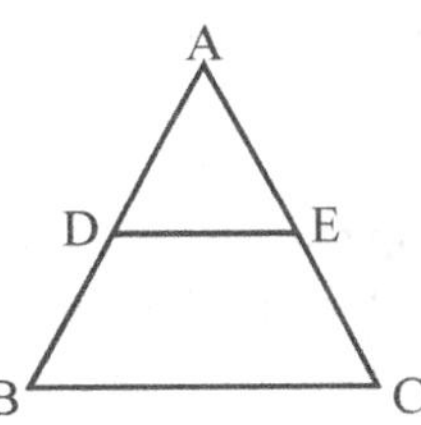

A. 2.25 cm
B. 4.5 cm
C. 3.4 cm
D. 5.1 cm

22. If AD is bisector of interior $\angle$A of a triangle ABC and AB = 10 cm, AC = 6 cm, BD = 12 cm, then CD = ?

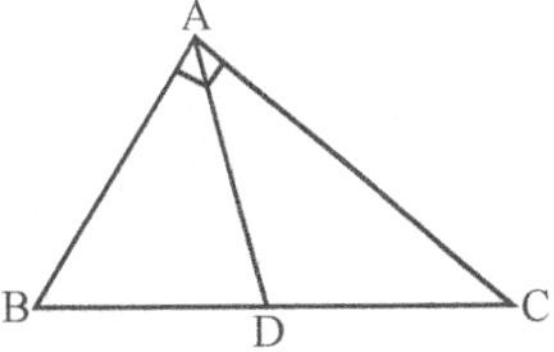

A. 8 cm
B. 7.2 cm
C. 10 cm
D. 16 cm

23. If $\angle A = 100°$, AB = AC, CD bisects, $\angle$ACB and BD bisects $\angle$ABC then values of x and y respectively are

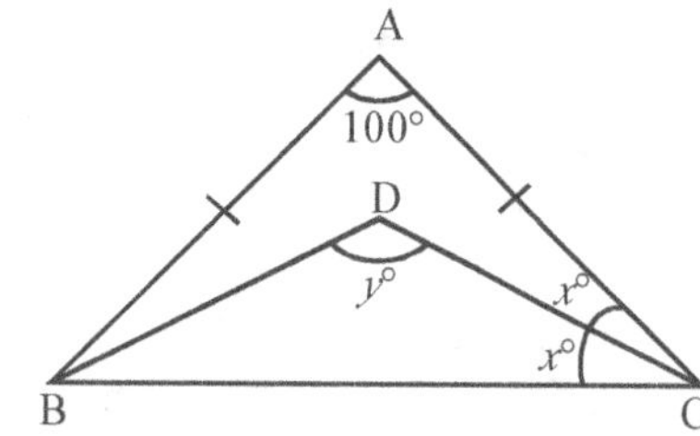

  A. 15° and 70°   B. 20° and 140°
  C. 10° and 160°   D. 20° and 125°

24. AD is a median of $\triangle$ABC. E is the mid-point of AD. BE produced meets AD at F.
The ratio AF : FC =
  A. 1 : 3   B. 2 : 1
  C. 1 : 2   D. None of the above

25. In $\triangle$ABC, AB = AC = 10 cm and BC = 16 cm. The length of median AD is
  A. 7 cm   B. 9.5 cm
  C. 10 cm   D. None of the above

26. Perimeter of a right $\triangle$ is 80 cm. Its sides could be
  A. 18 cm, 25 cm, 37 cm   B. 15 cm, 31 cm, 34 cm
  C. 16 cm, 31 cm, 33 cm   D. None of the above

27. In $\triangle$ABC, D is the midpoint of AB and E is mid point of AC. If area of $\triangle$ADE = 11 square units then area of quadrilateral $\triangle$BCE is

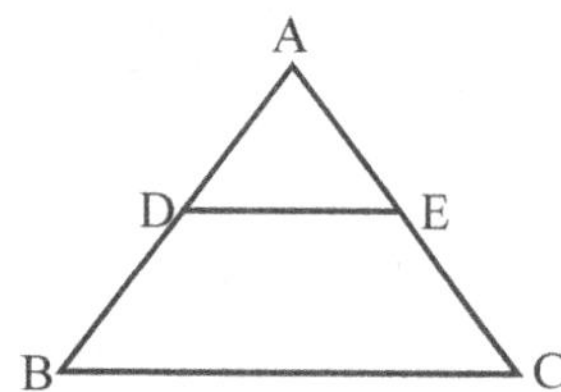

  A. 33 square units   B. 22 square units
  C. 44 square units   D. None of the above

28. In $\triangle$ABC, M is mid-point of BC. Length of AM is 9. N is a point on AM such that MN = 1unit. Distance of N from centroid of $\triangle$ABC is equal to
  A. 4 units   B. 3 units
  C. 2 units   D. 5 units

29. D, E and F are the mid-point of sides AB, BC and CA of $\triangle$ABC, then
area $\triangle$ABC : area $\triangle$DEF =

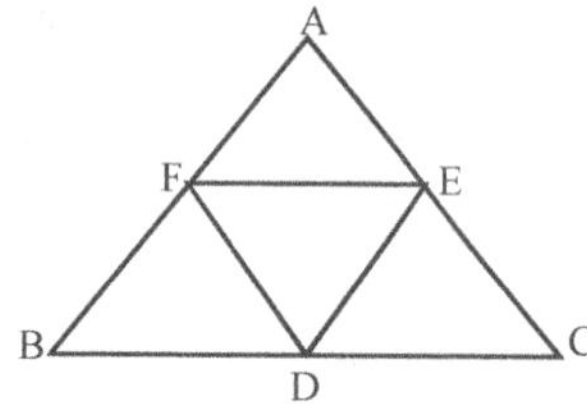

  A. 4 : 1   B. 1 : 4
  C. 2 : 1   D. 4 : 3

30. A line parallel to BC in $\triangle$ABC meets AB and AC in D and E respectively. If AD = $(4x - 3)$cm, DB = $(3x - 1)$cm, AE = $(8x - 7)$ cm, EC = $(5x - 3)$ cm, the admissible value of x is
  A. 1   B. 0
  C. 2   D. 3

31. If the ratio of the angles of a triangle is 2 : 3 : 5 then angles are:
  A. 36°, 54°, 90°   B. 18°, 36°, 126°
  C. 20°, 60°, 180°   D. 18°, 60°, 102°

32. If the two sides of $\triangle$ are perpendicular to each other then which of the following is satisfied:
  A. RHS   B. ASA
  C. SSA   D. SSS

33. If angle between two straight lines is acute angle, then angle between their prependiculars will be:
  A. acute   B. obtuse
  C. right angle   D. cannot be determined

34. If a point inside a triangle is equidistant from the three side of the triangle, then the point is:
  A. Orthocentre   B. Incentre
  C. Centroid   D. Circum centre

35. Which of the following statement is correct?
  A. Two triangles are always similar
  B. Two parallelograms are always similar
  C. Two rhombus are always similar
  D. Two squares are always similar

36. If a straight line drawn from the vertex of a triangle, parallel to the base of triangle bisect the exterior vertical angle, then the triangle is:
  A. equilateral   B. right-angled
  C. obtuse-angled   D. isosceles

37. Of all the triangles on the same base and between two parallel lines, the perimeter is least if the triangle is:
  A. isosceles   B. right-angled
  C. equilateral   D. obtuse-angled

38. The sum of length of altitudes drawn from any point inside a triangle, whose all sides are equal, to all three sides is:
  A. equal to side of triangle
  B. 1/3 of side of triangle
  C. 1/2 of side of triangle
  D. equal to perimeter of triangle

39. If the mid-points of base of a triangle is equidistant from the sides, then the triangle will be:
  A. equilateral   B. isosceles
  C. scalene   D. right angled

40. The orthocentre of an obtuse-angled triangle lies .... the triangle.
  A. outside   B. inside
  C. on smallest side of   D. None of these

ANSWERS

1	2	3	4	5	6	7	8	9	10
C	C	D	C	C	C	C	D	C	C
11	**12**	**13**	**14**	**15**	**16**	**17**	**18**	**19**	**20**
C	B	A	B	B	A	D	A	C	C
21	**22**	**23**	**24**	**25**	**26**	**27**	**28**	**29**	**30**
A	B	B	A	D	D	A	C	A	A
31	**32**	**33**	**34**	**35**	**36**	**37**	**38**	**39**	**40**
A	A	B	B	D	A	D	A	B	A

EXPLANATORY ANSWERS

10. According to eequstion

$\angle A = \angle D$ and $\dfrac{ar\,(\Delta ABC)}{ar\,(\Delta DEF)} = \dfrac{9}{25}$

Since, $AB = AC$ (given)   ....(*i*)

$DE = DF$ (given)   ....(*ii*)

Dividing (i) by (ii)

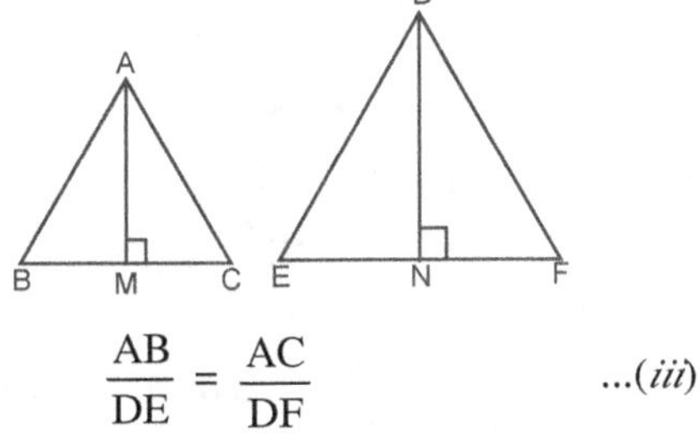

$\dfrac{AB}{DE} = \dfrac{AC}{DF}$ ...(*iii*)

Hence, $\Delta ABC \sim \Delta DEF$

[By SAS criterion of similar Δs]

In ΔAMC and ΔDNF

$\angle AMC = \angle DNF = 90°$

$\angle C = \angle F$ (because $\Delta ABC \sim \Delta DEF$)

$\therefore\ \angle AMC \sim DNF$ (By AA Criterion of similar Δs)

$\therefore\quad \dfrac{AC}{DF} = \dfrac{AM}{DN}$

and, $\dfrac{ar\,(\Delta ABC)}{ar\,(DEF)} = \dfrac{AC^2}{DF^2} = \dfrac{AM^2}{DN^2}$

$\therefore\quad \dfrac{AM^2}{DN^2} = \dfrac{9}{25}$

$\Rightarrow\quad \dfrac{AM}{DN} = \dfrac{3}{5}$

Hence required ratio = 3 : 5

11. $\dfrac{DG}{EG} = \dfrac{2}{3}\ \therefore\ \dfrac{DG}{DE} = \dfrac{2}{2+3} = \dfrac{2}{5}$

In Δ DGH and Δ DEF,

$\angle D = \angle D$

$\angle DGH = \angle DEF$

(Since, GH ∥ EF and DE is the transversal among corresponding angles)

$\therefore\quad \Delta DGH \sim \Delta DEF$

(By AA criterion of similar triangles)

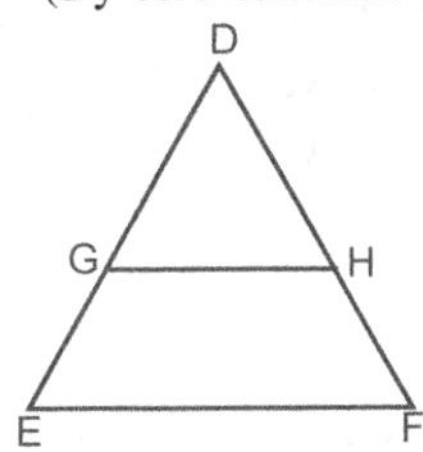

$\therefore\quad \dfrac{ar\,(\Delta DGH)}{ar\,(\Delta DEF)} = \dfrac{DG^2}{DE^2} = \dfrac{2^2}{5^2} = \dfrac{4}{25}$

12. Since, ratio of area of two similar traingles = ratio of square of corresponding sides

ratio of sides = 5 : 11

$\therefore$ ratio of their areas $= (5)^2 : (11)^2 = 25 : 121$.

13. From question,

$ar(\Delta ADE) = 9\ ar(\Delta ABC)$

or, $\dfrac{ar(\Delta ABC)}{ar(\Delta ADE)} = \dfrac{1}{9} = \dfrac{BC^2}{DE^2}$

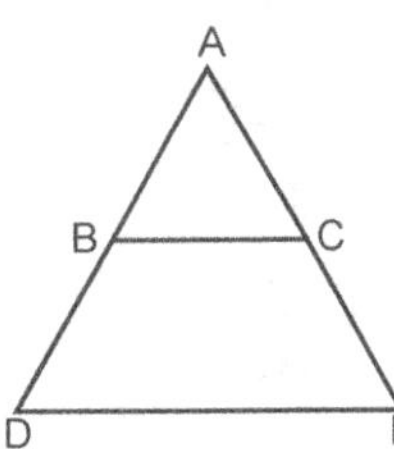

Hence, $\dfrac{BC}{DE} = \sqrt{\dfrac{1}{9}} = \dfrac{1}{3}$

14. From question,

In ΔABC, D is the mid-point of AB and DE is drawn parallel to BC and it meets at E on AC.

Since,   DE ∥ BC   (By B.P. Theorem)

$\dfrac{AD}{DB} = \dfrac{AE}{EC}$ ...(*i*)

also, $AD = DB$ ($\because$ D is mid-point)

$\therefore\quad \dfrac{AD}{DB} = 1$

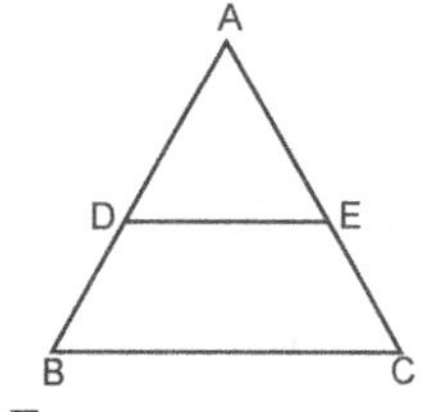

Now, $\dfrac{AE}{EC} = 1$ (From ...(i))

$\Rightarrow \quad AE = EC$

Hence, the line bisects the third line

15. According to questions

$$\angle B = \angle C \text{ (given)}$$

$\Rightarrow \quad AB = AC$ (i)

and, $BD = CE$ (ii)

Subtracting (ii) from (i)

$$AB - BD = AC - CE$$

$\Rightarrow \quad AD = AE$ (iii)

Dividing (iii) by (ii)

$$\frac{AD}{BD} = \frac{AE}{CE}$$

$\therefore$ DE || BC [By converse of BP Theorem]

Hence, option (B) is true.

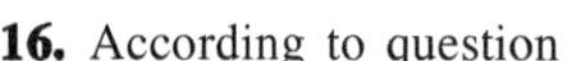

16. According to question

$$\angle A = \angle B$$

$\therefore \quad AC = BC$

[Sides opposite to equal angles of a triangle)

In $\triangle ABC$, DE || AB (given)

$\therefore \quad \dfrac{CD}{AD} = \dfrac{CE}{EB}$ (By B.P. Theorem)

or, $\dfrac{CD}{AD} + 1 = \dfrac{CE}{EB} + 1$ (Adding 1 to both sides)

or, $\dfrac{CD + AD}{AD} = \dfrac{CE + EB}{EB}$

or, $\dfrac{AC}{AD} = \dfrac{BC}{EB}$

or, $\dfrac{AC}{AD} = \dfrac{AC}{BE}$

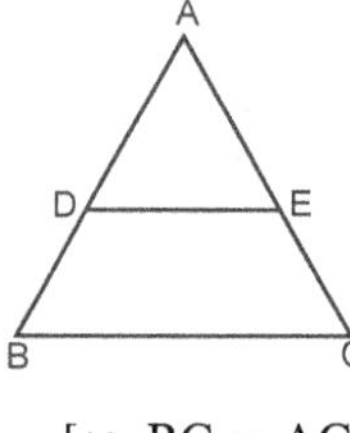

$[\because BC = AC]$

or, $\dfrac{1}{AD} = \dfrac{1}{BE}$; $AD = BE$

Hence, option (A) is true.

17. According to equestion,

$$DE || BC$$

$\therefore \quad \dfrac{AD}{BD} = \dfrac{AE}{CE}$

(By B.P. Theorem)

or, $\dfrac{4x-3}{3x-1} = \dfrac{8x-7}{5x-3}$

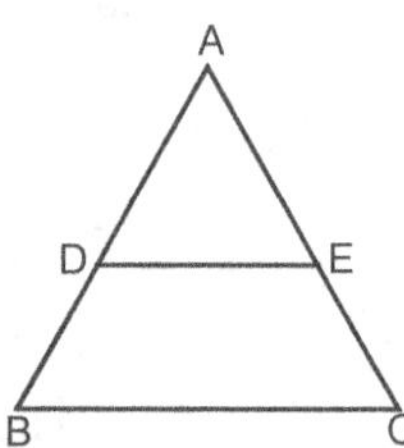

or, $24x^2 - 29x + 7 = 20x^2 - 27x + 9$

or, $4x^2 - 2x - 2 = 0$

or, $2x^2 - x - 1 = 0$

Again, $2x^2 - x - 1 = 0$

or, $2x^2 - 2x + 1 = 0$

or, $2x(x - 1) + 1\,(x - 1) = 0$

or, $(2x + 1)\,(x - 1) = 0$

$\therefore \quad x = -\dfrac{1}{2}, 1$

Hence obtion (D) is correct answer

18. As we know,

$$\frac{AD}{BD} = \frac{AE}{CE} \quad \text{(By B.P. Theorem)}$$

Let, $BD = x$

$\therefore \quad \dfrac{2.4}{x} = \dfrac{3.2}{4.8}$

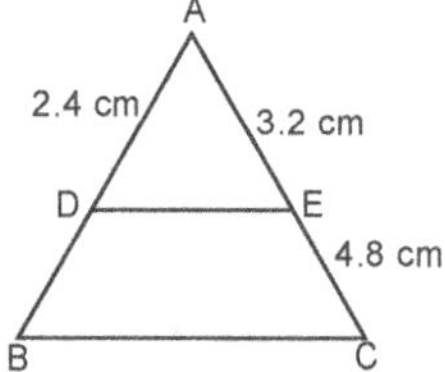

$\Rightarrow \quad 3.2x = 2.4 \times 4.8$

$\therefore \quad x = \dfrac{2.4 \times 4.8}{3.2} = 3.6$ cm.

19. $\dfrac{AD}{BD} = \dfrac{AE}{CE}$ (By B.P. Theorem)

$\therefore \quad \dfrac{2.4}{BD} = \dfrac{3.2}{4.8}$

$\Rightarrow \quad 3.2\,BD = 2.4 \times 4.8$

$\therefore \quad BD = \dfrac{2.4 \times 4.8}{3.2} = 3.6$ cm

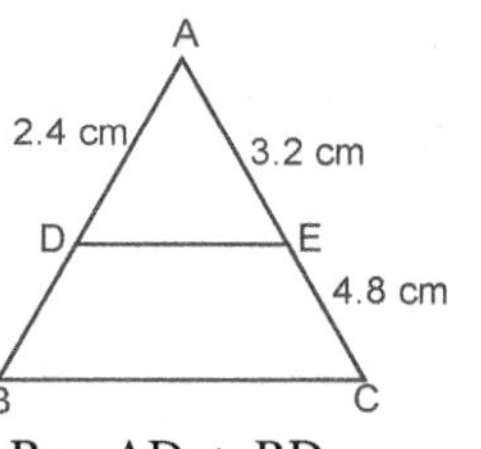

$\therefore \quad AB = AD + BD$

$\qquad\qquad = 2.4 + 3.6 = 6$ cm.

20. we know that,

$$\frac{AD}{AB} = \frac{AE}{AC}$$

$\Rightarrow \quad \dfrac{3}{8} = \dfrac{AE}{5.6}$

$\Rightarrow \quad AE = \dfrac{5.6 \times 3}{8} = 2.1$ cm.

21. $\dfrac{AD}{AB} = \dfrac{AE}{AC} \Rightarrow \dfrac{1.7}{6.8} = \dfrac{AE}{9} \Rightarrow AE = 2.25$ cm

22. $\dfrac{AB}{AC}=\dfrac{BD}{DC} \Rightarrow \dfrac{10}{6}=\dfrac{12}{CD}$

$\Rightarrow CD=7.2\,cm.$

23. $2x+2x+100=180° \Rightarrow x=20°$

In $\Delta BDC;$

$x+x+y=180° \Rightarrow y=140°$

24. Draw $DP\parallel BF.$

F is mid-point of AP and P is mid-point of FC.

Hence, $AF=\dfrac{1}{3}AC.$

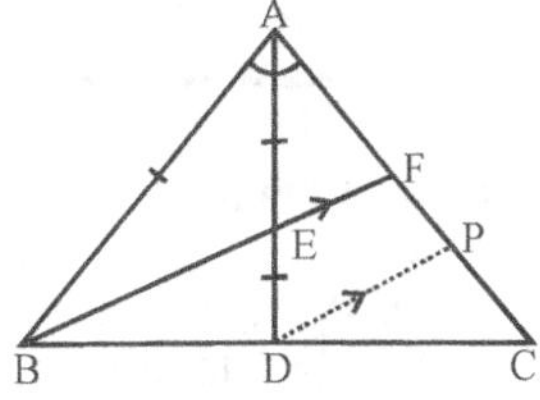

25. ΔABC is isosceles with AB = AC

Hence, AD is also the altitude of the triangle.

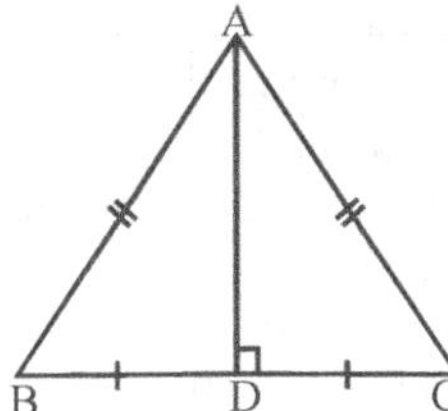

$DC=\dfrac{1}{2}\times16=8\,cm;$

AC = 10 cm

Thus, $AD=\sqrt{10^2-8^2}\;=6\,cm.$

26. $18^2+25^2\neq37^2;\;\;15^2+31^2\neq34^2$

$16^2+31^2\neq33^2$

27. D and E are mid-points of sides AB and AC respectively.

Hence, $ar\,\Delta ADE=\dfrac{1}{4}ar\,\Delta ABC$

$\Rightarrow\;\;ar\,\Delta ABC=44$ square units.

$ar\,\square DBCE=ar\,\Delta ABC-ar\,\Delta ADE.$

$=44-11=33\,$square units.

28. 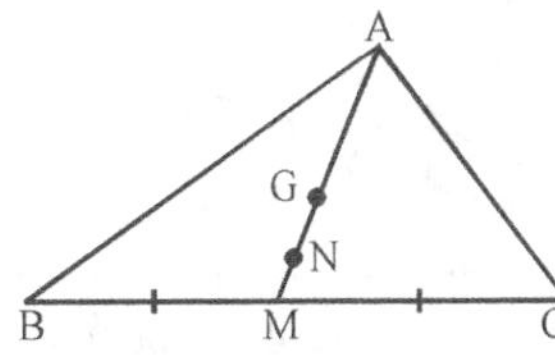

AM = 9 units

G is centroid of ΔABC

Hence, $AG=\dfrac{2}{3}\times9$ units $=6$ units

Hence, GM = 3 units

GN = 3 – 1 = 2 units

29. $ar\,\Delta DEF=\dfrac{1}{4}ar\,\Delta ABC \Rightarrow \dfrac{ar\,\Delta ABC}{ar\,\Delta DEF}=\dfrac{4}{1}$

30. 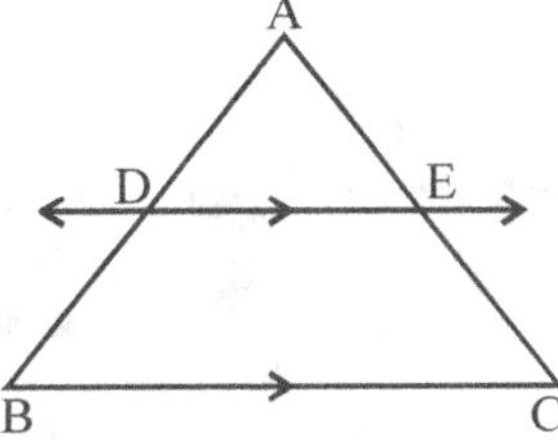

DE $\parallel$ BC.

Thus, $\dfrac{AD}{DB}=\dfrac{AC}{EC}$

$\Rightarrow\dfrac{4x-3}{3x-6}=\dfrac{8x-7}{5x-3}$

$\Rightarrow 20x^2-27x+9\;=24x^2-29x+7$

$\Rightarrow 4x^2-2x-2\;=0$

$\Rightarrow 2x^2-x-1\;=0$

$\Rightarrow (2x+1)(x-1)\;=0$

Thus, $x=1.$

31. Let the angles are $2x$, $3x$ and $5x$

$\therefore\;\;2x+3x+5x=180°$

[Sum of angles of a triangle]

or, $\quad\;\;10x=180°$

$\therefore\qquad\quad x=18°$

$2x=36°$

Hence, angles are $3x=54°$

$5x=90°$

33. According to figure,

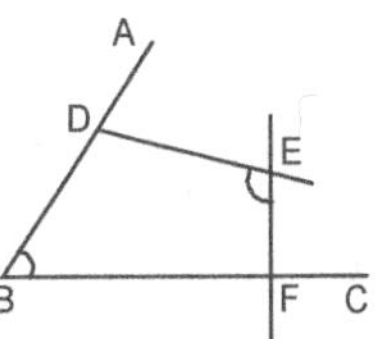

$\angle EDB=\angle EFB=90°$

$\because\angle EDB+\angle DBF+\angle EFB+\angle FED=360°$

or, $\quad90°+\angle DBF+90°+\angle FED=360°$

or, $\qquad\qquad\angle DBF+\angle FED=180°$

According to question,

$\quad\angle DBF$ is acute angle

$\therefore\;\angle FED$ is obtuse angle

★ ★ ★

9

Geometry : Circle & Tangents

A circle is a set of those points in a plane that are at a given constant distance from a given fixed point in the plane. The fixed point is called the **centre of the circle** and the constant distance of every point on the circle from its centre of called the **radius of the circle**.

Things to Remember

1. Locus of a point moving in a plane such that its distance from a fixed point in the same plane remains constant is called a circle.

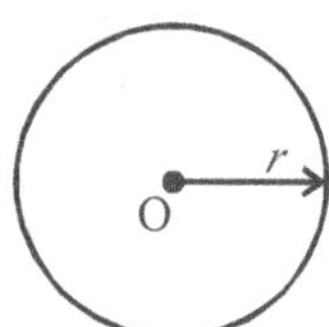

2. The fixed point O is called its centre and the constant distance r is called the radius.
3. The path traced by the moving point as described above is called the circumference of the circle.
4. The part of the plane containing the circle that consists the circle and its interior is called the circular region.

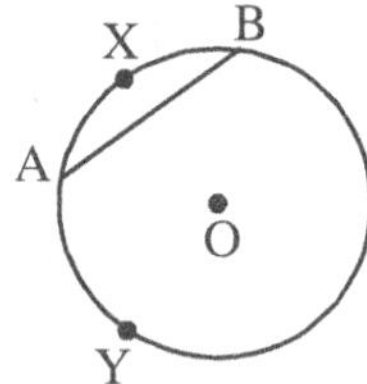

5. Line segment joining any two points on the circumference is called a chord of the circle. In the above figure AB is a chord of the circle.

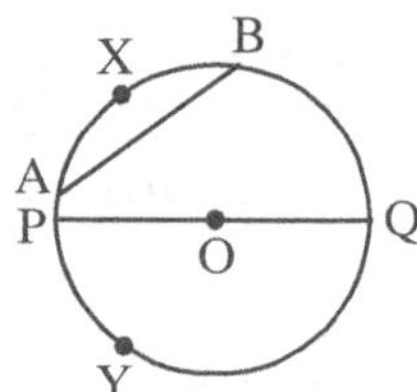

6. The chord passing through the centre of the circle is called its diameter.
   In the above figure PQ is a diameter of the circle.
7. Diameter is the longest chord of the circle.
8. Any fraction of the circumference is called an arc of the circle.
9. The remaining part of the circumference is called the alternate segment of the circle with respect to the arc.
10. An arc of a circle smaller in length than the semicircle is called a minor arc. In the above figure arc AXB is a minor arc.
11. An arc of a circle more in length than the semicircle is called a major arc. In the above figure arc AYB is a major arc.

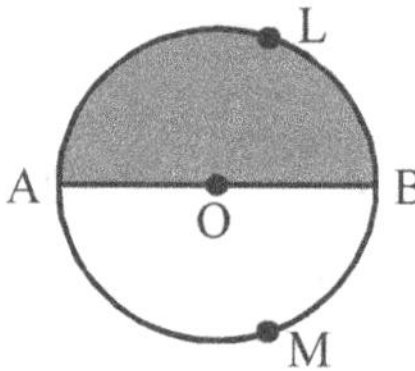

12. Diameter of a circle divides its circumference into two equal arcs. Each of them is called a semicircle.
13. The part of the plane containing the semicircle that consists the semi-circle, the enclosing diameter and its interior is called the semicircular region. In the above figure region ALB and region BMA are semicircular regions.

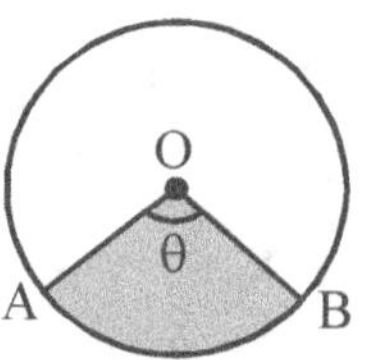

14. The angle formed by joining the end points of an arc to the centre of the circle is said to be the angle subtended by an arc at the centre of the circle. In the above figure, θ is the degree measure of arc AB.

15. The part of the plane containing the circle that consists of the arc enclosing radii and its interior is called the sector of the circle. In the above figure AOB is sector of the circle.

16. A chord of the circle other than a diameter divides the circular region into two unequal parts. Each of these parts is called a segment. The larger part is called the major segment and the smaller is called the minor segment.

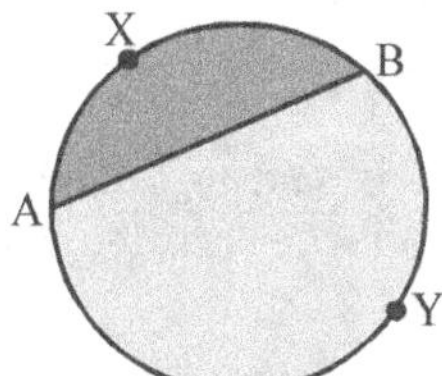

In the above figure segment AXB is a minor segment and segment BYA is the major segment.

17. Two circles in a plane are said to be concentric if they have same centre but different radii.

18. The chord formed by joining the end points of an arc of a circle is called its corresponding chord.

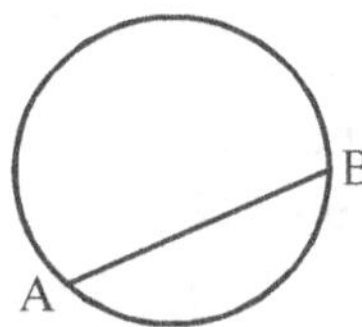

In the given figures chord AB is the corresponding chord of arc AB.

Important Theorems on Circles

1.

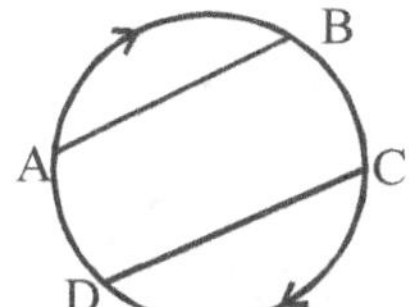

  (*a*) If two arcs of a circle are equal then their corresponding chords are also equal.

$$AB = CD \Leftrightarrow \text{arc} AB = \text{arc} CD.$$

  (*b*) If two chords of a circle are equal then their corresponding arcs are also equal.

2.

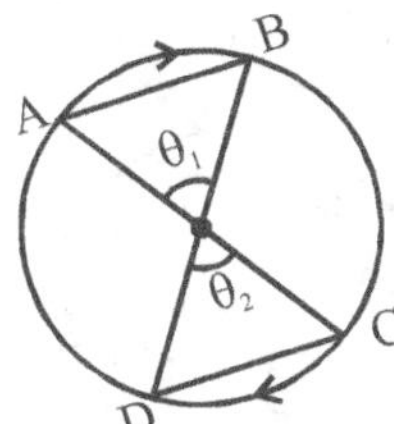

  (*a*) If two chords of a circle are equal then they subtend equal angles at the centre of the circle.

  (*b*) If two chords of a circle subtend equal angles at the centre of a circle then they are equal

$$AB = CD \Leftrightarrow \theta_1 = \theta_2$$

3.

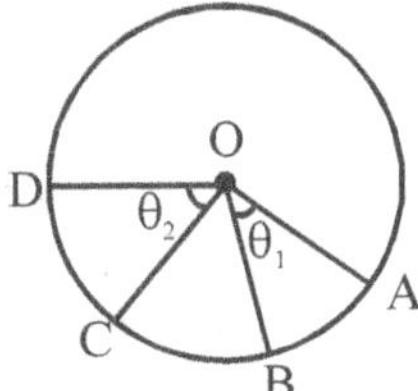

  (*a*) If two arcs of a circle have same degree measure then they are equal.

$$\text{arc } AB = \text{arc } CD \Leftrightarrow \theta_1 = \theta_2$$

  (*b*) If two arcs of a circle are equal then their degree measures are also equal.

4.

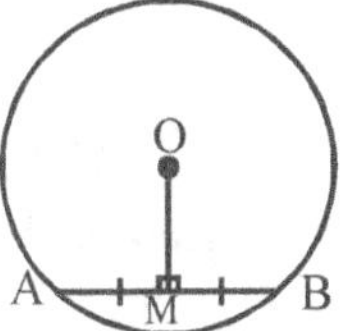

  (*a*) Perpendicular to a chord from the centre of the circle bisects the chord.

  (*b*) Line segment joining the centre of the circle to the mid point of the chord is perpendicular to the chord.

$$OM \perp AB \Leftrightarrow M \text{ is the mid point of } AB.$$

5.

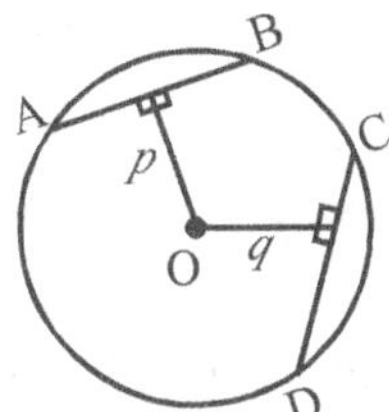

  (*a*) If two chords of a circle are equidistant from the centre of the circle, they are equal.

  (*b*) If two chords of a circle are equal then they are equidistant from the centre of the circle

$$AB = CD \Leftrightarrow p = q$$

6.

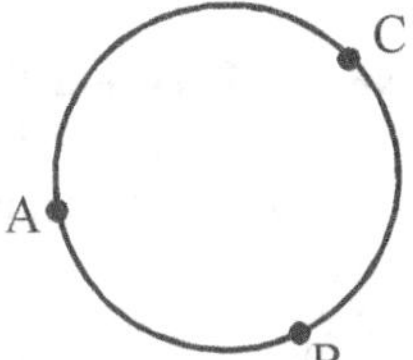

Through any three non collinear points, passes one and only one circle. A, B and C are three non-collinear points in a plane then one and only one circle passes through them.

7. Perpendicular bisector of a chord of a circle passes through the centre of the circle.

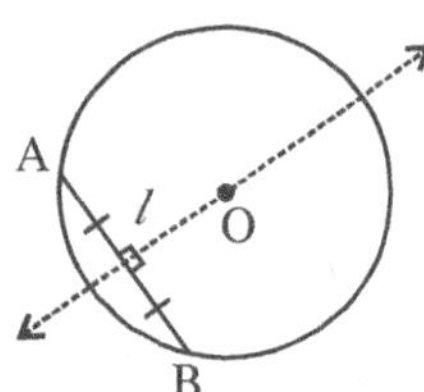

l is the $\perp$ bisector of AB

$\Leftrightarrow$ l passes through O.

8.

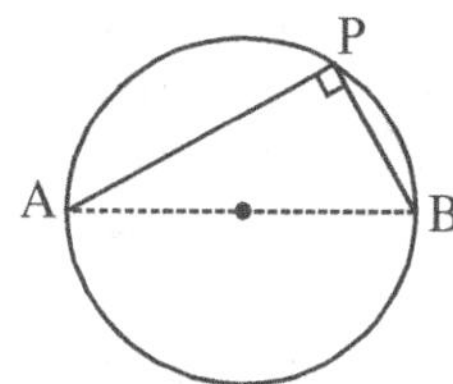

(*a*) **Theorem of Thales:** Angle in a semicircle is a right angle.

(*b*) If an arc subtends a right angle at any point in its alternate segment then it is a semi-circle.

$\overarc{APB}$ is a semicircle $\Leftrightarrow$ $\angle APB = 90°$

9. Angles in the same segment of a circle are equal

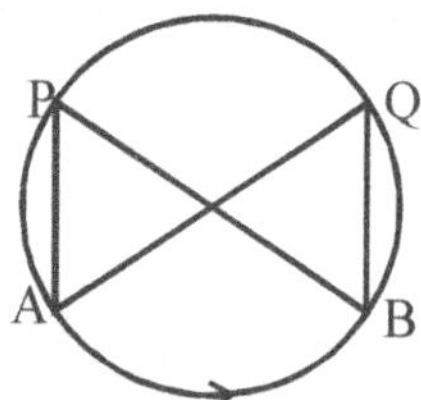

In the above figure $\angle APB = \angle AQB$

10.

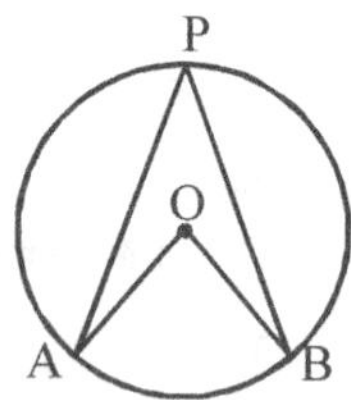

Degree Measure Theorem : Degree measure of an arc is twice the angle subtended by it at any point on the alternate segment of the circle with respect to the arc.

In the above figure $\angle AOB = 2\angle APB$

11. If a line segment joining two points subtends equal angles at two other points on same side of the line containing the two points then the four points are concyclic.

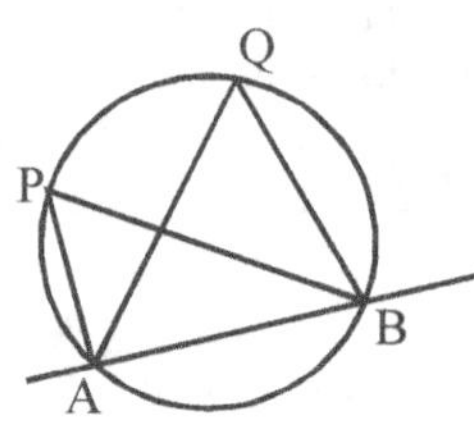

In the above figure $\angle APB = \angle AQB$, then A, B, Q and P are concylic.

Definition

A quadrilateral is said to be cyclic if all of its four vertices lie on the circle, ABCD is a cyclic quadrilateral.

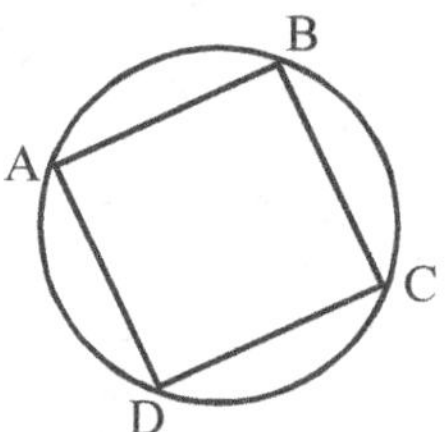

12. If in a quadrilateral the pair of opposite angles is supplementary then the quadrilateral is cyclic.

In the above figure

$\angle A + \angle C = 180°$ or $\angle B + \angle D = 180°$.

$\Rightarrow$ ABCD is cyclic quadrilateral.

13. Sum of each pair of opposite angles of a cyclic quadrilateral is 180°.

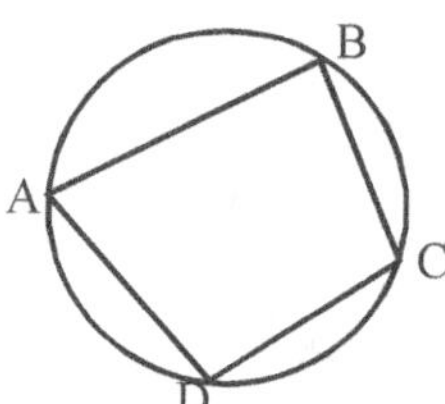

In the above figure

ABCD is cyclic quadrilateral

$\Rightarrow$ $\angle A + \angle C = 180°$ and $\angle B + \angle D = 180°$.

14. Exterior angle of a cyclic quadrilateral is equal to its opposite interior angle.

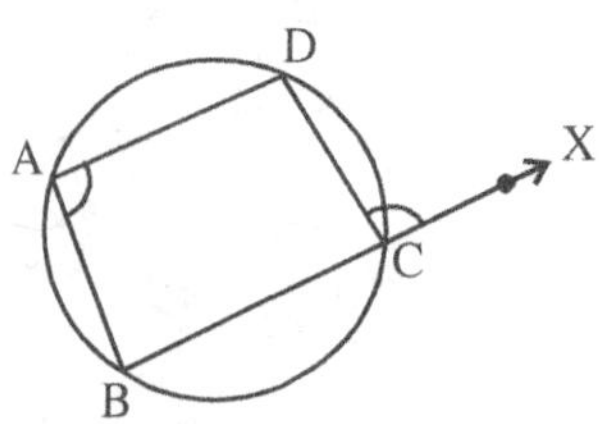

In the above figure $\angle DCX = \angle A$

MULTIPLE CHOICE QUESTIONS

1. AB and CD are two parallel chords of a circle such that AB = 5 cm and CD = 11 cm. If distance between them is 3 cm then radius of the circle is

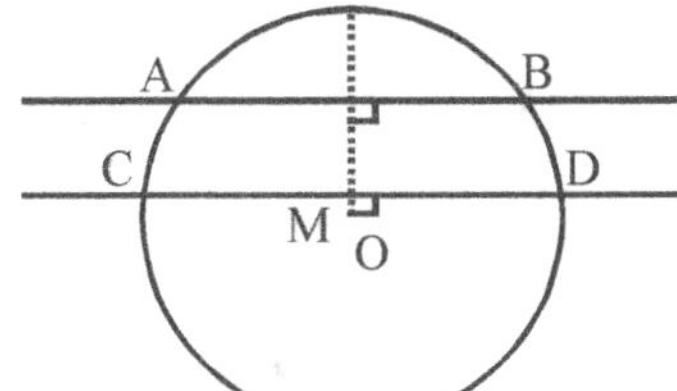

A. $2\sqrt{146}$ cm

B. $\sqrt{146}$ cm

C. $\dfrac{\sqrt{146}}{2}$ cm

D. None of these

2. The maximum number of common tangents to any pair of circles in the same plane is :
A. 4   B. 5
C. 2   D. 3

3. Find the length of a chord which is at a distance of 3 cm from the centre of a circle of radius 5 cm.
A. 2 cm   B. 6 cm
C. 8 cm   D. 10 cm

4. If AB and AC are two chords of a circle of radius 5 cm such that AB = AC = $4\sqrt{5}$ cm then the length of the chord BC is :
A. 8 cm   B. 8.4 cm
C. 9 cm   D. None of these

5. In the given figure AB is the diameter of the circle, PM bisects ∠APB then the measure of ∠ABM is :

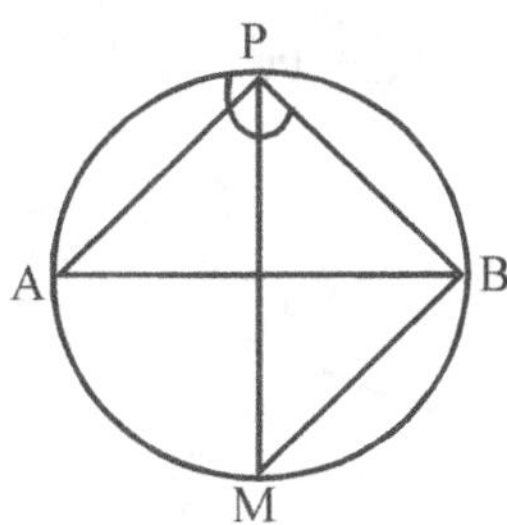

A. 45°   B. 30°
C. 15°   D. 60°

6. Determine the value of x in the figure given below.

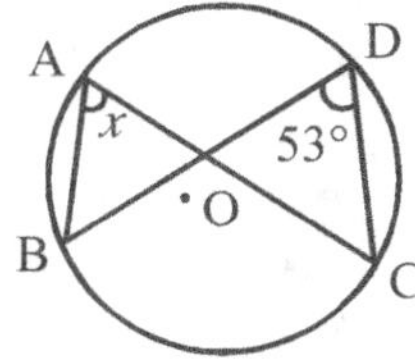

A. 53°   B. 106°
C. 26.5°   D. 100°

7. Determine the value of x in the figure given below.

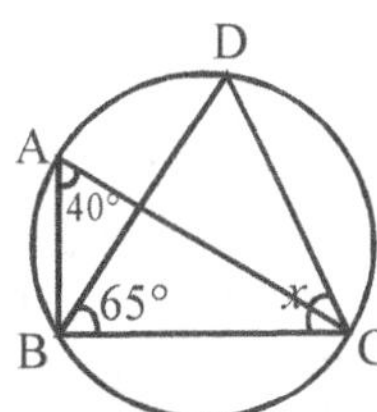

A. 40°   B. 75°
C. 65°   D. 105°

8. Determine the value of x in the figure given below.

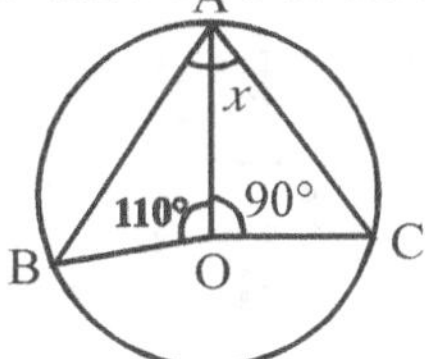

A. 80°   B. 100°
C. 90°   D. 110°

9. PQ is a diameter and PQRS is a cyclic quadrilateral. If ∠PSR = 150°, then measure of ∠RPQ is :

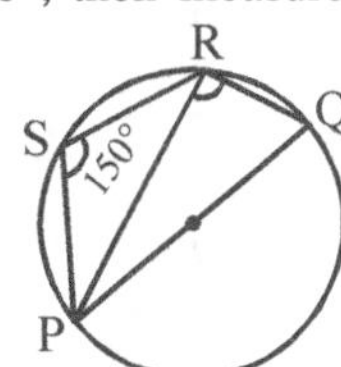

A. 90º   B. 60º
C. 30º   D. None of these

10. Determine the value of x in the figure given below.

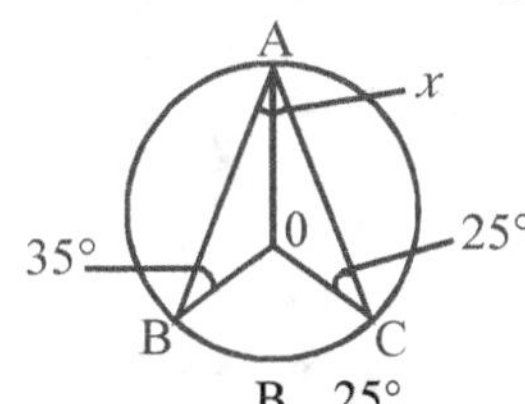

A. 35°   B. 25°
C. 30°   D. 60°

11. Determine the value of x in the figure given below.

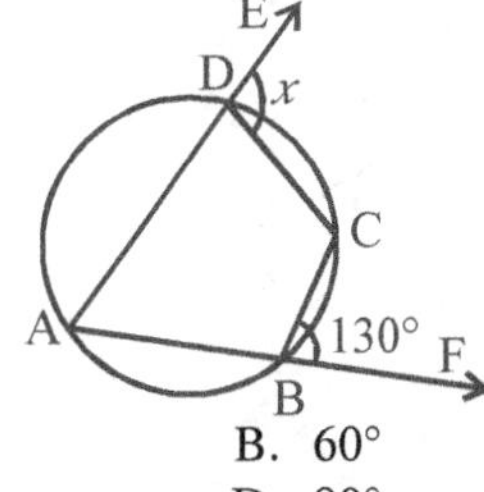

A. 65°   B. 60°
C. 50°   D. 80°

12. Chords AB and CD of a circle meet inside the circle at D. If PA = 4 cm, AB = 7 cm and PD = 6 cm then length of CD is :

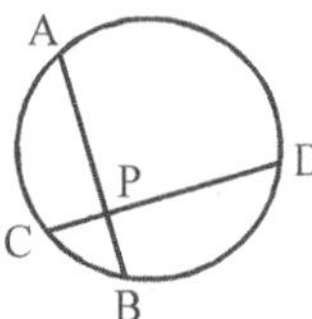

A. 8 cm   B. 6 cm
C. 2 cm   D. None of these

13. Chords AB and CD of a circle when product meet out side the circle at P, If AB = 4 cm; BP = 3 cm and CP = 14 cm then the length of CD is

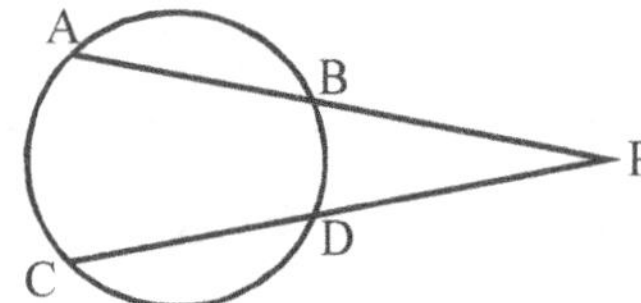

A. 3 cm   B. 4.5 cm
C. 6 cm   D. None of these

14. AB and CD are two parallel chords of circle such that AB = 10 cm and CD = 24 cm. If LM = 17 cm then the diameter of the circle is

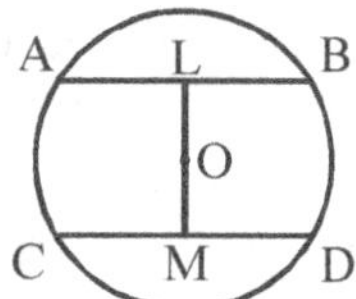

A. 13 cm   B. 26 cm
C. 14 cm   D. None of these

15. In the given figure determine the value of x.

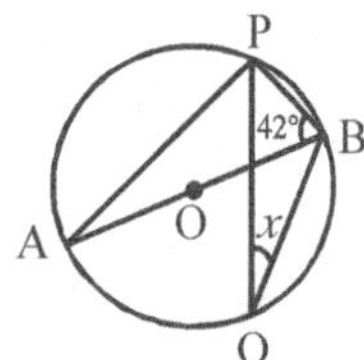

A. 48°   B. 42°
C. 60°   D. 38°

16. In the given figure determine the value of x.

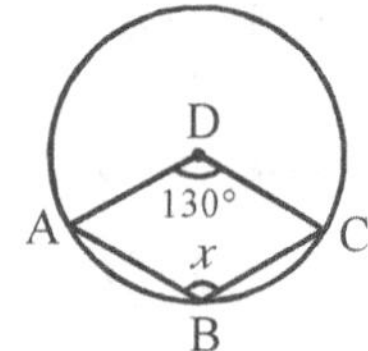

A. 90°   B. 115°
C. 130°   D. 65°

17. Find x

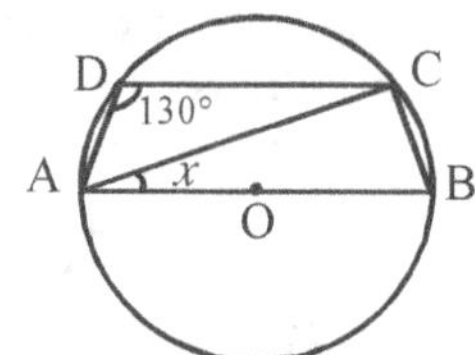

A. 40°   B. 50°
C. 30°   D. 60°

18. If O is the centre of the circle and ΔAOB is an equilateral triangle, then the measure of ΔACB is

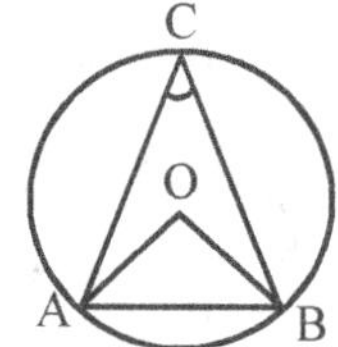

A. 60°   B. 30°
C. 90°   D. 75°

19. Find x if AO = 8.1 cm, BO = 5 cm, OC = 9 cm and OD = x cm.

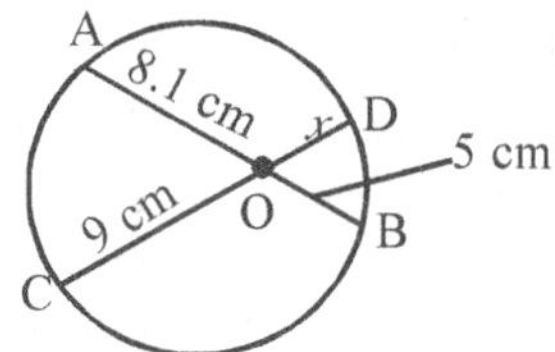

A. 4.1 cm   B. 4.1 cm
C. 4.2 cm   D. 4.5 cm

20. Find x if PA = 7 cm, PC = 6 cm, AB = 9 cm and CD = x

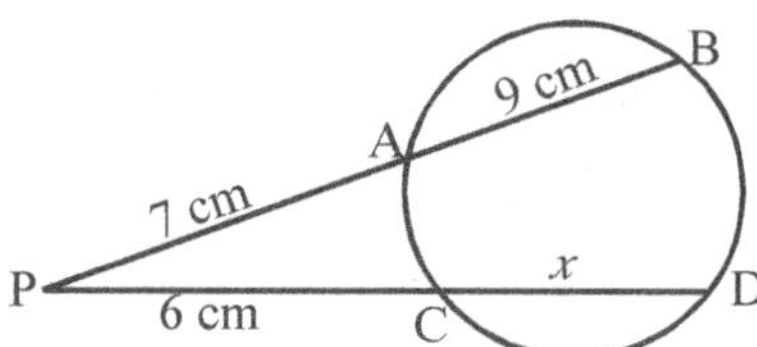

A. 12.0 cm
B. 12.6 cm
C. 12.66 cm
D. 12.67 cm

ANSWERS

1	2	3	4	5	6	7	8	9	10
C	A	C	A	A	A	B	A	B	D

11	12	13	14	15	16	17	18	19	20
C	C	D	B	D	B	A	B	D	C

EXPLANATORY ANSWERS

1. Let OM = x

Then $x^2 + \left(\dfrac{11}{2}\right)^2 = r^2$

and $(x+3)^2 + \left(\dfrac{5}{2}\right)^2 = r^2$

Then, $x^2 + 6x + 9 + \dfrac{25}{4} = x^2 + \dfrac{121}{4}$

$\Rightarrow 6x = 15$

$\Rightarrow \quad x = 2.5$ cm

Thus, $r^2 = (2.5)^2 + \dfrac{121}{4} = \dfrac{146}{4}$

$\Rightarrow r = \dfrac{\sqrt{146}}{2}$ cm

3. Length of chord = $2.\sqrt{5^2 - 3^2} = 8$ cm.

4. Let OP = x

and BP = y

Then $x^2 + y^2 = 25$

and $(5+x)^2 + y^2 = 80$

Solving these two, we get

$y = $ BP = 4 cm

Thus, BC = 8 cm.

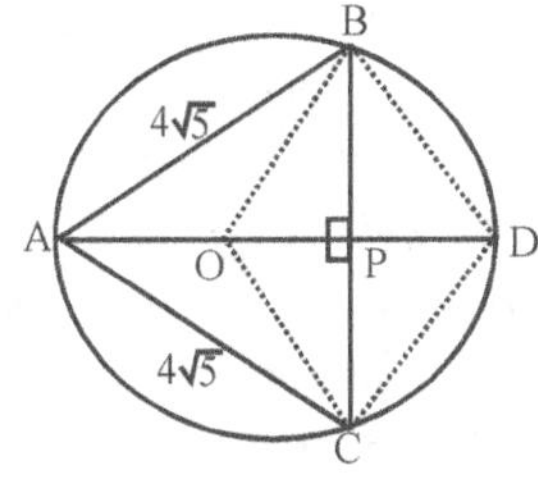

5. $\angle ABM = \angle APM = \dfrac{1}{2}\angle APB = \dfrac{1}{2} \times 90° = 45°$

6. As angle in the same segment are equal.
$x = 53°$

7. $x + 65° + 40° = 180°$

$x = 75°$

8. $x = \dfrac{1}{2}\left[(180° - 110°) + (180° - 90°)\right]$

$= \dfrac{1}{2}(70° + 90°) = 80°$

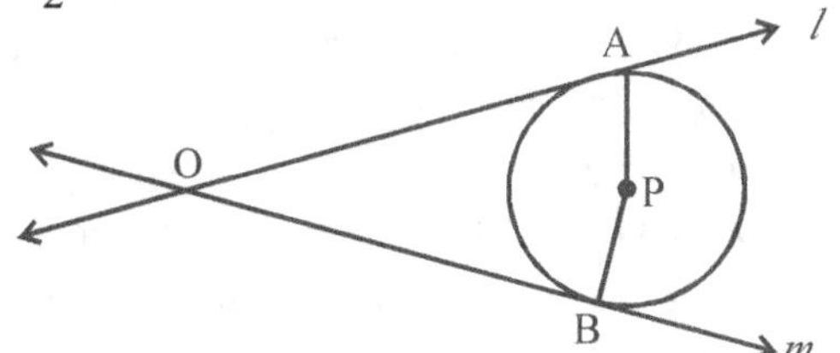

Let P be the centre of a circle touching l and m. Clearly, AP = BP.

Hence, P lies on angle bisector of $\angle AOB$. Hence, locus of P will be the angle bisectors of the angles formed by these intersecting lines.

9. $\angle PQR = 180° - 150° = 30°$

$\angle PRQ = 90°$ (Angle of a semicircle)

$\angle RPQ + 90° + 30° = 180°$

$\Rightarrow \angle RPQ = 60°$

10. $\angle OAB = \angle OBA (\because OA = OB)$

$\angle OAB = 35°$

Similarly, $\angle AOC = 25°$

$\therefore \quad \angle x = 35° + 25° = 60°$

12. Use $PA \times PB = PC \times PD$

$4 \times (7 - 4) = 6 \times PC$

$\Rightarrow \quad PC = 2$ cm

$CD = PC + PD = 2 + 6 = 8$ cm.

13. Use $PA \times PB = PC \times PD$

$\Rightarrow (4+3) \times 3 = 14 \times PD \quad \Rightarrow PD = 1.5$ cm

$\Rightarrow CD = PC - PD = 14 - 1.5 = 12.5$ cm.

14. Let OL = x. Then $OM(17 - x)$

Also LB = 5 cm, MD = 12 cm.

Then $x^2 + 25 = r^2$

and $(17 - x)^2 + 144 = r^2$

Solving these we get

$x = 12$ cm and $r = 13$ cm

Thus, diameter = $2 \times 13 = 26$ cm.

15. $x + 42° + 90° = 180°$

$\Rightarrow \quad x = 48°$

16. O is fixed

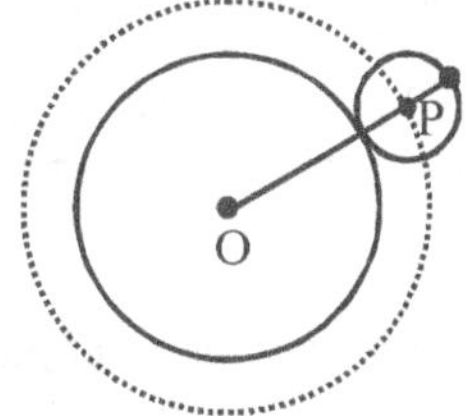

$OP = 4 + 3 = 7$ cm

As P moves a circle is traced out shown clotted.

18. $\angle ACB = \dfrac{1}{2}\angle AOB = \dfrac{1}{2} \times 60° = 30°$

PART–B: TANGENTS TO A CIRCLE

Secant

A line which interesects a circle in two distinct points is called a **secant** of the circle. In the fig. the line *l* intersects the circle in two distinct points A and B. The line *l* is a secant to the circle.

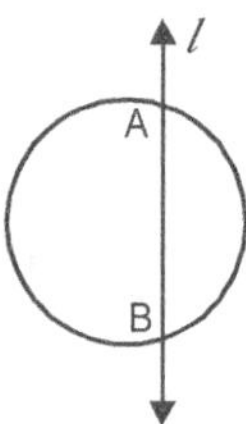

Tanget

A tangent to a circle is a line that intersects the circle at exactly one point.

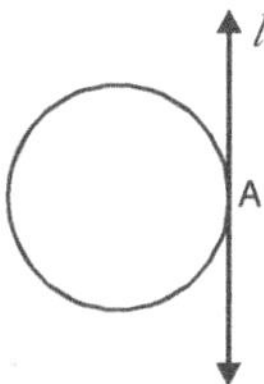

The point at which it meets the circle is called its point of contact and the line (tangent) is said to touch the circle at this point. In the figure, the line *l* meets the circle at only point A. Here A is the point of contact.

SOME IMPORTANT THEOREMS ON TANGENT

Theorem 1: *A tangent to a circle is perpendicular to the radius throught the point of contact.*

Given: A tangent AB to a circle C(O, *r*) with the point P as its point of contact.

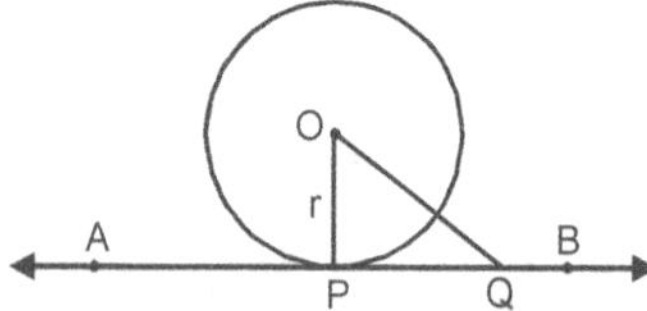

To prove: OP ⊥ AB.

Construction: Let Q be any point other that P, an AB. join OQ.

Proof: ∵ Q is a point on the tangent AB other than the point of contact P.

∴ Q lies in the exterior of the circle.

∴ OQ > OP

i.e., OP < OQ

Thus, of all the segments that can be drawn from the centre O to any point on the line AB, OP is the shortest.

We know that the shortest segment that can be drawn from a given point to a given line perpendicular from the given point to the given line.

Hence OP ⊥ AB.

Theorem 2: (Converse of theorem 1)

A line drawn through the end of a radius and perpendicular on it is tangent to the circle.

Given: A radius OP of a circle C(O, *r*) and a line APB perpendicular to OP.

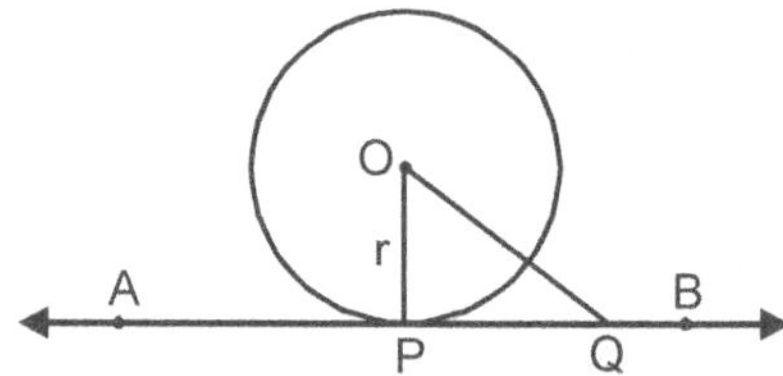

To prove: AB is the tangent to the circle at A.

Proof: Take a point Q, different from P, on line AB, since OP ⊥ AB, OQ > OP.

∴ The point Q lies outside the circle (since OP is the shortest line segment from O to AB).

Thus every point on the line AB, other P, lies outside the circle and therefore AB meets the circle only at the point P.

Hence AB is a tangent to the circle.

Theorem 3: *The lengths of the two tangents drawn from an external point to a circle are equal.*

Given: A is an external point to the circle C(O, r). AP and AQ are two tangent segments from A to the circle.

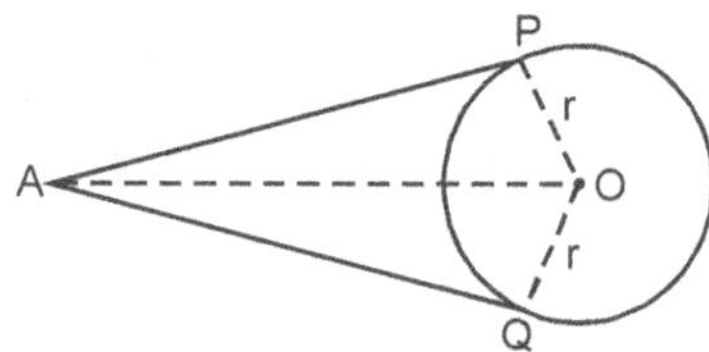

To prove: AP = AQ.

Construction: Draw line segments AP, OP and OQ.

Proof: A tangent to a circle is perpendicular to the radius through the point of contact.

∴ ∠OPA = ∠OQA = 90°

Now in right Δs OPA and OQA,

OP = OQ   [each = r]

OA = OA   [common]

∴ ΔOPA ≅ ΔOQA   [by RHS congruence rule]

∴ AP = AQ   [c.p.c.t.]

Ex. 1 : In Fig. chords AB and CD of the circle intersect at O. AO = 5 cm, BO = 3 cm and CO = 2.5 cm. Determine the length of DO.

Sol. Chorde AB and CD of the circle intersect each other at a point O lying inside

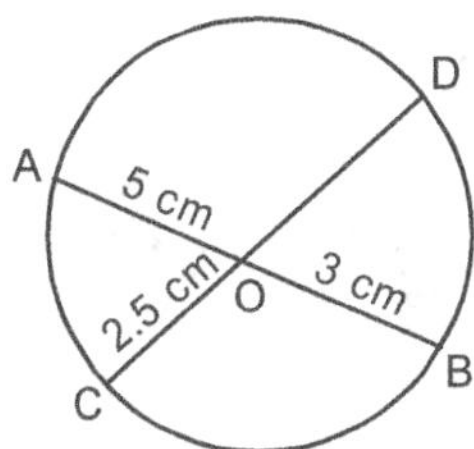

$\therefore$ OA × OB = OC × PD

[Rectangle formed by two parts of one chord is equal in area to the rectangle formed by the two parts for the other]

$\Rightarrow$ 5 × 3 = 2.5 × OD

$\therefore$ $OD = \dfrac{5 \times 3}{2.5}$ cm

        = 6 cm

Hence length of OD is 6 cm

Ex. 2 : In Fig., chords PQ and RS of a circle intersect at T. If RS = 18 cm, ST = 6 cm and PT = 18 cm, find the length of TQ.

Sol. Chords PQ and RS intersect at T.

$\therefore$ PT × TQ = RT × TS

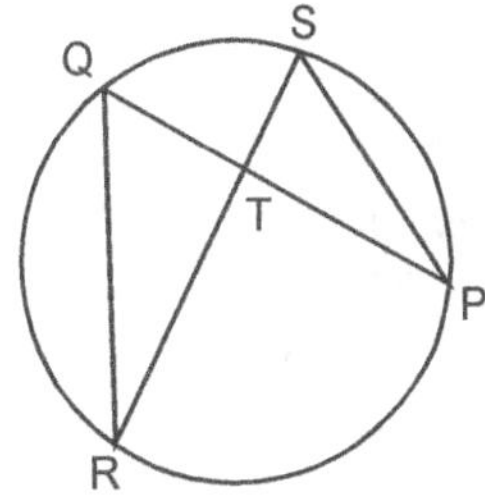

$\Rightarrow$ 18 × TQ = 12 × 6

[$\because$ RT = RS – ST = 18 cm – 6 cm = 12 cm]

$\Rightarrow$ $TQ = \dfrac{12 \times 6}{18} = 4$ cm

Hence the length of TQ is 4 cm.

Ex. 3 : In Fig., AB = 5 cm, BD = 4 cm, CD = 9 cm, Find DE.

Sol. In right $\triangle ADB$,

By Pythagoras theorem, we have

AD² + DB² = AB²

$\Rightarrow$ AD² + (4)² = (5)²

$\Rightarrow$ AD² = 25 – 16

                = 9 cm²

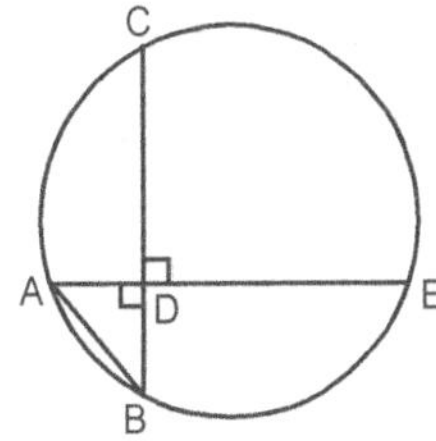

$\therefore$ $AD = \pm\sqrt{9} = 3$ cm.

Since two chords AE and BC of a circle intersect each other at the point D inside the circle.

$\therefore$ AD × DE = CD × BD

$\Rightarrow$ 3 cm × DE = 9 cm × 4 cm

$\therefore$ $DE = \dfrac{9 \times 4}{3} = 12$ cm.

Ex. 4. Find the value of x in Fig.

Sol. $\because$ Chords AB and CD of the circle, when produced meet at P

$\therefore$ PA × PB = PC × PD

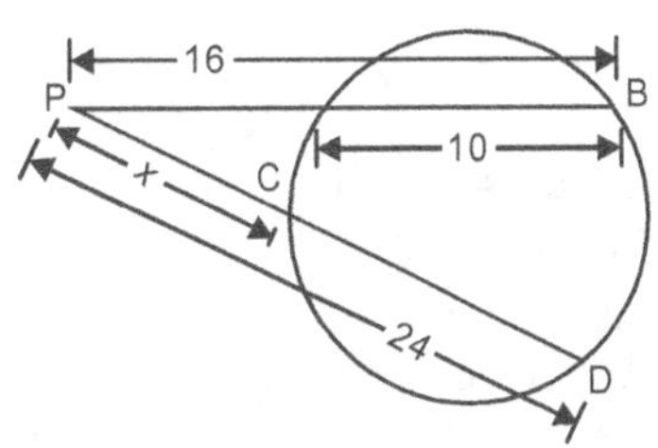

$\Rightarrow$ (16 – 10) × 16 = x × 24

$\Rightarrow$ 6 × 16 = x × 24

$\Rightarrow$ $x = \dfrac{6 \times 16}{24} = 4$

Hence $x = 4$.

Ex. 5 : In Fig., O is the centre of the circle. if PA = 12 cm, PC = 15 cm and CD = 7 cm, find the length of AB.

Sol. Chords AB and CD intersect each other at point P outside the circle.

$\therefore$ PA × PB = PC × PD

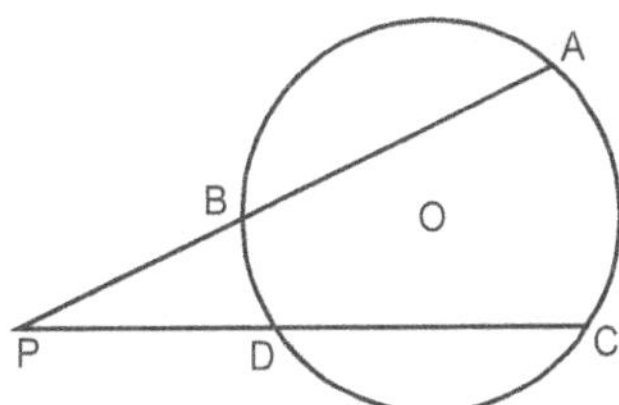

Since PA = 12 cm and PC = 15 cm

$\therefore$ 12 × PB = 15 × (PC – CD)

$\Rightarrow$ 12 × PB = 15 × (15 – 7)

$\Rightarrow$ 12 × PB = 15 × 8

$\Rightarrow$ $PB = \dfrac{15 \times 8}{12}$ cm = 10 cm

AB = PA – PB = 12 – 10 = 2 cm.

Ex. 6 : In Fig., chords AB and CD of the circle intersect externally at P. AB = 6 cm, CD = 3 cm, PD = 5 cm. Find PB.

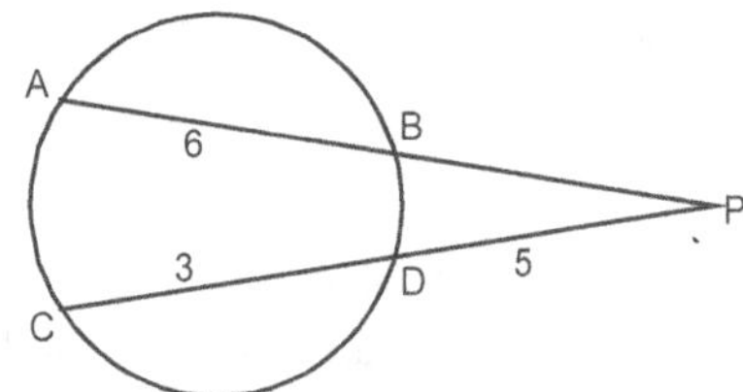

Sol. AB and CD are two chord of a circle intersecting each other at P outside the circle when produced

$$\therefore \quad PA \times PB = PC \times PD$$
$$\Rightarrow (AB + PB) \cdot PB = (CD + PD) \cdot PD$$
$$\Rightarrow \quad (6 + x)x = (3 + 5)5$$
$$\Rightarrow \quad 6x + x^2 = 40$$
$$\Rightarrow \quad x^2 + 6x - 40 = 0$$
$$\Rightarrow \quad x^2 + 10x - 4x - 40 = 0$$
$$\Rightarrow \quad x(x + 10) - 4(x + 10) = 0$$
$$\Rightarrow \quad (x + 10)(x - 4) = 0$$
$$\Rightarrow \quad x = -10, 4$$

Rejecting the –ve value of x, we get $x = 4$ cm.

Ex. 7 : In Fig. AB and DC are two chords of a circle, with centre O, which when produced meet at P. If PB = 8 cm, BA = 7 cm and PO = 14.5 cm, find the radius of the circle.

Sol. Let the radius of circle be x cm

PC = PO – OC = (14.5 – x) cm

PD = PO + OD = [14.5 + x] cm

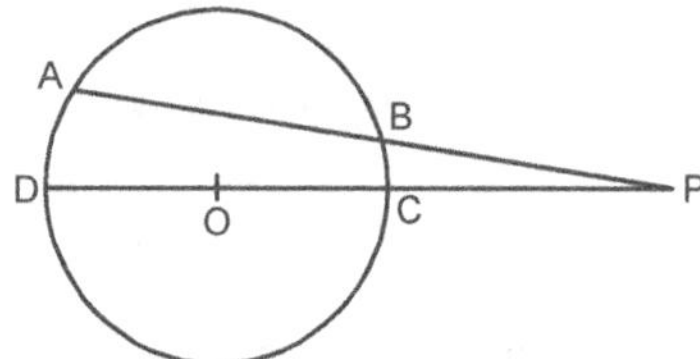

Now PB × PA = PC × PD
$$\Rightarrow 8 \times 15 = (14.5 - x)(14.5 + x)$$
$$[\because PA = PB + BA = 8 \text{ cm} + 7 \text{ cm} = 15 \text{ cm}]$$
$$\Rightarrow \quad 120 = (14.5)^2 - x^2$$
$$\Rightarrow \quad x^2 = 210.25 - 120$$
$$= 90.25 \text{ cm}$$
$$\Rightarrow x = \pm\sqrt{90.25} = 9.5 \text{ cm}$$

Hence radius of the circle is 9.5 cm.

Ex. 8 : If AB and CD are two chords which when produced meet at P and if AP = CP, show that AB = CD.

Sol. AB and CD are two chords. They are produced to meet at P

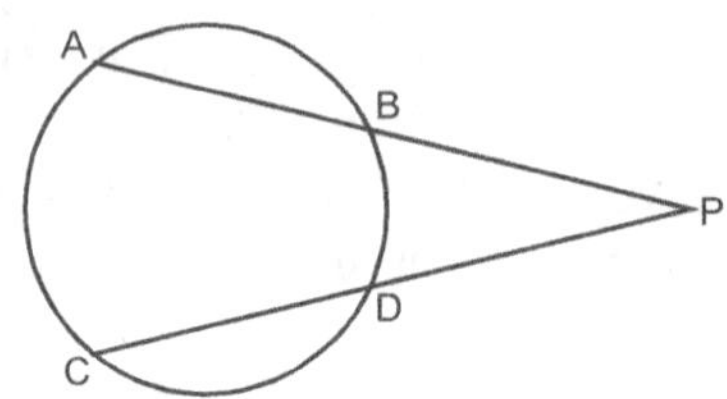

$$\therefore \quad PA \times PB = PC \times PD$$
$$\Rightarrow PB = \frac{PC \times PB}{PB} = \frac{AP \times PD}{AP} = PD$$
$$[\because PC = AP \text{ (Given)}]$$

Now AB = AP – PB
$$\Rightarrow \quad AB = CP - PD$$
$$[\because AP = CP \text{ (Given) and } PB = PD \text{ (Proved above)}]$$
$$\Rightarrow \quad AB = CD$$

Hence proved.

Ex. 9 : In Fig., find x.

Sol. Here PT is a tangent segment and PAB is a secant to a circle intersecting the circle at A and B.

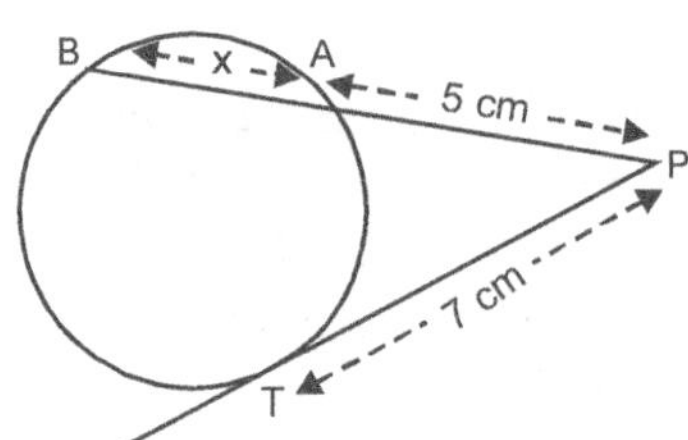

$$\therefore \quad PA \times PB = PT^2$$
$$\Rightarrow \quad 5(5 + x) = 7^2$$
$$\Rightarrow \quad 25 + 5x = 49$$
$$\Rightarrow 5x = 49 - 25 = 24$$
$$\Rightarrow \quad x = 24 \div 5 = 4.8 \text{ cm.}$$

Ex. 10 : In Fig., PT is tangent to the circle at T. PA = 4 cm and AB = 5 cm, find PT.

Sol. Since PAB is a secant to a circle intersecting the circle at A and B and PT is a tangent segment,

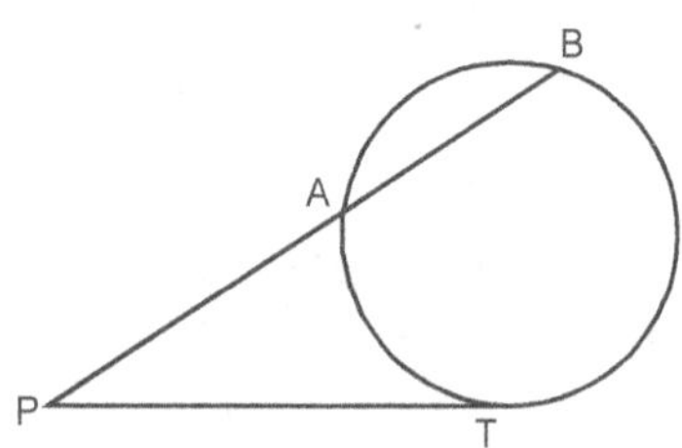

$$\therefore \quad PT^2 = PA \times PB$$
$$= 4 \times (PA + AB)$$
$$= 4 \times (4 + 5) = 4 \times 9 = 36 \text{ cm}^2$$
$$\therefore \quad PT = \pm\sqrt{36} = 6 \text{ cm.}$$

MULTIPLE CHOICE QUESTIONS

1. From a point Q, the length of the tangent to a circle is 24 cm and the distance from the centre is 25 cm. The radius of the circle is
A. 7 cm
B. 12 cm
C. 15 cm
D. 24.5 cm

2. In the given figure, if TP and TQ are the two tangents to a circle with centre O and that $\angle POQ = 110°$, then $\angle PTQ$ is equal to

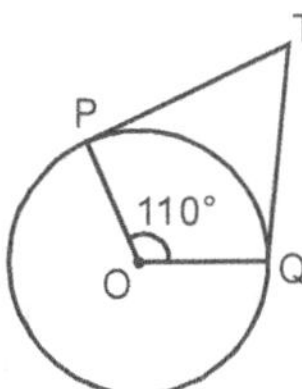

A. 60°
B. 70°
C. 80°
D. 90°

3. If tangents PA and PB from a point P to a circle with centre O are inclined to each other at angle of 80°, then $\angle POA$ is equal to
A. 50°
B. 60°
C. 70°
D. 80°

4. In Fig., a circle touches all the four sides of a quadrilateral ABCD whose sides AB = 6 cm, BC = 7 cm and CD = 4 cm. Find AD

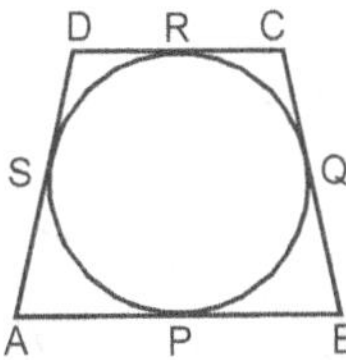

A. 2 cm
B. 5 cm
C. 3 cm
D. 4 cm

5. If AB, AC, PQ are tangents in the figure and AB = 5 cm. The perimeter of $\triangle APQ$ is

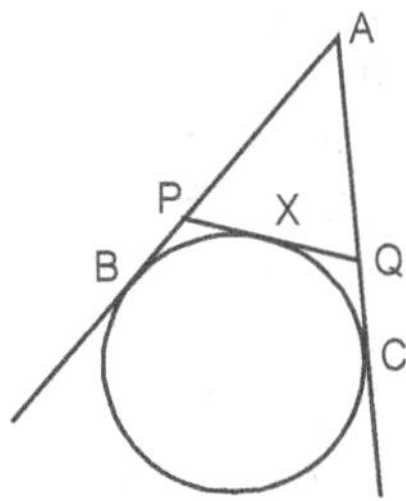

A. 8 cm
B. 6 cm
C. 10 cm
D. 5 cm

6. In Fig., a circle is inscribed within a quadrilateral ABCD. Given that BC = 38 cm, BQ = 27 cm and DC = 25 cm and that AD is perpendicular to DC. The radius of the circle is

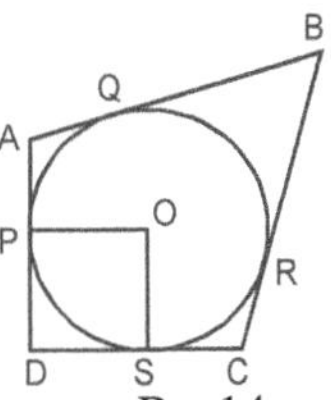

A. 10 cm
B. 14 cm
C. 8 cm
D. 12 cm

7. Two tangents are drawn to a circle from an external point A, touching the circle at the points P and Q. A third tangent intersects segment AP at B and segment AQ at C and touches the circle at R. If AQ = 10 units, then the perimeter of $\triangle ABC$ (in units) is
A. 22.0
B. 20.5
C. 20.0
D. 40.0

8. In Fig., two circles intersect each other at points P and Q. From A on line PQ, secant AMD for one circle and secant ASR for the second one are drawn. If AM = 3, MD = 5 and AS = 4, determine SR.

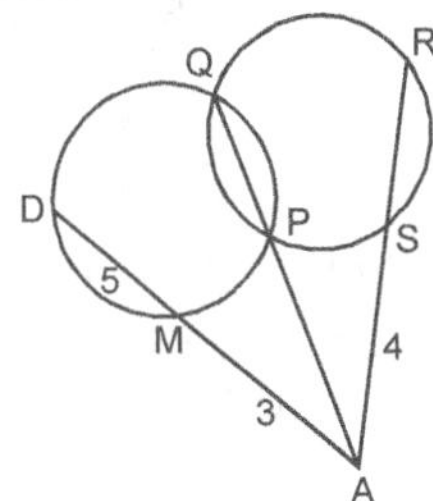

A. 2 cm
B. 4 cm
C. 3 cm
D. 1 cm

9. In the figure, KLMN is a cyclic quadrilateral and PQ is a tangent to the circle at K. If LN is a diameter of the circle. $\angle KLN = 30°$ and $\angle MNL = 60°$. Determine $\angle QKN$

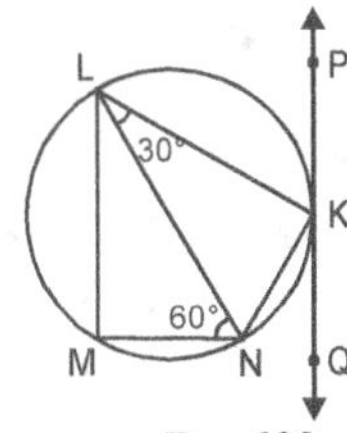

A. 30°
B. 60°
C. 90°
D. 100°

10. In the given Fig., PQ is tangent and O is the centre of the circle. Find EP is OP = 21, OQ = 9 and OM $\sqrt{80}$.

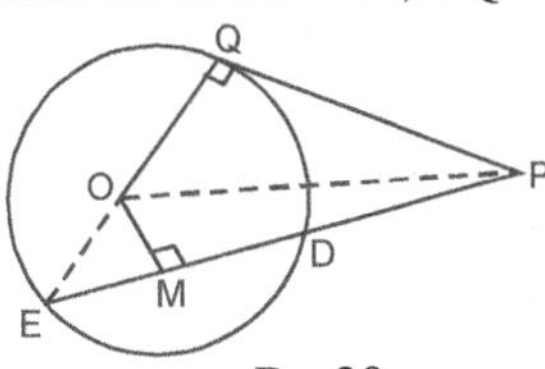

A. 10
B. 20
C. 30
D. 40

ANSWERS

1	2	3	4	5	6	7	8	9	10
A	B	A	C	C	B	C	A	A	B

EXPLANATORY ANSWERS

1. In rt. $\angle d$ $\triangle OTQ$,

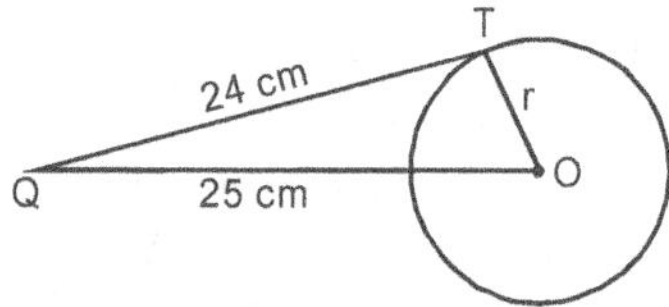

$$OT = \sqrt{OQ^2 - OT^2}$$
$$= \sqrt{25^2 - 24^2} = \sqrt{625 - 576}$$
$$= \sqrt{49} = 7 \text{ cm.}$$

2. Since $\angle POQ + \angle PTQ = 180°$
$$[\because \angle OPT = 90°, \angle OQT = 90°]$$
$\Rightarrow \qquad 110° + \angle PTQ = 180°$
$\Rightarrow \qquad \qquad \angle PTQ = 180° - 110° = 70°.$

3. Since $\angle APB = 80°$
$\qquad \angle AOB = 180° - 80° = 100°$
$\qquad \angle PAO = \angle PBO = 90°$
Since OP bisects $\angle AOB$

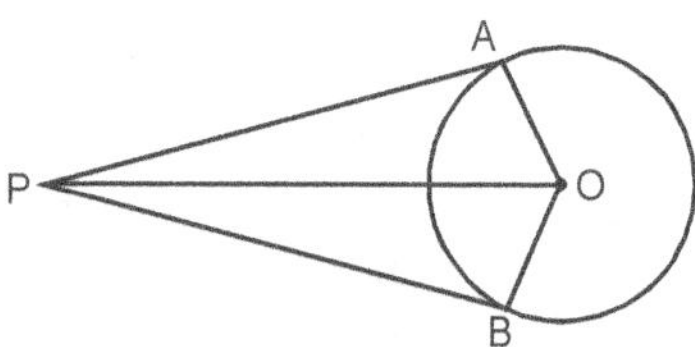

$$\angle AOP = \frac{1}{2}(100°) = 50°$$

i.e. $\quad \angle POA = 50°.$

4. $AD = AS + DS = AP + DR$
$$[\because AS = AP \text{ and } DS = DR]$$

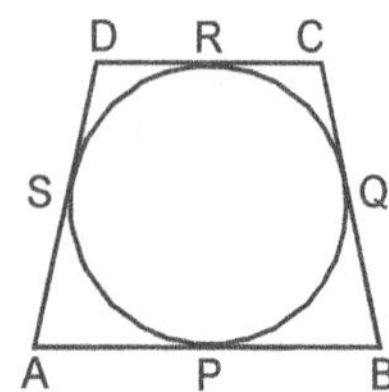

$= (AB - BP) + (CD - RC)$
$= AB + CD - (BP + RC)$
$= AB + CD - (BQ + CQ)$
$$[\because BP = BQ, RC = CQ]$$
$= AB + CD - BC = 6 + 4 - 7 = 3 \text{ cm.}$

5. Since AB and AC are the tangents from the same point A
$\therefore \qquad AB = AC = 5 \text{ cm}$

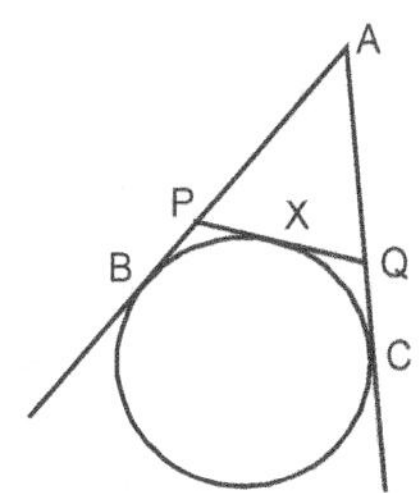

Similarly, $BP = PX$ and $XQ = QC$
Perimeter of $\triangle APQ = AP + AQ + PQ$
$= AP + AQ + (PX + XQ)$
$= (AP + PX) + (AQ + XQ)$
$= (AP + BP) + (AQ + QC)$
$= AB + AC$
$= 5 + 5$
$= 10 \text{ cm.}$

6. $\because$ Lengths of tangents drawn from an external point to a circle are equal

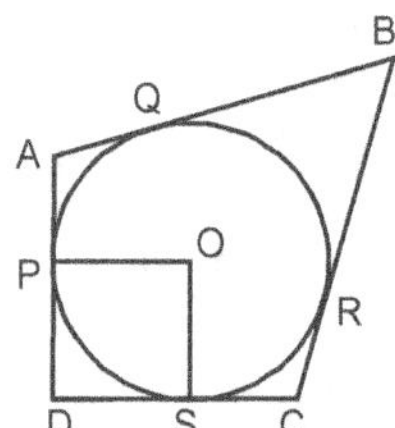

$\therefore \qquad BQ = BR = 27 \text{ cm}$
Let x be the radius of the circle
$\therefore \qquad OP = OS = PD = x$
$\qquad \qquad CR = BC - BR$
$\qquad \qquad \quad = 38 - 27$
$\qquad \qquad \quad = 11 \text{ cm}$
Now $\qquad CS = CR = 11 \text{ cm}$
$\qquad [\because$ Length of tangents from an external point to a
$\qquad \qquad \qquad \qquad \qquad \qquad \text{ circle are equal}]$
$\therefore \qquad \qquad DS = CD - CS$
$\qquad \qquad \qquad = 25 \text{ cm} - 11 \text{ cm}$
$\qquad \qquad \qquad = 14 \text{ cm}$
But $\qquad DS = OP = x = 14 \text{ cm.}$
Hence radius $= OP = 14 \text{ cm.}$

7. Since the tangents to a circle from an external point are equal in length

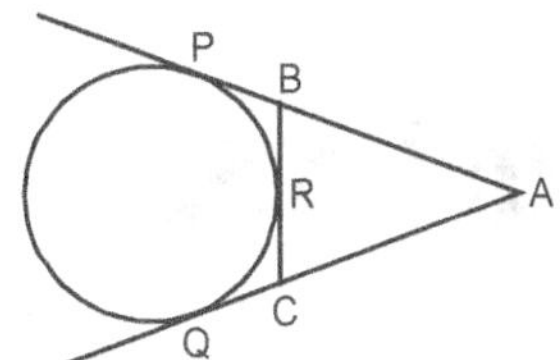

$$AP = AQ = 10 \text{ units}$$

and $\left.\begin{array}{l} BP = BR \\ CQ = CR \end{array}\right\}$

Adding these, we get,

$$BP + CQ = BR + CR = BC$$

Adding AB and AC to both sides, we get

$$BP + CQ + AB + AC = BC + AB + AC$$

$\Rightarrow (BP + AB) + (CQ + AC) = AB + BC + AC$

$\Rightarrow AP + AQ = \text{Perimeter of } \Delta ABC$

$\Rightarrow (10 + 10) \text{ units} = \text{Perimeter of } \Delta ABC$

$\therefore$ Perimeter of $\Delta ABC = 20$ units.

$\therefore$ (*iii*) is the correct answer.

8. In the larger circle, chord QP and chord DM intersect each other at the point A outside the circle

$\therefore \quad AM \times AD = AP \qquad\qquad ...(1)$

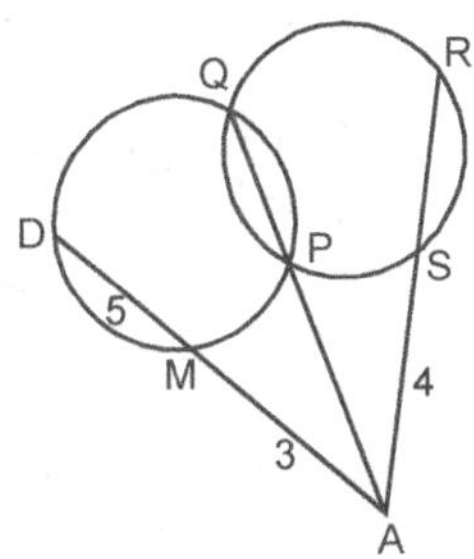

Again in the smaller circle, chord QP and chord RS intersect each other at the point A outside the circle.

$\therefore \quad AS \times AR = AP \times AQ \qquad ...(2)$

$\therefore \quad AM \times AD = AS \times AR \qquad ...(3)$

$$\text{[From (1) and (2)]}$$

Now $\qquad AD = AM + MD$

$$= 3 + 5 = 8$$

$\therefore$ From (3), $3 \times 8 = 4 \times AR$

$\Rightarrow \qquad AR = \dfrac{24}{4} = 6$

But $\qquad AS + SR = AR$

$\therefore \qquad 4 + SR = 6,$

$$SR = 6 - 4 = 2.$$

9. KN is a chord through the point of contact K.

$\therefore \quad \angle QKN = \angle KLN$

$$\text{[}\angle s \text{ in the alt. segment are equal]}$$

$$= 30°$$

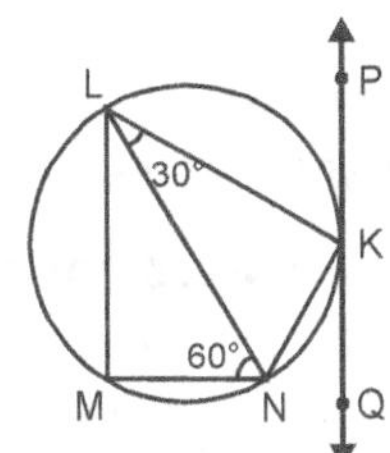

10. Join OQ and OE

In ΔOPQ, $m \angle OQP = 90°$

$\therefore \quad OQ^2 + QP^2 = OP^2 \qquad \text{[By Pythagoras Theorem]}$

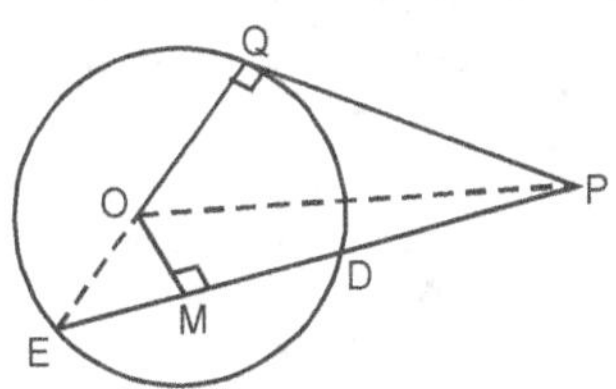

$\Rightarrow \quad (9)^2 + QP^2 = (21)^2$

$\Rightarrow \quad QP^2 = (21)^2 - (9)^2 = 360$

In rt. $\angle d$ ΔOME, $OM^2 + EM^2 = OE^2$

$\Rightarrow \qquad 80 + (EM)^2 = (9)^2$

$\Rightarrow \quad EM^2 = 81 - 80 = 1$

$\Rightarrow \qquad EM = +\sqrt{1} = 1$

$\therefore \qquad ED = 2EM = 2 \times 1 = 2$

Let $\qquad EP = x$

Then $\qquad PQ^2 = PD \times PE$

$$\text{[Tangent secant second point theorem]}$$

$\therefore \qquad 360 = (x - 2)x$

$\Rightarrow \qquad x^2 - 2x - 360 = 0$

$\Rightarrow \qquad (x - 20)(x + 18) = 0$

$\Rightarrow \qquad x = 20, -18$

But $\qquad x \neq -18$

Hence $\qquad EP = 20.$

✱ ✱ ✱

10

Geometrical Constructions

The process of making the various figures with the help of geometrical instruments is known as geometrical construction.

Some Important Constructions

Construction 1. *To draw the tangent to a circle at a point on it without using the centre of the circle.*

Given. A circle and a point P on it.

Required. To draw the tangent to the circle at P.

Steps of Construction :

1. Draw any chord PQ. Join P and Q to a point M in major arc (or QP minor arc PQ).

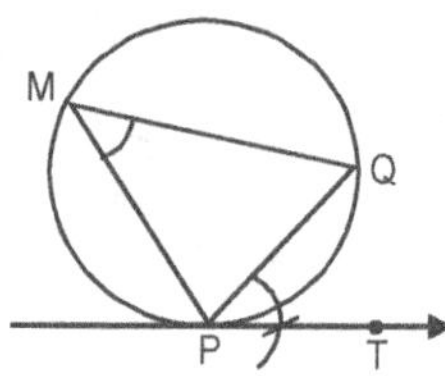

2. Draw ∠QPT equal to ∠PMQ and on opposite side of chord PQ.

Then, PT is the required tangent line at P.

Note. ∠QPT and ∠PMQ are ∠s in the alt. segments.

Construction 2. *To draw a tangent to a circle from a point outside the circle using its centre.*

Given. A circle with centre O and a point P outside it.

Required. To draw a tangent from P to the circle.

Steps of Construction :

1. Join OP and bisect it. Let M be the mid-point of OP.

2. With M as centre and MO as radius, draw a semicircle intersecting the given circle at Q.

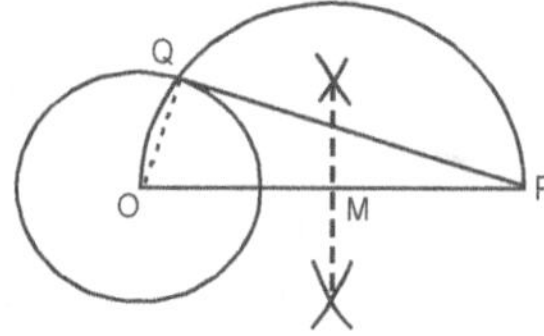

3. Join PQ.

PQ is the required tangent from P to the circle.

Note. If we join OQ, then we can observe that ∠POQ = 90° (Angle of a semi-circle)

⇒ PQ is perpendicular to OQ.

Construction 3. *To draw tangent to a circle from a point outside the circle without using it centre.*

Given. A circle and a point P outside the circle.

Required. To draw tangents from P to the circle without using its centre.

Steps of Construction :

1. Draw a secant PAB to the circle.

2. Draw the perpendicular bisector of line segment BP. Let M be the mid-point of PB.

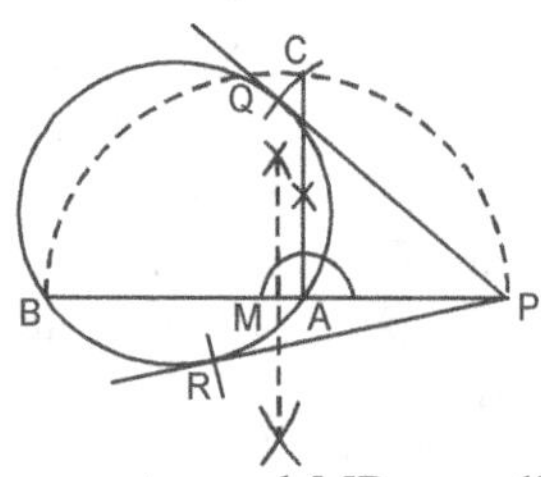

3. With M as centre and MP as radius, draw a semicircle.

4. Draw a line perpendicular to BP through A. Let it intersects the semi-circle at a point C.

5. With P as centre and PC as radius draw arcs to intersect the given circle at two points, say, Q and R.

6. Join PQ and PR.

The PQ and PR are required tangents.

Construction 4. *To construct incircle of the triangle whose sides are given to be a, b and c.*

Given. A ΔABC in which BC = a, CA = b and AB = c.

Required. To construct the incircle of the ΔABC.

Steps of Construction :

1. Construct the ΔABC in which BC = a, CA = b and AB = c.

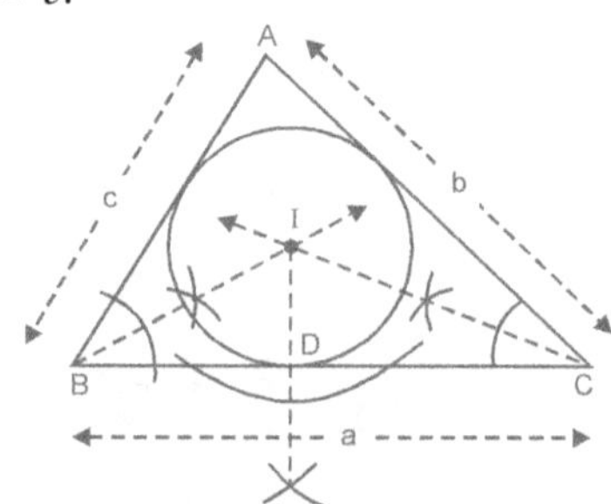

2. Bisect any two angles of the triangle, say ∠B and ∠C. Let the bisectors of these angles intersect at the point I. Then I is the incentre of ΔABC.

3. Draw ID perpendicular on the side BC (or on any other side)

4. With I as centre and ID, as radius, draw the circle.

Then this circle is the required incircle of ΔABC.

Construction 5. *To construct the circumcircle of the triangle with sides a, b and c.*

Given. A triangle ABC in which BC = *a*, CA = *b* and AB = *c*.

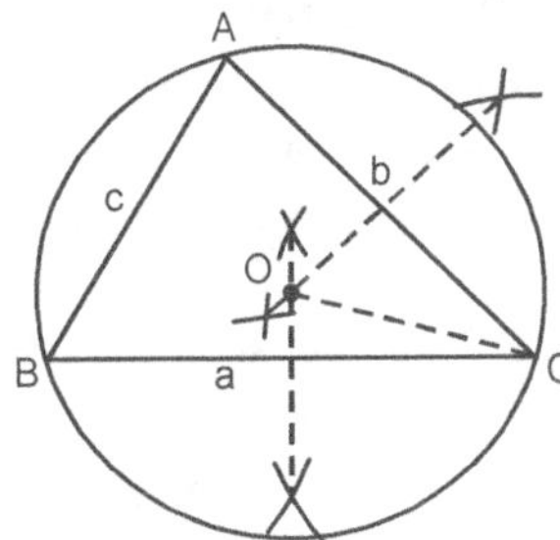

Required. To construct the circumcircle of the ΔABC.

Steps of Construction :

1. Construct a ΔABC with BC = *a*, CA = *b* and AB = *c*.

2. Draw the perpendicular bisectors of any two sides, say AC and BC, intersecting at O.

3. With O as centre and radius OC or OB or OA (circum-radius of ΔABC), draw the circle.

Then this circle is the required circumcircle of ΔABC.

SOLVED EXAMPLES

Ex. 1 : Construct a triangle ABC in which BC = 7 cm, ∠A = 60° and altitude through A is 3.7 cm. How many such triangles are possible? Write the steps of construction.

Sol. **Steps of Construction :**

1. Draw a line segement BC = 7 cm.

2. Construct ∠CBX = 60°.

3. Draw OB ⊥ BX intersecting the perpendicular bisector of BC at O.

4. With O as centre and radius OB or OC, draw a circle.

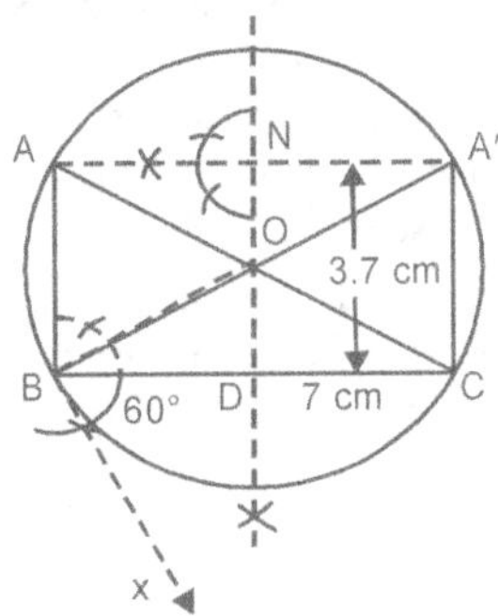

5. Cut DN = 3.7 cm.

6. Through N, draw ⊥ on DN intersecting the circle, at the point A and A′.

7. Join AB, AC and A′B, A′C.

8. ∴ ΔABC and ΔA′BC are the required triangles.

Hence the number of possible triangles = 2.

Ex. 2 : Construct a ΔABC in which BC = 6 cm, ∠A = 60° and altitude through A is 4.5 cm. Write the steps of construction.

Sol. **Steps of Construction :**

1. Draw a line segment BC = 6 cm and make an ∠CBP = 60° downwards.

2. Draw perpendicular bisector RQ of BC and perpendicular EB to BP. Let they intersect each other at O. Let M be the mide-point of BC.

3. With O as centre and radius = OB, draw a circle.

4. Mark a point L on RQ such that LM = 4.5 cm.

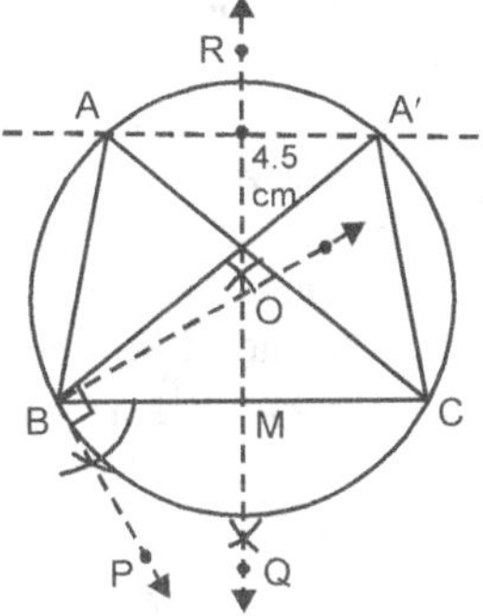

5. Draw a line *m* parallel to BC through L intersecting the circle, in two points say A and A′.

6. Join AB, AC and A′B, A′C.

Either of these Δ*s* ABC or A′BC is the required triangle.

Ex. 3 : Construct a triangle ABC in which BC = 4 cm. ∠A = 50° and the altitude through A is of length 3 cm. How many such triangles are possible? Take any one of the triangles and draw its incircle. Write the steps of construction.

Sol. **Steps of Construction :**

1. Draw a line segment BC = 4 cm.

2. Construct ∠CBX = 50°

3. Draw BE ⊥ BX intersecting the ⊥ bisector of BC at O.

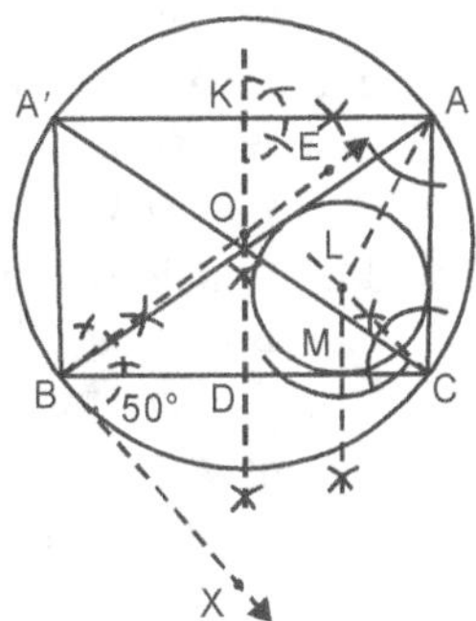

4. With O as centre and radius OB or OC, draw a circle.
5. Cut DK = 3 cm.
6. At K draw perpendicular A'A, intersecting the circle at the point A and A'.
7. Join AB, AC and A'B, A'C.
8. ΔA'BC and ΔABC are two required triangles.
9. For incircle, draw bisectors of ∠BCA and ∠CAB. Let the bisectors meet at L.
10. From L draw ⊥ to BC and let the perpendicular meet at M.
11. With L as centre and LM as radius draw the required incircle touching the sides of ΔABC.

Ex. 4 : Construct a triangle ABC in which BC = 6 cm, angle A = 45° and median AD = 5 cm.

Sol.   **Steps of Construction :**
1. Draw a line segment BC = 6 cm.
2. Make an angle PBC = 45° with the help of a protractor.
3. Draw the perpendicular bisector RQ of AB.
4. Draw BE ⊥ BP at B.
Let RQ and BE intersect at O.
5. Draw the circle with centre O and radius OB.
Then any angle in the major segment
$$= ∠PBC = 45°$$

6. Let RQ intersect BC to D then D is the mid-point of BC. Taking D as centre and 5 cm radius, draw arcs intersecting the circle in A, A',
7. Join AB, AC and A'B, A'C.
Then the required triangle is ABC or A'BC.

Ex. 5 : Construct a triangle similar to a given ΔABC such that each of its sides is $\frac{2}{3}$rd of the corresponding side of the ABC. It is given that AB = 4 cm, BC = 5 cm and AC = 6 cm.

Sol.   **Steps of Construction :**
1. Construct ΔABC, where BC = 5 cm, AB = 4 cm and AC = 6 cm.
2. Divide the base BC into three equal parts.
3. Mark C' on BC such that $BC' = \frac{2}{3}BC$.

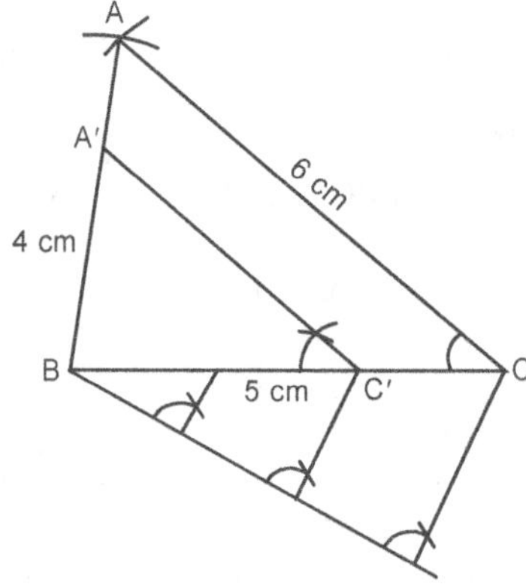

4. Through C', draw a line parallel to CA intersect AB in A'.
Here ΔA'BC' is the required triangle. It is similar to ΔABC.

MULTIPLE CHOICE QUESTIONS

1. A tangent to a circle is a line that intersect the circle in only:
A. two points
B. three points
C. four points
D. one point

2. A line intersecting a circle in two points is called:
A. tangent
B. secant
C. point of contact
D. None of these

3. The longest chord of a circle is called its:
A. radius
B. secant
C. diameter
D. tangent

4. A tangent PQ at a point P of a circle of radius 5 cm meets a line through the centre O at a point Q, so that OQ = 12 cm. Length PQ is:
A. $\sqrt{119}$ cm
B. 13 cm
C. 10 cm
D. 12 cm

5. In a right angled triangle hypotenuse is:
A. Any side of the triangle
B. Side opposite to right angle
C. Side opposite to acute angle
D. None of these

6. If the perimeter and area of a circle are numerically equal, then the radius of the circle is :
A. 6 units
B. π units
C. 4 units
D. 2 units

7. The area of a circle is 301.84 cm^2. Then its radius is:
A. 9.2 cm   B. 9.3 cm
C. 9.8 cm   D. 9.6 cm

8. If three altitudes of a triangle are equal then the triangle is :
A. Right angled   B. Equilateral
C. Isosceles   D. Scalene

9. The height of an equilateral triangle is :

A. $\dfrac{\sqrt{3}}{4} \times \text{Side}$ B. $\dfrac{\sqrt{3}}{2} \times \text{Side}$

C. $\dfrac{\sqrt{3}}{4} \times \text{Side}^2$ D. None of these

10. ABC is an isosceles right triangle. If AB^2 = 2AC^2 then right angle is at:
A. C
B. A
C. B
D. None of these

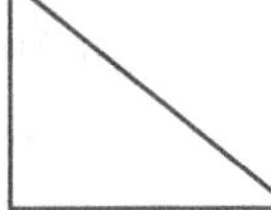

11. The length of an altitude of an equilateral triangle of side 2a is :

A. $\sqrt{2}\,a$ cm   B. $\sqrt{3}\,a$ cm
C. 2 cm   D. 1 cm

12. If $\angle$A = 100°, AB = AC, CD bisects $\angle$ACB and BD bisects $\angle$ABC. The values of x and y are:
A. 15° and 70°
B. 20° and 140°
C. 10° and 160°
D. 20° and 125°

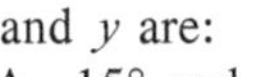

13. A perpendicular at the end of the radius of a circle is:
A. diameter   B. tangent
C. chord   D. anyline

14. ABC and BDF are two equilateral triangles such that D is the mid-point of BC. The ratio of the areas of triangles ABC and BDF is :
A. 2 : 1   B. 1 : 2
C. 4 : 1   D. 1 : 4

15. The exterior angle of a quadrilateral are x°, $(x + 5)$°, $(x + 10)$° and $(x + 25)$°, then value of x is :
A. 50°   B. 80°
C. 60°   D. 70°

16. The point equidistant from the three sides of a triangle is :
A. circumference   B. centroid
C. incentre   D. orthocentre

17. In $\triangle$ABC, AB = $6\sqrt{3}$ cm AC = 12 cm and BC = 6 cm. The $\angle$CAB and $\angle$ABC are:
A. 90° and 60°
B. 30° and 90°
C. 60° and 90°
D. 90° and 30°

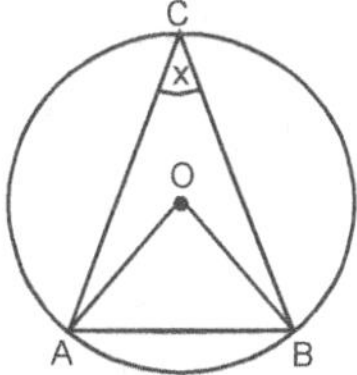

18. Chords AC and BD of a circle intersect each other, than the figure ABCD formed will be :
A. square   B. rectangle
C. parallelogram   D. quadrilateral

19. Sides of two similar triangles are in the ratio of 4 : 9 then area of these triangles are in the ratio :
A. 2 : 3   B. 4 : 9
C. 81 : 16   D. 16 : 81

20. In the given figure $\angle$AOB = 80°. The value of x is :
A. 10°
B. 25°
C. 40°
D. 160°

ANSWERS

1	2	3	4	5	6	7	8	9	10
D	B	C	A	B	D	C	B	B	A

11	12	13	14	15	16	17	18	19	20
B	B	D	C	B	C	B	B	D	C

EXPLANATORY ANSWERS

1. A line meeting a circle in one point is called a tangent to the circle.

2. A line, which intersects a cirlce in two distinct points is called secant of the circle.

3. Diameter is the longest chord in the circle.

4.

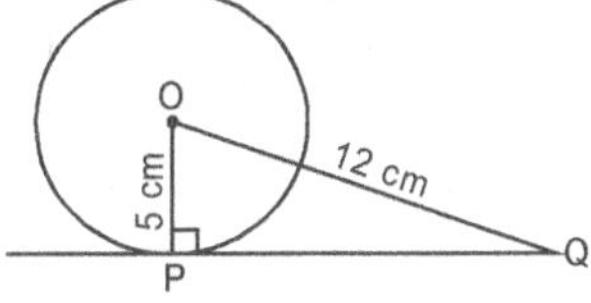

In $\triangle$OPQ,
$$PQ^2 = (OQ)^2 - (OP)^2$$
$$= (12)^2 - (5)^2 = 144 - 25$$
$$PQ^2 = 119$$
$$\therefore \quad PQ = \sqrt{119} \text{ cm.}$$

5.

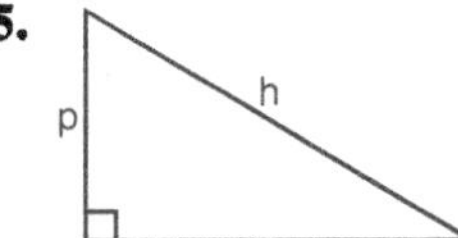

In any right-angled triangle hypotenuse is opposite to right angle.

6. From question,

circumference of circle = Area of circle

$$2\pi r = \pi r^2$$

$$\Rightarrow \quad r = 2 \therefore \text{ Radius} = 2 \text{ units.}$$

7. Area of the circle $= \pi r^2$

According to the question,

$$\pi r^2 = 301.84$$

$$\Rightarrow \quad \frac{22}{7} r^2 = 301.84$$

$$r^2 = \frac{7 \times 301.84}{22} = 96.04$$

$$\therefore \quad r = \sqrt{96.04} = 9.8 \text{ cm.}$$

8. If the altitudes of a triangle are equal then it is equilateral.

9. In $\triangle ABD$,

$$(AD)^2 = (AB)^2 - (BD)^2$$

$$= (a)^2 - \left(\frac{a}{2}\right)^2 = a^2 - \frac{a^2}{4}$$

$$AD^2 = \frac{3a^2}{4}$$

$$\therefore \quad AD = \frac{\sqrt{3}\,a}{2}$$

$\therefore$ Height of an equilateral triangle is $\frac{\sqrt{3}}{2} \times$ side.

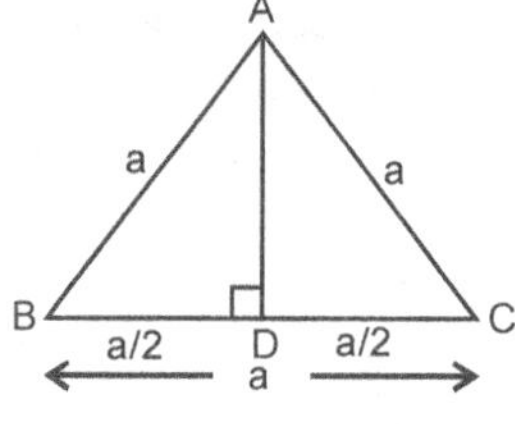

10. Let $\angle C = 90°$

In $\triangle ACB$,

$$(AB)^2 = (AC)^2 + (BC)^2$$

$$(AB)^2 = (AC)^2 + (AC)^2$$

$$AB^2 = 2AC^2$$

$$\therefore \quad \angle C = 90°.$$

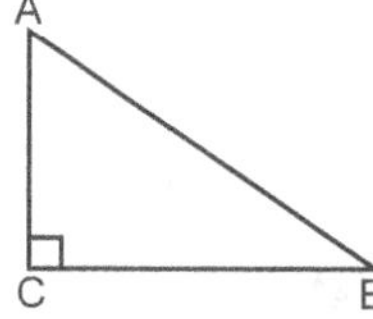

11.

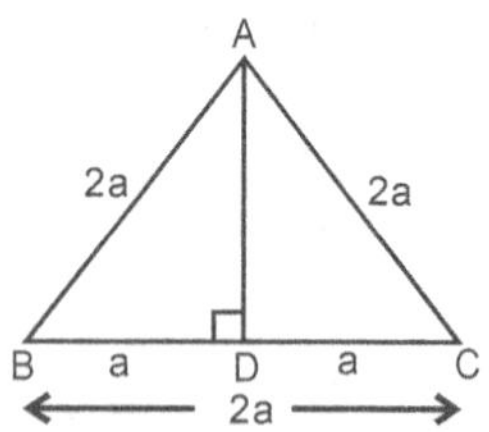

In $\triangle ABD$,

$$(AD)^2 = (2a)^2 - (a)^2$$

$$(AD)^2 = 4a^2 - a^2 = 3a^2$$

$$AD = \sqrt{3}\,a.$$

12. Since $AB = AC$

$$\therefore \quad \angle ABC = \angle ACB$$

$$\therefore \quad 2x + 2x + 100° = 180° \Rightarrow 4x = 80°$$

$$\angle x = 20°$$

In $\triangle DBC$,

$$x + x + y = 180° \Rightarrow 40° + y = 180° - 40° = 140°.$$

13. A tangent to a circle is at right angle to the radius.

14.

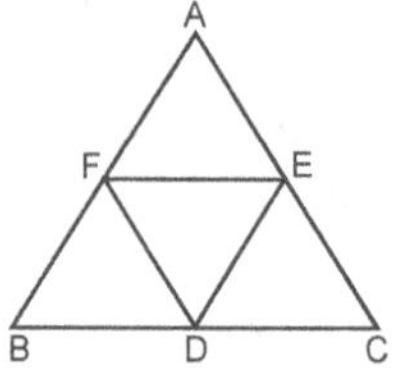

Draw DF $\parallel$ CA so that

$$\angle BDF = \angle BCA = 60°$$

$$\therefore \quad \angle BFD = 180° - 60° - 60° = 60°$$

$\therefore$ BDF is equilateral triangle.

$\therefore \triangle ABC \sim \triangle BDF$

$$\therefore \quad \frac{ar\triangle ABC}{ar\triangle BDF} = \frac{AC^2}{FD^2} = \frac{(2FD)^2}{FD^2} = \frac{4}{1}$$

$\therefore$ Required ratio is 4 : 1.

15. We have,

$$x° + (x + 5)° + (x + 10)° + (x + 25)° = 360°$$

$$4x + 40° = 360°$$

$$4x = 320°$$

$$x = 80°.$$

16. Point of concurrence of the right bisector of the angles of a triangle is called incentre.

17. In $\triangle ABC$

$$(12)^2 = (6)^2 + \left(6\sqrt{3}\right)^2$$

$$144 = 36 + 108 = 144$$

$\therefore \triangle ABC$ is right-angled triangle

$$\therefore \quad \angle B = 90°$$

$$\sin A = \frac{BC}{AC} = \frac{6}{12} = \frac{1}{2}$$

$$\Rightarrow \quad \sin A = \sin 30°$$

$$A = 30°$$

$\therefore$ The angles $\angle CAB$ and $\angle ABC$ are 30° and 90° respectively.

18. Chords AC and BD must pass through the centre of the circle and will intersect at the centre,

$\therefore \square ABCD$ is a rectangle.

19. $\because \triangle ABC \sim \triangle DEF$

$$\therefore \quad \frac{ar\triangle ABC}{ar\triangle DEF} = \frac{(4)^2}{(9)^2} = \frac{16}{81} = 16 : 81.$$

20. We have,

$$\angle AOB = 2\angle ACB$$

[Angle of the centre is twice at the angle of circumference]

$$80° = 2x \therefore x = \frac{80}{2} = 40°.$$

✱ ✱ ✱

11

Mensuration : Perimeter and Areas

SOME IMPORTANT FORMULAE

1.

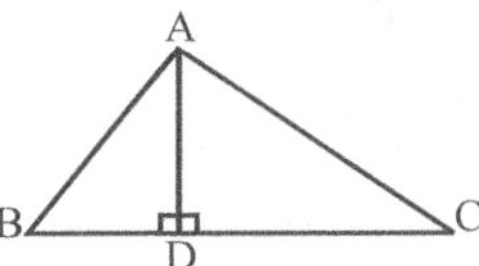

BC : base, AD : height corresponding to BC.

Area of $\Delta = \dfrac{1}{2} \times$ base $\times$ corresponding height.

$$= \dfrac{1}{2} \times BC \times AD$$

2.

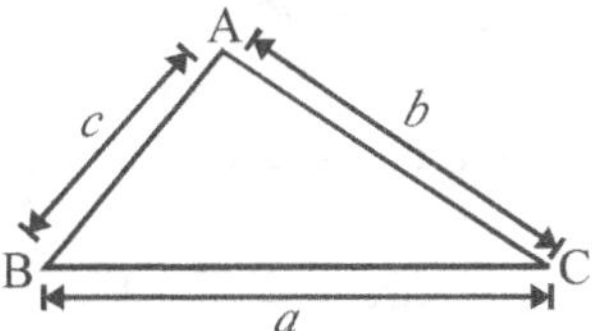

BC $= a$; AC $= b$; AB $= c$

Hero's formula

Area of $\Delta ABC = \sqrt{s(s-a)(s-b)(s-c)}$

where $s = \dfrac{a+b+c}{2}$

3.

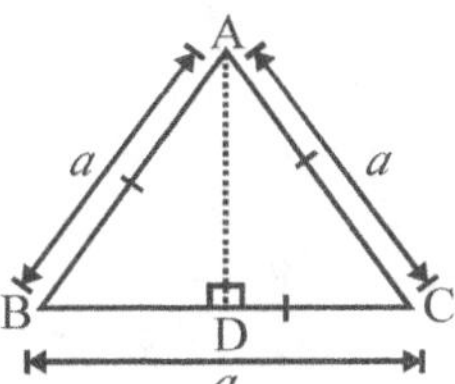

If Δ is equilateral with each of its sides equal to a

then each of the altitude $= \dfrac{\sqrt{3}}{2} a$

and area $\Delta ABC = \dfrac{\sqrt{3}}{4} a^2$.

4.

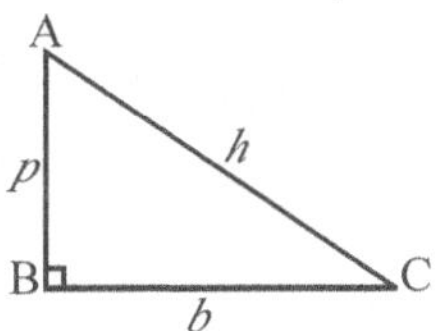

Right triangle

AB : p;   BC : b

The sides of the right Δ other than the hypotenuse are perpendicular p, and base b.

Area of right $\Delta = \dfrac{1}{2} \times b \times p$.

5. Trapezoid

A quadrilateral in which no two sides are equal or parallel is called a trapezoid.

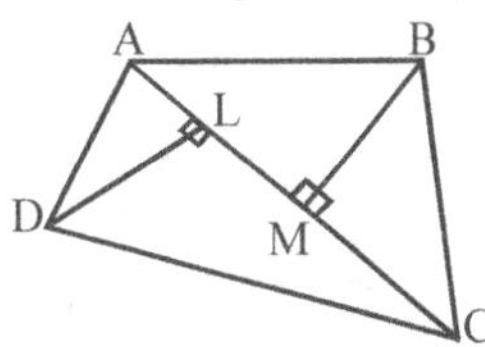

AC : diagonal

DL and BM are perpendiculars let fall on the diagonal from opposite vertices B and D. They are called offsets.

Area $\square ABCD = \dfrac{1}{2} \times AC \times (DL + BM)$

6. Trapezium.

A quadrilateral in which a pair of opposite sides are parallel is called a trapezium.

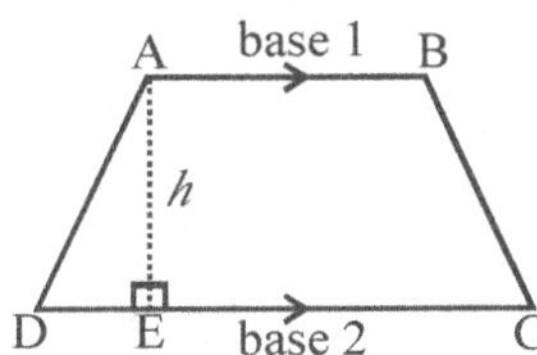

Area of trapezium ABCD $= \dfrac{1}{2} \times (AB + DC) \times h$

7. Parallelogram

A quadrilateral in which both pairs of opposite sides are parallel is called a parallelogram.

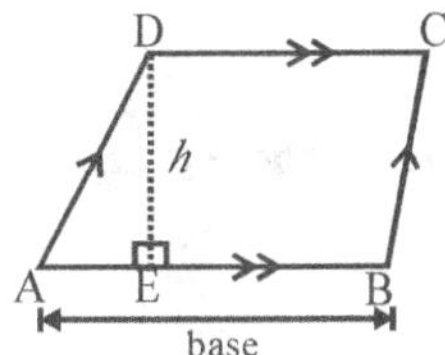

Area of parallelogram
= base × corresponding height

Area of $\parallel$ gm ABCD $= AB \times h$

8. Rhombus

A quadrilateral in which all sides are equal is called a rhombus.

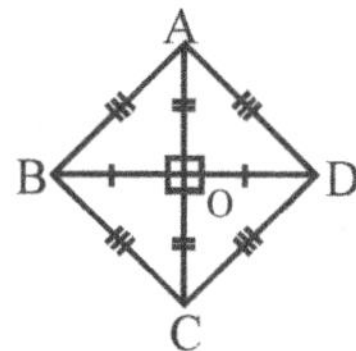 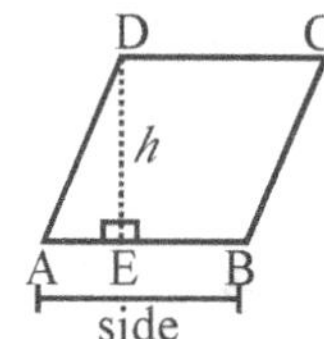

AC : diagonal$_1$; BD : diagonal$_2$;
AB : side (AB = a)   DE : altitude (DE = h)
Area of rhombus ABCD

$$= \frac{1}{2} \times AC \times BD = AB \times h$$

perimeter of rhombus ABCD

$$= 2\sqrt{AC^2 + BD^2} = 4 \times AB.$$

9. Rectangle

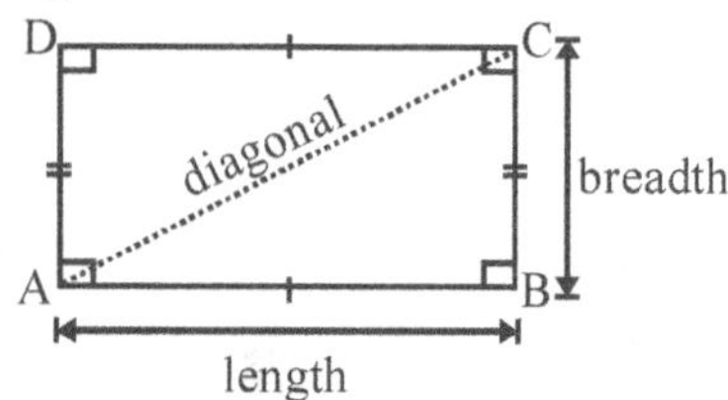

A parallelogram in which all interior angles are 90° is called a rectangle.

Perimeter of rectangle ABCD $= 2(AB + BC)$

Area of rectangle ABCD = AB × BC

Diagonal : $AC = \sqrt{AB^2 + BC^2}$

10. Square

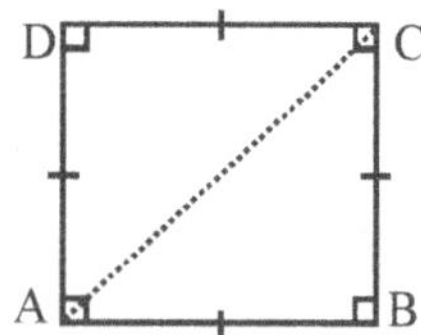

A rectangle in which adjacent sides are equal is called a square.

Perimeter of square = 4 × side

Area of square $= (\text{side})^2$

Diagonal of square $= \text{side}\sqrt{2}$

11. Circle, Semicircle and Quarter circle

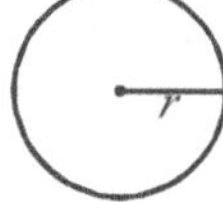

If O is the centre of circle, its radius is r and its

diameter is d then $d = 2r$, $r = \dfrac{d}{2}$;

circumference $C = 2\pi r = \pi d$

area $A = \pi r^2 = \pi \dfrac{d^2}{4}$

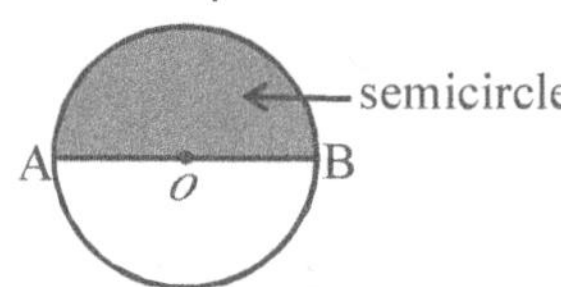

Area of semicircle $= \dfrac{1}{2}\pi r^2$

length of semicircular arc $\left(\widehat{AB}\right) = \pi r$

perimeter of semicircle $= (\pi + 2)r$

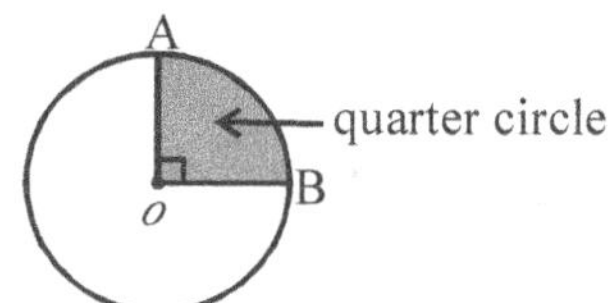

area of quarter circle $= \dfrac{1}{4}\pi r^2$

length of quarter circular arc $\left(\widehat{AB}\right) = \pi \dfrac{r}{2}$

perimeter of quarter circle $= \left(\dfrac{\pi}{2} + 2\right)r$

12. Concentric circles (Circular track or circular ring).

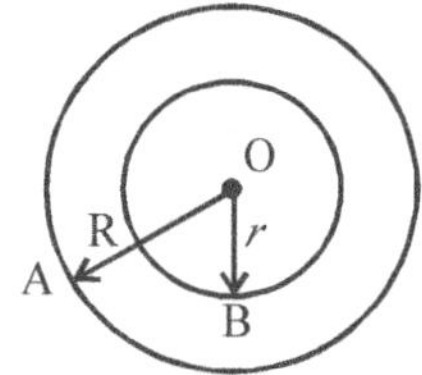

OA = R (outer radius)
OB = r (inner radius)

Area of circular track $= \pi\left(R^2 + r^2\right)$

13. Sector of circle

Length of arc :

$$AB = \frac{\theta}{360} \times \text{circumference of circle}$$

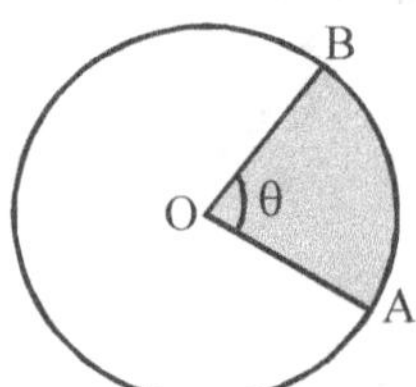

$\angle AOB = \theta$

Length of arc : $\widehat{AB} = \dfrac{\theta}{360} \times \text{circumference}$

$$= \frac{\theta}{360} \times 2\pi r$$

$$\text{Perimeter of sector} = 2r\left(\frac{\theta\pi}{360}+1\right)$$

$$\text{Area of sector} = \frac{\theta}{360} \times \text{area of circle} = \frac{\theta}{360} \times \pi r^2$$

14. Segment of circle

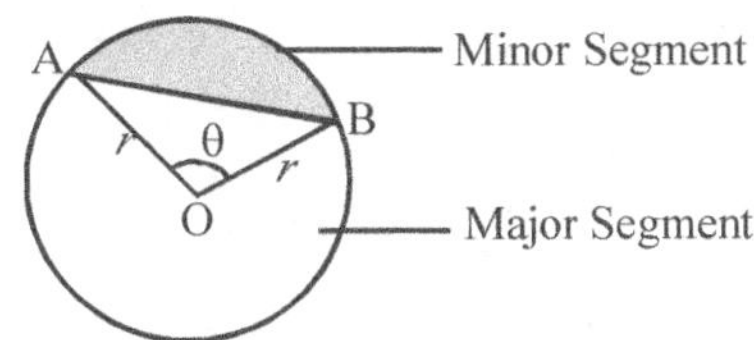

$$\text{Area of minor segment} = \frac{r^2}{2}\left[\frac{\theta\pi}{180} - \sin\theta\right]$$

Area of major segment = area of circle – area of minor segment

$$= \frac{r^2}{2}\left[\frac{(360-\theta)}{180}\pi + \sin\theta\right]$$

SOLVED EXAMPLES

Ex. 1 : A field in shape of a quadrilateral has one diagonal of length 10 m. Perpendicular to the diagonal from the opposite corners are of lengths 7 m and 5 m. The area of the field is :

A. $36\,\text{m}^2$ B. $60\,\text{m}^2$

C. $120\,\text{m}^2$ D. $30\,\text{m}^2$

Sol : Area of field $= \dfrac{1}{2} \times 10 \times (7+5)\,\text{m}^2$

$$= 60\ \text{m}^2$$

Ex. 2 : The area of triangle with sides 35 cm, 66 cm and 53 cm is :

A. 924 cm^2 B. 1386 cm^2

C. 693 cm^2 D. 1848 cm^2

Sol : $s = \dfrac{35+66+53}{2} = 77$

$$\text{Area of } \Delta = \sqrt{\begin{array}{c}77\times(77-35)\times(77-66)\\ \times(77-53)\end{array}}\ \text{cm}^2$$

$$= \sqrt{77\times11\times42\times24}\ \text{cm}^2$$

$$= 924\ \text{cm}^2$$

Ex. 3 :

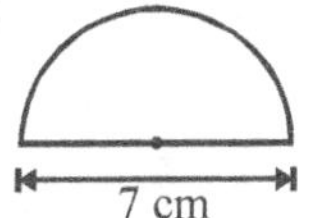

The area and perimeter of a protactor with base 7 cm are :

A. 6.5 cm^2 and 36 cm

B. 6.25 cm^2 and 36 cm

C. 6.125 cm^2 and 42 cm

D. 19.25 cm^2 and 18 cm

Sol : $r = \dfrac{7}{2}\,\text{cm}$

$$\text{Area} = \frac{1}{2}\times\frac{22}{7}\times\frac{7}{2}\times\frac{7}{2}\,\text{cm}^2 = 19.25\,\text{cm}^2$$

$$\text{Perimeter} = \pi r + 2r = \frac{22}{7}\times\frac{7}{2} + 2\times\frac{7}{2} = 18\,\text{cm}.$$

Ex. 4 : Sides of a quadrilateral are 9 cm, 40 cm, 28 cm and 15 cm. The angle between the first two sides is a right angle. The area of the quadrilateral is :

A. $312\,\text{cm}^2$ B. $280\,\text{cm}^2$

C. $306\,\text{cm}^2$ D. None of these

Sol :

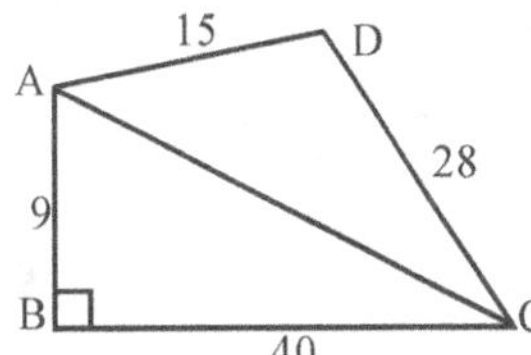

$$\text{Area } \Delta\text{ABC} = \frac{1}{2}\times 9\times 40\,\text{cm} = 180\ \text{cm}^2$$

$$\text{In } \Delta\text{ABC}; \text{AC} = \sqrt{40^2+9^2}\ \text{cm}$$

$$= 41\ \text{cm}$$

$$\text{In } \Delta\text{ADC}; \quad s = \frac{41+15+28}{2} = 42\ \text{cm}$$

Area ΔADC

$$= \sqrt{42(42-41)(42-18)(42-15)}\ \text{cm}^2$$

$$= 126\ \text{cm}^2$$

Area of quadrilateral

ABCD = (180 + 126) cm^2 = 306 cm^2.

Ex. 5 : The inner and outer radii of a circular track are 10 m and 14 m respectively. The total cost of levelling the track @ Rs 5/ m^2 and fencing the inner and outer boundaries of the track @ Rs 20/m is :

$$(\text{use } \pi = 3.14)$$

A. Rs. 4506.50   B. Rs. 4726

C. Rs. 4512.60   D. Rs. 4521.60

Sol : R = 14 m, r = 10 m

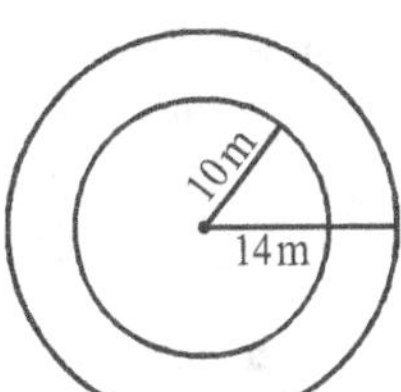

$$\text{Area of track} = 3.14\times(14^2-10^2) = 301.44\,\text{m}^2$$

cost of levelling
$$= \text{Rs. } 301.44 \times 5 = \text{Rs. } 1507.20$$

Perimeter of track $= 2 \times 3.14(14+10)\,\text{m}$
$$= 150.72 \text{ m}$$
Cost of fencing $= \text{Rs. } 150.72 \times 20$
$$= \text{Rs. } 3014.40$$
$$\text{Total cost } = 1507.20 + 3014.40$$
$$\text{Rs. } 4521.60$$

Ex. 6 : If the minute hand is 14 cm long: the area of the face of the clock swept between 12.10 a.m. and 12.25 a.m. is

A. $38.5\,\text{cm}^2$ B. $77\,\text{cm}^2$

C. $115.5\,\text{cm}^2$ D. $154\,\text{cm}^2$

Sol : The area swept is clearly a quarter circle.

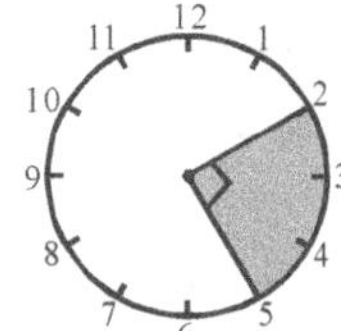

$$\text{Area } = \frac{1}{4} \times \frac{22}{7} \times 14 \times 14 \,\text{cm}^2 = 154\,\text{cm}^2$$

Ex. 7 : A chord of a circle of radius 6 cm subtends an angle of 60° at the centre of the circle. The area of the minor segment is :
(use $\pi = 3.14$)

A. 6.54 cm^2 B. 0.327 cm^2

C. 7.25 cm^2 D. 3.27 cm^2

Sol :

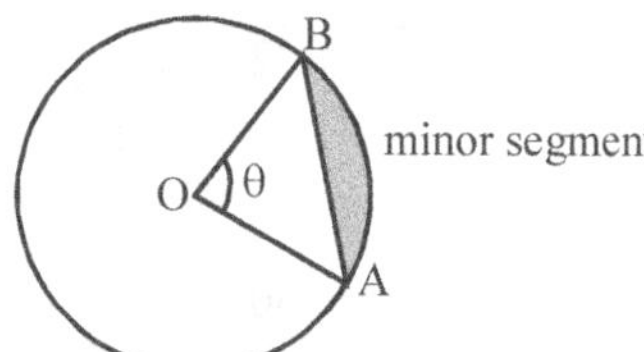

$$\theta = 60°, \quad r = 6\,\text{cm}$$

$$\text{Area of minor segment} = \frac{36}{2}\left[\frac{60 \times 3.14}{180} - \frac{\sqrt{3}}{2}\right]$$

$$= 3.27 \text{ cm}^2$$

Ex. 8 : The minute hand and the hour hand of a clock are 14 cm and 7 cm long respectively. The total distance covered by their tips in one day is

A. 24 m   B. 26 m

C. 22 m   D. None of these

Sol : In one day the minute hand covers 24 rounds while the hour hand covers 2 rounds.

Let radius of circular path covered by minute hand : $R = 14$ cm

and radius of circular path covered by hour hand : $r = 7$ cm

Total distance travelled $= 24 \times 2\pi R + 2 \times 2\pi r$
$$= 48\pi R + 4\pi r$$
$$= 4\pi(12 \times 14 + 7) \text{ cm}$$
$$= 4 \times \frac{22}{7} \times 175 \text{ cm}$$
$$= 2200\,\text{cm} = 22\,\text{m}$$

Ex. 9 :

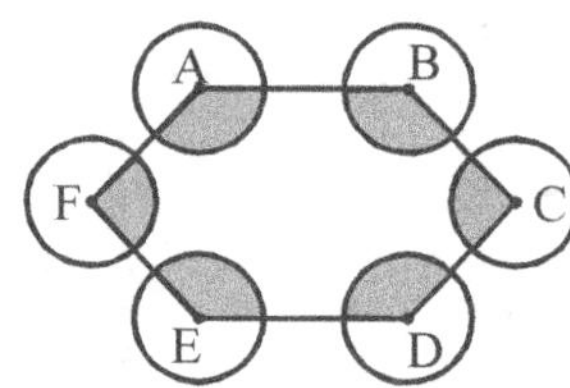

ABCDEF is a regular hexagon of side 3 cm. At each corner is drawn a circle of radius 1 cm. The area of the shaded part is :

A. 1.57 cm^2 B. 9.42 cm^2

C. 6.28 cm^2 D. 3.14 cm^2

Sol : Each angles $= \dfrac{180(6-2)°}{6} = 120°$

$$\text{Area of 1 sector} = \frac{120}{360} \times 3.14 \times 1^2 \text{ cm}^2$$

$$= \frac{3.14}{3} \text{ cm}^2$$

$$\therefore \text{ Area of 6 sectors} = 6 \times \frac{3.14}{3}\text{ cm}^2$$

$$= 6.28 \text{ cm}^2$$

Ex. 10 : A rectangular sheet of plastic has dimension 40 cm × 25 cm. 224 circular buttons of diameter 2 cm are cut out of this sheet. The area of the sheet left out is (use $\pi = 3.14$)

A. 593.28 cm^2 B. 296.64 cm^2

C. 444.96 cm^2 D. None of these

Sol : Area of sheet $= 40 \times 25 \text{ cm}^2 = 1000 \text{ cm}^2$

Area of button $= 3.14 \times 1 \times 1 \text{ cm}^2 = 3.14 \text{ cm}^2$

Area of 224 buttons $= 224 \times 3.14 \text{ cm}^2$

$$= 703.36 \text{ cm}^2$$

Area of sheet left out $= (1000 - 703.36)\text{cm}^2$

$$= 296.64 \text{ cm}^2$$

MULTIPLE CHOICE QUESTIONS

1. In a quadrilateral ABCD, AB ∥ CD and AD ⊥ AB. Also AB = 16 cm, DC = BC = 10 cm. The area of the quadrilateral is :
A. 26 cm^2 B. 54 cm^2
C. 52 cm^2 D. 104 cm^2

2. The parallel sides of a trapezium are 20 cm and 32 cm. Its non-parallel sides are 10 cm each. The area of the trapezium is :
A. 144 cm^2 B. 108 cm^2
C. 208 cm^2 D. 416 cm^2

3. The base of an isosceles triangle is 16 cm and its perimeter is 36 cm. The area of the triangle is :
A. 72 cm^2 B. 36 cm^2
C. 24 cm^2 D. 48 cm^2

4. Sides of a triangle are 8 cm, 15 cm and 17 cm. The altitude to the longest side is nearly :
A. 8 cm   B. 7.06 cm
C. 6.72 cm   D. 10.5 cm

5. The length of hypotenuse of a right-angled triangle is 5 cm and its area is 6 cm^2. The lengths of the remaining sides are :
A. 4 cm and 2 cm   B. 3 cm and 2 cm
C. 1 cm and 3 cm   D. 3 cm and 4 cm

6. The area of rhombus is 80 sq. cm and its perimeter is 80 cm. The length of its altitude is :
A. 2 cm   B. 8 cm
C. 4 cm   D. 2.5 cm

7. A field is in the form of a rhombus has each side of length 81 m and altitude 16 m. The side of a square field which has the same area as that of the rhombus is :
A. 20 m^2 B. 24 m^2
C. 26 m^2 D. 36 m^2

8. The area of a sector is 1/18th of the area of the circle. The sectorial angle is :
A. 18°   B. 36°
C. 10°   D. 20°

9. The arc of a circle, having measure of 18 degrees, has a length of 33 m. The circumference of the circle is:
A. 330 m   B. 660 m
C. 666 m   D. 1200 m

10. A sector of a circle with sectorial angle of 36° has an area of 15.4 sq. cm. The length of the arc of the sector is
A. 8.8 cm   B. 4.4 cm
C. 0.22 cm   D. 0.44 cm

11. The ratio of the two unequal sides of a rectangle is 1 : 2. If its perimeter is 24 cm, then length of diagonal is :
A. $\dfrac{2}{\sqrt{5}}$ cm   B. $\dfrac{3}{\sqrt{5}}$ cm
C. $4\sqrt{5}$ cm   D. $2\sqrt{5}$ cm

12. A rectangular sheet of acrylic is 50 cm by 25 cm. From it 60 buttons, each of diameter 2.8 cm have been cut out. The area of the remaining sheet is
A. 1260.82 cm^2 B. 880.4 cm^2
C. 630.4 cm^2 D. None of these

13. Area of circle A is 121 times the area of circle B. The ratio of the circumference of circle A to that of B is
A. 121 : 1   B. 1 : 11
C. 11 : 1   D. Cannot be determined

14. A circular disc of radius 7 cm has a sector of angle 45 degrees cut out. The area of the remaining part of the disc is
A. 134.75 cm^2 B. 144.75 cm^2
C. 269.5 cm^2 D. None of these

15. The minute hand of a clock is $\sqrt{21}$ cm long. The area described by the minute hand on the face of the clock between 7 am and 7.05 am is
A. 5.5 cm^2 B. 22 cm^2
C. 11 cm^2 D. None of these

16. A wire in the form of circle of diameter 42 cm is cut and bent to form a square. The side of the square is
A. 16 cm   B. 17 cm
C. 33 cm   D. 16.5 cm

17. A table cover 6 m × 3 m is spread on a table top. If 25 cm of the cover hangs all around the table then the cost of polishing the table @ ₹ 12 m^2 is
A. ₹ 165   B. ₹ 175
C. ₹ 180   D. ₹ 195

18. Diameter of semicircular protractor is 7 cm. Its perimeter is
A. 22 cm   B. 18 cm
C. 36 cm   D. 22 cm

19. The area of a quadrant of a circle whose circumference is 44 cm is
A. 144 cm^2 B. 175.76 cm^2
C. 38.5 cm^2 D. 154 cm^2

20. ΔABC is an equilateral Δ with area $36\sqrt{3}$ cm^2. The area of the inscribed circle is
A. 12π cm^2 B. 48π cm^2
C. 24π cm^2 D. 36π cm^2

21. AOBCA is a quadrant of a circle of radius 3.5 cm with centre O. P is adjoint on OB such that OP = 2 cm. The area of the shaded part is

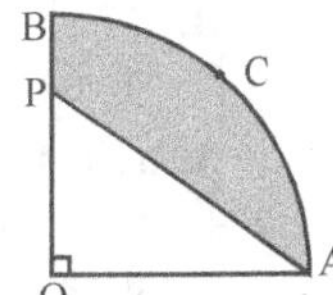

A. 12.25 cm^2 B. 6.125 cm^2
C. 12.5 cm^2 D. None of these

22. If the area of a circle is 346.5 cm². Its circumference is
A. 11 cm   B. 66 cm
C. 22 cm   D. 44 cm

23. The difference in the area of a square of perimeter 88 m and a circle with same circumference is
A. 166 cm²   B. 122 cm²
C. 133 cm²   D. 132 cm²

24. An iron washer is made by cutting out from a circular plate of radius 10 cm, a concentric circular plate of radius 6 cm. The area of the face of the washer nearly is (use $\pi = 3.14$)
A. 201 cm²   B. 206 cm²
C. 200 cm²   D. 204 cm²

25. Perimeter of a right angled triangle is 40 cm and length of its hypotenuse is 17 cm. The area of this triangle is
A. 30 cm²   B. 60 cm²
C. 120 cm²   D. None of these

26. One side of a right angled triangle measures 12 cm and the difference between the hypotenuse and the other side is 8 cm. The area of the triangle is :
A. 30 cm²   B. 15 cm²
C. 10 cm²   D. None of these

27. The length of the minute hand of a wall clock is 14 cm. The area swept by the minute hand in 7.5 minutes is
A. 63 cm²   B. 77 cm²
C. 57.75 cm²   D. 15.4 cm²

28. Diagonals of a rhombus are 5 cm and 12 cm long. Its perimeter is
A. 52 cm   B. 36 cm
C. 26 cm   D. 13 cm

29. If the side of a square is increased by 8 cm, its area increases by 120 cm². The side of the square is
A. 3.5 cm   B. 5.5 cm
C. 2.5 cm   D. 4.5 cm

30. A square and an equilateral triangle have equal perimeters. If the area of the triangle is $16\sqrt{3}$ cm², the side of the square is
A. 6 cm   B. $4\sqrt{2}$ cm
C. 4 cm   D. $6\sqrt{2}$ cm

31. Two circles touch externally. The sum of their areas is 130π sq. cm. and the distance between their centres is 14 cm. The radii of the circles are
A. 11, 3   B. 12, 4
C. 5, 8   D. 4, 6

32. A copper wire when bent in the form of a square, encolses an area of 484 cm². If the same wire is bent in the form of circle, the area enclosed by it is
A. 210 cm²   B. 616 cm²
C. 512 cm²   D. 54 cm²

33. In the given figure AOBCA resperesents a quadrant of a circle of radius 3.5 cm with centre O. The area of the shaded portion is

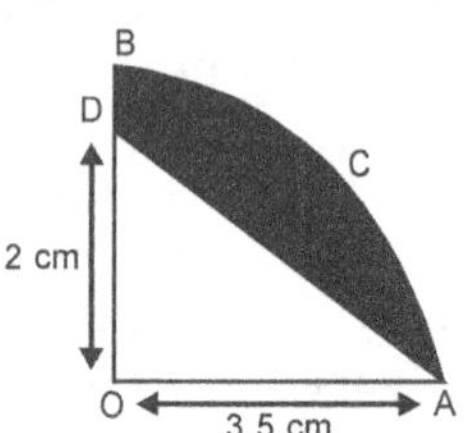

A. 5.25 cm²   B. 4.12 cm²
C. 6.125 cm²   D. 8.225 cm²

34. A bicycle wheel makes 5000 revolutions in moving 11 kms. The diameter of the wheel is
A. 70 cm   B. 50 cm
C. 35 cm   D. 28 cm

35. ABCD is a quadrant of a circle of radius 14 cm. With AC as diameter, a semi-circle is drawn. The area of shaded portion is
A. 56 cm²   B. 76 cm²
C. 88 cm²   D. 98 cm²

36. The minute hand of a clock is 10 cm long. The area of the face of the clock described by the minute hand between 9 AM and 9.35 AM is
A. 140 cm²   B. 183.3 cm²
C. 180 cm²   D. 175.3 cm²

37. It is proposed to add to a square lawn with each side 58 m, two circular ends, the centre of each circle being the point of intersection of the diagonals of the square. The area of the whole lawn is

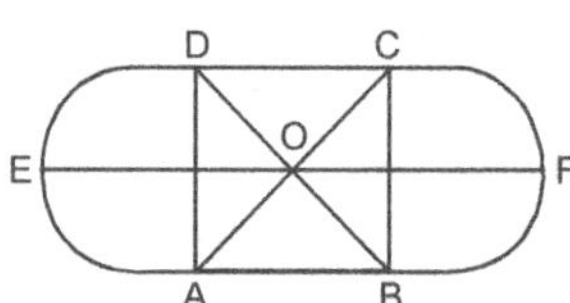

A. 415 m²   B. 4200 m²
C. 4319.5 m²   D. 4215.5 m²

38. There is a path all around outside a circular grassy field. If the radius of field be 20 metres and the area of path be equal to that of field, then the cost of paving the path with stones at the rate of ₹ 350 per sq. metres is
A. ₹ 2000   B. ₹ 2400
C. ₹ 3400   D. ₹ 4400

39. Find the ratio of areas of inscribed square in a semi-circle and a circle while the radii of circle and semi-circle are equal.
A. 2 : 5   B. 3 : 5
C. 4 : 5   D. 1 : 5

40. The perimeters of a circular and a square field are same. If the area of square field be 12100 sq. metres, the area of circular field is
A. 15200 m²   B. 15400 m²
C. 15600 m²   D. 15100 m²

ANSWERS

1	2	3	4	5	6	7	8	9	10
D	C	D	B	D	C	D	D	B	D
11	**12**	**13**	**14**	**15**	**16**	**17**	**18**	**19**	**20**
C	B	C	B	A	C	A	B	C	A
21	**22**	**23**	**24**	**25**	**26**	**27**	**28**	**29**	**30**
B	B	D	A	B	A	B	C	A	A
31	**32**	**33**	**34**	**35**	**36**	**37**	**38**	**39**	**40**
A	B	C	A	D	B	C	D	A	B

EXPLANATORY ANSWERS

1. 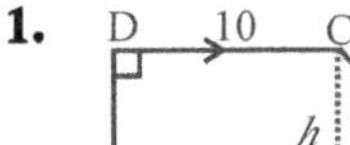

$BE = 16 - 10 = 6\,cm$

$h^2 + 6^2 = 10^2 \implies h = 8$

Area of $ABCD = \dfrac{1}{2}(16 + 10) \times 8\,cm^2$

$\qquad\qquad = 104\,cm^2$

2. 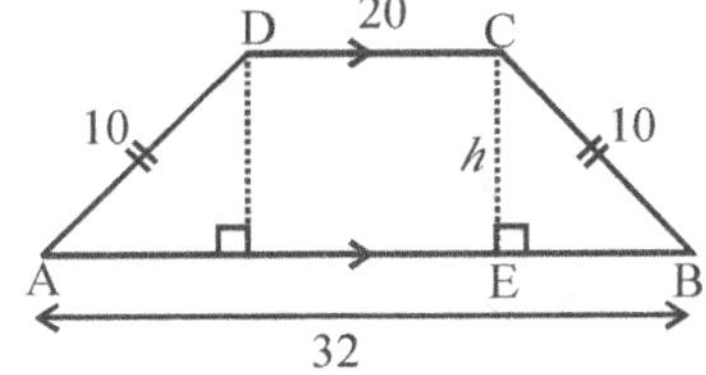

$BE = \dfrac{1}{2}(AB - DC) = 6\,cm$

$h^2 + 6^2 = 10^2$

$\implies h = 8\,cm$

Area of trapezium $= \dfrac{1}{2}(32 + 20) \times 8\,cm^2 = 208\,cm^2$

3. 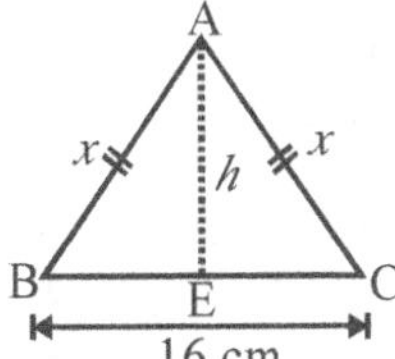

$x = \dfrac{1}{2}(36 - 16)\,cm = 10\,cm$

Now, $h^2 + 8^2 = 10^2$

$\implies h = 6\,cm$

Area of $\triangle ABC = \dfrac{1}{2} \times 16\,cm \times 6\,cm = 48\,cm^2$

4. $\langle 8, 15, 17 \rangle$ is a Pythagoras triplet

Area of triangle $= \dfrac{1}{2} \times 8\,cm \times 15\,cm = 60\,cm^2$

Now, $\dfrac{1}{2} \times 17 \times h = 60\,cm^2$

$\implies h \approx 7.06\,cm$

5. $\dfrac{1}{2}ab = 6 \implies ab = 12$

$a^2 + b^2 = 5^2$

$a + b = \sqrt{a^2 + b^2 + 2ab} = \sqrt{5^2 + 2 \times 12} = 7\,cm$

$a - b = \sqrt{a^2 + b^2 - 2ab} = \sqrt{5^2 - 2 \times 12} = 1\,cm$

$a = \dfrac{1}{2}(7 + 1) = 4\,cm$; Thus, $b = 3\,cm$.

6. Side $= \dfrac{80}{4}\,cm = 20\,cm$

Now, side $\times$ corresponding altitude = area

$\implies 20 \times h = 80 \implies h = 4\,cm.$

7. Area of square = Area of rhombus

$side^2 = 81 \times 16$

$side = \sqrt{81 \times 16}\,m = 9 \times 4 = 36\,m.$

8. $\dfrac{x}{360} = \dfrac{1}{18} \implies x = 20°$

9. $18° : 33\,m = 360° : x\,m$

$x = \dfrac{360 \times 33}{18} = 660\,m.$

10. $\dfrac{36}{360} \times \dfrac{22}{7} r^2 = 15.4 \implies r^2 = \dfrac{15.4 \times 5 \times 7}{11} = 49 \implies r = 7$

$C = 2\pi r = 2 \times \dfrac{22}{7} \times 7 = 44\,cm = 0.44\,m$

11. $L : B = 1 : 2$; $\qquad L = x, \qquad B = 2x$

$2(L + B) = 24$

$\implies 3x = 12 \implies x = 4$

Thus, two sides are 4 cm & 8 cm.

Diagonal $= \sqrt{4^2 + 8^2} = \sqrt{80} = 4\sqrt{5}\,cm.$

12. Required area
= Area of sheet − 60 × area of 1 button

$$=\left(50\times25-60\times\frac{22}{7}\times1.4\times1.4\right)\text{cm}^2$$

$$=(1250-369.6)\text{cm}^2 = 880.4\,\text{cm}^2$$

13. $\dfrac{\text{Circumference of A}}{\text{Circumference of B}}=\sqrt{\dfrac{\text{Area of A}}{\text{Area of B}}}=\dfrac{\sqrt{121}}{\sqrt{1}}=\dfrac{11}{1}$

14. Required area $=\dfrac{360-45}{360}\times\dfrac{22}{7}\times7^2$

$$=\dfrac{7\times11\times7}{4}=134.75\,\text{cm}^2$$

15. $r=\sqrt{21},\quad \theta=5\times6°=30°$

Required area $=\dfrac{30}{360}\times\dfrac{22}{7}\times21=5.5\,\text{cm}^2$

16. Perimeter of square = Circumference of circle

$$4\times\text{side}\;=\;\dfrac{22}{7}\times42=132$$

$$\Rightarrow \text{side} = 33 \text{ cm}$$

17. Area of table top $=5.5\times2.5\,\text{m}^2 = 13.75\,\text{m}^2$

Cost $=$ ₹ 12 × 13.75 = ₹165

18. $2r=7\Rightarrow\; r=\dfrac{7}{2}\text{cm}$

$$\overset{\frown}{AB}+AB=\left(\dfrac{22}{7}\times\dfrac{7}{2}+7\right)\text{cm}\;=18\,\text{cm}$$

19. $C=2\pi r=44\Rightarrow r=7\,\text{cm}$

Area of quadrant $=\dfrac{1}{4}\times\dfrac{22}{7}\times7^2 = 38.5\,\text{m}^2$

20. $\text{Side}^2\times\dfrac{\sqrt{3}}{4}=36\sqrt{2}\;\Rightarrow\;\text{Side}=12\,\text{cm}$

Semi perimeter $=\dfrac{12\times3}{2}=18\,\text{cm}$

Radius of the circle $=\dfrac{36\sqrt{3}}{18}=2\sqrt{3}\,\text{cm}.$

Area $=\pi\times\left(2\sqrt{3}\right)^2=12\pi\,\text{cm}^2$

21. Shaded Area = Area of quarter circle − Area of $\triangle POA$

$$=\dfrac{1}{4}\times\dfrac{22}{7}\times\dfrac{7}{2}\times\dfrac{7}{2}-\dfrac{1}{2}\times2\times3.5$$

$$=9.625-3.5=6.125\,\text{cm}^2$$

22. $\pi r^2=346.5\,\text{cm}^2$

$$\dfrac{22}{7}r^2=346.5\,\text{cm}^2$$

$$r^2=346.5\times\dfrac{7}{22}=110.25$$

$$\Rightarrow\; r=10.5\,\text{cm}$$

$$C=2\pi r=2\times\dfrac{22}{7}\times10.5=66\,\text{cm}.$$

23. Perimeter of sq = 88 cm

∴ side of sq = 22 cm

⇒ area of sq = 484 cm²

$C=2\pi r=88\Rightarrow r=14$

∴ Area $=\dfrac{22}{7}\times14\times14=616\,\text{cm}^2$

Difference in the areas = 616 − 484 = 132 cm²

24. R = 10 cm, $r = 6$ cm

Area of washer $=\pi(R+r)(R-r)$

$$=3.14\times16\times4$$

$$=200.96\,\text{cm}^2\approx201\,\text{cm}^2$$

25.

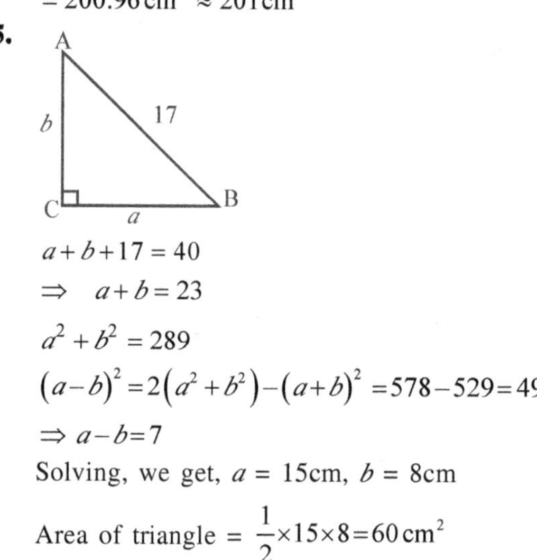

$a+b+17=40$

$\Rightarrow\; a+b=23$

$a^2+b^2=289$

$(a-b)^2=2(a^2+b^2)-(a+b)^2=578-529=49$

$\Rightarrow a-b=7$

Solving, we get, a = 15cm, b = 8cm

Area of triangle $=\dfrac{1}{2}\times15\times8=60\,\text{cm}^2$

26.

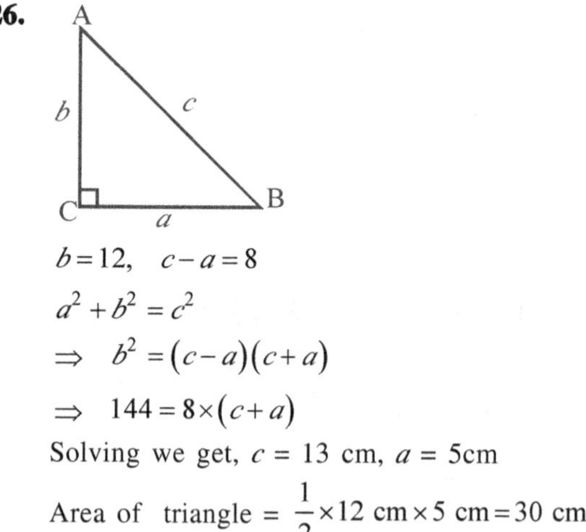

$b=12,\quad c-a=8$

$a^2+b^2=c^2$

$\Rightarrow\; b^2=(c-a)(c+a)$

$\Rightarrow\; 144=8\times(c+a)$

Solving we get, c = 13 cm, a = 5cm

Area of triangle $=\dfrac{1}{2}\times12\,\text{cm}\times5\,\text{cm}=30\,\text{cm}^2$

27. Required area $\dfrac{7.5}{60}\times\dfrac{22}{7}\times14\,\text{cm}\times14\,\text{cm}=77\,\text{cm}^2.$

28. Perimeter $=2\sqrt{d_1^2+d_2^2}$

$$=\sqrt{5^2+12^2}=2\times13=26\,\text{cm}.$$

29. $(x+8)^2=x^2+120$

$$\Rightarrow 16x=56\Rightarrow x=3.5\,\text{cm}.$$

30. Side of triangle $= \sqrt{\dfrac{4}{\sqrt{3}} \times 16\sqrt{3}} = 8\,\text{cm}$,

Perimeter $= 3 \times 8 = 24$ cm.

Side of the square $= \dfrac{24}{4} = 6\,\text{cm}$

31. Let the radii of the two circles be r_1 and r_2 respectively.

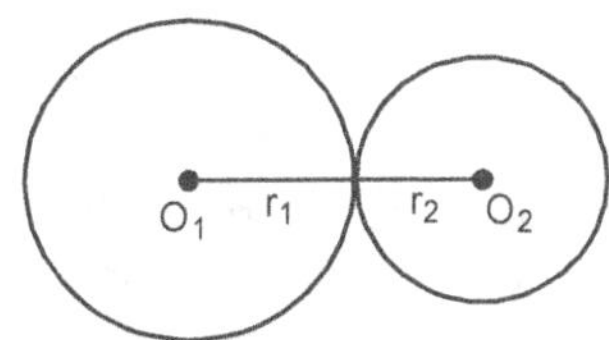

$\therefore$ They touch externally $r_1 + r_2 = 14$ ...(i)

According to the question,

$$\pi r_1^2 + \pi r_2^2 = 130\pi$$
$$\Rightarrow \quad r_1^2 + r_2^2 = 130 \qquad ...(ii)$$

Now, $(r_1 + r_2)^2 = r_1^2 + r_2^2 + 2r_1 r_2$

$14^2 = 130 + 2r_1 r_2$ [By (i) and (ii)]

$$\Rightarrow \quad 2r_2 r_2 = 196 - 130 = 66$$
$$\Rightarrow \quad r_1 r_2 = 33 \qquad ...(iii)$$
$$\therefore (r_1 - r_2)^2 = r_1^2 + r_2^2 - 2r_1 r_2$$
$$= 130 - 66 = 64$$
$$\Rightarrow \quad r_1 - r_2 = \sqrt{64} = 8 \qquad ...(iv)$$

Solving equations (i) and (iv) we have

$r_1 = 11$ cm and $r_2 = 3$ cm

32. Area of the square $= 484\ \text{cm}^2$

$\therefore$ Side $= \sqrt{484} = 22$ cm

Length of wire $=$ Perimeter of square

$$= 4 \times \text{side} = 4 \times 22 = 88\ \text{cm}$$

Let r be the radius of the circle

Then, circumference of circle $=$ Perimeter of the square

$\therefore$ $2\pi r = 88$

$$\Rightarrow \quad r = \dfrac{88}{2\pi} = \dfrac{88 \times 7}{22 \times 2} = 14\ \text{cm}$$

$\Rightarrow$ Area of circle $= \pi r^2 = \dfrac{22}{7} \times 14 \times 14$

$$= 616\ \text{cm}^2$$

33. Area of quadrant AOBCA

$$= \dfrac{1}{4}\pi r^2 = \dfrac{1}{4} \times \dfrac{22}{7} \times (3.5)^2 = 9.625\ \text{cm}^2$$

Area of $\triangle$AOD $= \dfrac{1}{2} \times \text{base} \times \text{height}$

$$= \dfrac{1}{2} \times 3.5 \times 2 = 3.5\ \text{cm}^2$$

$\therefore$ Area of the shaded portion $=$ Area of quadrant $-$ Area of $\triangle$AOD

$= 9.625 - 3.5 = 6.125\ \text{cm}^2$

34. Distance covered by the wheel in one revolution

$$= \dfrac{\text{Distance covered}}{\text{Number of revolutions}}$$

$$= \dfrac{11}{5000}\,\text{km} = \dfrac{11 \times 1000 \times 100}{5000}\,\text{cm} = 220\ \text{cm}$$

$\therefore$ Circumference of the wheel $= 220$ cm

or,   Let diameter $= d$ cm

$\therefore$ $\pi d = 220$ cm

$\therefore$ $d = \dfrac{220}{\pi} = \dfrac{220 \times 7}{22} = 70$ cm

35.

In the right angled triangle ABC

$$AC^2 = AB^2 + BC^2$$
$$\Rightarrow \quad AC = \sqrt{AB^2 + BC^2}$$
$$= \sqrt{14^2 + 14^2}$$
$$= \sqrt{2 \times 14^2} = 14\sqrt{2}\ \text{cm}$$

$\therefore$ Radius of semi-circle $= \dfrac{AC}{2} = \dfrac{14\sqrt{2}}{2} = 7\sqrt{2}$ cm

$\therefore$ Required area (shaded portion)

$=$ Area of ADCEA

$=$ Area of ACEA $-$ Area of ACDA

$=$ Area ACEA $-$ (Area of ABCDA $-$ Area of $\triangle$ABC)

$$= \dfrac{1}{2} \times \dfrac{22}{7} \times \left(7\sqrt{2}\right)^2 - \left[\dfrac{1}{4} \times \dfrac{22}{7} \times 14^2 - \dfrac{1}{2} \times 14 \times 14\right]$$

$$= \dfrac{1}{2} \times \dfrac{22}{7} \times 49 \times 2 - \dfrac{1}{4} \times \dfrac{22}{7} \times 14 \times 14 + \dfrac{1}{2} \times 14 \times 14$$

$= 154 - 154 + 98 = 98\ \text{cm}^2.$

36. Angle described by minute hand in 60 minutes $= 360°$

Angle described by minute hand in 35 minutes

$$= \dfrac{360}{60} \times 35 = 210°$$

$\therefore$ The area swept by the minute hand $=$ Area of sector where, $r = 10$ cm

and, $\theta = 210°$

$$= \dfrac{22}{7} \times 10 \times 10 \times \dfrac{210}{360}$$

$$= 183.3\ \text{cm}^2$$

37. Let ABCD be a square with side 58 metres.

Let its diagonals intersect at O,

Then OA $=$ OB $=$ OC $=$ OD and

$$\angle\text{AOD} = \angle\text{BOC} = 90°$$

With radius = $\dfrac{1}{2}$AC, arcs have been drawn namely AED and CBF

$\therefore$ Radius of each arc = $\dfrac{1}{2} \times$ diagonal

$$= \dfrac{1}{2} \times \sqrt{2} \times 58$$

$$= 1.41 \times 29 = 40.89 \text{ metres.}$$

$\therefore$ Area of whole lawn = Area of square ABCD + 2 × Area of segment with r where, $r = 40.89$ m and $\theta = 90°$

$$= 58 \times 58 + 2 \times \left[\dfrac{22}{7} \times (40.89)^2 \times \dfrac{90}{360} \right.$$

$$\left. - \dfrac{1}{2} \times (40.89)^2 \sin 90° \right]$$

$$= 33.64 + \dfrac{11 \times (40.89)^2}{7} - (40.89)^2$$

$$= (3364 + 2627.4 - 1671.9) \text{ sq. metres}$$

$$= 4319.5 \text{ sq. metres.}$$

38.

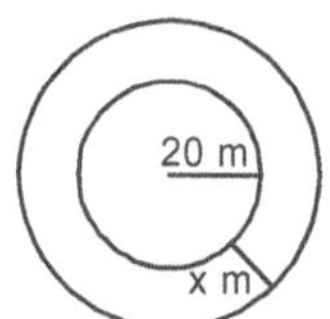

Area of circular field = $\pi \times$ (radius)^2

$= \pi \times 20 \times 20 = 400\,\pi$ sq. metres

Let the breadth of path be x m.

$\therefore$ Radius of outer circle = $(20 + x)$ metres

$\therefore$ Area of outer circle = $\pi (20 + x)^2$

$\therefore$ Area of path = $[\pi(20 + x)^2 - 400\pi]$ sq. metres

But, Area of path = Area of circular field

$\therefore \qquad \pi(20 + x)^2 - 400\pi = 400\pi$

$\Rightarrow \pi(400 + x^2 + 40x) - 400\pi = 400\pi$

$\Rightarrow \qquad\qquad x^2 + 40x - 400 = 0$

$$\therefore \qquad x = \dfrac{-40 \pm \sqrt{1600 + 4 \times 1 \times 400}}{2}$$

$$\left[\because \text{ For } ax^2 + bx + c = 0, = \dfrac{-b \pm \sqrt{b^2 - 4ac}}{2a} \right]$$

$$= \dfrac{-40 \pm \sqrt{2 \times 1600}}{2} = \dfrac{-40 \pm 40\sqrt{2}}{2}$$

$$= -20 + 20\sqrt{2}$$

[–is neglected as length can't be negative]

$$= 20\left(\sqrt{2} - 1\right) \text{ metres}$$

$\therefore$ Width of path = $20\left(\sqrt{2} - 1\right)$ m

Area of path = Area of field

$\therefore$ Cost of paving = $400 \times \dfrac{22}{7} \times 3.5$

$$= 400 \times 22 \times 0.5 = ₹\ 4400.$$

39.

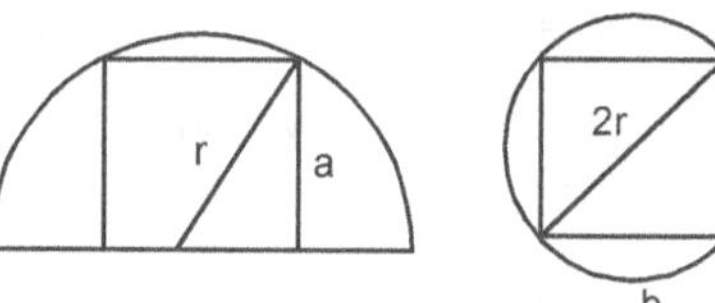

Let the side of square formed in semi-circle be a units and radius of semi-circle be r units

$$\therefore \qquad r^2 = a^2 + \dfrac{a^2}{4} = \dfrac{5a^2}{4}$$

$$\therefore \qquad a^2 = \dfrac{4r^2}{5}$$

For square inscribed in circle,

$$(2r)^2 = b^2 + b^2 = 2b^2$$

$$\Rightarrow \qquad 4r^2 = 2b^2$$

$$\Rightarrow \qquad b^2 = 2r^2$$

$$\therefore \qquad \text{Area} = b^2 = 2r^2$$

$$\therefore \quad \text{Required ratio} = \dfrac{\dfrac{4r^2}{5}}{2r^2}$$

$$= \dfrac{4r^2}{5} \times \dfrac{1}{2r^2} = \dfrac{2}{5} = 2:5.$$

40.

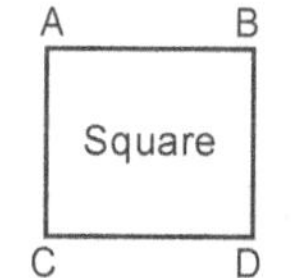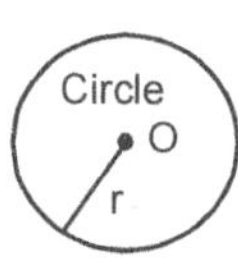

Area of square field = 12100 sq. metres

$\therefore \qquad$ Side of field = $\sqrt{12100}$ = 110 metres

$\therefore \qquad$ Its perimeter = 4 × side

$$= 4 \times 110 = 440 \text{ metres}$$

Since, perimeter of square field = perimeter of circluar field

$\therefore$ Perimeter of circular field = 440 metres

Let the radius of field be r metres

$\therefore \qquad 2\pi r = 440$

$$\Rightarrow \qquad r = \dfrac{440 \times 7}{44}$$

$$= 70 \text{ metres}$$

$\therefore$ Area of circular field = πr^2

$$= \dfrac{22}{7} \times 70 \times 70$$

$$= 15400 \text{ sq. metres.}$$

✳ ✳ ✳

12

Mensuration : Surface Areas and Volumes

The space occupied by an object is called volume. It is the measure of length, breadth and thickness of the object.

MENSURATION OF SOLID FIGURES

Cuboid

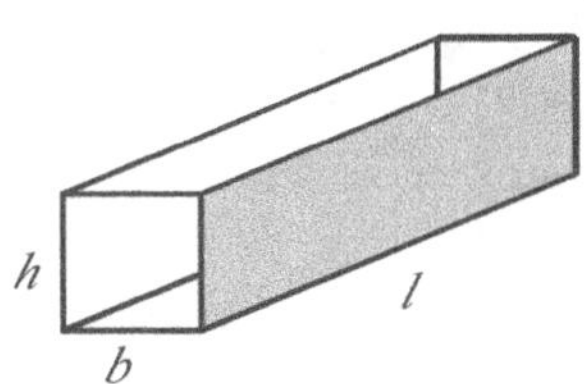

$TSA = 2[lb + bh + hl]$

LSA (area of 4 walls) $= 2 [l + b]$ H

$V = lbh$, Length of diagonal $= \sqrt{l^2 + b^2 + h^2}$

Cube

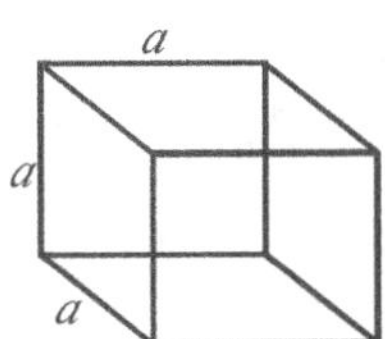

$TSA = 6$ (edge)^2, LSA (area of 4 walls) $= 4$ (edge)^2

$V = $ (edge)^3, Length of diagonal $=$ edge $\sqrt{3}$

Cylinder

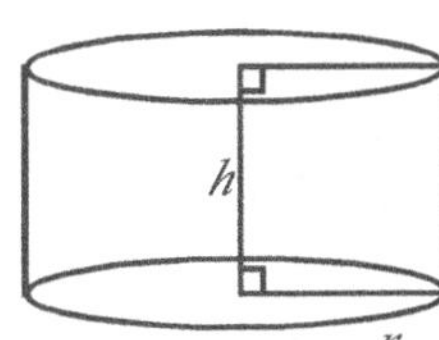

$CSA = 2\pi r h,\ TSA = 2\pi r (r + h)$

$V = \pi r^2 h$

Cone

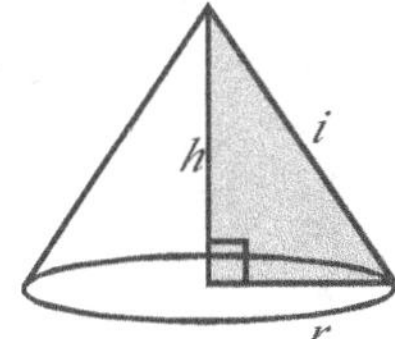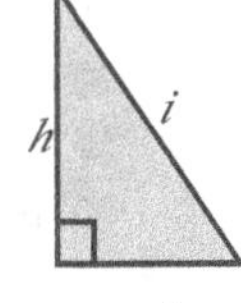

$r^2 + h^2 = l^2$

$CSA = \pi r l.\quad TSA = \pi r (l + r)$

$V = \dfrac{1}{3}\pi r^2 h$

Sphere

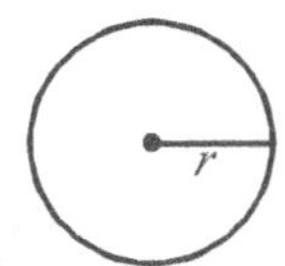

$SA = 4\pi r^2,\quad V = \dfrac{4}{3}\pi r^3$

Hemisphere

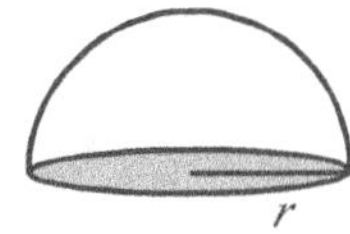

$CSA = 2\pi r^2,\quad TSA = 3.\pi r^2$

$V = \dfrac{2}{3}\pi r^3$

Hollow Cylinder

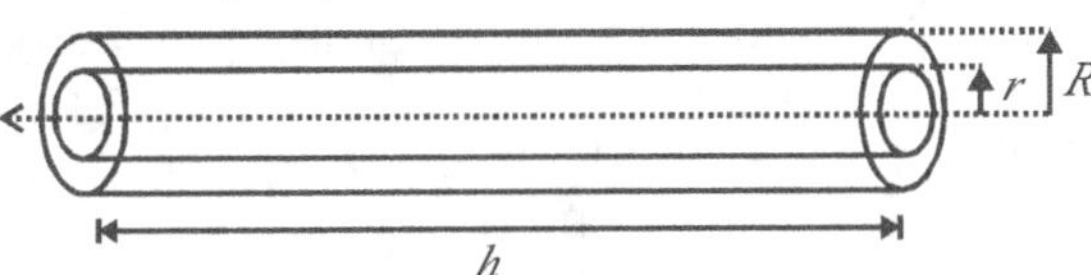

Volume of material of hollow cylinder $= \pi\left(R^2 - r^2\right) h$

Hollow Sphere

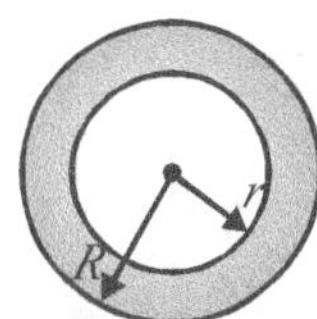

Volume of material of hollow sphere $= \dfrac{4}{3}\pi\left(R^3 - r^3\right)$

Capacity $= \dfrac{4}{3}\pi r^3$

Hollow Hemisphere

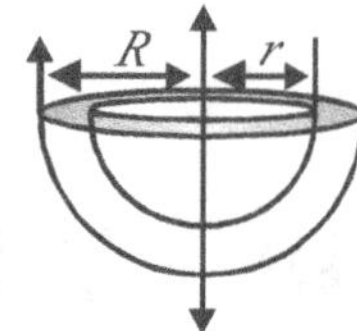

Volume of material of hollow hemisphere

$$= \frac{2}{3}\pi\left(R^3 - r^3\right)$$

Capacity $= \frac{2}{3}\pi r^3$

External $CSA = 2\pi R^2$,

Internal $CSA = 2\pi r^2$

$$CSA = \pi\left(R^2 + r^2\right), \quad TSA = \pi\left(3R^2 + r^2\right)$$

Frustum

If a cone is intersected by a plane parallel to its base the lower end so obtained is called a frustum.

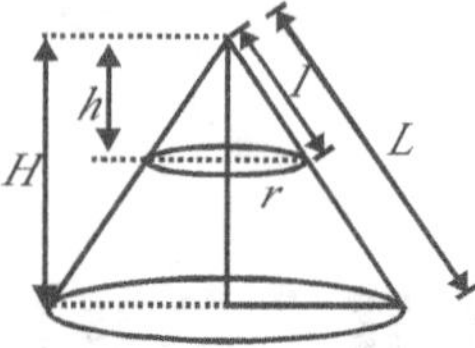

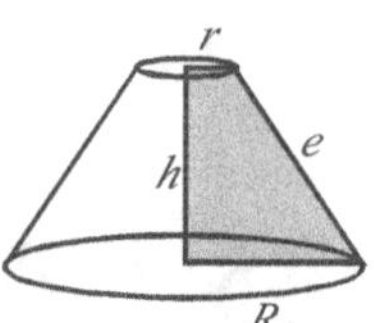

$$\frac{r}{R} = \frac{l}{L} = \frac{h}{H}$$

$$l = \sqrt{h^2 + (R-r)^2}$$

$$CSA = \pi(R+r)l, \quad TSA = \pi(R+r)l + \pi\left(R^2 + r^2\right)$$

$$V = \frac{1}{3}\pi h\left(R^2 + Rr + r^2\right)$$

$$V = \frac{1}{3}h\left(A_1 + A_2 + \sqrt{A_1 A_2}\right)$$

where A_1 is the area of the top surface and A_2 is the area of the bisected surface.

SOLVED EXAMPLES

Example 1 :

The length of canvas 2 m wide needed to make a conical tent of radius of base 4 m and height 3 m is ...... (use $\pi = 3.14$)

(a) 18.48 m   (b) 31.4 m
(c) 18.84 m   (d) 9.42 m

Sol : $l = \sqrt{4^2 + 3^2}$ m $= 5$ m

$CSA = \pi r l = 3.14 \times 4 \times 5$ m$^2 = 62.80$ m^2

Now, $l \times 2 = 62.80 \quad \Rightarrow \quad l = 31.4$ m

Example 2 :

A spherical ball made of iron has diameter 6 cm. If density of iron 8g/cm^3 then mass of the ball is nearly (use $\pi = 3.14$)

(a) 0.9 kg   (b) 0.8 kg
(c) 0.7 kg   (d) 0.62 kg

Sol : Volume of ball :

$$V = \frac{4}{3} \times 3.14 \times 3 \times 3 \times 3 \text{ cm}^3 = 113.04 \text{ cm}^3$$

Mass of ball = vol × density

$$= 113.04 \times 8 g$$

$$= 904.32 \text{ g} \approx 0.9 \text{ kg}$$

Example 3 :

A solid in shape of a frustum is 21 cm high. Its radius of top is 10 cm and diameter of bottom is 30 cm. The volume of the solid is

(a) 10,500 cm^3
(b) 10,450 cm^3
(c) 10,000 cm^3
(d) None of the above

Sol : Volume of frustum $= \frac{1}{3}\pi h\left(r_1^2 + r_1 r_2 + r_2^2\right)$

$$= \frac{1}{3} \times \frac{22}{7} \times 21 \times \left(10^2 + 10 \times 15 + 15^2\right) \text{ cm}^3$$

$$= \frac{1}{3} \times \frac{22}{7} \times 21 \times 475 \text{ cm}^3$$

$$= 10,450 \text{ cm}^3$$

Example 4 :

The length of longest pole that can be kept in a room 12 m long, 9 m broad and 8 m high, is ....

(a) 15 m
(b) 12 m
(c) 17 m
(d) None of the above

Sol : Length of largest pole $= \sqrt{12^2 + 9^2 + 8^2}$ m

$$\Rightarrow \sqrt{289} \text{ m} \Rightarrow 17 \text{ m}$$

Example 5 :

A cubical vessel can hold 1331 l of water. The length of side of the vessel in m is

(a) 11 m   (b) 1.1 m
(c) 0.11 m   (d) None of the above

Sol : $V = 1331 l = \dfrac{1331}{1000}$ m$^3 = \left(\dfrac{11}{10}\right)^3$ m^3

Side of cubical vessel $= \sqrt[3]{\left(\dfrac{11}{10}\right)^3}$ m $= 1.1$ m

Example 6 :
A cylindrical roller has a radius of 20 cm and is 77 cm long. The area travelled by this roller is 500 revolution is
(a) 1331 m² (b) 2000 m²
(c) 2660 m² (d) None of the above

Sol : Area levelled $= n \times CSA$

$$= 500 \times 2 \times \frac{22}{7} \times 20 \times 77 \text{ cm}^2$$

$$= \frac{500 \times 2 \times 22 \times 20 \times 11}{10000} \text{ m}^2$$

$$= 484 \text{ m}^2$$

Example 7 :
A hollow cylindrical pipe is made of iron. Its external and internal radii are 8 cm and 7 cm respectively and it is 35 cm long. If 1 cm³ iron weigh 8 g then the weight of the pipe is
(a) 13.25 kg (b) 13.2 kg
(c) 13.26 kg (d) 13.21 kg

Sol : Volume of material $= \pi\left(R^2 - r^2\right)h$

$$= \frac{22}{7}(8+7)(8-7) \times 35 \text{ cm}^3 = 1650 \text{ cm}^3$$

Weight $= 1650 \times 8 \text{ gm} = 13200 \text{ gms} = 13.2 \text{ kg}$

Example 8 :
A cylindrical tub of radius 16 cm contains water to the depth of 30 cm. A spherical iron ball is dropped into the tub. As a result the level of water rises by 9 cm. The radius of the ball is
(a) 10 cm (b) 6 cm
(c) 12 cm (d) None of the above

Sol :

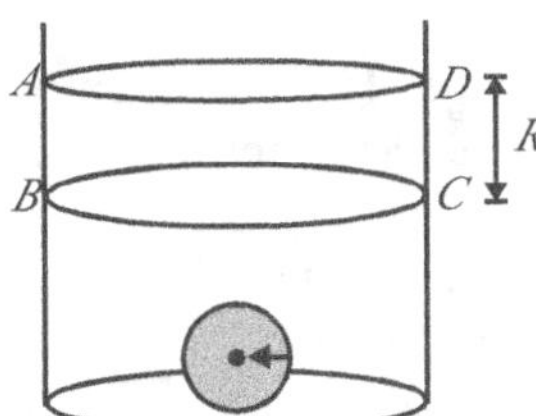

Volume of sphere = Volume of cylinder ABCD

$$\frac{4}{3}\pi r^3 = \pi R^2 h$$

$$\Rightarrow \frac{4}{3}r^3 = 16 \times 16 \times 9$$

$$\Rightarrow r^3 = 16 \times 16 \times 9 \times \frac{3}{4} = 1728 = 12^3$$

$$\Rightarrow r = 12 \text{ cm}$$

Example 9 :
A circus tent is cylindrical up to a height of 3 m and conical above it. If its diameter is 105 m and slant height of the conical portion is 53 m, then area of canvas needed to build the tent is

(a) 9730 m² (b) 9736 m²
(c) 9790 m² (d) 9735 m²

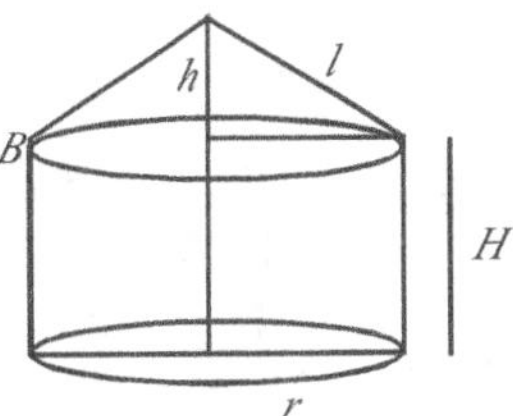

Sol : Area of canvas $= CSA$ of cyl $+ CSA$ of cone
$$= \pi r l + 2\pi r H$$
$$= \pi r\left(l + 2H\right)$$
$$= \frac{22}{7} \times \frac{105}{2}(53 + 6) \text{ m}^2$$
$$= 9735 \text{ m}^2$$

Example 10 :
Water flows at the rate of 7 m/min through a pipe with circular cross section of radius 2 cm. The volume of water which flows out of it in 10 minutes in litres is
(a) 44 l (b) 88 l
(c) 66 l (d) None of the above

Sol : Volume of water flowing out of the pipe
= Area of cross section × ratio of flow × time

$$= \frac{22}{7} \times \frac{2}{100} \times \frac{2}{100} \times 7 \times 10 \text{ m}^3$$

$$= 0.088 \text{ m}^3 = 0.088 \times 1000 \ l = 88 \ l$$

Example 11 :
The internal and external diameter of a hemispherical bowl are 12 cm and 10 cm respectively. The cost of painting the vessel all over @ ₹ 0.07/cm² is
(a) ₹ 26.25 (b) ₹ 50.52
(c) ₹ 25.26 (d) None of the above

Sol :

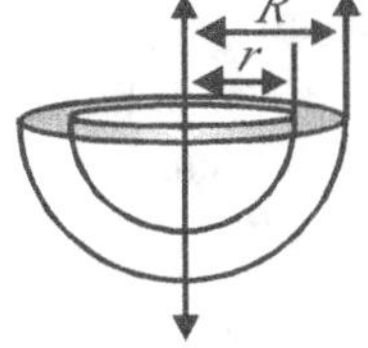

$$TSA = \pi\left(3R^2 + r^2\right)$$

$$= \frac{22}{7}\left(3 \times 6^2 + 5^2\right) \text{ cm}^2 = \frac{22}{7} \times 133 \text{ cm}^2$$

Cost $= ₹ \frac{22}{7} \times 133 \times \frac{7}{100} = ₹ 29.26$

Example 12 :
The volume of material of a hollow sphere with external radius 10 cm and internal diameter 6 cm is nearly.
(a) 4077 cm³ (b) 4070 cm³
(c) 4007 cm³ (d) 4073 cm³

Sol :

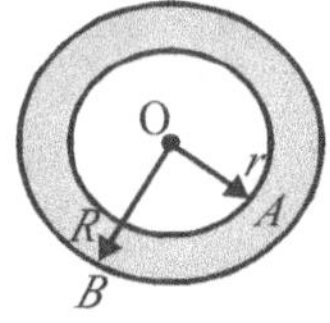

Volume of material $= \dfrac{4}{3} \times \dfrac{22}{7}\left(10^3 - 3^3\right)$ cm^3

$= \dfrac{4}{3} \times \dfrac{22}{7} \times 973$ cm^3 $= 4077.33$ cm^3 ≈ 4077 cm^3

Example 13 :

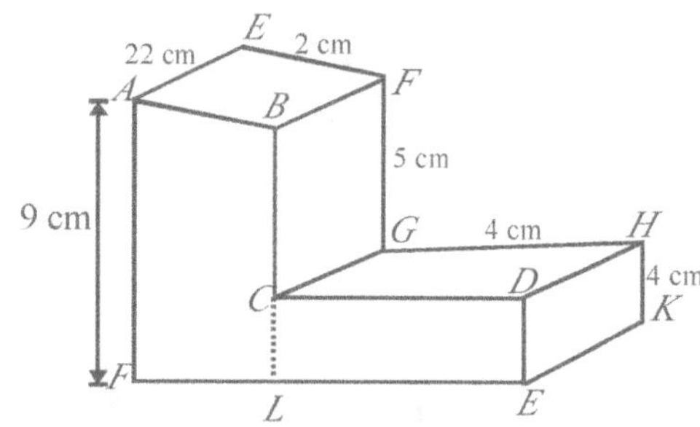

Volume of the solid shown above is

(a) 762 cm^2

(b) 784 cm^2

(c) 700 cm^2

(d) 748 cm^2

Sol : AF = (5 + 4) cm = 9 cm

DH = AE = 22 cm

volume of solid = volume of cuboid ABLF +

volume of cuboid CDEL

$= (22 \times 2 \times 9 + 4 \times 4 \times 22)$ cm^3 = 748 cm^3

Example 14 :

The number of spherical lead shots each 4.2 cm in diameter that can be obtained from a rectangular solid with diameter 66 cm × 42 cm × 21 cm is

(a) 750

(b) 3000

(c) 1500

(d) None of the above

Sol : Number of shots $= \dfrac{\text{volume of cuboid}}{\text{volume of sphere}}$

$= \dfrac{66 \times 42 \times 21}{\dfrac{4}{3} \times \dfrac{22}{7} \times \dfrac{21}{10} \times \dfrac{21}{10} \times \dfrac{21}{10}} = 1500$

Example 15 :

A hollow sphere of internal and external diameter 4 cm and 8 cm is melted and recasted into a cone of base diameter 8 cm. The height of the cone is

(a) 14 cm

(b) 15 cm

(c) 28 cm

(d) 30 cm

Sol :

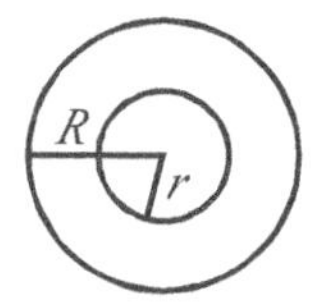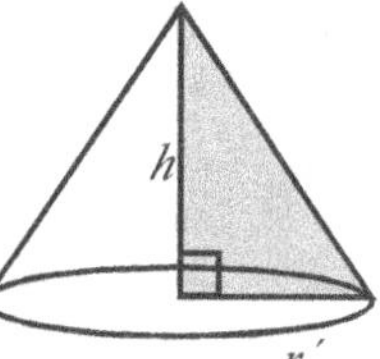

According to the question

$$\frac{1}{3}\pi r^2 h = \frac{4}{3}\pi\left(R^3 - r^3\right)$$

$$\Rightarrow \quad 4 \times 4 \times h = 4\left(4^3 - 2^3\right)$$

$$\Rightarrow \quad h = 14 \text{ cm}$$

MULTIPLE CHOICE QUESTIONS

1. The lateral surface area of a cube whose each side be 8 cm is:

A. 200 cm^2 B. 256 cm^2

C. 240 cm^2 D. 225 cm^2

2. The lateral surface area of cuboid whose length is 10 cm, breadth is 8 cm and height is 5 cm is:

A. 120 cm^2 B. 150 cm^2

C. 180 cm^2 D. 200 cm^2

3. Slant height of a cone is 13 cm and radius is 7 cm, its lateral surface area is:

A. 280 cm^2 B. 282 cm^2

C. 284 cm^2 D. 286 cm^2

4. The radius of a sphere is 3 cm its volume is:

A. 113.14 cm^3 B. 120 cm^3

C. 108 cm^3 D. 112.12 cm^3

5. The curved surface area of a right circular cylinder of height 14 cm is 88 cm^2. The radius of the cylinder is:

A. 2 cm   B. 1 cm

C. 3 cm   D. 4 cm

6. A rectangular sheet of paper 44 cm × 18 cm is rolled along its length and a cylinder is formed. The radius of the cylinder is:

A. 10 cm   B. 14 cm

C. 7 cm   D. 3.5 cm

7. The diameter of a garden roller is 1.4 m and it is 2 m long. How much area will it cover in one revolution?

A. 6.8 m^2 B. 8.8 m^2

C. 3.8 m^2 D. 5.8 m^2

8. A metal pipe is 77 cm long. The inner diameter of a cross section is 4 cm, then inner curved surface area is:

A. 900 cm^2 B. 960 cm^2

C. 968 cm^2 D. 964 cm^2

9. Curved surface area of a right circular cylinder is 4.4 m^2. If the radius of the base of the cylinder is 0.7 m, then its height is:

A. 2 m   B. 3 m

C. 4 m   D. 1 m

10. The radius and height of a cylinder are 7 cm and 15 cm respectively, then its volume is:
A. 2210 cm³
B. 2310 cm³
C. 2010 cm³
D. 2110 cm³

11. The circumference of the base of a cylinder is 132 cm and its height is 25 cm. The volume of the cylinder is:
A. 34650 cm³
B. 34640 cm³
C. 34450 cm³
D. None of these

12. The volume of a cylinder is 448π cm³ and height is 7 cm. The lateral surface area of cylinder is:
A. 252 cm²
B. 300 cm²
C. 352 cm²
D. 400 cm²

13. A cone of height 24 cm and radius of base 6 cm is made up of modelling clay. A child reshapes it in the form of a sphere. The radius of sphere is:
A. 1 cm
B. 2 cm
C. 4 cm
D. 6 cm

14. A 20 m deep well with diameter 7 m is dug up and the earth from digging is evenly spread out to form a platform 22 m × 14 m. The height of the platform is:
A. 2.5 m
B. 1.5 m
C. 1 m
D. 2 m

15. How many silver coins 1.75 cm of diameter and of thickness 2 mm, must be melted to form a cuboid 11 cm × 10 cm × 7 cm?
A. 1200
B. 1400
C. 1600
D. 1000

16. The diameter of the base of a right circular cylinder is 28 cm and its height is 21 cm. Curved surface area of the cylinder is:
A. 1540 cm²
B. 1648 cm²
C. 1848 cm²
D. 1548 cm²

17. The radius and height of a cylinder are 80 cm and 20 cm respectively. The ratio of total surface area to the lateral surface area of cylinder is:
A. 2 : 1
B. 3 : 1
C. 4 : 1
D. 5 : 1

18. The radii of two right circular cylinders are in the ratio of 2 : 3 and their heights are in the ratio of 5 : 4. The ratio of their curved surface areas is:
A. $\dfrac{3}{5}$
B. $\dfrac{5}{6}$
C. $\dfrac{4}{5}$
D. $\dfrac{8}{9}$

19. The volume of a cylinder of height 4 cm and total surface area 484 cm² is:
A. 612 cm³
B. 610 cm³
C. 616 cm³
D. 620 cm³

20. The circumference of the base of a cylinder is 12 m and its height is 77 m. The volume of the cylinder is:
A. 441 cm³
B. 882 cm³
C. 641 cm³
D. 782 cm³

21. The diameter of a sphere is 21 cm. Calculate its volume.
A. 4851 cm³
B. 4000 cm³
C. 2000 cm³
D. 3850 cm³

22. How many lead balls, each of radius 1 cm can be made from a sphere whose radius is 8 cm?
A. 312
B. 412
C. 512
D. 612

23. A spherical ball of radius 3 cm is melted and recast into three spherical balls. The radii of two of the balls are 1.5 cm and 2 cm. Find the diameter of the third ball.
A. 1 cm
B. 3 cm
C. 4 cm
D. 5 cm

24. Find the volume of a hemisphere of radius 63 cm. (π = 22/7)
A. 523.19 cm³
B. 520.91 cm³
C. 512 .91 cm³
D. 510.91 cm³

25. Three solid spheres of a lead are melted into a single solid sphere. If the radii of the three spheres be 1 cm, 6 cm and 8 cm respectively. Then radius of the new sphere is:
A. 2 cm
B. 3 cm
C. 5 cm
D. 9 cm

26. A circus tent is cylindrical to a height of 6 m and conical above it. If its diameter is 105 m and slant height of the conical portion is 50 m, then the total area of canvas required to build the tent is: (Use π = 22/7)
A. 10230 m²
B. 11230 m²
C. 14230 m²
D. 12340 m²

27. A toy is in the form of a cone mounted on a hemisphere of radius 3.5 cm. The total height of the toy is 15.5 cm. Then the total surface area is: (Use π = 22/7)
A. 214.5 cm²
B. 212.5 cm²
C. 210.5 cm²
D. 215.5 cm²

28. A military tent is in the form a right circular cone 21 dm in height, the diameter of the base being 4 cm. If 16 men sleep in it, find the average number of cu. dm of air surface per man.
A. 230
B. 550
C. 350
D. 250

29. A sphere of diameter 12.6 cm is melted and cast into a right circular cone of height 25.2 cm. Then the diameter of the base of the cone is:
A. 6 cm
B. 6.3 cm
C. 12 cm
D. 12.6 cm

30. What will be the cost of bricks at Rs. 350 per 1000 bricks if each of dimension 25 cm × 16 cm × 10 cm is needed to build a 24 m × 6 m × 0.4 m wall when 10% of the wall is filled with mortar?
A. ₹ 4000
B. ₹ 4500
C. ₹ 4536
D. ₹ 4636

31. Area of canvas needed to erect a right conical tent of height 12 m and a circular base having circumference 10π m is:
A. 60 m²
B. 65 m²
C. 120 π m²
D. 65 π m²

32. A well with inner diameter 8 m is dug 14 m deep. Earth taken out of it has been spread evenly all around it to a width of 3 m to form an embankment around the well. The height of this embankment is:
A. $6\dfrac{26}{33}$ m
B. $7\dfrac{26}{33}$ m
C. $4\dfrac{26}{33}$ m
D. $5\dfrac{26}{33}$ m

33. The paint in a certain container is sufficient to paint an area equal to 9.375 m². Bricks of dimension 22.5 cm × 10 cm × 7 cm are to be painted. The number of bricks that can be painted is:
A. 200
B. 100
C. 150
D. 50

34. The number of wooden cubical blocks of edge 20 cm that can be cut out from another cubical block of wood of edge 3 m 60 cm is:
A. 5382
B. 5832
C. 5283
D. None of these

35. A conical cup 36 cm high has diameter of base 28 cm. It is full of water. The water was poured into a cylindrical jar of radius of base 10 cm. The height of water in the vessel is:
A. 23.52 cm
B. 16.92 cm
C. 11.76 cm
D. 13.65 cm

36. A right circular cylinder and a sphere are of equal volumes and their radii are also equal. If h is the height of the cylinder and d is the diameter of the sphere then:
A. $\dfrac{h}{3}=\dfrac{d}{2}$
B. $\dfrac{h}{2}=\dfrac{d}{3}$
C. $2h=d$
D. $h=d$

37. A cylinder is circumscribed about a hemisphere and a cone is inscribed in the hemisphere such that its base coincides with the base of hemisphere. The volume of cylinder, volume of hemisphere and the volume of cone are proportional to:
A. 4 : 3 : 2
B. 2 : 3 : 1
C. 1 : 2 : 3
D. 3 : 2 : 1

38. A solid is hemispherical at the bottom and conical above it. The surface areas of the two parts are equal. The ratio of the volume of hemispherical part to that of the conical part is:
A. $2:\sqrt{3}$
B. 1 : 1
C. $1:\sqrt{3}$
D. $3:\sqrt{3}$

39. Height of a cone is increased by 200%. Its volume increases by:
A. 200%
B. 300%
C. 250%
D. 100%

40. A right circular cone has base radius 5 cm. If the radius is increased by 20%, without any change in height of the cone, then the percentage increase in volume is:
A. 44%
B. 40%
C. 25%
D. 22%

ANSWERS

1	2	3	4	5	6	7	8	9	10
B	C	D	A	B	C	B	C	D	B

11	12	13	14	15	16	17	18	19	20
A	C	D	A	C	C	D	B	C	B

21	22	23	24	25	26	27	28	29	30
A	C	D	A	D	A	A	B	D	C

31	32	33	34	35	36	37	38	39	40
D	A	B	B	A	B	D	A	A	A

EXPLANATORY ANSWERS

1. L.S.A. of cube $= 4a^2 = 4(8)^2 = 64 \times 4 = 256$ cm²

2. L.S.A. of cuboid $= 2(l + b)h$
$$= 2(10 + 8)5 = 180 \text{ cm}^2$$

3. L.S.A. of a cone $= \pi r l = \dfrac{22}{7} \times 7 \times 13 = 286$ cm²

4. Volume of sphere
$$= \dfrac{4}{3}\pi r^3 = \dfrac{4}{3} \times \dfrac{22}{7} \times (3)^3 = 113.14 \text{ cm}^3$$

5. $2\pi r h = 88$
$$2 \times \dfrac{22}{7} \times r \times 14 = 8 \Rightarrow r = 1 \text{ cm}$$

6. Circumference of the base = Length of the sheet
$$\Rightarrow 2\pi r = 44 \Rightarrow 2 \times \dfrac{22}{7} \times r \times = 44 \Rightarrow r = 7 \text{ cm}.$$

7. L.S.A of cylinder $= 2\pi r h = 2 \times \dfrac{22}{7} \times 0.7 \times 2 = 8.8$ cm².

8. L.S.A of cylinder $= 2\pi rh = 2 \times \dfrac{22}{7} \times 2 \times 77$

$$= 968 \text{ cm}^2.$$

9. $2\pi rh = 4.4 \Rightarrow 2 \times \dfrac{22}{7} \times 0.7 \times h = 4.4 \Rightarrow h = 1 \text{ m}.$

10. Volume of cylinder $= \pi r^2 h = \dfrac{22}{7} \times 7 \times 7 \times 15$

$$= 2310 \text{ cm}^3.$$

11. Volume of cylinder $= \pi r^2 h$

According to the question, $2\pi r = 132$

$$\Rightarrow 2 \times \dfrac{22}{7} \times r = 132 \Rightarrow r = 21 \text{ cm}$$

Volume $= \dfrac{22}{7} \times 21 \times 21 \times 25 = 34650 \text{ cm}^3.$

12. $\pi r^2 h = 448\pi$

$$r^2(7) = 448 \Rightarrow r^2 = \dfrac{448}{7} = 64 \Rightarrow r = 8 \text{ cm}$$

L.S.A of cylinder $= 2\pi rh = 2 \times \dfrac{22}{7} \times 8 \times 7 = 352 \text{ cm}^2.$

13. According to the question,

$$\dfrac{4}{3}\pi R^3 = \dfrac{1}{3}\pi r^2 h$$

$$4R^3 = 36 \times 24$$

$$\Rightarrow \qquad R^3 = 216$$

$$\therefore \qquad R = 6 \text{ cm}.$$

14. Volume of the earth dug out

$$= \pi r^2 h = \dfrac{22}{7}\left(\dfrac{7}{2}\right)^2 (20)$$

$$= 22 \times 7 \times 5 = 770 \text{ m}^3$$

Area of the platform $= 22 \times 14 = 308 \text{ m}^2$

$\therefore$ Height of the platform $= \dfrac{770}{308} = \dfrac{5}{2} = 2.5 \text{ m}.$

15. Volume of cuboid $= 11 \times 10 \times 7 = 770 \text{ cm}^3$

$$r = \dfrac{1.75}{2} = 0.875 \text{ cm}$$

$$h = 2 \text{ mm} = 0.2 \text{ cm}$$

Volume of one coin $= \pi r^2 h$

$$= \dfrac{22}{7} \times 0.875 \times 0.875 \times 0.2$$

$\therefore$ Required number of coins

$$= \dfrac{\text{Volume of the cuboid}}{\text{Volume of each coin}}$$

$$= \dfrac{770 \times 1000 \times 1000 \times 10 \times 7}{22 \times 875 \times 875 \times 2}$$

$$= \dfrac{35 \times 40 \times 40 \times 70}{35 \times 35 \times 2} = 40 \times 40 = 1600.$$

16. Diameter $= 28 \text{ cm}$

$r = 14 \text{ cm}, \; h = 21 \text{ cm}$

L.S.A of cylinder $= 2\pi rh = 2 \times \dfrac{22}{7} \times 14 \times 21$

$$= 1848 \text{ cm}^2.$$

17. $\dfrac{\text{Total surface area}}{\text{Lateral surface area}} = \dfrac{2\pi r(h+r)}{2\pi rh}$

$$= \dfrac{80+20}{20} = 5 : 1.$$

18. $\dfrac{S_1}{S_2} = \dfrac{2\pi(2)(5)}{2\pi(3)(4)} = \dfrac{10}{12} = 5 : 6.$

19. $2\pi r (h + r) = 484$

$$\Rightarrow \quad 2 \times \dfrac{22}{7} r(4+r) = 484$$

$$\Rightarrow \qquad r(4 + r) = \dfrac{484 \times 7}{2 \times 22} = 77$$

$$r^2 + 4r - 77 = 0$$

$$\Rightarrow \quad (r - 7)(r + 11) = 0 \Rightarrow r = 7 \text{ cm}$$

Volume of cylinder $= \pi r^2 h = \dfrac{22}{7} \times (7)^2 \times 4$

$$= 22 \times 28 = 616 \text{ cm}^3.$$

20. $C = 2\pi r$

According to the question,

$$2 \times \dfrac{22}{7} \times r = 12 = \dfrac{12 \times 7}{2 \times 22} = \dfrac{21}{11} \text{ cm}$$

Volume of cylinder $= \pi r^2 h = \dfrac{22}{7} \times \dfrac{21}{11} \times \dfrac{21}{11} \times 77$

$$= 2 \times 21 \times 21 = 882 \text{ cm}^3.$$

21. Diameter $= 21 \text{ cm}$

$$r = \dfrac{21}{2} \text{ cm}$$

Volume of the sphere $= \dfrac{4}{3}\pi r^3$

$$= \dfrac{4}{3} \times \dfrac{22}{7} \times \dfrac{21}{2} \times \dfrac{21}{2} \times \dfrac{21}{2} = 4851 \text{ cm}^3.$$

22. In the given Sphere :

radius $= 8 \text{ cm}.$

$V_1 =$ Volume of the sphere $= \dfrac{4}{3}\pi r^3$

$$= \dfrac{4}{3}\pi (8)^3 = \dfrac{2048}{3}\pi \text{ cu. cm.}$$

In the given Ball :

radius $= 1 \text{ cm}.$

$V_2 =$ Volume of the ball $= \dfrac{4}{3}\pi r^3 = \dfrac{4}{3}\pi(1)^3$

$$= \dfrac{4}{3}\pi \text{ cu. cm.}$$

Number of balls $= \dfrac{V_1}{V_2} = \dfrac{204}{3} \times \dfrac{3}{4\pi} = 512 \text{ balls}.$

23. Volume of the large ball of radius 3 cm

$$= \frac{4}{3} \times \frac{22}{7} \times 3 \times 3 \times 3 = \frac{792}{7} \text{ cm}^3$$

Total volume of the two smaller balls of radii 1.5 cm and 2 cm

$$= \frac{4}{3} \times \frac{22}{7} \times \frac{3}{2} \times \frac{3}{2} \times \frac{3}{2} + \frac{4}{3} \times \frac{22}{7} \times 2 \times 2 \times 2$$

$$\left[\because V = \frac{4}{3}\pi r^3 \right]$$

$$= \frac{4}{3} \times \frac{22}{7} \left(\frac{27}{8} + 8 \right) = \frac{143}{3} \text{ cm}^3$$

$\therefore$ Volume of the third ball

$$= \frac{792}{7} - \frac{143}{3} = \frac{2376 - 1001}{21} = \frac{1375}{21} \text{ cm}^3.$$

Let r be the radius of the 3rd ball.

$$\therefore \frac{4}{3} \times \frac{22}{7} \times r^3 = \frac{1375}{21}$$

$$r^3 = \frac{1375}{21} \times \frac{3}{4} \times \frac{7}{22} = \frac{125}{8}$$

$$\therefore \quad r = \sqrt[3]{\frac{125}{8}} = \frac{5}{2} \text{ cm}$$

Hence, diameter $= 2r = 2 \times \dfrac{5}{2} = 5$ cm.

24. $r = 6.3$ cm, $\pi = \dfrac{22}{7}$

Volume of a hemisphere

$$= \frac{\left(\dfrac{4}{3}\pi r^3 \right)}{2} = \frac{2}{3}\pi r^3$$

$$= \frac{2}{3} \times \frac{22}{7} \times \frac{63}{10} \times \frac{63}{10} \times \frac{63}{10} \text{ cm}^3$$

$$= \frac{4 \times 3 \times 63 \times 63}{5 \times 5 \times 10} \text{ cm}^3 = \frac{130977}{250} \text{ cm}^3 = 523.91 \text{ cm}^3.$$

25. Let r be the radius of the new sphere. Then

$$\frac{4}{3}\pi r^2 = \frac{4}{3}\pi (1)^3 + \frac{4}{3}\pi (6)^3 + \frac{4}{3}\pi (8)^3$$

$$\frac{4}{3}\pi \left[(1)^3 + (6)^3 + (8)^3 \right] = \frac{4}{3}\pi [1 + 216 + 512]$$

or, $\qquad r^2 = 729 = (9)^3$

$\therefore$ Radius of the new sphere $(r) = 9$ cm.

26. The tent has two parts :

(*i*) a cylindrical part and (*ii*) a conical part

(*i*) Curved surface area of cylindrical portion

$$= 2\pi r h$$

$$= 2 \times \frac{22}{7} \times \frac{105}{2} \times 6 \text{ m}^2$$

$$= 1980 \text{ m}^2$$

(*ii*) Curved surface area of conical portion

$$= \pi r l$$

$$= \frac{22}{7} \times \frac{105}{2} \times 50 \text{ m}^2$$

$$= 8250 \text{ m}^2$$

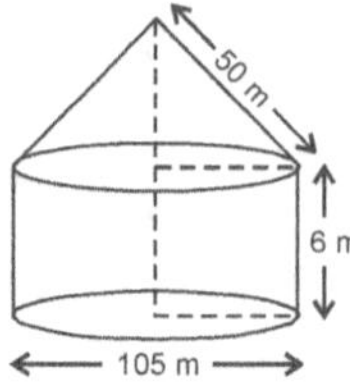

$\therefore$ Total area of canvas required to build the tent

= Curved surface area of cylindrical portion
     + curved surface area of conical portion

$= 1980 \text{ m}^2 + 8250 \text{ m}^2 = 10230 \text{ m}^2.$

27. $\because$ Radius of the hemisphere = 3.5 cm

$\therefore$ Radius of the base of the cone (r) = 3.5 cm.

Total height of the toy = 15.5 cm

$\therefore$ Height of the conical part,

$$(h) = 15.5 - 3.5$$
$$= 12 \text{ cm}$$

$\therefore$ Slant height of the conical part (l)

$$= \sqrt{r^2 + h^2}$$

$$= \sqrt{12^2 + (3.5)^2}$$

$$= \sqrt{144 + 12.25}$$

$$= \sqrt{156.25}$$

$$= 12.5 \text{ cm}$$

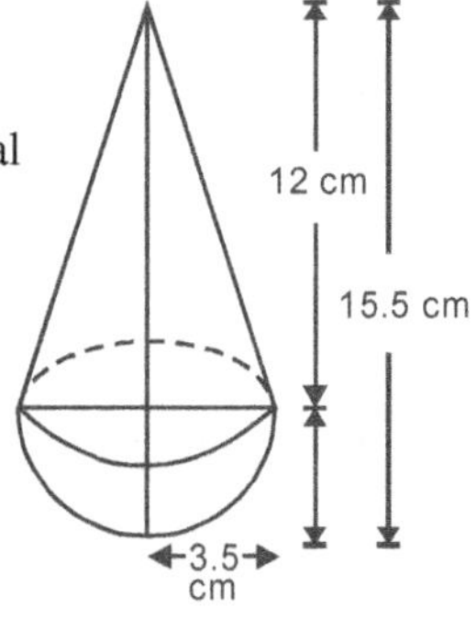

$\therefore$ Surface area of the conical part

$$= \pi r l = \frac{22}{7} \times 3.5 \times 12.5$$

$$= 11 \times 12.5 = 137.5 \text{ cm}^2$$

Surface area of the hemispherical part

$$= 2\pi r^2 - 2 \times \frac{22}{7} \times (3.5)^2$$

$$= 22 \times 3.5 = 77 \text{ cm}^2$$

$\therefore$ Total surface area of the toy

= Surface area of the conical part
     + Surface area of the hemispherical part

$= 137.5 + 77 = 214.5 \text{ cm}^2.$

28. Diameter of the base of the tent = 4 cm

$\therefore$ Radius of the base $(r) = \dfrac{4}{2} = 2$ m = 20 dm

Height (h) = 21 dm

$\therefore$ Volume of air in the tent $= \dfrac{1}{2}\pi r^2 h$

$$= \frac{1}{3} \times \frac{22}{7} \times 20 \times 20 \times 21 = 8800 \text{ dm}^3$$

$\because$ 16 men sleep in the tent.

$\therefore$ Average space per man $= \dfrac{8800}{16} = 550 \text{ dm}^3.$

$\therefore$ Average number of cu. dm of air surface per man
= 550.

29. Here $r = \dfrac{12.6}{2} = 6.3$ cm.

Volume of the sphere $= \dfrac{4}{3}\pi r^3$

$$= \dfrac{4}{3} \times \dfrac{22}{7} \times 6.3 \times 6.3 \times 6.3$$

Volume of the sphere = Volume of cone

$\Rightarrow \dfrac{4}{3} \times \dfrac{22}{7} \times 6.3 \times 6.3 \times 6.3 = \dfrac{1}{3} \times \dfrac{22}{7} \times 25.2 \times r^2$

$\Rightarrow r^2 = 6.3 \times 6.3$

$\therefore r = 6.3$ cm.

$\therefore$ diameter $= 12.6$ cm.

30. Here the length of the wall = 24 m = 2400 cm

Height of the wall = 6 m = 600 cm

Thickness of the wall = 0.4 m = 40 cm

Volume of the wall = 2400 × 600 × 40

$$(\because V = l \times b \times h)$$

$$= 57600000 \text{ cu. cm.} \qquad ...(i)$$

Volume of the wall filled with mortar is 10% of volume

$$= 57600000 \times \dfrac{10}{100}$$

$$= 5760000 \text{ cu. cm.} \qquad ...(ii)$$

$\therefore$ Volume of the wall occupied with bricks

$$= 57600000 - 5760000$$

$$= 51840000 \text{ cu. cm.} \qquad ...(iii)$$

Volume of 1 brick = (25 × 16 × 10) cu. cm.

$\therefore$ No. of bricks $= \dfrac{51840000}{25 \times 16 \times 10} = 12960$

But the cost of 1000 bricks = ₹ 350

$\therefore$ The cost of 12960 bricks

$$= ₹ \dfrac{350}{1000} \times 12960 = ₹ 4536.$$

31. $2\pi r = 10\pi \Rightarrow r = 5$m, $h = 12$m

$l = \sqrt{5^2 + 12^2} = 13$ m

C. S. A. $= \pi \times 5 \times 13 = 65\pi$ m².

33. Number of bricks $= \dfrac{9.375}{\text{S.A. of 1 brick}}$

$$= \dfrac{9.375 \times 10000}{2(22.5 \times 10 + 10 \times 7.5 + 7.5 \times 22.5)}$$

$$= \dfrac{93750}{937.50} = 100.$$

35. Vol. of cylinder = Vol. of cone

$\Rightarrow \pi \times 10^2 \times h = \dfrac{1}{3}\pi \times 14^2 \times 36$

$\Rightarrow h = 23.52$ cm

36. Volume of cylinder = Volume of sphere

$\Rightarrow \pi\left(\dfrac{d}{2}\right)^2 h = \dfrac{4}{3}\pi\left(\dfrac{d}{2}\right)^3 \Rightarrow h = \dfrac{2}{3}d \Rightarrow \dfrac{h}{2} = \dfrac{d}{3}.$

37.

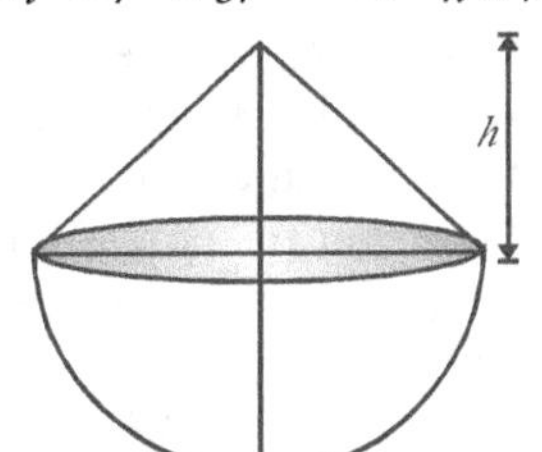

Clearly $h = r$

Volume of cylinder : Volume of semispheres : Volume of cone

$$= \pi\left(r^2\right)r : \dfrac{2}{3}\pi r^3 : \dfrac{1}{3}\pi r^2\left(r\right) = 3 : 2 : 1.$$

38. S. A. of cone = S. A. of hemisphere

$\pi r l = 2\pi r^2 \Rightarrow l = 2r$

Now, $h^2 = l^2 - r^2 = 3r^2 \Rightarrow h = r\sqrt{3}$

Now,

$$\dfrac{\text{volume of hemisphere}}{\text{volume of cone}} = \dfrac{\dfrac{2}{3}\pi r^3}{\dfrac{1}{3}\pi r^2\left(r\sqrt{3}\right)} = \dfrac{2}{\sqrt{3}}.$$

39. $\dfrac{V_2}{V_1} = \dfrac{\pi r^2(3h)}{\pi r^2 h} = \dfrac{3}{1}$

Thus, change in volume = 200%.

40. $\dfrac{V_2}{V_1} = \dfrac{\left(\dfrac{6}{5}r\right)^2 h}{r^2 h} = \dfrac{36}{25} = 1.44$

Increase = 44%.

✳ ✳ ✳

13
Statistics

INTRODUCTION

Sometimes we are required to describe the data arithmetically. The measures with which we do that are called Arithmetical Descriptors of Data. The name itself suggests that these measures describe the data arithmetically—for example, average age of a group, average height of a class, median score of the group or modal, collar size of a team. Because of the fact that these measures are representative of the group they represent, they are called Measures of Central Tendency—central because these are the measures around which the measures of all the members of the group gather around. Represented graphically, the graph of the observations of the group will be around and close to the measures of central tendency.

In the study of a population with respect to one in which we are interested we may get a large number of observations. It is not possible to grasp any idea about the characteristic when we look at all the observations. So it is better to get one number for one group. That number must be a good representative one for all the observations to give a clear picture of that characteristic. Such representative number can be a central value for all these observations. This central value is called a measure of central tendency or an average or a measure of locations. There are five averages. Among them mean, median and mode are called simple averages and the other two averages geometric mean and harmonic mean are called special averages.

The meaning of average is nicely given in the following definitions.

- "A measure of central tendency is a typical value around which other figures congregate."
- "An average stands for the whole group of which it forms a part yet represents the whole."
- "One of the most widely used set of summary figures is known as measures of location."

Hence, averages are "Statistical constants which enable us to comprehend in a single effort the significance of the whole", this definition is given by Professor Bowley; they give us useful information about the complete group. According to the **Father of Statistics** R. Fisher, "The inherent inability of the human mind to grasp in it's entirely a large body of numerical data compels us to seek relatively few constants that will adequately describe the data."

Hence a simple figure, which is used to represent the whole group, that must be a representative number, it is termed to be 'Measure of central tendency or the average.'

ARITHMETIC MEAN

The average or the arithmetic mean, or simply the mean when there is no ambiguity, is the most common measure of central tendency. It is defined as the sum total of all values in the sample divided by the number of observations. It is denoted by a bar above the symbol of the variable being averaged. Thus $\bar{X}$ stands for the mean, of X-values in the sample. If in a sample a particular X-value, say X_i occurs with frequency f_i ($i = 1, 2, \dots n$), its contribution to the total of X-values is $f_i X_i$. Thus, one can compute the mean of X-values by

$$\bar{X} = \frac{1}{N}(f_1 X_1 + f_2 X_2 + \dots + f_n X_n) = \frac{\sum_{i=1}^{n} f_i X_i}{N},$$

$$\text{where} \quad N = \sum_{i=1}^{n} f_i$$

When observations are classified into class intervals, as for continuous variables, individual observations falling into a class interval are not separately identifiable and the contribution of the individual observation from a class interval to the total cannot be calculated. To avoid this difficulty, it is assumed that every observation falling into a class interval has a value equal to the mid-point into which these observations fall. Such a procedure will not give the exact mean had one computed it from raw data and may require what is called corrections for grouping.

Harmonic Mean (H.M.)

Harmonic mean of a set of observations is defined as the reciprocal of the arithmetic average of the reciprocal of the given values. If $x_1, x_2 \dots x_n$ are n observations,

$$H.M. = \frac{n}{\sum_{i=1}^{n}\left(\frac{1}{x_i}\right)}$$

140

For a frequency distribution

$$H.M. = \frac{N}{\sum_{i=1}^{n} f\left(\frac{1}{x_i}\right)}$$

Example: From the given data calculate H.M. 5, 10, 17, 24, 30

X	$\frac{1}{x}$
5	0.2000
10	0.1000
17	0.0588
24	0.0417
30	0.0333
Total	0.4338

$$H.M. = \frac{n}{\sum\left[\frac{1}{x}\right]} = \frac{5}{0.4338} = 11.526$$

Geometric Mean (G.M.)

The geometric mean of a series containing n observations is the nth root of the product of the values. If $x_1, x_2 ..., x_n$ are observations then

$$G.M = \sqrt[n]{x_1, x_2 ... x_n} = \left(x_1, x_2 ... x_n\right)^{1/n}$$

$$\log GM = \frac{1}{n} \log\left(x_1. x_2 ... x_n\right)$$

$$= \frac{1}{n}\left(\log x_1 + \log x_2 + .. + \log x_n\right) = \frac{\Sigma \log x_i}{n}$$

$$GM = \text{Antilog} \frac{\Sigma \log x_i}{n}$$

For grouped data

$$GM = \text{Antilog} \left[\frac{\Sigma f \log x_i}{N}\right]$$

Example: Calculate the geometric mean of the following series of monthly income of a batch of families 180, 250, 490, 1400, 1050.

Solution:

x	$\log x$
180	2.2553
250	2.3979
490	2.6902
1400	3.1461
1050	3.0212
	13.5107

$$GM = \text{Antilog} \left[\frac{\Sigma \log x}{n}\right]$$

$$= \text{Antilog} \left[\frac{13.5107}{5}\right]$$

$$= \text{Antilog } 2.7021 = 503.6$$

Combined Mean

If the arithmetic averages and the number of items in two or more related groups are known, the combined or the composite mean of the entire group can be obtained by

$$\text{Combined mean } \overline{\overline{X}} = \left[\frac{n_1 \overline{x}_1 + n_2 \overline{x}_2}{n_1 + n_2}\right]$$

The advantage of combined arithmetic mean is that, we can determine the over, all mean of the combined data without going back to the original data.

Example : Find the combined mean for the data given below

$$n_1 = 20, \ \overline{x}_1 = 4, \ n_2 = 30, \ \overline{x}_2 = 3$$

Solution:

$$\text{Combined Mean } \overline{\overline{X}} = \left[\frac{n_1 \overline{x}_1 + n_2 \overline{x}_2}{n_1 + n_2}\right]$$

$$= \left[\frac{20 \times 4 + 30 \times 3}{20 + 30}\right]$$

$$= \left[\frac{80 + 90}{50}\right] = \left[\frac{170}{50}\right] = 3.4.$$

RELATIONSHIP BETWEEN ARITHMETIC MEAN, GEOMETRIC MEAN AND HARMONIC MEAN

If all the items in a series are the same the arithmetic mean, the geometric mean and harmonic mean are equal. If all the items in a distribution have the same value then,

$$\text{A.M.} = \text{G.M.} = \text{H.M.}$$

But if the size vary, as will generally be the case, mean will be greater than the geometric mean and geometric mean will be greater than the harmonic mean. This is because of the property of the geometric mean to give larger weight to smaller item and of the harmonic mean to give the largest weight to the smallest item. Hence,

$$\text{A.M.} > \text{G.M.} > \text{H.M.}$$

$$\text{G.M.} = \sqrt{\text{A.M.} \times \text{H.M.}}$$

MEDIAN

Median of a distribution locates a central point which divides a distribution into two equal halves, *i.e.*, it is the middle most value among a set of observations. Let us start with examples in a discrete case. Consider a data set having

5 distinct observations: 2, 4, 9, 12, 19 (arranged in ascending order). Here 9 is the middle most value since an equal number of observations are to its left and to its right. Thus, 9 is the median of the above observations. Consider another data set having 6 distinct observations: 3, 8, 15, 25, 35, 43. Here any point between 15 and 25 has the property that equal number of observations are to its left and to its right. Any point in the interval 15 to 25 may be used as a median. Conventionally we take the middle point of such an interval to define median uniquely. Thus 20 is the median of 3, 8, 15, 25, 35, 43.

When a data set has non-distinct observations-a situation more common in practice-difficulties may arise. In such situations, it may not be always possible to locate the middle most value or the central point that divides the distribution into two equal halves. For example, in the case of the data set having 5 observations 2, 9, 9, 12, 19 the value 9 is repeated twice. Thus, a formal definition of median is needed to overcome such difficulties.

A median of a distribution is a point or a central value such that at least 50% of the observations are less than or equal to it and at least 50% of the observations are greater than or equal to it. With this definition of median and the convention of taking the middle point of a class in which each point in a median, median of a distribution can always be specified uniquely Thus, median of observations 2, 9, 9, 12, 19 is 9 because 3 of the 5 observations (60%) are less than or equal to 9 and 4 of the 5 observations (80%) are greater than or equal to 9.

MEDIAN OF UNGROUPED OR RAW DATA

Arrange the given values in the increasing or decreasing order. If the number of values are odd, median is the middle value. If the number of values are even, median is the mean of middle two values.

By formula,

$$\text{Median} = \text{Md} = \left(\frac{n+1}{2}\right)^{th} \text{item.}$$

Example 1:

When odd number of values are given. Find median for the following data

25, 18, 27, 10, 8, 30, 42, 20, 53

Solution:

Arranging the data in the increasing order 8, 10, 18, 20, 25, 27, 30, 42, 53

The middle value is the 5th item *i.e.*, 25 is the median

Using formula,

$$\text{Md} = \left(\frac{n+1}{2}\right)^{th} \text{item} = \left(\frac{9+1}{2}\right)^{th} \text{item} = \left(\frac{10}{2}\right)^{th} \text{item}$$

$$= 5^{th} \text{ item} = 25$$

Example 2:

When even number of values are given. Find median for the following data

5, 8, 12, 30, 18, 10, 2, 22

Solution:

Arranging the data in the increasing order 2, 5, 8, 10, 12, 18, 22, 30.

Here median is the mean of the middle two items (*i.e.*) mean of (10, 12) *i.e.*,

$$= \left(\frac{10+12}{2}\right) = 11$$

$\therefore$ median = 11

Using the formula

$$\text{Median} = \left(\frac{n+1}{2}\right)^{th} \text{item} = \left(\frac{8+1}{2}\right)^{th} \text{item.}$$

$$= \left(\frac{9}{2}\right)^{th} \text{item} = 4.5^{th} \text{ item}$$

$$= 4^{th} \text{ item} + \left(\frac{1}{2}\right) (5^{th} \text{ item} - 4^{th} \text{ item})$$

$$= 10 + \left(\frac{1}{2}\right) [12 - 10]$$

$$= 10 + \left(\frac{1}{2}\right) \times 2 = 10 + 1 = 11$$

MODE

The mode refers to that value in a distribution, which occur most frequently. It is an actual value, which has the highest concentration of items in and around it.

According to Croxton and Cowden "The mode of a distribution is the value at the point around which the items tend to be most heavily concentrated. It may be regarded at the most typical of a series of values".

It shows the centre of concentration of the frequency in around a given value. Therefore, where the purpose is to know the point of the highest concentration it is preferred. It is, thus, a positional measure. Its importance is very great in marketing studies where a manager is interested in knowing about the size, which has the highest concentration of items. For example, in placing an order for shoes or ready-made garments the modal size helps because this sizes and other sizes around in common demand.

COMPUTATION OF THE MODE
Ungrouped or Raw Data

For ungrouped data or a series of individual observations, mode is often found by mere inspection.

Example 1:

2, 7, 10, 15, 10, 17, 8, 10, 2

$\therefore$ Mode = M_0 = 10

In some cases, the mode may be absent while in some cases there may be more than one mode.

Example 2:

1. 12, 10, 15, 24, 30 (no mode)
2. 7, 10, 15, 12, 7, 14, 24, 10, 7, 20, 10
$\therefore$ the modes are 7 and 10

RELATIONSHIP BETWEEN DIFFERENT AVERAGES

In a symmetrical distribution, Mean $\left(\overline{X}\right)$, Median (Med) and Mode (Z) will coincide, *i.e.,* Mean = Median = Mode. In an asymmetrical (skewed) distribution, these values will be different.

When the distribution is moderately skewed and has grater concentration in the lower values, $\overline{X} >$ Med $>$ Z (Mean > Median > Mode) it means the distribution is positively skewed (skewed to the right).

If the distribution concentrated in higher values, the tail is towards the lower values, then it is negatively skewed. In such cases, Z > Med > X (Mode > Median > Mean). As such there is a relationship in a moderately asymmetrical distribution between $\overline{X}$, Med and Z.

In a moderately asymmetrical distribution, the difference between $\overline{X}$ and Z is three times of the differences between $\overline{X}$ and Mode. Symbolically,

Mean – Median = 1/3 (Mean – Mode)
Mode = 3 Median – 2Mean
Median = Mode + 2/3 (Mean – Mode)
Mode = Mean – 3 (Mean – Mode)
Mean – Mode = 3 (Mean – Median)

It follows, that if any two values out of the three are given, the third value can be estimated by applying the above formula.

SOME IMPORTANT POINTS

❏ The algebraic sum of the deviations of the given set of observations from their arithmetic mean is zero.

❏ If all the observations of a series are added, subtracted, multilied or divided by a constant β, the mean is also added, subtracted, multiplied or divided by the same constant.

❏ A.M. of first n natural numbers is $\dfrac{n+1}{2}$

❏ Median is the positional average.

❏ The values which divide the series into a number of equal parts are called the partition value.

❏ Quartiles, Deciles and Percentiles are partition values.

❏ The various partition values viz., quartiles, deciles and percentiles can be easily located graphically with the help of a curve called the cumulative frequency curve or Ogive.

❏ Mode can be estimated graphically from a Histogram.

❏ Mode = 3 Median – 2 Mean

❏ In case of symmetrical distribution—
Mean = Median = Mode

❏ The logarithm of the G.M. of a set of observations is the arithmetic mean of their logarithms.

❏ If any one of the observations is zero, geometric mean becomes zero and if any one of the observations is negative, geometric mean becomes imaginary regardless of the magnitude of the other items.

❏ A.M. $\geq$ G.M. $\geq$ H.M. (the sign of equality holding if and only if all the n observations are equal.)

❏ $(G.M.)^2 =$ A.M. $\times$ H.M.

MULTIPLE CHOICE QUESTIONS

1. Measures of central tendency for a given set of observations measures
A. The scatterness of the observations
B. The central location of the observations
C. Both A and B
D. None of these

2. While computing the AM from a grouped frequency distribution, we assume that
A. The classes are of equal length
B. The classes have equal frequency
C. All the values of a class are equal to the mid-value of that class
D. None of these.

3. Which of the following statements is wrong?
A. Mean is rigidly defined
B. Mean is not affected due to sampling fluctuations
C. Mean has some mathematical properties
D. All these

4. Which of the following statements is true?
A. Usually mean is the best measure of central tendency
B. Usually median is the best measure of central tendency
C. Usually mode is the best measure of central tendency
D. Normally, GM is the best measure of central tendency

5. For open-end classification, which of the following is the best measure of central tendency?
A. AM
B. GM
C. Median
D. Mode

6. The presence of extreme observations does not affect
A. AM
B. Median
C. Mode
D. Any of these

7. In case of an even number of observations which of the following is median?
A. Any of the two middle-most value
B. The simple average of these two middle values
C. The weighted average of these two middle values
D. Any of these

8. The most commonly used measure of central tendency is
A. AM
B. Median
C. Mode
D. Both GM and HM

9. Which one of the following is not uniquely defined?
A. Mean
B. Median
C. Mode
D. All of these measures

10. Which of the following measure of the central tendency is difficult to compute?
A. Mean
B. Median
C. Mode
D. GM

11. Which measure(s) of central tendency is(are) considered for finding the average rates?
A. AM
B. GM
C. HM
D. Both B and C

12. For a moderately skewed distribution, which of he following relationship holds?
A. Mean – Mode = 3 (Mean – Median)
B. Median – Mode = 3 (Mean – Median)
C. Mean – Median = 3 (Mean – Mode)
D. Mean – Median = 3 (Median – Mode)

13. Weighted averages are considered when
A. The data are not classified
B. The data are put in the form of grouped frequency distribution
C. All the observations are not of equal importance
D. Both A and C

14. Which of the following results hold for a set of distinct positive observations?
A. AM $\geq$ GM $\geq$ HM
B. HM $\geq$ GM $\geq$ AM
C. AM > GM > HM
D. GM > AM > HM

15. When a firm registers both profits and losses, which of the following measure of central tendency cannot be considered?
A. AM
B. GM
C. Median
D. Mode

16. Quartiles are the values dividing a given set of observations into
A. Two equal parts
B. Four equal parts
C. Five equal parts
D. None of these

17. Quartiles can be determined graphically using
A. Histogram
B. Frequency Polygon
C. Ogive
D. Pie chart

18. Which of the following measure(s) possesses (possess) mathematical properties?
A. AM
B. GM
C. HM
D. All of these

19. Which of the following measure(s) satisfies (satisfy) a linear relationship between two variables?
A. Mean
B. Median
C. Mode
D. All of these

20. Which of he following measures of central tendency is based on only fifty percent of the central values?
A. Mean
B. Median
C. Mode
D. Both A and B

21. If there are 3 observations 15, 20, 25 then the sum of deviation of the observations from their AM is
A. 0
B. 5
C. –5
D. None of these

22. What is the median for the following observations?
5, 8, 6, 9, 11, 4.
A. 6
B. 7
C. 8
D. None of these

23. What is the modal value for the numbers 5, 8, 6, 4, 10, 15, 18, 10?
A. 18
B. 10
C. 14
D. None of these

24. What is the GM for the numbers 8, 24 and 40?
A. 24
B. 12
C. $8\sqrt{15}$
D. 10

25. The harmonic mean for the numbers 2, 3, 5 is
A. 2.00
B. $-\sqrt[3]{30}$
C. 2.90
D. –3 30

26. If the AM and GM for two numbers are 6.50 and 6 respectively then the two numbers are
A. 6 and 7
B. 9 and 4
C. 10 and 3
D. 8 and 5

27. If the AM and HM for two numbers are 5 and 3.2 respectively then the GM will be
A. 16.00
B. 4.10
C. 4.05
D. 4.00

28. What is the value of the first quartile for observations 15, 18, 10, 20, 23, 28, 12, 16?
A. 17
B. 16
C. 15.75
D. 12

29. The third decile for the numbers 15, 10, 20, 25, 18, 11, 9, 12 is
A. 13
B. 10.70
C. 11
D. 11.50

30. If there are two groups containing 30 and 20 observations and having 50 and 60 as arithmetic means, then the combined arithmetic mean is
A. 55
B. 56
C. 54
D. 52

31. The average salary of a group of unskilled workers is Rs.10000 and that of a group of skilled workers is Rs.15,000. If the combined salary is Rs.12000, then what is the percentage of skilled workers?
A. 40%
B. 50%
C. 60%
D. none of these

32. If there are two groups with 75 and 65 as harmonic means and containing 15 and 13 observation then the combined HM is given by
A. 65
B. 70.36
C. 70
D. 71

33. What is the HM of $1, \frac{1}{2}, 1/3, \ldots\ldots\ldots 1/n$?
A. n
B. $2n$
C. $\dfrac{2}{(n+1)}$
D. $\dfrac{n(n+1)}{2}$

34. An aeroplane flies from A to B at the rate of 500 km/hour and comes back from B to A at the rate of 700 km/hour. The average speed of the aeroplane is
A. 600 km per hour
B. 583.33 km per hour
C. 100 35 km per hour
D. 620 km per hour

35. If a variable assumes the values 1, 2, 3...5 with frequencies as 1, 2, 3...5, then what is the AM?
A. $\dfrac{11}{3}$
B. 5
C. 4
D. 4.50

36. Two variables x and y are given by $y = 2x - 3$. If the median of x is 20, what is the median of y?
A. 20
B. 40
C. 37
D. 35

37. If the relationship between two variables u and v are given by $2u + v + 7 = 0$ and if the AM of u is 10, then the AM of v is
A. 17
B. −17
C. −27
D. 27

38. If x and y are related by $x - y - 10 = 0$ and mode of x is known to be 23, then the mode of y is
A. 20
B. 13
C. 3
D. 23

39. If GM of x is 10 and GM of y is 15, then the GM of xy is
A. 150
B. Log 10 × Log 15
C. Log 150
D. None of these

40. If the AM and GM for 10 observations are both 15, then the value of HM is
A. Less than 15
B. More than 15
C. 15
D. Can not be determined

41. What is the value of mean and median for the following data:

Marks	5–14	15–24	25–34	35–44	45–54	55–64
No. of Students	10	18	32	26	14	10

A. 30 and 28
B. 29 and 30
C. 33.68 and 32.94
D. 34.21 and 33.18

42. The mean and mode for the following frequency distribution

Class interval	Frequency
350–369	15
370–389	27
390–409	31
410–429	19
430–449	13
450–469	6

are
A. 400 and 390
B. 400.58 and 390
C. 400.58 and 394.50
D. 400 and 394

43. The median and modal profits for the following data

Profit in '000 Rs.:	No. of firms:
below 5	10
below 10	25
below 15	45
below 20	55
below 25	62
below 30	65

are
A. 11.60 and 11.50
B. Rs.11556 and Rs.11267
C. Rs.11875 and Rs.11667
D. 11.50 and 11.67.

44. Following is an incomplete distribution having modal mark as 44

Marks	0–20	20–40	40–60	60–80	80–100
No. of Students	5	18	?	12	5

What would be the mean marks?
A. 45
B. 46
C. 47
D. 48

45. The data relating to the daily wage of 20 workers are shown below:

₹ 50, ₹ 55, ₹ 60, ₹ 58, ₹ 59, ₹ 72, ₹ 65, ₹ 68, ₹ 53, ₹ 50, ₹ 67, ₹ 58, ₹ 63, ₹ 69, ₹ 74, ₹ 63, ₹ 61, ₹ 57, ₹ 62, ₹ 64.

The employer pays bonus amounting to ₹ 100, ₹ 200, ₹ 300, ₹ 400 and ₹ 500 to the wage earners in the wage groups ₹ 50 and not more than ₹ 55 and not more than ₹ 60 and so on and lastly ₹ 70 and not more than ₹ 75, during the festive month of October.

What is the average bonus paid per wage earner?
A. ₹ 200
B. ₹ 250
C. ₹ 285
D. ₹ 300

46. The third quartile and 65th percentile for the following data

Profits in ₹ '000:	*No. of firms :*
less than 10	5
10–19	18
20–29	38
30–39	20
40–49	9
50–59	2

are
A. ₹ 33500 and ₹ 29184
B. ₹ 33000 and ₹ 28680
C. ₹ 33600 and ₹ 29000
D. ₹ 33250 and ₹ 29250

47. For the following incomplete distribution of marks of 100 pupils, median mark is known to be 32.

Marks	0–10	10–20	20–30	30–40	40–50	50–60
No. of Students	10	–	25	30	–	10

What is the mean mark?
A. 32
B. 31
C. 31.30
D. 31.50

48. The mode of the following distribution is ₹ 66. What would be the median wage?

Daily wages (₹)	30–40	40–50	50–60	60–70	70–80	80–90
No of workers	8	16	22	28	–	12

A. ₹ 64.00
B. ₹ 64.56
C. ₹ 62.32
D. ₹ 64.25

49. If the grouped data has open-end classes, one can not calculate.
A. median
B. mode
C. mean
D. quartile

50. Geometric mean of two numbers $\left(\frac{1}{16}\right)$ and $\left(\frac{4}{25}\right)$ is
A. $\left(\frac{1}{10}\right)$
B. $\left(\frac{1}{100}\right)$
C. 10
D. 100

51. In a symmetric distribution
A. mean = median = mode
B. mean = median = mode
C. mean > median > mode
D. mean< median < mode

52. If modal value is not clear in a distribution, it can be ascertained by the method of
A. grouping
B. guessing
C. summarizing
D. trial and error

53. Shoe size of most of the people in India is No. 7. Which measure of central value does it represent ?
A. mean
B. second quartile
C. eighth decile
D. mode

54. The middle value of an ordered series is called :
A. 2nd quartile
B. 5th decile
C. 50th percentile
D. all the above

55. The variate values which divide a series (frequency distribution) into ten equal parts are called:
A. quartiles
B. deciles
C. octiles
D. percentiles

56. For percentiles, the total number of partition values are
A. 10
B. 59
C. 100
D. 99

57. The first quartile divides a frequency distribution in the ratio
A. 4 : 1
B. 1 :4
C. 3 : 1
D. 1 : 3

58. Sum of the deviations about mean is
A. Zero
B. minimum
C. maximum
D. one

59. Histogram is useful to determine graphically the value of
A. mean
B. median
C. mode
D. all the above

60. Median can be located graphically with the help of
A. Histogram
B. ogives
C. bar diagram
D. scatter diagram

61. Sixth deciles is same as
A. median
B. 50th percentile
C. 60th percentile
D. first quartile

62. What percentage of values lies between 5th and 25th percentiles?
A. 5%
B. 20%
C. 30%
D. 75%

ANSWERS

1	2	3	4	5	6	7	8	9	10
B	C	B	A	C	B	B	A	C	D

11	12	13	14	15	16	17	18	19	20
D	A	C	C	B	B	C	D	D	B

21	22	23	24	25	26	27	28	29	30
A	B	B	C	C	B	D	C	B	B

31	32	33	34	35	36	37	38	39	40
A	B	C	B	A	C	C	B	A	C

41	42	43	44	45	46	47	48	49	50
C	C	C	D	D	A	C	C	C	A

51	52	53	54	55	56	157	58	59	60
B	A	D	D	B	C	D	A	C	B

61	62
C	B

***

14

Probability

The concept of probability is extremely important. It is extensively used in the development of all Physical Science and daily life events. The chance of happening of an event when expressed quantitatively is known as probability.

If an experiment results in $(m + n)$ mutually exclusive, exhaustive and equally likely outcomes and an event E can occur in m ways then probability of E is given as

$$P[E] = \frac{m}{m+n}$$

i.e., probability of an event is the ratio of favourable ways of that event upon total ways of the experiment

$$P[E] = \frac{\text{Favourable ways of event E}}{\text{Total ways}}$$

Thus, an event can occur in m ways and fails in n ways, this statement at times is given as odds in favour of the event E are n to m.

1. Random Experiment

If an experiment is conducted and its result is unpredictable, *i.e.*, its outcome can be one of the many outcomes, then such an experiment is called random experiment.

2. Sample Space

The collection of all outcomes of a random experiment in a form of set is called a sample space *e.g.*, if a die is thrown then the set S = {1, 2, 3, 4, 5, 6} is called a sample space.

3. Simple Event

Each outcome of an experiment is called a simple event.

4. Event

Any combination of simple events is called an event, it is denoted by E. **Example :** *If a card is drawn from a pack of cards, there are 52 possible outcomes, each of them is simple event and the card is a king is an event as it consists of four events. i.e., king of each unit.*

5. Mutually Exclusive Event

A set of events is called mutually exclusive, if the happening of one event excludes the happening of the other *e.g.*, tossing of a coin will result in either head or tail, happening of head excludes the happening of tail and vice-versa, if A and B are two mutually exclusive events then

$$A \cap B = \phi$$

6. Exhaustive Events

All the outcomes of the experiment put together are called exhaustive events as no other result outside this can happen as a result of this experiment.

7. Equally Likely Event

If any outcome of the experiment is not favoured or disfavoured compared to other outcomes they are called equally likely *e.g.*, drawing a card from a pack of cards result in 52 equally likely events.

8. Union of Events

If there are two events A and B in a sample space, if we write $A \cup B$ it means either of the event can happen and it is called A union B.

9. Intersection of Events

If both events happen simultaneously, it is written as $A \cap B$ and it is read as A intersection B.

10. Complement of the Event

The complement of event A contains all the outcomes of sample space except those of A it is denoted by $\overline{A}$ or A^C.

(*a*) **Addition Theorem:** For happening of either of two events A and B
$$P(A \cup B) = P(A) + P(B) - P(A \cap B)$$
If A and B are mutually exclusive, then
$$A \cap B = \phi \Rightarrow (A \cap B) = 0$$
Then $P(A \cup B) = P(A) + P(B)$

(*b*) **Multiplication Theorem:** If A and B are two independent events, then the probability of simultaneous occurrence is given as
$$P(A \cap B) = P(A) \cdot P(B)$$

(*c*) **Conditional Probability:** It is probability of the happening of one event with an assumption that another event has already happened if
$$P(A / B) = \frac{P(A \cap B)}{P(B)} \quad \text{here } B \text{ has happened.}$$
or, $P\left(\dfrac{B}{A}\right) = \dfrac{P(A \cap B)}{P(A)}$ here A has happened.

MULTIPLE CHOICE QUESTIONS

1. The probability of getting heads in both trials when a balanced coin is tossed twice, will be :

A. $\dfrac{1}{4}$ B. $\dfrac{1}{2}$

C. 1   D. $\dfrac{3}{4}$

2. Two cards are drawn at random from a pack of 52 cards. The probability of these two being aces is :

A. $\dfrac{1}{26}$ B. $\dfrac{1}{12}$

C. $\dfrac{1}{2}$ D. None of these

3. A card is drawn from a well shuffled pack of 52 cards, the probability of getting a queen of club or king of heart is :

A. $\dfrac{1}{52}$ B. $\dfrac{1}{26}$

C. $\dfrac{1}{13}$ D. None of these

4. A single letter is selected at random from the word "PROBABILITY" the probability that it is vowel is :

A. $\dfrac{3}{11}$ B. $\dfrac{4}{11}$

C. $\dfrac{2}{11}$ D. 0

5. The probability that leap year selected at random contains 53 Sunday is :

A. $\dfrac{7}{366}$ B. $\dfrac{26}{183}$

C. $\dfrac{1}{7}$ D. $\dfrac{2}{7}$

6. Three mangoes and three apples are in a box. If two fruits are chosen at random, the probability that one is a mango and the other is an apple is :

A. $\dfrac{2}{3}$ B. $\dfrac{3}{5}$

C. $\dfrac{1}{3}$ D. None of these

7. The probability of getting more than 7 when a pair of dice are thrown is :

A. $\dfrac{7}{36}$ B. $\dfrac{7}{12}$

C. $\dfrac{5}{12}$ D. None of these

8. Three letters are written to different persons and addresses on three envelopes are also written without looking at the address, the probability that the letters go into right envelopes is :

A. $\dfrac{1}{27}$ B. $\dfrac{1}{6}$

C. $\dfrac{1}{9}$ D. None of these

9. Three identical dice are rolled, the probability that the same number will appear on each of them is :

A. $\dfrac{1}{6}$ B. $\dfrac{1}{8}$

C. $\dfrac{1}{36}$ D. None of these

10. One die and one coin are tossed simultaneously the probability of getting 6 on die and head on coin is :

A. $\dfrac{1}{2}$ B. $\dfrac{1}{6}$

C. $\dfrac{1}{12}$ D. None of these

11. A card is drawn at random from a pack of 100 cards numbered 1 to 100, the probability of drawing a number which is a square is :

A. $\dfrac{1}{5}$ B. $\dfrac{2}{5}$

C. $\dfrac{1}{10}$ D. None of these

12. The probabilities of so solving a problem by three students A, B, C are $\dfrac{1}{2}, \dfrac{1}{3}, \dfrac{1}{4}$ respectively. The probability that the problem will be solved is :

A. $\dfrac{1}{4}$ B. $\dfrac{1}{2}$

C. $\dfrac{3}{4}$ D. $\dfrac{1}{3}$

13. The probability that a marksman will hit a target is given as $\dfrac{1}{5}$, then his probability of at least one hit in 10 shots is :

A. $1 - \left(\dfrac{4}{5}\right)^{10}$ B. $\dfrac{1}{5^{10}}$

C. $1 - \dfrac{1}{5^{10}}$ D. None of these

14. From a pack of cards two are drawn, the first being replaced before the second is drawn, the probability that the first is a diamond and the second is a king will be :

A. $\dfrac{13}{4}$ B. $\dfrac{4}{13}$

C. $\dfrac{1}{52}$ D. 52

15. Two cards are drawn successively with replacement from a well shuffled pack of 52 cards, the probability of drawing two aces is :

A. $\dfrac{1}{13}\times\dfrac{1}{13}$ B. $\dfrac{1}{13}\times\dfrac{1}{17}$

C. $\dfrac{1}{52}\times\dfrac{1}{51}$ D. $\dfrac{1}{13}\times\dfrac{4}{51}$

16. You are given a box with 20 cards in it, 10 of these cards have the letter *I* printed on them, the other ten have the letter *T* printed on them, if you pick up 3 cards at random and keep them in the same order, the probability of making the word *IIT* is :

A. $\dfrac{9}{80}$ B. $\dfrac{1}{8}$

C. $\dfrac{4}{27}$ D. $\dfrac{5}{38}$

17. In a box containing 100 bulbs, 10 are defective. What is the probability that out of a sample of 5 bulbs, none is defective?

A. 10^{-5} B. $\left(\dfrac{1}{2}\right)^5$

C. $\left(\dfrac{9}{10}\right)^5$ D. $\dfrac{9}{10}$

18. The chance of throwing an ace first only of two successive throws with an ordinary die is :

A. $\dfrac{1}{36}$ B. $\dfrac{5}{36}$

C. $\dfrac{25}{36}$ D. $\dfrac{1}{6}$

19. The mean number of heads in three tosses of a coin is :

A. $\dfrac{3}{2}$ B. $\dfrac{5}{2}$

C. $\dfrac{1}{2}$ D. $\dfrac{1}{8}$

20. The value of *P(2)* in a Binomial distribution when $P=\dfrac{1}{6}$ and $n=5$ is :

A. $\dfrac{3125}{7776}$ B. $\dfrac{250}{7776}$

C. $\dfrac{1250}{7776}$ D. $\dfrac{25}{7776}$

21. A die is thrown once. What is the probability of getting a number other than 3?

A. $\dfrac{5}{6}$ B. $\dfrac{1}{6}$

C. $\dfrac{2}{6}$ D. None of these

22. A die is thrown once. What is the probability of getting the number 5?

A. $\dfrac{2}{6}$ B. $\dfrac{5}{6}$

C. $\dfrac{1}{6}$ D. None of these

23. One card is drawn from a well shuffled deck of 52 cards. What is the probability of drawing an ace?

A. $\dfrac{1}{52}$ B. $\dfrac{1}{13}$

C. $\dfrac{4}{13}$ D. None of these

24. A box contains 3 blue marbles, 2 white marbles and 4 red marbles. If a marble is taken out at random from the box, what is the probability that it will be a white one?

A. $\dfrac{2}{9}$ B. $\dfrac{1}{9}$

C. $\dfrac{7}{9}$ D. None of these

25. 15 cards numbered 1, 2, 3, ... 15 are put in a box and mixed. One person draws a card from the box. Find the probability that the number in the card is a prime number.

A. $\dfrac{7}{15}$ B. $\dfrac{8}{15}$

C. $\dfrac{2}{5}$ D. $\dfrac{4}{5}$

26. 1000 tickets of a lottery were sold and there are 5 prizes on these tickets. If Saket has purchased one lottery ticket. What is the probability of winning a prize?

A. 0.002   B. 0.005
C. 0.05   D. 0.5

27. A bag contains 5 red balls and some blue balls. If the probability of drawing a blue ball is double that of a red ball, find the number of blue balls in the bag?
A. 5   B. 8
C. 10   D. 6

28. A box contains 20 balls bearing numbers 1, 2, 3, 4, 5, ... 20. A ball is drawn at random from the box. What is the probability that number on the ball is composite number?

A. $\dfrac{11}{20}$ B. $\dfrac{8}{20}$

C. $\dfrac{9}{20}$ D. $\dfrac{7}{20}$

29. In tossing a fair die, the probability of getting an odd number less than 4 is

A. $\dfrac{2}{3}$ B. $\dfrac{3}{4}$

C. 2   D. $\dfrac{1}{2}$

30. The probability of getting 9 with two dice is

A. $\dfrac{1}{36}$ B. $\dfrac{1}{27}$

C. $\dfrac{2}{9}$ D. $\dfrac{1}{9}$

ANSWERS

1	2	3	4	5	6	7	8	9	10
A	B	B	B	D	B	C	B	C	C
11	**12**	**13**	**14**	**15**	**16**	**17**	**18**	**19**	**20**
C	C	A	C	A	D	C	B	A	C
21	**22**	**23**	**24**	**25**	**26**	**27**	**28**	**29**	**30**
A	C	B	A	C	B	C	A	A	D

EXPLANATORY ANSWERS

1. Probability of getting head in one trial $= \dfrac{1}{2}$

∴ Probability of getting heads in both the trials

$= \dfrac{1}{2} \times \dfrac{1}{2} = \dfrac{1}{4}.$

2. Required probability $= \dfrac{^4C_2}{^{52}C_2} = \dfrac{4 \times 3}{52 \times 51} = \dfrac{1}{221}.$

3. Total ways = 52

There is one queen of club and one king of heart favourable ways = 1 + 1 = 2

∴ Required probability $= \dfrac{2}{52} = \dfrac{1}{26}.$

4. Total ways are 11, there are three vowels and one is repeated. So favourable case = 4

So, required probability $= \dfrac{4}{11}.$

5. In a leap year, there are 366 days, it means 52 full weeks and two days. These two days can be Mon., Tues.; Tues.; Wed.; Wed.; Thurs. Thurs.; Friday; Fri. Sat.; Sat.; Sun.; Sun.; Mon.

So, required probability $= \dfrac{2}{7}.$

6. Total ways $= {}^6C_2 = 15$

Favourable ways $= {}^3C_1 \times {}^3C_1 = 9.$

Reqd. Probability $= \dfrac{9}{15} = \dfrac{3}{5}.$

7. $P(8) + P(9) + P(10).$

8. Total no. of ways = 3! = 6 and favourable no. of ways = 1.

9. Total ways = 6 × 6 × 6 favourable ways are 6, *i.e.,*
(1,1,1) (2,2,2) (3,3,3)
(4,4,4) (5,5,5) (6,6,6)

So, required probability $= \dfrac{6}{6 \times 6 \times 6} = \dfrac{1}{36}.$

10. A die has 6 outcomes, coin has two. So, total ways = 6 × 2 = 12, favourable ways = 1.

So, required prob. $= \dfrac{1}{12}.$

11. Total ways = 100, Squares of following no's lie between 1 and 100, $1^2, 2^2, 3^2, 4^2, 5^2, 6^2, 7^2, 8^2, 9^2, 10^2$ which are 10 in number.

So, required probability $= \dfrac{10}{100} = \dfrac{1}{10}.$

12. $P(A) = \dfrac{1}{2}, P(\overline{A}) = \dfrac{1}{2}, P(B) = \dfrac{1}{3}, P(\overline{B}) = \dfrac{2}{3}$

$P(C) = \dfrac{1}{4}, P(\overline{C}) = \dfrac{3}{4}$

Problem will be solved if even one of them solve it. So, the first we calculate probability that is not solved

$P(\overline{A}) P(\overline{B}) P(\overline{C}) = \dfrac{1}{2} \times \dfrac{2}{3} \times \dfrac{3}{4} = \dfrac{1}{4},$

The required probability $= 1 - \dfrac{1}{4} = \dfrac{3}{4}$.

13. He will hit the target, $P(A) = \dfrac{1}{5}$. He will not hit the target, $P(\overline{A}) = \dfrac{4}{5}$. Probability that he will not hit the target in 10 shoots is $\left(\dfrac{4}{5}\right)^{10}$. So, at least once, target will be heat.

Required probability $= 1 - \left(\dfrac{4}{5}\right)^{10}$

14. The required probability

$$= \dfrac{^{13}C_1}{^{52}C_1} \cdot \dfrac{^{4}C_1}{^{51}C_1} = \dfrac{13}{52} \cdot \dfrac{4}{52} = \dfrac{1}{52}.$$

15. Required probability

$$\left(\dfrac{4}{52} \times \dfrac{4}{52}\right) = \left(\dfrac{4}{52}\right)^2 = \dfrac{1}{13} \times \dfrac{1}{13}.$$

16. As we have to consider order for IIT, the required probability

$$= \dfrac{10}{20} \times \dfrac{9}{19} \times \dfrac{10}{18} = \dfrac{5}{38}.$$

17. Probability of non-defective piece $= \dfrac{90}{100} = \dfrac{9}{10}$ in a sample of five none defective, the required probability

$$= \dfrac{9}{10} \times \dfrac{9}{10} \times \dfrac{9}{10} \times \dfrac{9}{10} \times \dfrac{9}{10} = \left(\dfrac{9}{10}\right)^5$$

18. $\therefore$ Probability of throwing an ace $= \dfrac{1}{6}$ and of not throwing ace $= \dfrac{5}{6}$. Hence, required probability

$$= \dfrac{1}{6} \times \dfrac{5}{6} = \dfrac{5}{36}.$$

19. We know that mean of binomial distribution is np here

$$n = 3, \ p = \dfrac{1}{2}. \ \text{So, mean } = 3 \times \dfrac{1}{2} = \dfrac{3}{2}.$$

20. For Binomial distribution, $p(r) = {}^nC_r p^r q^{n-r}$ Here,

$$p = \dfrac{1}{6}, \ q = \dfrac{5}{6}, \ n = 5, \ r = 2.$$

So, $p(2) = {}^5C_2 \left(\dfrac{1}{6}\right)^2 \left(\dfrac{5}{6}\right)^3 = \dfrac{1250}{7776}$.

21. Possible outcomes are 1, 2, 3, 4, 5, 6

$\therefore$ Required probability $= \dfrac{5}{6}$.

22. Possible outcomes are 1, 2, 3, 4, 5, 6
Favourable outcomes in this case is 5

$\therefore$ Required probability $= \dfrac{1}{6}$.

23. Possible outcomes = 52
Favourable outcomes = 4

$\therefore$ Required probability $= \dfrac{4}{52} = \dfrac{1}{13}$.

24. Total number of marbles = 9
Number of white marble = 2

$\therefore$ Required probability $= \dfrac{2}{9}$.

25. Total number of possible outcomes = 15
Favourable outcomes are 2, 3, 5, 7, 11, 13 = 6

$\therefore$ Required probability $= \dfrac{6}{15} = \dfrac{2}{5}$.

26. Total number of outcomes = 1000
Favourable outcomes = 5

$\therefore$ Required probability $= \dfrac{5}{1000} = 0.005$.

27. Let number of blue balls = x
Total number of balls = $5 + x$

Probability for a red ball $= \dfrac{5}{x+5}$

Probability for a blue ball $= \dfrac{x}{5+x}$

According to the question,

$$\dfrac{x}{5+x} = 2\left(\dfrac{5}{x+5}\right) \Rightarrow x = 10$$

$\therefore$ Number of blue balls = 10.

28. Possible outcomes = 20
Favourable outcomes are 4, 6, 8, 9, 10, 12, 14, 15, 16, 18, 20 = 11

$\therefore$ Required probability $= \dfrac{11}{20}$.

29. Total number of outcomes = 6
Favourable outcomes are = 1, 2, 3, 5 = 4

$\therefore$ Required probability $= \dfrac{4}{6} = \dfrac{2}{3}$.

30. Total number of possible outcomes = $6 \times 6 = 36$
Number of outcomes = 4

$\therefore$ Required probability $= \dfrac{4}{36} = \dfrac{1}{9}$.

✱✱✱

GENERAL AWARENESS

NATIONAL SYMBOLS

NATIONAL EMBLEM

State emblem of India is an adaptation from the Sarnath Lion Capital of Ashoka. It was adopted by the Government of India on January 26, 1950. In the adapted form, only three lions are visible, the fourth being hidden from the view. The wheel (Dharma Chakra) appears in relief in the centre of the abacus with a bull on the right and a horse on the left.

The bell-shaped lotus has been omitted. The words ''Satyameva Jayate'' meaning ''Truth alone triumphs'' are inscribed below the Emblem in Devanagari script.

NATIONAL FLAG

The National Flag of India is a horizontal tricolour of deep saffron (Kesari), white and dark green in equal proportion. In the centre of the white band there is a wheel in navy blue colour. It has 24 spokes. The ratio of the length and the breadth of the flag is 3 : 2. Its design was adopted by the Constituent Assembly of India on July 22, 1947.

NATIONAL ANTHEM

Rabindranath Tagore's song 'Jana-gana-mana' was adopted by the Constituent Assembly as the National Anthem of India on January 24, 1950.

Jana-gan-mana-adhinayaka jaya he, Bharata-bhagya-vidhata
Punjab-Sindh-Gujarat-Maratha-Dravida-Utkala-Banga
Vindhya-Himachala-Yamuna-Ganga Uchhala-jaladhi-taranga.
Tava subha name jage, Tava subha asisa mange,
Gahe tava jaya gatha,
Jana-gana-mangala-dayak, jaya he Bharata bhagya vidhata,
Jaya he, jaya he, jaya he, Jaya jaya jaya, jaya he.

NATIONAL SONG

Bankim Chandra Chatterji's 'Vande Mataram' which was a source of inspiration to the people in their struggle for freedom, has been adopted as National Song. It has an equal status with the National Anthem.

Vande Mataram
Sujalam, suphalam, malayaja-shitalam,
Shasya shyamalam, Mataram
Shubhrajyotsna,pulkita yaminim,
Phulla kusumita drumadalashobhinim,

Subhasinim sumadhura—bhashinim,
Sukhadam, Varadam, Mataram.

National Bird and Animal of India: Peacock and Tiger

National Aquatic Animal: Dolphin

National Flower: Lotus; **National Game:** Hockey

National Calendar: It was adopted on March 22, 1957. It has 365 days in the year and the first month of the year is Chaitra.

NATIONAL CALENDAR

It is based on the Saka era with Chaitra as its first month and a normal year of 365 days. It was adopted from March 22, 1957. Dates of the national calendar have a permanent correspondence with dates of Gregorian calendar as Chaitra I falls on March 22 in a normal year and March 21 in a leap year. In official communications, both Saka and Gregorian calendar dates are written. Months of the national calendar are Chaitra, Vaishakha, Jaishtha, Ashada, Shravan, Bhadra, Ashvina, Kartika, Margashirsha, Pausha, Magha and Phalguna.

NATIONAL ANIMAL

The magnificent tiger — Panthera tigris (Linnaeus) is the national animal of India. Tiger is found in several parts of the country and is known for its grace, strength, agility and enormous power. 'Project Tiger' was launched in 1973 to check their dwindling population in India.

NATIONAL BIRD

The Indian Peacock — Pavo Christatus (Linnaeus) is the national bird of India. It is a colourful, swan-sized bird with a fan-shaped crest of feathers on its head and a long-slander neck. The male species is more colourful with blue breast and a spectacular bronze-green train of around 200 elongated feathers.

National Flower—Lotus

National Tree—Banyan

National Fruit—Mango

National Currency—Rupee '₹' (One Rupee = 100 Paise)

National Aquatic Animal—Dolphin

BOOKS AND AUTHORS

Name of Book	Author	Name of Book	Author
Ain-e-Akbari	Abul Fazal	Arthshastra	Kautilya
Anand Math	Bankim Chandra Chatterjee	Coolie	Mulk Raj Anand
An Unknown Indian	Nirad C. Chaudhuri	Das Kapital	Karl Marx

Name of Book	Author	Name of Book	Author
Discovery of India	Jawaharlal Nehru	Neeti Shatak	Bhartrihari
Eternal India	Mrs. Indira Gandhi	Nehru and His Vision	Dr. K.R. Narayanan
Godan	Prem Chand	Old Man and the Sea	Ernest Hemingway
Gitanjali	Rabindranath Tagore	One World	Wendell Wilkie
Gora	Rabindranath Tagore	Panchtantra	Vishnu Sharma
Geet Govinda	Jayadeva	Paradise Lost	John Milton
Harsha Charit	Bana Bhatta	Ramayana	Valmiki (in Sanskrit)
Hindu View of Life	Dr. S. Radhakrishnan	Raghuvansham	Kalidas
India Wins Freedom	Maulana Abul Kalam Azad	Rajtarangini	Kalhan
Jobs of Millions	V.V. Giri	Ram Charit Manas	Tulsi Das
Jungle Book	Rudyard Kipling	Abhijnan Shakuntalam	Kalidas
Kamayani	Jai Shankar Prasad	Satanic Verses	Salman Rushdie
Kadambari	Bana Bhatta	Saket	Maithili Sharan Gupta
Life Divine	Sri Aurobindo	Speed Post	Shobha De
Last days of Netaji	G.D. Khosla	The God of Small Things	Arundhati Roy
Les Miserables	Victor Hugo	Treasure Island	R.L. Stevenson
Mahabharat	Veda Vyas	Twelfth Night	William Shakespeare
Macbeth	William Shakespeare	Train to Pakistan	Khuswant Singh
Mein Kempf	Hitler	Uttara Ram Charitra	Bhava Bhuti
Meghduta	Kalidas	Vanity Fair	W.M. Thackeray
Mother (Maa)	Maxim Gorky	War and Peace	Leo Tolstoy
Mother India	Katherine Mayo	Wealth of Nations	Adam Smith
My Experiments with Truth	Mahatma Gandhi	Wake up India	Annie Besant
My Presidential Years	R. Venkataraman		

INVENTIONS AND DISCOVERIES

Discovery	Discoverer	Discovery	Discoverer
Geographical Discoveries		Printing for the blind	Louis Braille
America	Columbus	Radium	Madame Curie
Brazil	Cabral	Telegraph	Samuel Morse
North Pole	Robert Peary	Television	J.L. Baird
Everest (Conquered)	Tabie Junko	Telephone	Graham Bell
Planetary Motion	Kepler	Wireless	G. Marconi
Hawaiian Islands	Captain Cook	X-rays	W.K. Roentgen
South Pole	Amundsen		
Solar System	Copernicus	**Mechanical**	
		Aeroplane	Wright Brothers
Chemistry and Physics		Bicycle	Macmillan
Atom Bomb	Otto Hahn	Computer	Charles Babbage
Atomic Theory	Dalton	Dynamo	Michal Faraday
Atomic Numbers	Moseley	Diesel Engine	Rudolf Diesel
Cosmic Rays	R.S. Millikan	Engine (Railway)	Stephenson
Dynamite	Alfred Nobel	Fountain Pen	Waterman
Electrons Theory	Bohr	Gramophone	Edison
Electricity (current)	Volta	Locomotive Power of Steam	James Watt
Electric Telegraphy (Code)	S. Morse	Helicopter	Brequet
Gravitation	Newton	Life Boat	Henry Greathead
Gas Light	Murdock	Microscope	Z. Jansen
Oxygen	J. Priestly	Printing Press	Gutenberg
Photography	L. Daguerre	Revolver	Colt

Discovery	Discoverer
Sewing Machine	Elias Howe
Thermometer	Fahrenheit
Transistor	W. Shockley
Typewriter	Sholes
Telescope	Hans Lippershey
Tank (Military)	Swinton
Medical	
Antiseptic Surgery	Lord Joseph Lister
Bacteria	Leeuwenhock
Circulation of Blood	William Harvey

Discovery	Discoverer
Homoeopathy (Discovered)	Hahnemann
Insulin	F. Banting
Penicillin	Alexander Flemming
Malaria Parasite	Dr. Ronald Ross
Stethoscope	Laennec
Vitamins	Funk
Anti-Rabies Treatment	Pasteur
General	
Nylon	Carouthers
Science of Geometry	Euclids

WORLD'S GEOGRAPHICAL SURNAMES

● City of Sky-scrapers—New York ● City of Seven Hills—Rome ● City of Dreaming Spires—Oxford ● City of Golden Gate—San Francisco ● City of Magnificent Buildings—Washington D.C. ● City of Eternal Springs—Quito (S. America) ● China's Sorrow—Hwang Ho ● Cockpit of Europe—Belgium ● Dark Continent—Africa ● Emerald Isle—Ireland ● Eternal City—Rome ● Empire City—New York ● Forbidden City—Lhasa (Tibet) ● Garden City—Chicago ● Gate of Tears—Strait of Bab-el-Mandeb ● Gift of the Nile—Egypt ● Granite City—Aberdeen (Scotland) ● Hermit Kingdom—Korea ● Herring Pond—Atlantic Ocean ● Holy Land—Jerusalem ● Island Continent—Australia ● Islands of Cloves—Zanzibar ● Isle of Pearls—Bahrein (Persian Gulf) ● Key to the Mediterranean—Gibralter ● Land of Cakes—Scotland ● Land of Golden Fleece—Australia ● Land of Maple Leaf—Canada ● Land of Morning Calm—Korea ● Land of Midnight Sun—Norway ● Land of the Thousand Lakes—Finland ● Land of the Thunderbolt—Bhutan ● Land of White Elephant—Thailand ● Land of Thousand Elephants—Laos ● Land of Rising Sun—Japan ● Loneliest Island—Tristan De Gunha (Mid-Atlantic) ● Manchester of Japan—Osaka ● Pillars of Hercules—Strait of Gibraltar ● Pearl of the Antilles—Cuba ● Playground of Europe—Switzerland ● Quaker City—Philadelphia ● Queen of the Adriatic—Venice ● Roof of the World—The Pamirs, Central Asia ● Sugar bowl of the world—Cuba ● Venice of the North—Stockholm ● Windy City—Chicago ● Whiteman's grave—Guinea Coast of Africa ● Yellow River—Huang Ho (China) ● Sickman of Europe—Turkey

CURRENCIES OF DIFFERENT COUNTRIES

Country	Currency
Australia	Australian Dollar
Bangladesh	Taka
Belgium	Euro
Britain	Pound (Sterling)
Myanmar	Kyat
Canada	Canadian Dollar
Germany	Euro
Iran	Rial
India	Rupee
Ceylon	Rupee
China	Yuan
Czech Republic	Koruna
Denmark	Krone
France	Euro
Pakistan	Rupee

Country	Currency
Poland	Zloty
Spain	Euro
Indonesia	Rupiah
Iraq	Dinar
Italy	Euro
Japan	Yen
Mexico	Peso
Netherland	Euro
European Union	Euro
Sweden	Krone
Switzerland	Swiss Franc
Turkey	Lira
U.A.E.	Dirham
U.S.A.	Dollar
Russia	Rouble

CAPITAL OF COUNTRIES

Country	Capital
Austria	Vienna
Afghanisatan	Kabul
Algeria	Algiers
Angola	Luanda
Australia	Canberra
Argentina	Buenos Aires
Bangladesh	Dhaka
Belgium	Brussels
Bolivia	Lapaz
Bulgaria	Sofia
Bhutan	Thimpu
Brazil	Brasilla
Canada	Ottawa
China	Beijing
Cyprus	Nicosia
Columbia	Bagota
Denmark	Copenhegan
Ethiopia	Addis Ababa
Finland	Helsinki
France	Paris
Germany	Berlin
Greece	Athens
Guatemala	Guatemala City
Hungary	Budapest
Iran	Tehran
India	New Delhi
Indonesia	Jakarta
Iraq	Baghdad
Italy	Rome
Ireland	Dublin
Japan	Tokyo
Kampuchea (Combodia)	Phnom Penh
Korea (North)	Pyong Yang
Korea (South)	Seoul
Kenya	Nairobi
Kuwait	Kuwait
Laos	Vientiane
Lebanon	Beirut
Mexico	Mexico City
Malaysia	Kualalumpur
Morocco	Rabat
Mozambique	Maputo
New Zealand	Welington
Netherlands	Amsterdam
Panama	Panama City
Portugal	Lisbon
Poland	Warsaw
Sri Lanka	Colombo
Sweden	Stockholm
Switzerland	Bern
Sudan	Khartoum
Sierre	Leone
South Africa	Capetown
Saudi Arabia	Riyadh
Spain	Madrid
Thailand	Bangkok
Turkey	Ankara
Russia	Moscow
Azerbaijan	Baku
Armenia	Yerevan
Latvia	Riga
Ukrain	Kiev
U.S.A.	Washington
U.K.	London
U.A.R.	Cairo
Vietnam	Hanoi
Zambia	Lusaka

INDIAN CITIES AND THEIR RIVERS

City	State	River
Agra	U.P.	Yamuna
Ahmedabad	Gujarat	Sabarmati
Allahabad	U.P.	Confluence of the Ganga, Yamuna, and invisible Saraswati
Alwaye	Kerala	Periyar
Kolkata	West Bengal	Hooghly
Cuttack	Odisha	Mahanadi
Delhi	Delhi	Yamuna
Haridwar	Uttarakhand	Ganga
Kanpur	Uttar Pradesh	Ganga
Ludhiana	Punjab	Sutlej
Lucknow	Uttar Pradesh	Gomati
Nasik	Maharashtra	Godavari
Patna	Bihar	Ganga
Srinagar	J & K	Jhelum
Surat	Gujarat	Tapti
Tiruchirapally	Tamil Nadu	Kaveri
Ujjain	Madhya Pradesh	Shipra
Vijayawada	Andhra Pradesh	Krishna
Varanasi	Uttar Pradesh	Ganga

WONDERS OF THE WORLD

Seven Wonders of the Ancient World: (1) the Pyramids of Egypt, built in approximately 2700 BC; (2) the Hanging Gardens at Babylon; (3) the temple of Artemis at Emphesus; (4) the statue of Zeus at Olympia; (5) the tomb of Mausolus at Halicarnassus, built in nearly 350 BC; (6) the Colossus of Rhodes, built in nearly 280 BC; (7) the Pharos Lighthouse at Alexandria.

Seven Wonders of the Medieval World: (1) the Colosseum of Rome; (2) the Great Wall of China; (3) the Porcelain Tower of Nanking; (4) the Mosque at St. Sophia (Constantinople); (5) Stonehenge; (6) the Catacombs of Rome; (7) the Leaning Tower of Pisa.

Seven New Wonders of the World: (1) Taj Mahal of Agra (India); (2) Pyramid at Chichen Itza (Mexico); (3) Machu Picchu (Peru); (4) Statue of Christ The Redeemer (Brazil); (5) Great Wall of China; (6) Roman Colosseum, Italy; (7) Ruins of Petra, Jordan.

STATES OF INDIA (CAPITALS, PRINCIPAL LANGUAGES)

States / Principal Languages	Capitals	States / Principal Languages	Capitals
■ Andhra Pradesh—*Telgu and Urdu*	Hyderabad	■ Maharashtra—*Marathi*	Mumbai
■ Arunachal Pradesh— *Monpa, Adi, Nissi etc.*	Itanagar	■ Meghalaya—*Khashi, Jayantia and Garo*	Shillong
■ Assam—*Assamese and Bengali*	Dispur	■ Manipur—*Manipuri*	Imphal
■ Bihar—*Hindi and Maithili*	Patna	■ Mizoram—*Mizo and English*	Aizawl
■ Chattishgarh—*Hindi*	Raipur	■ Nagaland—*Naga, Assamese and English*	Kohima
■ Goa—*Konkani*	Panaji	■ Odisha—*Odiya*	Bhubaneshwar
■ Gujarat—*Gujarati*	GandhiNagar	■ Punjab—*Punjabi*	Chandigarh
■ Haryana—*Hindi*	Chandigarh	■ Rajasthan—*Hindi, Rajasthani*	Jaipur
■ Himachal Pradesh— *Hindi and Pahari*	Shimla	■ Sikkim—*Sikkimese and Gorkhali*	Gangtok
■ Jammu & Kashmir— *Kashmiri, Dongri, Urdu, Ladakhi, Dardi and Pahari*	Srinagar	■ Tamil Nadu—*Tamil*	Chennai
■ Jharkhand—*Hindi*	Ranchi	■ Tripura—*Bengali, Tripuri and Manipuri*	Agartala
■ Kerala—*Malyalam*	Thiruvananthpuram	■ Uttar Pradesh—*Hindi*	Lucknow
■ Karnataka—*Kannada*	Bengluru	■ Uttarakhand—*Hindi*	Dehradun
■ Madhya Pradesh—*Hindi*	Bhopal	■ West Bengal—*Bengali*	Kolkata
		■ Telangana—*Telgu and Urdu*	Hyderabad

Union Territories / Principal Languages	Capitals	Union Territories / Principal Languages	Capitals
■ Andaman and Nicobar Islands— *Hindi, Nicobarese, Bengali, Malayalam, Tamil, Telugu*	Port Blair	■ Daman and Diu—*Gujarati*	Daman
■ Chandigarh—*Hindi, Punjabi, English*	Chandigarh	■ Delhi—*Hindi, Punjabi*	Delhi
		■ Lakshadweep—*Malayalam*	Kavaratti
■ Dadar and Nagar Haveli— *Gujarati, Hindi*	Silvasa	■ Puducherry—*Tamil, Telugu, Malayalam, English and French*	Puducherry

HIGH COURTS IN INDIA

Name	Year	Territorial Jurisdiction	Seat
Allahabad	1866	Uttar Pradesh	Allahabad (Bench at Lucknow)
Andhra Pradesh	1954	Andhra Pradesh / Telangana	Hyderabad
Bombay	1862	Maharashtra, Goa, Dadar & Nagar Haveli and Daman & Diu	Mumbai (Benches at Nagpur, Panaji and Aurangabad)
Calcutta	1862	West Bengal and Andaman & Nicobar	Kolkata (Circuit Bench at Port Blair)
Chhattisgarh	2000	Chhattisgarh	Bilaspur
Delhi	1966	Delhi	Delhi
Guwahati	1948	Assam, Nagaland, Mizoram and Arunachal Pradesh	Guwahati (Benches at Kohima, Aizawl and Itanagar)
Gujarat	1960	Gujarat	Ahmedabad
Himachal Pradesh	1971	Himachal Pradesh	Shimla
Jammu & Kashmir	1928	Jammu & Kashmir	Srinagar and Jammu
Jharkhand	2000	Jharkhand	Ranchi
Karnataka	1884	Karnataka	Bengaluru (Circuit Benches at Dharwar and Gulbarga)
Kerala	1958	Kerala & Lakshadweep	Ernakulam
Madhya Pradesh	1956	Madhya Pradesh	Jabalpur (Benches at Gwalior and Indore)
Madras	1862	Tamil Nadu & Puducherry	Chennai (Bench at Madurai)
Orissa	1948	Odisha	Cuttack
Patna	1916	Bihar	Patna
Punjab and Haryana	1966	Punjab, Haryana and Chandigarh	Chandigarh
Rajasthan	1949	Rajasthan	Jodhpur (Bench at Jaipur)
Sikkim	1975	Sikkim	Gangtok
Uttarakhand	2000	Uttarakhand	Nainital
Tripura	2013	Tripura	Agartala
Meghalaya	2013	Meghalaya	Shillong
Manipur	2013	Manipur	Imphal

HILL STATION

Station		State
1.	Almora, Mussoorie Nainital	: Uttarakhand
2.	Cherrapunji (Shillong), Khasi Hills (Shillong)	: Meghalaya
3.	Ooty, Kodaikanal Yereaud	: Tamil Nadu
4.	Dalhousie, Kassauli	: Himachal Pradesh
5.	Darjeeling	: West Bengal
6.	Gulmarg, Srinagar	: Kashmir
7.	Mahabaleshwar	: Maharashtra
8.	Mt. Abu	: Rajasthan
9.	Panchmarhi	: Madhya Pradesh
10.	Ranchi	: Jharkhand

NATIONAL PARKS

1. Corbett National Park : Nainital, Uttarakhand
2. Dudhwa National Park : Lakhimpur Kheri, UP
3. Kaziranga National Park : Jorhat, Assam
4. Kanha National Park : Jabalpur, Bhedaghat
5. Gir National Park : Rajkot, Junagarh, Gujarat
6. Guindy National Park : Guindy, Chennai, Tamil Nadu
7. Nagairhole National Park : Coorg, Karnataka
8. Bandipur National Park : Mysore, Karnataka

NATIONAL WILDLIFE SANCTUARIES

1. Dachigam Wildlife Sanctuary : Srinagar, Jammu and Kashmir
2. Sariska : Alwar, Rajasthan
3. Hazaribagh Wildlife Sanctuary : Hazaribagh, Jharkhand
4. Tiger Project : Sawai Madhopur, Rajasthan
5. Mudhumali Wildlife Sanctuary : Mudhumalia, Nilgiri, Tamil Nadu
6. Periyar Wildlife Sanctuary : Idukki, Kottayam, Kerala

HOLY PLACES IN INDIA

1.	Amarnath	Kashmir
2.	Ayodhya	Uttar Pradesh
3.	Badrinath	Uttarakhand
4.	Dwarka	Gujarat
5.	Haridwar	Uttarakhand
6.	Kancheepuram	Tamil Nadu
7.	Kedarnath	Uttarakhand
8.	Mathura	Uttar Pradesh
9.	Puri	Odisha
10.	Rameswaram	Tamil Nadu
11.	Tirupati	Andhra Pradesh
12.	Ujjain	Madhya Pradesh
13.	Varanasi	Uttar Pradesh
14.	Bodh Gaya	Bihar

SPORTS

Terms Associated With Sports :

Cricket : Ashes, Bye, Bodyline, Bowling, Break, Cover-point, Creases, Chinaman, Chucker, Drive, Duck, Follow on, Googly, Hit-Wicket, Hat-trick, Leg-before-wicket, Leg break, Leg-bye, Maiden over, No ball, Night-watchman, Runner, Run-out, Stumped, Silly-point, Slip.

Football : Handball, Corner kick, Dribble, Free Kick, Hat-trick, Off-side, Penalty Kick, Try, Throw in, Wembley.

Hockey : Bully, Carry, Corner kick, Corner, Penalty stroke, Off-side, Penalty, Roll in scoop, Sticks, Sudden death, Striking circle, Short Corner, Scoop, Tie-breaker, Under-cutting, Hat-trick.

Tennis : Backhand drive, Deuce, Fault, Half-volley, Net, Let, Volley, Smash, Service.

Billiards : Break, Cannons, Cue, Pot, Jigger, Scratch, In Bauk, In, Off.

Bridge : Dummy, Finesse, Grand-slam, Little Slam, Revoke, Ruff slam, Trump, Tricks, Vulnerable.

Volley Ball : Booster, Love, Service, Volley, Smasher.

Badminton : Smash, Drop, Let.

Chess : Check, Checkmate, Gambit, State-mate.

Golf : Bogy, Caddie, Hole, Links, Stymie, Tee, Put.

Polo : Chukker, Mallet, Bunder.

Baseball : Bunting, Diamond, Pitcher, Put-out, Strike, Home.

Boxing : Knockout, Punch, Upper-cut, Jab, Hook.

FAMOUS TROPHIES

Agha Khan Cup	Hockey
Beighton Cup	Hockey
Corbillion Cup	World Table Tennis (Women)
Davis Cup	Lawn Tennis
Duleep Trophy	Cricket
Durand Cup	Football
Ezra Cup	Polo
I.F.A. Shield	Football
Irani Cup	Cricket (India)
Jayalaxmi Cup	Table Tennis (Women)
Lady Rattan Tata Trophy	Hockey (Women)
Nehru Cup	Hockey (India)
Obaidullah Cup	Hockey
Ranji Trophy	Cricket (India)
Rangaswamy Cup	Hockey (India)
Rovers Cup	Football (India)
Santosh Trophy	Football (India)
Subroto Cup	Football
Thomas Cup	Badminton
Uber Cup	Badminton (Women)
Wellington Trophy	Rowing (India)

BIGGEST, LARGEST, TALLEST OF THE WORLD

Largest Desert	Sahara (Africa)
Biggest Palace	Palace of Parliament (Romania)
Tallest Statue	Statue of Budha (China)
Rainiest Place	Mowsynram near Cherrapunjee (Meghalaya, India)
Biggest Ocean	Pacific Ocean
Deepest Ocean	Pacific Ocean
Largest Telescope (Reflector)	Large Binocular Telescope (Arizona, USA)
Largest Mammal	Whale
Fastest Animal	Cheetah
Lightest Substance	Hydrogen gas
Longest River	Nile
Highest Waterfalls	Salto Angel Falls (Venezuela)
Tallest Animal	Giraffe
Largest Bird (Land)	Ostrich
Hardest Mineral	Diamond
Largest Delta	Sunderbans (W.B. India)
Largest Museum	American Museum of Natural History (New York)
Longest Day	June, 22
Shortest Day	December, 22
Biggest Army	People's Liberation Army, China
Largest Salt Water Lake	Caspian Sea
Highest Mountain Peak	Everest (8848 metre high)
Biggest Dam	Lloyd Dam (U.S.A.)
Longest Wall	Great Wall of China
Largest Peninsula	India
Largest Planet	Jupiter
Coldest Place	Polus Nedostupnosti (Antarctica −58°C)

Smallest Continent	Australia
Largest Lake	Caspian Sea
Deepest Lake	Baikal, 3200 ft.
Finest Harbour	Sydney Harbour
Smallest Planet	Mercury
Largest Continent	Asia
Planet nearest to the Sun	Mercury
Longest Highway Tunnel	Laerdal Tunnel (Norway)
Biggest Bridge	Danyang-Kunshan Grand Bridge (164,800 m), China
Highest Building	Burj Khalifa, Dubai
City largest (Population)	Tokyo
City Biggest in area	Mt. Isa (Australia)
City highest	Wen Chuan (China)
Country Biggest	Russia (17075000 sq. km.)
Electorate, Largest	India (over 80 crores)
Longest Epic	Mahabharat
Island, Biggest in the World	Greenland
Park Biggest	Central Park (New York, USA)
Population, Largest	China
Longest Railway Platform	Gorakhpur (India)
Swimming Course	English Channel

FIRST IN INDIA

Governor General of Independent India	— Lord Mountbatten
Commander-in-chief of free India	— General Roy Bucher
Cosmonaut	— Sq. Ldr. Rakesh Sharma
Field Marshal	— S.H.F.J. Manekshaw
Indian Governor General of Indian Union	— C. Rajagopalachari
Indian I.C.S. Officer	— Satyendra Nath Tagore
Indian to swim across English Channel	— Mihir Sen
Indian Women to swim across English Channel	— Miss Arti Saha
Man to climb Mount Everest	— Tenzing Norgay
Man to climb Mount Everest without Oxygen	— Phu Dorjee
Man to climb Mount Everest twice	— Nwang Gombu
Nobel Prize Winner	— Rabindra Nath Tagore
President of Indian National Congress	— W.C. Banerjee
President of Indian Republic	— Dr. Rajendra Prasad
Talkie Film	— Alam Ara (1931)
Test Tube Baby (Documented)	— Indira
Viceroy of India	— Lord Canning
Woman Minister of Indian Union	— Rajkumari Amrit Kaur
Woman Governor	— Mrs. Sarojini Naidu
Woman President of Indian National Congress	— Dr. Annie Besant
Woman Prime Minister	— Mrs. Indira Gandhi

Woman Speaker of a State Assembly	— Mrs. Shanno Devi
Prime Minister of India	— Pt. Jawaharlal Nehru
Muslim President of Indian Union	— Dr. Zakir Hussain
Speaker of Lok Sabha	— G.V. Mavlankar
Women to Climb Mount Everest	— Bachhendri Pal
Woman Judge in Supreme Court	— Mrs. Meera Sahib Fatima Biwi
Women Chief Justice of a High Court	— Smt. Leela Seth
The First Indian Weightlifter to Win bronze medal in Olympics	— Karnam Malleshwari (Sydney, in 2000)
World Chess Champion	— Vishwanathan Anand
India's First Woman Merchant Navy Officer	— Sonali Banerjee
The First Woman Air Vice-Marshal	— P. Bandopadhyaya
The First Indian to be appointed as United Nations Civilian Police Advisor	— Ms. Kiran Bedi
The First Women to be appointed Deputy Governor of Reserve Bank of India	— K.J. Udeshi
The First Indian Lady to win a medal in World Athletic Championship	— Anju Bobby George
The First Sikh Prime Minister of India	— Dr. Manmohan Singh

IMPORTANT DAYS

★ January

5-11	Road Safety Week
12	National Youth Day
15	Army Day
23	National Day of Patriotism
26	Republic Day
30	Martyr's Day

★ FEBRUARY

1-14	Oil Conservation Fortnight
14	Valentine's Day

★ MARCH

4	National Safety Day
8	International Women's Day
15	Consumers' Day
21	World Forest Day
22	World Day for Water
24	World Meteorological Day

★ APRIL

7	World Health Day
7-13	Handloom Week
14-20	Fire Service Week
18	World Heritage Day
22	World Earth Day

★ MAY

1	May Day
5	National Labour Day
8	World Red Cross Day

11	National Technology Day
15	International Day of the Family
17	World Telecommunication Day
24	Commonwealth Day
31	World No-Tobacco Day

* **JUNE**

5	World Environment Day
21	International Day of Yoga
26	International Day against Drug Abuse and Illicit Trafficking

* **JULY**

11	World Population Day

* **AUGUST**

1-7	World Breast feeding Week
10	Sanskrit Divas
15	Independence Day
20	Sadbhavana Divas

* **SEPTEMBER**

1-7	National Nutrition Week
5	Teachers' Day
8	International Literary Day
14	Hindi Diwas
23	World Deaf Day
27	World Tourism Day

* **OCTOBER**

2	✶ Gandhi Jayanti
	✶ International Day of Non Violence
	✶ Anti-Leprosy Day
4	World Animal Day
6	World Habitat Day (Ist Monday)
8	Indian Air Force Day
14	World Standard Day
15	International Day of Rural Women
16	World Food Day
24	United Nations Day
27	Infantry Day
28	World Thrift Day
31	Anti-Terrorism Day

* **NOVEMBER**

2	All Saints Day
14	Children's Day
15-21	National Cooperative Week
19-25	Quami Ekta Week
20	Child Rights Day
26	Constitution Day

* **DECEMBER**

1	World AIDS Day
3	World Day for the Disabled
4	Naval Day
7	Flag Day
8	SMRC Day
10	Human Rights Day
14	National Energy Conservation Day

PARLIAMENTS OF IMPORTANT COUNTRIES

Afghanistan	—	Shora
Britain	—	Parliament House of Commons, House of Lords
Denmark	—	Folketing
The Netherlands	—	States General
India	—	Sansad
Israel	—	Knesset
Iran	—	Majlis
Ireland	—	Airetann
Iceland	—	Althing
Japan	—	Diet
Norway	—	Storting
Russia	—	Supreme Soviet
Spain	—	Cortes
Sweden	—	Riksdag
U.S.A.	—	Congress Senate
Germany	—	Bundestag

MINERAL RESOURCES OF THE WORLD

Articles	Producers	Articles	Producers
Aluminium	China	Asbestos	Russia
Boxide	Australia	Chromium	South Africa
Copper	Chile	Cobalt	Congo (Kinshasa)
Diamonds	Russia	Gold	China
Iron-ore	Australia	Lead	China
Platinum	South Africa	Silver	Mexico
Silicon	China	Sulfur	China
Tin	China	Titanium	China
Tungsten	China		

TEN LARGEST COUNTRIES AND THEIR AREAS

Rank by Area	Country	Area (sq. km.)
1.	Russia	17,075,400
2.	Canada	9,976,139
3.	China	9,561,000
4.	U.S.A.	9,363,123
5.	Brazil	8,511,965
6.	Australia	7,686,848
7.	India	3,287,263
8.	Argentina	2,776,889
9.	Kazakhstan	2,724,900
10.	Algeria	2,381,741

PRESIDENT OF INDIA

He is the constitutional head of the Republic but not the real executive.

Qualifications: (1) Indian citizen; (2) age not less than 35 years; (3) should have qualifications for election to Lok Sabha; (4) should not hold any office of profit; (5) should not be a Member of Parliament or State Legislature.

Election: He is elected by the elected Members of Parliament and State Legislative Assemblies in accordance with the system of proportional representation by means of single transferable vote.

Powers: He makes appointment to all the Constitutional posts. He can address either House of Parliament and send message to them. He can summon and prorogue either House of Parliament and dissolve Lok Sabha. All Bills passed by Parliament must receive his assent to become an Act. He issues Ordinance when Parliament is not in session. No money Bill can be introduced in Lok Sabha without his recommendation. He can grant pardon, reprieve or remit punishment and he can commute death sentences. He can declare national emergency, state emergency and financial emergency.

VICE-PRESIDENT OF INDIA

The Vice-President acts as the ex-officio Chairman of Rajya Sabha and acts as the President when the latter is unable to discharge his functions due to illness, absence or any other reason, or till the election of a new President when a vacancy is caused by the death, resignation or removal of the President.

The Vice-President is elected by an electoral college consisting of the members of both Houses of Parliament in accordance with the system of proportional representation by means of the single transferable vote. He must be a citizen of India, not less than 35 years of age, and should be eligible for election as a member of the Council of States.

COUNCIL OF MINISTERS

Council of Ministers is to aid and advise the President in exercise of his functions. Prime Minister and other ministers are appointed by the President.

Cabinet: Every member of the Council of Ministers is not a Cabinet Minister. Cabinet is a small body consisting of only senior members of Council of Ministers. The Cabinet functions like the executive committee of the Council of Ministers.

PRIME MINISTER OF INDIA

Art. 74(1) of our Constitution states that the Prime Minister shall be at the head of council of ministers. He has the power of selecting and advising the President to dismiss them individually. He is the chairman of the cabinet. Art. 78 provides that it shall be the duty of the Prime minister –

- To communicate to the president all the decisions of the council of ministers relating to the administration of the affairs of the union and proposals for legislation.

- To furnish such information relating to the administration of the affairs of the union and proposals for legislation as the president may call for and

- If the President so requires to submit for the consideration of the council of ministers any matter on which a decision has been take by a minister but which has not been considered by the council.

THE SOLAR SYSTEM: SOME FACTS

Number of Planets: 8—Mercury, Venus, Earth, Mars, Jupiter, Saturn, Uranus and Neptune.

Largest most

Massive planet	Jupiter
Brightest planet	Venus
Brightest star	Sirius
Fastest orbiting planet	Mercury
Longest (Synodic) day	Mercury
Most moons	Jupiter (69)
Planet with largest moon	Jupiter
Greatest average density	Jupiter
Tallest mountain	Earth
Strongest magnetic fields	Jupiter
Most circular orbit	Venus
Shortest (synodic) day	Jupiter
Hottest planet	Venus
No moons	Mercury, Venus
Planet with moon with most eccentric orbit	Neptune
Lowest average density	Saturn
Greatest amount of liquid on the surface	Earth

THE EARTH: FACTS AND DATA

Composition of the Earth: Aluminium (0.4%), Sulphur (2.7%), Silicon (13%), Oxygen (28%), Calcium (1.2%), Nickel (2.7%), Magnesium (17%), Iron (35%)

Surface area	: 510100500 sq km
Land Surface (29.1%)	: 148950800 sq km
Ocean Surface (70.9%)	: 361149700 sq km
Type of water	: 97% salt, 3% fresh
Total area of water	: 382672000 sq km
Equatorial diameter	: 12753 km
Equatorial Circumference	: 40066 km
Polar Circumference	: 39992 km
Polar diameter	: 12710 km
Equatorial radius	: 6376 km
Polar radius	: 6335 km

Mass (estimated weight)	: 594×10^{19} metric tons
Mean distance from the Sun	: 149407000 km
Earth's orbit speed (around sun)	: 107320 kmph
Period of Revolution (round the sun)	: 365 days 5 hrs 48 min. 45.51 seconds
Time of Rotation (on its axis)	: 23 hrs 56 min 4.09 seconds
Inclination of the axis (to the plane of the ecliptic)	: 23°27'

PRINCIPAL MOUNTAIN PEAKS OF THE WORLD

	Mountains	Height in Metres	Range	Date of First Ascent
1.	Mount Everest	8,848	Himalayas	May 29, 1953
2.	K-2 (Godwin Austen)	8,611	Karakoram	July 31, 1954
3.	Kanchenjunga	8,597	Himalayas	May 25, 1955
4.	Lhotse	8,511	Himalayas	May 18, 1956
5.	Makalu I	8,481	Himalayas	May 15, 1955
6.	Dhaulagiri I	8,167	Himalayas	May 13, 1960
7.	Mansalu I	8,156	Himalayas	May 9, 1956
8.	Chollyo	8,153	Himalayas	Oct. 19, 1954
9.	Nanga Parbat	8,124	Himalayas	July 3, 1953
10.	Annapurna I	8,091	Himalayas	June 3, 1950
11.	Gasherbrum I	8,068	Karakoram	July 5, 1958
12.	Broad Peak I	8,047	Karakoram	June 9, 1957
13.	Gasherbrum II	8,034	Karakoram	July 7, 1956
14.	Shisha Pangma (Gosainthan)	8,014	Himalayas	May 2, 1964
15.	Gasherbrum III	7,952	Karakoram	Aug. 11, 1975

POPULAR NICK NAMES OF SOME FAMOUS PERSONALITIES

Andhra Kesari	T. Prakasam
Anna	C.N. Anna Durai
Bang Bandhu	Sheikh Mujibur Rehman
Bapu	Mahatma Gandhi
Bard of Avon	William Shakespeare
Chachaji	Jawaharlal Nehru
Desh Bandhu	C.R. Das
Frontier Gandhi	Khan Abdul Gaffar Khan
Fuhrer	Adolf Hitler
G.B.S.	George Bernard Shaw
Grand Old Man of India	Dadabhai Naoroji
Grand Old Man of Britain	Gladstone
Guru Dev	Rabindra Nath Tagore

Guruji	M.S. Golwalkar
Iron Man of India	Sardar Patel
Lok Nayak	Jayaprakash Narayan
Lady with the Lamp	Florence Nightingale
Lal, Bal, Pal	Lala Lajpat Rai, Bal Gangadhar Tilak, Bipin Chandra Pal
Little Corporal	Napoleon Bonaparte
Lokmanya	Bal Gangadhar Tilak
Mahamana	Pt. Madan Mohan Malaviya
Maid of Orleans	Joan of Arc
Maiden Queen	Queen Elizabeth I
Missile Man	A.P.J. Abdul Kalam

Man of Destiny	Napoleon Bonaparte	Punjab Kesari	Lala Lajpat Rai
Netaji	Subhash Chandra Bose	Shastriji	Lal Bahadur Shastri
Nightingale of India	Sarojini Naidu	Uncle Ho	Ho Chi Minh
Panditji	Jawaharlal Nehru	Wizard of the North	Walter Scott

FAMOUS INTERNATIONAL ORGANISATIONS, HEADQUARTERS AND YEAR OF ESTABLISHMENT

International Organisations	*Headquarters*	*Year of Establishment*
United Nations Organisations (U.N.O.)	New York	1945
International Monetary Fund (I.M.F.)	Washington	1945
World Health Organisation (W.H.O.)	Geneva	1948
Food & Agricultural Organisation (FAO)	Rome	1943
International Labour Organisation (ILO)	Geneva	1919
UNESCO	Paris	1946
International Court of Justice	The Hague	—
Universal Postal Union (UPU)	Berne	1874
International Civil Aviation Organisation (ICAO)	Montreal	1947
UNIDO	Vienna	1967
International Atomic Energy Agency (IAEA)	Vienna	1957
International Finance Corporation (IFC)	Washington	1956
United Nations Development Programme (UNDP)	New York	—
UNICEF	New York	1946
International Maritime Organisation (IMO)	London	1948
World Meteorological Organisation (WMO)	Geneva	1951
International Telecommunication Union (ITU)	Geneva	1947
Arab League	Cairo	1945
Commonwealth of Nations	London	1931
World Trade Organisation (WTO)	Geneva	1995
International Development Association (IDA)	Washington D.C.	1960
International Bank for Reconstruction and Development (IBRD)	Washington D.C.	1946
World Intellectual Property Organisation (WIPO)	Geneva	1967
Organisation of Islamic Conference (OIC)	Jeddah (Saudi Arabia)	1971
European Economic Community (EEC)	Geneva	1957
Red Cross	Geneva	1863
Interpol	Lyons	1923
Asian Development Bank (ADB)	Manila	1966
North Atlantic Treaty Organisation (NATO)	Brussels	1949
Association of South East Asian Nations (ASEAN)	Jakarta	1967

BHARAT RATNA AWARD WINNERS

1. Dr. S. Radhakrishnan	1954	**8.** Dr. D.K. Karve	1958
2. C. Rajagopalachari	1954	**9.** Dr. Bidhan Chandra Roy	1961
3. Dr. C.V. Raman	1954	**10.** Purushottam Das Tandon	1961
4. Dr. Bhagwan Das	1955	**11.** Dr. Rajendra Prasad	1962
5. Dr. M. Visvesvaraya	1955	**12.** Dr. Zakir Hussain	1963
6. Jawaharlal Nehru	1955	**13.** Dr. Pandurang Vaman Kane	1963
7. Govind Ballabh Pant	1957	**14.** Lal Bahadur Shastri	1966

15.	Indira Gandhi	1971	**31.**	Mrs. Aruna Asaf Ali	1997
16.	V.V. Giri	1975	**32.**	Dr. A.P.J. Abdul Kalam	1998
17.	K. Kamraj	1976	**33.**	M.S. Subbalakshmi	1998
18.	Mother Teresa	1980	**34.**	C. Subramaniam	1998
19.	Acharya Vinoba Bhave	1983	**35.**	Jaya Prakash Narayan	1999
20.	Khan Abdul Ghaffar Khan	1987	**36.**	Prof. Amartya Sen	1999
21.	M.G. Ramachandran	1988	**37.**	Pt. Ravi Shankar	1999
22.	Dr. B.R. Ambedkar	1990	**38.**	Gopinath Bardoloi	1999
23.	Dr. Nelson R. Mandela	1990	**39.**	Lata Mangeshkar	2001
24.	Rajiv Gandhi	1991	**40.**	Bismillah Khan	2001
25.	Sardar Vallabhbhai Patel	1991	**41.**	Bhimsen Joshi	2008
26.	Morarji R. Desai	1991	**42.**	C.N.R. Rao	2014
27.	Maulana Abdul Kalam Azad	1992	**43.**	Sachin Tendulkar	2014
28.	Jehangir Ratanji Dadabhai Tata	1992	**44.**	Madan Mohan Malaviya	2015
29.	Satyajit Roy	1992	**45.**	Atal Bihari Vajpayee	2015
30.	Gulzari Lal Nanda	1997			

ART AND CULTURE

☞ **Classical Dances**

Dance	State	Famous Artists
Bharat Natyam	Tamil Nadu	Yamini Krishnamurthy, Rukmini Devi Arundale, Swapna Sundari, Sonal Mansingh, Vaijanti Mala, Mrinalini Sarabhai, Chandralekha, Indrani, Ram Gopal, Bal Saraswati
Kathakali	Kerala	Gopinath, K.K. Nayar, Kunju-Kurup, T.K. Chandu
Kuchipudi	Andhra Pradesh/ Telangana	Sapna Sundari, Raja Reddy, Shobha Nayar, Radha Reddy, Vedantam Satyanarayan, Vimpanti Chinna Satyam.
Kathak	North India	Birju Maharaj, Gopi Krishna, Shambhu Maharaj, Sitara Devi, Vishnu Sharma, Durga Lal, Shobhana Narayan
Odissi	Odisha	Kelucharan Mahapatra, Indrani Rehman, Madhavi Mudgal, Pratima Bedi, Samyukta Panigrahi, Sonal Mansingh, Debudas
Manipuri	Manipur	Uday Shankar, Bipin Singh, Suryamukhi, Darohra Jhaveri

☞ **Famous Folk Dances**

State	Folk Dance	State	Folk Dance
Andhra Pradesh/ Telangana	Dandari, Banjara	Madhya Pradesh	Lota Nritya, Jawara
		Maharashtra	Tamasha, Dahi Handi, Gof, Deepak Dindi
Assam	Bihu, Keli Gopal, Sataria	Manipur	Dhol Cholam
Bihar	Chhau, Magahi, Durga dance	Meghalaya	Nongakarem
W. Bengal	Kirtan, Kalatri, Asweabadh, Brita, Kalidance	Nagaland	Bamboo dance
Chhattisgarh	Saila, Karama, Bhagoria	Odisha	Chhau, Maya Shabari, Dalachai
Gujarat	Garba, Rasalila, Tippani, Dandia,	Punjab	Gidda, Bhangra, Panihari
Haryana	Damyal, Lahoor	Rajasthan	Thumar, Kathaputali, Tera Tali
Himachal Pradesh	Dussehra dance, Hikat, Notio	Tamil Nadu	Terukalathu, Kabalatam, Kargam, Pulivesham
J&K	Dumhal	Tripura	Hazagiri
Jharkhand	Jhau, Ghumakudia, Jadur, Sarhul, Soharai, Karama, Vaima, Loojhari, Jat-Jatin, Vidayat	Uttar Pradesh	Rasalila, Nautanki, Thali, Dhurang, Jhumela, Huraka, Bol.
Karnataka	Yakshagan, Dolu Kunitha	Uttarakhand	Kajari, Karan
Kerala	Mohini Attam, Padayuni	Goa	Dhode Modini

MUSIC

Main Schools of Classical Music

- There are two main schools of classical music, namely, the Hindustani and the Carnatic. The Hindustani school of classical music is in vogue in north-western India, eastern India and northern parts of the South India.

Musical Instruments

- *They are:* Tabla, Mridangam, Pakhawaj, Chandai, Dholak, Veena, Sitar, Sarod, Gootuvadhyam, Sarangi, Flute, Nadaswaram, Shehnai, Shringi and Turahi.

FAMOUS INTERNATIONAL AIR SERVICES

Air Service	Name of Country	Air Service	Name of Country
Air India	India	K.L.M. Royal Airlines	The Netherlands (Holland)
British Overseas	Britain	Lufthansa Airlines	Germany
Airways Corporation		Iraqi Airways	Iraq
Trans World Airlines	America	National Airlines	Iran
Russian Airlines	Russia	Quantas Airlines	Australia
Japan Airlines	Japan	Hong-Kong Airlines	Hong-Kong
Pakistan International Airlines	Pakistan	Egypt Airlines	Egypt
Malaysia Airlines	Malaysia	Slovak Airlines	Slovakia
Royal Nepal Airlines	Nepal	S.I.A.	Singapore
Swiss Airways	Switzerland	Garuda Airways	Indonesia
Air France	France	Bangladesh Viman Sewa	Bangladesh
Kuwait Airways	Kuwait	Air Lanka	Sri Lanka
Pan American World Airways	America	Elitalia Airlines	Italy
		Air Canada	Canada

FAMOUS RELIGIONS, FOUNDERS, HOLY BOOKS & PLACES OF WORSHIP

Religion	Founder	Holy Books	Place of Worship
Hinduism	Hinduism has no one Founder. (This religion is based upon the religion of original Aryan Settlers)	Ramayan, Vedas, Puranas and Geeta	Temple
Sikh	Guru Nanak Dev	Guru Grantha Sahib	Gurdwara
Christianity	Jesus Christ	Bible	Church
Islam	Prophet Mohammed	Koran (Quran)	Mosque
Parsi	Zoroaster	Zend Avesta	Fire Temple
Jainism	Adinath Rishavdev	Jain Granth	Jain Temple
Buddhism	Gautam Buddha	Tripitaka	Buddha Temple
Jew	Moosa	Torah	Synagogue

INTELLIGENCE AGENCIES OF SOME PROMINENT COUNTRIES

Country	Intelligence Agency	Country	Intelligence Agency
India	Research & Analysis Wing (RAW), Intelligence Bureau (I.B.), Central Bureau of Investigation (C.B.I.)	U.S.A.	Central Intelligence Agency, Federal Bureau of Investigation
Pakistan	Inter Service Intelligence (I.S.I.)	Britain	Military Intelligence (M.I.)-5 and 6, Special Branch, Ultra, Joint Intelligence Organisation

Country	Intelligence Agency	Country	Intelligence Agency
Israel	Mosad	Iran	Sabak
Egypt	Mukhabarat	Iraq	Al-Mukhabarat
Japan	Nicho	Australia	Australian Security and Intelligence Organisation
Russia	K.G.B. (Komitel Gosudars-tvennoy Bezopasnosty) (Committee for State Security)	France	S.D.E.C.E.
Canada	Security Intelligence Service	Spain	C.E.S.I.D.
S. Africa	Bureau of State Security	Cuba	D.G.I.

SOME PROMINENT RACES OF THE WORLD

Races	Country	Races	Country	Races	Country
Veddas	Sri Lanka	Bantu	Central and South Africa	Lapps	European Tundra
Somaid	West Siberia				
Masai	East Africa	Tartars	Siberia	Hausa	Nigeria
Muree	New Zealand	Baddu	Arab's Desert	Kirghiz	Steppes (Russia)
Yakoot	Russian Tundra	Semang	Malaysia	Bushman	Kalahari Desert
Papuans	New Guyana	Eskimo	Canada, Tundra Region		
Pygmy	Congo Basin			Red Indian	North America

FAMOUS STRAITS OF THE WORLD

Strait	Between	Country
Malacca Strait	Andaman Sea and South China Sea	Indonesia
Palk Strait	Mannar and Bay of Bengal	India-Sri Lanka
Magellan Strait	Pacific and South Atlantic Ocean	Chile
Dover Strait	English Channel and North Sea	England-France
Berring Strait	Berring Sea and Chukasi Sea	Alaska-Russia
Sugaroo Strait	Japan Sea and Pacific Ocean	Japan
Sunda Strait	Java and Indian Ocean	Indonesia
Gibralter Strait	Mediterranean Sea and Atlantic Ocean	Spain
Harmuj Strait	Persia and Bay of Oman	Oman-Iran
Hudson Strait	Bay of Hudson and Atlantic Ocean	Canada

FAMOUS NEWSPAPERS OF THE WORLD

Newspaper	Place of Publishing	Language	Newspaper	Place of Publishing	Language
Daily News	New York (America)	English	Hindu, Hindustan, Times of India, Tribune, Statesman, Indian Express, Economic Times	India	English
Guardian	London (Britain)	English			
Pravada	Moscow (Russia)	Russian			
Al-Ahram	Cairo (Egypt)	Arabic			
Merdeca	Jakarta (Indonesia)	Indonesian			
Times	London (Britain)	English	Hindustan, Nav Bharat Times, Dainik Bhaskar, Dainik Jagaran, Punjab Kesari	India	Hindi
People's Daily	Beijing (China)	Chinese			
New Statesman	Britain	English			
Daily Mirror	Britain	English			

IMPORTANT BOUNDARY LINES

Boundary Line	Countries	Boundary Line	Countries
Durand Line	Pakistan and Afghanistan	Seigfrid Line	Germany-France
		24th Parallel	India-Pakistan
Hindenberg Line	Germany-Poland	17th Parallel	The line which defined the boundary between North Vietnam and South Vietnam before the two were united.
Maginot Line	France and Germany		
Mannerhein Line	Russia-Finland		
Mc Mahon Line	India-China		
Order Niesse Line	Germany-Poland	38th Parallel	North Korea and South Korea
Radcliff Line	India-Pakistan	49th Parallel	U.S.A. and Canada

SIGNALS/SIGNS AND MEANING

Signal/Sign	Meaning	Signal/Sign	Meaning
Red Triangle	Family Planning	White Flag	Treaty or Surrender
Red Cross	Medical Help	Yellow Flag	Vehicles with patients of contagious diseases
Red Light	Danger, 'Stop' for the movement of vehicles	Two Bones across with a Skull	Danger of electricity
Green Light	Go		
Olive Branch	Peace	Half mast flown Flag	National mourning
White Pigeon or Dove	Peace	Lotus and culture	Sign of civilization
Black Strip on Arm	(i) Opposition (ii) Sorrow	Wheel (Chakra)	Sign of Progress
		A blind folded woman with scale in hand	Sign of Justice
Black Flag	Opposition		
Red Flag	(i) Danger (ii) Revolution	Reversed flown	National calamity flag

NATIONAL EMBLEMS OF IMPORTANT COUNTRIES

Country	National Emblem	Country	National Emblem
America	Golden Rod	New Zealand	Kiwi, Fern Southern Cross
Australia	Kangaroo	Norway	Lion
Ireland	Shamrock	Nepal	Kukri
Italy	White Lily	Pakistan	Crescent
Israel	Candelabrum	Poland	Eagle
Iran	Rose	France	Lily
Canada	White Lily	Belgium	Lion
Great Britain	Rose	Bangladesh	Water Lily
Chile	Candor and Huemul	Mongolia	The Soyombo
Germany	Corn Flower	Russia	Double headed eagle
Japan	Chrysanthemum	Lebanon	Cedar Tree
Zimbabwe	Zimbabwe Bird	Sudan	Secretary Bird
Denmark	Beach	Syria	Eagle
Turkey	Crescent and Star	India	Lioned Capital
The Netherlands	Lion		

THE CONTINENTS OF THE WORLD

	Continent (2017)	Population	Yearly Change	Net Change
1.	Asia	4,478,315,164	0.95%	42,090,691
2.	Africa	1,246,504,865	2.5%	30,375,050
3.	Europe	739,207,742	0.05%	358,740
4.	Latin America and the Caribbean	647,565,336	1.02%	6,536,030
5.	Northern America	363,224,006	0.75%	2,694,682
6.	Oceania	40,467,040	1.42%	565,685
	World	**7,515,284,153**	**1.08%**	**82,620,878**

COMPUTER

The computer is the system of that electronic device through which various informations are processed on the basis of a definite set of instructions called program and mathematical (numerical) and non-mathematical both types of informations are processed.

The first mechanical computer was composed or fabricated by Blaise Pascal in 1642 and it is called Pascalene. But in 1833, Charles Babbage first time conceived an automatic calculator or computer. Charles Babbage is called the father of modern computer. Herman made an electronic tabulating machine based on punch cards which operates automatically.

In 1937, first mechanical computer mark-I was fabricated by Howard Akeen. The most outstanding contribution in the development of modern computer goes to John Wan Newmaan who brought the 2nd revolution in the area of computer in 1951. He discovered EDVAC (Electronic Discrete Variable Automatic Computer) and utilised the stored program and the binary number system in the computer.

FUNCTIONS OF COMPUTER

1. Collection and composition (input) of datas;
2. Storage of datas.
3. Processing of datas.
4. Retrieval or output of the proccessed informations and datas.

UNITS OF COMPUTER

1. Input unit.
2. Central processing unit–CPU.
3. External Memory unit.
4. Output unit.

The CPU of the computer is called brain of the computer and sometimes CPU is also called Micro Processor of the computer. The data is entered through the input unit in the computer and through the central processing unit with the help of External Memory Unit datas are arranged and processed. Ultimately by the output unit these datas or informations are issued or released.

PARTS OF COMPUTER

- **Monitor :** The monitor of the computer is like a television in which the picture appears in the form of doted points on the screen and these are called pixels.
- **Hard Disc and Floppy Disc :** The Hard Disc is the permanent disc in the computers while the Floppy Disc is the disc utilised when datas or informations are to be transferred from one computer to another.
- **Mouse :** The mouse of the computer is like the remote control of TV through which computer is directly regulated or controlled without utilising the key-board.
- **Printer :** The printer is a device which prints any documents or processed informations of the computer.

SOME HIGH LEVEL LANGUAGES

1. **FORTRAN :** This language was developed for solving the mathematical formulae very quickly and conveniently.
2. **COBOL :** This language was developed for the commerical purposes. For the processing of this language a group of sentences is selected called paragraph and all paragraphs composed are called a section, while all sections composed are called a division.
3. **BASIC :** In basic a definite part of the prescribed instruction is only inserted in the computer.
4. **ALGOL :** This was basically fabricated and designed for the complex algebraic calculations.

5. **PASCAL :** It is an amplified and modified form of ALGOL.

6. **COMAL :** This computer language is used for the students of secondary level.

7. **LOGO :** This language is used for children and kids for drawing Graphic line diagrams.

8. **PROLOG :** This language is developed in 1973 in France and this language is used for Artificial Intelligence which is capable and equivalent to the logical program.

9. **FORTH :** This language was invented by Charles Mure which is frequently used in all types of the works in the computer.

COMPUTER VIRUS

The computer virus is an electronic code which is used to abolish or erradicate the inclusive informations or programs of the computer. Some important computer viruses are Micheleanjalo, Dork Avangor, kilo, filip, Macmug, Scores, Casecade, Jeruslem, Date crime, Coloumbs crime, Internet virus, Pachcom, Pach EXE, COM-EXE, Marizuana, C-brain, bloody, Chenge Mungu and Desi etc.

COMPUTER NETWORKING

There are two types of networkings which are usually occur— Local Area Networking (LAN) and Wide Area Networking (WAN). By LAN all the computers of the same buildings are connected like the computers of university premises, computers of offices etc.

By WAN all the comptuers of a large area are connected like the computers of all the offices of a city or town etc. In India a very large computer network namely INDONET has been installing through which all the main towns and cities has to be interlinked.

COMPUTER TERMINOLOGY

- **Bit :** The bit is a unit of measurement of the electronic data. One bit is either 0 or 1 but not both. On composing 8 bits, 1 byte is formed.

- **Bug :** The Bug is the error in the computer program or system and its eradication is called Debug.

- **Byte :** Total eight bits compose a byte. Thus 8 bits = 1 byte.

- **CD-ROM :** A CD like of music CD in which data can be stored substantially called CD-ROM. In a CD with comparison to floppy extremely more datas can be stored but one problem in it is that one time recorded data can not be deleted or modified.

- **Chip :** It is a thin slice on which by a special mechanism a circuit is designed which is normally made from Silicon.

- **Memory System :** The place where computer data and program are temporarily kept is called Memory system. Usually memory is implied from RAM.

- **Modem :** The device which converts digital signals into analogue signals and vice-versa is called Modem.

- **RAM :** It is Random Access Memory (a place) where datas to be processed are kept temporarily and it is unstable memory.

- **ROM :** It is Read Only Memory and it is stable or Non-valatile memory which doesn't ended after power off.

- **Scanner :** It is a device through which graphic image is transformed to digital image and the scanners are of usually two types one desktop and another hand operating.

PROGRAMING

Computers perform phenomenal feats of calculation, but they do not do so in a complicated way. They actually carry out very simple operations, such as addition and subtraction. They achieve their fantastic computing power by carrying out these operations at incredible speed.

The programme, or set of instructions for operating the computer, is therefore written as a sequence of very simple steps. (See box below) Several computer languages have been developed for different applications, including BASIC, COBOL, FORTRAN and PASCAL. Writing programmes is very skilled and time-consuming work. But for most typical computer applications ready-written programmes are available, called "packages".

☞ **How A Programme Works**

Without a programme to tell it what to do and how to do it, a computer is unable to function. If, for example, you wanted to know how many times the word 'the' appears in this paragraph, or in the whole book, it would not be enough merely to put the text into a computer and then ask it how many times the word appears. For the computer to accomplish the calculations it has to be told what to do in simple steps. The instructions might be:

1. Scan the text until a space followed by 'T' or 't' is found.
2. If the next letter is not 'h', go back to step 1.
3. If the letter is 'h', is the next letter 'e'?
4. If not, go back to step 1. If it is, go to step 5.
5. If 'e' is followed by a space, add 1 to the total.
6. Go back to step 1.

A full computer programme for this operation would need to be broken down into even more simple steps, but a series of such programmes could enable a computer to analyse any amount of text in great detail.

DEFENCE

The Supreme Command of the Armed Forces is vested in the hands of the President of the Country. The responsibility for national defence, however, rests with the Cabinet. All important questions having a bearing on defence are decided by the Cabinet Committee on Political Affairs, which is presided over by the Prime Minister. The Defence Minister is responsible to Parliament for all matters concerning the Defence Services. All the administrative and operational control of Armed Forces are exercised by the Ministry of Defence. The three services – Army, Navy and Air Force function through their respective service headquarters headed by the chief of Staff.

COMMISSIONED RANKS IN DEFENCE SERVICES

Army	*Navy*	*Air Force*
General	Admiral	Air Chief Marshal
Lieutenant-General	Vice-Admiral	Air Marshal
Major-General	Rear-Admiral	Air Vice-Marshal
Brigadier	Commodor	Air Commodor
Colonel	Captain	Group Captain
Lieutenant-Colonel	Commander	Wing Commander
Major	Lt.Commander	Squadron Leader
Captain	Lieutenant	Flight Lieutenant
Lieutenant	Sub-Lieutenant	Flying Officer

INTERNAL SECURITY ORGANISATIONS OF INDIA

S. No.	Name of Organisation	Year of Creation	Headquarters
1.	Assam Rifles (A.R.)	1835	Shillong
2.	Central Reserve Police Force (C.R.P.F.)	1939	New Delhi
3.	National Cadet Corps (N.C.C.)	1948	New Delhi
4.	Territorial Army	1948	In different States
5.	Indo-Tibetan Border Police	1962	New Delhi
6.	Home Guard	1962	In different States
7.	Coast Guard	1978	New Delhi
8.	Border Security Force (B.S.F.)	1965	New Delhi
9.	Central Industrial Security Force (C.I.S.F.)	1969	New Delhi
10.	National Security Guard	1984	New Delhi
11.	Police	—	In different States

COMMANDER-IN-CHIEFS OF INDIA

1. General Roy Bucher   Jan. 1, 1948 — Jan. 14, 1949
2. General K. M. Kariappa   Jan. 15, 1949 — Jan. 14, 1953
3. General Maharaj Rajendra Sinhji   Jan. 15, 1953 — March 31, 1955
4. First Marshal of the Indian Air Force — Arjan Singh

FIRST CHIEFS OF STAFF OF INDIAN FORCES

1. General Maharaj Rajendra Sinhji (Army Staff)   April 1, 1955 — May 14, 1955
2. Vice Admiral R.D. Katari (Naval Staff)   April 22, 1958 — June 4, 1962
3. Air Marshal Sri Thomas Elmherst (Air Staff)   Aug. 15, 1947 — Feb. 21, 1950

ARMY INSTITUTES

1.	Sainik Schools upto +2 Level	18 places in India
2.	Rashtriya Indian Military College (prepare for entrance to N.D.A)	Dehradun
3.	National Defence Academy (three services)	Khadakwasla, Pune
4.	Indian Military Academy (Army)	Dehradun
5.	Officers Training Academy (3 services) Short Courses	Chennai
6.	National Defence College	New Delhi
7.	The College of Combat	Mhow
8.	The College of Military Engineering	Kirkee
9.	Military College of Telecommunication Engineering	Mhow
10.	The armoured Corps Centre and School	Ahmed Nagar
11.	The School Artillery	Deolali
12.	The Infantry School	Mhow and Belgaum
13.	College of Material Management	Jabalpur

AIR FORCE INSTITUTIONS

Air Force Academy	Hyderabad
Helicopter Training School	Hakimpet
Flying Instructors School	Tambaram, Chennai
The College of Air Warfare	Secunderabad
Air Force Administrative College	Coimbatore
Air Force Technical College	Jalahalli

DEFENCE PRODUCTION UNITS

1. Bharat Dynamites Ltd.	Hyderabad	8. Mazagaon Dock	Mumbai
2. Praga Tools	Hyderabad	9. Goa Shipyard	Marmugao
3. Mishra Dattu Nigam	Hyderabad	10. Hindustan Shipyard Ltd.	Vishakhapatnam
4. Bharat Electronics Ltd.	Bangalore	11. Hindustan Aeronautics Ltd.	Bangalore, Hyderabad,
5. Bharath Earthmovers Ltd.	Bangalore		Nasik, Koraput, Kanpur,
6. Heavy Vehicles Ltd.	Avadi, Chennai		Lucknow
7. Garden Reach Ship Builders and Engineers Ltd.	Kolkata		

☞ Indian Army Commands

Command	HQ Location	Command	HQ Location
Eastern Command	Kolkata	Western Command	Chandigarh
Northern Command	Udhampur	Southern Command	Pune
Central Command	Lucknow	Training Command	Shimla
South-Western Command	Jaipur		

☞ Indian Air Force Commands

Command	HQ Location	Command	HQ Location
Western Air Command	New Delhi	South-Western Air Command	Gandhinagar
Central Air Command	Allahabad	Eastern Air Command	Shillong
Southern Air Command	Thiruvananthapuram	Training Command	Bengaluru

☞ Indian Navy Commands

Command	HQ Location	Command	HQ Location
Eastern Naval Command	Vishakhapatnam	Western Naval Command	Mumbai
Southern Naval Command	Cochin		

☞ Missile and Other Weapons

Name	Class	Range	Name	Class	Range
✳ Agni I	SRBM	850 km	✳ Brahmos	Supersonic Cruise Missile	290 km
✳ Agni II	MRBM	2500 km			
✳ Agni III	IRBM	3500 km-5500 km			
✳ Agni IV *or* Agni II Prime	IRBM	4000 km	✳ Brahmos 2	Hypersonic Cruise Missile	290 km
✳ Agni V	ICBM	5000 km-6000 km	✳ Prithvi I	SRBM	150 km
✳ Agni VI	ICBM	8000 km-10000 km	✳ Prithvi III	SRBM	350 km
✳ Agni 3SL	ICBM	5200 km-11600 km	✳ Sagarika	SLBM	700 km-2200 km
✳ Dhanush	SRBM	350 km	✳ Shaurya	TBM	700 km-2200 km
✳ Nirbhay	Subsonic Cruise Missile	1000 km	✳ Astra	Air to Air Missile	80 km-100 km

MULTIPLE CHOICE QUESTIONS

1. Match List-I with List-II and select the correct answer from the codes given below the lists:
   List-I
   (*a*) Napoleon Bonaparte
   (*b*) Jean Jacques Rousseau
   (*c*) Croce
   (*d*) Madame Roland
   List-II
   1. 'A history is contemporary history'
   2. 'Liberty what crimes are committed in thy name'
   3. 'Man is born free but everywhere he is in chains.'
   4. 'I am the Child of Revolution'
   Codes :
	(a)	(b)	(c)	(d)
A.	1	2	3	4
B.	4	3	1	2
C.	3	4	2	1
D.	3	4	1	2

2. Abraham Lincon was elected the President of United States in:
   A. 1862 B. 1860
   C. 1875 D. 1855

3. Who was known as the 'Prince of Humanists'?
   A. Francisco Petrarch B. Dante
   C. Boccacio D. Erasmus

4. D-Day is the day when:
   A. Germany declared war on Britain
   B. US dropped the atom bomb on Hiroshima.
   C. Allied Troops landed in Normandy
   D. Germany surrendered to the allies

5. Whose teachings inspired the French Revolution?
   A. Locke
   B. Rousseau
   C. Hegel
   D. Plato

6. At a time when empires in Europe were crumbling before the might of Napoleon which one of the following Governor-Generals kept the British flag flying high in India?
   A. Warren Hastings B. Lord Cornwallis
   C. Lord Wellesley D. Lord Hastings

7. Which one of the following statements regarding Fascism in Italy is *not* true?
   A. The Fascists came to power as a result of popular uprising
   B. In 1926, all political parties except Mussolini's party were banned
   C. The Fascists suppressed the Socialist movement
   D. The Fascists were hostile to the Communists

8. The fall of Czar Nicholas-II is known as:
   A. Bloody Sunday
   B. Bolshevik Revolution
   C. February Revolution
   D. October Revolution

9. Industrial Revolution took place first in:
   A. France B. Germany
   C. United Kingdom D. Japan

10. The British Prime Minister at the outbreak of World War II was :
    A. Churchill B. Baldwin
    C. Attlee D. Chemberlain

11. The 'Great Depression' (1929) economic crisis was met by adopting the policy of
    A. Stimulus B. Marshall Plan
    C. New Deal D. Open Door

12. The slogan "No taxation without representation" was raised during the:
    A. American War of Independence
    B. Russian Revolution
    C. French Revolution
    D. Indian Freedom struggle

13. In the nineteenth century the people of Europe started moving from the villages to the cities due to the impact of :
    A. Epidemics
    B. War
    C. Industrialisation
    D. Population explosion in villages

14. The important cause of the Civil War in America was:
    A. Abolition of slavery
    B. Quest for freedom
    C. Industrialisation
    D. Rebellion by the native Americans

15. Industrial Revolution could not have come about without:
    A. Merchant capitalism
    B. The Enclosure Movement
    C. The services of the proletariat class
    D. An agricultural revolution

16. Consider the following statements :
    The French Revolution came about mainly due to the :
    1. Extreme poverty of the people
    2. Impact of the works of great writers
    3. Cruelty of the rulers
    4. Impact of impulsive reaction

Which of the above statements are correct?

A. 1, 2 and 4   B. 2 and 3
C. 1, 3 and 4   D. 1, 2, 3 and 4

17. Asia's oldest and largest Buddhist monastery is situated in :
A. Tawang (Arunachal Pardesh)
B. Lhasa (Tibet)
C. Trincomallee (Sri Lanka)
D. Ulan Bator (Mongolia)

18. Who was the main architect of the Russian Revolution?
A. Karl Marx   B. Lenin
C. Stalin   D. Tolstoy

19. V.I. Lenin is associated with :
A. Russian Revolution of 1917
B. Chinese Revolution of 1949
C. German Revolution
D. French Revolution of 1789

20. Which one of the following statements is *not* correct?
A. Voltaire believed in Natural Religion
B. Rousseau wrote *Social Contract*
C. Montesquieu authored *The Spirit of Laws*
D. Necker believed in 'General Will'

21. 6th April, 1930 is well known in the history of India because this date is associated with...........
A. Dandi March by Mahatma Gandhi
B. Quit India Movement
C. Partition of Bengal
D. Partition of India

22. Which ruler enforced the system of 'Price Control' in India?
A. Mohammad Tughlak
B. Razia Begum
C. Alauddin Khilji
D. Sher Shah Suri

23. The concept of 'Din-e-Elahi' was founded by which king?
A. Dara Shikoh   B. Akbar
C. Sher Shah Suri   D. Shahjahan

24. Who are supposed to be the earliest inhabi-tants of India? Where did they come from?
A. Aryans from Central Asia
B. Dravidians from Mediterranean
C. Negroids from Africa
D. Bhils and the Santhals from West Asia

25. The one chief characteristic of temple architecture of the Gupta Age was :
A. Absence of dome
B. Huge size
C. Beautiful carvings

D. absence of a covered courtyard for the gathering of worshippers

26. The Rigveda consists of :
A. 1000 hymns   B. 2028 hymns
C. 1028 hymns   D. 1038 hymns

27. The central point in Ashoka's dharma was :
A. royalty to kings
B. peace and non-violence
C. respect to elders
D. religious tolerance

28. The social evil which was conspicuously absent during ancient India was :
A. *Sati*-System   B. *Devadasi*-System
C. Polygamy   D. *Purdah*-System

29. Which, among the following, can be accepted as a novelty introduced by Mughal emperors to their buildings?
A. Domes   B. Minarets
C. Arches   D. Attached gardens

30. The first ruler of India who defeated Muhammud of Ghur was :
A. Mularaja II of Gujarat
B. Prithviraja Chauhan of Delhi
C. Jayachand of Kannauj
D. Parmaldeva of Bundelkhand

31. What important event happened in India in 1911?
A. Bengal was partitioned
B. Non-Cooperation movement was launched
C. India's capital was shifted from Calcutta to Delhi
D. Mahatma Gandhi presided over the Congress session

32. The first phase of the Congress Party (1885-1905) was characterized by its efforts to secure:
A. limited independence
B. complete freedom
C. Indianization of services
D. constitutional reforms

33. The Muslim League demanded a separate homeland for the Indian Muslims openly for the first time at its annual session held in Lahore in the year :
A. 1931 A.D.   B. 1936 A.D.
C. 1940 A.D.   D. 1941 A.D.

34. Under whose governorship did the East India Company secure the Diwani Rights in Bengal, Bihar and Odisha from Emperor Shah Alam?
A. Lord Cornwallis
B. Lord William Bentinck
C. Lord Clive
D. Lord Wellesley

35. The Simon Commission was generally boycotted by the Indian political parties. What was the reason for this general non-cooperation?
   A. the Commission aimed at dividing the people
   B. it was an 'all white' Commission
   C. it came after the Jallianwala Bagh carnage
   D. it was an eye wash

36. Aligarh Muslim University was founded by :
   A. Dr. Saifuddin Kitchlu
   B. Mohammad Ali Jinnah
   C. Sir Syed Ahmed Khan
   D. Maulana Mohammad Ali

37. Ibn Batutah was an African traveller visiting India during the time of :
   A. Alivardi Khan
   B. Ala-ud-din Khalji
   C. Iltutmish
   D. Mohammad-bin-Tughlaq

38. The battle of Wandiawash was fought in :
   A. 1726   B. 1760
   C. 1818   D. 1857

39. The abolition of *Sati* by government regulation was at the time of :
   A. Warren Hastings   B. Lord Wellesley
   C. Lord Bentinck   D. Lord Ahmerst

40. Pick out the wrong combination :
   A. Dilwara Temple : Mt. Abu
   B. Pashupati Temple : Kathmandu
   C. Padmanabh Temple : Bangalore
   D. Minakshi Temple : Madurai

41. Match the following:
   (a) Chanhudaro   (b) Kalibangan
   (c) Lothal   (d) Surkotada
   1. Alleged discovery of the skeleton of horse.
   2. Bead making.
   3. Traces of a dock and ship on seal.
   4. Evidence of ploughing the fields.
   The Correct code is :

	(a)	(b)	(c)	(d)
A.	2	4	3	1
B.	2	1	3	4
C.	1	2	3	4
D.	2	1	4	3

42. Match the Harappan settlements with the banks of rivers on which they were located :
   (a) Harappa   1. Ravi
   (b) Mohenjodaro   2. Indus
   (c) Ropar   3. Sutlej
   (d) Kalibangan   4. Ghaggar
   (e) Lothal   5. Bhogava

Codes :

	(a)	(b)	(c)	(d)	(e)
A.	1	2	3	4	5
B.	1	2	3	5	4
C.	2	1	3	5	4
D.	2	1	4	3	5

43. The Goddess 'Kannagi' whose many temples were erected during the 'Sangam Age' was the goddess of:
   A. Chastity   B. Love
   C. Prowess   D. Wisdom

44. The Jain goal of life is to attain deliverance from the fetters of mudane existence, the way to which lies through three jewels. Which one of the following was not included among the 'three jewels' of Jainism?
   A. Right faith   B. Right action
   C. Right knowledge   D. Right conduct

45. The most striking feature of the Ashokan pillar is polish. Name the Ashokan pillar which is considered to be the most graceful of all Ashokan pillars.
   A. Sarnath
   B. Rampurva
   C. Laurya-Nandangarh
   D. Rummindei

46. Which are the correct statements?
   1. The land grants, started in Satavahana period, paved the way for feudal developments in India.
   2. Silk and spices were the Chief Indian export articles of Indo-Roman trade.
   3. The Guptas issued the largest number of gold coins in ancient India.
   4. The first memorial of a 'SATI' dated 510 A.D. is found at Eran in Madhya Pradesh.
   A. 1 and 2   B. 1, 3, and 4
   C. 1 and 4   D. 1, 2, 3 and 4

47. Who among the following patronised the 'Gandhara' (Indo-Greek style) School of Art?
   A. Ashoka, the Great
   B. Harsha Vardhana
   C. Kanishka
   D. Chandragupta Vikramaditya

48. The Sultanate of Delhi had five ruling dynasties. The dynasty having longest and shortest period were :
   A. Ilbari and Khalji
   B. Tughlaq and Khalji
   C. Tughlaq and Sayyid
   D. Ilbari and Lodis

49. Which one of the following events took place at the last during reign of Muhammad-bin-Tughlaq?
   A. Introduction of token currency
   B. Increase of land-revenue in Doab
   C. Transfer of Capital from Delhi to Devagiri.
   D. Conquest of Khurasan and Iraq

50. The most learned medieval Muslim ruler who was well versed in various branches of learning including astronomy, mathematics and medicine was :
    A. Jalaluddin Khilji
    B. Sikander Lodi
    C. Ghiyasuddin Tughlaq
    D. Muhammad-bin-Tughlaq

51. The 'Sufis' had 12 silsilas. They propounded the idea of Union with God through:
    A. Love
    B. Rituals
    C. Fasts
    D. Prayers

52. Match the following:
    (*a*) Peshwa   1. Foreign affairs
    (*b*) Panditrao   2. Audit and accounts
    (*c*) Amatya   3. Providing grants to scholars
    (*d*) Sumant   4. General supervision
                     5. Military affairs
    Select the correct code :

	(*a*)	(*b*)	(*c*)	(*d*)
A.	2	3	4	5
B.	4	1	2	3
C.	4	3	2	1
D.	3	1	4	2

53. The Regulating Act of 1773 can be regarded as the first measure to :
    A. assert the right of British Parliament to legislate for India
    B. separate the legislature from the executive
    C. separate the judiciary from the executive
    D. centralise law-making

54. What was the exact constitutional status of the Indian Republic on 26th January, 1950?
    A. A Democratic Republic
    B. A Sovereign, Democratic Republic
    C. A Sovereign, Secular, Democratic Republic
    D. A Sovereign, Socialist, Secular, Democratic Republic

55. When the British obtained the grant of Diwani of Bengal, Bihar and Odisha they acquired the right to :
    A. maintain law and order in these territories
    B. administer civil justice and collect revenue in these territories
    C. collect revenue and establish revenue administration in these territories
    D. militarily defend these territories

56. Which of the following were responsible for the growth of nationalism in India during the British rule?
    1. Economic exploitation of India.
    2. Impact of western education.
    3. Role of the Press.

Select the correct answer using the codes given below :
Codes:
A. 1, 2 and 3
B. 1 and 2
C. 2 and 3
D. 1 and 3

57. Which one of the following nationalist leaders has been described as being radical in politics but conservative on social issues?
    A. G.K. Gokhale
    B. B.G. Tilak
    C. Lala Lajpat Rai
    D. Madan Mohan Malviya

58. Provincial Autonomy in British India was envisaged by the :
    A. Act of 1909
    B. Act of 1919
    C. Act of 1935
    D. Act of 1947

59. Dyarchy means :
    A. double government
    B. a government in which the centre is very powerful
    C. a government based on division of power between centre and provinces
    D. None of the above

60. The Indian National Congress observed 'Independence Day' for the first time on 26th January in :
    A. 1920
    B. 1925
    C. 1930
    D. 1947

61. ....is situated near the banks of Sabarmati River
    A. Bhavnagar
    B. Aurangabad
    C. Ahmedabad
    D. Rajkot

62. Sericulture is:
    A. science of the various kinds of serum
    B. artificial rearing of fish
    C. art of silkworm breeding
    D. study of various cultures of a community

63. The most abundant constituents of earth's crust are:
    A. Igneous rocks
    B. Sedimentary rocks
    C. Metamorphic rocks
    D. Granite

64. Indian Standard Time is based on:
    A. 80°E longitude
    B. 82½°E longitude
    C. 110°E longitude
    D. 25°E longitude

65. Tides in the oceans are caused by :
    A. Gravitational pull of the moon on the earth's surface including sea water
    B. Gravitational pull of the sun on the earth's surface only and not on the sea water
    C. Gravitational pull of the moon and the sun on the earth's surface including the sea water
    D. None of these

66. Nagarjunasagar Project is situated on the river:
A. Tungabhadra
B. Cauvery
C. Krishna
D. Godavari

67. The difference between the Indian Standard Time and the Greenwich Mean Time is:
A. – 3½ hours   B. + 3½ hours
C. – 5½ hours   D. + 5½ hours

68. Which of the following dams is not on Narmada river?
A. Indira-Sagar Project
B. Maheshwar Hydel Power Project
C. Jobat Project
D. Koyna Power Project

69. Which of the following statements is **not true** about the availability of water on the earth, the crisis for which is going to increase in the years to come?
A. About 97.5 per cent of the total volume of water available on the earth is salty
B. 80 per cent of the water available to us for use comes in bursts as monsoons
C. About 2.5 per cent of the total water available on the earth is polluted water and cannot be used for human activities
D. Possibility is that some big glaciers will melt in the coming ten-fifteen years and sea level will rise by 3-4 metres all over the earth

70. Which of the following is **not** a cash crop?
A. Jute   B. Paddy
C. Cashewnut   D. Sugarcane

71. Through which States does Cauvery River flow?
A. Gujarat, M.P., Tamil Nadu
B. Karnataka, Kerala, Tamil Nadu
C. Karnataka, Kerala, Andhra Pradesh
D. M.P., Maharashtra, Tamil Nadu

72. Indian Standard Time is the local time of 82½°E which passes through :
A. Guntur   B. Delhi
C. Allahabad   D. Kolkata

73. The 17th parallel defines the boundary between:
A. North and South Korea
B. USA and Canada
C. North and South Vietnam
D. China and Russia

74. During the period of south-west monsoon, Tamil Nadu remains dry because:
A. the winds do not reach this area
B. there are no mountains in this area
C. it lies in the rain shadow area
D. the temperature is too high to let the winds cool down

75. Which country does top in producing cocoa?
A. Ghana   B. Brazil
C. Ivory Coast   D. Nigeria

76. The biggest reserves of thorium are in :
A. India   B. China
C. The Soviet Union D. U.S.A.

77. The Girnar Hills are situated in which of the following states?
A. Gujarat   B. Karnataka
C. Madhya Pradesh D. Maharashtra

78. During December 22nd the sun is vertically over:
A. Tropic of Cancer
B. Tropic of Capricorn
C. The Equator
D. None of the above

79. Photosphere is described as the :
A. Lower layer of atmosphere
B. Visible surface of the sun from which radiation emanates
C. Wavelength of solar spectrum
D. None of the above

80. Broadly, there are three layers of the earth of the crust, the mantle and the core. The crust forms what percentage of the volume of the earth?
A. 0.5%   B. 2.5%
C. 7.5%   D. 12.5%

81. The grassland of Argentina is known as :
A. Pampas   B. Campos
C. Savanna   D. None of the above

82. Different seasons are formed because :
A. Sun is moving around the earth
B. of revolution of the earth around the Sun on its orbit
C. of rotation of the earth around its axis
D. All of the above

83. Eskers and Drumlins are features formed by:
A. underground water
B. running water
C. the action of wind
D. glacial action

84. Match List-I and List-II and select the correct answer using the codes given below the Lists :

List-I	**List-II**
(Rivers)	*(Towns)*
(a) Ghaghara	1. Lucknow
(b) Brahmaputra	2. Hoshangabad
(c) Narmada	3. Ahmedabad
(d) Sabarmati	4. Guwahati
	5. Ayodhya

	(a)	(b)	(c)	(d)
A.	4	5	1	2
B.	5	4	2	3
C.	5	4	3	1
D.	3	5	2	1

85. Which of the statements as regards the consequences of the movement of the earth is not correct?
A. Revolution of the earth is the cause of the change of seasons.
B. Rotation of the earth is the cause of days and nights.
C. Rotation of the earth causes variation in the duration of days and nights.
D. Rotation of the earth effects the movement of winds and ocean currents.

86. The world is divided into :
A. 12 time zones
B. 20 time zones
C. 24 time zones
D. 36 time zones

87. The 'Kiel' canal links the :
A. Pacific and Atlantic Oceans
B. Mediterranean Sea and Red Sea
C. Mediterranean Sea and Black Sea
D. North Sea and Baltic Sea

88. Match the following :

List-I		**List-II**
(a) Himadri	1.	Outer Himalayas
(b) Shivalik	2.	Inner Himalayas
(c) Himanchal	3.	Middle Himalayas
(d) Sahyadri	4.	Western Ghats

Codes:

	(a)	(b)	(c)	(d)
A.	1	2	3	4
B.	4	2	3	1
C.	2	1	3	4
D.	1	2	3	4

89. The term 'Regur' refers to:
A. Laterite soils
B. Black Cotton soils
C. Red Soils
D. Deltaic Alluvial Soils

90. Location of sugar industry in India is shifting from north to south because of:
A. cheap labour
B. expanding regional market
C. cheap and abundant supply of power
D. high yield and high sugar content in sugarcane

91. Consider the following statements :
1. Ozone is found mostly in the Stratosphere.
2. Ozone layer lies 55-75 km above the surface of the earth.
3. Ozone absorbs ultraviolet radiation from the Sun.
4. Ozone layer has no significance for life on the earth.
Which of the above statements are correct?
A. 1 and 3   B. 2 and 4
C. 2 and 3   D. 1 and 4

92. Match List-I with List-II and select the correct answer using the codes given below the Lists :

List-I	**List-II**
(Crops)	*(Producer)*
(a) Banana	1. Colombia
(b) Cocoa	2. Ghana
(c) Coffee	3. Jamaica
(d) Tea	4. Kenya

Codes :

	(a)	(b)	(c)	(d)
A.	2	3	1	4
B.	3	2	1	4
C.	3	2	4	1
D.	2	3	4	1

93. Darjeeling and Dharamsala would be the right places to visit if one wanted to get a clear view respectively of :
A. Kanchanjunga and Dhauladhar ranges
B. Nandadevi and Dhauladhar ranges
C. Kanchanjunga and Nandadevi ranges
D. Nandadevi and Nanga Parvat

94. Atmosphere exists because:
A. The Gravitational force of the Earth
B. Revolution of the Earth
C. Rotation of the Earth
D. Weight of the gases of atmosphere

95. Victoria lake is located in the continent:
A. Africa
B. Asia
C. North America
D. South America

96. The famous Lagoon Lake of India is :
A. Dal Lake   B. Chilka Lake
C. Pulicat Lake   D. Mansarover

97. Where are most of the earth's active volcanoes concentrated?
A. Indian Ocean   B. Pacific Ocean
C. Aral Sea   D. Atlantic Ocean

98. Through which of the following states does the river Chambal flow?
A. U.P., M.P., Rajasthan
B. M.P., Gujarat, U.P.
C. Rajasthan, M.P., Bihar
D. Gujarat, M.P., U.P.

99. Which country is called the sugar bowl of the world?
A. Cuba
B. India
C. Argentina
D. USA

100. The area covered by forest in India is about:
A. 46%
B. 33%
C. 23%
D. 21.54%

101. A closed economy is the one which :
A. does not permit emigration or immigration
B. permits emigration but no immigration
C. engages in no foreign trade
D. engages in no foreign and domestic trade or transit

102. In a developed economy the major share of employment originates in the :
A. primary sector
B. tertiary sector
C. secondary sector
D. any of the above

103. The Economic and Social Commission for Asia and Pacific (ESCAP) is located at :
A. Bangkok
B. Kuala Lumpur
C. Manila
D. Singapore

104. Commercial vehicles are not produced by which of the following companies in India?
A. TELCO
B. Ashok Leyland
C. DCM Daewoo
D. Birla Yamaha

105. In India, the Public Sector is most dominant in:
A. transport
B. steel production
C. commercial banking
D. organised term-lending financial institutions

106. The main argument advanced in favour of small scale and cottage industries in India is that:
A. cost of production is low
B. they require small capital investment
C. they advance the goal of equitable distribution of wealth
D. they generate a large volume of employment

107. The most serious economic problems of India are:
A. Poverty and unemployment
B. Stagnation, not poverty
C. Unemployment, not poverty
D. Underdevelopment, not poverty

108. Which of the following is not one of the three central problems of an economy?
A. What to produce
B. How to produce
C. When to produce
D. For whom to produce

109. If saving exceeds investment, the national income will:
A. fall
B. rise
C. fluctuate
D. remain constant

110. In which of the following industries in India are the maximum number of workers employed?
A. Sugar
B. Jute
C. Textiles
D. Iron and Steel

111. Terrace Cultivation is practiced mostly:
A. in urban areas
B. on slopes of mountains
C. on tops of hills
D. in undulating tracts

112. Which of the following is a Selective Credit Control method?
A. Bank Rate
B. RBI directives
C. Cash Reserve Ratio
D. Open market operations

113. Which of the following taxes is not shared by the Central Government with the States?
A. Union excise duties
B. Customs duty
C. Income tax
D. Estate duty

114. ICICI is the name of a:
A. Financial Institution
B. Chemical Industry
C. Cotton Industry
D. Chamber of Commerce and Industry

115. Structural Unemployment arises due to
A. Deflationary conditions
B. Heavy industry bias
C. Shortage of raw material
D. Inadequate productive capacity

116. Which of the following is the largest single source of the government's earning from tax revenue?
A. Corporation tax
B. Customs duties
C. Excise duties
D. Income tax

117. The largest public sector bank in India is:
A. Central Bank of India
B. Punjab National Bank
C. State Bank of India
D. Indian Overseas Bank

118. Which of the following statements best explains the term contraband goods?
A. Goods produced only for exports
B. Goods produced in joint sector only
C. Goods for the trading of which licence is not required
D. Goods that are forbidden, from export, import or even possession, by law

119. Price in the market is fixed by:
A. Stock exchange rates
B. The demand and supply ruling in the market at a particular time
C. The Finance Minister
D. None of the above

120. Devaluation of currency helps to promote:
A. National Income
B. Savings
C. Imports at lower cost
D. Exports

121. Balanced economic growth can be achieved only if:
A. All the sectors of economy grow at the same rate
B. Population growth is arrested
C. All the inter dependent sectors grow in harmony
D. Basic and heavy industries are assigned highest priority

122. Which one of the following contributes most to the National Income in India?
A. Agricultural Sector
B. Industrial Sector
C. Foreign Trade Sector
D. Tertiary Sector

123. 'MODVAT' stands for:
A. Ad Valorem tax on output
B. Deduction of cost of inputs from the value of output
C. Reduction in import duties
D. Imposition of tax on professions

124. Largest revenue in India is obtained from:
A. Excise duties
B. Corporation tax
C. Income tax
D. None of the above

125. The term 'devaluation' means:
A. Reducing the value of a currency in terms of another currency
B. Increasing the value of a currency
C. Revising the value of a currency
D. None of the above

126. Per capita net availability of pulses has shown a tendency of:
A. Increase over time
B. Decrease over time
C. Constant over time
D. First increase then decrease

127. National Income is the same as:
A. Net national product at market price
B. Net domestic product at market price
C. Net national product at factor cost
D. Net domestic product at factor cost

128. Which one of the following is not an example of indirect tax?
A. Sales tax
B. Excise duty
C. Customs duty
D. Expenditure tax

129. The major aim of devaluation is to:
A. encourage imports
B. encourage exports
C. encourage both exports and imports
D. discourage both exports and imports

130. Structural unemployment arises due to:
A. deflationary conditions
B. heavy industry bias
C. shortage of raw materials
D. inadequate productive capacity

131. When was the Family Planning Programme officially started in India?
A. 1950
B. 1952
C. 1956
D. 1962

132. When was the Reserve Bank of India nationalised?
A. 1947
B. 1949
C. 1950
D. 1951

133. Which of the following is *not* a feature of the Indian economy?
A. High rate of population growth
B. Disguised unemployment
C. Lowest rate of adult literacy
D. High rate of exports

134. The 'Relative Deprivation' approach for measuring poverty has been adopted by:
A. developing countries
B. developed countries
C. under-developed countries
D. None of the above

135. One of the main factors that led to rapid expansion of Indian exports is:
A. Imposition of import duties
B. Liberalisation of the economy
C. Recession in other countries
D. Diversification of exports

136. Sustainable economic development means an increase in the rate of growth of real:
A. total and per capita product
B. total and per capita product and level of literacy rate
C. total and per capita product and life expectancy at birth
D. total and per capita product, taking into account the cost of degradation of the quality of environment in this process

137. Functional unemployment occurs when:
  A. unemployed have no qualification for job
  B. people frequently change their job
  C. people were thrown out from job due to recession
  D. None of these

138. Which among the following does **not** have a 'free trade zone'?
  A. Kandla
  B. Mumbai
  C. Visakhapatnam
  D. Thiruvanantpuram

139. Sun Belt of USA is important for which one of the following industries?
  A. Cotton textile
  B. Petrochemicals
  C. Hi-tech electronics
  D. Food Processing

140. Commercial banking system in India is
  A. unit banking
  B. branch banking
  C. mixed banking
  D. None of the above

141. Who gives recognition to political parties in India?
  A. Parliament
  B. President
  C. Supreme Court
  D. Election Commission

142. The Quorum of the Legislative Council is :
  A. one-fourth of its total membership
  B. one-third of its membership
  C. one-tenth of its membership
  D. 25

143. The Indian Constitution is:
  A. federal
  B. unitary
  C. a happy mixture of the federal and unitary
  D. federal in normal times and unitary in times of emergency

144. Universal adult franchise implies a right to vote to all:
  A. adult residents of the State
  B. adult male citizens of the State
  C. residents of the State
  D. adult citizens of the State

145. When a resolution prefering a charge against the President has been passed by a specified majority in the House, it is sent to the other House for investigation. If, as a result of such an investigation, a resolution is passed through a specified majority by the other House, declaring that the charge has been sustained, the President shall leave his office. The specified special majority must not be less than :
  A. two-third of the members present and voting
  B. one-third of the members present and voting
  C. three-fourth of the members present and voting and two-third of the total membership

  D. two-third of the total membership

146. Which one of the following judicial powers of the President of India has been *wrongly* listed?
  A. he appoints the Chief Justice and other judges of the Supreme Court
  B. he can remove the judges of the Supreme Court on grounds of misconduct
  C. he can consult the Supreme Court on any question of law or fact which is of public importance
  D. he can grant pardon, reprieves and respites to persons punished under Union Law

147. The Vice-president of India can be removed from his office before the expiry of his term if :
  A. the Rajya Sabha passes a resolution by a majority of its members and the Lok Sabha agrees with the resolution
  B. if the Supreme Court of India recommends his removal
  C. the President so desires
  D. None of the above

148. The Chief Justice of a High Court in India is appointed by the :
  A. Governor of the State
  B. Prime Minister of India
  C. Chief Justice of the Supreme Court
  D. President of India

149. Which of the following statements is constitu-tionally not true about the passing of the Union Budgets, Railway Budgets and Finance Bill in India?
  1. Under the law, Finance Bill should be adopted by both the Houses of the Parliament within 45 days of its introduction.
  2. If the Finance Bill is not adopted within specified period, the government loses its authority to levy the taxes proposed in the budgets.
  3. In the absence of full budget, a vote-on-account gives the power to the government to spend.
  4. Government cannot raise revenues without a proper approval of the Finance Bill
  A. Only 2
  B. Only 3
  C. Only 4
  D. Only 1, 2 and 3

150. Normally, on whose advice the President's Rule is imposed in a State?
  A. Chief Minister
  B. Legislative Assembly
  C. Governor
  D. Chief Justice of High Court

151. Which Article of the Indian Constitution deals with Amendment procedure?
  A. Article 368
  B. Article 358
  C. Article 367
  D. All of these

152. Government is the agency through which the will of:
A. the state is expressed
B. the people is expressed
C. the head of the state is expressed
D. the majority is expressed

153. In a unitary system of government :
A. The centre is all powerful
B. The centre is weaker than the states
C. The centre and states stand at par
D. The states and centre are supreme in their respective spheres

154. In Cabinet System of Government the real executive authority rests with :
A. The Council of Ministers
B. The Prime Minister
C. The Constitution
D. The Parliament

155. The Head of the State under a parliamentary government:
A. is an elected representative
B. is a hereditary person
C. is a nominated person
D. may be any one of the above

156. In the event of a ministerial proposal being defeated on the floor of the legislature, under the parliamentary system :
A. the government waits for a general no-confidence motion
B. the minister concerned is taken to task by the Prime Minister
C. the minister is forced to resign
D. the whole Council of Ministers resign

157. The "due process of law" is an essential characteristic of the judicial system of:
A. UK   B. France
C. USA   D. India

158. Under the Constitution it is :
A. obligatory for the President to accept the advice of the Council of Ministers but is not obliged to follow it
B. obligatory for the President to accept the advice of the Council of Ministers
C. not obligatory for the President to seek or accept the advice of the Council of Ministers
D. obligatory for the President to seek the advice of the Council of Ministers if his own party is in power

159. Which one of the following statements is correct?
A. the Presiding Officer of Rajya Sabha is elected every year

B. the Presiding Officer of Rajya Sabha is elected for a term of two years at a time
C. the Presiding Officer of Rajya Sabha is elected for a term of six years
D. the Vice-President of India is the ex-officio Presiding Officer of Rajya Sabha

160. The introduction of "no confidence" motion in the Lok Sabha requires the support of at least:
A. 50 members   B. 70 members
C. 60 members   D. 80 members

161. The High Court comes under :
A. State List   B. Union List
C. Concurrent List   D. None of the above

162. Which one of the following has been wrongly listed as a Fundamental Duty of the Indian citizens?
A. to develop scientific temper, humanism and spirit of inquiry and reform
B. to work for raising the prestige of the country in the international sphere
C. to protect and improve the natural environment
D. to strive towards excellence in all spheres of individual and collective activity

163. Which one of the following is not a Fundamental Duty as outlined in Article 51A of the Constitution?
A. to abide by the Constitution and respect its ideals
B. to defend the country and render national service when called upon to do so
C. to work for the moral upliftment of the weaker sections of society
D. to preserve the rich heritage

164. The main characteristics of the Directive Principles of State Policy given in the Indian Constitution are :
A. not enforceable by any court
B. fundamental in the governance of the country
C. 'Like instruments, instructions, political manifesto and a code of moral precepts which have to guide governors of the country'
D. no law can be passed, which is opposed to these principles

165. Of the following which are true?
A. In a State, the Legislative Council is dominant with regard to non-financial bills and the Legislative Assembly with regard to financial (money) bills
B. Vidhan Parishad can virtually block legisla-tion even if the same is passed by the Vidhan Sabha
C. In case of a tie between the two Houses, the Governor is duty-bound to call a joint session of the two Houses to have the issue settled on a majority verdict

D. If a Bill is twice approved by the Vidhan Sabha, it becomes law even if rejected by the Vidhan Parishad

166. Which one of the following types of emergency can be declared by the President?
   A. Emergency due to threat of war and external aggresion
   B. Emergency due to break-down of constitu-tional machinery in a State
   C. Financial emergency on account of threat to the financial credit of India
   D. all the three emergencies

167. The chairman of which of the following parliamentary committees is invariably from the members of ruling party?
   A. Committee on public undertakings
   B. Public accounts committee
   C. Estimates committee
   D. Committee on delegated legislation

168. Which of the following is not a formally prescribed device available to the members of parliament?
   A. Question hour
   B. Zero hour
   C. Half-an-hour discussion
   D. Short duration discussion

169. Which of the following is not a tool of executive control over public administration?
   A. Power of appointment and removal
   B. Line agencies
   C. Appeal to public opinion
   D. Civil services code

170. If the Speaker of the State Legislative Assembly decides to resign, he should submit his resignation to the:
   A. Judges of the High Court
   B. Deputy Speaker
   C. Chief Minister
   D. Finance Minister

171. The Constitution of India provides for the nomination of two members of Lok Sabha by the President to represent:
   A. the Parsis
   B. men of eminence
   C. the business community
   D. the Anglo-Indian community

172. India is a Federal State because of:
   A. dual judiciary
   B. dual citizenship prevalent here
   C. share of power between the Centre and the States
   D. rigid Constitution

173. Residuary Subjects are those subjects which are:
   A. contained in the State list
   B. contained in the Union list
   C. contained in the Concurrent list
   D. not covered by any of the three lists

174. Which of the following writs can be issued, by the Supreme Court, to enforce Fundamental Rights?
   A. Writ of Habeas Corpus
   B. Writ of Mandamus
   C. Writ of Quo Warranto
   D. All of these

175. When the offices of both the President and the Vice-President of India are vacant, who will discharge their functions?
   A. Prime Minister
   B. Home Minister
   C. Chief Justice of India
   D. The Speaker

176. The Supreme Court tenders advice to the President of India on a matter of law or fact:
   A. on its own
   B. only when such advice is sought
   C. only if the matter relates to some basic issue
   D. only if the issue poses a threat to the unity and integrity of the country

177. Six months shall **not** intervene between two sessions of the Indian Parliament because :
   A. it is the customary practice
   B. it is the British convention followed in India
   C. it is an obligation under the Constitution of India
   D. None of the above

178. The States of the Indian Union can be recognised or their boundaries altered by:
   A. the Union Parliament by a simple majority in the ordinary process of legislation
   B. two-thirds majority of both the Houses of Parliament
   C. two-thirds majority of both the Houses of Parliament and the consent of the legisla-tures of concerned States
   D. an executive order of the Union government with the consent of the concerned State governments

179. The Basic Feature theory of the Constitution of India was propounded by the Supreme Court in the case of :
   A. Minerva Mills Vs. Union of India
   B. Golaknath Vs. State of Punjab
   C. Maneka Gandhi Vs. Union of India
   D. Keshavananda Vs. State of Kerala

180. Which one of the following writs is issued by a court in case of illegal detention of a person?
   A. Habeas corpus   B. Mandamus
   C. Certiorari   D. Quo-warranto

181. Name the instrument with the help of which a sailor in a submarine can see the objects on the surface of the sea.
A. Telescope
B. Periscope
C. Gycroscope
D. Stereoscope

182. 'HEMOPHILLIA' is the disease of ....
A. liver
B. blood
C. brain
D. bones

183. Vitamin A is abundantly found in ....
A. Brinjal
B. Tomato
C. Carrot
D. Cabbage

184. .... is not soluble in water.
A. Vitamin A
B. Vitamin B
C. Vitamin C
D. None of these

185. The blood vessels with the smallest diameter are called ....
A. capillaries
B. arterioles
C. venules
D. lymphatics

186. Out of the following .... has the greatest elasticity.
A. steel
B. rubber
C. aluminium
D. annealed copper

187. Cooking gas is a mixture of which of the following two gases?
A. Carbon Dioxide and Oxygen
B. Butane and Propane
C. Carbon Monoxide and Carbon Dioxide
D. Methane and Ethylene

188. The substance most commonly used as a food preservative is:
A. sodium carbonate
B. tartaric acid
C. acetic acid
D. benzoic acid

189. Normally, the substances that fight against diseases in human systems are known as:
A. dioxyribonucleic acids
B. carbohydrates
C. enzymes
D. antibodies

190. The SI unit of temperature is ....
A. Kelvin
B. Celsius
C. Fahrenheit
D. None of the above

191. One of the common fungal diseases of man is :
A. plague
B. ringworm
C. cholera
D. typhoid

192. A clear sky is blue because:
A. red light is scattered more than blue
B. ultraviolet light has been absorbed
C. blue light is scattered more than red
D. blue light has been absorbed

193. Jenner introduced the method of making people immune to :
A. small pox
B. rabies
C. cholera
D. polio

194. The largest cell in the human body is :
A. Nerve cell
B. Live cell
C. Muscle cell
D. Kidney cell

195. What is the device that steps up or steps down the voltage?
A. Dynamo
B. Conductor
C. Inductor
D. Transformer

196. The protein deficiency disease is known as :
A. Kwashiorker
B. Cirrhosis
C. Eczema
D. Clycoses

197. Iron deficiency causes :
A. rickets
B. anaemia
C. cirrhosis
D. goitre

198. Blood group of an individual is controlled by :
A. Haemoglobin
B. Shape of RBC
C. Shape of WBC
D. Genes

199. In a normal man the amount of blood pumped out by the heart per minute is about :
A. 1 litre
B. 3 litres
C. 4 litres
D. 5 litres

200. Red/green colour blindness in man is known as :
A. Protanopia
B. Deutetanopia
C. Both A and B above
D. Marfan's syndrome

201. The blue colour of the water in the sea is due to :
A. Reflection of the blue light by the impurities in sea water
B. Reflection of the blue sky by sea water and scattering of blue light by water molecules
C. Absorption of other colours by water molecules
D. None of the above

202. The image formed on the retina of the eye is:
A. upright and real
B. larger than the object
C. small and inverted
D. enlarged and real

203. Unit of loudness of sound is:
A. bel
B. decibel
C. phon
D. none of these

204. Oil rises up the wick in a lamp :
A. because oil is volatile
B. due to the capillary action phenomenon
C. due to the surface tension phenomenon
D. because oil is very light

205. The 'stones' formed in human kidney consist mostly of :
A. calcium oxalate
B. sodium acetate
C. magnesium sulphate
D. calcium

206. We hear the sound later, while the light is seen earlier:
A. because light's speed is more than that of sound
B. because lights travel in a straight direction while sound in a zigzag direction
C. because sound's frequency is lower than light
D. All of the above

207. Which part of an eye is transplanted?
A. Cornea   B. Retina
C. Iris   D. Sciera

208. The Universal donor group of blood is:
A. O   B. A
C. B   D. AB

209. The green colour of the leaf is due to :
A. Presence of Chloroplast
B. Presence of Chromium
C. Presence of Nicoplast
D. Presence of excess of oxygen

210. Voice of a child is more shrill than that of an elderly person because:
A. the pitch of the child's voice is higher than that of the person
B. the pitch is lower
C. the child is more energetic
D. None of the above

ANSWERS

1	2	3	4	5	6	7	8	9	10
B	C	D	C	B	C	A	C	C	D

11	12	13	14	15	16	17	18	19	20
C	A	C	A	A	D	A	B	A	D

21	22	23	24	25	26	27	28	29	30
A	C	B	C	D	C	B	D	D	B

31	32	33	34	35	36	37	38	39	40
C	D	C	C	B	C	D	B	C	C

41	42	43	44	45	46	47	48	49	50
A	A	A	B	C	D	C	B	B	D

51	52	53	54	55	56	57	58	59	60
A	C	A	B	B	A	B	C	A	C

61	62	63	64	65	66	67	68	69	70
C	C	B	B	C	C	D	D	D	B

71	72	73	74	75	76	77	78	79	80
B	C	C	C	A	A	A	B	B	A

81	82	83	84	85	86	87	88	89	90
A	B	D	B	C	C	D	C	B	D

91	92	93	94	95	96	97	98	99	100
A	B	A	A	A	B	B	A	A	D

101	102	103	104	105	106	107	108	109	110
C	B	A	D	D	D	A	C	D	C

111	112	113	114	115	116	117	118	119	120
B	B	B	A	D	A	C	D	B	D

121	122	123	124	125	126	127	128	129	130
C	A	A	B	A	D	C	D	B	D

131	132	133	134	135	136	137	138	139	140
B	B	D	A	B	D	B	D	D	C

141	142	143	144	145	146	147	148	149	150
D	C	D	D	D	B	A	D	C	C

151	152	153	154	155	156	157	158	159	160
A	B	A	A	A	D	C	B	D	A
161	**162**	**163**	**164**	**165**	**166**	**167**	**168**	**169**	**170**
B	B	C	B	D	D	C	B	B	B
171	**172**	**173**	**174**	**175**	**176**	**177**	**178**	**179**	**180**
D	C	D	D	C	B	C	A	D	A
181	**182**	**183**	**184**	**185**	**186**	**187**	**188**	**189**	**190**
B	B	C	A	A	A	B	D	D	A
191	**192**	**193**	**194**	**195**	**196**	**197**	**198**	**199**	**200**
B	C	A	A	D	A	B	D	D	A
201	**202**	**203**	**204**	**205**	**206**	**207**	**208**	**209**	**210**
B	B	B	B	A	A	A	A	A	A

1809

MANIPUR : A PROFILE

The word "Manipur" is being derived from the two Sanskrit Words "Mani" and "Pur", which literally mean 'A Jewelled Land' or 'The Land of Jewels'. Here "Mani" means Jewel and "Pur" means land or place respectively.

Surrounded by blue hills with an oval shaped valley at the centre, rich in art and tradition and surcharged with nature's pristine glory, Manipur lies on a melting pot of culture. It is birth place of Polo. This is the place where Rajashree Bhagyachandra created the famous Ras Lila, the classical dance of Manipur, out of his enchanting dream by the grace of Lord Krishna. Her folk dances reveal the mythological concept of creation of Manipur.

Having a varied and proud history from the earliest times, Manipur came under the British Rule as a Princely State after the defeat in the Anglo-Manipuri War of 1891. After independence of India in 1947, the Princely State of Manipur was merged in the Indian Union on October 15,1949 and became a full-fledged State of India on the 21th January, 1972 with a Legislative Assembly of 60 seats of which 19 are reserved for Scheduled Tribe and one reserved for Scheduled Caste. The State is represented in the Lok Sabha by two members and by one member in the Rajya Sabha.

Manipur extends between 23°50' and 25°42' latitudes north and between 92°58' and 94°45' longitudes east. It covers an area of 22,327 square kilometers and is bounded on the north by Nagaland, on the west by Cachar of Assam, on the east by Burma (Myanmar) and on the south by Mizoram and Chin state of Burma.

IMPORTANT FACTS

Capital	:	Imphal
Area	:	22327 sq.km.
Population (2011 Census)	:	28,55,794 (*Males*: 14,38,586; *Females*: 14,17,208)
Decadal Growth Rate	:	24.50%
Density of Population	:	128 (per sq. km.)
Literacy Rate	:	76.94%
Sex Ratio	:	985 (Females per 1000 Males)
Altitude	:	790 mtrs. above MSL (Imphal)
Latitude	:	23°50'N to 25°42'N
Longitude	:	92°58'E to 94°45'E
Rainfall	:	1467.5 mm (Avg.)
Rainy Season	:	May to October
Climate • **Summer**	:	14°C to 32°C
• **Winter**	:	0°C to 25°C
State Language	:	Manipuri
State Emblem	:	Kangla Sha
State Bird	:	Nongyeen

State Animal	:	Sangai
State Game	:	Manipuri Polo
State Flower	:	Siroi Lily
State Tree	:	Uning thou
Assembly Constituencies	:	60
Parliamentary Constituencies	:	2 (One for Inner and One for Outer)
Rajya Sabha Seat	:	1
National Highways	:	3(NH-39-Indo-Myanmar road, NH-53-New Cachar Road, NH-150-Jessami-Tipaimukh Road)
Districts	:	16-Senapati, Tamenglong, Thoubal, Ukhrul, Bishnupur, Chandel, Churachandpur, Imphal East, Imphal West, Jiribam, Kangpokpi, Kakching, Tengnoupal, Kamjong, Noney, Pherzawl.
Sub-divisions	:	66
Towns	:	51 *(Statutory towns 28, Census towns 23)*
Small Town Committees	:	33
Gram Panchayats	:	165
Largest District	:	Churachandpur
Smallest District	:	Bishnupur
Highly Populated District (2011)	:	Imphal West
Less Populated District	:	Tamenglong
Most Densily Populated District (2011)	:	Imphal West (998 persons per sq. km.)
Less Populated District (2011)	:	Tamenglong (32 persons per sq. km)
Major Religions	:	Hinduism, Christianity, Maibiasn
Major Festivals	:	Rath Yatra, Yaoshang (Dol Jatra), Christmas, Diwali, ID, Mahavir Jayanti, Lai Haraoba, Kut, Gan-Ngai, Cheiraoba
Major Cities	:	Imphal, Churachandpur, Kakching, Ukhrul, Andro, Bishnupur, Jiribam, Moirang, Moreh, Ningthoukhong, Thoubal, etc.
Largest City	:	Imphal
Major Tourist Places	:	Shaheed Minar, War Cemetery, Manipur Zoological Garden, Keibul Lamjao National Park, Kaina, Red Hill (Maibam Lok pa Ching), Loukoipat, Shree Shree Govindajee Temple, Phubala, Loktak Lake, Leimaram, Moreh, Tengnoupal, Andro, Khongjom, etc.
Major Crops	:	Wheat, Rice, Pulses, Paddy, Maize, Sugarcane, Potato, Mustard, etc.
Major Fruits	:	Pineapple, Banana, Papaya, Passion Fruit, Orange, Lemon, Mango etc.
Major Vegetables	:	Cabbage, Cauliflower, Peas, French Beans, Tomato, etc.
Major Spices	:	Green Chilli, Ginger, Turmeric, Corriander Seeds, etc.
Major Forest Products	:	Oak, Teak, Pine, Cane, Bamboo, Leihao, Uningthou, etc.
Major Import Products	:	Betel nut, Silk yarn, Pigs, Cotton thread, etc.
Major Export Products	:	Bamboo shoot products (orient food), ginger, pineapple, Maize, Mushrooms, etc.
Chief Rivers	:	Barak, Imphal, Khuga, Maklang, Ithai, Thoubal, Irang, Nambul, Chakpi, Sekmai, etc.
Major Minerals	:	Copper, Nickel, Chromite, Asbestos, Limestone, Lignite, etc.

ADMINISTRATION

Manipur in its wide territory of 22,327 sq. km. includes 16 districts. The name of districts are Imphal-East, Imphal-West, Senapati, Tamenglong, Thoubal, Ukhrul, Bishnupur, Chandel, Churachandpur, Jiribam, Kangpokpi, Kakching, Tengnoupal, Kamjong, Noney and Pherzawl. Number of Sub-divisions (2016) is 66. For the upliftment and development of the rural areas, the state is sub-divided into 34 community and Tribal Development Blocks and 33 small town committees. The Manipur Legislative Assembly consists of 60 seats out of which, 19 seats are reserved for scheduled Tribes, 1 for Scheduled Caste and 40 for General. Manipur has a two-tier panchayati Raj system. Gram Panchayat at the Village level and the Zila Parishad at the district level. There are about 165 Gram Panchayats and 4 Zila Parishads (the Imphal East Zila Parishad, the Imphal West Zila Parishad, the Thoubal Zila Parishad and the Bishnupur Zila Parishad) in Manipur.

Manipur sends 2 members to Lok-Sabha (Lower House of the Indian Parliament) and 1 member to the Rajya Sabha (Upper House of the Indian Parliament). Manipur was within the jurisdiction of the Imphal Bench of Gauhati High Court till March 25, 2013. Earlier, the Imphal Bench of Gauhati High Court came into existence on 21st January, 1972, the day Manipur attained its statehood. In March 2013, the then Chief Justice of India Altamas Kabir formally inangurated the Manipur High Court at Imphal and Justice Abhay Manohar Sapre was made the first Chief Justice of the Manipur High Court.

DISTRICTS AND SUB-DIVISIONS OF MANIPUR

Sl. No.	Name of District	Name of Sub-division		
1.	**Senapati**	1. Tadubi 4. Willong 7. Lairouching	2. Paomata 5. Chilivai Phaibung	3. Purul 6. Song-Song
2.	**Kangpokpi** (Bifurcated from the erstwhile Senapati District)	8. Kangpokpi 11. Kangchup Geljang 14. Lungtin	9. Champhai 12. Tuijang Waichong 15. Island	10. Saitu Gamphazol 13. Saikul 16. Bungte Chiru
3.	**Tamenglong**	17. Tamenglong	18. Tamei	19. Tousem
4.	**Noney District** (Bifurcated from the erstwhile Tamenglong District)	20. Nungba 23. Haochong	21. Khoupum	22. Longmei (Noney)
5.	**Churachandpur**	24. Churachandpur 27. Mualnuam 30. Kangvai	25. Sangaikot 28. Singngat 31. Samulamlan	26. Tuibuong 29. Henglep 32. Saikot
6.	**Pherzawl** (Bifurcated from the erstwhile Churachandpur District)	33. Pherzawl 36. Vangai Range	34. Thanlon	35. Parbung-Tipaimukh
7.	**Chandel**	37. Chandel	38. Chakpikarong	39. Khengjoy
8.	**Tengnoupal District** (Bifurcated from the erstwhile Chandel District)	40. Machi	41. Moreh	42. Tengnoupal
9.	**Ukhrul**	43. Ukhrul 46. Jessami	44. Lungchong-Maiphai	45. Chingai

Sl. No.	Name of District	Name of Sub-division		
10.	**Kamjong District** (Bifurcated from the erstwhile Ukhrul District)	47. Kamjong 50. Phungyar	48. Sahamphung	49. Kasom Khullen
11.	**Imphal East**	51. Porompat	52. Keirao Bitra	53. Sawombung
12.	**Jiribam** (Bifurcated from the erstwhile Imphal East District)	54. Jiribam	55. Borobekra	
13.	**Imphal West**	56. Lamshang 59. Wangoi	57. Patsoi	58. Lamphelpat
14.	**Bishnupur**	60. Nambol	61. Bishnupur	62. Moirang
15.	**Thoubal District**	63. Thoubal	64. Lilong	
16.	**Kakching** (Bifurcated from the erstwhile Thoubal District)	65. Kakching	66. Waikhong	

MUNICIPALITY

In Manipur there are altogether 9 municipalities which is headed by the Municipality Commission.

Sl. No.	Name of Municipal Council	Total No. of Wards
1.	Imphal Municipal Council	27
2.	Kakching Municipal Council	12
3.	Thoubal Municipal Council	18
4.	Jiribam Municipal Council	10
5.	Moirang Municipal Council	12
6.	Bishnupur Municipal Council	12
7.	Nambol Municipal Council	18
8.	Mayang Imphal Municipal Council	13
9.	Ningthoukhong Municipal Council	

NAGAR PANCHAYATS

There are 18 Nagar Panchayats in the state.

Sl. No.	Name of Nagar Panchayats	Total No. of Wards	Sl. No.	Name of Nagar Panchayats	Total No. of Wards
1.	Andro	12	10.	Heirok	12
2.	Lilong (Thoubal)	9	11.	Wangjing Lamding	9
3.	Lamshang	9	12.	Shikhong Sekmai	3
4.	Wangoi	12	13.	Yairipok	9
5.	Lamlai	9	14.	Sugnu	9
6.	Sekmai	9	15.	Oinam	9
7.	Thongkhong Laxmi Bazar	11	16.	Kakching Khunou	9
8.	Lilong (Imphal West)	9	17.	Kumbi	9
9.	Samurou	12	18.	Kwakta	9

HISTORY

PERIODS IN THE HISTORY OF MANIPUR

A careful study of a language may reveal a considerable amount of the historical events, the origin, migration, the art and culture of the people. Sir William Jones, a British judge in India in 1786 while studying the Sanskrit literature revealed that it bears a striking resemblance with other two ancient languages — Latin and Greek. The Sanskrit word for father 'Pitar' is astonishingly similar to the Greek and Latin 'Pater'. Similarly, Sanskrit 'Matar' Latin and Greek 'Mater' and English 'Mother' and Hindi 'Mata' share a considerable affinity. Two hundred years of linguistic research had provided evidences that one-third of the human race might have come from this Indo-European "common source", probably between 3500-2500 BC in the central Europe, from where people migrated to the West and East.

In case of the Meitei people, since there were no modern system of recording, where the sense of originality was always contemplated with the modern history, the reconstruction of the ancient manuscripts and languages has yielded a considerable knowledge on the history of ancient Manipur. The following is a brief history or Puwari of some prominent Meitei rulers with a view to bring out an understanding of the various developments in Meitei history, art, culture, tradition, sports, etc. The account is not complete but hope to provide an overall grasp on the history of Manipur.

The history of Manipur may be divided into four main periods: (i) **The Ancient period** (before Christ), (ii) **The early period** (1st-13th AD), (iii) **The Medieval period** (15-18th AD) and (iv) **The Modern period** (19-20th Century AD).

PRESENT MANIPUR

On 21 January 1972, Manipur was granted Statehood after several years of demand by All Manipur Students Union and several political organisations. The ceremony was performed at the Palace Polo ground in Imphal. In 1992, Meitei-lon (Manipuri) was included in the Eighth Schedule as one of the 22 official languages of India. Manipur has yet to see a proper road connection to the rest of India. Air transportations are provided from Kolkata, New Delhi, Gauhati and Silchar but much beyond the reach of commoners.

FAMOUS TITLES OF WELL KNOWN PERSONS

TITLE		NAME
❖ The Lion of Manipur	:	Bir Tikendrajit
❖ Mahakavi	:	Hijam Anganghal
❖ Melody King	:	Nongmaithem Pahari
❖ Melody Queen	:	Smt. Laishram Mema Devi
❖ Tarzan of Manipur	:	Irom Leikhendra
❖ Bob	:	Ralengnao Kathing
❖ Jananeta (leader of the people)	:	Hijam Irabot
❖ Kaksu	:	Meidigu Tonkonba
❖ Agayestha of the East	:	Atombapu Sharma
❖ Thangal General	:	Kangabam Chitananda Singha
❖ Leipok Keirungba	:	Leimapokpam Dev Singh

KINGS OF MANIPUR

Name	Period of reign (A.D.)	Number of Years/Months
❖ Nongda Lairen Pakhangba	33-154	121
❖ Khuiyoi Tompok	154-264	110
❖ Taothingmang	264-364	100
❖ Khui Ningonba	364-379	15
❖ Pengsiba	379-394	15
❖ Kaokhangba	394-411	17
❖ Naokhamba	411-428	17
❖ Naophangba	428-518	90
❖ Sameirang	518-568	50
❖ Wura Konthouba	568-658	90

Name	Period of reign (A.D.)	Number of Years/Months
❖ Naothingkhong	663-763	100
❖ Khongtekcha	763-773	10
❖ Keirencha	784-799	15
❖ Yaraba	799-821	22
❖ Ayangba	821-910	89
❖ Ningthoucheng	910-949	39
❖ Chenglie-Ipan-Lanthaba	949-969	20
❖ Keiphaba Yanglon	969-984	15
❖ Irengba	984-1074	90
❖ Loiyumba	1074-1112	48
❖ Loitongba	1122-1150	28

Name	Period of reign (A.D.)	Number of Years/Months
❖ Atom Yoiremba	1150-1163	13
❖ Iyanthaba	1163-1195	32
❖ Thayanthaba	1195-1231	36
❖ Chingthang Lanthaba	1231-1242	11
❖ Thingbai Shelhongba	1242-1247	5
❖ Puranthaba	1247-1263	16
❖ Khumomba	1263-1278	15
❖ Moiramba	1278-1302	24
❖ Thangbi Lanthaba	1302-1324	22
❖ Kongyamba	1324-1335	11
❖ Telheiba	1335-1355	20
❖ Tonaba	1355-1359	4
❖ Tabungba	1339-1394	35
❖ Lairenba	1394-1399	5
❖ Punsiba	1404-1432	28
❖ Ningthoukhomba	1432-1467	35
❖ Kyamba	1467-1508	41
❖ Koiremba	1508-1512	4
❖ Lamkhyamba	1512-1523	11
❖ Nonginphaba	1523-1524	1
❖ Kabomba	1524-1542	18
❖ Tangjamba	1542-1545	3
❖ Chalamba	1545-1562	17
❖ Mugyamba	1562-1597	35
❖ Khagemba	1597-1652	55
❖ Khunjaoba	1652-1666	14
❖ Paikhomba	1666-1697	31
❖ Charairongba	1697-1709	12
❖ Garibniwaj	1709-1748	39
❖ Chitshai	1748-1752	4
❖ Bharatsai	1752-1753	1

Name	Period of reign (A.D.)	Number of Years/Months
❖ Maramba	1753-1759	6
❖ Chingthangkhomba	1759-1762	3
❖ Maramba	1762-1763	1
❖ Chingthangkhomba	1763-1798	35
❖ Labanyachandra	1798-1801	3
❖ Madhuchandra	1801-1803	2
❖ Chourjit	1803-1813	10
❖ Marjit	1813-1819	6
❖ Takuningthou (Herachandra)	1819	1
❖ Yumjaotaba	1820	1
❖ Gambhir Singha	1821	6 months
❖ Jai Singha	1822	1
❖ Jadu Singha (Nongpok Chinslenkhomba)	1823	1
❖ Raghab Singha	1823-1824	1
❖ Nongchup Lamgaingamba (Bhadrasing)	1824	1
❖ Gambhir Singha (Chinglen Nongdrenkhomba)	1825-1834	9
❖ Chandrakirti (Ningthempishak)	1834-1844	10
❖ Nara Singha	1844-1850	6
❖ Debendra Singha	1850	3 months
❖ Chandrakirti (K.C.S.I.)	1850-1886	36
❖ Surchandra	1886-1890	4
❖ Kulachandra	1890-1891	1
❖ Churachand Singha	1891-1941	50
❖ Bodhachandra Singha	1941-1955	14

◀ IMPORTANT DATES IN MANIPUR HISTORY ▶

33 A.D. – The first king of Manipur was Pakhangba who reigned for 120 years.

154 A.D. – Khuiyoi Tompok ascended the throne and it is belived that during his reign 'Pung' (drum) was first invented.

264 A.D. – Taothing Mang ascended the throne.

568 – Wura Konthouba become a King.

1074 – King Loiyumba came to the throne during his reign many social reform took place.

1247 – Puranthaba became King and in his reign chinese invaded Manipur but was defeated.

1404 – Luwang Punsiba, who introduced the international game of Polo for the first time on the soil of Manipur, ascended the throne.

1467 – Kyamba, who was noted for his military and administration achievement ascended the throne.

1597 – Khangemba become a King and introduced first Manipur coins.

1704 – King Charairongba was initial into Vaishnavism with the result that Vaishnavism become state religion.

1714 – Garibaniwaj ascended the throne.

1736 – Garibaniwaj again with an army crossed Ningthee river and attacked and destroyed the town of Meyedu, on the bank of Yu river.

1762 – The first Alliance become Manipur and East India Company was made.

1765 – The second Burmese invasion took place.

1775 – Occurance of the worst flood known as 'Wang Khem Echao'.

1776 – Set-up the Govindajee Temple at Imphal by king Bheigyachandra.

1819 – 'Seven year Disertation' 1819 to 1825, Magazine wore a deserted look under the tyrancy of invading Burmese.

1826 – Making of the "Treaty of Yandaboo".

1833	–	Annexation of Jiribam to Manipur during the reign of Gambir Singh.
1834	–	The Kabaw Valley was handed over to Burma.
1885	–	First English school was established.
1891	–	The Government of India under the British declared war against Manipur; Yuvaraj Tikendrajit and General Thangal were executed by hanging at Pheida Pung (Present B.T. Park).
1904	–	First Nupeelal (Women's war against British)
1907	–	Manipur State Darbar was established to assist the Maharaja in the administration of Manipur.
1931	–	The hanging of Jadonang who was a great Zeliangrong leader.
1939	–	Nupeelal, i.e. Second Women's war against the misrule of the British and it continued for about 14 months.
1941	–	Maharaj Bodhachandra become the king of Manipur by succeeding to his father Chura Chand.
1944	–	The INA Flag Hoisted at Moirang.
1949	–	Merger agreement was signed between the government of India and Manipur.
1957	–	Manipur become one of the Union Territories under the Union Territories Act, 1956.
1960	–	Panchayati Raj System was introduced in Manipur.
1963	–	A Legislative assembly of 30 elected and 3 nominated was established under the Govt. of Union Territory Act, 1963; The AIR station of Imphal was inaugurated.
1967	–	President's Rule was imposed for the first time in Manipur.
1972	–	Manipur became a full fledged state.
1980	–	The Manipur university was established.
1987	–	TV transmission centre was opened.
1992	–	Manipur Language have included in the 8th Schedule of the Constitution of India by the 71st Amendment of Constitution.
1995	–	DD-2 metro channel of DDK-Imphal was opened.
1997	–	Divided the Imphal East & Imphal West District.
1999	–	The 5th National Games were held in Manipur. Manipur overall champion.
2000	–	Manipur Cup 2000, 5th International Invitation Polo Tournament at Imphal win Manipur Polo Team.
2002	–	The President of India APJ Abdul Kalam, inaugurated the 36 MW Heavey fuel based Power plant at Leimakhong, 20 Km from Imphal.
2004	–	Prime Minister Dr. Manmohan Singh handed over the Kangla Fort to the government of India.
2005	–	The first Chief Minister of Manipur M.K. Priyobrata passess away at his residence located in Konung Leikei at Palace Compound, Imphal.
2006	–	Former Chief Minister of Manipur R.K. Ranabir Singh passes away at his residence at Keishamthong Longiam Leirak, Imphal.
2007	–	Manipur gets second position in 33rd National Games held in Guwahati (February 9-18) with 51 gold, 32 silver and 40 bronze medals.
2008	–	The Manipur government has decided to construct 25 residential schools in the state with funding from the centre.
2009	–	Boxing icon M.C. Mary kom awarded with Rajiv Gandhi Khel Ratna award for 2008-09.
2010	–	Manipur won 18th Senior National Women's Football tournament.
2011	–	Manipur won Best State Award in 34th National Games-2011.
2012	–	Boxing icon M.C. Mary Kom won bronze medal in 2012 London Olympics.
2013	–	Chief Justice of India Altamas Kabir inaugurated the Manipur High Court on March 25, 2013.
2014	–	Seven Sportspersons from Manipur won medals (3 Gold and 4 Bronze) in Asian Games–2014 held in Incheon, South Korea.
2015	–	Binalakshmi Nepram wins L'oreal Paris Femina Women Awards 2015.
2016	–	Maurice Yengkhom and Chongtham Kuber Meitei got National Bravery Award; M.C. Mary Kom nominated in Rajya Sabha.
2017	–	BJP leader N. Biren Singh became new CM of Manipur.
2018	–	The Union Cabinet approved the ordinance of setting India's first National Sports University in Imphal.

GEOGRAPHY

Manipur has a total surface area of 22,327 sq. km. forming 0.7% of the total land surface of the Indian Union. It is situated between the parallels 23°50'N -25°42'N and the meridians 92°58'E - 94°45'E. It has a border of 854 km of which 352 km is international border with Myanmar on the east. The remaining 502 km long border separates her from the neighboring states of Nagaland on the north, Assam on the west and Mizoram on the south and the south west. Physiographically the land is divisible into a central valley and the surrounding mountains. The plain or the valley is approximately 2238 sq. km. accounting to 10% of the total state area. Out of this an area of 550 sq. km. is occupied by lakes, wetlands, barren uplands and hillocks. The valley is oval shape with a NNW-SSE orientation and has a gentle slope towards the south measuring 798 m above m.s.l. at the extreme north and 746 m above m.s.l. at the Southern end. The Imphal city stands at an altitude of 790 m above m.s.l.

GEOLOGY

Dayal and Duara (1963) outlined the classification of rocks in Manipur which is more or less in line with that of Oldham (1883) with some modifications after the views of Pascoe (1929) and Evans (1932). The geologic succession according to them is

Age	*Rock Type*
Recent to sub-recent	Alluvium
Oligocene	Barails
Intrusive rocks	Disang Series
Intrusive rocks (Cretaceous to early Eocene)	Surpentinities
Cretaceous	Axials

SEISMOLOGY

The hills of the whole zone of the eastern frontier of India including Manipur were built up during the late Pleistocene period and hence isostatic and seismic balances are yet to be attained. Manipur falls in one of the most seismically active zones of the Trans-Asiatic Earthquake Belt.

CLIMATE

Besides the influence by its locations around the latitudes just north of the Tropic of Cancer, the climate of the state is governed by the relief of land and the rain bearing winds viz. the South-West Monsoon in summer and the North-East Monsoon and the Mediterranean winds in winter. The eastern lowlands along the Indo-Burma border and the Western Assam Manipur border lowlands fall between the altitudes 30-100 metre above m.s.l. and thus reigned by a tropical climate. The Manipur Valley at a height of 780-800 metre above m.s.l. has sub-tropical climate while the higher reaches of the mountains surrounding the valley have a temperate climate.

RIVERS

Rivers along with other natural and man-made sources play an important role in irrigation in the state of Manipur. Irang, Barrak and Turel Achouba are some of the major rivers of the state.

Thoubal River : Thoubal river starts from Huimi hills of Ukhrul and flow westwards upto Yaingangpokpi and turning southwards, joins the Imphal river at Irong Ichin.

Iril River : It rises in the Lamkui and Kadam Hills of the north-eastern Mao. After flowing southwards, it joins the Imphal Rivers at Lilong area.

Barrak River : It is the biggest river of Manipur. Its source is 16 km east of Mao Police Station in Senapati District. Barrak, at its source is known as 'Sanglook'. It leaves Manipur area near Lalpur and flows towards Cachar, Assam. The Makru and the Irang are two main tributaries of this river.

Turel Achouba : Turel Achouba is also known as Imphal or Manipur river. It is the longest river of the state. Its source is Bolen Pat at 197 feet above sea level and 15 km from Kangpokpi area. It also joins the stream of Ningthee or Chindwin river of Burma in its way.

RIVERS IN HILL AREAS

Some of the important rivers of the hill areas of Manipur includes Makru, Barrak, Irang, Leimatak, Tuyungbi, Maklang, Chingai, Chalou, Taret Lok, Lokchao, Chakpi, Khuga and Tuivai river.

MAIN RIVERS : AT A GLANCE

River	Length (km.)	Aspect	Source	Destination
Barrak	84.39	West	Karong-Mao area	Brahmaputra River
Imphal	38	South	Bolen Pat in Kangpokpi area	Chindwin River
Iril	57.27	South	Lakhamai of Pural Block	Imphal River
Irang	28.13	South Western Block	Langka Chongjan area of Kangpokpi	Barrak River
Ithai	24.83	South	Selsi Thoubung area	Iril River

LAKES

The state of Manipur is characterised by numerous lakes. Many of them are also known for its scenic and aesthetic beauty. Loktak lake, the biggest of North East India, is also a part of Manipur. It is also famous for its great beauty.

LAKES IN HILL AREAS

There are two major lakes in hilly areas of Manipur. These are Kachouphung Lake in Ukhrul district and Zailad Lake in Tamenglong district.

MAIN LAKES : AT A GLANCE

Lakes	District
Loktak Lake	Bishnupur
Kharung Pat	Bishnupur
Heingang Pat	Imphal East
Kachouphung Lake	Ukhrul
Waithou Pat	Thoubal
Pumlen Pat	Thoubal
Utra Pat	Bishnupur
Zailad Lake	Tamenglong
Loushi Pat	Bishnupur
Ikop Pat	Thoubal
Ishok Pat	Bishnupur
Sana Pat	Bishnupur
Loukoi Pat	Bishnupur

WATERFALLS

Waterfalls		District
Barrak Waterfalls	:	Tamenglong
Sadu Chiru Waterfalls	:	Bishnupur
Khayang Waterfalls	:	Ukhrul
Leimram Waterfalls	:	Bishnupur
Dilily Waterfalls	:	Ukhrul

HILLS

- Cheirao-Ching
- Somrah
- Kanpum
- Mayangkhang
- Nupitel
- Khhunho Spurs
- Yomadoung
- Koubru Leikha
- Laison
- Kala Naga
- Chakka Nungba
- Chinganguba
- Kasom
- Kopru-Laimatol
- Nunjaibong
- Hawbi
- Thumion
- Bharuni
- Thangjing
- Sirohi Frar

CAVES

Caves	District
Tonglon	Churachandpur
Sangboo	Chandel
Tharon	Tamenglong
Khangkhui	Ukhrul
Hungdung Mangva	Ukhrul
Khukse	Churachandpur

PEAKS

Peaks	Height (m)	District
Leikot	2,832	Tamenglong
Tampaba	2,564	—
Mount Tenipu (Essau)	2,994	Senapati
Siroi	2,835	Ukhrul
Khayangbung	2,833	Ukhrul

Art and Culture

Folk Dances

Some Famous folk dances of Manipur are as follows:

Ras Lila : The Ras Lila, the epitome of Manipuri classical dance is inter-woven through the celestial and eternal love of Radha and Krishna as has been described in the Hindu scriptures and reveals the sublime and transcendental love of Krishna and Radha and the Gopies' devotion to the Lord. It is generally performed in an enclosure in front of the temple throughout the night and watched with a deep sense of devotion. Ras performances are seasonal and varied and performed at the temple of Shree Shree Govindajee in Imphal on the nights of Basanta Purnima, Sarada Purnima and Kartik Purnima and at local temples later. Ras performances are mainly of four types—Vasanta Ras, Kunja Ras, Maha Ras and Nata/Nitya Ras. At the temple of Shri Shri Govinda, Vasanta Ras is performed on the full-moon night of Hiyangei (November). After they are performed at the temple of Shri Shri Govinda, they are performed at any time of the year.

Nupa Pala : Nupa Pala which is otherwise known as Kartal Cholom or Cymbal Dance is a characteristic of the Manipuri style of dance and music. The initial movements of this dance are soft and serene, gradually gathering momentum. It is a group performance of male partners, using cymbals and wearing snow white ball-shaped large turbans, who sing and dance to the accompaniment of Mridanga, an ancient classical drum "Pung" as it is called in Manipuri. The Nupa Pala acts as a prologue to the Ras Lila dances, besides an independent performance too, in connection with religious rites.

Pung Cholom : Pung or Manipuri Mridanga is the soul of Manipuri Sankirtana music and Classical Manipuri Dance. Khuyoi Tompok who ruled over Manipur during (154-264 A.D) introduced the pung having only one beating face. Since then, it has developed to the present form of 'Meitei Pung with two beating faces. Today, 'Pung Cholom' which is a traditional dance form of the pung drummers has earned international acclamation for its charming artistic display.

Maibi Dance : During the festival of Lai-Haraoba which is an annual ritual festival of the Meiteis, the inhabitants of the valley of Manipur, the Maibis, the priestesses considered to be sprirtual mediums, trace through their dances the whole concept of cosmogony of the Meitei people and describe their way of life. Beginning with the process of creation, they show the construction of houses and various occupations of the people to sustain themselves. It is a kind of re-living of the way of life of the past.

Khamba Thoibi Dance : Khamba Thoibi dance is a duet of male and female partners, a dance of dedication to the sylvan deity, Thangjing of Moirang, is the depiction of the dance performed by Khamba and Thoibi, the hero and heroine of the Moirang episode of the hoary past. This, with the "Maibi" dance (Priestess dance), the "Leima Jagoi" etc. form the "Lai Haraoba" dance. The "Lai Haraoba" dance, in many ways, is the fountainhead of the modern Manipuri dance form. This dance is a part and parcel of Moirang Lai-Haraoba. It is believed that the legendary hero - Khamba, and heroin - Thoibi danced together before the Lord Thangjing, a celebrated deity of Moirang, a village in the South-West of Manipur which is known for its rich cultural traditions, for peace and prosperity of the land.

Some Important Tribal Dances of Manipur

1. Kabui Naga Dance
2. Tangkhul Naga Dance – *Tangkhul Hunting Dance, Tangkhul War Dance, Lakhahganui Dance i.e., Virgin Dance etc.*
3. Tarao War Dance etc.
4. Mao Maram Dance
5. Paite Dance – *Dak Lam, Jangta Lam, Phit Lam, Ton Lam and Silam Lam*
6. Thadou Kuki Dance

Folk Songs

Some famous folk songs of Manipur are as follows:

Wari Liba : It is an indigenous art form of telling stories prevalent in the State since the 17th century. The Mahabharata and the Ramayana are the themes of such story telling.

Khulang Ishei : Manipuri folk song is known as 'Khulang Ishei'. It is popular for its thematic and romantic contents. The folk songs are commonly sung by the rural folk and hill men at the time of harvesting, collecting firewood, hunting and fishing.

Khongjom Parva : It is a musical narration of the Battle of Khongjom fought between the Manipuris and the British in April 1891. Dhobi Leinou started singing Khongjom Parva by thumping his hands on the knee and some times used an empty tin to thump upon. The Khongjom Parva narrators glorify the Manipuris soldiers who sacrificed their lives for the sake of their motherland. Today the theme of singing Khongjom Parva includes the stories of Khamba and Thoibi, the Ramayana, the Mahabharata and the exploits of the kings of Manipur. The singer uses only a Dholak while singing.

Pena-Ishei : It is an ancient folk song of Manipur which is sung with a musical instrument called "Pena". This song narrates the popular stories of Manipur. Pena is a stringed musical instrument of Manipur. Its origin may be traced back to a hoary past. It is called Bena in parts of Assam. It is made up of two parts viz the penamasa and pena cheijing. Earlier, Pena was usually played by its player to invoke the gods and goddesses. But today, this musical instrument is played in musical concerts and other performances also.

Ougri : This is a very ancient type of song and sung usually in praise of Sun, Moon, Kings etc. It is mostly sung in Lai Haraoba festivals.

Moibung Esei : The conch music of Manipuri is quite distinct and extraordinary. An artist of it can blow two conches simultaneously producing enchanting music.

Nat Esei : It is a peculiar type of song composed and originated by the Manipuris. It is sung in both Manipuri and Bengali languages and the theme is usually of Hindu Gods and Goddesses.

Khubak Esei : This kind of song is performed by two sides of participants standing at opposite sides and facing at each other. The rhythmic clapping of palms is its accompanying music.

Khulang Esei : This kind of song is sung without any musical instrument and the theme of this type of song is related to love & romance. It is known as Heplee in archaic language.

TRADITIONAL MUSICAL INSTRUMENTS
1. Pung (Drum)
2. Kartal (Cymbals)
3. Pena (Sitar)
4. Manjira or Mandilla (Metal jingles)
5. Sipa (Flute)
6. Tingteila (Violin)
7. Mazo (Women's mouth-piece)
8. Khol (Drum), etc.

DANCE & CULTURE TRAINING INSTITUTES
- ○ Government Dance College (Shree Shree Govindajee Natanalya) – Palace Compound, Imphal.
- ○ J.N. Manipur Dance Academy – Near D.M. College Compound, Imphal.

MANIPURI STATE KALA AKADEMI
This Akademi was set up by the Government of Manipur in the year 1971. It is the first of its kind in the eastern region of India. It is an autonomous organization for the promotion and coordinating of cultural activities of the people of Manipur both of the valley and hills.

MUSEUM

MANIPUR STATE MUSEUM
This museum, located near the Imphal Pologround has a fairly good display of the state's heritage and a collection of portraits of Manipur's former rulers. Items of special interests are costumes, arms and weapons, relics and historical documents.

The Manipur State Museum was inaugurated by the late Prime Minister of India, Smt. Indira Gandhi on 23rd September, 1969. During 49 years, this Museum has become a fullfledged multipurpose Museum comprising of various Galleries like—Ethnology, Archeology, Natural History, Painting, Jallan, Children's Gallery and an open air gallery for housing the 78ft long boat called Hiyang Hiren (Royal boat).

Apart from the normal functions of Museum, it took up various activities like Museum awareness programmes, Conservation of Biological specimens, Cultural appreciation course, Science fairs, Thematic exhibition, Mobile exhibition etc.

Manipur State Museum has also taken up numerous sponsor programmes through National and International Museums.

IMPORTANT PLACES OF WORSHIP

All the communities and religions celebrate their respective religious festivals or days with devotion and unflinching commitment. Some of the major worship places are given below:

Kangla Temple	— 4th Assam Rifles Ground
Sanamahee Temple	— 1st Batalion, M.R.
Jain Digamber Temple	— Paona Road
Govindajee Temple	— Palace Ground
ISKON Temple	— Airport Road
Hanuman Thakur Temple	— Near Palace Ground
Gurdwar Temple	— Thangal Bazar
Jame Masjid	— Masjid Road
Hiyangthang Lairembi Temple	— Hiyangthan
M.B.C. Central Church	— Deulahland
Moirang Thangjing Temple	— Moirang

FESTIVALS

Manipur celebrates a number of peculiar festivals of its own with great pomp and joy. Some of them are:

Lai-Haraoba : Lai Haraoba is one of the most important indigenous ritual festivals celebrated by the Meitei community of Manipur. It is celebrated to propitiate and please the ancestral deities to get their blessings in return. It depicts the act of creating universe and its objects, and unveils the endless journey of universe through its ritualistic performances. It is celebrated in Manipur since time immemorial and is being continued till today.

Yaoshang (Dol Jatra) : Celebrated for five days commencing from the full-moon day of Phalgun (February/March), Yaoshang is the premier festival of Manipur. The Thabal Chongba, a kind of Manipuri folk dance in which boys and girls hold hands and dance away their blues in festive tube-lit ambience is an inseparable part of the festival.

Ratha Jatra : One of the greatest festivals of the Hindus of Manipur, the festival is celebrated for about 10 days in the month of Ingen (June/July). Lord Jagannath leaves his temple in a Rath locally known as Kang pulled by pilgrims who vie with one another for this honour.

Ramjan ID (The premier festival of Manipur Muslims) : Ramjan Id is the most popular festival of the Manipuri Muslims (Meitei Pangal) and is observed in the usual spirits of joy and festivities as in other Muslim world. Ramjan is the ninth month of Hijri year.

Kut (Festival of Kuki-Chin-Mizo) : It is an autumn festival of the different tribes of Kuki-Chin-Mizo groups of Manipur. The festival has been variously described at different places amongst different tribes as Chavang-Kut or Khodou etc. It is a happy occasion for the villagers whose food stock is bountiful after a year of hard labour. The festival is a thanks giving feasts with songs and dances in merriment and joviality for all, in honour of the giver of an abundant harvest, it is observed on the first day of November every year.

Gang-Ngai (Festival of Kabui Nagas) : Celebrated for five days in the month of Wakching (December/January), Gang-Ngai is an important festival of the Kabui Nagas. The festival opens with the omen taking ceremony on the first day and the rest of the days are associated with common feast, dances of old men and women and of boys and girls, presentation of farewell gifts etc. From 1997, it starts from January 21.

Chumpha (Festival of Tangkhul Nagas) : Chumpha, generally the festival of Tangkhul Nagas, is celebrated for seven days in the month of December. It is a great festival of Tangkhul Nagas. The festival is held after harvest. The last three days are devoted to social gatherings and rejoicing. Unlike other festivals women play a special role in the festival. The concluding part of the festival ends with a procession within the village.

Christmas (Festival of Christians) : The Christmas is the greatest festival of all the Christians of Manipur, observed for two days on December 24 and 25. Prayers, reading of Gospels, eating, singing of hymns, lectures on Christ, sports etc., form the major part of the festival. In some villages where the inhabitants are well-off, the celebration continues till January 1 on which the New Years day is also observed.

Cheiraoba (The Manipur New Year) : During the festival, people clean and decorate their houses and prepare special festive dishes which are first offered to various deities. Celebrated during the month of April, a part of the ritual entails villagers climbing the nearest hill tops in belief that it will enable them to rise to greater heights in their worldly life. The Pangals (Manipuri Muslims) also observe it.

Heikru Hidongba : Celebrated in the month of September, a festival of joy, with little religious significance along a 16 metre wide boat. Long narrow boats are used to accommodate a large number of rowers. Idol of Lord Vishnu is installed before the commencement of the race.

Ningol Chakouba : It is a remarkable social festival of the Meiteis. Married women of the family who were married to distant places come to the parental house along with her children and enjoy sumptuous feast. It is a form of family rejoinder to revive familial affection. The festival is also observed by the Pangals to a certain extent now-a-days. It is observed on the second day of the new moon in the Manipuri month of Hiyangei (November).

Lui-Ngai-Ni : It is a collective festival of the Nagas observed on the 15th day of February every year. This is a seed-sowing festival after which tribes belonging to the Naga group begin their cultivation. Social gathering, songs, dances and rejoicing highlight the festivity. The annual festival also plays a great role in boosting the morale and strengthening the bond of Naga solidarity.

Kwak Jatra : Goddess Durga is propitiated with pomp and ceremony in this festival. It is celebrated in the month of October and represents the victory of righteousness over evil.

FESTIVALS OF MANIPUR : AT A GLANCE

Festivals	Celebrated by	Time of Celebration
○ Lai Haraoba	Meiteis	May
○ Rath Yatra	Hindus	July
○ Yaoshang (Dol Jatra)	Hindus	February/March
○ Christmas	Christians	25th December
○ Mahavir Jayanti	Jains	April
○ Depawali	Hindus	October / November
○ Cheiraoba	Meiteis	April
○ Chumpha	Tangkhul Nagas	December
○ Gan Ngai	Kabui Nagas	16th January
○ Heikru Hitongba	Meiteis	September
○ Kwak Yatra (Durga Puja)	Hindus	September / October
○ Kut	Kuki Chin Mizos	November
○ Lui-Ngai-Ni	Nagas	15th February
○ Mera Nongma Panba	Meiteis	September
○ Ningol Chakkouba	Meiteis	November

SOME TRIBAL FESTIVALS OF MANIPUR

Tribes	Festivals
Anal	Sungkhomlkham, Mikhemphan, Ikam, Philthabla, Inhla, etc.
Aimol	Reeyan
Chothe	Inampeilin
Hmar	Butu Chonglawa
Kabui	Gan-Ngai
Kharam	Lamtoul Kalouh
Kuki	Chapchar Kut, Mimkut, Chavang Kut
Mao	Chithuni
Naga	Lui-Ngai-Ni
Tangkhul	Shimsak Kasa, Chumpha, Thisham, Yarra, Mangkhap, Luira, Darreo etc.
Thadou	Chon
Zeliangrong	Gudui Ngai, Rih Ngai

❑❑❑

CENSUS 2011

The Census of India 2011, is historic and epoch making being the second census of the twenty-first century. It reveals benchmark data on the state of abundant human resources available in the country, their demography, culture and economic structure at a juncture, which marks a centennial and millenial transition.

Census of India comprises of Population, Population-Density, Sex Ratio and Literacy. One of the important indices of population concentration in census is the density of population which is the number of persons per square kilometre. Sex ratio is the number of females per thousand males while a person aged seven, and above, who can both read and write with understanding in any language, is treated as literate.

The districts of the states play an important role in census. As an administrative unit, district assumes a lot of significance in the context of decentralized planning and implementation of various plans and programmes. Therefore, deciding on an appropriate size of a district in terms of population and geographical area is a vital and essential element in creating an effective administrative set up.

Census 2011 reveals that Tamenglong is the least populous district of Manipur while the Imphal West is the most literate district. Imphal West tops in the category of sex ratio, whereas child population (0-6) years is higher in Thoubal than any other district. Given below are the tables showing population, density, literacy rate etc. district wise for the entire state of Manipur.

POPULATION

Manipur : 2,855,794 (*Males:* 1,438,586 *Females:* 1,417,208)

Sl.No.	District	Population	Male	Female
1	Senapati	479,148	247,323	231,825
2	Tamenglong	1,40,651	72,371	68,280
3	Churachandpur	2,74,143	1,38,820	1,35,323
4	Bishnupur	2,37,399	1,18,782	1,18,617
5	Thoubal	4,22,168	2,10,845	2,11,323
6	Imphal West	5,17,992	2,55,054	2,62,938
7	Imphal East	4,56,113	2,26,094	2,30,019
8	Ukhrul	1,83,998	94,718	89,280
9	Chandel	1,44,182	74,579	69,603

DECADAL GROWTH RATE

Manipur (1991-2001) : 24.86%,   (2001-2011) : 24.50%

Sl.No.	District	1991-2001	2001-2011
1	Senapati	36.09	68.9
2	Tamenglong	29.23	26.1
3	Churachandpur	29.36	20.3
4	Bishnupur	15.27	13.9
5	Thoubal	23.87	15.9
6	Imphal West	16.70	16.6
7	Imphal East	19.49	15.5
8	Ukhrul	28.83	30.7
9	Chandel	66.62	21.9

SEX RATIO

District Wise Sex Ratio in Manipur (1971-2011)

Sl.No.	District	1971	1981	1991	2001	2011
1	Senapati	950	929	942	928	937
2	Tamenglong	1016	975	935	922	943
3	Churachandpur	976	929	931	993	975
4	Bishnupur	–	–	984	1004	999
5	Thoubal	–	–	980	998	1002
6	Imphal West	–	–	979	1007	1031
7	Imphal East	–	–	966	992	1017
8	Ukhrul	969	917	884	920	943
9	Chandel	975	935	913	986	933
	State	980	971	958	978	985

DENSITY

Manipur (2001) : 97; (2011) : 128

Sl.No.	District	2001	2011
1	Senapati	48	146
2	Tamenglong	25	32
3	Churachandpur	50	60
4	Bishnupur	420	479
5	Thoubal	708	821
6	Imphal West	856	998
7	Imphal East	557	643
8	Ukhrul	31	40
9	Chandel	36	44

LITERACY RATE

Manipur (2001)	: 70.50	Manipur (2011)	: 76.94
Males	: 80.30	Males	: 83.58
Females	: 60.50	Females	: 70.26

Sl.No.	District	2001			2011		
		Total	Male	Female	Total	Male	Female
1	Senapati	59.8	67.9	51.2	63.60	69.21	57.67
2	Tamenglong	59.2	68.7	49.0	70.05	76.09	63.69
3	Churachandpur	70.6	77.7	63.1	82.78	86.97	78.50
4	Bishnupur	67.6	79.6	55.7	75.85	85.11	66.68
5	Thoubal	66.4	80.4	52.5	74.47	85.00	64.09
6	Imphal West	80.2	89.2	71.3	86.08	92.24	80.17
7	Imphal East	75.4	85.5	65.3	81.95	88.77	75.32
8	Ukhrul	73.1	80.1	65.4	81.35	85.52	76.95
9	Chandel	56.2	64.3	48.0	71.11	77.78	63.96

❏❏❏

Multiple Choice Questions

1. What is the total area of Manipur?
   A. 22327 sq. km.
   B. 22223 sq. km.
   C. 22732 sq. km.
   D. 22237 sq. km.

2. In which year Manipur became the twentieth state of the Indian Union?
   A. 1970
   B. 1971
   C. 1972
   D. 1973

3. In Manipur Jadonang was hanged in August, 1931. Who was Jadonang?
   A. A great Naga leader
   B. A great Zome leader
   C. A great Zeliangrong leader
   D. A great Meitei leader

4. In which year revered king Pakhangba ascended the throne?
   A. 30 A.D.
   B. 31 A.D.
   C. 32 A.D.
   D. 33 A.D.

5. When was the Manipur Constitution Act passed?
   A. 1947
   B. 1948
   C. 1949
   D. 1950

6. In which year Nara Singha became the King of Manipur?
   A. 1832
   B. 1840
   C. 1844
   D. 1848

7. How many states touch the boundary of Manipur?
   A. 3
   B. 4
   C. 5
   D. 6

8. In which year was the Battle of Khongjom fought?
   A. 1885
   B. 1887
   C. 1890
   D. 1891

9. In which year did Manipur become a Union Territory?
   A. 1950
   B. 1955
   C. 1956
   D. 1960

10. When was Shillong Accord signed?
    A. 15 Oct., 1949
    B. 20 Sep., 1950
    C. 25 Nov., 1952
    D. 15 Aug., 1957

11. Who was the last King of Manipur?
    A. Maharaja Gambhir Singh
    B. Maharaja Tikendrajit Singh
    C. Maharaja Ranjit Singh
    D. Maharaja Purandar Singh

12. During the first world war, which King ruled over in Manipur?
    A. Maharaja Nara Singha
    B. Maharaja Garibniwaz
    C. Maharaja Chandrakirti Singh
    D. Maharaja Koineng Singh

13. During the reign of which King of Kangleipak was the title ''Manipur'' named after it?
    A. Maharaja Churachand Singh
    B. Maharaja Garibniwaz
    C. Maharaja Bhagyachandra
    D. Maharaja Chandrakirti Singh

14. What is the Capital of Manipur?
    A. Imphal
    B. Bishnupur
    C. Churachandpur
    D. Thoubal

15. What is the total number of districts in Manipur?
    A. Eight
    B. Sixteen
    C. Ten
    D. Twelve

16. What is the total population of Manipur as per the 2011 census?
    A. 30,48,756
    B. 28,55,794
    C. 32,27,309
    D. 22,18,960

17. When was the census started in Manipur?
    A. 1750
    B. 1752
    C. 1757
    D. 1760

18. When did Manipur come under the British rule?
    A. 12 April, 1891
    B. 12 March, 1890
    C. 10 May, 1885
    D. 5 June, 1860

19. How many District Councils are there in Manipur?
    A. Five
    B. Six
    C. Seven
    D. Eight

20. How many Legislative Assembly Constituencies are there in Manipur?
    A. 50
    B. 60
    C. 70
    D. 75

21. Which is the biggest river in Manipur?
    A. Iril
    B. Sekmai
    C. Barrak
    D. Nambul

22. Which one of the following is not a physical division of Manipur?
    A. Churachandpur
    B. Manipur Hills
    C. Manipur Valley
    D. Jiribam Plains

23. How many MLAs are elected from the Hill Districts to the Manipur Legislative Assembly?
A. 20   B. 25
C. 30   D. 35

24. In Manipur Assembly how many seats are reserved for Scheduled Tribes?
A. 15   B. 19
C. 25   D. 30

25. On what date Martyr's Day is observed in Manipur?
A. 10th August   B. 13th August
C. 15th August   D. 18th August

26. In which District Khangkhui Caves are located?
A. Chandel   B. Ukhrul
C. Senapati   D. Tamenglong

27. Which is the first Manipuri colour feature film?
A. Imagee Ningthem   B. Brojendrogi Luhongba
C. Langlen Thadai   D. Matamgi Manipur

28. Which is the first Manipuri feature film?
A. Ishanou   B. Khonjel
C. Saphabee   D. Matamgi Manipur

29. Who is the first Manipuri to win the Arjuna Award?
A. Dingko Singh   B. N. Kunjarani Devi
C. M.C. Mary Kom   D. Suraj Lata Devi

30. Who is the first Manipuri to win the Sahitya Academy Award?
A. Pacha Meeitei
B. N. Kunjamohan Singh
C. L. Samarendra Singh
D. A. Minaketan Singh

31. Who was the first woman MLA (Member of Legislative Assembly)?
A. Kim Gangte   B. W. Leima Devi
C. Hangmila Shaija   D. None of these

32. Who was the first Chief Minister of Manipur State?
A. M. Kaireng Singh   B. L. Thambou Singh
C. F.F. Pearson   D. R.K. Dorendra Singh

33. Who was the first Lok Sabha member from the Inner Parliamentary Constituency of Manipur?
A. L. Jugeswar Singh   B. L. Achaw Singh
C. S. Tombi Singh   D. M. Meghachandra

34. Who was the first Lok Sabha member from the outer Parliamentary Constituency of Manipur?
A. Rungsung Suisa   B. Rishang Keishing
C. Paokai Haokip   D. Yangmaso Shaiza

35. Heikru Hitongba festival was introduced in Manipur in :
A. 1778   B. 1775
C. 1779   D. 1772

36. Who was the first Governor of Manipur?
A. L.P. Singh   B. S.M.H. Burney
C. K.V. Krishna Rao   D. B.K. Nehru

37. Who was the first Rajya Sabha M.P. from Manipur?
A. Ng. Tompok Singh
B. L. Lalit Madhob Sharma
C. S. Krishnamohan Singh
D. Salam Tombi Singh

38. How many members represent Manipur in the Rajya Sabha?
A. 1   B. 2
C. 3   D. 4

39. How many members represent Manipur in the Lok Sabha?
A. 2   B. 4
C. 5   D. 7

40. In which year Manipur became a full fledged state?
A. 1970   B. 1972
C. 1973   D. 1974

41. When did the Gauhati High Court come into existence in Manipur?
A. 21-1-1972   B. 21-4-1970
C. 21-4-1971   D. 21-4-1973

42. In which of the following rivers does the Imphal river fall?
A. The Iril river   B. The Loktak lake
C. The Brahmaputra   D. The Chindwin river

43. In which year Imphal District was divided?
A. 1995   B. 1996
C. 1997   D. 1998

44. When was the "Khongjom War" fought in Manipur?
A. 23-7-1891   B. 23-6-1891
C. 23-4-1891   D. 16-9-1890

45. Who is the first olympian from Manipur?
A. P. Nilkamal Singh   B. N. Kunjarani Devi
C. H.L. Tangkhul   D. Thoiba Singh

46. 'Nongyeen' was declared as the State Bird of Manipur in the year :
A. 1986   B. 1987
C. 1988   D. 1989

47. The first Legislative Assembly was inaugurated in Manipur in :
A. 1961   B. 1962
C. 1963   D. 1964

48. In which lake the Sendra island is situated?
A. Loukai lake   B. Waithou lake
C. Ikop lake   D. Loktak lake

49. Which is the 'State Bird' of Manipur?
A. Tragopan   B. Ashangba
C. Nongyeen   D. Langmeidon

50. Who is the first sports person from Manipur to win a gold medal in the Asian Games?
A. N. Kunjarani Devi   B. Suraj Lata Devi
C. M.C. Mary Kom   D. Dingko Singh

51. In which year Manipuri language was included in the 8th schedule of the Indian Constitution?
A. 1990　　B. 1991
C. 1992　　D. 1993

52. Pamheiba was the most powerful kings of Manipur in whose reign the state reached the pinnacle as a powerful state. His original name was—
A. Madhuchandra　　B. Churachand Singh
C. Chandrakirti　　D. Garibniwaz

53. When did Doordarshan start in Manipur?
A. 30 April, 1990　　B. 30 April, 1991
C. 30 April, 1992　　D. 30 April, 1993

54. What is the percentage of land under the cultivation in Manipur to its area?
A. Nearly 10%　　B. Narly 20%
C. Nearly 30%　　D. Nearly 40%

55. Who is the poet of "Dustbin Amagi Warri"?
A. R. Constantine　　B. T.C. Hudson
C. T. Ibopishak Singh　　D. Vedaja Sanjenbam

56. How many recognised Tribal communities are in Manipur?
A. 30　　B. 32
C. 34　　D. 36

57. How many years Manipur remained as a part state and Union Territory?
A. Twenty　　B. Twenty one
C. Twenty two　　D. Twenty four

58. During the reign of which King in Manipur the first Telegraph line and Telegraph office were established?
A. Maharaja Chandrakirti in 1886
B. Maharaja Madhuchandra in 1801
C. Maharaja Yumjaotaba in 1820
D. Maharaja Churachand Singh in 1891

59. Which period was known as the "Dark Period" in Manipur?
A. 1730 A.D. to 1750 A.D.
B. 1755 A.D. to 1826 A.D.
C. 1650 A.D. to 1726 A.D.
D. 1820 A.D. to 1850 A.D.

60. "Manipur is the Jewel of India and Switzerland of the East". Who said this quotation?
A. Jawaharlal Nehru　　B. Mahatma Gandhi
C. Subhash Chandra Bose　　D. M. Kaireng Singh

61. Who introduced Polo in Manipur?
A. Thayanthaba　　B. Ebudhou Marjing
C. Garibniwaj　　D. Koiremba

62. Who introduced "Boat Race" in Manipur?
A. Thangbi Lanthabu　　B. Keiphaba Yanglon
C. Ninthou Punshiba　　D. Gambhir Singha

63. When did Hindu Priest Santidash Goshai come to Manipur?
A. 1550 A.D.　　B. 1600 A.D.
C. 1760 A.D.　　D. 1716 A.D.

64. When was Manipur State Film Festival started?
A. 1982　　B. 1983
C. 1984　　D. 1985

65. What is the state language of Manipur?
A. Manipuri　　B. English
C. Hindi　　D. None of these

66. In Manipuri week days 'Nongmaijing' is known as :
A. Monday　　B. Sunday
C. Tuesday　　D. Wednesday

67. In which year was 'Meitei Chanu' the first journal of Manipur published?
A. 1920　　B. 1922
C. 1924　　D. 1926

68. The number of Jila Parishads in Manipur is :
A. 3　　B. 4
C. 5　　D. 6

69. 'Chon Festival' is celebrated by which tribe of Manipur?
A. Aimol　　B. Kabui Naga
C. Thadou　　D. Kuki

70. How many alphabets were there in the original Meitei language?
A. 20　　B. 22
C. 25　　D. 27

71. When did Doordarshan's Metro Channel (DD2) start in Manipur?
A. December 23, 1995　　B. December 23, 1990
C. December 23, 1991　　D. December 23, 1992

72. The historic Kangla Fort Complex was formally handed back to the people of Manipur in the presence of the former Prime Minister Manmohan Singh on :
A. 20th November, 2004　　B. 20th November, 2005
C. 20th November, 2006　　D. 22nd November, 2006

73. When was the first "Nupi Lal" happened in Manipur?
A. 1904 A.D.　　B. 1905 A.D.
C. 1906 A.D.　　D. 1907 A.D.

74. In which district of Manipur can we find "DZUKU LILY"?
A. Imphal East　　B. Chandel
C. Senapati　　D. Thoubal

75. Which Manipuri scholar was called the "Agyestha of the East" by Smiti Kumar Chatterjee?
A. Shyam Sharma　　B. E. Nilakanta Singh
C. C. Joshua Thomas　　D. Atombapu Sharma

76. The founder of the Praja Sameleni was :
A. Hijam Irabat Singh　　B. Lalita Madhop
C. Elangbam Tompok　　D. Aaiga Bankabihari

77. Who is the author of the book 'Labangalata'?
A. Lucy Zehol   B. Khwairakpam Chaoba
C. M.K. Singh   D. E.W. Dun

78. The Sangai Deer is found at which National Park/wild life sanctuary in Manipur?
A. Sirohi
B. Keilam
C. Keibul Lamjao
D. Yaingangpokpi Lakchao

79. Tharon caves are located in which district of Manipur?
A. Chandel   B. Thoubal
C. Tamenglong   D. Senapati

80. What is the state tree of Manipur?
A. Teak   B. Pine
C. Parkia Javanica   D. Uningthou

81. Who become the first woman minister in Manipur?
A. R. Apabi Devi   B. Kh. Thoibi Devi
C. Kim Gangte   D. Khaidem Sakhi Devi

82. The state of Manipur lies between .... and .... east Longitude.
A. 80.20° and 84.35°   B. 92.58° and 94.45°
C. 75.10° and 60.20°   D. 96.20° and 99.13°

83. In which year Manipur Olympic Association was formed?
A. 1947   B. 1948
C. 1949   D. 1950

84. Who was the founder President of the Manipur Olympic Association?
A. Churachand Singh
B. R.K. Madhuryajit Singh
C. Kalachandra
D. Debendra Singh

85. Who was the founder of the ''Ningthouja Dynasty'' in Manipur?
A. Nongdalairen Pakhangba
B. Atom Yairemba
C. Keiphaba Yanglon
D. Nongchup Lamgaingamba

86. Who was the King of Manipur when the Burmese invaded in the year of 1819?
A. King Loyumba   B. King Marjit Singh
C. King Gambhir Singh   D. King Kiyamba Singh

87. Who was the first British Political Agent of Manipur?
A. George Gordon   B. Grimwood
C. Captain William   D. James Hednic

88. Who introduced ''Bell metal currency'' in Manipur?
A. Kyamba Maharaj
B. Maramba Maharaj
C. Khagemba Maharaj
D. Labanyachandra Maharaj

89. Porompat, Keirao Bitra and Sawombung are the sub-divisions of which district?
A. Churachandpur   B. Chandel
C. Imphal West   D. Imphal East

90. Who was the first non-Manipuri Chief-Minister?
A. Md. Alimuddin   B. F.F. Pearson
C. M.K. Priyobratta   D. Braj Kumar Nehru

91. Who introduced 'Vaishnavism' as a state Religion?
A. King Chingthangkhomba
B. King Koiremba
C. King Bhagyachandra
D. King Bharatsai

92. Who may be given the title of the ''First Modern Political Leader of Manipur?
A. Hijam Irabat Singh   B. L. Jugeswar Singh
C. Paokai Haokip   D. Ng. Tompok Singh

93. The first English Journal of Manipur 'Meitei Leirang' was published in :
A. 1965   B. 1969
C. 1972   D. 1975

94. Which is the first Health Journal of Manipur?
A. Chingtam   B. Sanaleibak
C. Meeyam   D. Meitei Maiba

95. Who was the first speaker of Manipur Legislative Assembly?
A. T.C. Tiankham   B. Sibo Larho
C. M. Koireng Singh   D. Tombi Singh

96. What is the literacy rate of Manipur as per the 2011 census?
A. 65.36 per cent   B. 72.16 per cent
C. 76.94 per cent   D. 75.24 per cent

97. What is the density of population in Manipur as per the 2011 census?
A. 128   B. 110
C. 132   D. 120

98. Who is the first Manipuri girl to become Miss East India?
A. Aparna Jhaveri   B. Bonnie Gurumayum
C. Gayatri Heisnam   D. Priyanka Kokila

99. The number of Universities in Manipur is :
A. 2   B. 3
C. 4   D 5

100. Manipur University was established in :
A. 1977   B. 1978
C. 1979   D. 1980

101. Board of Secondary Education, Manipur was established in :
A. 1972-73   B. 1974-75
C. 1976-77   D. 1978-79

102. Script of the Grand Prix award winning film 'Imagee Ningthem' is written by :
A. N. Kunjamohan   B. M.K. Binodini
C. A.K. Paul   D. L.R. Singh

103. 'Seven Years Devastation' (Chahi Taret Khuntakpa) covers the period from :
A. 1810 to 1816   B. 1819 to 1825
C. 1829 to 1835   D. 1827 to 1833

104. When did the Manipur State Archieves set up?
A. 1980   B. 1982
C. 1985   D. 1988

105. Who described Manipur as ''An oasis of comparative civilization amidst the Barbarians?''
A. James Hotten   B. William Ban
C. Alfred Lyll   D. George Linde

106. Who is known as Queen of Boxing in Manipur?
A. M.C. Meri Kom   B. N. Kunjarani Devi
C. Suraj Lata Devi   D. Brojeswari Devi

107. During the reign of which King of Manipur the ''Scout Movement'' was started in the state?
A. Maharaja Chalamba Singh
B. Maharaja Chura Chand Singh
C. Maharaja Bharatsai Singh
D. Maharaja Ching Thang Khomba Singh

108. What is the area of Kangla, the ancient palace of Manipur?
A. 240.56 acres   B. 350.16 acres
C. 237.62 acres   D. 290.48 acres

109. Who is the first chairman of Hill Area Committee?
A. P.K. Mohan   B. P.C. Mathew
C. E.P. Moon Jan   D. S.P. Henry

110. When was the first Community Development Block established in Manipur?
A. 1952   B. 1953
C. 1954   D. 1955

111. Keilam Wildlife Sanctuary is located in which district?
A. Churachandpur   B. Senapati
C. Thoubal   D. Ukhrul

112. How many airports are there in Manipur?
A. 1   B. 2
C. 3   D. 4

113. Which is the first railway station of Manipur?
A. Dimapur Railway Station
B. Jiribam Railway Station
C. Toubal Railway Station
D. Karong Railway Station

114. Where is airport of Manipur located?
A. Churachandpur   B. Tamenglong
C. Imphal   D. Chandel

115. What is the 'State Game' of Manipur?
A. Thang Yannaba   B. Mangjong
C. Lamjel   D. Sagol Kangjei

116. In which year 'Manipur Hockey Association' was formed?
A. 1976   B. 1977
C. 1978   D. 1979

117. The author of the book 'Bir Tikendrajit Road' is :
A. T.C. Hudson   B. Hijam Guno
C. Nilima Roy   D. Lal Dena

118. Who is the first Manipuri to appear on postage stamp?
A. Laishram Memma   B. Jugeswori Devi
C. Rani Gaidenlilu   D. Rashi Devi

119. Who is the first person from Manipur to receive the 'Padmashree'?
A. N. Kunjarani Devi   B. Irom Leikhendra
C. P. Neelkamal   D. Atombapu Sharma

120. The number of Industrial Training Institutes in Manipur is :
A. Four   B. Five
C. Six   D. Eleven

121. Manipur Handloom and Handicrafts Development Corporation was set-up in :
A. 1972   B. 1976
C. 1980   D. 1982

122. In which year was the Manipur State Museum established?
A. 1965   B. 1969
C. 1975   D. 1979

123. What is Manipuri Polo called :
A. Yubi Lakpi   B. Khong Kangjei
C. Mukna Kangjei   D. Sagol Kangjei

124. Who was the first Deputy Chief Minister of Manipur?
A. L. Jugeshwar Singh
B. M. Koireng Singh
C. Irengbam Tompok Singh
D. Yangmasho Shaiza

125. When was the 'Patriot Day'' observed at the first time in Manipur?
A. 1965   B. 1966
C. 1968   D. 1969

126. Which King introduced the system of 'Division of Labour'' in Manipur?
A. King Loyumba
B. King Marjit Singh
C. King Gambhir Singh
D. King Khagemba Singh

127. Who is the writer of the book ''Elisa Amagi Mahao''?
A. E. Nilakanta Singh
B. N. Kunja Mohan Singh
C. G.C. Tongbra
D. A. Minaketan Singh

128. When was the first "District Library established in Manipur?
A. 1950 B. 1952
C. 1955 D. 1958

129. R.K. Chandrajit Singh is related to :
A. painting B. writing
C. music D. sport

130. In which district of Manipur the highest hill mount Tenipu is situated?
A. Senapati B. Imphal East
C. Thoubal D. Bishnupur

131. The largest pineapple producer district of Manipur is :
A. Bishnupur B. Thoubal
C. Tamenglong D. Ukhrul

132. 'Manipur Film Society' was established in :
A. 1955 B. 1960
C. 1962 D. 1966

133. Which is the first Manipuri documentary film?
A. Maipak – the Son of Manipur
B. Meitei Pung
C. Chatldo Eidi
D. Yellhou Jagai

134. Who is the director of first Manipuri documentary film?
A. M.A. Singh B. Aribam Shyam Sharma
C. Devkumar Bose D. Oken Amakcham

135. The Number of National Highway passes through Manipur is:
A. 3 B. 4
C. 5 D. 6

136. When was the Jiribam Railway Station inaugurated?
A. 1990 B. 1982
C. 1987 D. 1992

137. The number of Post Offices (2011) in Manipur is :
A. 1200 B. 1394
C. 1060 D. 970

138. Which is the largest export-oriented agricultural product of Manipur?
A. Maize B. Rice
C. Cotton D. Wheat

139. Manipur State Kala Academy was established in :
A. 1965 B. 1970
C. 1972 D. 1975

140. What is the average height of Imphal valley above MSL (mean sea level)?
A. 790 metres B. 850 metres
C. 990 metres D. 1050 metres

141. Who started the festival of Kang-Chingba (Ratha Yatra) in Manipur?
A. Maharaja Jai Singh
B. Maharaja Madhuchandra
C. Maharaja Churachand Singh
D. Maharaja Gambhir Singh

142. The Meeteis were converted into Hinduism during the reign of which king?
A. King Garibniwaz B. King Maramba
C. King Marjit D. King Kyamba

143. When was the last independent war of Manipur fought against British?
A. 20th March 1875 to 25th June 1875
B. 24th March 1891 to 27th April 1891
C. 15th January 1890 to 25th February 1890
D. 10th May 1879 to 27 July 1879

144. What is the serial number of Manipuri as it is listed in the Eight schedule to the constitution of India?
A. 9th B. 10th
C. 11th D. 12th

145. The judges of Manipur High Court are appointed by :
A. The Chief Justice of India
B. The President of India
C. The Chief Minister of Manipur
D. The Governor of Manipur

146. The language spoken by the largest number of people in the Manipur is :
A. English B. Bengali
C. Hindi D. Manipuri

147. What was the old name of Senapati district?
A. Manipur East B. Manipur West
C. Manipur North D. Manipur South

148. What was the old name of Chandel district?
A. Central District B. Manipur West
C. Manipur East D. Tengnoupal

149. The ornament, which is worn around the neck by the Manipuri women, is called :
A. Khonanakpi B. Khuji
C. Khorau D. Kanberi

150. In which year Manipur was included on the Indian Railway Map?
A. 1989 B. 1990
C. 1991 D. 1992

151. As per the 2011 census what is the sex ratio in Manipur?
A. 985 B. 980
C. 975 D. 995

152. Loktak Project was commissioned in :
A. 1983 B. 1984
C. 1985 D. 1986

153. In which district of Manipur Zoological Garden is located?
A. Tamenglong B. Imphal
C. Churachandpur D. Bishnupur

154. Manipur Agro-Industries Corporation was set-up in :
A. 1989
B. 1990
C. 1991
D. 1992

155. The last Lieutenant Governor of Manipur was :
A. J.M. Raina
B. P.C. Mathew
C. D.R. Kohil
D. Baleshwar Prasad

156. Which King introduced Kwak Tomba religious ceremony in Manipur?
A. Khuiyoi Tompok
B. Keiphaba Yanglon
C. Khui Ningngomba
D. Chingthang Lanthaba

157. During the reign of which King in Manipur the game Yubi Lakpi first played?
A. King Thawanthaba
B. King Chingthangkhomba
C. King Lanthaba
D. King Ayangba

158. In which district of Manipur Khagemba's old palace was situated?
A. Bishnupur
B. Churachandpur
C. Chandel
D. Ukhrul

159. Jhaveri sisters are famous for :
A. Odissi Dance
B. Kathak
C. Manipuri Dance
D. Bharat Natyam

160. Manipur Theological college is located at :
A. Thoubal
B. Ukhrul
C. Imphal
D. Chadel

161. In Manipur INA Museum is located at :
A. Moirang
B. Nambal
C. Kakching
D. Lilong

162. Where is the state Museum of Manipur situated?
A. Chandel
B. Senapati
C. Imphal
D. Tamenglong

163. Who was Manipur's first MBBS Doctor?
A. Dr. Nanda Babu Roy
B. Dr. P.K. Rana
C. Dr. J.C. Arya
D. Dr. C.L. Mohan

164. Who was Manipur's first lady medical Doctor?
A. Manorama Devi
B. Thangjam Ongbi Bedamani Devi
C. N. Chidambara
D. Payal Ghosh

165. When was the first Operation Theatre opened in Manipur?
A. 1920
B. 1926
C. 1930
D. 1935

166. When was the first Hospital ward opened in Manipur?
A. 1925
B. 1928
C. 1930
D. 1931

167. Who was first Mr. Manipur?
A. P. Jugol
B. Irom Leikhendra
C. R. Shyam
D. Ranabir Meitei

168. Who is the Manipur's first Mr. India?
A. M. Gopal Sharma
B. K. Dilip Singh
C. Nongthongbam Maipak
D. M. Phanjoubam

169. Who is the author of the book "Manipur: The Jewel of India"?
A. E. Ishwarjit Singh
B. S.C. Joshi
C. L.R. Singh
D. H. Guno Singh

170. Who is the author of the book "Madhabi"?
A. Kh. Chaoba
B. R.K. Shitaljit
C. Dr. Komal Singh
D. Lal Dena

171. Who is the author of the book 'Mao : The Naga Tribe of Manipur?
A. Lorho Mary Maheo
B. Naorem Sanajaoba
C. R. Constantine
D. H. Bhuban Singh

172. Where is Nupee Lal Memorial Complex located in Manipur?
A. Imphal
B. Moirang
C. Churachandpur
D. Moreh

173. Ruins of Citadel was built during the reign of :
A. King Jai Singh
B. King Khagemba
C. King Marjit
D. King Chourjit

174. Ruins of Citadel was built in the year :
A. 1500 A.D.
B. 1550 A.D.
C. 1600 A.D.
D. 1611 A.D.

175. Where is Shree Shree Govindajee Temple located?
A. Bishnupur
B. Kongla Fort
C. Old Langthabal Palace
D. Ukhrul

176. Who is the first Manipuri Child to get the Best Child Actor Award?
A. Leikhendra Singh
B. Ranbir Goswami
C. Shyam Singha
D. K. Narsingha

177. A veteran freedom fighter and a great socio-religious leader, Rani Gaidenliu was a living goddess for the manipuri people. Name the great Prime Minister of India who described her as "the daughter of the hills and gave the title "Rani of her people".
A. Lal Bahadur Shastri
B. Pandit Jawaharlal Nehru
C. Smt. Indira Gandhi
D. Morarji Desai

178. Which is the first Manipuri magazine started in 1917-18?
A. Longtai
B. Wakhal
C. Meitei Leima
D. Athouba

179. Which was the first Manipuri book to be awarded with the Telem Ningol Atoibema Award in children's literature?
A. Sana Kakchao
B. Ithak Ipom
C. Jahira
D. Ima

180. Who is the first Manipuri to win the Sangeet Natak Akademi Award?
A. H. Atomba Singh
B. T. Amudon Sharma
C. Bipin Singh
D. M. Amubi Singh

181. Who is the first Manipuri to win a Gold Medal in Asian Games?
A. Ng. Dingko Singh
B. Sanamacha Chanu
C. N. Kunjarani Devi
D. M.C. Merrycom

182. Who is the first Manipuri to become a Union Minister?
A. Ng. Tompok Singh
B. R.K. Jaichandra
C. R.K. Dorendra Singh
D. N. Gouzagin

183. Who is the first Manipuri Film Actor?
A. Leikhendra Singh
B. Robindro Sharma
C. Aribam Shyam Sharma
D. M.A. Singh

184. Who is the first Manipuri Film Actress?
A. Gita Devi
B. Manorama Devi
C. Rashi Devi
D. Rashmi Devi

185. Who is the first Manipuri to win Rajiv Gandhi Khel Ratna Award?
A. Ng. Dingko Singh
B. Thaiba Singh
C. M.C. MaryKom
D. N. Kunjarani Devi

186. Who is the first Muslim Chief Minister of Manipur?
A. Md. Alimuddin Lilong Turel Ahanbi
B. Md. Abdul Qayum
C. Md. Ali Akbar
D. Javed Ahmed

187. Who is the first Manipuri Muslim Woman Advocate?
A. Noor Bano
B. Benazir Majumdar
C. Fatima Shaikh
D. Sabnam Noorani

188. What is the percentage of Muslim population as per 2011 census?
A. 22.40
B. 25.50
C. 8.40
D. 15.60

189. What is the area covered by the Manipuri Hockey field?
A. 200 × 20 Yards
B. 200 × 40 Yards
C. 200 × 60 Yards
D. 200 × 80 Yards

190. The historic 'International Polo Tournament' was held in Manipur in the year :
A. 1985
B. 1987
C. 1989
D. 1990

191. In which year Oak Tassar was introduced in Manipur?
A. 1973-74
B. 1975-86
C. 1977-78
D. 1980-81

192. Who built the famous Vishnu temple situated at Bishenpur?
A. King Kyamba
B. King Telheiba
C. King Tonaba
D. King Punsiba

193. Sirohi National Park of Manipur got its recognition by the government in the year :
A. 1990
B. 1998
C. 1999
D. 2000

194. In which year was Yaingangpokpi Lakchao Wildlife Sanctuary opened :
A. 1989
B. 1991
C. 1995
D. 1998

195. The Manipur State Museum was inaugurated by which Prime Minister of India?
A. J.L. Nehru
B. Indira Gandhi
C. Rajiv Gandhi
D. A.B. Vajpayee

196. In which year Manipur University was upgraded as a Central University?
A. 1990
B. 1992
C. 1994
D. 1998

197. Which is the largest and most important mineral resource of Manipur?
A. Chromite
B. Coal
C. Lignite
D. Limestone

198. What is the hydro-electricity potential of Manipur?
A. 1784 MW
B. 1700 MW
C. 1680 MW
D. 1480 MW

199. In which year the first Manipur Panchayati Raj Bill was passed?
A. 1972
B. 1975
C. 1978
D. 1980

200. In which year Manipur got its own High Court?
A. 2010
B. 2011
C. 2013
D. 2012

201. In which year the Indian Penal Code was first enacted in Manipur?
A. 1901
B. 1902
C. 1903
D. 1904

202. The number of Autonomous Hill District Councils in Manipur is :
A. 6
B. 9
C. 10
D. 12

203. The area covered by the Jiribam Rubber Farm is :
A. 800 hectares
B. 889 hectares
C. 900 hectares
D. 1050 hectares

204. Who was the Manipuri Muslim, popularly known as Japan Pitru?
A. Ali Akbar
B. Alauddin Khan
C. Naqi Ahmed Choudhary
D. Mehtab Ali

205. Which river flows from Manipur to Assam?
A. Barrak
B. Thoubal
C. Iril
D. Makru

206. Which is the largest grown agricultural product of Manipur?
A. Wheat
B. Maize
C. Rice
D. Orange

207. When was the old Cachar road constructed in Manipur?
A. 1530
B. 1532
C. 1534
D. 1536

208. Who constructed the old Cachar road?
A. Meidingu-Kabomba
B. James Johnstone
C. Yengkham Deksan Singh
D. J. K. Rajan

209. In which district was Khagemba's old palace situated?
A. Senapati
B. Churachandpur
C. Tamenglong
D. Ukhrul

210. Who was the first chief commissioner of Manipur?
A. Major General Rawal Amar Singh
B. Himat Singh
C. E. P. Moon Jan.
D. P. C. Mathew

211. Who was the first Lieutenant Governor of Manipur?
A. D. R. Kohli
B. Baleswar Prasad
C. J. M. Raina
D. E. P. Moom

212. Loktak Lake is located in which district?
A. Bishnupur
B. Thoubal
C. Ukhrul
D. Tamenglong

213. Kachouphung Lake is located in which district?
A. Ukhrul
B. Bishnupur
C. Thoubal
D. Tamenglong

214. Barak waterfalls are located in which district?
A. Tamenglong
B. Bishnupur
C. Ukhrul
D. Senapati

215. Sangboo cave is located in:
A. Chandel
B. Ukhrul
C. Churachandpur
D. Imphal East

216. Height of Leikat Peak is :
A. 2,832 m.
B. 2,760 m.
C. 2,560 m.
D. 2,960m.

217. As per the 2011 census, the urban population of Manipur is :
A. 8, 34, 154
B. 9, 50, 325
C. 7, 90, 660
D. 10, 10, 548

218. As per the 2011 census, the rural population of Manipur is :
A. 20, 18, 224
B. 16, 20, 360
C. 20, 21, 640
D. 17, 10, 660

219. The State Emblem of Manipur is:
A. Singda Dam
B. Komgla Shaa
C. Shree Govindajee Temple
D. Khang Khui Cave

220. Kamjong district came into existance in :
A. 2016
B. 2015
C. 2014
D. 2013

221. Which is the new district in Manipur?
A. Mao
B. Jiribam
C. Tamei
D. Moreh

222. As per the 2011 census which is the highly populated district in Manipur?
A. Thoubal
B. Bishnupur
C. Imphal West
D. Senapati

223. As per the 2011 census which is the less populated district in Manipur?
A. Ukhrul
B. Churachandpur
C. Chandel
D. Tamenglong

224. As per the 2011 census which is the most densely populated district in Manipur?
A. Imphal West
B. Thoubal
C. Bishnupur
D. Imphal East

225. As per the 2011 census which is the less densely populated district in Manipur?
A. Ukhrul
B. Tamenglong
C. Chandel
D. Churachandpur

226. What is the decadal growth rate (2001-11) of Manipur as per the 2011 census?
A. 20.01%
B. 25.02%
C. 24.50%
D. 32.03%

227. Which is the largest city in Manipur?
A. Kakching
B. Thoubal
C. Lilong
D. Imphal

228. Who is known as the "Lion of Manipur"?
A. Bir Tikendrajit
B. Hijam Irabat
C. Paona Brajabashi
D. Zilla Singh

229. Who is known as 'Mahakavi' in Manipur?
A. H. Guno Singh
B. Hijam Anganghal
C. Kh. Chaoba
D. Dr. Komal Singh

230. What is the hottest month in the State of Manipur?
A. July
B. August
C. September
D. June

231. Where is the headquarters of Imphal East district?
A. Porompat
B. Kirao Bitra
C. Sawombung
D. Jiribam

232. Where is the headquarters of Imphal west district?
A. Lamsang
B. Lamphelpat
C. Patsai
D. Wangai

233. How many Tribes are recognised by the Government of Manipur?
A. 30
B. 31
C. 32
D. 35

234. Manipur 'Statehood Day' is celebrated on :
A. 25th February   B. 13th August
C. 28th September   D. 21st January

235. 'Manipuri Language Day' is celebrated on :
A. 20th August   B. 28th September
C. 30th September   D. 12th September

236. 'Manipur Integrity Day' is celebrated on :
A. 25th September   B. 28th September
C. 23rd April   D. 25th February

237. When was the State Institute of Journalism established?
A. 15th May 1990   B. 16th June 1994
C. 19th October 1992 D. 20th July 1995

238. When was the Council of Higher Secondary Education, Manipur established?
A. 1990   B. 1991
C. 1992   D. 1993

239. Manipur Human Rights Commission, Lamphelpat was established on :
A. 20th June 1995   B. 27th June 1998
C. 11th May 1990   D. 15th June 1992

240. Bunning wildlife sanctuary is situated in which district?
A. Imphal East   B. Tamenglong
C. Chandel   D. Churachandpur

241. Which wildlife sanctuary has the largest area in Manipur?
A. Yaingoupokpi Lokchao
B. Keilam
C. Zeliad
D. Jiri Makru

242. Zeliad wildlife sanctuary is located in which district?
A. Chandel   B. Tamenglong
C. Bishnupur   D. Churachandpur

243. Which was the first English Journal of Manipur?
A. Meitei Leirang   B. Manipur Mail
C. Sangai Express   D. Manipur News

244. Who is the first Manipuri Film Producer?
A. Debkumar Bose
B. Karam Manmohan Singh
C. Kh. Pramodini
D. Aribam Shyam Sharma

245. Which was the first Manipuri Film to receive the President's Medal in the 20th National Film Festival?
A. Matamgi Manipur   B. Langlen Thadoi
C. Imagee Ningthem   D. None of these

246. First Arjuna and Rajiv Gandhi Khel Ratna Award winner for Manipur N. Kunjarani Devi is famous in which sport?
A. Cricket   B. Hockey
C. Weightlifting   D. Boxing

247. Suraj Lata Devi is related with which sport?
A. Hockey   B. Weightlifting
C. Boxing   D. Cricket

248. N. Dingko Singh is related with which sport?
A. Cricket   B. Football
C. Hockey   D. Boxing

249. Anita Chanu has fame in which sport?
A. Mountaineering   B. Football
C. Tennis   D. Cricket

250. The first National Games were held in Manipur in :
A. 1995   B. 1996
C. 1997   D. 1999

251. Who was the editor of the "Manipur Paojel" in 1939?
A. Keisham Kunjabihari Singh
B. George Gordon
C. Dr. Brown
D. Hijam Irabat

252. Of the whole India, how much area is covered by Manipur State?
A. $\dfrac{1}{132}$ B. $\dfrac{1}{147}$
C. $\dfrac{1}{180}$ D. $\dfrac{1}{165}$

253. When was the "Clapped song" sung first time in Manipur?
A. 1830   B. 1847
C. 1857   D. 1870

254. Which jail in Manipur houses drug exclusively?
A. Shajiwa Jail   B. Imphal Jail
C. Jiribam Jail   D. None of these

255. When was the Manipur State Transport established?
A. 10th July, 1948   B. 15th August, 1949
C. 13th May, 1950   D. 20th April, 1952

256. When was the Manipur State Transport become a Corporation?
A. 20th July, 1972   B. 14th December, 1978
C. 27th March, 1976   D. 16th November, 1976

257. When does Manipur observe "Save Boundary Day"?
A. August 4, 1987   B. May 6, 1987
C. July 4, 1987   D. October 10, 1987

258. When did the King Gambhir Singh die?
A. 1831   B. 1832
C. 1833   D. 1834

259. When was the second "Nupi-Lal" (Women war against British) took place in Manipur?
A. 1939   B. 1940
C. 1941   D. 1942

260. Where is the Pony Breeding Project established in Manipur?

A. Tamenglong District   B. Senapati District
C. Bishnupur District   D. Chandel District

261. When was the first Bank opened in Manipur State?
A. 1942   B. 1944
C. 1946   D. 1948

262. Manipur State Bank was opened in :
A. 1942   B. 1944
C. 1945   D. 1947

263. Who was the editor of the weekly jounral "Anouba Yug" in 1947?
A. Hijam Irabat Singh   B. George Gordon
C. R.K. Bhubonsana   D. Dr. Brown

264. During the reign of which king of Manipur the festival "Ningal Chackouba" was introduced?
A. Maharaja Tangjama
B. Maharaja Chandra-Kirti
C. Maharaja Garibnivaj
D. Maharaja Maramba

265. Who built the famous Lord Krishna temple situated in Imphal?
A. Nara Singha   B. King Surchandra
C. King Charairongba   D. King Kulachandra

266. When was the famous Lord Sanamahi temple built?
A. 1880 A.D.   B. 1885 A.D.
C. 1890 A.D.   D. 1891 A.D.

267. In which early part of the century Christianity came to Manipur?
A. 17th century   B. 18th century
C. 19th century   D. 20th century

268. Which song of Manipur is sung by only women?
A. Nat Ishei   B. Nupi Pala
C. Ougri   D. Pena Ishei

269. The creator of the Manipuri classical dance 'Ras Leela' was :
A. King Bhagyachandra Singh
B. King Chingthang Khomba
C. King Ningthou Khomba
D. King Madhuchandra

270. Nongthombam Maipak got the 'Mr. India' title in the year :
A. 1967   B. 1968
C. 1969   D. 1970

271. In which year Sougaijam Somorendra Singh became the first graduate from Manipur?
A. 1920   B. 1925
C. 1932   D. 1935

272. The Aimol, Purum, Kom, Koireng and Chiru are the sub-tribes of which tribe?
A. Konrem   B. Mao
C. Angami   D. Kacha Naga

273. Manipur Agro-Industries Coporation was set-up in :
A. 1992   B. 1993
C. 1994   D. 1995

274. What is the total area under cultivation of different crops in Manipur?
A. 2, 50, 000 hectares   B. 2, 60, 000 hectares
C. 2, 85, 000 hectares   D. 3, 00, 000 hectares

275. Which district is the largest producer of Sugarcane in Manipur?
A. Chandel   B. Imphal west
C. Bishnupur   D. Thoubal

276. Yangmaso Shaiza was the first tribal :
A. Chief Minister of Manipur
B. Chief Commissioner of Manipur
C. M.P. from Manipur
D. Governor of Manipur

277. How many seats are reserved for scheduled castes in Manipur?
A. 1   B. 2
C. 3   D. 4

278. "Manipur Municipality Act" was introduced in the urban areas of the state in the year :
A. 1971   B. 1973
C. 1976   D. 1978

279. The total area covered by the Manipur Valley is :
A. 1800 sq. kms.   B. 1843 sq. kms.
C. 1860 sq. kms.   D. 1875 sq. kms.

280. What is the height of Mount Tenipu?
A. 2910 metres   B. 2950 metres
C. 2970 metres   D. 2994 metres

281. With which country Manipur shares an international border?
A. Myanmar   B. China
C. Bangladesh   D. None of these

282. Mount Tenipu is located in which district of Manipur?
A. Tamenglong   B. Senapati
C. Thoubal   D. Bishnupur

283. Jananeta Irabat's birthday is celebrated on :
A. 20th October   B. 30th November
C. 30th September   D. 18th September

284. The biggest source of the state income of Manipur is :
A. Industry   B. Forest Resource
C. Agriculture   D. None of these

285. The State Anthem of Manipur was composed by :
A. B. Jayanta Kumar   B. K. Kunjabihari
C. A. Thambou Singh   D. Sagolsem Indramani

286. L.M.S. Law college stands for :
A. Lairenmayum Seibyasachi Law College
B. Lairenmayum Sobita Law College

C. Longjam Mani Singh Law College
D. Liberal Manipur Society Law College

287. Manipur's first eastern dam Khoupum Dam is situated on which river?
A. Imphal river   B. Manchandui river
C. Iril river   D. Nambul river

288. In which district Khoupum Dam is located?
A. Bishnupur   B. Thoubal
C. Ukhrul   D. Tamenglong

289. In which year was the Loktak Hydel Project commissioned?
A. 1980   B. 1981
C. 1982   D. 1983

290. Manipur's premier college Dhana Manjuri College (D.M. College) was established in the year :
A. 1946   B. 1947
C. 1948   D. 1949

291. In which part of Manipur bamboo forests are abundantly grown?
A. Eastern Part   B. South western Part
C. South Northern Part   D. Northern Part

292. Who is the author of the Jamini Gold Medal award winner novel "Khudol"?
A. Pacha Meitei
B. E. Nilakanta Singh
C. Hijam Guno Singh
D. A. Chitreshwar Sharma

293. Who was the author of the 18th century book called "Sana Manik"?
A. E. Sonamani Singh
B. R.K. Madhubir
C. Wahengbam Madharam
D. Sudhir Naoraibam

294. Who wrote "Elisa Amagi Mahao"?
A. Nilabir Sharma Shastri
B. Arambam Biren Singh
C. G.C. Tongbra
D. N. Kunjamohan

295. Padmashree Award winner author who translated 'Mahabharata' book in Manipuri is :
A. Ch. Kalachand Shastri
B. Birendrajit Naorem
C. Ningombam Sunita
D. N. Ibobi Singh

296. Luira is a festival of which tribe?
A. Thadou   B. Tangkhul
C. Kabui   D. Kuki

297. Which popular form of festival is observed by Kuki tribes?
A. Chumpha   B. Chavang Kut
C. Gan Ngai   D. None of these

298. Who was Manipur's first to get Lalit Kala Akademi Award?
A. T.A. Mudon Sharma
B. T. Kunja Kishore Singh
C. Th. Tombi Singh
D. Y. Gambhini Devi

299. In the reign of which king 'Heigru Hitongba' was started in Manipur?
A. King Irengba
B. King Chandra Kirti
C. King Surchand Singh
D. King Meidingu Loitongba

300. The game of 'Kong' flourished during the reign of :
A. King Ningthou Kongba   B. King Laitongba
C. King Keiphaba   D. King Khomba

301. How many gold Medals were won by Manipur in the Vth National Games?
A. 40   B. 45
C. 49   D. 55

302. R. K. Singhajit got Padmashree for his work in :
A. Dance   B. Literature
C. Drama   D. Education

303. As per the 2011 census which district have the highest literacy rate?
A. Imphal East   B. Imphal west
C. Bishnupur   D. Churachandpur

304. When was Manipur Human Rights Commission established?
A. 25th May 1995   B. 27th June 1999
C. 27th June 1998   D. 28th April 1996

305. As per the 2011 census what is the Males population of Manipur?
A. 1,438,586   B. 1,105,680
C. 1,516,123   D. 1,315,219

306. As per the 2011 census what is the Females population of Manipur?
A. 1,170,338   B. 1,417,208
C. 1,330,216   D. 1,175,670

307. The Kabaw Valley was handed over to Myanmar (Burma) in the year :
A. 1830   B. 1834
C. 1838   D. 1840

308. When was the first English school established in Manipur?
A. 1880   B. 1885
C. 1890   D. 1892

309. Why was Manipur Durbar established in 1907?
A. To assist the British in the administration of Manipur

B. To assist the Government of India in the administration of Manipur

C. To assist the Maharaja in the administration of Manipur

D. None of these

310. The Manipuri Kings who got title of KCSI (Knight Commander Service of India) are :
A. Chandrakriti and Churachand Maharaja
B. Surchandra and Churachand Maharaja
C. Budhachandra and Surchandra Maharaja
D. Chandrakriti and Budhachandra Maharaja

311. What is the full form of MOA?
A. Manipur Olympic Association
B. Manipur Oil Association
C. Manipur Organisation of Adults
D. None of these

312. In which year was 'Manipur women's Football Association' formed?
A. 1972   B. 1976
C. 1980   D. 1982

313. Who was the 'founder patron' of modern sports movement in Manipur?
A. Charairongba
B. Keiphaba Yanglon
C. Sir Churachand Singh
D. Bhadra Singh

314. Who is the author of the book 'My Experience in Manipur'?
A. Sir James Johnstone   B. Lucy Zehol
C. A.K. Paul   D. E.W. Dun

315. In Manipur 'Durga Puja' is locally known as:
A. Heikru Hitongba   B. Kwak Yatra
C. Yaoshang   D. None of the above

316. What is the height of Saheed Minar?
A. 45 feet   B. 50 feet
C. 55 feet   D. 60 feet

317. L. Nabakishore Singh got Padamshree for his work in:
A. Theatre   B. Literature
C. Dance   D. Herbal Medicine

318. Ksh. Thouranisabi Devi got Padamshree for her work in :
A. Nat Songkritan   B. Mountaineering
C. Cinema   D. Boxing

319. Where is Sainik School situated in Manipur?
A. Imphal   B. Bishnupur
C. Senapati   D. Ukhrul

320. Who is known as the 'Melody King' in Manipur?
A. R.K. Bhogen   B. Nongmaithem Pahari
C. S. Devabrata Singh   D. L. Lakpati Singh

321. Who is known as the 'Melody Queen' in Manipur?
A. Sabitri Heisnam   B. Y. Gambhini Devi
C. Laishram Mema Devi   D. Y. Ranjana Devi

322. Who is popularly known as the 'Jananeta' (leader of the people) in Manipur?
A. L. Jugeswar Singh   B. N. Tombi Singh
C. Paokai Hao Kip   D. Hijam Irabat

323. Which is the biggest Temple in Manipur?
A. Shree Shree Govindajee Temple
B. Vishnu Temple
C. Hanuman Thakur Temple
D. Radha Raman Temple

324. Which is the biggest cave in Manipur?
A. Khu Kse   B. Khang Khui Cave
C. Sangboo   D. Tonglon

325. How many tribal dialects are recognised by the government of India in Manipur?
A. 2   B. 4
C. 5   D. 6

326. Which is the highest rainfall area in Manipur?
A. Thoubal   B. Ukhrul
C. Tamenglong   D. Chandel

327. Which is the lowest rainfall area in Manipur?
A. Senapati   B. Imphal
C. Ukhrul   D. Churachandpur

328. Where is Orange Festival celebrated in Manipur?
A. Tamenglong   B. Ukhrul
C. Senapati   D. Bishnupur

329. The present 10+2+3 system of education was started in Manipur from the academic session of :
A. 1985-86   B. 1986-87
C. 1988-89   D. 1990-91

330. What is Jhum cultivation locally called in Manipur?
A. Mono   B. Kamlou
C. Pamlou   D. Tuwalu

331. How many small Town committees are in Manipur?
A. 20   B. 25
C. 33   D. 35

332. How many number of Municipalities are in the Urban areas of Manipur?
A. 9   B. 12
C. 16   D. 18

333. "INAMPEILIN" is the annual festival of which tribe of Manipur?
A. Maring   B. Tongkhul
C. Chothe   D. Tarao

334. What does 'MASLSA' stand for?
A. Manipur State Legal Services Authority
B. Manipur State Legal Society Authority
C. Manipur Strong Legal Society Association
D. None of these

335. When was the status of chief commissioner upgraded to Lieutenant Governor in Manipur? .
A. 1968　　　　　　　B. 1969
C. 1970　　　　　　　D. 1971

336. Who is the first Manipuri Women Film Producer?
A. Sabitri Heisnam
B. Y. Ranajana Devi
C. Khaidem Sakhi Devi
D. K. O. Thouranisabi Devi

337. Manipur State Gazette was first launched in the year :
A. 1929　　　　　　　B. 1930
C. 1931　　　　　　　D. 1932

338. Who was the first Teacher (Manipuri) to have taught in School?
A. Mayanglambam Purna Singh (1893)
B. Ch. Kalachand Shastri (1860)
C. R.K. Jhalajit Singh　　(1870)
D. G. Surchand Sharma (1880)

339. Who was the first Director of Education in Manipur?
A. M.S. Sharma (1960-61)
B. S.D. Bahuguna (1958-59)
C. C. Kirti Singh (1972-73)
D. K.C. Tongbra (1975-76)

340. Which lake is known as the "Kohinoor of Manipur"?
A. Zailad Lake　　　　B. Kachouphung Lake
C. Loktak Lake　　　　D. Kharung Lake

341. What is the oldest salt mine (brine) in Manipur?
A. Ningel salt mine
B. Sikhong salt mine
C. Chandrakhong salt mine
D. Waikhong salt mine

342. Where is rubber grown in Manipur?
A. Kakching　　　　　B. Jiribam
C. Nambal　　　　　　D. Machi

343. When does the "Manipur Plantation Crops" establish?
A. 1985-86　　　　　　B. 1990-91
C. 1979-80　　　　　　D. 1981-82

344. Where is the hottest place in Manipur?
A. Tengnoupal　　　　B. Moirang
C. Jiribam　　　　　　D. Kakching

345. Who was the first person to set up NCC in Manipur?
A. L.H. Harnet　　　　B. H. Tombi Singh
C. P.K. Suisy　　　　　D. P. K. Behring

346. Who is the first Manipuri Chief Justice ?
A. P. Jugal
B. R. K. Manisama Singh
C. Ranbir Meitei
D. K. Sanatomba

347. The district of Manipur which is known as the birth place of Christianity in the state is :

A. Thoubal　　　　　　B. Senapati
C. Ukhrul　　　　　　　D. Chandel

348. The Number of tea gardens in Manipur is :
A. 4　　　　　　　　　B. 6
C. 10　　　　　　　　　D. 12

349. In which year Oak Tassar Project was introduced in Manipur?
A. 1971-72　　　　　　B. 1975-76
C. 1973-74　　　　　　D. 1978-79

350. Bir Tikendrajit Singh's crusade was against the :
A. Chinese　　　　　　B. Japanese
C. Burmese　　　　　　D. Britishers

351. Takhel Khong (Tripura Canal) was Constructed by :
A. Khabomba　　　　　B. Punsiba
C. Telheiba　　　　　　D. Bharatsai

352. Manipur state Durbar was established in :
A. 1905　　　　　　　B. 1906
C. 1907　　　　　　　　D. 1908

353. In which district Nungba Sub-division is located?
A. Thoubal　　　　　　B. Jiribam
C. Noney　　　　　　　D. Ukhrul

354. How many Nagar Panchayats are in Manipur?
A. 15　　　　　　　　　B. 16
C. 17　　　　　　　　　D. 18

355. When was the war of Independecne or the Anglo-Manipur war held?
A. 1890　　　　　　　B. 1891
C. 1895　　　　　　　D. 1897

356. When did the Chandel district come into existence?
A. May 13, 1974　　　　B. July 6, 1977
C. June 10, 1978　　　　D. Septerber 5, 1980

357. When was the 'Fast Tract Court' established in Manipur?
A. October 5, 2001　　　B. November 6, 2002
C. January 7, 2003　　　D. July 5, 2001

358. When did Manipur Sales Tax Act & Rules come into force?
A. December 10, 1990　　B. June 5, 1980
C. May 20, 1985　　　　D. August 6, 1995

359. Manipur Public Service Commission was formed in :
A. 1972　　　　　　　B. 1973
C. 1974　　　　　　　D. 1975

360. Who was the first chairman of the Manipur Public Service Commission?
A. S. K. Behring
B. G. B. K. Hooja
C. K. L. Sharma
D. P. Krishnamohan Singh

361. Who was the first secretary of the Manipur Public Service Commission?
A. Ch. Abhijit Singh
B. Ph. Shyamananda Sharma
C. Karam Goura Kishore Singh
D. Ch. Dhanbir Meitei

362. When was the Manipur Science & Technology Council established?
A. 1980
B. 1985
C. 1988
D. 1990

363. What is the total area of Manipur under forest cover?
A. 16000 sq km.
B. 16538 sq km.
C. 17346 sq km.
D. 17503 sq km.

364. How many Gram Panchayats are there in Manipur?
A. 150
B. 155
C. 161
D. 165

365. Thanlon is located in which district?
A. Pherzawl
B. Imphal West
C. Senapati
D. Tamenglong

366. Phungyar is located in which district?
A. Bishnupur
B. Thoubal
C. Kamjong
D. Chandel

367. The book 'Fragments of Manipuri Culture' was written by :
A. E. Nilakanta Singh
B. G. K. Ghosh
C. R. K. Shitaljit
D. M. K. Binodini

368. The book 'Ima' was written by :
A. L. Premchand
B. Hijam Angahal
C. Lucy Zehal
D. E. W. Dun

369. The book 'Sur Vigyan' recognised by the state government as a text book for music in Manipur is written by :
A. H. Guno Singh
B. E. Nilakanta Singh
C. Laishram Memma
D. R. K. Madhubir

370. In Manipur who was popularly known as Bob?
A. Birendrajit Naorem
B. Aribam Shyam Sharma
C. M. A. Singh
D. Ralengnao Khaling

371. Who is known as the 'Father of Manipuri Dance and Style'?
A. Guru Amubi Singh
B. Guru T. Amudon Sharma
C. Guru Bipin Singha
D. Guru L. Kaireng Singh

372. Who is honoured with the title 'Nritya Rani'?
A. L. Ibemhal Devi
B. Elam Indira Devi
C. H. Ngangbi Devi
D. Darshana Jhaveri

373. Who is the first recipient of the Manipuri children's literature award named 'Telam Ningal Atoibema Award'?

A. R. K. Bhubonsana
B. S. Surchand Sharma
C. M. Kirti Singh
D. M. K. Binodini Devi

374. Which place is called the 'Rice Basket of Manipur'?
A. Kumbi
B. Kwakta
C. Kakching
D. Samurou

375. The Meitei language has its own script. The name of script is :
A. Meitei Mayek
B. Devnagari
C. Sabrai
D. None of these

376. Which of the following highways did not pass through Manipur?
A. NH-39
B. NH-53
C. NH-150
D. NH-35

377. The total length of National Highways in Manipur is :
A. 850 kms.
B. 900 kms.
C. 1745 kms.
D. 1000 kms.

378. Who was the first General Secretary of the Manipuri Sahitya Parishad established in 1935?
A. Hijam Irabot
B. Gokulchandra Singh
C. Laitman Yaima
D. A. Thambou Singh

379. Sirohi National Park is located in which district of Manipur?
A. Imphal East
B. Chandel
C. Tamenglong
D. Bishnupur

380. Where is 'Khansari Sugar Factory' located in Manipur?
A. Khangabok
B. Iraishemba
C. Kabowakching
D. Kadamtala

381. Where is 'Mechanised Dye House' located in Manipur?
A. Iroishemba
B. Takyel
C. Loitang Khunou
D. Kabowakching

382. Around which plant all Manipuri marriage ceremonies are conducted?
A. Sirai Lily
B. Pineapple
C. Tulsi
D. Orange

383. The Gostha Lila dance of Manipur is also known as :
A. Panshenba
B. Manshenba
C. Sanshenba
D. None of these

384. Which is the biggest festival celebrated by the Kabui Naga tribe of Manipur?
A. Gan Ngai
B. Kut
C. Cheiraoba
D. Chumpha

385. Manipuri folk dance 'Thabal Chongba' is associated with which festival?
A. Lai Haraoba
B. Yaoshang
C. Rath Yatra
D. Heikru

386. How many types of Kauna are available in Manipur?
A. Two
B. Three
C. Four
D. Five

387. How many types of 'Yenpak' are used by the people of Manipur?
A. Four   B. Six
C. Three   D. Seven

388. Who was the last Chairman of Manipur Territorial Council 1957?
A. M. Koireng Singh   B. S. Meenakitan
C. Dr. P. Kamal   D. Vimal Laishram

389. Who wrote 'Bor Saheb Ongbi Sanatombi' and 'Nungairakta Chandramukhi'?
A. E. Sonamani Singh   B. M. K. Binodini
C. N. Ibobi Singh   D. G. C. Tongbra

390. Which was Manipur's first book to be awarded Sahitya Academy (National) Award?
A. Imphal Amasugn Magi Ising— Nugsheetki Phibam
B. Aseibagi Nitaipog
C. Ngabongkhao
D. Kalenthagi Leipaklei

391. "Naga Lui Ngaini" which is a festival of Naga people relates to :
A. New year   B. Seed sowing
C. Harvesting   D. None of these

392. "Phait Lam, Dak Lam, Silam Lam" are the dance forms of :
A. Mao Maram   B. Paite
C. Tangkhul   D. None of these

393. The 55 feet high Monument of Shaheed Minar was constructed by well- known sculptor :
A. M. Priyo Kumar
B. Mohit Paul
C. Ramesh Paul
D. Mahendra Mani Singh

394. Who among the following sportpersons is nominated in Rajya Sabha in 2016?
A. N. Kunjarani Devi   B. Suranjoy Singh
C. N. Dingko Singh   D. M.C. Mary Kom

395. What was the former name of the present Paona Bazar of Manipur?
A. Sardar Bazar   B. Maxwell Bazar
C. Prem Bazar   D. Ongbi Bazar

396. Manipur's biggest masjid 'Sardar Bazar Jama Masjid' was constructed in the year :
A. 1890   B. 1896
C. 1875   D. 1885

397. Which of the following is not associated with Ratan Thiyam, the noted Director?
A. Chakravyuha   B. Uttar Priyadarshini
C. Urubhangam   D. Jamadarin

398. Meitram Bir Award is given in the field of :
A. Manipuri Drama   B. Sport
C. Education   D. Social Service

399. The first treaty of Anglo Manipuri Alliance was signed in the year :
A. 1750   B. 1755
C. 1758   D. 1762

400. In which year the 'Treaty of Yandaboo' was made?
A. 1820   B. 1830
C. 1826   D. 1840

ANSWERS

1	2	3	4	5	6	7	8	9	10
A	C	C	D	A	C	A	D	C	A
11	**12**	**13**	**14**	**15**	**16**	**17**	**18**	**19**	**20**
A	C	B	A	B	B	C	A	B	B
21	**22**	**23**	**24**	**25**	**26**	**27**	**28**	**29**	**30**
C	A	A	B	B	B	C	D	B	A
31	**32**	**33**	**34**	**35**	**36**	**37**	**38**	**39**	**40**
C	C	A	B	C	D	A	A	A	B
41	**42**	**43**	**44**	**45**	**46**	**47**	**48**	**49**	**50**
A	D	C	C	A	D	C	D	C	D
51	**52**	**53**	**54**	**55**	**56**	**57**	**58**	**59**	**60**
C	D	C	A	C	B	C	A	B	A
61	**62**	**63**	**64**	**65**	**66**	**67**	**68**	**69**	**70**
B	C	D	C	A	B	B	B	C	D
71	**72**	**73**	**74**	**75**	**76**	**77**	**78**	**79**	**80**
A	A	A	C	D	A	B	C	C	D
81	**82**	**83**	**84**	**85**	**86**	**87**	**88**	**89**	**90**
A	B	A	B	A	B	A	C	D	B
91	**92**	**93**	**94**	**95**	**96**	**97**	**98**	**99**	**100**
C	A	B	D	A	C	A	B	A	D
101	**102**	**103**	**104**	**105**	**106**	**107**	**108**	**109**	**110**
A	B	B	B	C	A	B	C	D	A

111	112	113	114	115	116	117	118	119	120
A	A	B	C	D	A	B	C	D	D
121	122	123	124	125	126	127	128	129	130
B	B	D	C	D	A	B	D	A	A
131	132	133	134	135	136	137	138	139	140
B	D	A	C	A	A	B	A	C	A
141	142	143	144	145	146	147	148	149	150
D	A	B	A	B	D	C	D	A	B
151	152	153	154	155	156	157	158	159	160
A	A	B	D	C	C	A	B	C	C
161	162	163	164	165	166	167	168	169	170
A	C	A	B	B	D	B	C	B	C
171	172	173	174	175	176	177	178	179	180
A	A	B	D	B	A	B	C	A	D
181	182	183	184	185	186	187	188	189	190
A	B	B	C	D	A	B	C	D	D
191	192	193	194	195	196	197	198	199	200
A	A	B	A	B	C	D	A	B	C
201	202	203	204	205	206	207	208	209	210
D	A	B	C	A	C	D	A	B	A
211	212	213	214	215	216	217	218	219	220
B	A	A	A	A	A	A	C	B	A
221	222	223	224	225	226	227	228	229	230
B	C	D	A	B	C	D	A	B	C
231	232	233	234	235	236	237	238	239	240
A	B	C	D	A	B	C	C	B	B
241	242	243	244	245	246	247	248	249	250
D	B	A	B	A	C	A	D	A	D
251	252	253	254	255	256	257	258	259	260
A	B	B	A	B	C	A	D	A	B
261	262	263	264	265	266	267	268	269	270
C	D	A	B	C	D	D	B	A	D
271	272	273	274	275	276	277	278	279	280
A	A	A	C	D	A	A	C	B	D
281	282	283	284	285	286	287	288	289	290
A	B	C	C	A	A	B	D	D	A
291	292	293	294	295	296	297	298	299	300
B	C	C	D	A	B	B	C	A	B
301	302	303	304	305	306	307	308	309	310
C	A	B	C	A	B	B	B	C	A
311	312	313	314	315	316	317	318	319	320
A	B	C	A	B	C	D	A	A	B
321	322	323	324	325	326	327	328	329	330
C	D	A	B	D	C	D	A	B	C
331	332	333	334	335	336	337	338	339	340
C	A	C	A	B	C	D	A	B	C
341	342	343	344	345	346	347	348	349	350
A	B	D	C	A	B	C	B	C	D
351	352	353	354	355	356	357	358	359	360
A	C	C	D	B	A	A	A	A	B
361	362	363	364	365	366	367	368	369	370
C	B	C	D	A	C	A	D	C	D
371	372	373	374	375	376	377	378	379	380
C	B	A	C	A	D	C	A	A	A
381	382	383	384	385	386	387	388	389	390
A	C	C	A	B	A	C	A	B	A
391	392	393	394	395	396	397	398	399	400
B	B	C	D	A	B	D	A	D	C